The Checkbook

Charles E. Merrill

THE
CHECKBOOK

*The Politics and
Ethics of Foundation
Philanthropy*

CHARLES MERRILL

Oelgeschlager, Gunn & Hain, Publishers, Inc.   Boston

Two previous titles have been published by Charles Merrill:

The Walled Garden: The Story of a School

The Great Ukrainian Partisan Movement:
And Other Tales of the Eisenhower Years

International Standard Book Number: 0-89946-217-0

Library of Congress Catalog Card Number: 86-17937

Printed in the U.S.A.

Oelgeschlager, Gunn & Hain, Publishers, Inc.
131 Clarendon Street
Boston, MA 02116

Library of Congress Cataloging-in-Publication Data

Merrill, Charles E.
  The Checkbook.

  Includes index.
  1. Endowments. 2. Philanthropists. I. Title.
HV16.M47 1986   361.7   86-17937
ISBN 0-89946-217-0

The author gives his recognition to Elizabeth Smith-Eisenhauer, production manager, for bringing this book to completion.

Composed in Monotype Caledonia by the Anthoensen Press, Portland, Maine

To Robert and Doris Magowan

Przepraszam wielkie pytania
za małe odpowiedzi.

"Pod jedną gwiazdką"

I apologize to big questions
for small answers.

"Under a Certain Little Star"

Sounds, Feelings, Thoughts:
Seventy Poems by Wisława
Szymborska

CONTENTS

The Checkbook

CHAPTER ONE

The Charles E. Merrill Trust

A man was on his way from Jerusalem when he fell in with robbers, who stripped him, beat him, and went off leaving him half dead. It so happened that a priest was going down by the same road; but when he saw him, he went past on the other side. So too a Levite came to the place, and when he saw him, he went past on the other side. But a Samaritan who was making the journey came upon him, and when he saw him was moved to pity. He went up and bandaged his wounds, bathing them with oil and wine. Then he lifted him to his own beast, brought him on to an inn, and looked after him there. Next day he produced two silver pieces and gave them to the innkeeper, and said, "Look after him; and if you spend any more, I will repay you on my way back." [Luke 10:30–35]

INTRODUCTION

The tale of the Good Samaritan seems a reasonable beginning for any study of philanthropy, and it has two aspects worth discussing. The Samaritan was an outsider. The humiliations he had experienced rendered him sensitive to the suffering of another. The priest and the Levite belonged to the Establishment. They were off on an important deal and did not want to be late, did not want to mess up their clothes, and trusted the System to, somehow, get around to looking after this welfare case.

The Samaritan invested adequate resources in taking care of his task. In fact, he did more than was strictly necessary. He left that extra money with the innkeeper. The Samaritan was not only a responsible man—he had class.

The important detail remains, however, of the Good Samaritan as outsider.

Theodore Roosevelt, the first American president to show any concern for the environment, had been a sickly young man sent out west to the Dakotas for his health. With his thick glasses, squeaky voice, and cowboy costume, he would stride into a saloon to order, I suppose, a lemonade, and all the real guys would crack up at his Eastern accent and silly appearance. Because he wasn't a Real Guy with an unquestioning Paul Bunyan/John Wayne assumption that animals are to shoot and trees to cut down, Roosevelt had some distance on the West. Out of that came an awareness that unless steps were taken to protect water, land, wildlife, forests, these inexhaustible natural resources wouldn't last much longer—for which awareness he was scorned as a meddling Easterner.

Another outsider was Julius Rosenwald. As son of a Jewish immigrant, he was sensitive to the exclusion of blacks from the American Dream, which had brought him to the top of Sears Roebuck but which offered them very little, starting with the first step up any ladder, an adequate education. It was not an issue that bothered 99 percent of regular Americans, who knew that Negroes were too dumb to make any use out of booklearning, and feared that if they did it would unfit them for their proper careers as cotton pickers. Between 1917 and its termination in 1932, the Rosenwald Fund helped build 5,300 rural schools for blacks plus dozens of urban high schools when the southern state governments saw this not at all as their responsibility. Rosenwald's preoccupation with Negro education was just the sort of thing one might expect of a Jew.

It was not nice Germans who opposed Hitler's conquest of Europe nor nice Americans who opposed the war in Vietnam. It was neurotics and troublemakers. When nice people turned against those wars, it was not because the wars were evil but because the home team was losing.

When one tries, therefore, to examine philanthropy and the history of the Charles E. Merrill Trust, a typical foundation, one is left with a paradox. Significant philanthropy must play the role of both Good Citizen and Damn Nuisance. It supports the institutions that serve society and hold it together, that educate the next generation, that give the bits of pleasure which make daily life worthwhile. Because it operates without the constraints of a state agency, private philanthropy can act with freedom and precision, within different limits of time. It can support cancer research at Sloan Kettering without the spasmodic funding and maddening restrictions of federal policy. It can write a check for the repair of poor overused Central Park when the city has literally run out of funds for such a purpose. Because its priorities are not limited by national boundaries, it can decide to repair a Gothic cathedral in England or fund an Indian co-op in southern Chile.

> When you reap the harvest of your land, you shall not reap right into the edges of your field; neither shall you glean the loose ears of your crop; . . . You shall

leave them for the poor and the alien. I am the Lord your God.   [Leviticus 19:9–10]

The Good Citizen, the Righteous Man, was honored, in every society. In sixteenth-century Turkey such a man endowed a *vakif* with estates sometimes as far west as Hungary, quite a modern type of foundation that made itself responsible for the religious education of poor boys, the maintenance of a walled khan for the shelter of travelers, an insane asylum where the troubled could quiet their spirits by listening to the splash of water in a marble fountain. The Good Citizen is not the Texan who reckons up his worth by the length of his car.

Nevertheless, you cannot become seriously involved in philanthropy and escape the ridiculous status of Theodore Roosevelt with his Eastern worries about elk and antelope, or of Julius Rosenwald the Jew. If you see a critical problem too intensely, if you go beyond the accepted limits of social concern, you cease to be the Righteous Man honored at the high table. You become a do gooder, a nigger lover, a parlour pink who hangs out with long-haired men and short-haired women. Your old buddies wonder whether you might possibly be a Samaritan.

The Samaritans came from the class too inferior to be carried off by the Chaldeans to Babylon, after the collapse of the Hebrew uprising of 586, along with the pillars of society, the media personalities, and the skilled technicians. They stayed behind in Palestine, intermarried with non-Jews, became sloppy in their religious observances, and were despised as mongrels when the nice people returned from Babylon after Cyrus the Persian smashed the Chaldeans. There were narrow Samaritan quotas at all the good schools in Jerusalem. You wouldn't want your daughter to marry one. Jesus was once again sticking his elbow into the ribs of the Establishment by holding up a Samaritan as his example of a Good Man.

Accordingly, in the Charles E. Merrill Trust's twenty-three years of working life and in the pages of this book, the question that came up again and again was the conflict between our self-assumed role of Good Citizen and the occasions when we sought to go beyond that and be something more, or less. We trustees had to face, or evade, the contradiction that the money that permits generosity isolates the givers from the reality of suffering and turns any fundamental alleviation of suffering into a threat to that ownership of money.

This book is not simply the history of one foundation that spent a little over $114 million in twenty-three years. It also tries to look at what is meant by Philanthropy and its relations both to the Establishment that supplies its resources and to the bramble-patches of the society that asks its help. In short, what did we spend all that money on and why? And, more difficult to answer, what did we accomplish?

CHARITY AND MR. MERRILL

Measuring the goals and values of this charitable foundation has to begin with the realities of life in small town Florida and Amherst College which set the basic direction of Charles E. Merrill. He had grown up in Green Cove Springs, a little town on the St. John's River in northern Florida, listening to the yarns of the aging Confederate veterans seated outside the barber shop. His mother's father and his father's father had both fought at Vicksburg, in opposite armies. From the Wilson side there were tales about plantation life in Mississippi: his mother's Faulknerian brothers and sisters, the aunt jilted by a salesman from Natchez, the aunt who became spelling champion of Arkansas, the godly uncle killed by lightning on his way to church. Old Mr. Merrill, as lieutenant in Sherman's army, had been court-martialed (in family legend) for refusing to burn down the house of a widow standing in the way of the march through Georgia. After the war he had brought his wife and boy from Ohio to start an orange farm in Florida, and on Sundays, still Northerners, he and his wife would walk barefoot, shoes in hand (for they were poor) to teach in two black churches.

Son and daughter of these two veterans met at Maryville, a small Presbyterian college in eastern Tennessee, where my grandfather was studying to be a doctor. Dr. Merrill became a respected, overworked physician in Green Cove Springs who charged three dollars for a delivery, five if a servant had to row him to the other side of the St. John's River, but forgot the bills of his patients, white or black, who could not pay.

My father was restless in this limited world and went North to college at Amherst, arriving there in September 1904 with just about everything against him. He was 5'5", he spoke with a Southern accent, he had little money, and his mother accompanied him. In later years he accepted the myths that other people told about his wonderful years at college, and he made some up himself. He was popular and charming, unfailingly successful with women, a brilliant student and great athlete. A favorite story was of himself as varsity quarterback, so light that two halfbacks could pick him up and hurl him over the helmets and shoulder pads of the players struggling beneath him until some great fist would reach up and grab the little hero and dash him to the ground.

Reality was more painful. He was humiliated by his poverty. The sale of two lots in West Palm Beach, Dr. Merrill's one bit of capital, had paid his first tuition bill; his mother's income from two rooming houses, one white, one black, was the source of a little money from home. My father was not proud of his position as business manager for a boarding house, and when he sold secondhand clothes he felt that friends bought them because they felt sorry for him. A course in English he liked, another on the truth of re-

vealed religion, where the professor set out to destroy the students' faith in
the first semester and rebuild it in the second. He dropped out of Amherst
after two years, went to law school at the University of Michigan, dropped
out there, went to Wall Street. He possessed the abilities to work hard, be
charming and trustworthy in the eyes of his employers, make a quick math-
ematical analysis of a complicated problem, reach decisions rapidly and hold
onto them without looking back: "If I made a decision fast I was right 60
percent of the time; if I made a decision carefully I'd be right 70—but it
wasn't always worth it." He made a million dollars, went broke when the
market collapsed, and came back to make it again.

His love of Amherst came after graduation. He attended every reunion,
not simply those of '08, and came to know the alumni from the classes far
before his—President Coolidge (who was offered a job at Merrill Lynch when
he left office but was afraid of what had happened to Grant in similar circumstances) was one such—and eventually those much younger. He admired
the leadership in finance and law that Amherst produced, the ambitious
young men it attracted, and he was quick to help those who lacked money
for their education. He was loyal to his old college friends and sensitive to
the way those who had not found it felt threatened by his success. In the
pressures of his own life, he came to see the college and the town around it
as a place of calm, dignity and beauty in its elm trees and white houses, part
of an older America like the little Florida towns where he had grown up.
Amherst gave Mr. Merrill his lifelong belief in the value of education, and
his loyalty to the college had an almost religious love to it.

He was very personal in his loyalties. The three most important people in
his life were his mother, his sister, and his daughter, and what was of concern
to them was of concern to him.

He was attracted by those whom he considered strong and good individuals. He greatly admired an Episcopal minister named Donald Aldrich, who
tried to run the Church of the Ascension on lower Fifth Avenue (my father
and his second wife Hellen were then living in a house on West 11th Street
that would be blown up fifty years later by an affluent female revolutionary
experimenting with explosives) as if it were a small town church, visiting the
sick and the shut-in, directing the money of his vestrymen to the needs of
poor families, keeping the church open twenty-four hours a day every day of
the year. In my father's last years he became friends with the doctor who
was his heart specialist, Samuel Levine, who had been born in Poland and
went through Harvard on a newsboy's scholarship and who used to swap
stories with the old man of what it was like to start out from the bottom.
Before he died, my father had the honor of establishing a chair at Harvard
Medical School in Dr. Levine's name.

He admired the British. For their sufferings in the First World War (it was always a loss for Dad that although he had been an advanced combat instructor at Kelly Field outside San Antonio, Texas, he had never gone overseas; in fact, he had even made the gesture of trying to volunteer, he said, for the American expeditionary force that went to Siberia). For their stolidity during the depression, their respect for a job well done and for the rules of class difference, the rules of weekend life at country homes and, of course, for their acceptance of sacrifice when war came again in 1939. One of the few men he disliked for moral reasons was Joseph Kennedy, not just because of some of the ways by which Kennedy had made his money, but because when he was ambassador he refused to believe that the British would fight or could win. In 1940 the three children of a Liverpool doctor came to live with him until the end of the war.

He scorned unnecessary regulations. One time around 1931 he was trying to reach Denver before his beloved sister Edith died. When a snowstorm grounded his airline plane in Cheyenne, he strode into the staff room and offered $1,000 in cash (he always carried a full wallet) to whoever would fly him to Denver. One pilot handed the bills to a friend to keep for him, or his widow, and in an open-cockpit biplane like the ones my father had flown in 1918, they took off through the storm, flying just above the hillcrests, every so often glimpsing a beacon in the valley. The Federal Aviation Administration was chartered to outlaw flights like that.

He liked novel ideas. He encouraged the careful organization of alumni giving at Amherst, and in judging any school would measure the loyalty of its alumni in their willingness to tithe themselves for it. Perhaps the first serious "think tank" in this country was at the summer sessions at The Orchard, the great white house in Southampton that he gave to Amherst in the early 1950s, where experts from business, universities, and government would meet together in an atmosphere of intensity and leisure to discuss economic problems.

The money that paid for the foundation came out of new approaches to traditional enterprises, like the raising of finance capital and the selling of food. Charles Merrill believed that a brokerage firm should be open (Merrill Lynch was the first firm to issue public financial statements), democratic (he had a fantasy of vans ringing bells like Good Humor wagons, parked at suburban curbsides, so that housewives could buy stocks on their way to the grocery), large enough to take advantage of economies of scale, its decisions supported by thorough research, and its executive staff specially trained. When the war and the postwar boom brought Wall Street out of its doldrums, Merrill Lynch had the new ideas to grow rapidly.

Out of a contract for Merrill Lynch to serve as underwriters for Safeway Stores, a Western grocery chain headquartered in Oakland, California, my father became fascinated by the whole process of food distribution. How could prices be cut and profits increased by integration, the firm establishing control of its own trucking and warehousing, setting up its own bakeries and breweries and coffee processing plants trying ever new methods of display and administration, publishing the *Family Circle* as a free magazine designed to meet the needs and set the tastes of the resourceful housewife? The store managers worked eighty-hour weeks but received rich bonuses for their successes. After his inspection tours Dad would write a letter to each manager who had been his host, congratulating him for the attractive canned pea exhibit and cautioning him about the meat, which looked a bit stale.

One result of Safeway's expansion was the destruction of the traditional mom-and-pop corner grocery, inefficient perhaps but independent. Another result of this enlargement of scale for every part of the food business was the replacement of the family farm by the agricorporation. In the same way, the expansion of Merrill Lynch meant the taking over of local brokerage firms, often quite old and reputable ones, by this giant corporation on Wall Street. My father played an important role in the concentration of the American economy, though that aspect of his career he did not discuss.

His involvement with giving started with responsibilities towards his mother's family, the Wilsons of Mississippi, who were always in need, and whose doctors' bills, mortgage payments, legal bills rich-Charlie-Merrill-who-lived-in-New York was willing to help meet. Early on he made sizable annual gifts to Amherst, to his parents' college of Maryville. He loaned money to dozens and dozens of young men for their education and usually forgot to ask for repayment. He wasn't much interested in female education though he was generous to the daughters of his old friends when they needed help. When my sister, my brother, and I were children, Dad used to send Christmas checks to the *Herald Tribune* Fresh Air Fund in our names—I remember how excited I was to see my name in the newspaper—to get us started in the habits of giving.

> If Charlie Merrill made his money out of the free enterprise system, and if the Trust which he established received and continues to receive most of its funds from the two companies which he established and built up, then we have no right to support individuals or programs whose main objective is to attack these companies or the economic system of which they are a part.

> He who pays the piper calls the tune.

That statement became almost an incantation at each meeting to veto appeals the more conservative trustees thought were in contradiction to Mr. Merrill's way of thought. The statement was logically correct. He was satisfied with his prejudices and liked to get his way. He had a hot temper and could be a frightening adversary but respected backbone, logic, and facts. He was intrigued by new ideas and elegant solutions to complicated problems.

Most of the time, he was pragmatic enough to adapt his thinking to the demands of a given situation—a line of reasoning I employed in our arguments about social policy.

Mr. Merrill was afraid that he belonged to the last generation of millionaires. The taxes and regulations fostered by the New Deal would prevent both the accumulation and retention of capital, and millionaires, like snow leopards, would become extinct. What they could contribute to the creativity and diversity of society would be lost.

> Glory be to God for dappled things—
> For skies of couple-colour as a brinded cow;
>
> . . . .
> All things counter, original, spare, strange
> Whatever is fickle, freckled (who knows how?)
> With swift, slow; sweet, sour; adazzle, dim;
> He fathers-forth whose beauty is past change: Praise him.

That complicated sonnet, *Pied Beauty*, by Gerard Manley Hopkins, offers an ideal for foundation policy. If God has created, or allowed to develop, a world of astounding diversity, with condors and orchids and snow leopards, it is in this interrelated beauty that He expresses His will. If through selfishness and stupidity men kill off all birds except the sparrow, starling, and herring gull and limit themselves to being computer programmers, file clerks, and police informers, then there is less proof that God exists.

Pluralism is not a word that my father's generation employed. It is a concept that he understood, though. America included Green Cove Springs and Amherst as well as Wall Street. It included scholars and artists and doctors as well as businessmen. Whatever his own beliefs, he was interested in what other people had to offer, and he gave the trustees of his foundation the authority to work out their own set of values. There are a lot of fine things we might have accomplished out of those resources if we had possessed better discipline and a more coherent sense of direction—which we didn't. But we did evolve, I think, an ideal of pluralism, a respect for things counter, original, spare, strange that we could strengthen and preserve and which would have interested the man who had supplied the money.

THE CAST OF CHARACTERS

Every man is a friend to him that giveth gifts. [Prov. 19:6]

When you die and try to get into Heaven, St. Peter will not waste his time asking about your petty personal vices and virtues. He will simply ask how you helped spend the money of the Rockefeller Foundation.

The anonymous caution to an anonymous trustee of that great foundation has realism to it as well as charm. What was done with the resources of the Merrill Trust came out of the personal lives of the individuals involved. We learned, usefully or negatively, from what we lived, from our childhoods, our service in the war. A man who has had to work his way through school holds a different attitude toward poverty—whether the man without a job goes on welfare because he drinks or because a textile corporation has moved its factories to Taiwan—than the man whose father paid for all his bills. To assume that a foundation, or university, corporation, government agency runs on interchangeable parts like a Chevrolet is self-delusion. If it is the truth, then that is worse.

When Charles E. Merrill died in October 1956 at the age of seventy he had already provided generously for his children and friends. His will stated that his residual estate of $35 million was to supply the capital of a charitable trust to last for twenty years. He appointed five trustees: Winthrop Smith, his long-time business associate, as chairman; Sam Marks, a Florida lawyer who had been his high school classmate; his son-in-law Robert Magowan, who was head of Safeway Stores in Oakland, California; Charles Cole, the president of Amherst College; and myself, his oldest son. We were men who had known him and his values, men whom he had known and trusted.

I became chairman after Win Smith died. My first contact with my father's world, my first historical memory, had been of the crash of 1929, when my questions "Where did all the money go? Who has it now?" went unanswered. During the 1930s I gave my loyalty to the New Deal and remember the disappointment that, despite all his acumen in business, my father seemed to have no awareness of any need for change in society or even action. If people became poor when the business cycle sagged, that was just that.

One August I paid a visit to the 3,000-acre plantation—Wildwood—in the Mississippi Delta that he had bought near his mother's birthplace of Lexington. The Young Master rode along the cotton fields, old black women would stop my horse and say that they had been my daddy's nurse, and I gave them a quarter. In the summer just before the war broke out I took a long European trip as far east as Warsaw and Bucharest. On a rainy Sunday afternoon in Vienna I walked through the Stadtpark, past rows of empty green benches and then a yellow one with four people seated silently on it which reminded me, in a way, of Mississippi. As an infantryman at the landing at Salerno I was lightly wounded—my union card.

After the war and graduation from Harvard, I taught at a boys' boarding school outside of St. Louis that I had helped start and, for perhaps the richest year of my life, was a Fulbright teacher in Austria. At the end of two years in Paris, I spent a week in Warsaw as it was emerging from the worst of the Stalinist years, which made a lasting impact upon my ideas of state and society. At the same time as the Merrill Trust was being organized, I opened my own school—Commonwealth—in Boston, and my daily experience teaching 125 three-dimensional adolescents (and helping to raise five children) was the reality by which I measured the theories of education.

My contact with blacks, in the South and in Boston, was part of my reality. How we whites acted toward this minority was a measure of American society. At the same time racial conflict forced upon Americans the need to make a conscious effort to change their basic assumptions, to face reality around them and inside themselves that a lucky people like the Danes would never need to know. Similarly, it is only by personal contact with dictatorships like Nazi Germany, Communist Poland and Czechoslovakia, Brazil and Turkey—I collected them—that one keeps aware of what freedom means. The architecture and music from the past, which my wife and I enjoyed so intensely in postwar Austria, must be preserved for the future. This presents a complicated linking of obligations: to the musicians, to the children taught to sing and fall in love with Mozart and Schubert, and to the hoodlums out on the streets and in bombing planes who will destroy what doesn't mean anything to them. So long as it did not become too timid about taking risks, a foundation like ours could recognize the complexity of society and work for change and justice.

Our first chairman was Winthrop Smith, an old and trusted Amherst friend of my father's, who was then head of Merrill Lynch. A practical, shrewd, kindly man with a clear mind, he was the one who steered the Trust, with the help of Henry Happel, our legal counsel, through incorporation and set up our administration. Since the Trust owned such a large part of Merrill Lynch, the Internal Revenue Service intended to tax its income, and our attorneys said that it would take from one to two years to get a bill through Congress allowing any exemption. Smith let Frank Boyden, headmaster of Deerfield Academy, which was one of the major beneficiaries, suggest to his old friend John McCormack, Speaker of the House in Eisenhower's administration, what was needed, in a bill passed that allowed all (unnamed) charitable trusts incorporated within a certain narrow time range to be so privileged. There was an implied quid pro quo involving, perhaps, massive support of a home outside Boston for wayward girls that McCormack's old friend, Cardinal Cushing, was then pushing, and which we slipped up on.

A second trustee was Sam Marks, friend of my father since their days at Stetson Academy together, a suspicious old man who lived in furnished rooms despite his wealth and whose social and intellectual interests were limited to a fifty-mile radius of Greater Jacksonville. He was angered by his colleagues' ideas ("We don't need to have the Jews come down and tell us how to treat the Niggers" is one remark I remember), but his contacts with Judge Knott ("Judge knott lest ye be judged" was a quiet joke that cheered Happel during the eighteen years of his service) in the interpretation of the Trust in Florida courts made him someone to treat carefully. An increase in his commission as executor of Mr. Merrill's estate, a post he shared with my sister, was related to his resignation as trustee in 1960, and Doris Magowan replaced him.

Charles Cole was president of Amherst at the time, and he felt that he had been put on the board by my father to safeguard the college's interests. He had earned a Ph.D. at Columbia in French history and retained a scholar's commitment to details of intellectual life—good libraries, fellowship programs to help serious students build a career, conferences to allow professionals to share ideas—and though he sided with me in my concern for Negro education, he was affronted by black nationalism's rejection of objective learning.

After leaving Amherst, and after two years with the Rockefeller Foundation in work related to Mexican wheat production, Dr. Cole was appointed by President Kennedy to be ambassador at Santiago. He acquired a great loyalty and respect for Chile and was intensely involved in its sufferings.

Cole loved western Massachusetts, its colleges and schools, the corporate life of its small towns, the efforts to preserve its meadows, woods, and rivers. His greatest love was fishing, which led him into every form of conservation, the crisis of the Atlantic salmon and the osprey, ecological struggles around Seattle, his last home. His fantasy was that if he could have maintained his Chilean contacts, our foundation might have backed a great project to stock those gorgeous mountain rivers, just like the ones Charlie had fished in Norway and Newfoundland, with salmon.

My brother-in-law, Robert Anderson Magowan, grew up in Philadelphia, where his father was a railway station master, and went to school at Kent in Connecticut under Father Sill, a place he admired tremendously for the simplicity and sincerity of its Christian discipline. Bob worked his way through Harvard, went to work for Macy's at the bottom of the depression, and worked for my father at Safeway and Merrill Lynch after he married my sister. During the war he was an intelligence officer on the aircraft carrier *Cowpens* in the Pacific. In 1953 the new administration sent him on a team to Saigon and Hanoi as a responsible Republican layman to make a personal evaluation of Indo-Chinese viability. "It is a corrupt, demoralized society—we should have nothing to do with the place" was his report.

In 1955 he became president of Safeway Stores. The company was in shambles. His predecessor was a brilliant but doctrinaire individual who had led Safeway into devastating price wars that had brought it to the verge of bankruptcy and also into a major criminal antitrust lawsuit. The expertise Magowan lacked with the grocery business was made up for by his insight, instincts, gutsiness to force change, and the realism, when he made a major

error, to admit it and change policy. He drove his subordinates there as hard
as he drove himself. He believed in the free enterprise system. If the money
the foundation spent came from that system, he argued, it was not our task
as trustees to back individuals who opposed it.

RAM had two sets of memo pads—one displaying a ram's head with a
frown and one with a smile. An executive's future at Safeway would depend
on the proportion of smiling versus frowning rams addressed to him.

In his loyalties Bob was probably closer to my father than were any of the
rest of us. He involved the foundation in that whole world west of the Rockies
and radiating out from San Francisco and Stanford University. He was proud
of his role of Good Citizen (though he did not use the term) of his city, and
of his support of the Mormon institutions in Utah and Idaho that received
the loyalty of so many Safeway executives. He was sensitive to social structure,
to the interlocking network of family and friends, colleagues and employees,
as well as of institutions that held society together and must be given support.
Henry Happel, the Trust's lawyer, described him as "impulsive, mercurial,
and a man of business who believed in the tenets of Horatio Alger and not
those of the Great Leap Forward or even Martin Luther King." He and I
clashed often and unhappily over racial and political issues, yet some of our
most important grants towards black needs—the first $100,000 to the United
Negro College Fund and the million dollars given through Stanford and Harvard business schools to support the training of black entrepreneurs—were
his proposals.

Doris Magowan joined the board after we negotiated old Sam Marks off
it. The most rewarding year of my sister's education had been the one she
spent at seventeen in Florence. It was at a traditional finishing school, but
the young ladies were immersed in Renaissance art and architecture, and for
Doris it started a lifelong love of art and a sympathy with Italian culture that
broadened later to French and English. With the opportunities this trust-
eeship gave her, she could contribute to every part of San Francisco life—
the De Young Museum, the opera and symphony and ballet, the concerts of
sacred music at St. Luke's, the botanical garden and the architectural society,
the hospitals and children's homes and youth agencies. In her girlhood well-
to-do families didn't concern themselves as much with the formal education
of their daughters as they would twenty years later, but Doris had the ability
to educate herself, and these foundation contacts led her further into new
fields perhaps than they did the rest of us: into hospital administration and
medical research, historic and nature conservation. She was particularly interested in the National Trust's conservation programs for historic houses and
gardens in England.

In Doris's love of beautiful and traditional things, there was a great sense
of responsibility. What we have been given we must help to pass on. Edu-

cation means learning not to take things for granted. She tried to share this belief with younger women who had the same privilege of money and time. Working for the foundation gave each of us a chance to say thank you for what we had particularly enjoyed: a cathedral in England, an opera performance, a friendship with a fine human being, and Doris's own enthusiasm for this privilege humanized our meetings.

Win Smith was replaced in 1961 by Donald Regan, then head of Merrill Lynch's Philadelphia office and soon to be president and chief executive officer of the firm. He had grown up in Cambridge and after graduating from Harvard had joined the Marines, rising to the rank of major in the anti-aircraft artillery, surviving the worst battles of the western Pacific. When the war ended he joined the new executive training program at Merrill Lynch that my father had thought out, and all his business life had been spent with the firm; in 1954, at thirty-five, he became the youngest partner in the firm's history.

Regan was one of the most brilliant men I ever met, with intellectual keenness expressed in a business framework, not the academic one I was used to. He had a clear, tough, cold, fair mind, with a breadth of view, a sensitivity to historical change I had not found in my father's friends. He was not only a Catholic but a Democrat, not usual among Merrill Lynch executives. In 1964, though supporting both presidential candidates, the firm leaned toward Johnson. In reply to my surprise: "LBJ gives us what we want. Goldwater would just rock the boat." If you clashed with him, as I did, you had better be sure of your facts. At the same time he found life a great source of enjoyment: becoming chairman of the board of the University of Pennsylvania, going to the White House to confer with Johnson and Carter, engaging in two weeks of talks with Japan's top corporate leadership, telling brash new Arab financiers what manners they would have to accept if they were going to stay in for the long haul, winning both the respect and the fear from men in that same profession. Regan's reward for this ability to see large problems clearly was to be appointed Secretary of the Treasury and later Chief of Staff at the White House by President Reagan. As the *New York Times Magazine* (January 5, 1986) stated, he reveled in the fact that he had risen to the pinnacle of success through aggressive gambles, bold ambition, and the fact that his critics had consistently underestimated his bureaucratic shrewdness, even cunning.

"I don't get ulcers—I give'em."

Don was fascinated by the way things worked and used the foundation for grants going into the millions to fund every sort of program to improve skills in administration. He had a sympathy for struggling Catholic colleges and hospitals and, despite Merrill Lynch's role and his own role in centralizing America's economic life into fewer and fewer larger and larger units, he went out of his way to look for obscure, vulnerable Appalachian and Midwest schools that stood for the independence and self-reliance of an older America.

As he described himself (*New York Times,* April 18, 1982): "I have a knack of being able to see things ahead of other people, and being right about what I see more often than not—sometimes wrong but never in doubt." He was not an economist, he stated, but a chooser of options.

For the last three years of the foundation, after Charlie Cole's death, the Magowans' third son, Peter, became trustee. He had been educated at Stanford, Johns Hopkins, and Oxford, been intrigued for a while by the State Department and the CIA, but entered Safeway, survived the brutal moving about by which American corporations dehumanize their executives (seven moves in ten years), and became chairman and chief executive officer in 1979 at thirty-seven. Toughened by long experience of bargaining with Safeway's unions, he involved himself in practical ways with minority needs, and partly out of his affection for his father-in-law, became interested in the problems of old people. He was concerned that too many Americans were caught up in unrealistic liberal criticisms and did not comprehend the problems and usefulness of business.

After Don Regan retired, my wife, Mary Merrill, who had also influenced very many of my own decisions, served as trustee for our final meeting. She was interested in textiles, libraries, theatre, archaeology, conservation, the problems of older women, and the value of small institutions run by people who could make their own decisions.

Our administrator for the entire life of the Trust was David Thomas, associate dean and eventually head of the Cornell School of Business and Public Administration. He was born in a West Texas town of 900 people, in arid, barren, harsh, violent country 200 miles north of Lyndon B. Johnson's hometown. The men were sunburned, grim, and muscular, but no matter what they had done during the week, they gathered without fail in the fundamentalist churches on Sunday morning. "One memory that stubbornly remains in my mind," Thomas wrote, "is of riding a horse in August 1932 in 114 degree heat looking for stray cattle and desperately trying to identify any talents I had that would get me away from there." He was the only one of the eight youngsters in his high school class to go on to college, Texas Technological in Lubbock. "College and I were compatible. Also, there I did not have to care for cattle." He became a combat staff intelligence officer in the Air Force, and was wounded at Iwo Jima while taking aerial photographs of Japanese installations against curtains of antiaircraft fire. In 1956 he obtained a Ph.D. at the University of Michigan in accounting, finance, and economics.

Dr. Thomas was a reserved, methodical, courteous man with strong feelings that he rarely showed. He was able to deal with the salesmen on foot and on paper (eventually 12,000 a year) who came to his office, and he ran the office that processed these grants at an expense average of 2.8 percent—a record for foundation administration. He became immunized to their arguments, for the rhetoric of salesmanship destroys the mind, but he retained a respect for and interest in people who accomplish something, who are straightforward and realistic and do not welch on their agreements. Dave went out of his way to study the questions we had to be knowledgeable about: New York City's sociology, Jewish sectarianism, juvenile delinquency and overpopulation, museums and women's colleges. He talked with cardinals and wrote careful reports to share with us what he had learned. He retained a prejudice against Texans for the narrowness of their interests and their self-aggrandizement. He respected scholarship and had a special sympathy for Jewish research proposals that reached him. He got along easily with blacks, but the bombast of black militancy that hit Cornell when he was acting dean of the business school and the timid confusion of the university's administration brought him the worst days of his professional life.

Nancy Culligan ran the office in Ithaca and held off paralysis and apoplexy from those 12,000 yearly appeals. She began working for Dr. Thomas as an eighteen-year-old fresh out of high school. American society suffers from the disease of credentialism: what degrees do you hold? Hers were energy, good sense, resourcefulness, and the ability to learn.

What did those decision makers basically care about? Each one of the 5,000 appeals we acted upon evoked some response that mixed intellectual interest, justice, compassion, self-concern, propriety. We were not the faceless bourgeois beloved of Marxists. But if one sought beyond an impersonal interest in elephants or diabetes research, what would one find? Preservation of the bell-shaped curve?

A good society can accept minorities of the poor and the rich at the two extremes if there are not too many of them. Society makes minimum concessions to the poor in education, health care, shelter, nourishment, and some countries (Sweden, New Zealand) handle this better than others (Brazil, the United States). The rich are able to look after themselves and rig the system to their benefit so they get a private room at Mass. General.

But what can allow the great majority of people in the middle—John Adams's home owners, Thomas Jefferson's independent farmers—to believe that they have a stake in society? Is the answer a society that helps the able and hard working to get ahead through education, that offers ways to express religious values, that allows a sharing of civilization's culture, that offers medical care not as charity nor as the luxury of the rich, but as something one can plan ahead for? Is there a place for both freedom and security? If you play by the rules, are you reasonably rewarded?

At all the discussions about whether to say yes or no, there were invisible young men present in the same room, the young men who had been des-

perately anxious to get out of small-town Florida, the lackluster streets of
Philadelphia and North Cambridge, the Texas cattle ranch at 114-degree
heat. When my father was a boy his four-year-old sister Mary fell sick and
died because her father the doctor did not have money for the medicines, or
the equipment and skill that might have saved her—a loss he never forgot,
just as he never forgot the humiliation (he came back over and over to that
word) of being poor at Amherst.

DAY BY DAY

Seize each opportunity to be useful with rapturous assiduity.   [Cotton Mather]

O for the reign of universal benevolence! I want to make all mankind good and
happy.   [Mr. Fanton in William McGuffy's *Newly Revised Eclectic Reader*,
1834]

In their sphere [the foundations] have an obligation of standardsetting, of lifting
hearts and hopes. As in the case of great concert artists, it is not sufficient that
they arrive at the performance on time, play in key, and remember to thank
their accompanist.   [Waldemar Nielsen, *The Golden Donors*]

Saul Alinsky, the radical community organizer from Chicago, liked to tell the
story of a wealthy Italian immigrant who, dying without heirs, willed all his
money to his native village south of Naples. He didn't endow a clinic or a
school. He just left X million dollars to be divided equally among every man
and woman in the village. As any sociologist will warn you, this would end
in a saturnalia. The ignorant peasants would spend it all on fiestas, weekends
in Naples, bright red cars, and then, the windfall thrown away, would face
the hangover of wasted opportunities.

Not true. With few exceptions the villagers spent their funds wisely: paying
off a mortgage, buying a tractor, repairing the roof, sending a bright boy off
to school, visiting the children in Chicago—objectives that the family had
been discussing for years. Alinsky took pleasure in describing the indignation
of social workers who saw these bumpkins spend their undeserved riches in
such sober ways, without ten lire put out in professional consultation. And
for the villagers, they had not only enriched their lives through these windfalls
and made their village a more humane place to live in, they had acquired a
new confidence from this proof that they knew how to manage their lives
effectively.

Alinsky's irreverence towards sociologists, his respect for the good sense
of ordinary people, made this story a favorite of mine. He also illustrated the
patterns of judgment, good and bad, of the Charles E. Merrill Trust. With
few exceptions, we did not hire outside experts to examine a field or a project

we were considering nor to evaluate what we had accomplished. That might have been a sensible expenditure of money, wiser in the long run than our insistence in keeping down administrative costs: burning candles to our ikon of 2.8 percent. We also rejected almost any articulation of priorities from within the committee. As academics, Charlie Cole and I drew up lists of how we might decide upon the most important institutions or the most rational ways of facing, meeting by meeting, the different needs of a major problem. It never worked.

Any line of policy that suggested constraint was listened to and then ignored. The trustees would select a general field: we ought to take care of major Protestant and Jewish seminaries, Canadian universities because most American foundations ignore them, the major zoos, symphony orchestras, black colleges, drug programs, population control agencies; and at each of the twice-yearly meetings Dave Thomas would present a write-up of an example or two from these categories. There were appeals from Merrill Lynch vice-presidents—for a wife who was head of the Ladies' Guild of St. Mary's Hospital in Cincinnati—and from Safeway branch managers in Salt Lake City. There were appeals from business colleagues of Bob Magowan and Don Regan, from old friends of Doris Magowan, former students of Charlie Cole and myself. And from screwballs and salesmen so importunate that we promised $5,000 just to get them the hell out of the office.

This form of scattered, ad hoc, old-boy-network way of doing business is despised by critics of establishment foundations as the reason why their expenditures, on the whole, don't have much effect. To an extent I agree—and so would the other Merrill trustees.

On the other hand, the second lesson from Alinsky's village tale is that life is not rational. It cannot be planned out too carefully. The corporation executives, social workers, Communist officials who place a rigid grid of expectations upon the exasperating (and sometimes entertaining) complexity of human life cause a lot of misery and often muck up adequate solutions that would probably have appeared if people had been left alone. In my own reasoning, in this six-year task of writing what I first thought would be a rather simple book, I go back and forth between a belief in discipline and an acceptance of serendipity.

If we had concentrated on the field of low-cost urban housing, on development projects in the black South or in Mexico to prevent their refugees from scrambling into our cities, on projects to upgrade academic excellence and social responsiveness within 200 different public and parochial high schools, we might have accomplished something tangible we could point to with pride.

We couldn't. We were restricted, to a certain extent, by the structure of Mr. Merrill's document and the conservatism of his social values. We were restricted by the differences of the five trustees' political convictions, social priorities, and intellectual and esthetic tastes. And along with having to survive in a society where a large number of people knew that we controlled a large amount of money and wanted very much to share it, we were sustained perhaps by a sort of realistic modesty. We would try to make sensible decisions. We would listen to another trustee's proposal and try to understand the reason behind its importance to him. If we made some dumb mistake, we hoped that the money was not completely wasted, and we would try to do better next time.

Waldemar Nielsen's *The Big Foundations* (commissioned by the Twentieth Century Fund and first published in 1972 by Columbia University) is an excellent study of the thirty-three American foundations with assets exceeding $100 million. Nielsen criticizes these foundations for their timidity, lethargy, self-serving and self-praise, as well as often simple mismanagement. The Merrill Trust was well run and honestly run, but I recognize ourselves in his criticisms.

We issued no reports. We were unimpressed by the theory of accountability. It was *our* money. Annual reports would have exposed us to even more seagulls squalling around the stranded whale. We scorned the glossy-brochure puffery of other foundations praising their social goodness. Now I believe that a report every two or three years would have been useful in forcing us to measure what we had done and might do. A rule that no single trustee could serve for more than five years at a time would have encouraged wider and fresher participation.

Against Mr. Merrill's admonition and our own warnings, we did scatter our grants. This looseness increased after 1970, partly because we were moving into new fields—environment, arts, drugs (we cut back on seminaries and black projects)—where small grants would be applicable, even though inflation had reduced the value of a $10,000 check. We felt bruised by the constant demands for gifts. Earlier on we had set up a rule that three years must pass before a second grant to the same institution would be considered. This obstructed sustained support of what was important but protected our freedom of action from the greedy. There were days when I was running my school with my left hand while trying to appease or deflect those applicants. We began to doubt our judgment.

Because we got tired of our disagreements and disillusioned by the major decisions we had collaborated on—"As soon as we launch one of those big birds off the drawing board we get hit by its clay feet"—the solution was a system of quotas. If $1.5 million might be available next meeting, that meant $300,000 apiece. In a way the Trust became a confederation of five semi-autonomous mini-foundations.

That form of decentralization—"self-indulgent anarchy!"—was easy to criticize, but it met reality. It also allowed us to integrate our own patterns of giving: the institutions might be many in number but fitted coherent categories. We respected one another's concerns, formed alliances: Charlie Cole and I collaborated on Latin America, my sister and I on the environment.

Of course, once we had liquidated that angry redneck, old Sam Marks, the two wealthy businessmen, two academics, and the founder's daughter comprised the Establishment board resented by radicals and populists, rich and poor, for its predictable commitments: the standard Northeastern colleges, preparatory schools, and seminaries, major hospitals, museums, symphonies, two or three libraries, the United Negro College Fund, Planned Parenthood, a few of the older settlement houses and agencies like the Fresh Air Fund, the Foreign Policy Association, Westminster Abbey and the American Hospital in Paris, Audubon. That's it!

Forty percent of this trust's income had to go to eight named beneficiaries: Amherst received half that amount (eventually over $12 million, almost all put into endowment) and Deerfield Academy in western Massachusetts received a quarter (about $5.5 million), with smaller fractions going to Stetson University in Florida (whose preparatory school Mr. Merrill had attended), Kenyon College in Ohio (because he respected its president), and four hospitals (St. Luke's and New York in New York City, Saint Mary's and Good Samaritan in West Palm Beach). The remaining 60 percent of income was divided equally among education, religion (10 percent Protestant, 5 apiece Catholic and Jewish), and established charitable, scientific, or religious institutions with a substantial portion of such funds to be devoted to medical and surgical research. The first measurement of any appeal was whether it helped people to help themselves. That insistence upon responsible individuals, the Protestant ethic, marked Charles E. Merrill's whole philosophy and supplied, I would say, the focal point of twenty-three years of trustee argument.

Outside of these category percentages, the only two formal limitations were that the moneys of the Trust should all be disbursed within twenty years (Mr. Merrill distrusted self-perpetuating bureaucracies) and a rule that any institution had to be in operation for at least three years before it could be considered. He trusted a track record more than he did promises. In actuality, therefore, there were no legal restrictions to whatever decision the trustees chose to make, which turned out to be the strength and the weakness of the Trust in its twenty-three years of operation.[1]

I hated to see all those millions in income going to Amherst and Deerfield (though the percentages fell when we were distributing capital), but in reality those required categories did not limit our freedom. In fact, the required

1. When Merrill Lynch stock went public in 1972 and our capital tripled, briefly, the trustees asked court permission to extend its life to twenty-five years.

Catholic and Jewish 5 percent opened doors that a committee like ours would never have noticed: Catholic women's colleges and Latin American cooperatives, Jewish services to the aged and the last dictionary of Yiddish.

Categories are not important. It is the sensitivity and precision in seeking out some institutions rather than others within any category that make the difference between standard and unusual foundations. The very procedures adopted by foundations to protect administrative tidiness against each day's ravening army of kooks and deadbeats—the office on the fortieth floor, the steely-eyed receptionist, the large wastebaskets and printed rejection letters—will ensure B+ efficiency but not A-level creativity.

How wide is a foundation's screen? What sort of people do the trustees know? An officer or trustee of an imaginative foundation should resemble the old-fashioned newspaperman who hung around bars and followed up intriguing remarks until he landed The Story, even if in the meantime his wife had gone home to her mother. The pressures we resented so much—the letter from a former employee or student, the cheerful invitation to lunch (you can get a good lunch for $25,000), the carefully random remarks at a party—all were means of breaking the limitations of administrative order. Our children became a conduit. In the early 1970s it seemed important to persuade young people that their opinions were respected. One Magowan son was an ornithologist, a second was involved in the theatre, a third, through his wife, in Israel. My oldest son lived in Salt Lake City and made contact with a counterculture world that had little in common with what Safeway's Mormon vice-presidents knew.

What sort of appeal did we turn down? Most from Texas. A new medical center near Los Angeles called the City of Hope with a brochure as pretentious as the name. Requests, at first, from Yale, Wesleyan, Cal Tech, and MIT because their vast endowments would demean our standard $25,000. Institutions that had too parochial an appeal: individual churches and camps, private academies in the South set up to evade integration, the scholarship fund of the Serbian Eastern Orthodox Church. The March of Dimes. A blind charismatic whose life's dream was to build a great monument to Stonewall Jackson. Public television, a bottomless pit.

The name of the Association for the Study of Abortion scrubbed that. Was the Environmental Defense Fund involved with Ralph Nader, hurting Merrill Lynch's relations with General Motors? The National Rifle Association's youth self-reliance project sounded plausible, but none of us could stomach the Association. In 1966 the Delta Ministry asked us to help purchase an abandoned Air Force base in Mississippi to create a town for dispossessed agricultural workers and a job training center for young adults on their way to Chicago and Detroit. An inspired idea, but it did not touch our trustees.

Bob Magowan was intrigued by Harding College in Searcy, Arkansas—

"the West Point of the ultra-right"—for its aggressive defense of the free enterprise system, but he agreed not to propose it if I did not put up the Black Panthers.

Americans are proud of their allergy to theory—we aren't French intellectuals—but our foundation's fifty or more meetings were torn by arguments over quite abstract theories.

For example, do you back winners or losers? Do you establish a scholarship program for the best students in West Palm Beach or Sacramento, the best artists in East Los Angeles or Harlem? Don't waste $10,000 to salvage a birth-injured child or heroin addict. Write him off. Society, whether represented by the Charles E. Merrill Trust or the City of New York, does not have infinite resources. Put your money where it will do the most good. Or, does concern for the insulted and injured show a compassion that makes all society more humane? Even the winners need to know that when they become losers they are not expendable.

Are you sympathetic to nostalgia or to change? Do you look back to a simpler America and give money to Berea College in mountain Kentucky? Should you support beleaguered ethnic neighborhoods in Chicago and renovation of beautiful old buildings? Private wealth which is not forced to give rational justification for everything it does can indulge itself in this form of nostalgia which allows continuity and diversity instead of leaving society at the mercy of the bulldozer. A wholesome way of expressing nostalgia may immunize society against pathological nostalgia, the sort of Shintoism that is the worship of oneself, the fundamentalism that seeks refuge in rigid symbols: the flag, the church where Mother prayed, Our Kind of People, the old neighborhood which maybe never existed, and whose defense may in reality be a disguise for very up-to-date prejudice.

A foundation's policy towards blacks—and add the Spanish-speaking—is the surest way for measuring its attitude towards change. A reactionary foundation makes an annual grant to the United Negro College Fund just to stay out of trouble. A conservative one contributes to the Harlem School of the Arts, Morehouse College, an Urban League job-training program because it knows that only by giving opportunity or hope to this troublesome minority can there be any hope of stability for whites as well as blacks. A liberal foundation brings new cadres—a Marxist term—into the ruling class, not as symbols, but in numbers large enough to redirect the values of society. Any program like this costs big money and after a while begins to step on people's feet who happen to be friends or customers of the trustees.

And if one goes further and allies oneself with radicals who feel that society is so brutal, exploitative, or corrupt that mere local improvements and changes in leadership are inadequate, then one gets in real trouble. Radicals are usually poor administrators, make vulgar noises, put in their own pockets

the funds supplied by the gullible ("Why not, it's owing us!"), have run-ins
with the police. How does one respect the independence of radical leaders,
their anger, their freedom to learn by making their own mistakes and still
not be taken for a fool? Foundations should talk more seriously about class
conflict than they do. Do programs directed towards helping the poor serve
essentially as cosmetics ("See, isn't the American system a nice one after
all?"), as safety valves (co-opting radicals[2] with good jobs, offering a few isolated symbols of change), or are they meant to accomplish something of importance? At whose expense? With what ultimate goal?

A third theoretical conflict comes between the followers of Harold Ickes
or Harry Hopkins. In *Roosevelt and Hopkins,* Robert Sherwood gives a fascinating picture of the conflict between the two men within the leadership
of the New Deal. Ickes as Secretary of the Interior was responsible for the
major investments: dams, highways, housing projects. He believed in ex-
haustively researching the needs, making meticulous plans, retaining meticulous control. He was proud of the Department of the Interior's record of
spending hundreds of millions of dollars with little waste, almost no corruption, and with a relative absence of blatant politics. The only drawback was
that if these public works were being constructed to give jobs to men out of
work right now, those unemployed died of starvation before the checks got
written and the shovels handed out.

Harry Hopkins, director of the Works Progress Administration, had a different sort of mind: impatient, impassioned. Things had to be built—a play-
ground, a post office, a road—*now*. Men had to have jobs and people had to
eat. The priority was speed. If the project wasn't always carefully planned,
if a certain amount of money found its way into private pockets, if jobs were
handed out through channels that supported the Democratic party, well, that
was that. The priority was to have the unemployed member of society be
given a useful job, pushing a wheelbarrow, painting a post office mural (artists
eat too) as quickly as possible.

All of us are either Ickesians or Hopkinists, or both at different times.
Where does a foundation plan things and ask careful questions, and a year
later ask to see what the money accomplished? Where does it stress imagination, sympathy, a rapid response, and make mistake after mistake?

The most important conflict involves the ways Democracy is defined. Is it
the will of the majority or the rights of the minority? Democracy means both,
of course, but which do you emphasize? Rich people stress the rights of the
minority, and their definition of the state is the institution that protects the
rich against the demands of the poor. Or, on the other hand, is the state's
function, as in Sweden and New Zealand, to equalize the discrepancies of

2. Leroy Jones called them "poverty pimps."

income, services rendered, and style of life between rich and poor at the price of high taxation and all-encompassing controls? The American compromise is to encourage a responsible generosity whereby the wealthy are encouraged by tax credits and emulation—Mellon and his museum, Morgan and his library—to meet in a more haphazard way society's needs. The American system allows an opportunity not only to the inspired nut but also to the idea that does not fit the state budget and its carefully bargained-out set of priorities.

These questions bring our discussion to the Tax Reform Act of 1969, which represented this century's major assault on foundation autonomy.[3] "Foundations have long been aware of their political vulnerability. But with the characteristic insensitivity of aristocratic institutions to new social trends, they have consistently misconceived its basis. They have tended to attribute it to 'public misunderstanding' of their good works or their 'lack of constituency,' ignoring the fact that they are highly visible examples of special privilege accorded to the very rich by an inequitable tax system that is increasingly resented by the general public."[4]

This Wright Patman Act (its other name) was a long time coming and represented a wide range of complaints. One was concern over excessive involvement of foundations in business and the manipulations by them to serve various private purposes of the donors. If, upon his death, a wealthy entrepreneur could lock up his company's stock holdings within a foundation, then his heirs, both family and corporate, continued to control the business instead of seeing their power dissipated by taxation, and by withholding the payment of any substantial income to charity as long as possible, they could retain this control indefinitely.

Another concern was a cumulative resentment against the indiscriminate hodgepodge of tax exemptions. In 1965 it was estimated that the Internal Revenue Service was monitoring the exemptions of 400,000 nonprofit organizations and 700,000 subsidiaries.[5] This keeps up taxes for ordinary people by eroding the tax base[6] and proves the point that the wealthy possess the resources to get around the theory of progressivity at the legislative level by skilled lobbying and at the enforcement level by skilled legal counsel.

The Merrill Trust tried to maintain a low profile during this controversy, though Henry Happel, our lawyer, made many trips to Washington. Perhaps

3. Most of this material comes from Nielsen's *The Big Foundations.*

4. Nielsen (p. 365), attributed to Louis Survey in *Life* (August 15, 1969).

5. Nielsen (p. 369), attributed to Marion Fremont-Smith, *Foundations and Governments* (New York: Russell Sage Foundation, 1965), p. 407.

6. A common cause for the collapse of Chinese dynasties was that the emperors traditionally assigned exemption from taxes in perpetuity to their wives' relatives. When too many exemptions had accumulated, the people rebelled, and a new emperor was chosen who wiped the board clean, except for his own in-laws.

too much of our capital was in Merrill Lynch stock, but essentially representatives of the Patman Committee considered us Good: (1) we had a firm termination date; (2) we had low administrative costs—that 2.8 percent which Waldemar Nielsen felt condemned us to triviality; and (3) we avoided withholding income in order to turn it into further capital. By 1966 returns the Trust ranked 120th in assets among American foundations, but by total value of grants it was 45th. The main impact of the bill upon our grant-making policy was to make us even more cautious. When I proposed one more controversial black project, I was warned that the I.R.S. would cause trouble. We individual trustees could be fined for improper behavior and the Trust lose its charter.

The Budget Reform Act of 1985, first presented by the former Merrill trustee Donald Regan when he was Secretary of the Treasury, presents another set of problems. By reducing the highest tax upon income to 38 percent from the 70 percent of a few years ago, it offers less incentive to the very wealthy to make tax-deductible gifts to charity. By denying to all taxpayers credit for the first 2 percent of charitable giving, it hurts institutions like churches supported by a large number of small gifts from ordinary people. A law this important comes at a time when nonprofit institutions are already in trouble.

A trustee's work was always interesting, and through the foundation we met unusual individuals and found ourselves involved in institutions and crusades we would never otherwise have known. We talked endlessly about our terminal date: how could we be sure that we had Done Something Significant? We were surprised to have lasted as long as 1981. Exciting new projects did show up: a feminist group in New York that was attacking the porno industry, a one-man crusade for animal rights against unnecessary cruelty by lab testing and food processing, a Chinese exchange program at a Mennonite college in Indiana. Nevertheless, it was clear that we were becoming tired, and showed it by becoming bureaucratic and cranky.

As I was recently rereading *The Conservative Mind* by Russell Kirk, first published in 1953, which went on to become the intellectual foundation of the Right's counterattack upon establishment Liberalism, I was struck by our unconscious identification with Edmund Burke—namely, his *Reflections on the Revolution in France*, his *Appeal from the Old to the New Whigs*, and his diatribes against Jean-Jacques Rousseau (an insufferable upstart with a bladder problem that made him so ill at ease in society that he sought refuge in sentimental abstractions). Burke expressed a complicated conservatism that seemed re-expressed in the conversations at Palm Beach and Southampton.

He had an affection for the proliferating variety and mystery of traditional life as distinguished from the narrowing uniformity and egalitarianism and the utilitarian aims of most radical systems. Civilized society requires orders and classes. The only true equality is moral equality. Property and freedom are inseparably connected. Tradition and sound prejudice provide checks upon man's anarchic impulse. Innovation is a devouring conflagration more often than it is a torch of progress. The state is a divinely ordained moral essence, a spiritual union of the dead, the living, and those yet unborn. To follow a shallow notion of human perfectability in order to wrench it from its traditional patterns would be to cause immoderate harm.

How very true.

CHAPTER TWO

The Private School?

First to find a spacious house and ground about it fit for an academy and big enough to lodge a hundred and fifty persons . . . all under the government of one who shall be thought of desert sufficient and ability to do all or wisely to direct and oversee it done.

Milton, *Of Education*

In large and small ways the Merrill Trust funded almost fifty private boarding schools for a total of $9.4 million, thirty of them in New England accounting for $8.7 million, including $5.5 million that went to Deerfield Academy. The Trust funded eighty or more day schools, mainly near Boston, New York, and San Francisco, for a total of $3.3 million. Receiving $350,000 were eleven day schools, where the grants went primarily for black students (see Chapter 5, under *Black and White*). It includes grants to Jewish schools and Catholic schools serving what I would call the typical private school clientele. That adds up to $12.7 million for about 125 institutions.

That amount does not include the $420,000 given to large parochial schools in New York, Chicago, and San Francisco which served more or less the same type of families as the public schools did. Our aid to public schools, in the form of teacher training programs and cultural services like Young Audiences, came to about $650,000.

Breaking down the Merrill Trust's investment in primary and secondary education on the basis of social class, as comprehensive a measurement as I can think of in looking at these statistics, we gave about $12.7 million to

education of students from the middle class and about $1.1 million to those
from the lower-middle and working class. Even omitting that huge Deerfield
gift, this is a larger investment in private precollege education than for most
foundations of our size ($114 million total expenditure). What did that money
accomplish? We strengthened a number of institutions, allowed them to be
more democratic, and set higher standards in the range of students they
accepted. We gave money for faculty salaries so that tuition and scholarships
were not subsidized, as all too often, by the salaries that the teachers and
their wives in their worn tweeds were willing to accept. Money went too for
libraries and laboratories, new plumbing and wiring, art supplies, administrative reorganization, sports facilities, experiments with new ideas in curriculum, community service, international outreach.

Many individuals as well as institutions were aided. Were we merely
strengthening class privilege? In the United States, whose democratic school
system is in crisis, should we not have spent that $12.7 million, imaginatively
and forcefully, in support of public schools?

THE BOARDING SCHOOL

Our twelve most favored boarding schools were Deerfield—$5,545,000;
Kent—$1,176,000; Ethel Walker—$380,000; Wooster—$182,000; Williston
Northampton—$176,000; Groton—$150,000; Northfield-Mount Hermon, St.
Mark's, and Taft—$115,000 each; Emma Willard in upstate New York and
Lawrenceville in New Jersey—$80,000 each; Nyack Boys School—$95,000.

The origins of such schools and their place in American education are complex enough that it is hard to state exactly why families send their children
there and why foundations give them money. The Episcopal boarding
schools—Groton, St. Paul's, St. Mark's—modeled themselves deliberately on
an English model, with a mix of religion and money, discipline and tradition
that would create as rapidly as possible institutions based upon and creating
caste. It took money and Groton plus Harvard to create a gentleman. Two
of the three alone were insufficient.

Another origin was the New England academy, a day school partly supported by the local town but which also included boarders, and examples of
these were Deerfield and the two Phillips Academies at Andover and Exeter.
When a Massachusetts law in the 1920s forbade any public subsidy of such
academies, Deerfield almost collapsed. It was the tremendous need of its
headmaster, Frank Boyden, to find alternative sources of backing for a school
which had never had wealthy patrons that supplied the energy to put Deerfield into the varsity group. There was also around Philadelphia a Quaker
tradition that created Germantown Friends and George and their followers.

Schools originated on the funding of a single wealthy man or a group of families because the local public schools had poor academic standards, sloppy discipline, or too many members of unrespected ethnic groups. Boarding schools exist, as in Dickens's novels, to take care of unwanted children whose parents prefer to go on Caribbean vacations, have a divorce, or put on someone else's shoulders their son's alcohol habits and their daughter's coming-home hours. In a state like Oklahoma, when I first started to teach in 1946, to say one's daughter was away at boarding school could be code that she was pregnant.

In the 1980s a stated goal of the left wing of the Labour Party was to abolish the nonstate schools. It is no longer enough to dilute their homogeneity with large numbers of students on government scholarships as has been true since 1945. Out of their influence, more than from any other source, come the class barriers that imprison English society, the argument runs, and there is no chance of building a democracy with understanding and respect going beyond class until these schools are destroyed.

The truly snobbish American schools were never important enough to be taken seriously. An opulent campus filled with the sons of millionaires seems ridiculous, not threatening. It is true, nevertheless, that the assumptions of these boarding schools, which place upon their adolescent students a deliberate isolation from the ordinary world of the public high school, gave these places a quality of caste. "We want them to grow into people like ourselves," their parents silently said, and the result is the "preppy," with his special rules of behavior, dress, manner, accent, who never tries too hard but assumes that he is entitled to a first-class ticket to whatever worthwhile event life offers.

The god of these schools was sports. And yet a school like Deerfield, where I went for three years, was humane about the devotion. If we were ordered to attend the varsity football and basketball matches, so also was there a team for every boy in school, down to the lowest two-left-feet level, with a tiny paragraph in *The Scroll* to mention his winning goal. There were other respected channels—the debating and glee clubs, the paper, an increasing range of offerings in the arts—where a boy with any skill and drive could make a name for himself and learn the skills of speaking in public or meeting a deadline that he might employ all of his life.

The schools all had some involvement with Protestant observance. At Deerfield this meant sermons on "make Jesus Christ your shortstop in the baseball game of life," but also a lifelong remembrance of twenty or so hymns, the ones we sang at the Sunday evening services led by Mr. Boyden, that I was grateful for. At its worst, compulsory religion could be one more force for conformity, like the courses in Marxist-Leninism in Communist schools. It indulged the histrionic extravagance of the headmaster: how many Groton

boys grew up to think of God as Endicott Peabody! As John Verdery of Wooster described his efforts to portray God's concerns for His world, it was hard
not to make Him sound like the headmaster of an Episcopalian boarding
school. But for my brother-in-law, Father Sill of Kent formed his understanding of Christianity: a sense of responsibility for others and for the community,
a need to look further than oneself, a definition of what was a good human
being.

Accordingly, one great appeal of the boarding school at its theoretical best
was to expose boys (and though there were girls' schools, it was essentially,
in America as in England, a male institution) to men of high caliber. Carlisle's
phrase that an institution is the lengthened shadow of a great man was used
and overused to justify a hagiography not to be equaled until the communist
and third-world nations after 1945: the Great Man, in tweed or clerical robes,
with a ho-ho-ho that only Episcopalians employ, with an ability to deliver
Truth from the mountain and a total lack of interest in what did not come
within his tradition.

With Frank Boyden I was exposed to a master. He grew in memory compared to heads I met later on, so anxious to please, to be in step with the
latest social or psychological fad. He knew his own values, he stressed an
integrity of character hard to define that I think stuck with his boys, a readiness to deliver the goods as they were rather than as they were promised to
be. Mr. Boyden and his wife (an ungainly, almost blind woman who taught
math and chemistry, loved music, extended kindness to marginal boys, and
showed a humorous lack of awe towards her husband) were beyond criticism.
There was only one rule, to please The Head, and there was no way to oppose
him, as much as if we lived in East Germany.

Plato, India, Poland, Tanzania offer other insights to these schools. The
starting point for the sons of millionaires who would grow up to run Dad's
business were Books VII and VIII of *The Republic*, the education of the philosopher kings, and the discipline of athletics, of mathematics and dialectic,
the control of sex, the emulation by the young of the old.

Interestingly enough, the second step is India. India was, in a way, a great
boarding school ruled by English prefects. The Indian Civil Service was a
creature of classics scholars who trained the Guardians, the head boys of
Charterhouse and Shrewsbury, who went out and ruled the natives in an
upright, honest, disciplined way, as respectful of their customs and weaknesses as they were of the twelve-year-olds in the first form.

It was not until after 1945 when I made a number of visits to Eastern
Europe that I realized how these communist states and the new nations of
Asia and Africa modeled themselves after New England boarding schools.
There were the same totalitarian societies: no one could stand up to the will

of the headmaster. All this is being done for your own good. The socialist countries, like the boarding schools, had different personalities and different levels of control. Mount Hermon, like Poland, accepted a greater give to the system than did Groton or Romania, Nyerere of Tanzania believed in an ideal of service similar to Father Sill's of Kent. With his cigars and love of baseball and getting everyone out to cut sugar cane, Castro would have been interchangeable with any one of a dozen headmasters. Both types of institutions were bothered by Jews, girls, and intellectuals. Their chapel talks were almost interchangeable in the sins they warned of, pounding their fists upon the lectern or whispering the awful syllables of masturbation and revisionism.

These closed societies, however, could not protect themselves from a changing world. By the 1970s American schools were badly hurt. In my own school, Commonwealth, any fourteen-year-old knew more about the details of drug use than I did. It established a zone of mistrust that hurt the whole community, whether the administration turned itself into a police state or tried to look the other way. The new black students did not fit in. Some played ball with the system and sang in the glee club and let themselves be made captains of the varsity teams. Others felt driven to fight and deride the liberals who played up to them and the conservatives who tried to discipline them. And girls—Plato and Mr. Boyden were right: they confused the system and would not give the brainless loyalty that boys did.

And yet it was a powerful figure like Bruce McClellan of Lawrenceville, the last, by the 1980s, of the great headmasters, with a stature, longevity, and authority that his ill-at-ease peers lacked, who saw a reality that the system served. No matter what the feminists argued, in contemporary America it was the father image that was fading, through divorce, through the demands of careerism, the time spent in getting a doctorate or going to conferences, through the family disruptions as Dad was moved from Portland to Peoria. Maybe the headmaster and the best of the teachers at these schools gave a sense of manly forcefulness, perhaps even joy, that American society lacked.

Let's go further. If the threat to America is the domination of unequal wealth, then the private school that gives better education to the children of the wealthy simply perpetuates privilege. The trustees of the Merrill foundation were defending a class position. Our scholarship grants helped the unfortunate or less affluent members within that class—the children of teachers, ministers, army officers, widows, divorcees—priced out of the market as tuitions climbed over $8,000. And because the American ruling class is often intelligent, wealthy individuals and foundations made sizable gifts to bring in outsiders—children of Negroes and immigrants, factory workers and tradesmen, because those outsiders make the schools realistic and interesting for their own children and because such a policy appealed to their concepts of justice and democracy. An effective society has to run on more than cynical self-interest.

Or, if you *are* cynical, an endowment that allows Andover to accept the bright son of a Negro janitor or a Jewish tailor and reject the dumb soft son of a Scarsdale stock broker has co-opted the potential leadership of the opposition. A bright youngster like that, who will keep on getting scholarship aid through college and graduate school, serves the system which has treated him well. In a crisis America may respond better than Britain or France did in 1940 just because its leadership class is more able and diversified.

On the other hand, if the real danger to American democracy, as Alexis de Tocqueville concluded back in the 1830s, comes from egalitarian conformity, then the exclusiveness of private schools, even in their totalitarian versions, has a role to play if that snobbery is based on higher standards and a respect for independence, not simply money and manners.

Excellence is a cheapened word. It is always interpreted to be whatever the speaker can do well. Somewhere along the line, however, a youngster who is going to amount to anything in life has got to be challenged by that concept, and not simply in sports. What can the mind accomplish, not in rote skills but in analysis and imagination, the dealing with precise and subtle shades of meaning, the joy of learning as opposed to "Will it be on the test?" What can the *will* accomplish when it is so much easier to quit? What is the freedom of learning as expressed by teachers who are excited by what they do and are unafraid?

Deerfield Academy, Deerfield Massachusetts, 1959–1983—$5,500,000. Deerfield is a wealthy, well-equipped, well-run school in western Massachusetts. It possesses handsome resources, including a million-dollar hockey rink, a $1.8 million library and a wonderful $2.8 million science building. There has always been a heavy atmosphere of money, but a generous scholarship policy does leaven the class mix, and the homogeneity of dress and manner, the schoolboy democracy of homework, sports, jobs for everyone like waiting on tables or putting up and taking down the bleachers do militate against snobbery. Most of the faculty in my day were competent rather than distinguished, and there was little encouragement for a critical intellect in the classroom, but any fine teacher was honored.

Deerfield is still the story of one man, Frank Boyden, and my father's friendship with Mr. Boyden was the reason for that amount of money given the school. Any evaluation of the school is so tied up with Boyden, and Boyden's life is so involved with myth, that an objective analysis of Deerfield is surprisingly difficult to reach. It began in 1799, as the official seal states, one of those little academies all over New England, partly supported by fees, partly by town appropriations. Boyden came there in 1903, right out of Amherst, as teacher, coach, janitor, and principal, and made a name for himself by accepting boys—rowdies, poor students, boys who had never accomplished anything—whom successful schools would not touch, and by demanding the best from them. The boys acquired a strong loyalty to their school and their headmaster, became proud of themselves and wanted him to be proud of them. Despite the homogeneity of their attitudes, Deerfield boys had a moral backbone, a drive to make something of themselves different from the standard preppy.

Boyden built his dormitories, his classroom building, his gym by the gifts he won from wealthy friends like my father. The thin little wiry man with his flat New England accent would curl up in an armchair and tell yarns about the local eccentrics, gradually drift around to the great job the school was doing, and conclude with "Charlie, you've just got to help us!" My father, who admired any star performance, would laugh and respond by writing a check of five digits.

As a boy grew older, he came to notice the instruments of control (I figured out once that a student's whereabouts were checked sixteen times a day) and the meticulous planning that insured the spontaneity of those handsome boys in their tweed jackets. But since the seniors were encouraged to believe that it was they and the Head who ran the school, they rarely noticed who were expendable. The expendables were the teachers' families, ignored or exploited as the Head's was; the young teachers, who monitored the dormitories and turned off the lights and picked up trash, and if they did not find pleasure in coaching, might have wondered what they were doing with their lives; day students, sons of Polish farmers and French-Canadian factory workers who barely existed save in sports; and below them, their homely sisters, retained for a while to please the rich old women who had given the science building, untouchables.

Deerfield responded in varied ways to history. During World War II the boys dug potatoes and picked apples for the local farmers, the graduates became ensigns and pilots. A fair number were killed. In the long afternoon of Mr. Boyden's last years, change was carefully monitored: more art—yes, new mathematics—no. Negroes? It wouldn't be fair unless the boy was just right, and the school waited patiently for a Perfectly Qualified Negro to present himself. Girls? They would alter what Deerfield stood for. Pot smoking? It didn't exist.

As he became older and called the boys by their fathers' names, secret committees of senior staff would meet to make the decisions that the Head did not care to. There was always one reason or another, like an important new building, to postpone his departure. He was almost eighty-five when he did leave, and he died a year later. His successor, David Pyncheon, who came from St. Louis and stayed for about ten years, lacked a commanding public presence though he was more honest than the old man in facing up to the realities of that alienated time, and after a couple of efforts to open the academy to girls, was encouraged to resign. He was followed by Robert Kaufmann, also a nonalumnus, who held an MBA and had received his training in Harvard's administration. Kaufmann was realistic about Deerfield but valued as well as deplored the archaic isolation. Boys are forced to grow up too fast, he believed. They are pushed too hard. It does no harm for them to act young when they *are* young and follow noisy loyalties to things that are appropriate to sixteen-year-olds.

Could that $5.5 million have been better used? Probably. Boys should have stable, happy boyhoods. I did during my three years at Deerfield and made close friends and met a number of men I admired, who taught me well and were kind to me. But so much is taken for granted at such a place: the versions of reality offered to its students, the expectations for the future, the learning to be obtained in the $2.8 million science building and $1.8 million library. For maintaining a going concern, Deerfield and schools like it do a workmanlike job. If Deerfield is a better run, more honest and humane version of a totalitarian society like Czechoslovakia, it is also not unlike IBM or Merrill Lynch. Deerfield graduates do well in such corporations. The habits of leadership, responsibility, straightforwardness, teamwork, concern for more than just yourself that were pounded into them as schoolboys keep them from being like the operators in the Watergate soap opera. Extra resources like that $5.5 million allowed better salaries for teachers and scholarships which spread the opportunities around more fairly and meant that the local values were not purely those of rich kids. If an Establishment exists in this country, Deerfield is the quintessential establishment school.

But if the society that is based upon institutions like Deerfield and our great corporations, is *not* a going concern, if it really doesn't work either justly or efficiently, these ex-schoolboys are not going to be the people who ask the important questions or propose the critical alternatives. I have always respected the school, but after each visit I come away with the same troubled thoughts.

Kent School, Kent, Connecticut, 1959–1981—$1,176,200. Kent School was founded in 1906 by Father Sill of the Order of the Holy Cross of the Episcopal Church in order to serve the ideals of simplicity of life, self-reliance, and directness of purpose. Its famed self-help system meant that boys rose at 6:00 P.M. to sweep the dorms and classrooms, wash the dishes, and mow the lawns. There were no uniform tuition fees; each family paid what it could afford, a secret figure known only to the headmaster. Father Sill believed in Christian community. Kent's western boundary was a looming mountain that must have cut off the sunshine by early afternoon, its eastern was a fast-flowing river whose bridge the boys were forbidden to cross. There were no away weekends. The masters taught and coached at low salaries and with few more liberties than the boys. For Bob Magowan from Philadelphia, with tremendous energy and ambition and little money, who chose Kent because he had been told it would get him into Harvard and let him make a success out of his life, that discipline suited those dreams. It was absolutely what he wanted.

The school continued to believe in the ideal of soundly educated Christian citizens, including, by 1960, girls (admitted into a new campus two miles away, so they wouldn't be too disturbing). The study of theology was required in each grade. Merrill money went for new science-math and audiovisual facilities, for renewal of outmoded and inadequate facilities, for endowment, scholarships, salaries, and a headmaster's discretionary fund, and in 1972 $1 million for construction of a Robert Magowan athletic facility with a gymnasium, indoor tennis court, and swimming pool, a blessing for morale during the long winters.

How to keep raising money for endowment, the headmaster worried on my visit there, for salaries and for scholarships when ever-rising costs cut the flexibility in tuition that was the heart of the school? How to graduate young men and women with some loyalty to the church, which seemed to be dying throughout the West? Where did Kent discipline and Christian ideals fit into a permissive society?

Ethel Walker School, Simsbury, Connecticut, 1961–1980—$380,000 in six grants. Ethel Walker, which my sister Doris attended, received the major support given to any girls' school. It was an over-sheltered, over-structured school in her day, a sort of female military academy. The students were not allowed to speak with boys, and were supposed to report their own misdemeanors or "sins" like whispering in study hall, by putting them on a little piece of paper in a box for one of the prefects to read. Too many sins and one was forbidden to go to the Pettibone Inn for lunch on Sunday, the ultimate deprivation.

Nevertheless, Doris Magowan, who always valued self-discipline, felt that the school taught her to organize her time, to think ahead, to make decisions for herself. The girls slept on sleeping porches, even in winter. Making the bed on a Saturday morning, with fresh starched sheets, was a torture, though a younger girl with a sweet tooth might be bribed with a Hershey bar to do the job instead. Miss Hewitt, the headmistress, had no intention of making the school easy. Girls were expected to take their obligations seriously— studies, sports, posture. One result of these expectations was a deep sense of loyalty to the school and to each other, with friendships made that, for my sister, lasted her entire life.

The Merrill Trust grants went toward the library, dormitory renovation, scholarships, endowment, and in 1972 one grant of $250,000 in the hands of an able new head went to modernize and restructure the school: to offer salaries that would allow hiring a different sort of young teacher, to offer scholarships to bring in a wider range of girls. In the early 1970s girls' schools seemed terminal, but a change in thinking allowed the strong ones to be seen as places where a girl could speak her mind, learn leadership, and not simply defer to boys in a still very sexist society.

Miss Porter's School, Farmington, Connecticut, 1976—$15,000 to a similar school and a traditional rival of Ethel Walker, a grant for scholarships to maintain educational standards and admit a wider range of girls. Miss Porter's was a pretty standard place in composition and values, and yet in 1983 it took on a new headmistress who was one of the most spirited, imaginative, resourceful professionals I met, a sign of the capacity for re-creation that American institutions seem to hold on to.

Wooster School, Danbury, Connecticut, 1959–1980—$182,000 in nine grants. For the Merrill trustees Wooster School was one man, John Verdery, an Episcopal priest who was its headmaster for almost thirty years, the son-in-law of my father's family minister at the Church of the Ascension in New York. Wooster always had thin financial resources, which meant low salaries, a shabby plant, often quite ordinary students who had to be accepted if their families could pay full tuition, an unremitting pressure upon the boss to raise money for each month's bills.

These limitations did not bother Mr. Verdery. His intense Christian commitment made other things unimportant. The boys (girls came in 1974) at Wooster were not very interesting students perhaps, but they were interesting human beings, and the headmaster was concerned about how they got along with their fathers and learned understanding, confidence, self-discipline, and modesty. He was not concerned by curriculum, though his faculty were. He worked hard to upgrade the academic quality of the school—using our grants for construction and renovation and scholarships, library books, and lab equipment—though he was always suspicious of the self-esteem that more successful schools assumed out of their Ivy League college placements. Wooster avoided the caste assumptions of Groton and St. Paul and the meritocracy of superschools like Andover and Exeter. What he wanted was for his boys to be able to see a Christian faith as the framework of their lives in success and failure. Jewish students were always asked to share the services, in the hope that his strong but humane Christianity would lead them to a greater desire to understand their own tradition.

What was important didn't have to cost a lot. Wooster accepted Negroes in the fifties, before most other private schools did, was hurt by their surly

militancy of the late sixties, which Verdery told himself was a need to free
themselves from gratitude and subserviency. As the school became more heterogeneous, with Hispanics and Orientals, the black-white confrontation became less sharp. Wooster also became involved in a long-term relation with
a town in the Vaucluse. The students stayed with local families and attended
the local lycée, escaped the role of tourists, added a French dimension to the
way they looked at life. Verdery sought to involve the school with Danbury
and Waterbury, manufacturing and bedroom towns. An Upward Bound program brought in disadvantaged local children, and the school's new art building brought in adults.

Our long-term backing of Wooster was what a foundation should do. The
school was small enough (around 200/300) and financially constrained enough
so that our modest though steady support gave strength, security, and room
for experiment. We made that investment out of respect for the school's leader
and his belief in what Christianity should mean in education. Some things
one should take seriously. Other things are not important. That is the lesson
youngsters should learn, and not be led astray by buildings, endowment size,
and the names of colleges that the seniors get into.

Williston Northampton School, Easthampton, Massachusetts, 1960–1980.
This is the name chosen by Williston Academy and Northampton School for
Girls when they merged in 1971. To the separate schools and that partnership
we made a series of grants between 1960 and 1980 that totaled $175,000. In
his involvement with the institutions of western Massachusetts, Charlie Cole
concerned himself about these two weak schools. Through aid to better management, debt retirement, and specific needs like the library, he felt that the
Trust could serve the same purpose it had with Wooster.

The questions of quality and purpose are hard to deal with. By any standard, both places had been close to collapse. Write them off?—a reasonable
conclusion. And yet the measurements that an outsider would employ—College Board scores and college placement, deficit and endowment, faculty
salaries—would miss a detail like the large number of students from Polish,
Irish, French-Canadian working-class families attending Williston on scholarships that the school really could not afford. For them the school was a step
up the ladder worth sacrifice to their parents, and in turn they added a reality
that the children of businessmen and college professors would never have
gained at Deerfield. By the help of gifts like ours a basic structure had been
maintained. When better leadership and more money came along at the end
of the 1970s, larger enrollment, better academic and salary standards, a good
theater program could be built upon that structure. Williston was no elite
establishment, but it was a well-run school.

Groton School, Groton, Massachusetts, 1960–1981—$150,000 for scholarships and $47,500 to support a classics teacher's archeological projects in Greece. Groton was one of the earliest and most famous of the Episcopal boarding schools and under the great Endicott Peabody was dedicated to thorough college preparation and Christian values in Spartan living conditions. The totalitarian stamp of its daily life—cubicles and cold water, church services and Latin verse—made Groton strangely similar to the most hardline Eastern European regimes. For its approximately 300 students there was an endowment of $17 million. It attracted good headmasters and good teachers. It accepted Negroes, though I have a memory of its elegant dining hall with one silent, well-groomed black boy at each table. (Suppose two of them had sat together or made a racket?) Our grants were requested by Peter Magowan, a graduate who respected the school highly, including its able, humane administration, which wanted the money put towards scholarships for middle-income families, so that Groton would not be a school just for the rich and the poor.

It is hard to evaluate the Trust's decisions. Groton is a good school. A certain kind of boy and now girl can obtain an excellent education there and not be over-affected by the fact that family wealth is the basic common denominator of the kids who attend. Williston Northampton was in much greater need of that $150,000, but did it have the leadership to make best use of a lot more money? Should we have given to neither and put an extra $300,000 into Wooster (though Verdery never pushed us for large gifts and was proud of the school's tradition of doing a decent job with ordinary funding)? I don't know.

St. Mark's, Southborough, Massachusetts, 1962–1981—$115,000 in six grants for faculty salaries, the construction of a music and art center, renovation of the auditorium, support of the summer drama program, and scholarships for Protestant students. Another one of the Magowan sons had gone there, a young man interested in theater, where the school was strong and went out of its way to share its rich facilities with the local community.

St. Paul's, Concord, New Hampshire, 1975–1981—$35,000. St. Paul's is the third member of this league, though lack of family contacts meant that we supported it—for library acquisitions and for a $30 million capital drive—less. It began in 1856. The school is known for its advanced sections, constant academic challenge. "The aims are what they always have been: the informal and friendly supervision of every boy in all his activities." Twenty-five percent of its 500 students receive financial aid. Forty of them belong to minority groups. Money is needed to maintain this scholarship percentage and to strengthen recruitment by alumni committees as far away as Germany and Japan. The library has 50,000 volumes and the endowment is $46 million.

The school runs an excellent summer program for New Hampshire high school students. All that money may not spoil St. Paul's kids, but does it trouble the more perceptive ones with an over-obvious conclusion, as at Deerfield, that one cannot do anything effective in education without that amount of capital?

Taft School, Watertown, Connecticut, 1965–1978—$116,000. Under the leadership of John Esty, Taft involved itself imaginatively in trying to look at the problems facing administrators and teachers. Esty believed that only the strong independent schools would survive over the next twenty-five years and therefore should plan carefully, whether in determining architectural needs in order to avoid the usual wasteful ad hoc building, or in obtaining departmental funds for experimentation with new techniques and materials and sending teachers to professional meetings.

The Trust financed a summer program in the new math for elementary school teachers and students at a time (1965) when large numbers of frightened teachers had to be retrained from a mathematics that stressed computational skills to one that was conceptual and verbally abstract, where children and teachers of a lower economic and less articulate class might end up in confusion. $4,500 in 1970 went for a summer program in curriculum and bibliography for courses in black culture and on ways to help white middle-class teachers meet the problems raised by black working-class students.

Northfield Mount Hermon, East Northfield, Massachusetts, 1960–1971—$115,000. Northfield for girls had been started in 1879, Mount Hermon for boys in 1881. When they merged in the 1960s, they formed the largest private boarding school in the country. The two schools had a strong Christian tradition based on a heavy-handed fundamentalism interpreted by the once famous Dwight L. Moody. Students came from modest backgrounds, and there was a tradition of community work around campus including the management of a dairy farm. The school was known for a good summer program, to which the Trust gave $15,000 in 1964 to help expand it to serve public school students. The two sprawling campuses had a run-down, costly physical plant, and a tradition of generous scholarships had meant a low salary range. As times became harder the difficulties of recruitment for an institution that large meant lower admission standards.

Northfield Mount Hermon made a serious commitment to admitting a sizable number of black students and under Howard Jones was one of the founders of A Better Chance's scholarship program. Jones was also alert to the changing values that young people set for education: what you *feel* is as important as what and how you *think*. You prove the value of your education by what you do as a complete human being. And what you learn *outside* the classroom may be more important than what you learn inside. In 1971 the Trust put up $35,000 to strengthen these non-academic offerings: volunteer service at a nearby old people's home, foreign study in France, Germany, and Spain, off-campus programs of forest reclamation, urban experience in Springfield, wintertime wilderness camping and climbing, work as teaching assistants both at Northfield and at public schools.

New programs like those at Northfield Mount Hermon were sometimes hastily slapped together in the early 1970s, and yet the school unwilling to experiment and to trust its students in problematical situations risked losing their allegiance. The American establishment had so obviously botched things in Vietnam, in its treatment of nonwhite and poor people at home, in its lack of visible values worth respecting, that a school *had* to distance itself from the status quo. The aggressive militancy of the new black students reduced some administrations to jelly, others to rage, and yet headmasters and teachers who showed that they were willing to listen, learn, and change, were willing to say what they didn't know as well as say what they believed in were able to win, in time, the respect of those opponents and ride out the worst years.

Emma Willard School, Troy, New York, 1965–1976—$81,000. Emma Willard is one of the oldest private schools in the country, founded in 1821 to give women the liberalizing influence of an education then available only to men. In 1819 Emma Willard herself presented to the New York State Legislature a plan for women's education adapted to women's nature and duties combining a course of scientific and philosophic training with the study of the arts that was considered a blueprint for the women's colleges to follow. It achieved its status as a national institution under the leadership of Eliza Kellas, 1911–1942, "years of almost motionless administration." I first saw Emma Willard toward the end of Miss Kellas's rule, when the Deerfield glee club was bused to Troy for a joint concert and dance. Miss Kellas and Mr. Boyden sat in armchairs at the edge of the dance floor, a young teacher behind each to be sent to warn any couple holding each other too close. Styles changed, and William Dietl, headmaster during the 1960s, once had the senior class stand in white dresses in a large circle on the lawn till down out of the sky he came in a helicopter to hand each girl a yellow jonquil.

In all the pressures for change, a girls' school was painfully vulnerable. It was too easy to do what seemed popular and expedient and accept merger with a boys' school. If one believed in separate education, other than from merely tradition, then one had to say *why* clearly and forcefully enough for girls to understand. Schools had to discover sources of value outside their students' own experience, which meant accepting black and less affluent girls, not as symbols but in numbers able to change the community as well as be changed by it, an often painful process. It meant a deliberate search for useful projects in the discouraged city of Troy, for a study program abroad, or the enjoyable adventure of an exchange program with Thatcher, a school for rich boys in California. How to build a varied community where a young woman can establish, articulate, and defend the rationale for her belief? Blacks must not hear only black voices, whites must not see only white and male heroes.

Emma Willard, with $7 million for 305 students in 1976, was the most heavily endowed girls' school in the United States, but thirty-seventh on the list of all independent secondary schools. Trying to decide what it really wanted to be—a school where Oklahoma businessmen sent their strong-willed daughters, and yet more than that, trying to find its own administrators who were both sensitive and efficient—Emma Willard had confused periods during the 1970s.

Lawrenceville School, Lawrenceville, New Jersey, 1965–1973—$85,000. One of the oldest, richest, best boarding schools, Lawrenceville was well led by strong, long-lasting headmasters: Allan Healy in the thirties and forties, Bruce McClellan for the last twenty-five years. It was built upon the English house system of small dormitory units, providing a society for a boy to belong to, and its teaching upon the conference plan with small sections seated around large oval tables, where a shy or poorly prepared boy could not hide and where a teacher could not simply give a lecture. My brother, James Merrill, a graduate of Lawrenceville who always respected the training he received there, particularly in English, urged these grants to improve the library, now the main resource of the school with new emphasis upon independent study rather than upon textbooks.

Nyack Boys' School, Southampton, New York, 1963–1970—$95,000. Nyack must qualify among the dozen boarding schools that received major funding, although it was a third-rate place run by an adventurer who called himself Colonel. It had bought The Orchard, the great estate and beautiful white house that my father had owned for twenty-five years and then given to Amherst as home of the Merrill Center for Economic Study, and our grants went to repair the picket fence and the roof, maintain the gardens and the library paneling, replace the trees, and pay some of the bills. The Colonel had a showy rendering of a gymnasium with a Lincoln Continental parked in front that was drawn to spearhead a great funds drive, but there was a limit to how far one could operate on chutzpah alone, and in 1972 the school folded and the Colonel disappeared.

The two best-known independent schools in the country are the Phillips Academies of Exeter and Andover. They are so wealthy and arrogant that

the Trust saw no reason during our first ten years to give them our usual
grants, but the schools offer leadership to American education and have always had strong headmasters.

Phillips Academy, Exeter, New Hampshire, 1969–1978—$75,000. Our first
$25,000 in 1969 was to participate in a $25 million capital drive, the second
to purchase library material to improve student skill in research (documents,
census records, reprints), the third to improve the athletic department.

Exeter was famous for its faculty, which operated at a level of teaching
and scholarship closer, often, to college standards than to a secondary
school's. With Andover it collaborated in setting up a well-run study year in
Rennes (Brittany) and Barcelona. It tried to involve its students in imaginative
social work programs in summer and term time. Its ambitious summer courses
for public school students had a valuable long-range stimulus upon youngsters
who afterwards just wouldn't accept the ordinary fare they had been willing
to tolerate. The magnificent endowment of $60 million allowed the school to
accept or reject anyone it pleased, to bring in a democratic spread of Negro,
working-class, foreign boys (and then girls) of ability and energy, and to hold
its charges to about 60 percent of what other schools were forced to demand.
Exeter and Andover exemplified the meritocratic ideal, and a well-armored
child got a lot out of the place. If you were shy and could not prove your
accomplishments to an intensely critical environment, you might become an
unhappy kid indeed.

Phillips Academy, Andover, Massachusetts, 1975, 1978—$40,000. Andover
had 1,170 students, a library with 100,000 volumes, and an endowment of
$65 million, adequate reason for our grade B foundation to ignore the place.
Theodore Sizer, who replaced John Kemper (one of the 1960s' leading headmasters), held the belief that adolescents learn best in a variety of educational
environments, and persuaded us to back a program that would bring in public
school students to study intensive short-range courses concentrating on one
subject: Russian, oceanography, astronomy, theater, African history. The experiment would show how much a youngster can learn in a concentrated time
and also illustrate cooperation between public and private schools. At $100
a week, the fee was within the range of parents unable to afford private
school. Our money was to help give permanence to the idea.

Some Other New England Schools

Pomfret School, Pomfret, Connecticut, 1964–1980—$70,000. Two grants
went to support the summer session for Negro and Puerto Rican boys from
Hartford, another to plan for academic changes with money used to hire a

full-time curriculum design specialist (is that necessary?). Our $10,000 grant in 1980 went for the teacher intern program. Pomfret's administration had become sensitive to the most damaging long-range effect of the teacher job crisis. If there are no longer any jobs available in education, if young teachers without seniority are being let go no matter what their quality, and if when old Mr. Chips falls dead shoveling snow his post is abolished, no twenty-year-old worth his salt will consider teaching a field worth choosing. Only a second-rater—the traditional individual not good enough to do anything better—will want to teach. By the end of the 1970s the fall-off in entry level quality was already showing up in the public schools. What sort of education will our children's children receive? Pomfret felt that if special funds might be obtained, the school could continue to make room for beginning teachers, benefit from their energy and new ideas, and give them the experience and recommendations for landing a second job.

Worcester Academy, Worcester, Massachusetts, 1962–1979—$40,000. We made four small grants to Worcester for scholarship aid and improvements because my father had gone there for a year in 1903 on his way to Amherst. The Florida boy had hated that rough, cold, dingy school. One of his roommates had been a quadroon, assigned, he was sure, in order to humiliate him. Prostitutes used to pick up varsity football players on their way back from practice. Mr. Merrill had a healthy scorn for nostalgia.

The modern Worcester was proud of its urban affairs program of internships with local businesses and agencies and state legislators as a way to give students an exposure to the real world. By the end of the seventies the Academy felt that good management had allowed it to come through an era where independent schools had been severely challenged and where many of the weaker ones died.

Stowe School, Stowe, Vermont, 1974—$10,000 towards purchase of new property. Stowe had been started as a co-ed boarding school in 1961 for the children of families weakened by divorce, absenteeism (parents away on interesting jobs or fun vacations), or lack of care. The children were cynical and hurt, ready to drop out or sell out. How was it possible to help kids grow through their failures as well as their successes, and learn how to face and solve their problems? Like many schools, Stowe began when the beauty, skills, and responsibility of rural living, modeled after Putney in Vermont, were the ideal, Thoreau the inspiration. By the late sixties, the city was where the action was. Coming to terms with black values and black demands was the task, drugs and rock music were the ways by which young people challenged, withdrew from, or mocked the adult world. Meanwhile the town of Stowe had returned into a ski resort with hedonistic values much more alluring than anything a school could offer. John Hardy, the founder and head-master, was trying to build a new campus on a high plateau backing into thousands of acres of wilderness, hoping to avoid the architectural styles of neo-penal or monumental.

Mountain School, Vershire, Vermont, 1976—$10,000. Mountain School was started in 1963 by a Quaker couple named Connard to stress hard work, self-reliance, community, the understanding of nature. The students raised pigs, sheep, black Angus, apples, and vegetables for their food and cut wood for their heat. Dartmouth was near enough for culture, and along with regular courses there was an annual focus subject like China, Vermont, energy. A major emphasis, however, was upon what one made with one's own hands. The Connards were a decent, thoughtful couple with a personally evolved idea of what an education should offer a young person. One's response upon meeting them was a conviction that people like this must somehow find a niche in the standardized pattern of American education. With just thirty students, however, the school was not in good shape either in finances or admissions, and in the summer of 1982 it closed down.

Peacham School, Peacham, Vermont, 1977—$5,000. Peacham started out of the wreckage of a traditional local academy that died in 1971, in a town too small to have its own high school and too far from other towns to relish the solution of busing. Most of the students are not college bound, and there-fore have a need for work co-ops and apprenticeships to help them make constructive career decisions. There is a tough outdoor survival program in both warm and winter weather, also an interesting emphasis upon theater, including tour performances, to teach these inarticulate, isolated small-town youngsters how to act in public. Each year there is also a program of foreign films shown at the academy to reach both students and town people.

A foundation should look for schools like Mountain and Peacham as well as Harlem Prep and not just write out checks to Groton and Exeter.

Outside New England

Purnell School, Pottersville, New Jersey, 1972–1976—$25,000. This small school for girls has a close family atmosphere and concern for each girl as an individual, a deliberate alternative to the highly competitive college prepar-atory school. The building of student confidence, not just high testing scores, should be a measure of a school's success. Purnell is proud of its strong studio and performing arts departments and its immersion approach in foreign languages.

There were times in my own pressured, competitive school that I envied the approach of Purnell. And yet without the discipline of pressure and competition, a student may be haunted by the fear that she can function only in a protected environment, and may never become aware of the strengths that she does possess. A non-pressured school can also become dull.

George School, Newtown, Pennsylvania, 1965–1976—$25,000. George, with 300 boarding and 200 day students, in Bucks County outside Philadelphia, is one of the leading Quaker schools. Only 20 percent of the students are of Quaker background, but the aim is to follow Quaker ideals of simplicity and service as well as the tradition of academic and social innovation. An example of this was the work camp started in Germany right after 1945. African and Asian as well as black American students found a welcome at George. The school also ran the first teenage volunteer project involving mental patients at a state hospital. Money was obtained from the Trust for services such as summer study, trips to professional conferences, workshops, opportunities for theater, music, and travel. Such crucial luxuries for faculty enrichment and advancement cannot be funded out of general revenue.

Western Reserve Academy, Hudson, Ohio, 1971—$25,000 for scholarships for Appalachian students. Western Reserve is a solidly established, wealthy school, one of two midwestern boarding schools honored with an endowed faculty chair by the Independence Foundation. Involved early on with the black scholarship program for A Better Chance, in 1970 it started a new program for white boys from the mining and farming communities in southwest Ohio and West Virginia. Rural boys adapt better than urban blacks to boarding school life, and the poverty and destructiveness of their environment are certainly no less.

Colorado Rocky Mountain School, Carbondale, Colorado, 1972—$25,000. Colorado Mountain is a small (125) co-ed school aiming to provide college-bound youngsters with the inner resources which Americans have lost through easy living. Demanding work programs (ranching, construction, maintenance chores) and demanding sports (rock climbing, kayaking, wilderness survival) go along with off-campus volunteer work (hospital, veterinary clinic, museum) and academics.

Thacher School, Ojai, California, 1972–1979—$75,000. Started in 1889, Thacher is the oldest boarding school in California and the first with a national reputation, in fact almost the oldest private school west of the Mississippi. All ninth graders own their own horses, and riding, polo, and camping are an important part of Thacher life. Scholarship funds were sought to attract students of wider social and income groups, although the administration wished to stay small (under 200) in order to hold on to quality. A humane touch was the belief that quality of academic work was more important than quantity: students need time to reflect and to pursue their own interests outside the classroom, not just fill every available minute with homework.

Athenian School, Danville, California, 1968–1978—$55,000 for construction and debt retirement. Athenian opened in 1965. Its founder, Dyke Brown, was a vice-president of the Ford Foundation and a lawyer involved with inner-city kids in trouble but was shocked by the bored delinquency he witnessed in affluent Scarsdale. He wanted to build a school committed to intellectual excellence, self-government, responsible physical work. To pursue that concept of independence, he envisaged four individual campuses around a core of central facilities and set up an ambitious program of mountaineering and map trekking in the High Sierras plus term-long city internships. The handsome campus ran up high debt-carrying charges, and the school was probably overstaffed and overcommitted to its democratic scholarships, which forced some pressured fund-raising.

THE SCHOOL-COLLEGE SCHOLARSHIP PROGRAM

The foundation's trustees met twice a year, in March at the Magowans' house in Palm Beach, in September at their house on the ocean at Southampton, Long Island. When we broke for drinks and lunch, the favorite topic was the stock market, but there always came a moment of introspection: Were we doing as good a job as we should? Was this what the Old Man would have wanted? He was always concerned about individuals, my sister stated. Could we think up a project that would have a direct impact upon the lives of individual human beings? Out of those questions in 1966 evolved the Trust's school-college scholarship program.

We would choose eight boarding schools, not the best (Exeter, Andover, Lawrenceville), nor the richest (Choate, Groton, St. Paul's), but decent places with a reputation for social concern: Bob Magowan's Kent, Northfield Mount Hermon, Williston (second rate at that time but Charles Cole thought it had potential), Governor Dummer, Taft, Emma Willard (the only girls' school), Wooster, whose headmaster we admired, The Hill in eastern Pennsylvania. These schools would choose a boy or girl, though Kent and Northfield Mount Hermon as co-ed were given two scholarships. In fact the inclusion of girls at all was almost an afterthought, and twenty-one girls to thirty-nine boys went through the program. The students were to come out of the tenth grade of public or parochial school, neither poverty stricken nor too often of minority background, but they were to be young people of character and potential leadership, qualities that my father valued over outstanding intellect. After all, really bright kids will always be noticed. Then, upon graduation from preparatory school, these students would continue to be backed by us through whatever college they chose.

We would put up $1,500 a year at secondary school, $1,000 a year at college, where financial aid was considered easier to obtain, plus $100 a year for books, theater and concert tickets (to teach the value of little luxuries), a one-time $800 for foreign travel, for a total of $8,400 per person.

There was a spareness to the concept: a program unburdened by administrative overhead and the agonies of selection committees. Once a year we would mail off the checks to the schools and colleges, and they, not us, would have responsibility for those students.

I was the supervisor. The students progressed, repeated (yes, we put up an extra $1,000 for a third year at school), quit, re-enrolled, were expelled, transferred from college to college in those restless years, dropped out for a year to find themselves. My image of the process came to be of the Japanese banquet where a platter of little live crabs covered with a bell jar is brought to the table, the bell is lifted, and the crabs scurry in all directions.

Given the American suspicion of intellect, we made a mistake in downplaying that criterion. Some schools recruited big dumb varsity athletes. We paid for hapless kids who burrowed like moles into the bottom quarter of their class, with good money thrown after bad as they blundered along. Well, we said we didn't insist on Success, and those were troubled years. The swinging Jewish-Indian girl from Seattle had a pert brightness. The farm girl from northern Minnesota was ambitious and wholesome. Both left Kent after less than a semester, homesick and lovesick. Keith's mother was a home economics teacher in Rhode Island who desperately wanted a chance for her son. He was a muscular, popular, well-meaning boy. He tutored black kids in Springfield, joined the drama club, couldn't understand why teachers got so uptight about his grades. "It's a sign of the times. We have done too much for this boy!" his guidance counselor exploded after Keith had more or less graduated and went for a while to Rutgers and then drifted off to a Negro college in North Carolina.

One can look for the desire to serve. Barbara was one of six children in a family farm in upstate New York, played the flute, was interested in social work or occupational therapy. From Emma Willard she went on to the University of Rochester, was badly hurt in an auto accident in early 1972, but was touched by the concern shown by what she had thought was a huge, impersonal institution. Our travel money paid for a stay at a Christian community in Switzerland, and that helped rebuild her confidence; back at Rochester she worked with children with learning disorders.

A sense of purpose. Stuart came from a tiny community in coastal Maine where his father was a bookbinder. He had always been interested in science, graduated at the top of his class from Northfield Mount Hermon, went on to Dartmouth—"I sure made lots of mistakes"—majored in aquatic ecology, took a course in oceanography, used our travel money for a trip to Hawaii, where the marine life was totally different from Maine's.

Determination. Sharon came from West Dennis, Massachusetts, where her father was pressman at the *Cape Cod Times*. The family had so little money that she assumed responsibility for paying all the Northfield costs out of her summer earnings as a motel cleaning girl. At first she hated the University of Massachusetts for its lack of discipline but learned how to grow up and deal with that. Her mother fell seriously ill, which meant more duties at home and lower grades. Our extra money allowed the adventure of being a student teacher—"another name for slave labor!"—at the American International School at Düsseldorf—"but I think I learned a great deal."

An ability to enjoy life. Paul's mother was a nurse at a state hospital in St. Paul. His counselor said the boy demanded more from his teachers, asked more questions than a public school could satisfy. At Taft he went on a French program to Arcachon, a town on the Bay of Biscay, where he lived with a butcher's family and their seven children. Adjustment to that highly structured family unit was rough—"When I said I drank milk everyone laughed"—but he started making friends with the smallest children. He went back home to the University of Minnesota, used our extra funds to start a record collection, supported himself as a bus driver, had a religious conversion and taught one summer at a Bible camp. Then he met Jennifer. "Marriage is the greatest thing that has happened to me in a long time!" He planned to teach in high school and some day write famous novels.

Intellectual distinction. Jean's father was a professor of religion at Randolph Macon, whose salaries were as low as those at any other women's college in the South. "She is able to make full use of everything her teachers can offer her at Kent," the counselor reported. There were so many things—music, her responsibilities on the student council, her senior paper on Language and Learning—each day to give herself to. At Chapel Hill she won honors in political science and sociology, learned how to use the computer, used our money to study modern history and German literature at the University of Marburg: "Living alone in a foreign land is not easy, but it is allowing me a sense of confidence and direction."

Was the program a success? It cost over $500,000. Jacqueline, whose parents were textile workers in Monetta, South Carolina—"a mature girl whose singleness of purpose her peers are apt to lack"—I met while she was at Smith. We talked about her course in constitutional law, her internship at the mayor's office at Northampton, and her coming semester in Washington. She was a modest, straightforward, realistic young woman. If one has money, what better way to spend it?

I did not meet Beverly, "a shy gentle Negro girl with a refreshing honesty," who found her first year at Penn so confusing with all the conflicting responsibilities to herself, to society, and as a black woman. Ken broke his pelvis playing hockey. Rhys tore his shoulder muscle badly in football—schoolboy athletics may build character but they sure destroy bodies. Leigh spent the summer playing the guitar and singing in Vermont bars. Edna took a year off from studying to be a psychiatric social worker in order to write poetry. John, who was black, flunked out of Harvard from overinvolvement in political action, in 1970, the year to be overinvolved—but perhaps learned to work more steadily at the University of South Carolina later. Michael, one of four children of a utility lineman in Essex, Connecticut, whose Wooster counselor thought was the most promising boy in the program, deferred entrance to Miami University to get a job on a freighter and then quit school entirely to go to Holland and, like Peter the Great, study shipbuilding.

Would it be worthwhile to track down these sixty men and women and ask how the generous Merrill scholarships changed their lives and benefited society? I doubt it. Someone could report back on Success ("Out of humble beginnings I am now a lawyer and live in Scarsdale") and keep silent about Failure ("I drink too much and get on badly with my wife"). Is the silly kid who started a great autobiographical novel at twenty-two and is now working with retarded children a failure because his income is so small or a success because he is doing something useful? I don't know. The project forced us to acquire some knowledge of what it means to grow up in this country.

DAY SCHOOLS

Every day school headmaster has wished that he could have better control over his students' lives and remove them from a chaotic, brutal, indulgent home situation. In a boarding school young people might enjoy a more consistent discipline. Some parents, whether corporation executives, university professors, feminist artists, or janitors, just aren't made for the job. The value of the day school is the reverse of that coin. Children spend the day arguing with their teachers and then go home to argue with their parents. They aren't locked into a totalitarian society. Teachers and headmasters can shut the door behind them. There's a good deal to be said for all the odd ways by which children learn, whether it's sitting around the supper table with their parents or riding to school on the subway.

New York City and Philadelphia and on South

St. Bernard's, 1959–1981—$155,000. Four of the five Magowan sons attended St. Bernard's, a well-run school for younger boys that the family respected tremendously. In Mr. Westgate, an Englishman educated in Manitoba, at Oxford, and at Harvard, it had attracted a strong-minded headmaster who saw that sort of school as serving the most impressionable, varied years of a boy's life. The attitudes, work habits, and basic approaches to other people are shaped then. Our nine different grants went for all sorts of purposes, but Mr. Westgate was most concerned about the need to raise faculty salaries. The salaries were low, and even a dedicated teacher could not afford to stay at St. Bernard's after he had started a family, with the result that a lot of the headmaster's time was spent looking for replacements. Only 6 percent of the 300 students received financial aid, and that in turn meant too narrow a range of families.

St. Bernard's was a fine school and the years its boys attended *were* their most impressionable ones, but those impressions were restricted to a society of little boys in navy blue blazers from nice families, and the assumptions learned there might be costly ones.

Spence School, 1970–1980—$150,000. A school (with now about 500 students) that Doris Magowan had attended, which we backed for its commitment to teaching girls high-quality math and science. In cooperation with Columbia and New York University, with the help of visiting teachers known to be innovators, and after visits by the science faculty to twenty other schools, Spence put together an integrated, accelerated science program from kindergarten to twelfth grade. In 1973 the Trust helped fund a computer program that Spence planned to share with other schools, costs including summer training for faculty. With natural curiosity, a carefully thought-out curriculum, and an assumption that there was no limit to what any normally bright girl might learn, it was an exciting place.

Stony Brook School, Easthampton, New York, 1970—$15,000. An interesting place established by parents dissatisfied with the public schools on the eastern half of Long Island. The intellectual stress was upon progress and motivation rather than content. Children moved at their own speed in the ungraded courses and received reports rather than marks. There was a deliberate effort to attract a wide mix, with IQs ranging from 89 to 149, including the children of farmers and migrant workers as well as doctors and lawyers. Many children went on to college, but it was not a priority.

An important conclusion: in America's commitment to children of the inner city, let us not forget those in small towns and on farms who are apt to be just as deprived.

Montclair Kimberley Academy, Montclair, New Jersey, 1976, 1981—
$20,000. A large composite school with 1,000 students on its three separate
campuses. Our money went towards a new science lab and, more important
because harder to fund, faculty development: training in improved teaching
techniques, new enrichment programs, computer literacy. The computer revolution is too important to be left to technicians and game players. How can
biology students, for example, be taught to fit together a varying range of
statistics on water availability, pollution, population, and business growth to
make a rational estimate of what life in New Jersey might be like in 2001?

Jacksonville Episcopal High, Jacksonville, Florida, 1971—$35,000 towards
a $3 million campaign. This appeal was referred by Hellen Plummer, Charles
E. Merrill's second wife, a native of Jacksonville. It is considered one of the
leading schools of northern Florida, important within the life of St. John's
Cathedral, whose dean has tried to keep the church involved in the city rather
than seeking refuge in the suburbs. (This had even included a biracial retirement community for elderly people of modest income.) Dean Parks was
committed to this school started in 1967 and aiming towards an enrollment
of 1,000. The funding was delayed until the first board of trustees could agree
on a philosophy of racial integration. By 1971 the president of the student
body (and co-captain of the football team) was black and so was an honor
graduate of 1971 who had won one of Mt. Holyoke's most generous scholarships. The school was considered a success in every way except financially.

Boston and New England

Commonwealth School, Boston, Massachusetts, 1962–1983—$1,695,000 in
fifteen grants. Half a dozen of these Merrill Trust grants went for specific
purposes: scholarships, salaries, our biracial Urban School in the summer of
1964, a headmaster's discretionary fund, library purchases. Most of the
money, however, including two residual grants in 1982 and 1983 totaling
$220,000, went into endowment. As a foundation executive I had always
played down endowment: one takes care of the needs of today, the future
can be handled as it comes. As a headmaster I was grateful for this support
which gave my school its guarantee of survival, independence, and quality.

I started Commonwealth in 1958 with two major goals. The first was to
interpret and transmit the heritage of the past for the use of the future, a
conviction that came to me out of my year as a Fulbright teacher in postwar
Austria. The students I taught had an ability to get by on very little. They
had, however, a heritage of musical richness, above all in opera—*Don Gio-
vanni, Figaro, Fidelio, Rosenkavalier*—and Austria's resilience came, in large
part, from its culture. Later, in 1957, I spent a week in Warsaw. I spoke to

more people that week, I felt, than in my two preceding years in Paris, and about what was most important: war, freedom, religion, the meaning of art. These men and women had an intense conviction of the value of the *Will*, to stand up to the Germans, who had wanted to wipe out the city, and to the Russians, who had seen it as a docile provincial capital within the Soviet Union. One held to a faith in the spirit when there was little else. Could some of this ability to transcend the suffering of history be offered American youngsters?

Another goal was to educate an elite, as the Jesuits and Communists did, who out of native ability, hard work, and good teaching would learn the skills to lead society. By sheer good fortune, Sputnik had just been orbited around the earth, and this feat had been interpreted as a victory for Soviet technology and education over an America whose schools were lost in the morass of life-adjustment courses. Here was exactly the school to fill that vacuum! And in honest discussions of sex, socialism, and religion we would make use of our freedom.

When times became bad, these noble goals seemed pretentious. The pressures of race conflict, the shame of Vietnam, the wilderness of drugs and the new sexual standards, the fear of unemployment, the fear of nuclear war weighed upon our students and led to alienation, even to despair. I was willing to settle for a school that would allow children to lead stable, sensible lives and be able, in Sigmund Freud's great recipe for mental health, to love and to work.

I became less and less interested in curriculum. One hires the best teachers one can and leaves them alone. Nor is one method—progressive or conservative, authoritarian or free—better than another, so long as both sides are well handled. And no single point of view dominates the institution. I originally felt that Russian would be our most useful language. To my chagrin, Latin became more important because we seemed to hire outstanding classics teachers. During the troubles around 1970 we held the kids' allegiance because we had strong, generous men and women in the arts.

During the 1960s we led the other schools around Boston in our commitment to opportunity for black students. For almost fifteen years half of our scholarship budget went to that 10 to 12 percent, but when the new militancy blew up at the end of the decade, this commitment merely meant a highly visible block of students who gave no value whatsoever to the ideals of a liberal education that we professed. I don't remember much joy in those years, though our classes moved along competently and most of our graduates were pretty well put together and went on to useful careers.

By the mid-1970s the struggle for female equality became the field that demanded the most thoughtful response. One summer I reread my Bible and Plato to try and see from a woman's point of view what they said. We started exchange programs with an Irish and a French school. We insisted that every senior take a month's special project—in a lab, a nursing home, an architect's office—to force some contact with the Real World, some experience in looking for a job and working with adult strangers. We had a "strong" college placement record because the kids were well taught, knew how to work, and showed an interesting self-awareness, but more and more intensely I came to hate this subservience to Success. One person gets into Harvard and his life has meaning. The next one is turned down and everything is sham.

Who benefited from this school? The boys and girls (most of them) who went there, and the Trust endowment allowed us to accept almost any applicant we really wanted, whether he could pay $5,000 or less than $500. Anyone else? In our odd mix of serious work and high spirits, we offered useful competition to the older schools around us, sometimes encouragement to other teachers. Did we offer anything to Boston's public schools? We creamed off some of their student leadership, black and white. We made it easier for liberal families to attack Boston's racism because their own children were safely into our nice private school.

What was it worth? I kept asking myself that. What we demanded and offered in academics and in art were, at their best, first rate. At its best, the school had a moral and social concern that elicited a practical idealism from its children, in big ways (organizing an antinuclear rally), in small ways—a tradition of kindness to vulnerable people. There was a sense of freedom: you could say what you believed and others would listen to you.

Roxbury Latin, West Roxbury, Massachusetts, 1975—$10,000. Roxbury Latin is the ultimate Boston school. Founded in 1645, it has an endowment of $5.5 million for its 260 students, and its tuition accordingly holds at about half that of other schools. It had been run for centuries on a pattern of hard work, stiff competition, rigorous athletics, and a Harvard placement tradition. A headmaster who had tried to liberalize that pattern in the early 1970s was brutally fired by the board of trustees. At its worst, it was overpressured, rigid, but it was a part of Boston's history where old families sent their sons to make sure they developed a backbone, and where an Irish contractor on his way up could insure that Kevin rose higher than his dad. Washington Jarvis, an Episcopal priest, became headmaster in the mid-1970s, facing the problem of how to prepare his boys for a changing society and also to set moral and academic standards at a time when people preferred to do things more comfortably.

Buckingham Browne and Nichols, Cambridge, Massachusetts, 1971, 1977—$25,000 for capital needs. When the two traditional Cambridge schools, Buckingham for girls and Browne and Nichols for boys, merged in the early 1970s, they formed the largest (900) independent school in greater

Boston. A strong sports program helped and hurt it, for many second-class athletes resented the time they spent sitting on the bench, and too many of the staff had been hired first as coaches, then as teachers. The headmaster, Peter Gunness, who had come to the job from Harvard's admissions office, was faced with the duties of upgrading academics, trying to break through the self-centered, taking-life-for-granted assumptions of his students, who called themselves liberal because that allowed them to criticize everyone else. How to measure, how to attain a morally responsible society by the way one handles each day's ordinary chores—perhaps by genuine commitment to international education (in Russia and Zambia as well as Europe) and by practical outreach to the city community.

Concord Academy, Concord, Massachusetts, 1970, 1977—$45,000. Concord had always had a strong reputation for high-level academic and artistic achievement, a strong community atmosphere. It was hurt by its success, with a homogeneous atmosphere of pretty girls with Fair Isle sweaters, shoulder-length, honey-colored hair (and ski slope noses, as Commonwealth's Jewish girls remarked), and affluent parents. And though it was a well-run school, it suffered a high turnover of leadership in the 1970s. (Trustees lost sophistication and expected too much too soon, one colleague remarked. A headmaster's life lasted as long as an infantry lieutenant's in Vietnam, or a razor blade's: they use you till your edge is gone and then throw you away.)

Dana Hall School, Wellesley, Massachusetts, 1973—$5,000. Dana Hall had suffered a slow cumulative sag with the symptoms of lowering College Board averages and college placement results, increasing deficits, a discouraged faculty, and a routine, slow-moving administration. In the mid-1970s, though, the board hired a public school principal named Patricia Wertheimer, who had made a name for herself in handling a dangerous race crisis in Princeton, to try and turn the place around. I was intrigued by the day-to-day decisions of the process, the conflicting demands of money for a new teacher or a new boiler, admissions of a better girl needing financial aid or a richer girl not as bright, the use of hard work, cajolery, threats ("You trustees get me X thousand dollars for better salaries or I quit!"), patience, temper at each stage of the rebuilding process. The grant I obtained to support Mrs. Wertheimer was petty, and after a couple of years more she left, but a worthwhile foundation policy should be to look for exactly these tough-minded, unglamorous, turn-around leaders.

Identity—the School We Have, Concord, Massachusetts, 1972—$25,000. This school was started at the worst period of the youth crisis by a professor of psychiatry at Boston University. He sought to build an adolescent-centered environment in which creative but nonconforming and also disturbed young people could become involved with therapists, artists, craftsmen in an environment where they got interested in *something*. With group and encounter therapy, with professional drug therapy, they might strengthen themselves and be able to return to regular schools, or learn a skill like pottery, cabinet making, or car repair. It was a halfway house for students in crisis who could not be reached by the standard educator.

Shady Hill School, Cambridge, Massachusetts, 1960, 1975—$40,000. Shady Hill is probably the best-known primary school in New England for its long tradition of academic innovation and the bright imaginativeness of its daily life. It had been sponsored originally by the families of Harvard faculty, and parental labor as the substitute for cash had been turned into a way of life. The campus, a collection of little houses, one for each grade, was charming but run down and costly. Salaries were so low that the headmaster, like a medieval king with his barons, had little actual control over his senior staff. The school was quick to experiment, with the new math, the open classroom and integrated day from Leicestershire in England, with a year built around a central subject like the fourth grade being Greeks, new courses like "What Is Man?," a strong apprentice teacher program (graduates just out of college who paid to be worked very hard), use of its facilities by inner-city children. A voluntary graduated giving program tried to enforce a sliding scale of payment according to family income so that the school could admit up to 25 percent black students.

Some troubling details arose out of the very excellence of Shady Hill: a certain complacency, and among its graduates who had been exposed to wonderful education since kindergarten a certain flute-playing preciousness and surfeit.

Cambridge Friends School, Cambridge, Massachusetts, 1965–1981—$35,000. Friends had been founded by a former teacher from Shady Hill aiming to express the Quaker belief that there is good in every man which, given the right conditions, can find expression in daily life: "There is a desperate need in Cambridge and all over the world for human beings to learn to trust an inner rightness and not to be afraid to speak out." There was a stress on simplicity and democracy, on low tuitions so that young families could afford to come, on avoiding the competitiveness of other Boston private schools, on outreach to the hostile North Cambridge community around it. Reality was difficult. Local kids broke in to vandalize and steal. The stress on good thoughts meant that the students became intellectually soft, and respect for the group meant that they lost self-reliance. Yet there was a strong effort to be a force for community integration in that unhappy neighborhood, to try out new ways of teaching.

One headmaster spent a week in jail for participation in a sit-in at a New Hampshire nuclear power plant—a worthwhile contribution to children's education.

California and Elsewhere

Because of the Magowans' involvement in that state, the Trust made grants to around thirty California private schools, primary and secondary, religious and secular, in all the variety for which the state is famous.

Town School, San Francisco, 1964–1991—$45,000. Town is the largest (390) nonsectarian, primary boys' school in California and stresses scholarship, citizenship, and leadership. It was established in 1939 with stiff admissions standards and a need of constant fund raising by the headmaster to modernize and rebuild the plant, improve the library, expand scholarships, and build endowment so that pressure might be taken off the need for constant raises in tuition.

Bridgemont High School, San Francisco, California, 1981—$5,000. A new (1975) school, pointedly stating that it is not remedial or alternative or for kids in trouble but is directed towards students ready to make decisions about themselves, students dissatisfied with the intellectual relativism of their teachers and the rowdiness, sexuality, drug use, academic indifference, violence, and intimidation of their fellow students. In fact to create the old-fashioned American high school with "an atmosphere of serious serenity." Those words have different meanings according to who is using them, but one wishes the adventurers well.

St. Paul's School, Oakland, California, 1979, 1981—$15,000. A coed Episcopal school with almost 50 percent of its students from ethnic minorities and receiving financial aid.

York School, Pacific Grove, California, 1963–1981—$80,000 in seven grants. York was started in the late 1950s by a Hungarian refugee, a Benedictine monk who became an Episcopalian. At the beginning he was headmaster, teacher, janitor, and secretary. Salaries were low and since at first 20 percent of the boys came from families of public school teachers, tuition stayed low and scholarship commitments (40 percent for a while) high. For a time Merrill grants represented all the scholarship funds which came in. Despite this lack of underpinning, the school was able to establish and maintain high academic standards.

Cate School, Carpinteria, California, 1969–1981—$75,000. Established in 1910 near Santa Barbara, Cate was described as intensely pressured academically in order to maintain its reputation as one of the strong preparatory schools of the West. The Trust gave $40,000 in 1972 to help finance construction of a fine arts building with a 400-seat auditorium, audio and photographic facilities, radio station, and art galleries and studio. Californians think big, but I question that mega-complex, and not simply for its cost and debt. A high-priced facility produces nervousness about theft, vandalism, and mistakes. It prevents students and teachers from making do with some gymnasium-dining hall that can be turned into a theatre with imaginative lighting and carpentry. It encourages a conviction that if one spends enough money one becomes creative.

Crossroads School for the Arts and Sciences, Santa Monica, California, 1981—$10,000. A school established in 1971 to give equal importance to academic and artistic training, placed in a former factory building in an industrial sector of Santa Monica. Its two most recent courses were computer literacy and classical Greek. A primary policy had been to avoid the "star thing"—at this school the super-talented kid is just one of many. A strong scholarship program ensured a heterogeneous student body. All older students participated in community work, particularly with children and the elderly.

San Ramon Valley Christian Academy, Danville, California, 1980—$15,000 to provide a Christian education for 114 children, kindergarten through six, operating in the Community Presbyterian Church. At a time when both public and Catholic parochial schools are closing, one new Christian school a week is opening in California—the fastest growing educational movement in the United States. It has a Bible-centered curriculum designed to challenge the children to think. Discipline is administered with love in order to develop obedience, respect, and responsibility. The headmaster, who holds a doctorate from Columbia, was principal of three Juvenile Court schools before coming to San Ramon.

River School, Charleston, West Virginia, 1981—$10,000. This new primary school whose headmaster came from Francis Parker in Chicago is a mainstream liberal place, child oriented, and mildly experimental. What is unusual is its location in the middle of fundamentalist West Virginia where the local public school superintendent was involved a few years earlier in burning improper books. As the corporate executive community is too transient to take much interest, most parents come from Charleston's medical and university community. Because this means a homogeneous student body and because families will endure a thirty-mile commute each way to place their children in a school so unusual for the region, scholarship funds are badly needed.

San Ramon Valley Christian and River School make an interesting pair. As an educator I have been concerned by the metastasis of the Christian schools that combine fundamentalist theology, social conservatism and often racism, an icon-worshipping nationalism, and a heavy-handed discipline to encourage an unquestioning conformity. The delights of diversity and the reality of complexity are alien to them. One can imagine how precious are the qualities of intellectual self-reliance, the freedom to question, and the absence of fear that liberal parents in West Virginia exile seek in the River School. That atmosphere I tried to build in my own school. Our one formal rule—don't roller skate in the hallways—said, essentially, don't be a damn fool, act sensibly, and show concern for the rights of others (and work hard). Out of that injunction came the disciplinary structure. Show generosity towards outsiders. Learn to trust yourself in new situations.

Liberalism in decay, of course, as it was in the years around 1970, left our poor kids in a jungle. For many of them only two laws remained: don't criticize blacks, and don't rat on another kid to an adult. They distrusted their parents and teachers but would trust the stranger who sold them dope in Harvard Square.

I remember one girl who applied to Commonwealth in order to go to the bathroom. She couldn't at her present public school because the bathrooms were the turf of girls buying, selling, and using drugs. Couldn't a teacher interfere? If a teacher barged into the girls' john, she might well be sued for child molestation. And the principal would not back her up because the school board, in that spineless community, would not back him up. Accordingly, one accepts the Christian Academy, which knows Right from Wrong and enforces a tightly integrated world of virtue that includes dress code, short hair, salute to the flag, prayers in the classroom, formal courtesy, and biology textbooks that state that you cannot actually prove that God did not create the world. Discipline is administered with love. If the boss at San Ramon Valley Christian Academy had previously been principal of three Juvenile Court schools, he might have known what he was talking about.

CATHOLIC SCHOOLS

Although the Merrill Trust showed inadequate concern for public schools, it invested a lot of money in parochial schools and in the training, through Catholic colleges and universities, of men and women who taught in the public schools. A convent of the Sacred Heart occupying a Tudor mansion in

Winnetka and a factory-sized institution on Chicago's West Side for the children of immigrants are both parochial schools. The standards vary, and the worst schools can be awful, with a cloying religiosity, a blinkered distrust of new thoughts, panic at any expression of sexuality, and tight-fisted authoritarianism. On the other hand, church authority may be a counterweight to the totalitarianism of public opinion. It was the cardinal of St. Louis who ordered racial integration in his schools three years before the Supreme Court ruling of 1954. In Boston, I met non-Catholic black parents who enrolled their children in parochial schools because they trusted the discipline and sense of purpose. And for the new immigrants from Latin America, the Caribbean, and Indo-China, as for the old immigrants from Ireland, Italy, Poland, and Quebec, these front-line schools offer the first step in the Americanization of their children.

Roman Catholic Archdiocese of New York, 1969—$50,000. This major grant came out of a *New York Times* article on the crisis of the city's parochial system with its 430 elementary and high schools and 216,000 students. Since the construction of the Erie Canal and the 1847 potato famine, the Catholic Church of New York has had an Irish stamp. All but one of its presiding bishops has been of Irish background, and it is described as proud and rigid and shaped by the moral rigor and theological pessimism of Irish Catholicism.

Parishes are apt to be set by ethnic origin rather than by neighborhood, with the latest wave being Spanish-speaking—in 1970 one-third, in 1980 one-half. The Irish, Italian, and German congregations are being pushed out to Staten Island, the Upper Bronx, and then to Westchester and Long Island, resulting in financial crisis as middle-class white congregations are replaced by black and Hispanic ones. Because Cardinal Spellman put almost a half billion dollars into construction between 1939 and 1967, the Archdiocese is property-rich and cash-poor, and all income goes into operating expenses. The archdiocesan high schools alone run an annual deficit of $2.5 million. Teaching nuns are declining in number and lay teachers demand higher salaries. There is an intense need to retain schools in slum neighborhoods and there, of course, the cost to the archdiocese is the highest.

A young Jesuit priest, Anthony Meyer, chose these schools for us, using standards of leadership and need. Donald Regan supported the grant because so many of Merrill Lynch's faithful female employees were parochial graduates.

Cardinal Hayes, Brooklyn,—$15,000—held 2,400 boys of Italian, Polish, Czech, Ukrainian, Cuban, Puerto Rican, and Negro background. Ninety percent of the senior class in 1968 had gone on to college. Funds were needed for library expansion, audiovisual equipment, sports dressing rooms, and data-processing equipment.

Bishop Dubois, Harlem—$15,000— had 500 boys, 37 percent nonwhite. Fifty percent enter college, and the other 50 percent are educationally deprived and have serious reading problems. A professional reading program with special teachers and lab equipment was needed in order to cut the dropout rate.

Cathedral, on Lexington Avenue in Manhattan but with annexes in Harlem, South Bronx, and Greenwich Village, totaling more than 3,500 girls, received $20,000. The thirty-six different national backgrounds present a complicated language background, and an electronic speech lab was needed to help the girls and then their parents speak correct English. Also proper equipment to train students in computer key-punching.

Xavier High, New York, 1972—$25,000. Originally established to serve Catholic immigrant families, this school in lower Manhattan has a long tradition of response to community education needs such as adult evening education, a high school equivalency program, and an institute of industrial relations. Boys are accepted on scholarships to prepare them for entrance into the academic public and private high schools of the New York area.

St. Peter's Preparatory School, Jersey City, 1976—$15,000. This school serves an inner-city population of poorer whites and an increasing number of blacks and Hispanics. It runs a free summer school program for boys finishing seventh grade and tutorial assistance in the eighth grade to help minority students. Ninety-five percent go on to college. In a survey of sixty-five U.S. cities to measure education opportunities, Jersey City ranked sixty-fifth. In a city with 15 percent unemployment, even the low Catholic tuition was hard to meet.

Mount Carmel-Holy Rosary Consolidated School, New York, 1977—$15,000 for this primary school of 300 Italian, Hispanic, and black children in East Harlem. The rooms hold thirty to forty-three pupils apiece, and approximately fifty are handicapped or learning disabled and require special care. Our grant went to establish a resource center for diagnosis and remedial work with a teacher specially trained in learning disabilities. It also went to recruit aides from the neighborhood in order to raise the level of help and understanding.

Inner-City Scholarship Fund, New York, 1978—$10,000 for funds to allow poor children to attend parochial schools in certified poverty areas throughout the city. These scholarships provide opportunity for underprivileged children, and by strengthening the schools in Harlem, South Bronx, West Side, Midtown East, and the Lower East Side provide greater stability for these deprived areas.

Cardinal Spellman High, Bronx, New York, 1981—$25,000. This place came to my attention from a Williams dean who said that even if previously good New York schools like Peter Stuyvesant could no longer offer their top 1 percent students to a college like Williams, other strong working-class schools did exist. Because of good leadership, a dedicated faculty, discipline, and an immigrant parent body who took education seriously, Spellman, in the North Bronx, was one of them. Each year four or five seniors won placement and financial aid at Williams.

This seemed worth following up. Cardinal Spellman was organized in 1959 and currently enrolls 2,250 boys and girls. Admission is by competitive exam. Twenty-eight percent of the students are black or Hispanic. Ninety percent of graduating seniors go on to college, and nearly 80 percent of the faculty have master's degrees. What would they like? The school had never received an offer like ours, and the principal had to touch base with his different departments before we received a shopping list: one Apple II computer and software; video tapes for Kenneth Clarke's *Civilization*; one helion neon laser for experiments in optics; two microfilm readers for use with periodicals references in library; one microfilm reader-printer for preparing transcripts; special assembly programs from the Metropolitan Opera, Lincoln Center, and New York City Ballet traveling groups; aid to twenty needy students to help defray costs of tuition and books; and tuition aids to faculty for summer study.

There is a program that any foundation trustee could work out with a public or parochial high school. It will allow a wonderful sense of accomplishment.

Immaculata High School, Chicago, Illinois, 1971—$15,000. Sister Mary Trinetta, a teacher at Immaculata who back in the 1920s had worked for E. A. Pierce (one of the companies that eventually merged into Merrill Lynch) sent this appeal. Immaculata opened around 1920 and had an enrollment of about 1,000 girls, the daughters of policemen, firemen, janitors, and taxi drivers who wanted something better than the public schools. The students came from large families whose parents found it more and more difficult to pay tuition, and many girls helped by working in the library, the cafeteria, or by cleaning the classrooms. The old nationalities were Germans, Italians, Irish, Ukrainians, and Poles. The new were Cubans, Mexicans, Chinese, Japanese, Laotians, and Haitians. There was special teaching for foreign students with language handicaps as well as tutoring for slow learners. The school was trying to raise money for closed-circuit TV equipment for a rapid reading and comprehension program. Parents say they chose Immaculata because it is well run and has a good plant, good teachers, and good training in moral values.

There are lots of large parochial schools like Immaculata, but I found the letters from Sister Mary Trinetta very moving in that struggle to keep the school alive. Eight Catholic high schools had recently closed in Chicago, the Catholic schools are closing down in Massachusetts, and the public schools in all our cities are unprepared to take on the new burdens.

University of San Francisco High School, 1978–1981—$65,000. In 1978 $25,000 was given to establish Summerbridge, an enrichment and skills program for attracting and preparing able public school students for entrance into the seventh grade, and $25,000 in 1981 for scholarship aid to maintain the impetus of that program. $15,000 was given in 1979 for faculty salaries— so important in a city so expensive.

St. Ignatius Preparatory School, San Francisco, 1969–1971—$60,000. A large (1,185), long-established (1855) Jesuit school with an energetic, responsible alumni body and a strong community commitment that includes work with retarded children and the nearby Jewish home for the aged.

National Catholic Welfare Conference, Washington, D.C., 1964, 1965— $22,700. Between 1940 and 1964 there had been a 129 percent increase in enrollment among parochial pupils compared with 53 percent in public schools. Untrained people moved to the top where they operated busily and inefficiently. There was a need not only to improve math and science instruction but also to train principals and superintendents through conferences, workshops, and seminars and to establish standards for accreditation.

PUBLIC SCHOOLS

When the trust began operations, Charlie Cole insisted that one of our priorities should be support of the public schools, particularly in teacher training. In our first years we appropriated almost $300,000: $70,800 through Atlanta University for black social science teachers; $210,000 through the Wharton School of Finance, University of Pennsylvania, for summer study in economics; $75,000 to the American Council of Learned Societies, New York City, as fellowships for high school language teachers to study abroad; $11,500 to Amherst College in 1962 to help finance the development of a new 11th grade American history course, stressing the use of primary sources and the in-depth study of eight or ten major periods in American life; and $10,000 in 1964 to the Massachusetts Council for Public Schools, Boston, to support their process of helping local school systems gain accreditation and solve operating problems.

By the mid-1960s that priority went out of focus for us, perhaps because the issue of better education for public school children became involved in— got lost in?—the more dramatic demands of new opportunities for blacks, and we put our money into scholarship programs or, particularly in the Boston area, into alternative schools (described in *Black and White*). But where we were attracted to a special school system or a special problem that seemed valuable we continued an involvement.

National Association for Independent Schools, Boston, Massachusetts, 1972—$20,000. One of the most controversial reforms in American education was the Leicestershire open classroom idea. Tried out first in England, this was an effort to free up the schools' over-disciplined procedures. A group of children, sometimes of two different grades, would work under two or three teachers in the same large classroom where the work was centered on the task not the bell system. The result might either be chaos or a greater willingness and alertness, with pupils willing to learn out of their own interests.

The National Association for Independent Schools ran four-week workshops for 3,000 elementary teachers on the open classroom as a way to bring new life into a system as traditional as that of Massachusetts and also as a way for public and private school teachers to work together.

Cambridge School Department, Cambridge, Massachusetts, 1972— $25,000. Cambridge had a typical mediocre school system: politically controlled and unresponsive to either the needs of the community or of the children in the classroom. The efforts of a mixed group of parents and teachers, black and white, to provide an alternative to this suddenly became realistic with a new professional (as opposed to political) superintendent of schools and a city council and a school committee receptive to change. An alternative public school was established in a new building of the existing Martin Luther King School in a racially and economically mixed neighborhood.

The National Association for Independent Schools, which approached the Merrill Trust for this grant, saw the project as a way to strengthen teacher training and to establish one model school within a typical city community. $15,000 went to fund a one-month workshop for teachers, administrators, and parents to learn new ideas and also to get to know each other; $10,000 went for new equipment that the Cambridge budget could not afford despite its $12 million annual size.

I cannot think of a more important way for foundations to spend their money, and one notices, of course, how rarely it is done, both for service to one specific community and as a political leverage and example for others.

Reading is Fundamental, Washington, D.C., 1976—$20,000. This low-budget project, started by Mrs. Robert McNamara in 1966, sought to attract children to cheap, interesting, and relevant paperbacks that they were allowed to keep. Children in the inner cities, in Appalachia and Indian reservations, and in hospitals and reformatories were the targets. A statistic often employed, but without much done about it, is that twenty million Americans cannot read a want ad.

Orton Society, Towson, Maryland, 1980—$25,000 for a more scientific approach to the same problem: the study, treatment, and prevention of problems in a specific language disability. Dyslexia, word blindness, is the inability to learn and use language skills in a manner consistent with a child's intellectual and social potential and carries over destructively into adult life. Orton tries to sensitize schools and families and to train teachers. An unanswered question is why more boys than girls are affected, a discouraging fact the high proportion of prisoners who are dyslexic—that initial frustration at school setting off a lifetime of hostility to society.

New York City School Volunteer Program, New York, 1978—$15,000. Nearly 1,200 volunteers in 312 schools throughout the five boroughs are involved with individual instruction from kindergarten through twelfth grade. At least 400 principals have shown interest in starting and expanding this program, and there is a need to supply additional teacher coordinators and enlarge black participation. Results have been higher reading scores and greater motivation and interest in school work.

National Committee for Citizens in Education, Columbia, Maryland, 1979, 1980—$35,000. This group sought to improve the quality of education for students in the public schools, primarily by involving parents responsibly in their children's schooling. Intelligible, jargon-free information and technical assistance were offered to 325 affiliated parents and citizen groups. The Committee offered advice on how to monitor legislation on education, get the most out of a PTA, ask the right questions, and avoid the traditional passivity of American society.

Sad to read how any reform movement within the public schools uses *jargon-free* as almost the first adjective about its work. Why are educationists taught to employ that tortured dialect?

American Association for Gifted Children, New York, 1981—$10,000. The Association was started in 1946 to meet the needs of talented children, especially those gifted in the arts and humanities. There was cooperation with the AMA and the Academy of Pediatrics to learn best how to meet their psychological and emotional needs. The egalitarian prejudices of children and teachers are affronted by unusual ability, and the unfortunate individual is humiliated unless given some protection.

For the cultural enrichment of public school children the Trust gave $95,000 to Young Audiences' New York and Boston centers; $10,000 to the Grand Monadnock Arts Council for small-town schools in southern New Hampshire (described in *Culture*); and $20,000 to *Urban Gateways*, Chicago, Illinois, 1975, 1981. Urban Gateways sponsored a Talent Development Program to aid the academic and social development of children through exposure to art; to artists brought into the public and parochial schools; and to cultural centers like the Art Institute, Field Museum, Chicago Symphony, and Goodman Theatre. The Program sought to reach exceptionally talented teenagers and to broaden their horizons, providing skills training and creating communities where they could share their interest and overcome their sense of isolation. Merrill money went for small grants for lessons, instrument rentals, an annual New York tour for seniors, concert tickets, and performances at member schools.

Brookside School, San Anselmo, California, 1981—$10,000 for aid to forty learning and physically handicapped children at this public school whose parents must raise private funds to pay for services no longer supplied by the state. My eleven-year-old granddaughter, partly deaf from meningitis, was one of the children who received these special services, and I was grateful that our Trust could help meet this need. One is left troubled, however, by the thinking that supports a Proposition 13½ that ends the services a democratic society should take for granted. Marin County possesses enough well-to-do families to raise alternative funds and who become usefully politicized in the process. How about children in poor counties? What will be the long-range impact on their lives of these mean economies?

CONCLUSIONS

In the $12.7 million that the Merrill Trust gave to 125 private schools, boarding and day, primary and secondary, one might argue about criteria and argue for more or less concentration, but the real argument is whether, instead of all that money to Deerfield, Kent, and San Ramon Valley Christian Academy, we should have given far more grants to specific public schools and the needs of public school teachers and their pupils.

When I used to show visitors around Commonwealth School and talk about what we offered in science or art or the teachers' sabbatical policy that I was particularly proud of, or pass a couple of youngsters studying silently by themselves at the top of a stairway, I inevitably received the protest of what a shame that only this small, privileged group of boys and girls could benefit from the atmosphere of stimulus, concern, and trust. And then there was the broader question of wasn't it my duty, if I believed in democracy, to invest the money, energy, and skill that went into serving those 125 or so students at Commonwealth into serving ordinary students in the Boston public schools, whose needs and desires were great and who received so very little?

That is the question. The answers that the private school establishment gives—look at these kids who win the Martin Luther King scholarships, look at the way our new methods have been copied, look at the leadership our graduates give American society—are not as significant as that establishment would like you to think. Fundamentally, private schools serve privilege in this country and in the Soviet Union, though the academies attended by children of high officials are not called by that name. Exceptions, like those scholarship grants, go just so far.

Accordingly, a new responsibility for foundations, which they have traditionally avoided, may be to invest serious money and thought into our country's public schools. The mid-1980s are an apt time for launching a major shift in policy.

Americans, both average citizens and professionals, seem in agreement that our schools, particularly the secondary schools, are in poor shape. The troubled introspection coming out of this conclusion may support a readiness to consider major changes, as did the similar malaise after Sputnik, which seemed to prove that Soviet technology and schooling were superior to our own.

The situation may be worse than our pessimists believe. A 25 percent rate of white teenage unemployment, 50 percent among minority teenagers, and perhaps 65 percent among minority dropouts mean that a large proportion of young American males are going no place and, with the slow dying of smokestack industry, never will go any place. Going to school has ceased to have any relevance to their future. If teachers have nothing to offer these sullen, dangerous young men, our recourse is to hire more police.

The reform movements being touted today may make things worse. The crusade against mediocrity is a covert war on equality. There is vindictiveness about the new elitism: Don't worry about blacks—they had their chance! The traditional American high schools had to juggle, and it was never easy, their often conflicting social and academic responsibilities. Poor kids can't be written off. The new excellence is a technocratic goal to be measured by objective testing—above all else by the SAT scores. If these scores aren't on their way up, taxpayers and people in authority won't be interested in whatever else the school stands for. And, last, the drive for excellence is an authoritarian, top-down reform such as a new president of General Motors or a new minister of education in Czechoslovakia would shove through. The school principals, as much as the teachers and students, are expected to obey and comment only when asked to.[1]

In making any commitment to public schools, a foundation might begin with its own version of the shopping list offered to the Merrill Trust by Cardinal Spellman High: video tapes of *Civilization*, assembled programs of good music and theater, new lab and office equipment and library books, and subsidy for faculty summer study. How about money earmarked to improve lunchroom food and to hire extra help to keep the bathrooms cleaner? It is squalor as well as noise, crowding, depersonalization, boredom, and potential violence (qualities that schools share with jails) that turn off so many youngsters. At a school I know in New Hampshire, a local corporation has funded an 8:00 A.M. volunteer math class for good students. If a rule for giving might be that what is offered to bright kids should be matched by equal value for dumb kids, how about other special classes in remedial reading and math? Adolescent illiteracy is not going to be cured by temper tantrums but by skilled (usually expensive) professional service with small classes. Hiring well-educated young mothers, who need to work at home, as paper correctors to English and social science teachers will allow writing assignments to be set once or twice a week, impossible now for a suburban teacher with an average pupil load of 120 or an inner-city teacher whose load may go up to 175.

Money is needed to expand the health services to include classes and face-to-face counseling on diet (to counter self-destruction by junk food), obesity (lethal for self-image), and alcohol and drugs (parents are so panicked by drugs that they evade the scourge of teenage alcoholism). These approved goals would in turn supply cover for a low-profile program of sex counseling: avoidance and treatment of venereal disease, contraception, or a quiet discussion with a girl who has realized she is pregnant and wants to learn the options before she tells her parents. The most important single step to keep marginal adolescents out of a life of poverty and dependency is to cut down teenage parenting. The right-to-lifers who wage a holy war on abortion show little practical concern for prevention or for support afterwards to the young mother and baby that would help her put her life back together. Sex is a hot topic for school administrators, but your foundation's money could hire a

1. For more on this subject, see the excellent article by Joseph Featherstone in the August 14, 1984, edition of *The Boston Phoenix*.

hygienist who, once the grapevine reported that she was no-nonsense, know-ledgeable, kind, and did not tell tales, would have troops of boys and girls show up at her door.

Instead of giving all one's scholarship grants to colleges, why not channel five or ten thousand a year through a school you have come to trust? The principal may know who are needy and deserving seniors, and such funds strengthen his hand in trying to back academic values. A trust with legal expertise could show a whole school district how to set up a 501(c)(3) foundation as a channel for gifts from local business and individuals who could be persuaded by the examples described of the ways that extra funds would benefit their community's children.

In dealing with Cardinal Spellman, the Merrill Trust was clearly involved with a model school. My correspondence with them revealed this, and we had that recommendation from the Williams dean. At the same time, I feel it is important not to get hung up on quality. Children are children. They are of equal worth whatever their SAT scores. A conversation with a college admissions professional can tell you a lot about comparative status, but there is nothing wrong with simply choosing the high school nearest your home or a dozen schools within your city. Start small. Give yourself time to know the people you are dealing with and give them time to trust you and learn what you are aiming at. School administrators are (usually with justification) suspicious. It also takes time for them to develop confidence and imagination. But if the principal is worth dealing with, make sure that he or she, with input from teachers and students, is the one who makes the decisions, not the superintendent. When you establish a reputation as someone with sustained, intelligent concern for schools (an exclusive club to belong to), then higher officials will want to make your acquaintance, listen to your suggestions, and offer you their own requests, which may be quite sensible. But remember that your objective is not only to serve the needs of students and teachers but to defend the concept of democracy, which is not really all that healthy in the American educational system, or anywhere else.

If the Merrill Trust could have spent the $5 million allotted to Deerfield in ways like these, think of what we might have accomplished! And yet what private foundation, however wealthy, can put up the money to pay for what is really necessary: smaller class sizes and higher teacher pay? And more important than money, grant trust and autonomy to the classroom teachers?

CHAPTER THREE

Amherst and Others

I want to help relieve the tensions which develop in young men
from a lack of funds to carry out their education. During my high
school and college years I felt a burden of pressure almost too heavy
for me to bear.

[Charles E. Merrill, in a letter to Frank L. Boyden of Deerfield]

Perhaps half of the Merrill Trust grants in every field were somehow involved
with education, but our major investment was in the liberal arts college. That
was what we knew best. As we made our first grants in 1959, we began with
the places each one of us knew: Colby and Bates in Maine, Reed in Oregon,
Morehouse in Georgia, and Mount Holyoke in Massachusetts. From the beginning, we agreed that we would not concentrate on "the best" but would
take seriously any institution that seemed to be moving ahead, played a responsible role in its community, or served a specific clientele as did Springfield
College in western Massachusetts, which trained for careers in youth leadership (with ex-prisoners, for example), physical education, and service to the
aged and retarded.

We also agreed that our concerns would be the institution, not the program.
Many foundations are self-indulgent in funding special programs—Asian
studies, community outreach—and then they quit and leave this new commitment upon the general budget. Others are too refined to be interested in
bricks and mortar. On the whole, we gave money to meat-and-potatoes
needs: financial aid, salaries, and libraries. Guilford College in North Carolina wanted money for a new gymnasium, which did not interest us, but
their administration felt that such a building was important for morale and
recruitment, and we accepted the argument. The late 1960s and early 1970s
were the time of baby-boom applications and of commitments to a rapid

increase in the numbers of blacks on campus, and we joined in new construction and new scholarship programs. It was the time for grandiose performing arts centers—later on for computer projects. As national values and our own changed, we shifted from large scholarships for working class students to partial ones for middle class and often specifically small-town students, which revealed, of course, less concern for black needs.

Amherst put almost all of the $12 million it received from us into endowment. On the whole, however, we reasoned that if today's needs were met rationally, tomorrow would take care of itself.

What did we accomplish? If the grant was to repair the roof on Founder's Hall the answer is easy. If the money went for scholarships, the dean of students wrote an upbeat letter about Imogene's service with crippled children and did not mention that Ignatz had been dropped for selling dope. The $25,000 to Stanford in 1969 for Mexican-American students opened a specific door that could then be kept open by general revenues. The $100,000 to Brown in 1979 for retaining untenured younger staff met a particular crisis that was a serious threat to faculty morale and the university's academic quality—and to the future of the teaching profession. Otherwise the giver is left with the assumption that if the chosen institution is well run the money will be well used, probably true 90 percent of the time.

How did we judge the quality of these colleges? Dr. Thomas, the Trust's administrator, wanted to know whether the student body was intellectually alive or passive and listless. Is it fashionable to study? Our questions became increasingly bureaucratic, but some factual criteria were useful.

First of all are the Scholastic Aptitude Test averages. Next, the number of National Merit Scholars in the freshman class. Then, out of these freshmen, what percentage remain to graduate and to go on to graduate school? Also important were faculty salaries at different ranks and the percentage of faculty holding doctorates. This figure has ambiguous value. Too low shows intellectual thinness; too high may simply reveal an overly academic institution too unimaginative to search out more interesting measurements. A mediocre scholar at a mediocre university earns a doctorate of purely statistical value. I proposed asking the percentage of who were alcoholics and who were divorced.

Other measurements are book and market value of endowment, library size, and the budget (last year and five years ago) for library acquisitions. Those two figures are the most useful you can employ for sizing up the intellectual commitment of a school. Also, the percentage of alumni who contributed last year and the average size of the gift. My father thought that information crucial. Alumni who became teachers and ministers could not afford gifts as large as bankers, but if the percentage was low it meant that the alumni did not care much for their old school, and maybe justifiably.

Nevertheless, the Primal Fact, right or wrong, is the SAT averages.[1] As a professional for thirty-three years, I looked at that detail first. Other professionals angrily disagree. SATs discriminate against inarticulate proletarian and minority youngsters. They favor the middle class who read, who go to schools where they are encouraged to speak, are assigned difficult books, and write papers where mistakes are explained and accurately corrected. They favor children from families that eat dinner together and share discussions about politics and daily life. The child does poorly from a home where English is not spoken, where father or mother is too tired or angry to answer questions, where each member eats in silence watching TV, who sits passive and bored in a large classroom, and who talks only with his peers in Youthspeak and has been given no skills for measuring words and the ideas that come from words: causation and result, analogy and exception, and essence and irrelevance. Again, in mathematics the student drilled in computation and formulas lacks the problem-solving skills and the ability to analyze and abstract that win good SAT scores.

Let's face it, average American life at home, in the classroom, and on the streets does not encourage intellectual potential.

The scores worsened from the late 1960s on. Each sociologist had a favorite reason: television replacing books, undisciplined progressive teaching, and less talk between adults and children as family ties loosened. How about rising unemployment? Demoralized parents became brutal, frightened children dulled. The most obvious cause was ignored by conservatives: the vast new numbers taking the tests out of working class and minority backgrounds. Any institution, whether Wesleyan University or Commonwealth School, which admitted a sizable percentage of such students, became a more interesting and worthwhile institution thereby but saw those precious averages slump. A grade B school forced by economic and demographic hardship into accepting just about any applicant who can pay will also show lower averages.

At any rate, colleges and universities received a total (including the $12 million to Amherst but excluding funds given to divinity, law, medical, and business schools of often the same institutions) of about $30 million. This figure includes $2,160,000 to twenty-three black institutions even if they are discussed separately under *Black and White*. Nineteen million went to institutions in New England.

New England

Amherst College, Amherst, Massachusetts, 1959–1982—$12,300,000. This support was the most that the Merrill Trust gave to any institution. One of

1. December 1985: real estate values in wealthy Washington suburbs whose local high schools had outstanding SATs might average $20,000 above similar communities elsewhere.

the foundation's original trustees, was, accordingly, Charles Cole, then president of Amherst. My father respected his judgment and probity, even if Dr. Cole had moved the college in directions different from Mr. Merrill's standards—admitting more Jews, upgrading academic standards and faculty influence, weakening the power of the fraternities, and expressing skepticism about the values of the Republican Party—and Cole saw one of his functions on our board to be defender of Amherst interests.

Amherst represents success. Harvard is bigger, better known, even richer, more heterogeneous, more "brilliant," with an artistic, critical flavor Amherst lacks, but both schools have the same arrogance, the same conviction that no other place is as good and that their graduates are the men who run and should run this country. The best American corporate lawyers—including Negro lawyers who handled the NAACP's critical cases under Thurgood Marshall in the 1940s and 1950s—bankers, college presidents, ambassadors had started out at Amherst. Or, if they were not the best, they were the men who had gotten what they wanted to get. Commonwealth School sent a black graduate to Amherst who complained about the insufferable elitism of his classmates, but he went on to win a fellowship to the University of Kyoto (Amherst always valued its connections with Japan), graduated from Michigan's law school, and started his own elite career at a government agency in Washington.

The $12 million given to the college from 1959 to 1982 was put into endowment, and this Merrill money represents 10 percent of its total. What does Amherst do with its resources? If it is the outstanding college in the United States, what does that mean? That question makes Amherst people ill at ease. Nevertheless, Amherst is one of the last colleges in the country that practices "aid-blind" admissions: if the admissions office accepts a high school senior, the decision is made almost entirely on merit (plus points as an alumnus child or from interesting details: i.e., as medievalist from Wyoming versus pre-med from New York City). When the acceptance has been made, then the admissions and financial aid committees confer on what size scholarship the youngster needs. The family's cash is not a relevant question. The American dream still exists.

More money buys better students and teachers. Granted. But where, so far as American society is concerned, is the repayment for this gold-plated distinction? First of all, Amherst has the strength to set its own standards. It does not have to follow the fads. It can stress the importance of getting its students to think, to see a complex problem through a mix of disciplines, and to make use of a faculty/student ratio small enough that an able upper classman can form a close intellectual friendship with a professor. American universities have always turned out beautifully trained specialists, but a young executive out of Amherst may have been sure enough of himself not to major in computer analysis but in history, biology, poetry, mathematics, and he may therefore have the imagination to see his corporation's problems in the round.

Amherst has the freedom to take gambles. In 1971 its new president, William Ward, just three months in office, sat down at an Air Force base near Holyoke to protest the Cambodian bombing and got himself arrested, which turned off the alumni but was an expression of what a confident head could risk. The admissions director does not have to play things safe with valedictorians who have 750 College Board scores but can look for some odd sort of intellectual quirkiness or moral strength. (Like everybody else, they began to take in young women too, but weren't exactly sure what to do with them.) The black students Amherst accepted in the 1960s and 1970s made a lot of noise, partly to see how far they could push the college, but they had the strength and received the education so that ten and fifteen years later they played leadership roles in their institutions and communities.

To come from an elite institution may mean a guaranteed arrogance and the ability to see the world only through one's own frame of reference, like English gentlemen and Prussian landowners. Or it can mean generosity, modesty, and realism. Having been treated so well, one can turn around, as my father did, and help others. To be convinced of one's superiority can allow a sense of honor. One isn't for sale.

If the arguments are *not* true, of course, then that $12 million investment simply helped a number of lucky individuals get ahead faster and better.

Williams College, Williamstown, Massachusetts, 1960–1979—$210,000. Williams wasn't Amherst, and given the composition of our trustees, received a patronizing regard: really quite good in its own way. Our gifts went toward a named chair in history and public affairs, scholarships, special capital drives, and a gift in honor of the Trust's attorney, Henry Happel. Perhaps because it was stereotyped as rich, conservative, and homogeneous, Williams made a determined effort to change its policies, admitting Jews, artists, women (that was seen as a clever idea—women paying the same tuition but majoring in fields like poetry and French, which do not require expensive equipment), and downgrading the frats. It experimented with new admissions criteria that stressed a student's individual qualities rather than Board scores and class rank, favoring public over private school applicants (less well trained but more self reliant) and starting a pre-freshman summer program to meet the needs of black and Hispanic students.

Though never as good as Amherst, of course, Williams was an interesting school that showed the value of being such a firm part of the Establishment. Each year it received, without having to lift a finger, the legacies of its old graduates and their widows in a way that newer institutions could never match.

Wesleyan University, Middletown, Connecticut, 1967–1980—$103,400.
Wesleyan, the third of the Little Three, had less prestige than Amherst and
Williams—"a creative inferiority complex" was the local phrase—and was
hurt on its applications to us by its reputation of having a huge endowment
from wise or lucky investments in IBM, Xerox, and educational publications:
$150 million or $107,000 per student in 1967. When that year, however, the
incoming president was Edwin Etherington, former head of the American
Stock Exchange, Don Regan thought it impolitic for us to ignore a college of
such quality. Probably no other institution in the Northeast had made such
overall improvement since 1945, and many of the new approaches that became standard procedure for other colleges had been first tried out at Wesleyan. It had initiated an integrated program for freshmen to expose them—
in letters, social studies, and quantitative studies—to the ideas that have
shaped world cultures as well as to break down the rigidity of the traditional
departments. Under its College Plan, selected students at Wesleyan can pursue independent study with formal work suspended (as at Oxford and Cambridge) in favor of colloquia, tutorials, and the writing of many papers. A
Center for Advanced Studies invited distinguished scholars, artists, professionals on campus. Graduate programs were established, including a few
doctorates where Wesleyan felt itself strong enough. Students were involved
in policy decisions. In its interest in Asian and African cultures, Wesleyan
was almost the first mainline institution to broaden its range of inquiry there.

With all this money and with strong, energetic leadership, there came a
frightening breadth of choice—a problem Emory University was to face in
1979 when it received a $100 million gift from the Woodruff Foundation.
Where to go: higher wages, better financial aid? The averages were already
high, and no college wants a reputation as a soft touch. Schools of law and
medicine, new Ph.D. programs: those would change Wesleyan's essential
quality of a liberal arts college. Negroes? In 1969 Wesleyan did start a generous scholarship program for blacks, but there were too few motivated, disciplined, well-prepared black students on the market, as all too many schools
learned. Such a program meant a large number of new students, no matter
what signs of brains and ambition they might show, absolutely unprepared
for college-level work, and who hid their lack of confidence by aggressive
contempt for all the college stood for and for their white liberal classmates.
It is not always fun to have lots of money.

At any rate, the Merrill Trust checked off its obligation by $15,000 in 1967
for the World Music Center, where students learned about Indian, Japanese,
and Indonesian music. In 1977 we gave $50,000 for scholarships. Costs had
increased, the fabled endowment had shrunk, more students needed financial
aid, and an operating deficit has been projected for just under $1 million.
Wesleyan was having to look for money just like everyone else. In 1980 we

made a final grant of $25,000, again for scholarships and by 1982 Wesleyan ended its policy of aid-blind admissions, which marked the close of an era.

That November 1980 appeal, however, caused a colorful crisis at the Charles E. Merrill Trust. The preceding spring there had been a demonstration by students and faculty to demand the divestiture of endowment stocks in American corporations doing business in the Republic of South Africa, and the university's board had agreed. Bob Magowan insisted that South Africa was a more reliable anti-communist ally than a lot of the silly nations that liberals favored and that an administration so spineless as to give in to impudent demands was not one we should back.

South African investment is a complex issue. In the 1970s one found American blacks who argued, against white liberals, that American corporations served the needs of black Africans. They paid higher salaries, placed African workers into skilled jobs that national corporations would not, and were allowed by the government to test out changing racial customs in experiments too risky for any domestic outfit. By 1980 the climate had changed. The economic suffering of African workers was less important, in their and in American eyes, than the need to hold a united front against a brutal and also insecure regime anxious to win international recognition. Moreover, the overemphasis by American academics upon this issue was not, as my brother-in-law stated, a sign of their arrogant strength, but of their weakness. To harry their different boards of trustees—and it was surprising to learn how many institutions, from Princeton to Berkeley, had taken similar stands on divestiture—was the *only* political policy that the fading Left could unite upon. And, as presented in the arguments before the final vote, to go back on our expressed interest in this appeal because of Wesleyan's stand on South Africa might expose not only the headmaster of Commonwealth School but also the president of Merrill Lynch and the former and present chief executives of Safeway Stores to embarrassment.

Colby College, Waterville, Maine, 1959–1977—$263,000. Charlie Cole saw Colby as the sort of college that our foundation should concentrate upon, and the $100,000 in 1959 to help put up a new administration building was one of our first big grants. Colby, Bates, and Middlebury had been coeducational at a time when almost no other New England colleges were, modest places but with importance in northern New England. They possessed self-respect, identity, and solid leadership, where the sort of help we might offer would have a tangible effect.

In 1952 Colby moved from its old (since 1818) location in grubby Waterville to a new hilltop campus, put up a series of brick buildings, and made a conscious effort through one capital drive after another to enlarge its student body, endowment, and library, and improve its faculty and academic offerings. It had two able presidents, Seelye Bixler and Robert Strider, while the Merrill Trust was connected with it, and óur later grants went for faculty salaries, a student health center, a science development program, scholarships, and purchases for the art museum. Colby's isolation could become deadening over the long winters as one looked out at the snow-covered hills of central Maine. One way to counteract this was the January term for independent study off campus, started in 1962 and copied by other colleges. Another was to strengthen the arts. There were few cultural facilities nearby for students to patronize, but the college had its own symphony orchestra, an excellent small museum specializing in New England painting, and a good art department. We made Colby one of our $10,000 art purchase grants in 1972 in recognition of this strength.

Bates College, Lewiston, Maine, 1960–1977—$170,000. Bates, founded in 1863 to serve the talented poor from the rural villages and farming communities of Maine, was one of the first American colleges to grant degrees to women. I first heard of it as the alma mater of Benjamin Mays, a poorly prepared Negro student from South Carolina who learned that by desperate hard work he could hold his own against Yankees and who went on to become president of Morehouse College. Its president during the 1950s and 1960s was so conservative that he never started construction of a new building until all the financing was in hand, which meant that the campus was dishearteningly shabby, and when a library eventually got built, it cost twice as much as it might have. Salaries, tuition, endowment, and morale were low. For students from private schools like my own, it had been the fifth-choice insurance application in case every other hope failed, but for graduates of small-town Maine high schools it offered a useful education.

On Dr. Cole's advice we allotted $30,000 for general purposes in 1960 and $25,000 in 1962 to help fund a public broadcasting station in cooperation with Colby and Bowdoin. At the end of the 1960s a new president, Hedley Reynolds, who had been dean of faculty at Middlebury, took over and launched a determined effort to upgrade the college: building, at last, the new library (to which we gave $30,000), reorganizing its approach to learning with off-campus courses like marine biology on the coast or social studies in Harlem, setting up honors courses and a junior year abroad, encouraging student participation in discipline and policy making, and using a whole new level of salaries and sabbaticals to build a strong faculty. Reynolds sought to bring in more blacks and also French Canadians from industrial towns like Lewiston. They were the bottom rung of the local ladder, and he tried to build the prestige of French culture through films, through artists from Montreal at campus events to which townspeople were invited, and through summer fellowships to France. By the late 1970s even strong private school seniors found Bates a choosy college to deal with.

Over-sensitive critics fault the American college president's preoccupation with fund raising—the desperation leading to a final coronary as he scrambles to meet the great Ford challenge. I met more than I cared to of those sad, frantic creatures. Nevertheless, that same task could also be an outlet for honest creativity. In orchestrating a capital campaign between 1976 and 1984 where President Reynolds raised $21 million for Bates, with the bringing up of alumni leadership to share in responsibility; the search for the wealthy few and organization of the many; appeals to local corporations; involvement of governors and senators (easier in Maine and Tennessee than in New York); and foundation negotiations of a subtlety, timing, and decisiveness that Metternich admired—that's art! And the rewards in endowment, art center, and olympic-sized pool are matched by the rewards of achievement, independence, pride, and a conviction that in meeting the needs of this provincial institution, the battle-scarred president is also facing up to the needs of contemporary American education.

The rule of a foundation is not only to back the changing, growing institution but also the first-rate executive, and it was in recognition of Reynolds's determination that I obtained an $85,000 grant in 1977 for scholarships to small-town students from Maine. Forget the lavish summer resorts on the coast. Inland Maine is as poor as Mississippi, and if the college was not going to be one more school serving a homogenized suburban clientele, that special responsibility had to be recognized.

Bowdoin College, Brunswick, Maine, 1969–1976 — $59,600. Bowdoin was Maine's oldest college, far wealthier than its two competitors. On one of my college placement trips that took me to Brunswick, I remember asking the director of admissions what he considered his strongest and weakest departments, a condescending question. "Listen, mister," he replied, "a pretty ambitious type of student comes to this college. No matter what graduate school or career they elect, we have to be sure they're prepared"—a professional reply.

Bowdoin took special efforts to recruit a new type of black student in the late 1960s, one of them a senior (born in Tennessee, whose mother ran a beauty parlor) from Commonwealth. He organized the college's first Afro-American society, which sought to assert itself by having every black student in Bowdoin march together to Brunswick's blood bank. A traditionalist like Dr. Cole felt that this new preoccupation meant the danger of overlooking the sort of Maine student (sons of ministers, teachers, librarians, farmers)— who made up 23 percent of the enrollment, but of whom 80 percent (1969 figures) required financial aid—so both our grants went for young men from rural and coastal areas. In the early 1970s the college, like so many others, went co-ed, and the mystique of Maine made Bowdoin so popular that it became harder, for a while, for even the ablest girl to enter there than Radcliffe.

Dartmouth College, Hanover, New Hampshire, 1971, 1977—$93,500 (plus $90,000 to the medical school). Dartmouth, like the Maine colleges, benefited from the Merrill trustees' nostalgic (and mildly racist) but realistic concern for the young men from the New Hampshire mill towns, backwater Maine lumber towns, and the barren counties south of the Canadian border whose isolation and despair were as crippling as anything to be found in New York City or Mississippi but were not part of America's culture of concern. Under President Kemeny, a Hungarian-born Jewish mathematician, Dartmouth was trying to free itself from its hipflask, coonskin coat, *Wall Street Journal* stereotype, showing a new interest in blacks (eighty-two entered in 1969), a renewed interest in Indians, building a strong department of Latin American studies, and an imaginative school of engineering.

Harvard University, Cambridge, Massachusetts, 1959–1981—$1,796,000. Harvard received support from the Merrill Trust in a dizzying complexity of ways: Widener Library, $150,000; the University itself for the capital campaign of 1979, $270,000; the Graduate School of Education, $90,000; Graduate School of Business Administration, $100,000 for training in business management for black students; Divinity School, $205,000 for fellowships for working ministers, women's studies, and general support; Medical School, $60,000; Graduate School of Public Health, $485,000. The Fogg Museum received $10,000 to help mount an exhibit of Jacob Van Ruisdael and $25,000 to support an archeological dig on the Aegean coast of Turkey. $20,000 went in 1977 to support the Center for Renaissance Studies at the Villa I Tatti in Florence. The Peabody Museum received $20,000 for its Peruvian textile collection and the Arnold Arboretum $25,000 for the publication of scholarly papers. To this add on $270,000 to Radcliffe College for support of part-time graduate study.

A foundation could spend its entire lifetime wandering philanthropically around the satrapies of Harvard's empire. If one really believed in the value of an elite, could one evade the logic that would compel the giving of all one's money to Harvard?

Magowan, Regan, and myself had all graduated from the World's Greatest University, which encourages a calm superiority not granted elsewhere, but also a love-hate response renewed with each appeal for money. When I arrived in the fall of 1938, my dismay, after considering myself the-brightest-boy-at-Deerfield, was to realize that no matter what field I claimed as my own, there were dozens of classmates who knew far more than I did. In the fall of 1940 after the Germans had beaten the French and English, and it was not simply the Nazi armies but the Nazi values that would control the future, I took a course under Carl Joachim Friedrich on the theories of constitutional democracy. He was trying to free his students from fundamentalist absolutes, where the abstractions of freedom just did not square with the realities of attacks from Left and Right. A democratic principle might indeed fail, but if one re-examined the priorities and changed the language and the time-frame of action, and jettisoned parochial details in order to win new allies, then the principle might be quite capable of winning again. It was a quality of scholarship I never forgot.

During the McCarthy ordeal Harvard was a leader in defending independent thought. Under the Kennedy administration it was a source of exciting new leadership. Through the eyes of my former students I could see where the same challenge of new ideas and new horizons and the demand to deliver the best that one was capable of still (for most of them) existed. Commonwealth School's first senior to be accepted there was a black Washingtonian, from a family whose annual income was $2,000 (not much even in 1961), who went on to organize the Afro-American Society and eventually became a lawyer in Virginia and Zimbabwe. There was never a question but that for a young man of his ability and drive the doors would open.

Of course, there are other points of view. "You are educated by the wonderful atmosphere"—that is, don't expect too much from the teaching. The famous professor doesn't teach the course. He is on a consulting engagement in Washington; he is working on his book (his secretary is working on his book); he is doing research at his villa in the Alps. When the war in Vietnam was new, many of the professors were excited to be sent on missions to Saigon and to be treated as equals by generals. When the war got ugly, they opposed it mainly by words and became angry and frightened when their students fought its ugliness in violent ways. I taught too many faculty children at my school and learned something of the bitterness of sixteen-year-olds whose families had been written off as father disappeared to earn his Ph.D.—which by the 1980s didn't mean much.

At its best, however, Harvard was preoccupied not only in training leadership for the future but also in setting standards within each field—law, medicine, public and business administration, science, and the liberal arts— that would respond to changing needs and changing values, which would ask the important questions and be concerned about long-range results. It was an exciting place to deal with.

Yale University, New Haven, Connecticut, 1962–1981—$407,900 (plus

$75,000 to the Divinity School). Our first grant to Yale went to the Law School's program for bringing students from newly independent African nations to study American legal concepts and procedures. The second, in 1970, shortly after the college started to admit women, was $50,000 in scholarship aid to *male* students, an example of Establishment petulance under the threat of change. The conservative alumni whom Bob Magowan knew considered President Kingman Brewster a weakling too willing to give in to antiwar, black, feminist demands—one reason why he left before the end of the capital campaign. Yale was also a victim of McGeorge Bundy's conviction (when president of the Ford Foundation) that colleges should take greater risks in the investment of endowment capital (those who did not might receive less support), which caused the university—and Ford—to lose its shirt when the market turned down. Brewster was replaced by Bartlett Giamatti, a young scholar in medieval and Renaissance literature, and we made an unrestricted gift of $300,000 in 1978 to help him develop his priorities, a gift any new president would treasure.

Brown University, Providence, Rhode Island, 1962–1981—$220,000 (including $25,000 to Pembroke and $25,000 to the medical school). Our first grant to Brown was to strengthen the graduate school. At this period of rapid expansion of America's education industry, there was a need to increase the flow of Ph.D's. Brown was one of the universities equipped to share this responsibility at a rather low incremental cost. It had a good graduate faculty, several distinguished scholars, adequate libraries, excellent science laboratories, and an electronic computer. Enrollment was low, however, because of limited fields of specialization and insufficient fellowship funds.

In 1972, we gave $50,000 for graduate fellowships earmarked for blacks. Brown had made a strong commitment, and in just four years, from 1968 to 1972, the number of black men and women at Brown had gone from 85 to 417. The National Defense Education Act fellowship program for black graduate students allotted in 1972 only 25 percent of the funds it had given in 1967, and Brown was trying to make up the slack and to serve the large numbers of blacks just beginning to leave undergraduate institutions. This was clearly a program we should have continued to support. By the 1980s, of course, all those optimistic statistical curves had turned down, and the fall in the numbers of black students, graduate and undergraduate, at institutions like Brown had become dangerous.

From 1946 to 1966 Brown's president had been Henry Wriston, a strong figure with a nationwide reputation. Then came a decade of mediocre leadership that led to lowering of academic standards, muddled dealing with black and feminist demands, poor relationship with alumni, and erosion of financial resources. Brown still had a famous name, but the outer as well as the inner world was beginning to learn about the reality.

The arrival of Howard Swearer, a specialist in Soviet studies who had been president of Carleton from 1970 to 1977, brought a happy change. In fact, his decisiveness, clarity, and energy were so evident from his first days in office that he faced the dangerous expectations of the entire university that here was the man who would turn the entire game around, right away. He tightened up the administration, cut costs, improved fundraising, and rapidly made Brown almost the most popular and hardest to enter university in New England.

I had known and admired Swearer at Carleton and felt, as with Hedley Reynolds at Bates, that the foundation's job was to search out and back any genuine leader in this troubled time and demoralized profession. Dr. Swearer saw the crisis in American education as even more serious at the faculty level than at the student. The 1960s had brought a great expansion of young college graduates into teaching and by the early 1970s blacks and women too. Now the country was cutting back: the student age group was smaller, the federal government had reduced its funding, and the economic climate was chillier. Sometimes this led to sensible thrift, but except in the departments leading to law, medicine, business, accounting, computers, and certain fields of science, the retrenchments were threatening the institutions and the whole commitment to education. In 1974 Reed College advertised an opening in English and received 1,000 applications! If untenured younger staff (particularly among the black and female newcomers) are dropped, only the elderly remain. New federal rules raising the retirement age from sixty-five to seventy made the situation only more rigid. In this atmosphere of stagnation and low morale, teaching rapidly ceases to attract top-notch new members.

By the mid-eighties Brown would have a number of retirements out of the age group that entered teaching in the years after 1945. A large gift would allow Dr. Swearer to hold on to the best young staff until those openings developed, offering two-year contracts in the multidisciplinary new fields like law and liberal arts, Renaissance studies, and biomedical ethics. $100,000 in 1979 went to strengthen that initiative.

At our final meeting in 1981, Mary Merrill, a Brown alumna, obtained a $20,000 grant to purchase books in history. A 66 percent increase in annual book acquisition funds from 1969 to 1978 was buying 25 percent fewer books. All teaching, learning, and research revolve around a strong library.

Hampshire College, Amherst, Massachusetts, 1968–1980—$2,025,000. We gave $2 million in two grants in 1968 and 1972 to help establish Hampshire College in western Massachusetts. Hampshire had been on the drawing boards for ten years. It was a cooperative venture among the other schools of the area—Amherst, Smith, Mt. Holyoke, and the University of Massachusetts—and the new college could avoid unnecessary expenses and be able to survive on tuition payments alone by sharing their surplus resources, for example, in fields of foreign languages, history, and physics. It would break free from the traditional boxes of departments, course credits, and grades, and students could move through the college at their own speeds, subject only to passing three different examinations that would prove their competency and maturity. Student course choices would be tailored to their individual needs; in fact, they would be encouraged to look beyond the college, whether in a course whose activity would be at some welfare agency in Springfield or in a semester's work at some totally nonacademic endeavor. Because of courses taken at the neighbor institutions and less emphasis upon formal classroom work, the college could afford a much smaller teacher-to-student ratio—1 to 16—than usual. All staff, moreover, including the president, would be on term contracts, therefore avoiding that disease of mediocrity—fixed tenure. An old business associate of my father, Harold Johnson, had become fascinated by the project. When his original $6 million plus $3 million from the Ford Foundation, our first million gave the impetus to the college's start.

Hampshire may be the last liberal arts college launched in the United States. There may not be that much money available to start new colleges any more. Demographic changes mean that there is no longer a surplus of eighteen-year-olds—a fact obvious to any college president who bothered to look at population statistics during the great boom of the sixties, though few did. And this country has lost its optimism that education will ensure a better society. So, if the Merrill Foundation helped found the last college, it is interesting to see what that meant.

Hampshire suffered from two historical accidents. First of all, it had been planned during a period of optimism when people did not believe in sin or failure. There was no mechanism—"don't judgmentalize"—for flunking, for getting rid of, or even, at first, for confronting someone who did no work or who just sat on his bed and smoked pot and plucked on his guitar. This lack of accountability led to a Peter Pan atmosphere where not only did things not get done, but a mystique was created of not getting things done. The college divorced itself from artificial Western time ("the train for Berlin leaves at 14.05") and accepted an Eastern and Youth Culture time ("when Allah wills") where it was vulgar to speak of deadlines. Secondly, the college opened shop at the peak of democratic anti-authoritarianism. To avoid any possibility of X giving an order to Y, the process of decisionmaking at every level was so bounded by committee meetings, appeals, procedures, and popular review that, again, to expect results ran counter to the Zeitgeist. And, paradoxically, the emphasis upon a curriculum shaped to the personal needs of each individual led to a badly overworked faculty, whose energies were expended on face-to-face counseling all day long, and a lonely student body, despite all the rhetoric of community, because they shared so little with each other.

And yet, despite the maddening fuzziness of its corporate personality, Hampshire was well administered, hired some fine faculty, and attracted students who at their best were learning better how to deal with American reality than the go-getters a couple of miles away at Amherst. For example, if one were interested in mental illness one worked in a mental hospital and, rather than study Freud, studied law so as to be able to set off a class action suit against it for improper management. Even if the college was dominated by with-it, Youth Culture ideas, it was possible to point out accomplishments that were imaginative as well as foolish. In order to work for better New England food self-sufficiency at a time of rising transportation costs, Hampshire's thrust in economics symbolized itself in an experimental sheep farm at the edge of the campus. This provoked its share of wisecracks, yet the climb in fuel costs allowed doubts about the accepted economics of a nation-wide distribution system. Small-scale sheep-raising suited New England geography and also a new ethic where people were no longer locked into one career: the exteacher pays his rent as a computer programer but adjusts his work hours in order to manage a farm. The agony of Detroit's auto industry showed that doing-things-as-before was not necessarily the road to survival.

The Ship of Fools ambiance could be exasperating. Middle-class kids from Scarsdale pretended they were proletarians, medieval villagers, or Angolan freedom fighters, and as representative of nineteenth-century values on the board of trustees, I used to bang my cane angrily at all this narcissistic non-sense. Even when Hampshire students had sensible things to say—and they were bright folk exposed to stimulating teaching—their goofy appearance and youthspeak kept them from being listened to. Those disguises, of course, were a deliberate way of keeping the Establishment at a distance. The students who rejected outside rules came to establish, by costly trial and error, their personal rules. The rejection of corporate control had as by-product the 30 percent of alumni who were running their own businesses five years after graduation.

The raucous style was also a nose-thumb to the correctly groomed class who had led America through ten years of war in Vietnam, an economy that produced unemployment and hunger despite its executives' self-praise, and above all the madness of nuclear posturing. Not even the silliest, pot-soaked weirdo would dare to talk about "winning" a nuclear war. Real insanity wore three-piece suits.

Hampshire was planned and started in good times when there seemed a bottomless supply of both money and students and then, with little tradition of mutual trust, had to face the bad times that started for colleges in the mid-1970s. Under pressure, institutions and individuals become narrow and frightened, and take refuge in tradition. Or they can move in other directions, become more objective and imaginative, and rethink the premises they used to take for granted. There was no purpose whatsoever in creating one more standard liberal arts college in the Northeast, an imitation of Middlebury without its resources.

Eisenhower College had been exactly that. As its name suggests, it stood for traditional values, and when it opened in upstate New York a little before Hampshire did, it received patronage from wealthy businessmen and famous generals. But men like that were really not interested in education, and the college, outside of its commitment to wholesomeness, did not stand for anything special. Once the novelty wore off, and money and students became hard to get, Eisenhower tottered, let out cries for help, and died.

A student is smart to obtain a haircut as well as precise facts before he goes off for an interview. Academic and administrative standards can be tightened, as they were under the leadership of Adele Simmons, who had campaigned for the presidency when seven months pregnant, an approach that suited Hampshire's style. The very fragility of the college, however, forced it to hold onto its sometimes dangerous reputation for new ideas. Either it kept questioning and taking risks or it didn't stand for anything at all.

Boston University, Boston, Massachusetts, 1960–1981—$96,000 (plus $25,000, School of Theatre; $30,000, Dentistry; $25,000, Medicine). Boston University is a large (30,000) university of mixed strengths and heterogeneous student body, a balance to Amherst and Hampshire. Starting in the late 1950s, a sustained effort was made to collect its schools scattered all across Boston into one campus along the Charles River. This massive construction program was paid for by low salaries and high tuitions. The faculty was rated in many departments as excellent, the bureaucracy callous, and the student body alienated in its grubby, dangerous Kenmore Square environment. What did give a sense of purpose to that community was universal dislike of its president, John Silber. In 1970 he had been brought from the University of Texas at Austin, where he had been a distinguished chairman of the philosophy department, and given the charge of raising academic standards and balancing the annual budgets. He accomplished these two tasks, with an arrogant joy in infuriating every single slice of the university. Silber had little interest in winning supporters or allies, but a humane president might have been unable to hold together such a fractious institution.

St. Michael's College, Winooski, Vermont, 1963–1968—$60,000. St. Michael's had been started as a boy's academy in 1904 by French priests from

Mont St. Michel exiled by the anticlerical government "for solid religious instruction and wholesome moral training of poor boys." Then it became a Catholic liberal arts college and was coed in 1970. Of the students it appealed to from French-Canadian Vermont rural and small-town families, for whom it was the first step up the ladder, 45 percent needed financial aid. It was the sort of struggling institution that appealed to Don Regan, especially in its effort, supported by our last grant of $25,000, to attract a new class of student by building up its offerings in business administration.

Marlboro College, Marlboro, Vermont, 1962–1980—$145,000. Marlboro had been started in 1946 on a 300-acre Green Mountain campus in southern Vermont, but it held only a handful of students and was clearly moribund when Thomas Ragle, an English teacher from Phillips Exeter, took over in the late 1950s. I came to know Ragle and strongly admired his dedication to learning, to the ideal of a democratically run institution, and above all, to that particular little college which became his cross. He obtained five grants from our foundation for the library, science building, theatre, activities center (badly needed during the long winters), salaries, and debt reduction. Without knowing Ragle and his visionary belief in Marlboro's role in the pluralistic mix of American education—"If there is a Berkeley at one end of the spectrum, there should be a Marlboro at the other"—the other trustees voted grudgingly for these proposals. The student body barely exceeded 200. In 1981, when Ragle resigned, the financial picture, admissions picture, and academic qualifications of incoming students were as critical as they had ever been. What was the place actually worth? Did it justify the tremendous efforts to keep it alive?

It was a good school for bright students with flawed records and for those older than average who knew what they wanted. Admissions standards were low, but a high level of performance, particularly in writing, was demanded once the students got in, and Ragle went far to prove the objectivity (examination committees of outside professionals) of the honors awarded to the best. The staff doggedly accepted their low salaries because they trusted the boss and respected one another. Marlboro was too small to be eligible for the federal grants and low-cost loans that allowed Hampshire's rapid expansion, and therefore the construction costs meant a staggering debt whose service charges threatened the college's survival. Ragle was convinced that if only the debt could be removed, Marlboro was economically viable. It stood for a student's active involvement in his own education, and through the town meetings in democratic self-government. Some fields—English, philosophy, art, theatre, and biology—were strong, others nonexistent. Perhaps the major contribution of Marlboro to the lives of the people who touched it was simply the fight to keep it alive: trustees, faculty, and students. No one could take for granted that the college, despite its fine qualities, would survive. Each year came the same battle to raise money and to find students. The American system throws its institutions upon the community. Fighting for the life of such an institution is one way of showing what citizenship means.

Trinity College, Hartford, Connecticut, 1959–1978, $235,000. "A third-rate place, now second rate and improving greatly since 1945," Dr. Cole wrote from the president's desk at Amherst College to recommend the Foundation's first grant. The elitism was typical of our interoffice memos, but so was our resolution to support an institution that showed direction and confidence, and not stick with established successes. Right after the war, a determined young president, Keith Funston, had brought new leadership to this small, under-capitalized, local college, and by 1959 its trustees agreed that upgrading Trinity's library resources was the most effective way to maintain its intellectual momentum. Most of the funding came from the Andrew Mellon Foundation, but we helped toward the purchase of the Watkinson Research Library, a local treasure of lovely old books, especially in Americana, and our subsequent grants remained in the field of library operations and endowment.

Enrollment, endowment, College Board scores, number of library books, and percentage of minority students—all the statistics by which the profession measures progress (plus a strong new theatre department) showed a steady strengthening over the next twenty years: a good college for smart, conservative students.

Clark University, Worcester, Massachusetts, 1965–1979, $80,000 Clark, a meat-and-potatoes institution in one of the world's dullest cities, has some odd distinctions: Sigmund Freud lectured there on his one visit to the United States, Robert Goddard did pioneer research on rocket propulsion there, it possessed one of the nation's strongest departments in geography. It gave a respectable education to the children and grandchildren of Irish, Italian, Greek, and Polish immigrants. Dr. Cole backed its first application out of respect for the college's efforts to upgrade itself. During the 1970s I came to know its new president, Mortimer Appley, and was impressed by his realism and thoughtfulness.

Clark had three presidents during its first eighty years and three during the eight years preceding 1975. It acted foolishly during the fat 1960s and overbuilt, overstaffed, accepted unqualified students, and as times got bad ran up whopping deficits. Dr. Appley was trying to rationalize staff, a miserable task since the job market was so tight that every dismissal was appealed and re-appealed indefinitely, and the students occupied the president's office for two weeks to protest dropping a radical young economics instructor.

Ninety-five percent of Clark's faculty had doctorates, over 80 percent were tenured. Both figures were too high in Dr. Appley's eyes, and revealed an aging, conservative, rigid faculty structure that prevented any creativity unless one could raise special funds to hire younger staff, persuaded veterans to retire early, or paid Mafia killers to rub out half the full professors. Money was needed to competitively modernize the dowdy plant and to attract older students to replace the diminishing pool of nineteen-year-olds. He desperately wanted $2.3 million to permit the flexibility dear to any college president: to purchase a unique collection of manuscripts that might have just come on the market, to support an intriguing new student or faculty project, or to bring on campus a distinguished scholar—to escape for a moment the terrible vise of the budget.

Technical Schools

In a section called "Economic growth and industrial retardation" in *The First Industrial Nation* (Methuen, London, 1969), Peter Mathias describes the way that Britain's industrial supremacy began, unnoticed, to fail as early as the 1880s. The British had been the masters of the world in invention and production, and at each level of the process relied upon the apprenticeship system—"Can you be as good as your Old Man?"—to train new craftsmen and engineers. The Germans, coming from behind, were not burdened by the dead hand of success, and were willing to experiment with new concepts and techniques in Britain's own field of shipbuilding and to explore fields like electrical engineering and chemistry that the British ignored. The British were proud that their machines were so well built that they still functioned after eighty years. By that time the design was obsolete and could not possibly compete with German models.

The American industrial-educational system alternates in the same cycles of complacency and panic. Sputnik, the Soviet satellite that circled the earth in 1958, forced a usefully agonized set of comparisons between the Soviet and American education systems: their discipline, thoroughness, and breadth compared with our superficiality.

The failure of our auto, steel, and electronics industries by 1980 against Japanese competition has forced another cycle of introspection. The remedies are seen in back-to-basics rigor, a longer school day and year, better paid teachers, and stress on science and math. Much of this is useful, but those who loudly urge us to catch up are those who were quite willing to vote at every level for funding cut-backs that forced larger class sizes; the dropping of undemocratic courses in calculus and foreign languages; and the shrugging off of the whole costly process of classroom interaction built on analysis, debate, independent study, and skilled writing, which cannot be carried on by harried, exploited teachers.

At its best the American system can beat Russian or Japanese competition, no matter how hard they overwork their students, because we are willing to trust our individual teachers and students to argue out a problem no matter where it takes them. They are not bound into a straitjacket of ideology or syllabus. But American educational quality is not going to have a chance when a policy of neglect is followed by frantic catch-up.

Rensselaer Polytechnic Institute, Troy, New York, 1967, 1979—$35,000. Rensselaer (1824) was America's first scientific and engineering school. In putting too much emphasis upon purely practical approaches, it fell behind leaders like M.I.T. and Cal Tech, which stressed theory and intellectual breadth. Our two grants went for library and classroom resources in the humanities and social sciences.

Pratt Institute, Brooklyn, New York, 1977—$27,000. Pratt was started in 1887 to replace or supplement apprenticeship as a way of passing on vocational skills, particularly in architecture and engineering. A $6.3 million capital campaign was seeking to expand library resources, upgrade the learning resource core in the School of Architecture, and renovate the oldest art school building in New York City.

Rockefeller University, New York City, 1971—$75,000. Rockefeller was a purely graduate university, a large number of its students being postdoctoral fellows, and this grant was to encourage scientific study of the highest quality at a time when government funding was already moving away.

Virginia Military Institute, Lexington, Virginia, 1981—$15,000. One might well ask why, at a time when the military profession was being drowned in money, a foundation like ours at its last meeting should make such a grant. Donald Regan had by now moved to Washington as Secretary of the Treasury and requested this for library acquisitions. Future army officers might be exposed to interesting books on economics, history, and art. This is called compromise.

California Institute of Technology, Pasadena, California, 1972, 1976—$125,000. An earlier appeal had been rejected because Cal Tech was too rich, but Don Regan and Bob Magowan felt it unwise to ignore a school that important, and in 1972 we made an unrestricted gift of $100,000. (Is there an ultimate memory bank somewhere that keeps track of every foundation's virtue and debit points?) Despite its $129 million endowment, there was need of free funds for research projects of younger faculty members.

Cal Tech chose to remain small (786 undergraduates and 615 Ph.D. candidates in 1972) with stress on quality rather than size, small classes, and no artificial barriers between the fields of knowledge. There had been a recent expansion into the social sciences but always a stress upon fundamentals and upon the issues that become the basis for further studies. In 1976 we gave $25,000 toward new laboratories in cellular biology and chemistry. Inflation and reduced federal funding threatened Cal Tech's continued preeminence, and it had launched a $141 million campaign, one of whose goals was to examine the surfaces of the cell for the understanding of cell disorders and diseases, their basic functions, and their malfunctions in cancer.

The president at this time was Harold Brown, who had been Lyndon Johnson's Secretary of the Air Force, much involved with nuclear weapon research (a moral problem of our elite scientific institutions?).

New York and the Central States

Bard College, Annandale-on-Hudson, New York, 1965–1979—$81,000. Bard was started in 1880 to prepare young men for the Episcopal ministry, but for some reason caught the revolution of our times sooner than any other similar college. Though it always retained a good academic name, its lurid reputation in discipline along with deficits and low faculty morale almost closed its door in the early 1960s. It was a warning, which few heard, of what was to come. The stress on ideas and on independent study weakened contact between an excitable, atomized student body and the institution. Out of the sexual freedom came a lack of any commitment to group activities: "Why work on the school newspaper when you can study in your girlfriend's bedroom?"

Reamer Kline, an Episcopal minister, became president and brought about improvement, which let our trustees feel by 1965 that Bard was worth supporting. Our second grant of $36,000 in 1970 was to back an institutional and research program in environmental science, making use of the college's half-mile stretch of Hudson River pollution. Our last $25,000 was toward the $6 million capital drive where a young president, Leon Botstein, was trying to build a basic endowment and make Bard a cultural resource for the entire community. An interesting recruitment gimmick was to promise applicants an immediate yes/no decision when they came to the college, with their records, for an interview. If one could trust the standards of the admission committee, this might be a counterweight to the paranoia among high school seniors.

University of Pennsylvania, Pennsylvania, 1975–1980—$2,890,000. Don Regan was chairman of the university's board of trustees 1974–1978 when the greater part of these grants were made (in 1963–1972, at his urging, we had given $1,125,000 to Penn's Wharton School of Finance), but the negotiations had been between him and the university, with the Merrill trustees not consulted, and it was not until 1982 (after the Trust had ended) that $1,650,000 was designated as the Donald T. Regan Loan Fund and $100,000 as a challenge grant to annual giving.

Any form of financial aid is useful, and low-interest university loans, at a time when government loans have been cut, are better than high-interest commercial loans. A loan fund keeps renewing itself and is certainly appropriate for students going through business and law school into high-income professions. In medicine, however, a large debt forces young doctors into high-return medicine that may not be the same as good medicine, and in undergraduate years a fear of debt will frighten away minority and working-class students as well as those headed for nursing, social work, the ministry, or other fields that promise limited income. If the details of this proposal had been debated with us trustees, I am sure we would have insisted that a third or a half be allotted to outright grants.

Haverford College, Haverford, Pennsylvania, 1970, 1977—$60,000. These two grants were for scholarships to black and Puerto Rican students in the effort to go from 2 percent to 13 percent of incoming freshmen. Haverford stressed independence in intellectual and social life, academic rigor, and imagination. Its small size (650 in 1970 and 890 in 1977) was compensated for by extensive cooperation with its neighbors, particularly Bryn Mawr. It was proud of its Center for Non-Violent Conflict Resolution, which ran programs in innercity and suburban Philadelphia. In the 1970s its Quaker president, John Coleman, took a leave of absence to work as a dishwasher, his way to express the need for intellectuals to understand what is meant by labor.

Swarthmore College, Swarthmore, Pennsylvania, 1963–1977, $99,800. A lot of critics reacted negatively to the activism and irreverence of Swarthmore students. More objectively, the college could be faulted for overworking them. Its intensity meant that some people just never left the campus, and its small size meant that you had to eat breakfast within eyesight of your ex-love. Despite the overwork it had a sparkling atmosphere and made you wish you were young enough to be going to college again.

Don Regan pursued a number of special interests in education, and one of these was Pennsylvania colleges. At each meeting he presented what he saw as a sturdy, responsible place with some special angle of service.

Dickinson College, Carlisle, Pennsylvania, 1965–1979—$70,000. We gave four small grants to this traditional, conservative college that was making a tangible effort during these years to raise its academic standards.

Franklin and Marshall College, Lancaster, Pennsylvania, 1969–1980—$100,000. Founded in 1787, Franklin and Marshall is the nation's fourteenth oldest college. We participated in its capital drives to strengthen academic programs, improve salaries, share African studies with nearby Lincoln University, build an arts center, and maintain its Commonwealth Scholars Program for students from rural Pennsylvania high schools. No other college unattached to a medical school sent a higher proportion of its graduates into medicine, a favorite statistic.

Bucknell University, Lewisburg, Pennsylvania, 1970–1979—$120,000.

Lafayette College, Easton, Pennsylvania, 1970–1980—$50,000.

Lehigh University, Bethlehem, Pennsylvania, 1970, 1977—$55,000. A university with a strong record in science, engineering, business, and economics, with new programs in urban affairs, marine and environmental studies. Regan was intrigued by a course on Fundamentals of Business for liberal arts students as well as courses termed High Immediate Relevance: effects of federal training and poverty programs on ghetto life, cryogenic engineering, and thermal pollution.

Alliance College, Cambridge Springs, Pennsylvania, 1972—$35,000. This college, sponsored by the Polish National Alliance, was another discovery by Regan in his fascination with the diversity of American education. With a tiny endowment and 58 percent of its students on financial aid, it served the children of Polish coal-miners and steel-workers. Our gift went for recreation and sports facilities so needed in this remote Appalachian setting.

University of Pittsburgh, 1961–1979—$75,000. I was introduced to the university through Richard Rubenstein, a friend who was then director of its Hillel Center, who felt that small grants for teaching and research in the humanities had a disproportionate impact at such an institution where money and prestige went to the practical fields. Three grants totaling $40,000 were parceled out in small sums but provoked keen competition, served as a catalyst for a smarter tempo of academic work, and were prized as recognition of a part of the university usually ignored. It was the Foundation's first exposure to the surprising value of small sums used for a high-quality purpose limited in range but free in choice.

These grants also led me to an acquaintance with Edward Litchfield, who had been hired as chancellor in 1955 to change the nature of the university. He was a man of imagination, energy, optimism, and charm who set out to reorganize administration and curriculum, upgrade faculty and student body, change the role of women in education, and draft plans for a stupendous $250,000,000 research and cultural center that would make Pittsburgh a combination of Athens and Augustinian Rome, as fast as possible. By the late 1960s he had bankrupted the university and crippled himself with a coronary. Those the gods destroy they first make mad.

Appalachia and the South

Charles E. Merrill's Florida and Mississippi background gave him a Southern point of view in looking at his country. He was sensitive about Southern poverty and the way that Southern values were looked down upon by Northeasterners. If one basic tenet of the Trust was a respect for Pluralism, then that implied a respect for regionalism, a refusal to accept a homogenized America all watching the same television programs and shopping at the same shopping malls.

Davis and Elkins College, Elkins, West Virginia, 1972—$35,000. Davis and Elkins was located in an impoverished mountain area and yet attracted a wide range of students. It made a higher faculty expenditure per student than any other college in West Virginia, and though its financial aid budget had gone from $74,000 in 1965 to $480,000 in 1971, high costs had pushed tuition out of reach of local students. Accordingly, there was a new effort to reach foundations such as ours, which made its grants (as to many other Appalachian colleges) under the category of religion, for Protestant students, since that category had less pressure upon it than did education.

Berea College, Berea, Kentucky, 1960–1981—$135,000. Berea is the archetypal Appalachian college and has played this public relations angle with skill, appealing to the nostalgic affection by city folk for an older, simpler America. It was one of my father's favorite charities. Berea had been founded in 1855 to supply the educational opportunities for Southern mountain people, and, protected by its isolation, accepted women and blacks at that early date. Even in 1960, 90 percent of the students came from 230 mountain counties of eight southern states. No tuition was charged and the cost was defrayed by a high endowment ($23 million in 1960, $69 million in 1973), gifts, and the college's famous work program. In fact, a student who does not have financial need, even as an alumnus child, is excluded. Every student was expected to put in ten hours minimum a week in the library or dining hall, with the farm animals or at the craft shops. This kept down expenses (as did low salaries) and reinforced the sober realism of the student body.

Our grants went for salaries, construction, and curriculum reorganization that demanded retraining of faculty to be able to handle the new interdisciplinary courses, and strengthening of the Afro-American Studies Program. The college was also trying to fund a program to recruit students of Appalachian background now in Cleveland, Detroit, and Chicago.

It is tempting to keep alive a traditional America by giving money to a college like Berea, and with generous support this heritage becomes a creative one instead of something twisted up in resentment and self-pity.

Warren Wilson College, Swannanoa, North Carolina, 1967, 1974—$50,000. Warren Wilson had gone from a Presbyterian boarding school to a two-year, then a four-year college, and our first grant went to complete that process. It had a required work program (fifteen hours a week) like Berea's to pay for room and board, which involved a farm and the use of heavy machinery and skills in plumbing and landscape gardening. There was a high student dropout rate from poor preparation, low family cultural background (SAT averages around 440), and financial stress. Religion is considered important, and each student is expected to perform a major service program before he graduates: painting a neighbor's house, cataloguing a rural library, assisting in a hospital. Despite the limitless practicalities of the college's needs, it had received a couple of massive gifts for an arts center and an ambitious international scholarship program. In 1974, 21 percent of the 388 students came from foreign countries, which allows an extensive language program with Hindi, Japanese, Arabic, and Swahili for training younger Americans for service abroad.

Fascinated by Appalachian myth and reality, I visited Warren Wilson in 1983. Why should a student choose that isolated, limited (though beautiful) community instead of the resources of a public university at the same price, I asked the students and staff I met. "It's friendly—people care about you— I like the foreign touches, and I went on a program to Germany—They take religion seriously—People don't throw money around"—were some answers. In the library was an exhibit of the life of Bertolt Brecht, the German communist writer, and announcement of a festival of Eastern European films. Neither of these would probably have been permitted at a state school.

Maryville College, Maryville, Tennessee, 1959–1980—$357,000. Both my father's parents went to Maryville, a small Presbyterian college in eastern Tennessee founded in 1819. Charles Morton Merrill arrived a year later than he had planned. A frost had destroyed his father's orange trees on the farm beside the St. John's River, south of Jacksonville, and my great-grandfather had taken his son's savings to rebuild the grove. When he did get to college, he fell in love with Octavia Wilson, who came from a cotton plantation outside Lexington, Mississippi, and whose father had been captured at Vicksburg while Lieutenant Merrill was serving under Grant on the other side. My father, always sentimental about his family, left Maryville $50,000 in his estate, and one of the Trust's first grants was $25,000 in 1959 for salaries.

It is hard for Northeasterners to understand a Southern college like Maryville. One can be touched by its friendliness—"That's the first quality we look for in a teacher"—and then see the intellectually deadening quality of those unvarying smiles, and later on see the judgment, backbone, and clear-eyed knowledge of the world expressed in a different accent. One notes the low SAT averages, low tuitions ($2,400 total cost in 1970, at Morehouse's level, and even then half the students needed financial aid) that simply supplied no revenue to be worked with, low salaries, and poor library. It takes time to understand the role that the college plays in the region (where 60 percent of the graduates go into teaching, church, and social work) or its tradition, in a part of the world dominated by the Klan, for intellectual freedom and social diversity.

In 1969 we gave $50,000 to be used for either library construction or salaries, and in 1971 $250,000 as a scholarship fund named for Charles Morton and Octavia Wilson Merrill for students planning to enter the fields of science or medicine.

A final grant of $25,000 in 1980 went towards a faculty sabbatical program. Of this faculty, almost 25 percent had been there over twenty years, but 40 percent for four years or less. The two groups had quite different needs. For the older teachers money was needed to help them update knowledge of their own field, to develop a new area of competence, or to gain familiarity with new teaching methods. For the younger, fresh out of graduate school and its overspecialization, they needed to develop courses that cut across disciplinary lines. Nervous undergraduates want more tangibly career-related courses, but just because college education is so much more costly and its practical rewards less evident, they also want courses that are genuinely thought provoking. What they will not accept is business-as-usual academics: lecture notes with twenty years' dust on them, unrelated to the agonized world outside the classroom. This unexpected, nonbudgeted $25,000 had to be sliced precisely to meet the competitive needs of new teachers and veteran teachers, but it was an opportunity to prove to the faculty how seriously the administration regarded them.

The college was in trouble. During his long administration President Copeland had strengthened it academically, but when Wayne Anderson (a man whose interests were in administration) replaced him in 1977, finances were in critical shape. The campus had been built for 1,000, but enrollment stood around 650. SAT averages had fallen below 500. The admissions office had to fill beds, but these students had to have the ability and drive to be worth teaching. The president had to raise money and cut costs, but would Maryville retain the intellectual and moral distinction to make it worth keeping alive? The alternatives, except for a Vanderbilt or a Duke here and there, are the large state institutions, reasonably effective if you don't expect too much but not designed to meet a young person's idealism or dream of excellence.

The solution, of course, is the capital campaign—toward Century III—of 1979–1984, like the one at Bates, which took on a religious intensity as it doggedly put together one grant after another to reach $12 million. So many sources of money exist in our bizarre country if one has imagination, connections, and tenacity, and the efforts to harvest these funds from Alcoa (which owned a plant nearby), Tennessee Valley Authority, Blount County alumni, and all the other well-wishers supply a network of faith that the standard sociologist cannot comprehend. The harvest included a 47 percent raise in faculty salaries, doubling of financial aid, greater support for international students and a Center for Campus Ministry, a new (of course) computer lab, a wood-burning energy system, and eliminating accumulated deficits, balancing the budget, and doubling the endowment. You won't find anything like that in the Soviet Union.

University of Richmond, Richmond, Virginia, 1975—$15,000. This gift was made at Don Regan's urging to help construct a new university commons for the 7,000 students. In 1964 the university was given $40 million worth of A. H. Robins Company stock plus a further matching gift of $10 million.

College of the Ozarks, Clarksville, Arkansas, 1972—$40,000. An appeal came to us somehow from this desperate Presbyterian college founded in 1834. It offered courses in teaching, business, medical technology, and secretarial preparation. Tuition and room and board came to a total of $1,500 per year, but 55 percent of the student body still needed help in meeting that figure. The Merrill money was to be doled out at ten grants a year for four years. Arkansas ranks forty-nine in the United States in per capita income.

These two grants make for useful discussion on policy. We gave to University of Richmond because it was rich, to College of the Ozarks because it was poor. The Virginia school had nearly all the money it needed. The Arkansas school had standards so low, one might argue, that our large gift did not make all that much difference. But if a function of charity is to restore some equilibrium between rich and poor, powerful and weak, we should have taken that $15,000 from Richmond and sent it on down to Clarksville.

All too often we avoided hard value decisions by giving money at both extremes, to Harvard and University of Bridgeport, and to the Sierra Club and the Pacific Legal Foundation representing developers and timber interests whose enemy was the Sierra Club. Don Regan and Bob Magowan moved more easily within the business world when this foundation made generous gifts to their peers' favorite charities. True for Charlie Cole and myself in the academic world. But there must also be formal standards of justice that condition what you do.

Washington and Lee University, Lexington, Virginia, 1959–1977—
$105,000. Washington and Lee met old Sam Marks' idea of what a good school
should be, and one of our initial grants was $50,000 to increase faculty
salaries.

Guilford College, Greensboro, North Carolina, 1972–1980—$60,000. Guil-
ford (1838 as a boarding school, 1888 as a college) was a sleepy Quaker college
pulled up during the long administration of Grimsly Hobbs who, with the
help of the Dana Foundation, improved student and faculty quality, salaries,
buildings, and library. He sought to involve the college with the Greensboro
community, setting up a downtown evening center for adults, inviting bright
high school students on campus, and establishing a cooperative program with
other Greensboro colleges. Our first two grants went to restore Founders Hall
and to help give Guilford competitive attraction by adding a field house to
the gym.

The Quaker atmosphere can be frustrating as well as strengthening, as I
saw while teaching at Guilford for three weeks in 1983. Quiet goodness turns
into complacency, intellectual tolerance into good-natured vagueness. "This
is a nurturing institution," and "I was terribly confused when I came here,
I needed a place like that" were remarks I heard more than once and had
to be matched against the total allegiance to competitive success at other
institutions. There were other standards, including the effort to break the
ghetto walls of youth culture in close contacts students had with a large retirement community at one end of the campus, a primary school at the other.
An ambitious foreign study program existed in England and Germany (East
as well as West), and the third Merrill grant went to fund faculty and student
exchange at Tezukayama University in Tokyo.

Guilford is a liberal enclave in a tense community affected by fundamentalist Protestantism, the big money conservatism behind Senator Helms, the
Klan tradition among the blue-collar workers of its textile and furniture factories. Greensboro was the scene of the first civil rights sit-in in 1960 and of
a murderous shoot-out between Klansmen and Communists in 1979. The
Quaker response has been to establish a working tradition of nonviolence, to
offer mediation that both sides could trust, to try and change the attitudes of
policemen through its Law Enforcement Education courses (for example, on
the Black Family and Society) that a large proportion of regional police have
taken, and to work in active support of the public schools.

Guilford is not financially strong. North Carolina has too many colleges and
a shrinking student-age population, and these second-rank institutions compete by lowering admissions standards and offering concessions in scholarships that weaken their resources even further. The situation is not a healthy
one, and the most positive step might be for the weakest faction—public

and private, black and white—to close down. The regional colleges that possess intellectual, social, and moral standards of value—Maryville, Berea, Guilford, Warren Wilson, Morehouse, and Spelman—must insist that these standards are not compromised away in the name of survival. And foundations like the Merrill Trust must show more discrimination and more commitment in whom they back as times get worse.

John B. Stetson University, DeLand, Florida, 1959–1981—$1,630,000. Stetson University, whose high school my father had attended before he went to Amherst—"Charlie, I think that your personal strengths would be better appreciated in the North than down here," the principal said as he expelled the young man who had just dropped a cracker box filled with water from a fourth story window on a professor whom he had mistaken for a friend—was a named beneficiary in our charter. Old Sam Marks, a classmate of my father's, thought highly of Stetson—"the Harvard of the South"—and had us allot $100,000 extra in 1959 for faculty salaries. From my visit there in the early 1960s, I remember the detail that because of a rich old Baptist trustee, the students were forbidden clutch-and-hug dances, though they could hold hands and walk around the gym floor together in time to the music.

University of Florida, Gainesville, Florida, 1976—$25,000 to help meet a challenge grant by the National Endowment for the Humanities to include material out of the humanities within the curricula of the schools of law, business administration, and engineering to try and instill sensitivity towards ethical values into future professional leaders.

An impressive variation in this approach occurred in July 1983 when a federal judge ordered a commodities operator found guilty of market rigging to pay $1.4 million to the University of Nebraska to establish a chair in Ethics. What a wizard idea for educational financing: drug dealers building chemistry labs and gangsters funding seminars in nonviolence.

Palm Beach Atlantic College, West Palm Beach, Florida, 1977–1981— $65,000. Bob Magowan had a high respect for this college. He appreciated its lack of pretentiousness (the campus began as two converted office buildings and a hotel), the stress on volunteer community service as part of the curriculum, and the stress upon teaching practical job skills. Eighteen percent of the 400 students were black or Hispanic, and there were thirty to forty black women learning to become secretaries. The college filled a serious need in this job-sensitive time.

Emory University, Atlanta, Georgia, 1966—$25,000 (plus 1977, $20,000 to School of Business Administration). Our grant was part of a $25 million campaign to meet the education needs of a fast growing area: for program enrichment and new buildings, endowment of salaries, and scholarships. Emory's financing through Coca Cola largesse was responsibly employed: in scientific research, a first-rate medical school, and a school of theology that prepared more men for the ministry than any Methodist seminary in the nation. Its sizable foreign enrollment helped pave the way for cooperation later with the local black colleges and then the acceptance of black students. It could be dangerous, however, for a relatively weak institution to cooperate too closely with a neighbor as rich and powerful as Emory. The latter could offer so much more money to any black student or teacher it wanted (its physical resources were so superior) that a Morehouse or Spelman was in danger of being turned into a vassal.

Then in 1979 Emory received a $100 million gift from the Woodruff Foundation. One can think of all sorts of valuable things to do with ten or twenty million, but even for a large university, what could one do with a hundred? The ethics of university management are based upon the assumption that one must always try harder (giving by alumni and parents) and show self-restraint (faculty, administration, and students) because there is never as much cash as needed. If there is lots and lots of money around, that attitude changes to "What's in it for me?" And for an institution burdened with such riches, what level of dialogue on any level is it possible to carry on with one's peers?

Tulane University, New Orleans, Louisiana, 1961, 1964—$55,000 (plus $130,000 for Tulane Medical Center and School of Public Health and Tropical Medicine). Tulane ranks with Vanderbilt, Emory, and Duke as one of the leaders of Southern education. In 1950 a program had been launched to improve the university's national standing, on the decision to spend what was needed now, while looking for new money. Thirty million dollars was taken in 1953–1963 from endowment to improve physical plant; increase graduate enrollment; step up research activities; and upgrade faculty, student body, and library. Annual expenditures for book acquisitions rose from $239,000 in 1952 to $717,000 in 1963. Our first grant was to support that gamble, our second for the Latin American Program. This involved a reorganization of Colombian medical education, publishing the bilingual InterAmerican Review, archeological study, and orientation for United States and Latin American students going in both directions.

Midwest

Carleton College, Northfield, Minnesota, 1960–1977—$207,000. Carleton was the midwest college to which we gave our largest discretionary support.

It seemed able to combine strengths that in other places were mutually exclusive. There was a rich cultural life and also the friendliness of a traditional,
midwestern, small-town campus. The corporate sense of a responsible community went along with a surprisingly cosmopolitan student and faculty body.
A liberal intellectual atmosphere was matched by efficient professional
administration. On a visit one was impressed by the caliber of the people in
charge, starting with the president, at the time of my visits in the mid-1970s,
Howard Swearer, who went on to become head of Brown.

I also saw the college through the eyes of one of my former students, a
bright, high-strung Jewish girl from Cambridge who'd been in tears because
she was turned down by Radcliffe and had to go to Squaresville. Then she
discovered that her courses demanded the best work she was capable of, that
her classmates, even if their accent was different, were just as bright as she
ever thought she was, and that she could play her cello in the college's symphony orchestra. In the house for French-speaking students where she lived,
no doors were locked, and when she walked home from the library at 11 P.M.
she didn't have to feel afraid.

There was a strong academic program, whether in a traditional course on
Chaucer or an interdisciplinary one like Modern American Society, an effort
to reach liberal arts students with computer programing so they would not
be locked out of a useful new language. In partnership with other midwestern
colleges, Carleton students could study at the Argonne National Laboratory
outside Chicago; the Wilderness Field Station on the Canadian border; urban
education at Chicago University; or foreign programs in Liberia and India,
London and Kyoto. The faculty was hard-working and stressed teaching over
research, with an expectation too that a professor be willing to share in
courses outside his field or take part in the orchestra or weekend cross-country
ski trips.

The Foundation had made two small grants for financial aid in the 1960s,
$7,000 for contemporary art purchases in 1974, then in 1977, $150,000 for
scholarships to small-town students. Over two-thirds of Carleton's almost
1,800 students received some form of financial assistance through jobs, grants,
and loans. This Merrill grant had our standard aim to strengthen the college
by allowing it to accept more high-quality students whose parents could not
afford full tuition. (As the director of admissions stated, the college needed
1,800 students to stay in shape economically but only 1,500 if it wanted to
maintain proper academic standards.) The main purpose of that large gift
was to help Carleton remain close to its original clientele of students from
midwestern small towns, who badly needed its diversity, culture, and intellectual freedom and who gave the campus a special flavor not found in the
standard mix from Scarsdale and Winnetka.

These students, not simply from Duluth and St. Paul but also from Winoma and Sleepy Eye, often had a better sense of identity and of their place in society, President Swearer argued, and were more self-reliant. They appeared less jaded, more imbued with what used to be called the Protestant Ethic, and exposed their peers from metropolitan areas to different perspectives.

Grinnell College, Grinnell, Iowa, 1963–1978—$122,000. Grinnell was founded in 1846 as the first four-year liberal arts college west of the Mississippi. It had rapidly expanded from 1946 to 1950 in order to accommodate returning veterans. Then with the loss of students again during the Korean War, the college started to run severe operating deficits, with a cumulative total by 1954 of $500,000. This was met by stringent economy measures that hurt morale and caused student withdrawals, which in turn were met by one desperate fund drive after another. One $4 million gift in 1956 started to turn things around, plus half a million from Ford, and a $2.6 million successful capital campaign.

Grinnell is an appealing college. Its study of American history and society is bound up in involvement with local government in the town of Grinnell and state government in Des Moines. There was a high-class string quartet playing at the arts center when I made my visit in 1963, and good student art hung on its walls. The new chemistry building was impressive. Because the college was small, any outgoing student had personal contact with his professors, and because the faculty were imaginative, there was an interest in combining scientific and economic, ethical, and esthetic approaches in examining a given topic. There was the same effort as at Carleton to break small-town confines and place its students for a term at the Milwaukee Repertory Theatre or a science program in Costa Rica.

The changes coming out of the 1960s were harder for these traditional rural colleges than for the city ones. As the kids started making experiments, there weren't experienced role models around to say that one sort of drug was no big deal whereas another could be a killer. When it hit, the drug scene was like the coming of measles to Hawaii. No immunity had been built up. When Grinnell started admitting innercity black students, there was no heterogeneous, cosmopolitan society able to absorb one more set of newcomers. These blacks saw nothing in common that they shared on this campus and staked out a corner of the student union building where they played soul music at top volume and smoked pot and dared any white to mess with them.

The Merrill Foundation still said it believed in the values of small-town America and made its last grant of $50,000 in 1978 to serve students from there. Eighteen-year-old students, however, no longer believe in these values, and by the 1980s, despite all the resources of a large endowment, enrollment, and with it morale, had fallen.

Macalester College, St. Paul, Minnesota, 1972, 1979—$65,000. Macalester received generous support from the DeWitt Wallace Foundation, which allowed impressive investments in plant and financial aid but led to dependence on one strongly opinionated source of funds. Macalester saw itself as a liberal arts college within an urban environment, made good use of the social and artistic resources of the Twin Cities, and developed a strong international program (one of my former students joined the Yugoslav semester and eventually found herself married and permanently settled in Zagreb). The college made a commitment to racial opportunity and went from 3 percent minority enrollment in 1968 to 14 in 1971. This led to worse strains than it could manage and frightened away the Wallaces. In the late 1970s, as a financial remedy, Macalester began to recruit Arab and Iranian students, which brought along a different set of strains, and one full-time workman was employed to paint out the hostile graffiti written on the walls every night.

Lawrence University, Appleton, Wisconsin, 1972—$40,000. Two undergraduate colleges, a music conservatory, and an institute for paper chemistry were formed into Lawrence University by 1964. It was proud of its academic standards, the quality of its music, and its belief in diversity threatened by the monolithic development of public institutions. In its financial aid policy, the administration tried to juggle responsibility to its traditional midwest constituency, its new commitment to blacks (minority students went from nine in 1965 to sixty-seven in 1971), the struggle to keep student indebtedness at a tolerable level, and a balanced budget. Lawrence was the first college I knew to send up warnings about the alarming rise in student debt.

Oberlin College, Oberlin, Ohio, 1969–1972—$35,900. Oberlin (1835) was the first coed college, the first to accept blacks, and one of the first to have a music conservatory. In academics Oberlin is probably the leading liberal arts college of the Midwest and should have received more support from our foundation than it did. That elitist intellectuality and small-town isolation when the cities were where it was at, the new breed of black student (no longer the children of Negro professionals: white people with brown skins— "oreos") meant an ugly tension, including a bad drug scene during The Troubles. Oberlin was always a liberal college (Ohio neighbors liked to gossip about the morals of its students and the politics of its professors), but traditional liberalism was even harder put than conservatism to stand up to the times' almost nihilistic radicalism.

Goshen College, Goshen, Indiana, 1975–1980—$65,000. Goshen is a Mennonite College of about 1,000 students in northern Indiana. I was first attracted to it by its student service trimester, whereby just about every student put in a period of sustained work in a foreign country. A resourceful boy, teaching at a village school in Haiti, found himself assuming the role of midwife because he knew how to learn. Nursing students at a badly run clinic in Nicaragua were gradually able to bring in correct standards of hygiene and administration because they knew what they were talking about. In Poland there was a special program where Goshen students worked on family farms and taught English in rural schools. The Mennonites were welcome in Poland because they worked hard and did not drink and took their hosts' Catholicism seriously. In Costa Rica they were praised by a cabinet minister because they set the example of educated, middle-class students working with their hands and living by moral standards.

The returns were tangible too in what the students brought back. For example, Goshen education majors, who practice taught in the schools of Elkhart County, had all had previous experience teaching in Central American villages. The trimester program also brought the college approximately fifty students a year from Ethiopia, Mexico, Taiwan, and Germany. Most of our three grants went to support this foreign service program—the last $20,000 to help launch an exchange with Sichuan University in Chengdu, western China, without any involvement with the U.S. Embassy and the first Chinese-American exchange at the undergraduate level.

Goshen is a sober, reserved place (dancing, drinking, smoking are not allowed on campus) where students come mainly from midwestern small towns, although there are Mexicans, Puerto Ricans, and blacks from Chicago and Gary. The endowment is less than $2 million. Part of this poverty stems from the peculiarities of Mennonite belief. The sect began in sixteenth-century Switzerland out of an insistence on tolerance—no person should be forced to follow the rule of any church unless he believed in it—against the compulsions of the Calvinists. Biblical allegiance, enjoyment of music, and a sober style of life meant a worldwide spread of communicants (Pennsylvania, Russia, Paraguay) and a new interest in countries as diverse as Indonesia, Ghana, and Brazil in this church group that did not have the colonialist wealth or aggressiveness of the better-established denominations. In this country, the Mennonites (and Goshen) are too theologically conservative to obtain support from the foundations who take their cue from the World Council of Churches, but because they are socially liberal and nonfundamentalist, they do not receive support from right-wing Texas money. It does have a handsome new library and a theatre in the process of construction. What impressed me, however, on my tour through an inadequate science building was not simply the enthusiasm and intelligence of the professor, who had come to Goshen from Princeton, but the sophisticated precision of the physics equipment built mainly by the students because the college lacked the resources to buy it. As a daily diet, that conservatism might become oppressive, but what a resource for a country to possess institutions like this that follow their own values and don't have to be like every place else!

St. Olaf, Northfield, Minnesota, 1978—$20,000. St. Olaf, with almost 3,000 students, is the largest, private, liberal arts college in Minnesota. It was founded in 1874 by Norwegian pastors, farmers, and businessmen, and 58 percent of its student body is still Lutheran. Its most famous professor was Ole Rolvaag, author of the tragic novel of immigrant farmers, *Giants in the Earth,* who taught there around the turn of the century. Among recent grants from the usual foundations—Kresge, Lilly, Mellon—was $50,000 from the Royal Norwegian government. Our money went to Lutheran scholarships, although the college's main fundraising impetus was for endowment (then a bit over $6 million) to help support faculty development and curriculum renewal, and meet the unending pressures of inflation.

Suomi College, Hancock, Michigan, 1977—$15,000. This junior college is the only Finnish-established college in the United States, significant for the study and preservation of an ethnic heritage and a resource used by the Smithsonian, the State Department, and the White House for hospitality to Finnish visitors (President Kekkonen in 1976) and for preparation for Americans going in the other direction. Suomi ran an interesting oral history project to capture the lore of the Great Lakes mining region. Our grant went towards establishment of a Finnish-American Studies Center whose resources would be shared with other institutions.

Hope College, Holland, Michigan, 1968–1980—$90,000. A significant business acquaintance of Don Regan's pressed us for five grants—for needy students of the Reformed Church—to this college started by Dutch immigrants in 1852. One of my students had chosen it because she was fed up with the self-importance of Boston intellectuals and because she could not afford anything more expensive, had heard it took academics seriously, and felt that within its small size (1,800) she might stand out. Not religious herself, she respected Hope's Christian perspective, but by the end of four years its limitations had her ready to explode.

Fifty percent of the students came from families earning less than $15,000 per year; over 70 percent received some financial aid. Hope involved itself with local industry in the training of Mexican-American blue-collar workers, developed a Chicano studies program, and extended itself into a cooperative program with black high schools in Alabama.

Washington University, St. Louis, Missouri, 1967, 1972—$55,000. During the nine years when I lived in St. Louis, Washington, except for its medical school, was an undemanding local institution. With a distinguished president in Thomas Eliot and a major capital drive in 1965–1970 for $70 million achieved with the help of $15 million from Ford, the university moved ahead strongly: recruiting an abler and more national student body; downgrading its fraternities; putting more emphasis on social, intellectual, and artistic commitments; enrolling more blacks.

Bradley University, Peoria, Illinois, 1968, 1980—$35,000. Bradley, known for its basketball team, had its campus in Peoria, home of Caterpillar tractor, on whose board of directors Bob Magowan served. The university received corporate funding from Caterpillar, Westinghouse Air Brake, Pabst, and Hiram Walker but was trying to broaden this support and improve its image. The Merrill Foundation gave $25,000 in 1968 to the Speech and Hearing Sciences Center whose cleft palate, brain damage, hearing, and laryngeal speech clinics served 2,000 children in central Illinois per year.

Kenyon College, Gambier, Ohio, 1959–1981—$1,025,000. Kenyon was a named beneficiary in Mr. Merrill's trust charter because of his friendship and respect for Gordon Chalmers, its president during the 1940s and 1950s. It had had a fine academic reputation, particularly in English ($15,000 in 1980 went to strengthen the *Kenyon Review*), but its rural isolation hurt it at a time when students looked for city life, and by the late 1970s it had ceased to have much significance even in the Midwest.

The West

University of Colorado, Boulder, Colorado, 1981—$50,000. In this grant $30,000 went to attract dynamic outside speakers for a newly established two-year residential liberal arts college within the university, and $20,000 went to aid integrated and personalized education by computer through well-tested instructional software. There should be better ways in the 1980s to spend $50,000.

Reed College, Portland, Oregon, 1959–1976—$165,000. Charlie Cole was always impressed by Reed's academic distinction, based upon excellent teaching and stiff demands. It led the nation in percentage of Rhodes Scholarships per capita, of graduates going on to a doctorate in science, and of women in advanced science education. It was a pacesetter and a gadfly in an area dominated by large public universities, although as the nation became more radical, Reed, a left-wing enclave in Portland, began to seem conservative in its old-fashioned commitment to the liberal arts. This primary role of academic excellence was threatened by inadequate financing. The best new students,

particularly those from the lower-middle class with a strong scientific potential, went elsewhere for better financial aid. Our grants funded scholarships
and salaries. Only 50 percent of freshmen remained to graduate, a sign of
Pacific Coast restlessness.

Whitman College, Walla Walla, Washington, 1964–1979—$65,000. "Whit-
man does have potential, but it has only recently discarded a feeling of isolation and begun a long-term program of improvement. Until about 1960
change was strongly resisted by the faculty. Whitman was good enough and
what was being done at Harvard, Yale, and elsewhere was meaningless to
the state of Washington. Progress had been made since 1945, and there was
no need to go further." That in 1964 was our first report on this provincial
institution, which had been noticed, shaken up, and challenged by a major
Ford grant in 1962. Our grants were scattered: to strengthen the art department, to encourage English and drama, and for minority scholarships.

Seattle Pacific College, Washington, 1976—$30,000 for a science learning
center. Seattle Pacific had been started in 1891 by the Free Methodists to
meet the needs of the evangelical Christian community, and even in the 1970s
there were parietal rules, required church attendance and Bible study, and
a prohibition of tobacco and alcohol. Graduates go into medicine, nursing,
social work, or Christian ministry, but in 1960 it received an award as a leader
in physics. Afraid of going into debt, the college scrapped its plans of building
a $6 million Science Learning Center and instead recycled at half the cost
an empty factory building at the edge of the campus. Recycled materials were
used in design and construction with an exposed energy delivery system uti-
lizing different forms: wind, solar, the burning of college wastes, and a computerized system to decide which would be used each day. Mobile labs were
designed to be plugged in at the center or transported for use at marine,
desert, and mountain locations. Equipment was housed in the ceiling and
could be pulled down when needed instead of being fixed on the floor. Merrill
trustees were leery of hardcore evangelism, but this sort of imaginativeness
was too rare to pass up.

Alaska Pacific University, Anchorage, Alaska, 1980—$10,000. This grant,
our only one in Alaska, was to the state's only private four-year university.
Of Alaska's best students, 60 percent attend college outside the state, and
fewer than 15 percent return. Fewer than one-third of Alaska high school
graduates go on to college as opposed to about half nationally.

*University of San Francisco, San Francisco, California, 1961–1980—
$110,000* (plus $65,000 for the University High School). This university was

started in 1855 by the Jesuits, was destroyed in the 1906 fire, rebuilt, and now is a major part of the city's educational establishment. Our first $25,000 began as part of a capital campaign to improve the intellectual quality of the School of Theology, then drifted into the hands of the Department of Psychology to help priests work with mental health programs, and then to offer psychological counseling to priests.

Stanford University, Stanford, California, 1960–1983—$2,175,000. The Trust's main investment in Stanford—though $1,660,000 of this went to the Graduate School of Business and $75,000 to the School of Medicine—was to support its claim as the leading private university west of the Mississippi. In his love-hate relationship with Harvard, Bob Magowan saw Stanford as its West Coast counterbalance. The style was different, with a California flavor of sunny outdoor walkways, the students of Oriental background, and the acres and acres of parking lots, but the intellectual leadership was a serious one.

In 1969 we gave $25,000 for financial aid to Mexican-American and American Indian students. In 1976, $50,000 went for expansion of the library, and $300,000 went in 1981–1983 (Stanford was one of three residual beneficiaries of the Trust) for Magowan Scholarships. The financial aid problem at Stanford, as at every other university, expressed itself at two different levels. As tuition and other costs steadily rose, the average middle-income family was forced to send its children to Berkeley. This change threatened the democratic breadth within the student body that had always been taken for granted and once gone would mean quite a different set of assumptions. The university had also made a newer commitment to open its gates to working class students, largely of black and Mexican-American background, who needed much bigger grants and who should not be excluded again as the federal government lost interest and times became hard.

That $300,000 to Stanford is what I mean by establishment philanthropy. Genuine conservatism begins with a concern for institutions that give leadership to society and that hold it together and respond in wholesome ways to demands for change. Money like that opens doors for young men and women who assume, as they ought to assume, that if they have brains and character and work hard they will be helped to obtain a first-rate education that will start them off to making a good life for themselves and to serving and changing society. If our country stands for anything, it stands for this.

Claremont Group, Claremont, California—$270,000: Pomona College, 1969, 1972—$35,000. Pomona was the oldest (1887) and best-known institution of the Claremont Colleges in the distant suburbs of Los Angeles where the decision had been made to establish a series of cluster colleges, patterned after Oxford and Cambridge, each with a separate administration and corporate personality but sharing the same facilities (library, auditorium, utilities) and cultural offerings. Our two grants to Pomona were for scholarships to Hispanic students and for the purchase of contemporary art. *Scripps College, 1976—$10,000* for scholarships. Scripps is the only women's institution in Claremont, with special strengths in art and languages and with heavy pressure to maintain its financial aid responsibilities. *Harvey Mudd, 1959, 1977—$80,000.* The scientific school within the Claremont complex, Harvey Mudd was started in 1955 to produce engineers trained in the physical sciences and scientists trained in engineering, stressing basic rather than applied science in order to educate leaders able to grow within their fields instead of being fettered to an outmoded technology. *Southern California School of Theology, 1965–1980—$95,000. Claremont Graduate School, 1963, 1968—$50,000* for construction.

University of California at Santa Cruz, Santa Cruz, California, 1968, 1980—$680,000. The Trust's major involvement with public universities was its grant to Santa Cruz. Out of the troubles of 1964 at Berkeley and the beginning of student militancy, the University of California regents had worked out an imaginative alternative. Instead of the antheap approach of Berkeley, ULCA, or Davis, it would found a university composed of residential colleges. Each would have 500 to 700 students and its own eating facilities, but more than being a purely residential facility as at Harvard or Yale, it would have its own intellectual personality like the colleges at Oxford and Cambridge. The extra cost of these smaller and more agreeable units would be met by obtaining private support: $500,000 from the Trust towards the construction of Merrill College, plus $150,000 to endow its library and visiting lectures and student ventures.

Santa Cruz had a beautiful campus among the redwoods near Monterey, the ocher hills behind, the ocean in front. It was easy to poke fun at its youth culture inmates who consumed pot and Zen and meditated in the lotus position as they watched the sun set over the Pacific, but there was a generous, reasonably serious, personal commitment to study. The university chapel was a spacious flower and vegetable garden on a hillside where students and faculty worked in silence.

Without our trustees knowing this ahead of time, Merrill College was handed the mission of concentrating upon the problems of poverty and the Third World. At first that attracted fuzzy middle-class radicals, similar to those at Hampshire, who attended classes taught by Indian and African guest professors. Later on, a tougher, less academic black and Chicano element began to show up. In pursuit of its concern for the needs of the poor and to free its students from that redwoods isolation, Merrill College encouraged its members to take part in social action. The most vivid example of this was the effort of the United Farm Workers under Cesar Chavez to unionize migrant workers in the grape and lettuce fields. A prime target of UFWOC, for its support of the farmers who believed in the open shop, was Safeway Stores. This led Bob Magowan to protest to the Board of Regents that Merrill College students were receiving academic credit for picketing Safeway.

That became a complicated, no-win situation. The anger between young people and old people, the worsening financial crisis within the whole California education system, and a more conservative and less generous climate of opinion made Santa Cruz a football. Each year a new rumor came along of what fate was destined for it. A pity, for it promised to be one of the country's best state universities, and private givers have a responsibility to those students lacking the money for private institutions.

In 1980, out of increasing concern for the needs of California's Chicano population, the Trust made a grant of $30,000 for the recruitment of Hispanic students. Merrill College's provost, Rafael Guzman, was anxious to steer those easily discouraged students toward more serious long-range goals than the community colleges could supply and made a special effort to reach the young women, whose education received so little respect in that macho world.

University of Southern California, Los Angeles, California, 1972–1978—$175,000. The university was an important institution within the area of both Merrill Lynch and Safeway interest and was the oldest, largest university in the West. $100,000 in 1972 was given toward construction of a new interdisciplinary research facility for the study of urban problems. Since 1945, new cities grow too quickly while old cities decay at their cores. USC, in the heart of Los Angeles, which contains all the major urban problems, had great academic and physical growth since 1960, and more than $200 million had been raised in gifts and pledges from private sources. $25,000 in 1978 went to the School of Business Administration for financial aid within the Food Marketing Management Program.

Deep Springs College, Deep Springs, California, 1972—$20,000. Deep Springs was founded in 1917 by Lucien Nunn, Telluride gold mine owner and electric power visionary, who was fascinated by the idea of combining manual and intellectual labor. Students work half a day on the cattle ranch and half a day in the classrooms and library. Those who rank in the top one percent of the College Board scores and who show evidence of character and leadership are invited to join this austere, isolated junior college that the students legally own. A small alumni body plus the impact of inflation upon endowment had forced this appeal for outside funds.

WOMEN'S EDUCATION

> On the whole, America has educated its girls quite well. It has done a less good job in the education of women. [Mary Bunting]

> An educated woman makes me nervous. [Charles E. Merrill]

These two remarks are the opposite sides of the same coin. Mr. Merrill was generous to the daughters of his friends when they needed tuition money their widowed mothers could not supply. He gave to Smith and Mount Holyoke, whose girls had always been the dates of Amherst men. He enjoyed the intelligent women he met in his last years, many of them European, as if wit and originality could not be found among the wives of his business associates. He respected force of character: the spunk his grandmother showed in running, barely out of her teens, the Wilson plantation after her husband had been drafted into the Mississippi state militia. But a process of education that trained objective, independent minds upset the old man's concept of the proper relationship between the sexes. And though the Merrill Trust gave well over $4 million to institutions and educational programs serving women and girls, there was always ambiguity in the decisions as to whether this was exactly what Mr. Merrill would have wanted.

During the years when the Trust operated, it became harder to define what was a women's institution or women's education. Vassar, Connecticut, Bennington, Skidmore, and Sarah Lawrence were accepting men. Wesleyan, Yale, Princeton, Dartmouth, Williams, and Amherst were accepting women. Pembroke had been absorbed totally by Brown, Kirkland by Hamilton, Radcliffe partly by Harvard. Chatham and Goucher had set out on that path and then reversed direction.

These changes, mainly of the 1970s, led to intense discussion of the definition of women's education and a new interest for young women in women's history and in the stories of their mothers and grandmothers. They gave a new drive to the lives of women (true in part for the lives of blacks) that made white males and their institutions seem less interesting.

A foundation like ours became nervous whenever it sensed itself drawing too far from Establishment consensus, of being trapped into posing questions whose answers we might not care for. Blacks and women are not always sure if they want to be discussed under the same topic heading, but some of the issues of their education have a similar colonial quality. British writers on the West Indies often mentioned how black children in the primary grades were on a par with their white classmates. As they came into adolescence, however, they fell behind, became sullen and frustrated, and eventually dropped out. This was interpreted as proof of innate inferiority toward the problems of abstract thinking and the inability to accept discipline or deferred enjoyment.

A more humane critic might interpret this failure as the result of both racial groups refusing to tolerate an individual success that would call into question the established relationships between black and white. Higher education for the lower class could be accepted, even encouraged so long as it did not amount to anything much. Black women could accept this compromise and take jobs as teachers and nurses; black men could not.

Traditional female education could also go in many directions so long as it did not make men nervous. This could be the total vacuity of schools we read about in Dickens and Charlotte Brontë: French conversation, piano, embroidery, and theatricals. The aim was to learn how to win and hold a husband, to keep from associating with the wrong people, and, at the bottom line of every disciplinary system, to make sure nobody got pregnant. As Alexis de Tocqueville, visiting this country in the 1830s, wrote home to his sister: "How are American women supposed to occupy themselves once they are married—by staying home and admiring their husbands."[2]

Young ladies at Sweet Briar might study French literature or even economics so long as it made no difference. After graduation they might work for a couple of years teaching school, serving as receptionist in Daddy's office, or helping the poor. Then marriage to a rising young businessman, maintenance of a proper style of consumption and behavior, and the raising of children to replace themselves. (How did such students react to the revolutionary 1960s: by letting their Bermuda shorts go unpressed?) Another colonial approach, as at Mount Holyoke, was to train women for sexless ghetto careers, as teachers, librarians, social workers, missionaries—where they could do Good Works, but so far removed from what was important that they were not threatening.

The colonial period was coming to an end in the 1970s. Abigail Adams' great statement to her husband—"John, we will not hold ourselves to be bound by the laws in which we have no voice or representation"—was quoted again and again. Women sought to make changes in the most basic relations between men and women in the home and in the workplace and to expand the whole range of career choice. Male-dominated institutions with power and money like the Charles E. Merrill Trust made concessions to changing values or supported neutral institutions whose female members could use these extra resources as they saw fit, or made angry gestures like that $50,000 for male students at Yale.

Smith College, Northampton, Massachusetts, 1963–1977—$433,600. Smith is the richest and probably best women's college in the United States and in the world. Its endowment is higher than Amherst's. Though it cannot match Amherst's arrogance, it poses to a foundation like ours the same ques-

2. Quoted in Richard Reeves *American Journey,* p. 309.

tion as an elite institution: what leadership in American education and society justifies that level of wealth, and the appeals for further support?

The college has had a long tradition of excellence: in science, foreign languages, history, art, in the caliber of its teachers and students, in its tradition of hard work, in the quality of its facilities, and in its social concern. It administers one of the oldest and best-run junior year abroad programs.

In 1971 the Trust gave $50,000 for library development; in 1973 $100,000 for improved facilities in physical education. A by-product of the feminist movement was new interest in sports for women; and Smith's facilities were crowded, worn, and obsolete.

Thomas Mendenhall, the president who had overseen the major changes of the 1960s and early 1970s, was replaced in 1975 by Jill Conway, an Australian-born historian from the University of Toronto. Mrs. Conway was determined to use the troubled times, as demands for changes in the status of women were being worked out in an increasingly discouraged economic climate, as a way of demonstrating the importance of Smith's leadership. To begin with, as fees rose, sustained aid from the federal government became more chancy, and weaker colleges cut back in their scholarship offerings, it was crucial for Smith to hold to its traditional standard that any student good enough to be admitted would receive the financial aid she needed. In 1977 the Trust sought to strengthen the new president's position by making a grant of $250,000 for scholarships.

Don Regan appointed Mrs. Conway the first woman director of Merrill Lynch, an occasion for much self-congratulation. The new member used the post as a way to educate herself on the bond market, worked closely with the college's investment committee, and from 1976 to 1983 doubled the endowment from $80 to $160 million.

If, unlike most other colleges, Smith had strengthened its resources to such an extent, what were the priorities for all this money? First, to define women's education at a time when, at least superficially, the feminist objectives had been met. Second, to restore morale and a sense of mission to the faculty when, all over the globe, the teaching profession became increasingly undervalued. Third, to communicate the values of a liberal education to potential applicants.

Women's education in the English-speaking countries had followed two quite different goals. One was to train women to be a redemptive force and a spiritual influence within a brutal society, a point of view that expresses itself in the tradition of volunteerism. The other was to train women to rise in that society: to become Merrill Lynch's next chairman of the board. Smith should be a repository of knowledge and influence about volunteerism. It should restructure social science research so that female responses were seen as normative, not deviant. It should possess the confidence not to lose itself in each feminist fad.

As fellowships for sabbatical and postdoctoral study dried up, it was necessary to put special fund-raising efforts into faculty support, to increase
teachers' effectiveness, and prove how seriously the college valued them.
Problems are to be met primarily by investment in faculty. For example, like
every other college, Smith is faced by declining skill in writing. Young people
today have no practical experience—in sustained reading or in writing diaries
or letters home—in finding a formal voice. To rebuild this skill, first step is
to teach the faculty how to teach writing. Faculty, from all departments, are
paid to attend such workshops. Next step is then to train students to tutor (at
the same wages as they would receive for work in the dining hall or library)
their peers.

If it becomes clear that the president knows her own mind and has engi-
neered a tangible rise in intellectual standards, then she acquires the authority to take on unpopular decisions. This means, for the sake of the college
and the profession, trying to bring in first-rate younger teachers by encouraging the departure of less than first-rate senior staff. Some popular people
do not get tenure. Some older people may be helped (pushed) to choose early
retirement. Such astringency is not the enjoyable side of leadership, but it
can't be avoided if one is going to maintain a good school.

Who are the students to enter a college like this? The great majority of
high school girls do not want a women's college. The intense, silent competitiveness and the dorm atmosphere on weekend nights for the girl who
doesn't have a date don't help sales. Nationwide the population of eighteen-
year-olds is declining, their parents have less money, and the present government is not much interested in education. The majority of colleges compete for a shrinking market by lowering their standards. Mrs. Conway backed
a contrary policy of cutting the number of incoming freshmen and replacing
them by older women, transferring into sophomore or junior year, many from
community college, and 40 out of these 160 were women on welfare. It is a
costly policy, but foundation support was obtained, and the new students,
though poorly prepared, were intelligent, hardworking, and tremendously
motivated—a realistic and inspiring example to their younger peers.

If certain colleges have money, attainment, and pride that are the marks
of an elite institution, then there are ways to utilize these resources and stand
for something.

Mount Holyoke College, South Hadley, Massachusetts, 1959–1980—
$410,000. The college is the creation of one woman, Mary Lyon, who opened
Mount Holyoke Female Seminary in 1837 to give poor young women the
opportunity for Christian and intellectual training. As she writes about her
life and thoughts, quoted in Sidney MacLean's essay in *Notable American*
Women, how modern her remarks sound: the teachers she had who "talked

to ladies as if they had brains," the failure in financing one of her projects "from good men's fear of greatness in women," her wrestling with male panic that if women were educated, who's going to bake the pies. From the beginning, the students shared in maintenance work in order to cut costs and acquired a cheerful camaraderie out of working together. Classes were conducted by topic and discussion rather than by rote. In her writings over and over comes up the same phrase: "We are trying a new experiment."

Mount Holyoke was never as large, rich, or classy as Smith. It was traditionally famous, along with Wellesley and Goucher, as a teacher of teachers, with particular strength in science, and ranked ninth in the United States for the proportions of female graduates going on to doctorates. Our first $75,000, 1959–1963, went towards construction costs of an expansion program. Richard Gettell, president then, saw Mount Holyoke threatened by the very improvements which made it such an exciting place to be in. As the good high school graduates became better educated, they demanded more from colleges, which had to upgrade their faculties and therefore desperately raided each other's best teachers. Salaries climbed rapidly during the 1960s, which was rough on the more fragile institutions, sorely pressed by competition from wealthier state universities, and Gettell feared that rising tuition would price Mount Holyoke out of its traditional role as a college for the daughters of teachers, ministers, and social workers.

The Trust gave $300,000 during 1976–1980 towards the Winthrop H. Smith Chair of Economics, named for the man who had replaced Charles E. Merrill as head of Merrill Lynch and had been a trustee of the college as well as first chairman of the Merrill Trust. During the 1970s female colleges were both threatened and buoyed by the rising feminist movement. Young women demanded the training that fitted them for new leadership openings and showed this by pushing for entrance into the colleges where they could share classroom and daily life with men. Mount Holyoke had to emphasize a less popular line of reasoning. Free, perhaps for the first time, from the stereotypes of a male-dominated society, its students were more than twice as likely to major in the sciences and mathematics as women at coeducational institutions. Women held every position of leadership and executed every decision. The Winthrop Smith Chair, oriented towards the administration of complex organizations—the sort of career field in business, government, and nonprofit institutions that women are entering now—was part of this process.

Mount Holyoke always held a commitment to serving minority students. At my own school I was almost embarrassed by the fact that it was our black seniors, all of them needing large scholarships, who applied, not full-pay white girls who preferred coed institutions. Laura Gonçalves, who was born in the Cape Verdes (and whose mother had been kept illiterate so she wouldn't write to boys), came to Commonwealth from Dorchester High, saw her self-esteem shatter as she received barely passing grades, but doggedly built up the skill and confidence that eventually earned her a place at Mount Holyoke. From there she went on to medical school at Brown, part of her lifelong ambition to become a doctor and then return, at least for a year or two, to the islands to show other girls what they could make out of their lives.

Laura was sustained by her sense of purpose. Other minority students felt totally displaced in this isolated, white, female community and hated Mount Holyoke despite all the help they received. Elizabeth Kennan, who became president in 1979 (a medieval scholar, not an MBA, as one might have expected then), felt it important to remind the community that Mary Lyon had started the college to serve exactly that same deprived young woman. Who could be more alienated from American society than an educated woman of the nineteenth century? What changes in curriculum (every student must study one third-world culture), what new teachers (like Shirley Chisholm, the black ex-congresswoman), and new cultural groups (a black theatre and dance company called Shades of Expression that became very popular) could show both white and nonwhite students how the college was trying to change?

Could one escape elitism not into a leaden egalitarianism but into realism and even humility? Could one persuade young women, now being told by every message they read and hear that it is their duty to put themselves first, to listen to their natural inclinations to justice and generosity and be willing, every so often, to sacrifice individual attainment for the general good, which means volunteer work in Springfield's slums or Belchertown's mental hospital?

Bryn Mawr College, Bryn Mawr, Pennsylvania, 1964–1976—$125,000. Traditionally the most demanding of the women's colleges, Bryn Mawr is famed for its academic rigor, its blue stocking pride, and its high-minded commitment to social service of its graduates. Not all of this appeals to the average high school girl. An early president made the unfortunate statement, "Only our failures marry." (Study might be made of the relation between contraceptives and higher education for women; there was a third choice to the traditional alternatives of mother or nun.) Even late in the 1960s each incoming freshman was advised to bring her own tea set.

Low salaries caused a loss of faculty during the 1950s, and in trying to catch up, the college fell behind on new construction and financial aid. A Ford promise in 1962 of $2.5 million if Bryn Mawr could raise $7.5 million launched the first building program since the 1930s. The Trust's first $25,000 went towards that goal. $50,000 in 1971 went towards modernization of the rather rigid, old-fashioned curriculum and to improve cooperation with nearby colleges, another $50,000 in 1976 for financial aid to girls from middle-income families.

Bryn Mawr never tried to be popular, but the feminist rejection by the late 1970s of so many of the easy assumptions of American society brought a new respect from young women for a college that had such firm values.

Wellesley College, Wellesley, Massachusetts, 1974, 1977—$88,000. Wellesley is the college usually compared to Bryn Mawr. Its wealth (endowment over $100 million by the mid 1970s) turned off the Merrill trustees for a while, but one had to respect its long tradition of excellence in science education (aided by a partnership with MIT) and its community strength and pride. Fifty-five percent of alumnae contributed every year—the highest rate of any women's college. Forty-two percent of all undergraduates received scholarship aid. A girl of quality was never turned down for financial reasons. Wellesley had a good reputation for the way it treated its students—in counseling, in job placement, and in sensible flexibility when someone got in trouble. There was a sense of community—not the atomization that appears in all too many colleges.

Vassar College, Poughkeepsie, New York, 1970–1981—$55,000. Vassar was founded in 1885 by a successful brewer to insure a good education for his daughter. It started to take men in 1969 after deciding not to affiliate with Yale (as one of the first males stated: "Think of having 2,000 older sisters!"). It has always been a well-endowed, well-run school in its gloomily handsome brick buildings. The Trust gave $35,000 in 1970 for faculty salaries; and $20,000 in 1981 towards the purchase, with James Merrill's help, of the Elizabeth Bishop papers for the college's manuscript collection that included so many important women writers. The competition was Harvard's Houghton Library, which claimed its convenience for scholars. The Merrill Trustees felt that the papers would have more importance to Vassar than to Harvard, a gift that was owed to a women's college, even though Bishop always insisted she was A Poet, not A Female Poet.

Sarah Lawrence College, Bronxville, New York, 1961–1981—$110,000. Sarah Lawrence was started in the late 1920s as an experimental college that would develop the talents and needs of the individual. There were no required courses; reports were given on a student's work rather than grades; and there was emphasis upon the creative arts, small classes, practical fieldwork, and complete student self-government. A low endowment and a high faculty-student ratio meant a high tuition, a fact which in itself attracts a certain type of student, and poses a problem of how to compensate for that— by scholarships (the Trust gave $80,000 for these) to attract middle-income and a few token minority students and by programs that will expand the interests of this over-articulate, self-absorbed student population.

The president we dealt with, Charles De Carlo, got off to a bad start by asking for $1 million, but his background as an IBM executive gave him an objectivity in looking at the college's needs and a clarity of administration to back up what was important: the spirit of demanding the highest possible commitment by teachers and students. De Carlo drove himself to the limit as a fund-raiser for new buildings and for faculty and scholarship endowment. Men were also accepted but, more importantly, Sarah Lawrence was one of the first colleges to make a serious effort, for both intellectual and financial reasons, to recruit older students into its Center for Continuing Education. This was helped by the college's suburban location but also by the ability to see specific needs and the resourcefulness then to meet them. For example, in the rapidly expanding medical fields attracting older women, an M.A. program was offered in human genetics (research and counseling for Tay Sachs disease, sickle cell anemia, diabetes) and in patients' rights: how to be an effective ombudsman and keep patients and their families from being chewed up by hospital machinery.

In the latter 1970s Sarah Lawrence was hurt by the lesbian stereotype that a certain style of feminism encouraged and the fact that its high tuition made it too easy for any candidate able to pay full freight just to walk in. In 1970 its SAT Verbal 695 ranked with Radcliffe's (but Radcliffe's math was almost as high while Sarah Lawrence's was 600). Five years later, Sarah Lawrence had a Verbal 580 (Math 540) that, even if SAT scores throughout the country were dropping, was a token of weaker standards.

Bennington College, Bennington, Vermont, 1970, 1979—$45,000. Our second grant, $20,000 in 1979, was illustrative of the college's problems and of the Foundation's: to be used for students from disadvantaged and minority backgrounds and from middle-income families. Given the cost—over $10,000 by 1979, over $15,000 by 1984—some families chose Bennington (or Sarah Lawrence) as they would choose a Mercedes, just because it was expensive, from a mix of consumerism and radical chic where the stereotype was a girl wearing jeans and a leopard skin coat. There was a time when spark, energy, and pride could go beyond these contradictions, and where the girls shared creativity in the classroom with a nine-week winter project that might include teaching drama in a women's prison. The tension between that beautiful Vermont campus and the work terms created something of value.

Then the mandate of heaven passed from the country campus. The isolation was not good for the girls. Nor for the faculty: to make up for low salaries a male of any masculinity, the cliché repeated, could have a pretty free run among his students. It was no longer as easy to be avant garde when almost every college was experimenting with work terms, individualized instruction, no grades, and no rules. Gale Parker, president in the mid-1970s, usefully challenged the self-serving passivity of liberal academe but gave such an example of undisciplined, high-strung leadership that she made the college a figure of fun. And by the late 1970s the campus was torn by rumors, as with Antioch, of whether the place could survive.

So, back to our grant. What black or Spanish-speaking girl should consider Bennington, even if all expenses were free (even with a generous scholarship she'd be staggered by the cost)? Ditto for any disadvantaged student, on display as a sociological curiosity. A middle-income student could find a better college at a lower cost. That bit of cash would have no positive impact upon either institution or individual.

Wells College, Aurora, New York, 1968–1978—$85,000. Wells, which had been bankrolled by the founder of Wells Fargo and American Express, appealed to Charlie Cole as a traditional WASP institution with loyal alumnae, a good curriculum and student body, and, in 1969, an able new president. Could support from our foundation help maintain morale, a sense of identity and purpose to this small but well-run college so that it was more than just a source of dates for Cornell frat parties? Our gifts went for renovation and in 1978 for support of the college's energy conservation program. The rise in oil prices was devastating northeastern schools, and Wells sought to finance this pilot project to show what a small college with modest capital and limited technical staff could do to improve its management. This involved sophisticated energy surveillance procedures, awakening sensitivity (briefer showers), altering building usage and the college calendar during winter, not only to save $40,000 a year but also to serve as a model for democratic decision-making that involved the entire community in its plans and procedures.

Wells was in trouble. The SAT verbal had fallen a hundred points in ten years. Enrollment, 700 in 1973, was 500 in 1978. High school girls weren't interested in isolated all-female places. Eisenhower, Kirkland, Windham, and Franconia were examples of other northeastern liberal arts colleges that had closed since 1975. Good leadership and a conviction of what one stood for that could be shared with potential students and givers were needed to keep a decent place like this going.

Kirkland College, Clinton, New York, 1969–1973—$80,000. Kirkland did not survive. Chartered in 1965, it was the first independent, eastern women's college to be started since Sarah Lawrence and Bennington—part of a fantasy of cooperative cluster colleges around Hamilton and an alternative (as at Claremont) to simply increasing the size of the host institution. In Sam Babbitt, Kirkland had an energetic, thoughtful president. Its spark and its lively young women were a useful stimulus to ivy-wreathed (1812) wealthy Hamilton (to which the Trust gave $95,000), whose trustees put up half a million as seed money and later extended $1 million in a line of credit. Academically, Kirkland sought to break the departmental strait-jacket, apportioning its courses among the broad divisions of knowledge (humanities, social sciences, arts), brought in courses like child psychology and music that complemented Hamilton's, and worked for more independence and flexibility, more cooperation between teacher and student.

1968 was not a good year for starting a college. The high student attrition of those times meant overuse of such gimmicks as guest seniors and awarding degrees in absentia, which weakened its repute. And if you had only $100,000 in financial aid to award then, how would you apportion it? $1,000 or $2,000 apiece to the daughters of teachers and social workers, a known constituency that would increase numbers and improve academic quality? No, at that time you had to give out most of your aid in $5,000 units to black girls from New York City, most of them poorly prepared, unable to accept the rules of this rural liberal campus, and absolutely unable to show gratitude or respect to the college that was desperately trying to serve them. The first valedictorian was a black student who felt compelled to denounce the entire community as frauds.

The Trust gave $50,000 for scholarships and $30,000 for debt retirement. By then Kirkland was already in serious state from the high debt service on its $16 million campus. Forty-seven percent of the students were requiring financial aid. Good management and a good pattern of gift giving were not sufficient. The college launched a $28 million drive for endowment and plant amortization, but that rapidly proved unrealistic, and the Hamilton trustees began to fear that those who did give to Kirkland might essentially be their own clientele. Kirkland asked for further credit from Hamilton, which was refused, and after harsh words and agony, the college closed, all its assets and liabilities assumed by Hamilton, which through that process became coed.

What are the lessons? Think small, build cheap, don't fool around with high-risk, high-need applicants? And avoid the vision and excitement that sustain a new institution?

Wilson College, Chambersburg, Pennsylvania, 1977—$20,000. Wilson almost failed. It had been recommended as a serious Establishment place, and our grant went to strengthen the field of religious studies. Many of its students went on an Indian semester in Mysore. It took part in a Central Pennsylvania consortium with Dickinson, Gettysburg, and Franklin and Marshall in order to widen offerings and cut costs, but in such a consortium the weakest institution may find itself drained away. By 1977 enrollment was down to 285 though an anonymous donor had just given half a million, and a new president had been hired to rebuild. In 1979, while a group of students sang the college hymn in the rain, weeping, outside the building where the trustees were voting to close up shop, the heart stopped beating. Later the board reconsidered and allowed the college to limp on into the 1980s.

Why does a college become terminal? When? When do trustees and friends make even deeper sacrifices to increase their support? When do they cut their losses and quit? When is the team strengthened (as I think was true with Marlboro), through its showing of loyalty, resourcefulness, and tenacity, in fighting for survival? When is it simply scarred and embittered? The institutions that fail are not necessarily the worst.

Wheaton College, Norton, Massachusetts, 1968–1981—$85,000. Charlie Cole led us to this college, a long-established (1834), serious, underfinanced place near Boston, without much prestige or glamor, despite the fact that the wife of the president of Reader's Digest had graduated from there and had brought in big money from the conservative DeWitt Wallace Foundation. Between 1955 and our first gift in 1968, the enrollment had climbed from 500 to 1,100, faculty salaries had doubled, library holdings had tripled, and $7 million worth of buildings had been erected. Our gifts went mainly for improving the library.

An intellectual problem of a Wheaton was that the female faculty were so heavily involved in teaching and administration that they lacked the energy and resources (and the college could not fund an effective sabbatical program) to keep up-to-date and grow. It was to serve women teachers at colleges like Wheaton, when hard times were making academic competition ever more cut-throat, that the Mary Bunting Institute at Radcliffe committed itself to providing opportunities for advanced study.

Simmons College, Boston, Massachusetts, 1973, 1977—$60,000. Simmons could be compared with Clark, Bates, and Trinity as an unglamorous, useful college, perhaps the first women's institution to blend training in liberal arts with practical skills. It was the first to have a collegiate program in social work, one of the earliest in nursing and library science, the first to offer part-time degree programs for women trying to deal also with family responsibilities, and was a prime mover in the new field of continuing education. It had a record of good administration and was proud of the fact that during the optimistic fifties and sixties it did not overextend itself in programs or construction. The reverse side of this sobriety was a worn and inadequate physical plant and not enough apparent spark to stand up, in hard times, to competition from low-tuition state colleges. A $6.7 million science building, to offset the traditional weakness of female colleges in science, a new library, an aggressive effort to upgrade salaries and financial aid were efforts at change in the seventies under an able new president, William Holmes. Our first grant went to strengthen Simmons' outreach to black students, the second—like almost all of our scholarship grants by then—to middle-income students, where even $500 might make the difference to a pressured family.

Newton College of the Sacred Heart, Newton, Massachusetts, 1974—$40,000. This Catholic college was trying to take advantage of the new career aggressiveness among women that Simmons was serving, and our gift was to strengthen a program in developing business and money management skills among older women. It was an interesting idea, but too many other things were going wrong, and the college closed a year or two later.

Barnard College, New York, New York, 1959, 1967—$50,000. Barnard is perhaps the best known city college for women and is proud of its academic achievements. It has trod a fine line between practical cooperation with Columbia, its parent institution, and the danger of being swallowed by that powerful neighbor.

Hunter College, New York, New York, 1977—$25,000. In 1961 Hunter was absorbed administratively into the City University of New York but continued to operate undergraduate programs with a degree of autonomy. Because it was assumed that state and federal governments gave generous aid to working-class students, help from foundations like Merrill was needed, in our trustees' reasoning, for middle-class students, which carries of course its own racial overtones. And by the eighties neither group was receiving much support.

Chatham College, Pittsburgh, Pennsylvania, 1966, 1971—$55,000. Chatham, the fourth oldest (1869) women's college in the United States had been an undemanding place for nice girls from western Pennsylvania, but in the sixties, led by an able president, Edward Eddy, made a strong effort to upgrade itself. The book acquisitions budget went from $11,000 in 1961 to $34,000 in 1964. Salaries rose an average of 50 percent from 1961 to 1965. Alumnae contributions in the same period went from 30 to 50 percent. There was a strong volunteer and political service program, an active involvement with the life of the city, including its political campaigns, increasing cross registration with Carnegie Mellon and the University of Pittsburgh, and in the yearbook (to show the importance of academics) the only detail placed under a graduate's picture was the title of her senior thesis.

Another side of the picture of course is that even during this period of improvement, only 60 percent of entering freshmen stayed to graduate. The older students became restless on their pretty, suburban campus, and went off to coed colleges or marriage. By 1970 came a strong movement among the students to have Chatham become coed. Then with a realization that they had a special place worth respecting, the students reversed themselves and voted down the idea. The struggle for identity and a sense of purpose never ends of course, but there are a lot of practical things one can do to improve an institution, and the pride that comes with that may carry it across the next rough time.

Goucher College, Towson, Maryland, 1963–1980—$85,000. Goucher was opened in 1885 in Baltimore, and World War II caught it in the middle of a move to suburban Towson. Our first $25,000 in 1963 was for aid to students interested in teaching but also to finance the education of older students, women who had raised their children and now wanted to complete their B.A. or earn a teacher's certificate in elementary education. It was one of the first such programs that became so popular ten years later (and which we backed on the graduate level at Radcliffe), and the suprised reaction at Goucher, to be repeated over and over elsewhere, was the positive impact upon the younger students by the motivation and seriousness of these older peers.

Goucher shared courses with Johns Hopkins and was burdened with the same restlessness as at Chatham of students who wanted MEN available, all the time. An exchange partnership with Mills, on San Francisco Bay, which we helped fund in 1971, added a little glamor to this well-run but meat-and-potatoes place. The Trust also gave $10,000 in 1972 for the purchase of contemporary graphics from area artists, a way to show respect for an interesting department.

Our last $25,000 went for science equipment. Goucher shared the same troubles of every underendowed college, and it is tempting for an institution in trouble to put every dollar it can lay its hands on into operating expenses: fuel oil, roof repairs, and financial aid as a way to lure in a few more bodies. Rhoda Dorsey, the president, was particularly proud of Goucher's reputation in science. Despite its small size, about 700, it stood twenty-second among all undergraduate institutions in the percentage of female graduates going on to the doctorate. The small size meant that the science students worked directly with their professors, with every piece of equipment the labs possessed. A girl headed towards graduate school in chemistry, geology, physics, or medicine knew why she would choose Goucher; and President Dorsey felt that the college should play to its strengths. Our money went for a fluorescent and an infrared spectrophotometer, a microprocessor, and a liquid scintillation counter.

Randolph-Macon Women's College, Lynchburg, Virginia, 1968–1977—$29,800. Most of this money went to match a Ford grant. Randolph Macon was the first Southern women's college to receive a *ΦBK* chapter, shared a faculty exchange program with a group of women's colleges in India, and had recently expanded its offerings in international studies including the first year-long program among any colleges of its kind in Africa. It is a serious college but with a homogeneous student body and a small endowment.

Sweet Briar College, Sweet Briar, Virginia, 1964–1973—$70,000. Sweet Briar was respected and well run; and the grants we gave for the library, scholarships, and renovations of Benedict Hall were well used, but the un-questioning values of this college for nice girls from affluent families made me wonder what good was served by our money. I wished that our $70,000 had gone to Spelman or even Goucher instead. Horses played an important role on campus; many of the girls kept their own. The two big social events were the prom weekends at Princeton and the University of Virginia, and a great deal of thought went into clothing, logistics, and probably ethics in preparation for them. Along with Smith and Vassar, Sweet Briar had a strong junior-year program (which included women from other colleges) in Paris, and one used to see their wholesome students at the Comédie and Opéra.

Scholarship funds went to the grateful daughters of teachers and ministers. The college benefited from a wider range of students, but when feeling cyn-ical I asked myself, what did those girls receive? Teaching in French and literature (from professors who in 1970 earned less than those at Morehouse) was better than what they would have received at most state institutions, certainly, but would not the basic impact have been the gulf between their lack of privilege and what the richer girls enjoyed? Unless they were quite mature, would they not have been fitted into the slot of "Oh, I only wish I could" or the more wholesome "To hell with it!"

Agnes Scott College, Decatur, Georgia, 1969—$25,000. A serious college of Presbyterian background with a high academic reputation in its region, a tradition of strong student involvement in decisionmaking, courses shared with Emory, and a high endowment and low salaries. From his fascination with how to run things better, Don Regan included in our grant the suggestion that the board of trustees investigate whether the college would be better off with an enrollment larger than its 760.

When I visited Agnes Scott in the mid-1960s, in my role as chairman of the Morehouse board of trustees, it was not yet accepting Negro students but did invite a distinguished professor of French from Morehouse to lecture. One rationale for this cautious "movement" was to do nothing that would stir up the hornets' nest of public school integration. Rich schools like Emory and Agnes Scott would eventually offer scholarships to black applicants that Morehouse and Spelman could not match, but those pioneers paid a high price.

Mills College, Oakland, California, 1960–1980—$125,000. Mills, started as a young ladies' seminary in 1852, is the best-known women's college west of the Mississippi. Easton Rothwell, president in 1959, set about to upgrade the curriculum with new courses in arts, sciences, and non-Western studies; dropped vocational offerings; raised salaries; and brought in new faculty (one-third of whom are involved professionally in Asia). The college became increasingly strong in the social sciences, for in a way the San Francisco Bay area is one great social laboratory.

Radcliffe-Harvard, Cambridge, Massachusetts, 1964–1978—$300,000. Our major involvement with graduate education for women came through Radcliffe. In 1963 I had called upon its president, Mary Bunting, with the pretentious question of what was the best way for the Merrill Trust to help American education. She had been waiting years, it seemed, for exactly that question. As she saw it, the greatest bottleneck was the interrupted graduate education of women. They have come out of good colleges with fine records; they have entered graduate school with ambitious and realistic hopes. Then their husbands transfer to another spot; they have one child and then another; they lack the time and money, the energy and ability to concentrate, and finally the confidence and sense of purpose. Like women throughout history, they see those hopes turn into lost dreams and settle for far less or live vicariously the lives of their husbands and children.

That doesn't have to be true, Mrs. Bunting went on. The frustrations of a woman's life can also be her strengths. If she finishes graduate education in her thirties, her knowledge and judgment are superior to whatever they might have been in her twenties. The obstacles that made competitive success harder might free her from slavery to success. A medical practice or a piece of research might be important for its own sake, not because it won prizes. And the means to open those doors to her need not be too costly. First of all, the university graduate programs must be willing to accommodate her special needs so that she be allowed to take two courses a year rather than four. Add to this some money toward tuition, for child care, plus that precious title of Radcliffe Fellow, which stood for identity, status, pride, a refusal therefore to interrupt a workday to take her husband's suit to the cleaners.

It was impossible not to be carried away by Mrs. Bunting's enthusiasm. In 1964 the Trust made its first grant of $30,000 for part-time graduate study. When I came back a year later she showed me letters from the first fellows, and I saw their intense joy at having their work taken seriously while protected from interruptions by this formal title—the letters from women so far away that they could never participate in such a program but heartened to know that other women were benefiting: "It gave me courage!" In 1967 we made a second grant of $100,000 with the caveat that only 40 percent of the sum would go to students at Radcliffe-Harvard; the rest to students at any graduate school in Massachusetts, Connecticut, or Rhode Island. A final $100,000 was given in 1969.

By then other foundations were also interested, other universities were experimenting with similar plans, and the growing feminist movement was protesting those same issues of wasted human resources. The Radcliffe Institute with its small, efficient private studies and workrooms was the dream of any woman who had ever sought to free herself from daily chores to accomplish something of value. The money went a long way, doled out precisely, without waste.

In 1978, when Matina Horner had become president of Radcliffe College, that after its merger with Harvard had become little more than the Institute, now named after Mrs. Bunting, the Schlesinger Library on women in American society, and an alumnae association, the Trust gave a further $40,000. This was for fellowship support for older women at colleges like Wheaton who were so fully committed to their daily responsibilities of instruction and administration that they had no opportunity to keep abreast of developments in their field. At a time when almost all teaching jobs were at risk, such women had no chance to keep themselves competitive.

In 1979 we made a grant of $30,000 to Harvard Divinity School for another type of need. By that year women's interest in religious education had come to mean that 51 percent of the students in the regular Master of Divinity ordination program were female, and yet there were only three or four female faculty members in the school and no tenured professor. On the one hand, female students were offering an energy, a dedication that the church desperately needed. On the other, they were chafing angrily at a Christian tradition[3] and an institutional inertia where Truth, as defined by the usual Harvard professor, was a white, male, middle-class, middle-aged, and (if he was in the Divinity School) German-trained version of the term. Our grant went towards salaries of female instructors, library books of relevance to women, and financial aid for female students—a program that later on received much greater funding from Ford and Rockefeller.

These five grants to Radcliffe-Harvard were among our most important. Three hundred thousand dollars is nothing special, but shows the impact that private philanthropy can make at the right time and in the right place.

CONCLUSIONS

I thought of this topic of women's education and indeed about the whole history of the Merrill Trust in July 1984 when Geraldine Ferraro was nom-

3. The words of St. Paul in I Tim. 2:12: But suffer not a woman to teach nor to usurp authority over the man, but to be in silence.

inated as Walter Mondale's running-mate. After the death of her father, an immigrant from southern Italy, her mother became a seamstress, sewing little buttons on wedding dresses to pay the tuition for her daughter at Marymount School in Tarrytown (to which the Merrill Trust gave $10,000 in 1981). Upon graduation Geraldine obtained a full scholarship to Marymount Manhattan College on East 71st Street ($15,000 in 1977, again financial aid). There are better colleges than Marymount Manhattan (SAT V460, M439), one of the countless Catholic schools that Don Regan presented to us; but for the ambitious, intelligent, fatherless, almost penniless Italian-American girl, it was exactly what she needed and she made good use of the opportunity.

You can't tell when and where a Ferraro turns up. She may not necessarily be in the top 5 percent of some ultimate scholarship program. But if enough chances are offered, other able, ambitious, and—one hopes—generous, young people like her are given a chance. Don't draw your rules too tight.

What sensible suggestions about foundation funding might one offer in this conclusion to the long chapter on higher education?

1. Don't fund computer labs. Other millionaires will do that. Don't build one more multimillion-dollar performing arts center. Put bricks-and-mortar money into repairing the ills caused by deferred maintenance. Repair the leaking roof, buy a heating system, and repaint the dorms. Earn a small bronze plaque stating that four hundred rotting window frames were replaced in memory of your mother.

2. Look for leadership. If the education industry is going through hard times, a fair proportion of its troubles is its own damn fault. In fat times professors were as self-indulgent and college heads as wasteful as Pentagon generals. The schools overbuilt, tangled themselves in overadministration, started up programs whose consequences they did not reason out, and accepted words for deeds. Can you find a president with a convincing picture of the relation of his institution to American society and to the current needs of American education? How is he dealing with the paralysis of committee management and the rigidity of departmentalism? Does he have relatively humane ways of getting rid of older professors in order to hire better, younger ones?

Our trustees were always impressed by good leadership when they ran across it: James Hester at New York University, Theodore Hesburgh at Notre Dame, Benjamin Mays at Morehouse during the 1960s; Jill Conway at Smith, Hedley Reynolds at Bates, Howard Swearer at Carleton and Brown, Donald Stewart at Spelman, and Hugh Gloster at Morehouse during the 1970s.

3. Under the pressures of less money and the demand for vocational practicality, the intellectual capital of most colleges is running thin. I am cynical about support for new doctorates because American education has suffered more than it admits from the narrowness and triviality of doctoral research.

Nevertheless, we must be training a new generation of scholar-teachers to replace those who are retiring or who dropped out in the 1970s to go to business school.

For example, our foreign areas programs have badly eroded over the past fifteen years. Departments in Latin America, the Near East, Africa, Japan and China, the Soviet Union, even Western Europe are inadequately staffed in history, in current economics and society, certainly in languages, to remedy the amateurism and self-centeredness that hobble American relations with the outside world. And it isn't just a matter of training up high quality Brazilianists. Those Brazilian experts should know what's going on in the conflict between tradition and modernism in Mexico and Argentina, and even Nigeria and Turkey. The red-hot specialist has caused our country no end of trouble. And, if possible, support these graduate studies by grants rather than loans so that the newly minted professional is not forced into the career slot that simply gives the quickest chance to pay off that mountain of tuition debt.

4. Find an institution with a commitment to doing what it can to prevent nuclear war between the United States and the Soviet Union. That sounds pretentious. Nevertheless, beyond the presentation of one more nightmare of children dying from radiation and the world freezing in blackness, there is a need of an institutional structure for seminars or conferences on options for compromise, studies of negotiations, and of the lethal militarization of our planet. Americans, neither worse nor better than Russians, need to be exposed to objective history. A college, helped by your funding, could also exploit what study/travel possibilities exist within the Soviet Union, Nicaragua and Cuba, and East Germany and Czechoslovakia so that Americans learn to deal with reality and not simply good guy/bad guy abstractions.

5. *Equality.* This is not a popular ideal in the 1980s. We have returned to Social Darwinism, a shopworn Calvinism where those who haven't made it— individuals, institutions, classes, races, and nations—reveal their lack of God's election by their lack of success. But in the choice of what colleges to support, a foundation should be able to work out some coherent line of thought on the relationship between wealth and need. If you believe in the leadership supplied by Harvard and Amherst, support specific projects, of course, that appeal to you. $25/50,000 makes little impact there whereas the same amount can back Goucher's strength in science; the international programs at Goshen, Kalamazoo, or Warren Wilson; or give body to the emergency loan fund at Spelman. Responsible philanthropy cannot allow black institutions of historical value like Fisk, Atlanta University, or Talladega to die, as they are at risk of doing now. And whatever their academic quality may be, the desperately poor population served by the College of the Ozarks in Arkansas, Miles in Birmingham, Rust in Mississippi, and Alliance in the Polish Alleghanies makes it reasonable for a foundation trustee to visit one

or two such places, try to judge their strengths and resourcefulness, and make a five-year commitment the administration can count on. Moreover, most foundations like our own gave far too little attention to the state institutions, from the universities on down to the community colleges.

By the mid-1980s for every institution from Yale to Morehouse, money is needed, at every level possible, in financial aid to the colleges through minority programs like Aspira and the United Negro College Fund and through high schools or to individuals. The Reagan budget has set lower ceilings on how much any student may receive in federal funding and on the income limit of any family eligible for low-interest loans. Ostensibly, this is to free up more money for new missile systems and the production of nerve gas. Everyone, including college students, has to share the financial sacrifices entailed. A healthier economy will allow these government reductions to be offset, to an extent, by larger contributions by corporations and individuals.

Perhaps. A belief in the conspiracy theory of history is usually the sign of a vulgar mind. Just the same, I worry about the influence of the conservative ideologues in favor today, and not just in our own country, who distrust excessive education as a threat to their version of the Good Society.

"Billions for equal opportunity, not one cent for equal outcome" is the ultimate quotation from *Losing Ground*[4] by Charles Murray, which may be the flight plan of the second Reagan administration. The new elitism, going beyond the old-timey slogan that book learning spoils a good bean picker, shows particular contempt for all those Martin Luther King scholars who wanted equality of results (useful diplomas) without distinction or even equality of effort. That type of phony is expendable. Nevertheless, what these ideologues really fear is the Martin Luther King scholar who worked till midnight night after night; who earned an honest education with his own blood, sweat, and tears; and who now wants to use it to change society. That's the sort of student, of any background, whom the crowd now in authority wants to squeeze out of the colleges, universities, and graduate schools so that they do not acquire threatening ideas and skills—and power. That level of competition disturbs the natural balance of society. Clean-cut American youth should be offered a hand (as the Merrill Trust did with its scholarships for small-town aspirants to Bowdoin and Grinnell); but not everybody—no matter what their SAT scores—deserves higher education. The old tradition that college is basically the privilege of young men whose fathers can pay the bills is not yet dead.

4. Charles Murray, *Losing Ground* (New York: Basic Books, 1984), p. 233.

CHAPTER FOUR

Religion

What doth the Lord require of thee, but to do justly, and to love mercy, and to walk humbly with thy God? [Micah 6:8]

Mr. Merrill's taste in religion was conservative. He would have wanted the trustees to look for places like the Church of the Ascension in New York with the same warmth of pastoral concern given by his friend Donald Aldrich. He would have wanted us to care about Protestant seminaries and the Catholic colleges that educated priests and football players, nurses, nuns, and faithful secretaries, the homes for orphans and wayward girls. His knowledge of Jewish institutions was more abstract, but all gentiles respect the Jewish love of scholarship, their brilliance in medicine, and their care for the aged.

As in the other categories, Mr. Merrill left the trustees free to work out their own priorities, which in those years from 1958 to 1981 involved us with an intensity of religious challenge and change that few periods in history could match and which the nervously secular foundations missed.

The two men who set their stamp on that time were John XXIII and Martin Luther King, Jr.

At last there was a pope able to see all Christians as equals and able to respect each human being's right to approach God in his own way. In every detail by which the Catholic church reached its followers, this shrewd, perceptive, kindly old man sought to bring the church into Today—the Aggiornamento. He reminded people who had little to do with any church that religion was a relevant dimension for looking at the world, and the message he proclaimed encouraged Christians, and Jews as well, to stand by each other in the struggles of that decade.

King put a simple, inescapable demand to white America: if you claim to believe in Christianity and democracy, you must change your basic attitudes towards people of color. Otherwise, as Gandhi challenged the British, your deepest beliefs are just words, are lies. King gave new life to the prophetic tradition. He gave a warning that the church was not simply fighting for the rights of blacks, it was fighting for its own soul, its self-respect, and whatever sense of mission it retained.

How do five ordinary individuals respond to such a challenge? The answers seem more clear now than when we foundation trustees were making the decisions. There was, as usual, a lot of housekeeping to put money into: churches and clergy for the new suburbs, support to parochial students and teachers in the crowded classrooms of those baby-boom years, support for an endless mix of small-town Protestant and Catholic colleges that might help a traditional America respond to modern times, support for the large Catholic universities in attaining higher, broader standards, and help for timid schools to reach out to minority students. Also, there was completing the great Episcopal cathedrals in Washington and San Francisco, repairs for half a dozen cathedrals in England, commissioning a stained glass window, or replanting a cloister garden. That is one way the church serves each generation of its people.

What did our foundation do in the hard new fields: the church and the city, the church trying to deal with the demands of blacks, of migrant workers, of frightened white ethnics, and of desperately alienated young people destroying themselves with drugs? Sometimes we understood the new language, sometimes we didn't. For a while my oldest daughter was involved with a radical crowd in San Francisco. One day she and her friends went over to the Oakland army base and lay down in front of the main entrance to block a truck convoy taking soldiers to a ship bound for Vietnam. For five minutes they halted the war. Then MPs arrived to drag them away, and she was put in jail. That was my closest contact with an appropriate religious response to those times.

In the 1980s Americans face a schism between two totally opposed Protestant churches. The liberal clergy try to adapt themselves to all the different social changes and accept obligations to women, fur seals, welfare families, illegal aliens, and Sandinistas; distance themselves from what ordinary Americans find acceptable; and at 3 A.M. despair lie awake and ask what are they doing. They discuss ways to initiate dialogue with the Russians; they can't talk with fundamentalist Protestants who live a mile away.

> God Guts Guns
> Keeps America Free
> (1983 bumper sticker)

The fundamentalists live by opposite rules, with a picture of contemporary history that sure doesn't square with page one of the *New York Times*. Apocalypse represents the future as a mythic small town represents the past. They are unperturbed by their alliance with wealth and are convinced that Jesus and his friend God are Americans. Sin is narrowed to abortion and homosexuality, and their abstract sense of righteousness includes little compassion for the poor and humiliated. Yet they have a fighting spirit, a sense of who they are that their liberal opponents have lost.

Does the black church, as spoken for by Jesse Jackson in 1984, have a mediating role to play, standing for justice and also God's immediacy? What might a foundation with a Christian commitment do now?

What were the Jewish issues of those years?

The most important was the hardest for Christians to comprehend: the devastating impact of the Holocaust. (Including the lack of concern within the anti-Nazi gentile world, beginning with Churchill and Roosevelt, in taking any steps to save its victims.) The God who made a covenant that He would protect His people if they were loyal to Him had failed.

Easier to deal with is the new reality of Israel. The land of the Bible lies under a Jewish flag and is protected by its soldiers and by American dollars. A traditionalist like Louis Finkelstein, chancellor during the 1950s and 1960s of Jewish Theological Seminary in New York, worried about these symbols of authority and violence that would have the Jewish homeland function at the moral level of, for example, Argentina. For other Jews the very amorality of Israel was their pride. Jews were no longer confined in a helpless "spirituality" that asked gentiles to be nice. If someone hurt them, the Israeli army would strike back twice as hard.

A third issue was the troubled relationship with blacks. An outsider like Julius Rosenwald was sensitive to black suffering as mainstream Americans were not. A later generation saw blacks as allies in the common struggle against injustice. But as blacks became more radical they resented Jewish tutelage and identified with the humiliation suffered by Palestinians. If this rift were allowed to deepen, both sides would lose.

A foundation like the Merrill Trust had the most to offer, of course, in strengthening Jewish society and identity in the Diaspora: its institutions of caring, the training of new leadership, and the rebuilding of culture. Perhaps because we were outsiders, our foundation, unconnected to any single group within Jewish life, was able to move with impartiality and played a useful role.

PROTESTANT SEMINARIES

> Foolish and unlearned questions avoid, know that they do gender strifes.
> [II Timothy 2:23]

In 1979 the Trust gave $35,000 to create and install a great stained glass altar window at St. John's Episcopal Church in Southampton in honor of Mr.

Merrill, a beautiful piece of work in the summer colors of sea and sky and sand dunes, the one piece of art we ever commissioned. Otherwise, in religion as in every other field, we placed our major funds in education: $2.5 million to Protestant seminaries training the servants and leaders of tomorrow's church, something we were equipped to do because we were not committed to any one denomination and, unlike too many foundations, were not precluded from religious involvement. In trying to decide whether seminaries should express traditional belief, which gives consistency and steadiness, or change to meet new needs of the times with all the risks of pop think and jive talk, we backed both groups.

Northeast

Andover Newton Theological School, Newton Center, Massachusetts, 1959–1978—$250,000. Andover Newton is the oldest (1807) Protestant graduate school of theology in the United States. Most of our grants went to improve faculty salaries. In 1959 there were 15,000 vacant Protestant pulpits; 70,000 churches needed to be built in the next ten years to absorb 28 million additional members. Andover Newton's enrollment went from 145 in 1953 to 500 in 1969, and in the early 1960s, Andover Newton was expanding faster than any accredited seminary in the country. The cost of theological education, however, had doubled in each decade from 1940 to 1970.

Andover Newton had always been sensitive to contemporary needs. It started the first program in pastoral psychology and clinical training and was one of the first to organize an intern plan of supervised field experience during the school year and summer vacations, where a seminarian would begin his education by working as a hospital orderly. When Pope John XXIII unleashed the spirit of ecumenism, Andover Newton began to enroll large numbers of Catholics.

Graduates of Andover Newton became chaplains in prisons and universities; involved themselves in the civil rights and peace movements even at the risk of going to jail and in the urban ministries that started in Detroit, Chicago, and Philadelphia; worked with Catholic partners; worked out new relationships between liturgy and the arts, including jazz; and built bridges to young people in the coffeehouse movement.

Episcopal Divinity School, Cambridge, Massachusetts, 1959–1980—$135,000. By tradition Episcopal Theological (as was its name from 1867 to its merger with Philadelphia Divinity School in 1974) was one of the country's leading seminaries. This strength gave the confidence that allowed frankness in discussing its needs in the school's six different appeals to the Merrill Trust and that illustrated the problems of Protestant seminaries in general.

Their distinction always rested on a fragile base. Salaries and scholarships were low (in the mid 1960s the average salary of a full professor at Episcopal was $9,700, and the highest financial aid award was $500), which meant that the seminary could not really compete for the best teachers and students. In 1965 the average undergraduate record of entering seminarians was B–. Too many of the schools of religion were mediocre because the Church was no longer attracting the best young men and because theological education was not in touch with changing times. Episcopal needed to take advantage of the vast recent improvement in education at the secondary and university level, upgrade its curriculum, and expand its field work program.

A seminary had to share the resources of similar institutions, rather than compete with them or isolate itself from them. Episcopal Theological School (ETS) had a long tradition of cooperation with Harvard Divinity School; all courses in the history of religion, for example, were taken at Harvard; and its students could use the vast resources of Widener Library. In 1968 the staff and student body of the Jesuit Seminary of Weston College moved to the ETS campus. The formation of the *Boston Theological Institute*, a consortium of seven Protestant and Catholic schools (to which the Merrill Trust gave $30,000 in 1971), fitted into this pattern, especially in sharing field education programs in prisons or welfare agencies and teaching chaplaincy skills in the Boston-area hospitals.

There was a responsibility also to look at the changing needs and goals of ministers at different states in their lives. In 1963 the Trust gave $25,000 to retrain middle-aged parish ministers. In 1980 we gave $30,000 to reach a new type of student, often ten years older than the seminarians of the 1960s, often female, with little formal sectarian allegiance or experience, impatient with details but with a much more mature, personally intense religious commitment. In the mid-1970s enrollment had fallen and weak finances threatened the survival of the seminary itself. If it was to stand for anything, it had to be through changing with a changing church.

Berkeley Divinity School, New Haven, Connecticut, 1966—$25,000. Berkeley didn't make it. We had put off action on a 1965 appeal because it seemed moribund, but Charlie Cole visited the place and felt that despite its poor facilities, low salaries, and lack of scholarship funds, the closeness to Yale's resources, its competent staff and decent leadership made it worth supporting. There were fewer than 100 full- and part-time students, however, and within a few years the school was closed down by the Episcopal Church.

Union Theological Seminary, New York, New York, 1960–1972—$150,000. Union had the reputation of being the most urban and socially and internationally committed of the top-flight seminaries. Paul Tillich, Harry Emerson Fosdick, and Henry Sloane Coffin had been its faculty members, but the most influential was Reinhold Niebuhr, whose combination of liberal sociology and orthodox theology made him the leading Protestant intellectual of the 1930s and 1940s.

The Merrill Trust gave $50,000 in 1960 for salaries, $25,000 in 1961 for the Program of Advanced Religious Studies to attract young men of promise from foreign countries, and $50,000 in 1972 as a participant in the fund-raising campaign of the Seven Theological Schools.[1] The last great contribution to such seminaries had come in the early 1950s when John D. Rockefeller Jr. gave $20 million for the strengthening of theological education, a gift so large that it scared away other philanthropists. The new capital campaign was to underpin salaries and financial aid, build endowment to allow stability, take care of deferred maintenance, and encourage a few new ideas.

Union was a leader in ecumenical partnership with the Catholics in the 1960s and increasingly with Jewish Theological Seminary in the 1970s. Its lack of connection with any denomination gave it more freedom and less support.

Harvard Divinity School, Cambridge, Massachusetts, 1963–1979— $205,000. Harvard College was established in 1636 from "a dread of leaving an illiterate ministry to the Churches when our present ministers shall be in the Dust." But since it expected of all early New England colleges to produce ministers and Christian gentlemen, Harvard saw no reason until 1811 for a formal divinity school "to give every encouragement to the serious, impartial, unbiased investigation of Christian truths." Although it had begun as a Unitarian seminary, Harvard was, like Union, nondenominational and so academically intellectual that a student interested in the parish ministry was apt to feel a second-class citizen. By the mid-1900s it had become almost the weakest of the university's graduate schools, and rebuilding the Divinity School as well as the School of Education were two of Nathan Pusey's accomplishments while president. A succession of outstanding and diverse deans in Samuel Miller, Krister Stendahl, and George Rupp provided the leadership.

The Trust made three grants totaling $100,000 between 1963 and 1967 to retrain parish ministers, a program we duplicated at other Protestant and Jewish institutions. (Post-graduate education is wasted on the young, who are fed up with reading books and writing papers and what they see as the marginality of student life.) A minister who has been involved in his parish for ten years, however—drained, trivialized, cut into thinner and thinner slices by the obligations of the vestry committee, the capital fund drive, meetings

1. Harvard, Union, Chicago, Yale, Notre Dame, Vanderbilt, and the Graduate Theological Union at Berkeley.

of the youth club, the young adults' club, the senior citizens' club—desperately hungers for a chance to study, to learn about new frontiers and talk with his peers, to read Augustine and Luther again, and go with his wife to the museums and theatre that don't exist in Ottumwa. A wide mix of men and women were involved, from Nova Scotia to Hawaii, from small-town, suburban, and city parishes, who also served a valuable role towards the seminarians who appreciated their contacts with older professionals.

In 1972 we gave $50,000 as part of the Seven Theological Schools Campaign, one of the first grants in that drive and a way of attracting attention from other foundations. Big corporations do not support theological education; nor do government and the large foundations. The alumni are poor, and the denominational churches give only to their own seminaries. Those major seminaries train the teachers, leaders, opinion formers, and scholars, but not the parish ministers. In every field one looks at—business and politics, education and career choice, identity and life style—what used to be taken for granted doesn't go anymore, and looking back to a nostalgia-wrapped past offers no useful guideposts. In order to build a wholesome, responsible future society, one must strengthen the leadership of seminaries like these that are the backbone and forward thrust of American Christian life.

The 1980s saw a larger proportion of students headed for ordination rather than teaching, and with the cutback in federally supported low-interest loans for graduate students, Harvard seminarians were driven into isolation and exhaustion by longer and longer job hours to pay their bills. And for the new young dean, George Rupp, his priority was to reduce the proportion of tenured faculty from 90 percent to 60 percent in order to give himself the freedom to hire younger teachers and train the leadership of 2001.

Yale Divinity School, New Haven, Connecticut, 1962, 1972—$75,000. Yale University was founded in 1701 "to train men for public employment both in church and civil state." Yale received $50,000 in 1972 for the same Seven Theological Schools drive and $25,000 in 1962 for scholarships for the program of Religion and the Arts. By the time that all too many students reach divinity school they are already in debt, heavily involved in part-time jobs, and headed toward careers with such low salaries that a debt perfectly manageable for a doctor or lawyer will wear upon them all their lives. Outright grants are the only humane way of financing religious education.

School of Theology, Boston University, Boston, Massachusetts, 1970— $25,000. This school's most famous graduate, of course, is Martin Luther King, Jr. That was not totally an accident, since half the doctorates in religion awarded to Negroes in the period of 1952–1967 were earned at Boston University. Howard Thurman, another black alumnus of Morehouse College, was its dean during most of that time. The school built a strong record in the field of clinical pastoral education and in the new ministries of service to the city.

New York Theological Seminary, New York, 1969–1981—$130,000. New York Theological was a run-down, out-of-it seminary when George Webber became president in 1968. Rather than trying to improve standards and finances within the traditional academic style, Webber, who had been one of the founders of the East Harlem Protestant Parish after World War II, decided to go in a different direction, dedicating it to the mission of Christ in an urban world and willing to aim towards this goal by whatever path he could find. One approach was to set up a Metropolitan Intern Program offering classroom and field work in city problems to students from other seminaries, Catholic and Protestant, as well as to practicing ministers. Another, which became increasingly important, was to certify black and Puerto Rican storefront pastors, men with an intense experience of city life but who needed more formal training. New York, known as a Catholic and Jewish city, had a Protestant population up to 30 percent by 1970—80 percent black, 10 percent Hispanic. New York Theological was one of three seminaries in the United States meeting needs of the Spanish church.

Eventually the seminary came to specialize in continuing education for clergy and laity: young and old, black, Hispanic, white and Asian, innercity and suburban, mainline and storefront—a religious expression of the pluralism that should be the mark of any democratic society. By 1981 enrollment had risen to 600 highly motivated, mature students who saw classroom study as relevant to their work. And because the seminary had such fragile resources, its cost accounting had to be very precise, with tuition able to cover 70 percent of costs (as against 9 percent at ninety other seminaries).

At the beginning of Webber's administration the Merrill Trust was the only foundation interested. Our money went for operating costs, new programs, and then, as the seminary achieved a little stability, for endowment.

Chicago and the South

Chicago Theological Seminary, Chicago, Illinois, 1964, 1973—$50,000. This seminary is the oldest (1855) institution of higher education in Chicago. It was open to all denominations from the beginning, and in 1902 was the first in the United States to award a B.D. to a woman. It specialized in training parish ministers. All too often a minister keeps himself busy running a small-time religious club while the mainstream of life sweeps by untouched. A seminary should be a center for theological education for the entire church, carrying out a missionary role between involvement and reflection. The students serve with practicing ministers in both innercity and suburban locations.

Lutheran School of Theology, Chicago, Illinois, 1965—$25,000. Lutheran School of Theology was a 1962 consolidation of four existing midwestern seminaries. Our grant went toward its location upon a new site, within walking distance of the University of Chicago—an acceptance of the metropolitan city and the secular university by an essentially conservative and small-town church. The Lutherans form a church that can be identified by each group's origin: German, Swedish, Norwegian, Danish, Finnish, or Slovak. Now, however, it is part of a new expansion into general American life (the fourth largest Christian group after Roman Catholics, Baptists, and Methodists) and the largest Protestant body worldwide. Today the Missouri Synod brings in the most new members, conservative, self-reliant German and Scandinavian midwesterners. Lutherans are also the chief Protestant supporters of parochial schools. Since 1957 there has been a concern for going beyond the role of Good Samaritan toward becoming a conscience for society as a whole.

Protestant Episcopal Theological Seminary, Alexandria, Virginia, 1962–1978—$125,000. For a century after its founding in 1823, this seminary existed on the edge of collapse (during the Civil War its campus was taken over by the Union Army as a hospital), with low salaries and run-down buildings, and little progress until the 1920s when a full complement of students allowed the administration to use tuition funds to strengthen the faculty. In the nineteenth century it had a strong missionary tradition (China, Japan, Liberia, Greece, Brazil) and always played a strong role in the administration of the Episcopal Church, providing bishops, deans, and headmasters. In 1953 it merged with Bishop Payne Divinity School, a black institution, and has the largest (177 in 1978) and most diversified student body of any Episcopal seminary.

Protestant Episcopal received this generous support (for salaries, a center of Christian education for lay people, and new library construction) from our foundation because certain trustees saw it as a counterweight to Union and Harvard. Nonetheless, the schools that northerners label as conservative would in their own regions be valuable centers of responsible liberalism with a Southern accent.

School of Theology, University of the South, Sewanee, Tennessee, 1962–1979—$65,000 (plus $30,000 to the University to strengthen the arts). On the outskirts of the campus is a sign stating that the university was burned down by northern soldiers in 1863. (The buildings were rebuilt with contributions from English churches and the library with books from Oxford and Cambridge.) A large percentage of Southern Episcopal ministers train at this small (eighty-five students), isolated, homogeneous seminary.

Divinity School, Vanderbilt University, Nashville, Tennessee, 1971, 1972—

$80,000. We gave $150,000 to the University, half of it to the new Graduate School of Management, which Don Regan admired, but the Divinity School, unknown in the parochial Northeast, clearly seemed a place worth supporting. Since 1914, when it cut its ties to the Methodist Church, Vanderbilt has been the only major nondenominational, university-based theological school in the South. $30,000 in 1971 went to support of the field education program to develop self-awareness and social awareness among the students through work at a crisis call center; within business and industry; and in hospitals, prisons, and asylums. $50,000 in 1972 was again part of the Seven Theological Schools campaign that went toward a $6 million figure for faculty appointments, for training leadership in the black churches, for student aid (including $500,000 for black students), and for field and continuing education.

Vanderbilt has shared its resources with Fisk, but how disheartened must be the black students who come from that shabby campus to see the riches that the white world takes for granted.

Florida State University, Tallahassee, Florida, 1972–1979—$80,000. This state university had a surprisingly strong ecumenical program of advanced religious study and research, and in 1972 we gave $35,000 to finance graduate fellowships in religion. The Department of Religion offered a Ph.D. in humanities with a major in religion (one of three such programs in the United States) and attracted scholars in the religions of Africa and Asia, as well as Christianity and Judaism. With all financial assistance from the state of Florida diminishing, there was need for private support.

In the mid-1970s, Florida was the fastest growing state in the union, part of the United States' monumental shift in population. The Department of Religion at Florida State was a center of intellectual leadership in a very conservative, business-oriented region that usually supports only the most practical university departments like engineering, economics, and health. These Merrill Fellowships ($25,000 in 1976) were a useful drawing card for attracting good students and teachers at a time when other graduate opportunities were being cut back.

$20,000 in 1979 went to the Center for a program in Modern Jewish History and Thought, financed in 1978 by the National Endowment for the Humanities for a demonstration course on the Holocaust. The South's population explosion extends to Jews also, and this program shared with the University of Florida in Gainesville was the only one in advanced Jewish studies (outside one at Duke/Chapel Hill) in the entire South and Southwest.

California

Graduate Theological Union, Berkeley, 1966–1981—$155,000 (plus $200,000 to member schools). The Graduate Theological Union was founded in 1962 as a consortium of six Protestant and three Catholic schools of religion in order to strengthen their intellectual and physical resources. Certain facilities are shared: the bookstore, registrar's office, and the library, as well as courses at the Ph.D. level at both Berkeley and Stanford. The Union also provides a structure for new centers to be shared by the members, for example, in Judaic, Buddhist, black urban, Hellenistic, and women's studies. Our grants went for improving the library, computer operations, fund-raising, and scholarships in what is probably the most comprehensive, ecumenical educational complex in the world.

Southern California School of Theology, Claremont, California, 1965–1980—$95,000. The School of Theology (1885) was originally Methodist and took on many different names, auspices, and homes before it joined the Claremont campus in 1957. Its first president, Ernest Colwell, had been president of the University of Chicago and was an experienced, cultured man with a drive to establish a strong seminary willing to experiment with entrants unsure as to whether they were committed to the ministry. The school grew rapidly; established a strong pastoral care program in the Los Angeles area with hospitals, jails, and asylums; made a strong commitment to work among black, Hispanic, and Japanese minorities; and shared an Asian studies program with another seminary. In the chaos of Southern California, Colwell and his successor, Gordon Michalson, saw their duty as trying to build a school of religion that would stand for intellectual objectivity and social responsibility as well as Christian commitment. As a new school with only a tiny endowment, it was to endure incessant fund-raising and increasing annual deficits until the institution became old enough to start benefiting from legacies. Our grants went for library construction, operating expenses, faculty salaries, and the last one was to encourage Mexican-American students. East Los Angeles is one of the great Spanish-speaking cities of the hemisphere with a tremendous need for leadership, both religious and secular.

Religion and Education

Christian Faith and Life Community, Austin, Texas, 1959, 1961—$32,000. By the end of the 1950s, Protestant involvement in higher education was running into two serious difficulties. The first was financial. The costs of supporting a college were becoming too high for even the wealthy churches. Moreover, an increasingly secular student body was no longer held by denominational loyalties, and those who took Christianity seriously wanted sharpness that the tepid church-related colleges could not meet.

Christian Faith and Life sought an alternative as a residential community, held together by study and worship, attached to but not part of the huge, dynamic University of Texas, setting itself the two tasks of religious training of the laity and the search for a philosophy of church mission in a changing world. This alternative was the dream of one man, Jack Lewis, a Presbyterian minister and former Navy Chaplain who chose Picasso's *Guernica* as the religious symbol of the twentieth century. It hung in almost every classroom and hallway of the Community building, to destroy traditional Christian sweetness by its scream of horror and to try and force students to reach themselves and God in less protected ways. By 1961 more than thirty-five colleges and universities were using material and ideas that had been tested out originally in Austin. It was such efforts as this to bring Christianity alive on campus and to free it from its Eisenhower pieties that provided the religious foundations for the revolutionary civil rights and antiwar movements a few years later.

Council on the Study of Religion, Philadelphia, 1973—$20,000 to fund a pilot project on the academic study of religion in community colleges. The rapid growth of community colleges during the 1950s and 1960s was an important development in American and Canadian higher education. Their new students were whites of blue-collar and ethnic families who saw college not as a source of interesting learning but as a step up the economic ladder. The community college becomes an idealistic hope and an intellectual slum, a mediocre continuation of a mediocre high school in order to keep the kids off the job market for a couple of years because they don't know what else to do. But the colleges can also widen their intellectual horizons and help them grope for what makes sense. Thoughtful, questioning courses in religion might be rewarding.

Fellowship of Christians in Universities and Schools (FOCUS), Wallingford, Connecticut, 1973—$15,000. For twelve years FOCUS sought to provide ways in which the Christian message could be heard by young people questioning established faith, values, and traditions. FOCUS felt that drug abuse, promiscuity, apathy, and disregard for authority came from the existentialist, nihilist ideologies in the literature, films, and music to which young people are exposed. Leadership, to express another point of view, is looked for in private schools, and yet their moral and religious authority is eroding. Merrill money went towards salary of a full-time director to help organize Christian-oriented house parties, a Cape Cod bike trip, a "Skis and Skeptics" winter sports party, and faculty conferences.

The Trust received hundreds of similar appeals. Most we turned down. They have their place. Many adolescents are fed up with smart-set values and are attracted by wholesomeness if they don't lose too much status thereby and if the message isn't put across too heavily. My feeling, however, is that establishment Christians confuse symptoms with disease. The spread of drug use is a disease, of course, and no nation or ideology is making headway against it save for Khomeini's Iran, where anyone involved is shot within twenty-four hours of apprehension. But unless our nation is really worth moral respect, unless our religious leaders bear witness against injustice and idolatry—pouring pig's blood over draft files during Vietnam was one such act[2]—in often costly ways, then patriotism, and Christianity are just routines and no young person worth his salt will waste time on them. When genuine service is demanded (through the work camp ideal, for example) young men and women will respond generously, but they demand a strong ideology, not only of service to the poor but of contempt for the self-indulgent and prejudiced. One way for a Christian to stimulate serious discussion might be to remove the stars and stripes from the chapel.

Epworth Ministry, Knoxville, Tennessee, 1972—$15,000. Within a 150-mile radius of Knoxville are fifty-nine colleges and universities with 90,000 students. Most of these serve a poor white student from coal, factory, and mining towns. Epworth is a cooperative ministry with Methodist, Episcopalian, Presbyterian, and Catholic members, and Merrill funds were requested for office and staff to help conduct discussions on questions that concerned college and church: the jobs available in that region, education as preparation for job, the relations between jobs (textiles, strip mining) and health (black and brown lung disease), and politics and environment. How might these colleges serve their area better, what new social structures need to be built, and how can young women share child care better so that they can go to school? (This type of consciousness-raising in personal and community needs is unknown in Appalachia.)

CATHOLIC

> For if the trumpet give an uncertain sound, who shall prepare himself to the battle?   [I Corinthians 14:8]

How much did the Charles E. Merrill Trust give to Catholic institutions? Well, what is a Catholic institution? A gift to Georgetown University for scholarships for Catholic freshmen comes within the Catholic category. How about a gift to its library's science collection? In what category is the Catholic city hospital with its Jewish doctors and Negro patients? Perhaps we gave $5 million to institutions that might be called Catholic and that are found in this book within the chapters on education, medicine, social welfare, and international.

2. An update: throwing bottles of Chivas Regal through the windows of Mercedes?

What is the Catholic church? In America it has traditionally been the church of the poor and the immigrant. The millowner was Protestant; his employees were Catholic. The closeness to this immigrant background gave a democratic seriousness to the church. Yet the individual church might be ruled with complete autocracy by its priest, dominating his parishioners and his faithful nuns, isolating them from the secular world outside, and over him at the top of the pyramid was the prince of the church in his bishop's palace.

The Catholic church supplies an alternative power position in American life that can be infuriating and/or wholesome for non-Catholics. In the imperialist war that right-thinking, progressive Protestants forced upon Spain in 1898 in order to free Cuba, the church was one of the few institutions that stood aloof. There is also a Catholic version of Shintoism, the worship of one's own nation, and Cardinal Spellman blessing Kevin and Michael and Tony (the men who make up America's infantry regiments) spoke as the expression of a seamless church-state authority as they left for the crusade in Vietnam. At the same time, the most intense opposition to that war came from members of the same church.

The issue of contraception and abortion has intensely troubled Catholic life and its alliances with the outside world. Traditionally the growth of population had a balance built into it: the Irish mother had six or eight children but a couple died early; one became a priest or nun, a maid in London, a soldier in India; two went to America; and two stayed home to oppose Protestant power by their peasant tenacity. When they became middle class they accepted middle-class values, in Dublin as well as Chicago, and opted for an automobile rather than lots of children. But how about the desperate countries of Africa and the Latin World, where the church's denial of contraception means a population out of control, a Colombia doubling in less than twenty-five years? The Pope insists on no compromise. People are more than ambitious careerists or frantic consumers. They are human beings with souls.

What is the meaning of a *soul?* If one cannot understand that word, one looks at the church as an art historian or as a sociologist but as an outsider. The other word is *eternity.* The liberal hope is that the church does not mean what it says. Often that is right: a sensible expediency sets up other priorities. But if a pope or a priest does mean what he says, whether soul or eternity, then it is the alliance with Protestant or Jewish liberal or with the state that is merely expedient. Sometimes, of course, that level of intransigence can be magnificent, and the state draws back, unwilling to cart the Polish or Brazilian cardinal in his embroidered robes off to jail.

Education, social justice, and democratic self-expression are valuable by-products, but they don't come first. The priests and nuns who take these objectives too seriously find themselves leaving the church. And the church may break or bleed to death by standing too firmly (rigidly?) for traditional values. The contradictions of human life are more visible in the Catholic world than in the Protestant and Jewish world because the message is more sharply stated.

Our major investment in a Catholic church changing under John XXIII's leadership was in education. A sentence by David Thomas examining Fordham University's 1967 appeal gave a summary of that tradition: "Up to the early 1960s Fordham provided education for the sons of the parish faithful and protected the virtue of its youth by closing its doors to the non-Catholic world." There was little Catholic intellectual distinction in the United States, and the competition of the contemporary world was to be feared and avoided. The changes coming then at Fordham were illustrative of changes in most Catholic schools: the addition of Protestant and Jewish professors and even clergy in the faculties of philosophy and theology, the building of a coordinate women's college, and new approaches in pedagogy—all leading to a determination to turn away from the intellectual and spiritual isolation that had characterized its history. As the new president, Father Leo McLaughlin, stated in 1967: "Fordham will pay any price, break any mold to achieve her function as a university."

The Trust put a lot of money into the modernization of schools and hospitals with Fordham's needs: money for library books and science equipment; for advanced education of faculty; for training in new administrative methods; and for scholarships to allow the traditional Irish, Polish, and Italian lower-middle-class students to get ahead and to bring in new blacks, Hispanics, and Orientals.

The Trust's support of Catholic schools and colleges; its involvement with city life; with black and Hispanic needs, and with the handicapped, troubled, and aged is described elsewhere.

Our Lady of Poland, which Southampton's Polish farmers and tradesmen attended, including some of my sister's employees, received $20,000 in 1970 for repair of the school's roof, renovation of the convent, and debt retirement.

Beyond aid to parochial schools training teachers, nurses, and the Catholic laity, we backed institutions educating priests and nuns or serving them in their relations with society, specific religious orders, and institutions of Catholic scholarship.

Gray Nuns of the Sacred Heart, Philadelphia, 1962–1973—$45,000. Most of this money went to train sisters in service and administrative skills in their work in homes, neighborhoods, and public institutions where they must deal with the aged and sick, addicts, and the broken in spirit.

Center for Applied Research in the Apostolate, Washington, 1968— $25,000. In the new process of reform and renewal after Vatican II, there came hopes for a new era of Christian cooperation. There was need, however, to examine issues such as the changing role of the clergy and laity, dimensions of interfaith cooperation, and the commitment of U.S. dioceses to the world-wide mission of the church. Specifically, this meant the effort to keep parish priests up-to-date and practical and to look at the changing role of sisters, parish councils, and school boards.

Community of Cistercians of the Strict Observance, Berryville, Virginia, 1979—$25,000. The Trappist monks of this Benedictine reform group, orig-inating in twelfth-century Dijon, sought to be self-sufficient through agricul-ture and animal husbandry and held to a regimen of prayer, solitude, silence, and manual labor. The twenty monks of the Berryville community had re-cently expanded into baking and sold their bread through Safeway Stores. Their self-reliance and respect for work appealed to Bob Magowan, and our money went toward construction of a new infirmary, dormitory rooms, re-fectory, and kitchen.

Next Step, San Francisco, 1970—$25,000. By 1970, when 4,000 priests left in a single year, the increasing departure of priests and sisters from the Roman Catholic Church had become a hemorrhage. Often it was the most able, the most sincere who quit, in rejection of celibacy, of routine institutional chores as less meaningful than direct social welfare work, of an overbearing hier-archical authority, and of the constraints of doctrine over individual freedom.

And yet these fugitives had little money, few skills, and were naive about how to adjust when they left their protected, privileged church position. Father James Mundell, whom the Trust had served at his mission with the Chol Chol Indians, had built fifteen schools and a canning factory in southern Chile, but had been traumatized by his return home. He felt that the United States was a selfish island of luxury and that his church was unresponsive to the needs of the poor. He became a farmhand, then a real estate broker. When Dave Thomas met him in Ithaca in 1969, he was selling pots and pans from door to door. From there, however, he went on to a job in Los Angeles that involved him in helping other exreligious merchandise church-learned skills in the second-job market.

Next Step was perhaps the best-known such group, serving former clergy (both Catholic and Protestant) in the Bay Area, which had become a mecca for displaced clergy of all faiths. It helped them deal with loneliness and fear and helped them evaluate their skills and translate them into meaningful jobs.

Athenaeum of Ohio (Mount St. Mary's Seminary of the West), Cincinnati,

1976—$20,000 to back the Second Vocation Priesthood program. One of the reassuring signs in Catholic life of the mid-1970s was that the significant decline of enrollment in the priesthood by young men was being offset by applications by older men, many of whom had been debating the decision for ten or twenty years. Money was needed for financial aid, recruitment, academic tutoring, and psychological counseling.

House of Affirmation, Whitinsville, Massachusetts, 1979—$5,000. This group was setting up branches in Boston, St. Louis, California, and England to meet precisely the problems of a troubled clergy. It sought to heal and reconcile the lives of priests and other religious professionals no longer able to be effective in their work and to reach out to them through emotional and spiritual counseling before they left the church in despair.

THE CHURCH AND THE CITY

Woe unto them who crush my people to pieces and grind the faces of the poor. [Isaiah 3:15]

What is the role of the church within society? Is it to comfort the insulted and injured? Is it to change the forces in society that cause insults and injuries? At whose expense? But when Jesus said he had come to preach good news to the poor, that good news was not simply that he was the Messiah come to save their souls. His coming might actually change their lives today. Jesus was not a social reformer or a revolutionary—thousands of bishops and hundreds of popes have stressed that point, yet Jesus never states that he absolutely isn't a revolutionary. Upsetting the money changers' tables in the temple courtyard was a rash gesture. Accordingly, there is always a dimension of the uncertain in any Christian act. The argument can always be escalated if someone presses too hard.

In the Baptist gospel of our first trustee, my father's old-time school pal Sam Marks, Jesus had come to preach the Word. That was that. He couldn't understand why our religious projects should be the ones to involve so much disagreement.

When the Foundation started to operate in 1958, the role of the church in the city was the front line of Christian responsibility. We made many grants in the Protestant and Catholic categories to the city church, about a million dollars, and we had our most troubling arguments about what that meant.

East Harlem Protestant Parish, New York, New York, 1958–1964— $185,000. The parish had been started in the 1950s by a group of young ministers trying to reach the Puerto Rican population living in the East Har-

lem area of Manhattan. The Catholic Church involved itself little in their
needs. The storefront churches of Adventists and Jehovah's Witnesses supplied an intense evangelical message but did not concern themselves with
the linkage between man and society. The core of Parish activity was the
Bible study meetings in the members' homes: what did Jesus say, what was
the significance of his message to life in East Harlem, and how could Christians act together to set the goals and the methods of working out that message? The problems around them were pretty awful—bad housing, poor jobs,
crime and police, hostile and largely useless schools, and heroin (a reality on
every East Harlem street)—adding up to an awareness of being despised and
of being unable to deal with their own needs or to supply any future for their
children.

Where to begin? One starts with finding out the levers of power and who
turns the levers—who actually is supposed to enforce a housing law stating
a landlord's obligations in keeping down rats—and then learns how to acquire
the power that makes the lever-turners listen. From the beginning, a primary
aim of these young ministers was to work themselves out of a job, teaching
their parishioners how to deal with their own problems: administrative, social, and theological.

During the first half of the sixties, the East Harlem Protestant Parish was
the most influential of the urban church groups, and the conclusions of its
spokesmen became accepted wisdom for serious Christians who followed the
same mix of leftist social thought and conservative theology.

First, if the metropolitan city is the most destructive expression of twentieth-century life, it is in the city also where the Christian counterattack must
take place.

Second, when the Christian church seeks to redeem urban life, it is fighting
for its own life. Protestant Christianity in particular follows a style set by the
farming community, small-town and suburb, Christmas-basket and summer-
camp, that has no relevance to the cities that express our century, not simply
in New York and London, but in São Paulo, Mexico City, Cairo, Jakarta, and
Lagos, growing at geometrical speed all over the world. The private search
for salvation, everyman's solitary journey, is as out of touch with real need
as the self-protecting, self-indulging suburban home is from the agony of
innercity life. And the suburban pastor who busies himself frantically with
committees all day long is hiding his innermost conviction that nothing he
does is relevant to human needs and God's will. The hostile city may be too
strong. The church may fail. But the battle is a real one. There is less chance
for self-delusion and of kidding oneself that out of nostalgia and architecture
one has built a Christian society.

Third, if the city's challenge is more than any individual can meet, if the
solutions offered by secular society simply become the next generation's

problems—the great housing project that was supposed to bring decent shelter to the poor turns into a monstrosity that must be destroyed by dynamite—then pragmatic, cheerful American theology is not good enough. One is left with a somber awareness of man's limitations. One tries out all sorts of tools—rent strike, boycott, demonstration, campaign—that may accomplish practical results and also teach the congregation to work together and trust each other. Nevertheless, salvation, if it comes, will be through God's grace. Human victories will only be temporary, partial ones. Perhaps in that way one does not expect impossible things out of a political victory. One does not give total allegiance to a charismatic leader. One is less cast down by one's failures and failings.

The Merrill Trust made seven grants to the Parish for the narcotics prevention program (in 1960, before the white middle class had heard of heroin), the family retreat center in the country, a clinic, training of parishioners to carry out broader responsibilities, ministers' salaries, and construction of a new church.

Inner-City Protestant Parish, Cleveland, Ohio, 1960–1967—$78,000. This Cleveland program was modeled after East Harlem. The Trust's first grant of $28,000 in 1960 went to train students, mainly from Oberlin's Graduate School of Theology, to work in low-income, mixed-race urban areas. Cleveland is a city of southern Negroes, Appalachian whites, Puerto Ricans, Italians, Poles, and Yugoslavs. The student interns would apprentice at a parish church but live in a group ministry to avoid the loneliness of such a life.

$25,000 in 1961 went to finance construction of a new church, one of the few new ones in the inner city, whose gym would be useful for local kids and which would be a meeting place for local and old people. $25,000 in 1967 towards construction of another church in Hough, a terrible ghetto area of poverty and delinquency. This new building was next to a community college whose facilities it would share, a bridge between college and community. Up to 80 percent of black males there sixteen to twenty-one were unemployed— this was in 1967, when the United States was close to "full employment." And in housing two thousand units had been built to replace five thousand: "Urban renewal means Negro removal."[3] Hough had been the scene of a destructive riot in 1966, like Watts and Rochester in 1965, Newark and Detroit in 1967, and Washington and Boston in 1968. Did these riots alienate white allies, or did they provoke whatever real concessions to black city needs that Lyndon B. Johnson's Great Society was willing to make? Probably both.

Board of Missions of the Methodist Church, New York, 1968—$30,000 to

3. A slogan first used in the early 1950s in St. Louis, when blacks voted down the bond issue that white liberals thought was such a progressive idea.

finance the Metropolitan Urban Service Training facility. This program, run by another graduate of East Harlem, George Webber (who was to become head of the New York Theological Seminary dedicated to training city-oriented ministers), was organized under Methodist auspices to prepare Christians for work in urban America. While teaching the discipline and testing the methods to achieve change, the program sought to force its students and their congregations to face the reality of Christian paternalism and to be ready to accept the conflict situations that were the only genuine vehicles of change.

One approach was the Metropolitan Intern Program where students would live in New York City for a year, finding their own jobs and homes, while attending two seminars a week on the topics of how does Christian faith provide a frame of understanding in secular culture and what is the relevance of the church to metropolis. Another was a joint program with a few Protestant and Catholic seminaries to supply intense exposure to city life and extended to liberal arts graduates headed towards secular careers.

Ecumenism and the Fight Against Racism

Community Renewal Society, Chicago, Illinois, 1962, 1964—$35,000 to finance the Urban Training Center: to convey a living religion to poor, badly housed, troubled people and to teach middle-class seminarians to understand the city and to survive in it. If you had only five dollars in your pocket, could you manage to get by for a week: what sort of jobs as dishwasher or delivery boy could you land, where would you sleep, whom would you talk to? What new picture of yourself might you acquire?

Board of National Missions of the United Presbyterian Church, New York, New York, 1964, 1966—$27,000. $15,000 in 1964 went towards community organization work in southwest Chicago to stop neighborhood deterioration and to help both sides respond decently to the expanding black population. A caucus of Presbyterian ministers in 1960 had tried to oppose housing segregation and work for physical betterment and also tried to get their white and black parishioners to share in the decisionmaking as an expression of Christian citizenship. One result was cooperation between twenty-seven Protestant and eleven Catholic parishes.

These social action projects presented to the foundation's trustees had reached me through George Todd, a Presbyterian minister I had known at the East Harlem Protestant Parish. Todd's "radicalism" had irritated my colleagues to such an extent that he had proposed in 1966 a studiedly noncontroversial appeal for $12,000 for "the Beautification of the Church in the City."

United Presbyterian Church, New York, New York, 1966—$25,000 for a Community Services Center in San Diego. This city was a port of entry, or dumping ground, for Mexicans, southern blacks, and Indians, with every social ill of the urban world: housing in disrepair, poor trash facilities, no recreational facilities—fear, hatred, conflict. A serious riot had been averted in 1965, at the time of Watts, by the courage of a Presbyterian pastor, but what could be done through the church to prevent explosion? What sort of cooperation between different churches, innercity and middle-class, what plans for emergency welfare services to new families, what better pastoral care and better education, and what new program of self-help and community development could be worked out—with limited resources—as fast as possible?

This appeal also came to us through George Todd, who had left East Harlem and was working in Social Action at Presbyterian headquarters. He respected the resourcefulness of the leadership in this San Diego crisis but resented the fact that emergency funds could be obtained from the church and from foundations like ours only to avert an explosion of violence, not at any adequate level, nor from any determination to clean up the basic problems. This help from the church was a sort of holding action to deliver enough tangible improvements to defuse the worst anger until something better turned up. Probably, however, nothing would.

New England Conference of the Methodist Church, Boston, Massachusetts, 1963–1965 $54,000. $29,000 went to strengthen the church's understanding of and service to the people dislocated by the massive process of urban renewal in Boston's West End. One part of the area was the medical complex around Massachusetts General Hospital; a second was the giant new Government Center with its offices of federal, state, and city agencies. A textbook example of the destructiveness of urban renewal was the leveling of the old West End, a disadvantaged but viable, mixed community, to make room for showy high-rise apartments.

Jack Russell, the minister trying to organize this West End project, felt that the church should not hide in the bedroom suburbs and tried to involve seminarians in a halfway house for MGH patients and in neighborhood programs for people on the edges of all this construction. The city planners seemed to have some moral commitment in trying to protect the urbanity of the area, but the dynamics of change left little behind to work with.

$25,000 went to the Methodist Bishops' Housing Action Charitable Corporation for work in the South End. The South End was a poor, racially mixed part of Boston with serviceable but crowded and deteriorated housing. Methodist money went for down payments on houses, then quite cheap, for remodeling costs, and for guaranteeing mortgages by the families who took over the property. Jack Russell pushed us hard in this project, asking for at least $50,000 a year to meet the losses due to urban renewal projects and highway construction, supply new jobs and job-training benefits provided by such work, and encourage banks and other foundations to enter a high-risk field like this. It was also important to act fast before speculators were drawn into this fast-changing area and drove up prices to resell the gentrified buildings to middle-class fugitives from the suburbs. This form of scattered, small-unit improvement, offering decent, low-cost housing and encouraging tenants to become houseowners, would have exactly the opposite effect of the giant government projects that concentrated all the weakest families in one complex.

After four appeals by Russell, however, our trustees became tired of his importunity. We involved ourselves in only two other housing proposals—noted below.

Connecticut Housing Investment Fund, Waterbury, Connecticut, 1973, 1977—$30,000. Sponsored by The Ford Foundation as well as insurance companies like Aetna and Travelers, this program helped poor and minority families buy houses by loaning them down payment and second-mortgage money and by offering help in the mechanics of location and funding.

Cooperative Metropolitan Ministries, Boston, Massachusetts, 1973—$25,000 toward the housing needs of the Hispanic community of Roxbury and North Dorchester.

These three projects added up to a bit over $100,000. I subsequently came to feel that a sustained involvement with housing might have been the most creative focus that the Merrill Trust found. As the Methodist project in the South End showed, such an investment had three crucial results: It did something to meet the crying need for low-cost housing, a crisis in every part of our country (and the world) whether one talks of inner cities or small towns in New Hampshire. It provided adequate workmanship in construction and utilities; some concern for privacy, comfort, and beauty; and rentals and opportunities for purchase that can be fitted into a low income budget—homes that embody these qualities are desperately needed. The variety of labor skills needed in construction makes it the most practical way of giving jobs and job training, whether one is dealing with middle-aged craftsmen or high school dropouts. Moreover, a network of buildings being rehabilitated can be an effective way of bringing cohesion and wholesomeness to a city neighborhood.

A private foundation like ours might have worked in a variety of regions and offered start-up capital both in outright grants or revolving loan funds for low-cost mortgages or mortgage guarantees. We might have backed groups actually getting things done and not being paralyzed by the deadly bureaucracy. One cannot comprehend the logic of empty lots and adequate, solid buildings boarded up (except for junkies and squatters) until vandals or arsonists hired by developers burn them down. For a while the Urban Homestead project, halfheartedly sponsored by the federal government, seemed promising whereby a family might take title for a small sum on an abandoned house seized for nonpayment of taxes and then pay for it with their own sweat. By the 1970s, however, the buildings were almost beyond salvage and the neighborhoods became too dangerous. Charity money should go into the main needs, providing housing and jobs, and not be spent trying to patch up the evils caused by the lack of both.

Synagogue Council of America, New York, New York, 1960—$20,000 to help fund a human relations project in Catholic parochial schools in New York, Boston, Washington, and Pittsburgh; to discuss what is meant by prejudice; and to look for ways to better understanding.

Union of American Hebrew Congregations, New York, New York, 1960— $25,000 to support work of its National Commission on Social Action, examining issues of human equality and respect for individual dignity in civil rights, housing, and interfaith relations. Two hundred of these congregations were in the South, and this program sought to prepare their leaders to make a positive impact upon community affairs.

Brotherhood Synagogue, New York, New York, 1961—$5,000 toward support of a house of worship in Greenwich Village shared by Presbyterians and Jews, with a joint family counseling service, brotherhood programs in schools, and a visit, at Bonn's request, by both congregations to West Germany.

Union of American Hebrew Congregations, Chicago, Illinois, 1964— $15,000 to finance work in community development led by Rabbi Robert Marx. Marx had been unusually active in working with Protestants and Catholics and was at this date forming a Jewish Council on Urban Affairs to occupy itself with urban renewal, the development of recreation and education facilities, the improvement of public school standards, and the encouragement of intergroup cooperation. In sum, to resolve conflicts and obsessions. Rabbi Marx was the finest example of the Jewish-Negro alliance that was such an important part of American liberalism and was to shred apart by the end of the decade.

Our grants to different United Jewish Appeals are covered in the Jewish subheading, and yet many of this blanket organization's chapters, particularly ones in Chicago, Seattle, and San Francisco, were strongly involved with jobs and housing to innercity people of any background.

When I was a student at Harvard in 1940 and exposed to the realities of a city new to me, Boston's battle line—in Dorchester, Roxbury, Mattapan, and Jamaica Plain—was Catholic and Jewish. These were the two sides in the afternoon fights as the boys walked home from school. The Jews, however, have left the hard parts of Boston—and Chicago, Cleveland, and Philadelphia—as much as the Protestants have, and the battle line is Catholic and Negro.

National Catholic Conference for Interracial Justice, Chicago, Illinois, 1964, 1967—$45,000. Organized in 1960, the Chicago Interracial Council was one of sixty throughout the United States to promote better understanding among racial groups within and beyond the Catholic community. In 1963 it had sponsored a four-day meeting on religion and race in Chicago with leaders from all three religious groups. From this conference there had come a concerted effort to expand teaching on race in the parochial schools. Our $20,000 in 1964 had funded the tour of three teams of nuns who traveled around the country to conduct institutes of human relations on race, poverty, and the city. In that spirit a Lutheran-Catholic elementary school was established in Chicago and efforts for biracial summer schools and camps. Our second grant, $25,000 in 1967, went towards setting up pilot schools of both races, courses in urban problems for Catholic sisters, and exchange programs between Catholic and Negro colleges.

George Wallace became a national political figure when his racist arguments won intense Polish Catholic support in Milwaukee's South Side. Martin Luther King Jr.'s worst confrontation had come not in Birmingham, Alabama, but with Poles and Lithuanians in westside Chicago. The church leaders saw this worsening confrontation and were trying to do what they could to replace hatred with understanding, humanity, and discipline.

Roman Catholic Archdiocese of Boston, Boston, Massachusetts, 1970, 1974—$25,000. Both small grants went to the Planning Office for Urban Affairs run by Fr. Michael Groden. The first was concerned solely with the needs of the parochial schools, which educated one-third of Boston's children. The mediocrity of Boston's public schools was the main reason for the importance given to parochial ones, and yet the size of the parochial system was a major reason why the public schools received inadequate backing. A decline in financial support, inflation, the shortage of religious personnel, and higher salaries demanded by lay teachers had put the system into crisis. Was it possible by intelligent leadership to consolidate these schools where necessary, train parents as aides, improve the curriculum and teaching, and show greater respect for the children's cultural identity? The community having highest priority was East Boston, 80 percent of its 40,000 inhabitants of Italian origin, with the schools needing to show a total change in style, content, and quality of operation.

$10,000 in 1974 went to prepare for the coming crisis caused by court-ordered bussing. If the Irish in South Boston and Charlestown and the Italians in East Boston could be given a more positive understanding of their own background, they might be more generous to rival groups. Students and parents might be taught useful political skills (how to conduct a meeting, conduct an opinion poll, or make a photo-journalistic report of a community), offer some stabilizing influence to public school families, and head off the violence coming with forced integration.

It didn't work. Buses with black children rolled through mobs of yelling, rock-throwing whites. South Boston and Charlestown Highs stationed cops with clubs, guns, and radios on every floor. The liberals who said they believed in integration sent their children to private schools like Commonwealth. Without the desperate Catholic planning, however, in Boston, Chicago, and elsewhere, things might have been worse.

United States Catholic Conference, Washington, D.C., 1971—$30,000 for use by the National Center for Urban Ethnic Affairs. A protest by Don Regan and Bob Magowan that the Merrill Trust was too involved with purely non-white poverty had led me, via a *Reporter* article, to Monsignor Gino Baroni. He had come from an immigrant family of coal-miners and steel-workers, had been educated at Catholic University and Notre Dame, had come to know King, and after the murder had been desperately involved trying to keep his own Washington neighborhood from blowing apart. White radical students and blacks, as Baroni reasoned, have some idea of who they are and what they want, but not his people, whose sufferings are inarticulate and unnoticed.

He spoke for what he termed the PIGS—Poles, Irish/Italians, Greeks and Slovaks—the blue-collar people in the northern industrial cities, the people who benefited from the New Deal and fought in our country's infantry. These were the people who felt betrayed in the Vietnam agony, passed over by the blacks, ignored by the Anglo-Saxon power structure, and ineligible for poverty programs while their neighborhoods deteriorated and their children were hurt and alienated. They were exploited by demagogues like George Wallace and Spiro Agnew and stereotyped as hard-hat racists. There was a need therefore to give these second- and third-generation Americans a positive self-image, show them how to attain better schools and political influence, and how to reach out to blacks and the Spanish speaking as poor people like themselves and not just "niggers" and "spics."

Merrill money would be used for leadership training, the building of prototype organizations, and awareness groups.

Catholic Charities of the Archdiocese of New York, New York, 1965—
$20,000. Cardinal Spellman felt that the disease of poverty had first to be
fought within the family. The breakdown of the family kept children from
being able to learn anything at school, involved them in delinquency, and
prevented them from being able, as adults, to earn a living or lead stable
lives. He sought money for increased family and vocational guidance, long-
term homemaker services when mother was ill, special training for parochial
teachers in Harlem to recognize mental illness, and a new emphasis on trying
to rehabilitate problem families into at least minimal working order so that
the children could be reunited with them instead of being put out for foster
placement.

Quite unlike Cardinal Spellman's approach to poverty was Saul Alinsky's.
Alinsky, who had grown up in South Chicago out of Russian Jewish background, had started his organizing career in the Polish community around
the stockyards area and by the 1960s involved himself in black urban neighborhoods, usually as an ally of Catholic and Protestant church groups. He
had a low opinion of black militants, whom he saw as drunk with words,
Afros and dashikis and Swahili names, who frightened white liberals with
their anger and acted to make a big name for themselves or line their own
pockets. He thought even less of most white liberals as unable to come to
grips with the reality of the lives of the poor, afraid of confrontation and
hard work, and afraid of letting the people they came to help run their own
show.

Alinsky was an arrogant, often foul-mouthed, but fascinating man intrigued
by his own historical stature—and indeed he did become the prophet for all
radical organizers with a tremendous joy in conflict and also a surprisingly
sweet-natured concern for the working out of democratic values in different
situations. His concept was that effective radical action could be the alternative to the frustration and despair that led to violence. Even simple people
essentially know what they want, and the task of the outsider organizer is to
set the highly visible first goal, whether police brutality or overpricing at the
supermarket, and then show local people how to go on to the next goal. In
the process of working together for these concrete rewards, they learn the
skills of leadership and cooperation and build a new image of themselves as
able to direct their own destiny.

I met him in Chicago around 1964, we became rather good friends, and I
helped get backing for perhaps half a dozen projects he was involved with,
although the other trustees never really trusted him. Alinsky, more than any
other social leader of the 1960s, had the clearest picture of the linkage between means and aims in meeting urban needs.

Catholic Interracial Council of Rochester, Rochester, New York, 1965—Rejected. Rochester, known for its high-technology industries like Xerox and Kodak, was unprepared for the disastrous riots of 1964. The black rioters, unskilled, often unemployed, recent immigrants from the South, with inadequate housing and few social services, felt that the city offered them nothing and that the only way to attract attention was violence. In collaboration with the Catholic Interracial Council, the Board of Urban Ministry, which represented 150 Protestant, Orthodox, and Polish National Catholic churches, invited Saul Alinsky to come to Rochester as a consultant.

His approach was first to identify small, visible organizations that could be persuaded to cooperate with each other by discussing a specific problem, and then to encourage these groups to unite. The task of organization—and the need to pay for the rather pricy services of Industrial Areas Foundation: people don't value what they don't pay for—is a means of raising confidence and morale, to pressure landlords, merchants, and public officials to deal fairly with the problems of urban renewal, health services, transportation, jobs, and voter registration. "A democracy lacking in popular participation dies of paralysis" was Alinsky's most quoted statement.

This appeal was rejected by our foundation's trustees as hostile to the Rochester power structure and therefore to the world of Merrill Lynch, Pierce, Fenner and Smith.

Rochester Area Council of Churches, Rochester, New York, 1966—$15,000. In a way this was selling the same horse under a different name. The Board of Urban Ministry was trying to coordinate urban strategy of all its member churches in liaison with community welfare agencies. It sought to meet the massive housing dislocations caused by urban renewal and expressway construction ("White men drive cars through black men's bedrooms!"), meet the problems ignored or worsened by federal antipoverty programs, and conduct educational programs for laymen to force the point that the church was fighting not only for the soul of the ghetto but for its own.

A city like Rochester, with a population of 325,000, would be a test case in shaping urban values throughout the nation.

Catholic Charities, Diocese of Kansas City, Kansas City, Missouri, 1965—$25,000 for community organization. Kansas City's inner city had all the standard symptoms of urban pathology: poor housing, broken homes, juvenile delinquency, wasteful use of leisure time, and an all-pervading sense of lack of any meaning in life. People are turned into things. Bishop Lawrence McNamara felt that efforts to help like Cardinal Spellman's in New York are doomed to fail because the individuals concerned have not had a part in bringing these programs about. Unless the poor can make themselves heard, passivity leads to total alienation.

Like Alinsky, Bishop McNamara believed that the very act of organization gave people some new respect for themselves. They learn the concept and techniques of problem solving, learning how to utilize the agencies and laws that do exist, and creating community self-help organizations. There was extensive cooperation between Catholics, Episcopalians, and Presbyterians in the city, and this ecumenism persuaded the Trust to agree to two grants of $25,000 apiece.

Alinsky argued that to crystallize issues into confrontation, which in turn led to practical negotiation, was actually a way of reducing the likelihood of violence. A person can reach for his rights in an orderly and organized way instead of striking out in blind rage. The logic was hard, however, for the suburban property-owners to grasp: they heard only the angry words—and they were not convinced that innercity blacks had rights. The people threatened by criticism of unethical merchants, intransigent police, and lack of voting registration among the poor included, it seemed, every single Merrill Lynch customer, and their complaints to Don Regan caused the second grant in 1966 to be cancelled.

United Church of Christ of Greater Kansas City, Kansas City, Missouri, 1967—$30,000 for construction of a day-care wing on the new St. Mark's Church. This was an unusual biracial church that came to our attention from the previous Kansas City involvement, one run jointly by Catholics, United Church of Christ, Episcopalians, and Presbyterians. Protestants and Catholics have shared worship facilities on military bases and college campuses, but St. Mark's was the first city parish that the two faiths jointly sponsored. The shared efforts in trying to meet Kansas City's social problems had heartened a Presbyterian minister named Kenneth Waterman into believing it possible to take the next step. The sacraments within the different services were held separately, though some sermons and prayer services were common, but the responsibilities of spiritual counseling, religious education, home care services, youth and elderly activities, job placement and social action were shared. The church served about 15,000 residents, mainly black, with a large number on welfare and in public housing. The new day-care facility would free the mothers for work.

The aim of the church was to serve the neighborhood and to stress leadership and independence. It was an unusual, heartening institution. One asks why is this the only example.

Industrial Areas Foundation, Chicago, Illinois, 1969—$35,000 for the National Training Institute. Alinsky, who could be charming when he tried, won the temporary support of Bob Magowan, which led to this large grant to the training institute he had organized within his Industrial Areas Foundation.

Generous, spirited young people needed to be offered a more practical channel for their beliefs than the usual noisy, ineffectual mass demonstration. They should learn the realities of city life, its power structure, the common and conflicting needs of its citizens, and the techniques of stimulating useful action. This would be a way to institutionalize the Master's principles. Not too much came of this, however, and Alinsky died a few years later.

First Presbyterian Church of Chicago, Chicago, Illinois, 1970—$20,000 for the Community Education Center. This project was a disaster. One of my former students had gone to the University of Chicago, had become a part of the militant world and found herself (because she could write, figure, and didn't steal) executive secretary of the Blackstone Rangers, a two-thousand-member gang in South Chicago. Police, uptown newspapers, and probably most middle-class Negroes saw them as hoodlums, but the Black P. Stone Nation, as its members called themselves, gave an identity and a set of loyalties to its young men. My friend Margot admitted their brutality, needed for survival in that brutal world, but saw the Nation as supplying the only structure the community possessed. At her urging I had put up money of my own, using the First Presbyterian Church as a tax-exempt channel, to bankroll an eatery, a dry cleaners, and a bookstore as opportunities for these young men to move up in the world.

This was clearly a project I could not sell to our trustees, but I thought they might accept a program also sponsored by First Presbyterian to serve children expelled as hopeless by the Chicago schools. One can imagine how awful the kids must have been, but after all, they were only eight or nine, and that is young to be written off. The Church wanted money for a counseling, tutoring, and health program to civilize these kids so that they could reenter the public schools.

My fault, a serious one, was not to inform my colleagues that I had used the same channel for my own backing of Stone projects—I was sure that that would end any chance of winning their support for the out-of-school children's program, which seemed important. The story eventually hit the *Tribune* headlines as "Merrill Lynch Money Funds Black Killers," and every customer in Chicago phoned Don Regan to demand what the hell was being done with his money. I was asked to testify before the City Council as to why I was so gullible and also to explain my rule-breaking before a special meeting of the Foundation.

What were the lessons? First, if trustees of an institution are divided politically, as we were, they must abide by their own rules and not try to put across extremist positions, right-wing, left-wing, or disguised as something else. Second, the Black P. Stone Nation was undoubtedly a tribe of hoodlums. Its maximum leader, Jeff Ford, then in jail for homicide, was involved in a wide variety of rackets including drug running, extortion, and prostitution. If I had been less hasty I could have found out more of these facts myself. Third, one of the justifications for backing the Stones was that in their own chaotic, brutal way their leaders were trying to channel the raging frustration of young black males, the most dangerous subcaste in American society, into some sort of economic and political organization that could have potentially revolutionary overtones. This was the reason for the intensity of opposition from police, *Tribune*, and Daley machine, who would have been less hostile to standard criminal activity. Accordingly, police were apt to attack the Stones' legitimate business activities and their pathetic little stores more strongly than their gangster actions.

What does one do with the young black unemployed that terrorize every American city? Anything that deals with more than one percent of that caste will involve so much money, in such odd ways, that a large amount of it will be stolen. They are so poorly educated that it is hard for them to start in at any level. Antidrug programs just treat the symptoms and don't do even that effectively. "Lock 'em up and throw away the key!" always an appealing idea, means, at the unit cost that maximum security prisons are running now, more than thirty thousand dollars per year, a statistic that the law-and-order crowd do not publicize. Little business programs, little training programs, little experimental programs like sending ghetto hoodlums to Outward Bound camps in Maine—all of which our Foundation supported—are doomed to failure because such small numbers are employed and because the graduates return to the same diseased city they came from. Any effort to reach large numbers or to change the framework to allow jobs, housing, and a chance to build a future worth joining becomes political, and anything political can only be revolutionary, or seem revolutionary. The desperate ask for surprisingly modest concessions, but they do make a lot of noise.

What are the solutions? Police, jail, methadone, neglect (so long as blacks kill just each other), television, or labor camps? Soviet history takes great credit for the reeducative process during the 1920s of salvaging the Bezprizornia, or homeless orphans, left over in the wake of the Revolution and the Civil War. A new social organization and iron revolutionary discipline were able to bring back these young people as productive workers. And if it did not work, when the hard-core hooligans proved intractible, they were, out of sight, apt to be shot.

Our Foundation avoided hard-core urban projects, where one radical proposal out of sixty on that meeting's agenda jeopardized[4] three or four liberal

4. The basic rule of committee politics is that no member may win or lose too often. If you really want a controversial proposal passed, arrange to place two or three troublemakers that seem to be your choices on the list ahead of that one. When they have been indignantly voted down, your partners then owe you a victory.

proposals with more chance of doing what they claimed to do. We put money into noncontroversial drug programs and settlement houses, a few delinquency and prison projects, and parochial schools for the lower middle class.

Federation of Protestant Welfare Agencies, New York, New York, 1973, 1976—$60,000. $25,000 had gone here in 1973 to establish resident councils in Federation-affiliated homes for the aged, but the $35,000 in 1976 was used to sustain agencies faced with cutbacks in city funds. As New York tried, more or less, to avoid bankruptcy, the institutions of civilized life—parks, libraries, agencies—were either to be funded by private sources or be allowed to die. The Protestant Welfare Agencies were trying to meet two problems: a reduction of subsidy from the city and a need to offer new services previously supplied by the city agencies. Here was a desperate issue as the fabric of city life decayed, and a group that we should have supported at a more sustained level.

Urban Commitment from 1976 On: Return of Hard Times

Lutheran Metropolitan Ministry Association of Greater Cleveland, Cleveland, Ohio, 1976—$15,000 for service to the unemployed and their families. This meant working with exprisoners on probation (counseling, food, clothing, furniture) and with Appalachian families in West Cleveland, rehabilitation of innercity housing, and job training for Vietnam veterans. The most serious problem was long-range structural unemployment. Jobs have simply ceased to exist as corporations move their factories to Brazil, Mexico, and South Korea, where labor costs are 20 percent, 10 percent of the costs in Ohio. This form of unemployment can be devastating to previously secure families and demands careful counseling as well as retraining and placement in the change from manufacturing to service jobs. The Protestant tradition of personal responsibility does not fit with dis-industrialization and leads to silent drinking and then terrible family violence.

Pilgrim Lutheran Church, Portland, Oregon, 1981—$10,000 to further the work of an ecumenical group of pastors from twenty churches, Catholic and Protestant, to strengthen families and communities that had previously relied on government-sponsored programs. The stress is now upon self-help: can senior citizens, for example, help take care of a welfare mother's children while she goes off to work?

St. Stephen's Episcopal Church, Boston, Massachusetts, 1980—$15,000. St. Stephen's was the financial channel for six Protestant and Catholic churches trying to meet the economic, social, and spiritual needs of the Spanish-speaking in Boston. "Jesus is the only answer!" is a cruel statement when the parishioners must endure unemployment, poor housing, poor city services, and lack of any political power. At the same time, the efficiency of a good welfare agency is not going to change an individual's sense of loneliness, confusion, and meaninglessness. The Christian message has always been to be both.

Roman Catholic Archdiocese of Boston, Boston, Massachusetts, 1976–1980—$35,000 to the Planning Office for Urban Affairs. The first two grants went toward operating expenses and the summer jobs program of the Columbia Point Cultural Center. Columbia Point wins a prize as one of the country's worst housing projects. Bleak, wind-swept, cut off from the city by a major expressway, it sticks out into Boston Harbor, a dump for unsuccessful and despised blacks and Hispanics. Vandalism and theft caused the closing of the stores that were opened there to serve the community. Transportation is difficult and costly. The one profitable activity is dope selling. A community health center started under the aegis of Tufts Medical School opened in 1970, financed partly by the Merrill Trust, with an aim of developing community leadership through uneducated but forceful, responsible older women, but was abandoned within a couple of years under the threat of violence.

A cultural center did open and precariously stayed open, led by two young black former Tufts students to give tutoring and counseling to high school students; to serve as a structure for some minimum cultural, medical, and legal services; and for cooperative food purchasing, transportation, and child-care services. Marauding whites from South Boston came across the expressway to shoot up the place; marauding blacks vandalized, stole, and burned. $10,000 in 1979 went for a teenage summer jobs program to help keep idle youngsters out of trouble at a time when no such money was coming from government plus money to pay salaries to a few men and women in their twenties who had come out of the project and managed to get ahead and might serve as role models.

$10,000 in 1980 went into a more general project of the Planning Office to work out multilevel approaches to Boston's problems: obtaining new housing in underutilized old buildings, training teams of mothers of both races to be parent representatives at public schools to head off friction, and setting up job banks for high school graduates.

Diocese of Worcester, Worcester, Massachusetts, 1977—$10,000 for the Urban Ministry Commission. The Commission was a coalition of clergy and lay people developing service and self-help programs directed toward Polish, Irish, and French-Canadian communities. Programs of the 1960s had been directed towards blacks and Hispanics. White ethnics felt themselves ignored and forgotten and were left with their run-down neighborhoods and dying factories, unemployment, arson, vandalism, and juvenile delinquency. The Commission believed that with capable leadership these people could learn how to solve real problems and create a sense of community: to pressure absentee landlords to pay taxes and keep up their buildings; to pressure banks to invest their money in the innercity communities (not the suburbs), and to pressure the city to repair streets, install lights, clean up parks.

Massachusetts Community Center, Boston, Massachusetts, 1977—$15,000 to help Fair Share set up a neighborhood organization in Roslindale.

Massachusetts Fair Share, Boston, 1977—$15,000 for start-up costs of a Springfield branch office.

These two secular projects are included under the category of the Church and the City because they are similar to other church-sponsored projects and because Fair Share, to the surprise of its left-wing staff members, found itself allied to Catholic groups. Its leader, Michael Ansara, had been a Harvard militant during the 1960s who came to the conclusion that student radicalism was a dead-end street. All too theoretical, it was led astray into violent and useless gestures, preoccupied, often gullibly, with black issues, scornful and totally ignorant of the problems of the white working class. Its feminist militants were apt to drift off into politicized lesbianism.

Ansara set himself to build an organization that would serve these voiceless whites in practical ways: housing, jobs, neighborhood security, and city services. Out of these bread-and-butter campaigns, might come, in the best spirit of Saul Alinsky, a sense of direction that would head in turn to a comprehension of social change and of the specific ways by which government, business, and media affected their lives. The ultimate goal was an active rather than a passive way of looking at life and emancipation from the sense of being controlled by a faceless *Them*. As an old-fashioned Marxist, Ansara sought to persuade his Catholic and to a certain extent black and Hispanic clientele to concentrate on political and economic, as opposed to racial, issues. It wasn't necessary to like your neighbors, but if you understood how your problems— and hopes—and theirs were essentially the same, you could build alliances, starting with the first step of keeping white and black boys from getting arrested for fighting each other.

These unhappy white families Ansara saw as people who had tried to play by the rules: they raised their children; went to church; fought in the wars; worked hard; endured poverty but in neighborhoods where people, including teacher, cop, priest, even the judge, knew each other; stood by each other in trouble; and showed compassion towards each other's failings. But dad's experience in World War II hadn't prepared them for what happened to Kevin in Vietnam. Dad drank; Sean was into heroin. They had always been poor, but now they felt despised by the media and by liberals who said they sympathized with blacks and in reality never had anything to do with them. The old neighborhoods were run by strangers from downtown. None of the rules were valid anymore. By social organization might it be possible to give such people a sense that, to a certain extent, they still had control over their lives?

It was a shame when this pragmatic, often creative alliance between radicals and Catholics was (deliberately?) ruptured by introduction of the abortion issue in the 1980s.

Family Counseling and Guidance Center, Boston, Massachusetts, 1976, 1978—$25,000. This Catholic service sought to offer professional help in family conflict and depression, for those who could pay and those who could not. The services were being broadened to include non-Catholics and toward adolescents but at a time when church and state funding was being eliminated and when severe economic times were increasing the number of patients. Growing middle-class unemployment was putting families who used to be secure under pressures that they were just not equipped to meet. Parental alcoholism and violence were the most visible first symptoms, but the Center needed funding to deal with adolescents and children whose troubles would get far worse if they were not dealt with now.

Wall Street Ministry, New York, New York, 1968, 1969—$20,000. Here was an American expression of the worker priest movement, the clerics endeavoring to enter not the factories but the executive offices of Wall Street firms. The movement was started in 1965 by Trinity Church at the corner of Broadway and Wall, whose director sought to close the distance between clergy and laity. Like the Jesuits of another tradition, its ministers spoke with bankers, stockbrokers, and business executives about ethics (standards of truthfulness for securities salesmen, sexual harassment), social change (equal hiring of blacks and women, responsibility to the labor force if a plant is to be closed), competition, and long-range goals. One pamphlet widely circulated by the ministry was entitled "My Job is Tedious and Meaningless." It placed four seminarians as summer clerks in large firms and asked them to keep diaries of their spiritual experiences. It made a survey of job satisfaction among 1,600 employees of one large firm.

If the ministry retained the readiness to cause trouble—the Quaker ideal of speaking truth to power—such a project would be invaluable, and not just on Wall Street.

International Christian Leadership, Washington, 1968—$15,000. This group sponsored breakfast meetings of important men to come together in small groups in the spirit of Christ, to build a camaraderie, a common spiritual bond that would transcend politics and economic considerations. A group in Seattle focused on the question of corruption in government, and one in Washington focused on ways to make Congress more morally sensitive. The Leadership sought to hold a world conference every two years.

I cannot imagine a more trivial way of wasting money. These breakfasts might be enjoyable, but as soon as anyone asked the members to do something or even to raise unpopular questions, I can see them tiptoeing out of the room.

JEWISH

> Learn to do well; seek judgment, relieve the oppressed, judge the fatherless, plead for the widow.   [Isaiah 1:17]

Because Charles E. Merrill felt that his financial career had benefited so much from Jewish customers, his will stated that 5 percent of the Foundation's income should go to Jewish charities. This category was different from our Protestant and Catholic ones. None of the Trustees were Jewish. We saw that world as outsiders: through our friends and colleagues, through our sympathies and interests, but not as insiders with an insider's knowledge or loyalties. In the Holocaust the Jewish world had suffered the greatest tragedy of modern times, and in Israel had a whole country that was its special responsibility, but Judaism did not encompass whole regions or ethnic groups in deep poverty, as was true with Protestant Appalachia and the black cities of the North, or with Catholic industrial cities and the hemisphere crisis of the Spanish-speaking poor. Jewish need was special—the troubled teenager into drugs, the troubled single-parent family, and the ailing and lonely old person. Because Judaism is a religion based on culture and history, we were involved in the support of schools and seminaries and cultural and historical societies with little first-hand knowledge of our own to help us reach decisions.

About $1 million of the $4 million total went to different charitable and service agencies, almost a million to federations like the United Jewish Appeal (UJA) often quite deliberately chosen in cities where a prominent Merrill Lynch customer might win prestige for himself as well as for the generous firm—Atlanta, Baltimore, Cincinnati, Cleveland, Los Angeles, Miami, and St. Louis. In every Jewish city the UJA funds and coordinates the agencies from day-care centers to nursing homes. The most sensitive link is probably the young people's clubs for wholesome recreation and serious discussion within a Jewish setting: $35,000 to the Jewish Center of Greater Buffalo for construction of the new activities building so that adolescents don't smoke marijuana or fall in love with gentiles. The UJA can also be its own reason for being, an empire of committee meetings, newsletters, phonathons that build stairways for the ambitious to the speaker's table at the annual banquet.

We gradually formulated a policy that we would try to support scholarly and cultural institutions that did not attract popular support. Moreover, when we started by the 1970s to include Israeli projects, we deliberately stressed ones that involved Arabs, not simply because Merrill Lynch had offices in Beirut and Teheran, but because all too often American Jewish philanthropy gives automatic support to the most hard-line, hawkish elements within Israeli society without ascertaining whether this intransigence is the best policy for American interests or even Israel.

Jewish Theological Seminary of America (JTS), New York City, New York, 1959–1980—$275,000. Of the $800,000 that went to seminaries and in support of the professional needs of rabbis, JTS received the largest support. This was partly out of my respect for its chancellor, Dr. Louis Finkelstein, who had edited an Encyclopedia of Judaism (my first formal exposure to Jewish history) and who seemed to stand for a particularly pure, sweet level of piety where the Law is not constraint but a means to liberation from the tyranny of the trivial and the selfish. He was concerned about *bringing in*, not *keeping out*, and we helped support projects of his and his successor, Gerson Cohen, to fund fellowships not only for scholars and rabbis (including $35,000 in 1965 for the retraining of rabbis who had been away from the seminary for ten years or more) but also to invite Dean Farunzafar of the University of Teheran as visiting scholar and Protestant students from Union Theological Seminary.

Hebrew Union College, Cincinnati, Ohio, 1959–1978—$125,000. With pedantic care we tried to give equal support to the three religious divisions within Judaism. If JTS was the leading Conservatory seminary, Hebrew Union, part of the nineteenth-century German culture of the Ohio valley, was the leading Reform seminary, and our five gifts went to support students preparing for the rabbinate and doctorate.

Dropsie University, Philadelphia, Pennsylvania, 1967–1978—$50,000. Dropsie, not well known outside the Jewish community, is respected within. It offers work at the graduate level only, mainly for Ph.D. candidates, who are apt to be mature students with families to support and therefore needing financial aid. As more of the larger American universities began to offer courses in Hebraic studies, there came an increasing need for Dropsie graduates as professors, as well as staff members at Jewish teachers' colleges. Merrill money also went to help in the microfilming of what remained of the major Hebrew libraries of Hungary and Poland.

Hebrew Culture Foundation, New York, New York, 1966–1979—$65,000.
This foundation, whose chairman, Milton Konvitz, was a professor of law at
Cornell, sought to create and enrich centers of Hebrew civilization at universities ranging from Columbia to West Virginia. From the expanding interests of both Jews and Christians in archaeology, the impact of Israel and
the Arab states upon current history, the uncovering of ancient languages
like Akkadian and Ugarit, the ecumenical movement and the contributions
of Protestant theologians like Niebuhr and Tillich, came a growing demand
for both scholars and library resources. All administrative services at the
foundation were volunteered, which meant no overhead costs, and all moneys
raised were invested in the actual processes of starting these new centers.

National Foundation for Jewish Culture, New York, New York, 1968—
$25,000 to finance a study of the teaching of Judaica at American colleges
and universities and to train Jewish scholars for university teaching. Before
1955 there were fewer than ten full-time such teachers outside of the seminaries; by 1968 there were seventy-five. Judaism had been an immigrant
culture—what was it now? What will be the manpower needs of such programs over the next ten or twenty years? What funding will be needed; what
are goals to be sought?

For many of these grants we were advised by a long-time friend of mine,
Richard Rubenstein, who had begun his career as director of Hillel at Harvard, eventually became professor of religion at Florida State in Tallahassee,
and who enjoyed his reputation as a thorny critic of the establishment. Dr.
Rubenstein argued against competing with the wealthy UJA supporters and
for targeting our grants to the scholarly, often immigrant institutions that
were the bedrock of Jewish society.

Reconstructionist Rabbinical College, Philadelphia, Pennsylvania, 1965–
1972—$67,000 for scholarships, library needs, and endowment. This college
started as an effort to transcend the barriers of Orthodox, Conservative, and
Reform, irrelevant now after the Holocaust, the work of an inspired leader
named Mordecai Kaplan. It sought to reach Jewry's drop-outs through intermarriage and indifference that the regular groups could not cope with, but
it did not win support. It stayed small and isolated and was threatened by
the State of Pennsylvania with losing accreditation because its endowment
was inadequate. Should one continue support of a struggling institution or,
given its precariousness and the high unit cost of teaching its few students,
back the winners?

Jewish Teachers' Seminary and People's University, New York, New York,
1964–1972—$55,000. The seminary was an old-fashioned and self-consciously working-class school that did not train rabbis but accepted high school

graduates from low-income families and gave an education in Judaism in its historical, spiritual, and social manifestations in Yiddish as well as Hebrew and English.

Spertus College of Judaica, Chicago, Illinois, 1965–1976—$55,000. Spertus is an interesting place. Confronted by declining enrollment and rising costs in the 1960s, its management decided to concentrate on Jewish and Hebrew studies as a common resource for the entire Chicago area, offering 200 different courses for the eleven institutions of this consortium to which its 600 students go for courses in the humanities and sciences. The result was high-quality education at much lower costs. The cooperation between Spertus and the University of Illinois meant the first degree in Jewish studies ever to be offered at a public university.

Yeshiva University, New York, New York, 1968—$25,000 to finance a three-year program of interpreting and evaluating the legal literature of Judaism, the Talmud. More than translation is needed of this great tradition that includes the earliest writings on the issues of self-incrimination and judicial review, the right to privacy, and the right to work.

Does Talmudic learning have any beyond a museum value? It is in fact destructive of intellect with a half-semester course on the correct wording of a bill of divorcement, a whole lecture on whether it is advisable for the prayer said at dawn really to be said at midnight, and of commentaries upon commentaries where Rabbi Ben-David of Grodno proved that Rabbi Yitzak of Lublin did not know what he was talking about.

And yet the Talmud represents far more than nostalgic nit-picking. It rejects absolutes. Each statement is made by a specific rabbi upon a specific occasion. The subtleties of the commentaries match the dangerous subtleties of life. When the Jews were surrounded by a gentile world of such arbitrary violence, it was by their leaders' meticulous attention to detail and to the possible that humane life was preserved—after all, if one delayed the dawn prayer until sunrise and then was attacked by cramps or a robber. . . . A whole series of rabbinic legends centers upon Moses' slaying of an Egyptian for mistreating a Hebrew (Exodus 2:12). Israeli militants quote that verse to justify counterviolence against the Arabs. Not so, insist the scholars. That killing by Moses is hedged around by an aura of such dread. The language of the legends makes it into such a special event that it just cannot be exploited by one murderer to justify the killing of another. Jewish tradition is not simply at the mercy of German destructiveness and American neglect but of the brutal pragmatism of Israelis who worship their army and consider God as minister of propaganda. Care for the Talmud is a way to protect a fragile but tenacious part of the human spirit: a worthy commitment by a gentile foundation that believes in pluralism.

Brandeis University, Waltham, Massachusetts, 1961–1979—$240,000.
Brandeis is the only general Jewish university in the entire country. In fact,
one of the reasons for its beginning immediately after World War II was not
simply as expression of Jewish creativity at the end of a terrible period of
history but as a way for the Jewish community to make its own contribution
to American higher education that had served Jews well. Its first president,
Abram Sachar, was a virtuoso of fund-raising. He could design one six-sided
structure and have it known as six separately named buildings besides a seventh larger name for it as a complex. Professorships were named at a price—
$250,000—which made them appealing bargains for donors, though the result
was that the remainder of the cost had then to be met out of general revenues.
The faculty had stars in fields like biochemistry, Semitic languages, and many
of the social sciences—so-so folk sometimes elsewhere.

At one level was the stereotype of the genius and the neurotic revolutionary, but the college was sustained by meat-and-potatoes students: the valedictorian of Long Island City High who came, at the serious sacrifice of his
parents, to prepare for a career as lawyer or dentist and who was impatient
of any turmoil that hampered that process. The Trust gave $65,000 to train
scholars in Judaica and $175,000 earmarked "for students of the Jewish faith."
Our last grant of $50,000 was to be divided between partial scholarships for
middle-class students, priced out of the market at Brandeis as everywhere
else, and a few (very few) larger grants to the new Russian applicants, all of
whom knew as their plane left Moscow airport that they were headed straight
for that one university where they would be greeted with open arms and
given all the financing they asked for.

B'nai B'rith Hillel Foundation, Washington, D.C., 1962–1976—$120,000.
A 1962 grant of $20,000 provided college faculty with time and money for
studying Jewish history and culture. B'nai B'rith served the religious, cultural,
and counseling needs of Jewish students at 243 colleges and universities in
the United States and Canada at the time. An earlier appeal in 1960 had
been rejected by Dr. Cole, whose Amherst experience had made him see the
group as separatist. Nevertheless, B'nai B'rith served a purpose as interpreters of the Jewish tradition to the academic world, where so many of its
Jewish faculty and students had little contact with their own background. If
in the growing dissatisfaction with secularism there was the need to express
a 4,000-year tradition in contemporary terms, it was also necessary to see the
similarity and differences between Jewish and Christian values so that in an
atmosphere of tolerance the Jewish contribution was not simply swallowed
up. The 1976 grant went to fund lectures on Biblical, Holocaust, Israeli, historical, and religious topics. (*The Jewish Chatauqua Society,* New York City,
received $40,000 in 1967, 1972 for the same purpose.)

In 1969 an appeal was made for $35,000 for a program to reach dissident

Jewish students on university campuses. These students were alienated from the Jewish establishment, were involved in the New Left, in the crisis of Vietnam, the black revolution, and were a source of disruption, chaos, and anti-Semitism. How would it be possible to persuade these rebels to respect Jewish traditions and not to tear the campuses apart? The project was postponed and then forgotten, just as well, for the student agony of that year could not really be touched by the well-meaning earnestness of B'nai B'rith.

In 1967 we gave $60,000 to provide retraining and advanced study for rabbis and Hillel directors, similar to our program at Harvard and Episcopal Divinity School. To go straight from college to graduate school is to run learning into drudgery. Next to alcoholism, no disease is more destructive to intellectuals than the pursuit of the Ph.D. The generous scholar has traded in his youth, lost his hair and waistline, ruined his eyes, and left his wife a secret drinker and his children alienated and cynical because that old degree was so obviously more important to father than they were; and when at last he did receive his union card, his magic key, he was so narrowly enmeshed in his topic, so cut off from the rest of the world and any sympathy towards other humans, that he was really of no value as a teacher.

On the other hand, formal learning can be a longed for dream of the rabbi who has run a thousand meetings where the budget committee disputed over whether to use social action money for roof repair or the mortgage, shepherded hundreds of gawky pubescents through Bar Mitzvah recitations, asked men he scorned for more money than they wanted to give, ate and overate at banquets, and defended his support of Mrs. K over Mrs. Y as president of Hadassah, with a life of ceaseless care: phone calls at midnight from a parishioner afraid of death, talks with a boy on drugs, and a girl pregnant, until a coronary, a silent suicide—if no busybody doctor inteferes—frees him. To be able to study again, to recharge his mind so that he no longer preaches by computer with the same few buttons pressed to bring forth the same anecdotes, aphorisms, and quotations. The half a million or more dollars our Foundation invested in such retread fellowships, for rabbis and Protestant ministers, and for high school and college teachers, businessmen and doctors, was one of our best policies. In addition to this B'nai B'rith grant:

Synagogue Council of New York, New York, New York, 1961—$20,000 for reeducation of rabbis in the fields of counseling and administration where their old seminary-earned skills might seem obsolete.

Jewish Theological Seminary, New York, New York, 1965—$30,000 for further education of rabbis who have been away from the seminary for ten years or more.

Central Conference of American Rabbis, New York, New York, 1973, 1979—$40,000 for mid-career counseling.

We supported institutions that tried to preserve and disseminate Jewish culture.

Leo Baeck Institute, New York, New York, 1967, 1971—$25,000 for the cataloguing of its library. The Institute was established in 1955 to study all available materials on the history of German-speaking Jews: diaries, family papers, manuscripts of famous and ordinary people, photographs, tapes, and eyewitness accounts—what remains after the Nazi destruction.

Yivo Institute for Jewish Research, New York, New York, 1966, 1971—$35,000 to support research on the American Jewish community since the 1870s. Although most American Jews are descendants of immigrants from Eastern Europe, there are only limited facilities in American universities for the study of this culture.

American Jewish Historical Society, New York, New York, 1967–1977—$15,000 to build an archive of films made in Polish studios during the 1930s.

Young Men's and Young Women's Hebrew Association (YMHA), New York, New York, 1969, 1977—$35,000. The YMHA in particular was a center of Jewish cultural and social life in the city with its lectures, poetry readings, library, children's classes, and dance.

Jewish Museum, New York, New York, 1971, 1977—$45,000. This museum has a rich collection of historical and contemporary art and strongly involved itself in community life with children coming for classes in Bible archaeology and old ladies for classes in ceremonial needlework.

Judah Magnes Memorial Museum, Berkeley, California, 1972—$20,000. It was dedicated to the documentation of the influence of Jews on the development, character, and culture of the West, and who played a role out of all proportion to their numbers. The Museum was proposed to the Merrill Trust by Mortimer Fleishhacker, one of the leaders of San Francisco's Jewish community.

Institute for Yiddish Lexicology at CCNY, New York, New York, 1965–1972—$40,000. A poignant cause to which we made three grants, though there was no logical reason to justify our support. In 1953 the Institute had begun a ten-volume project to preserve the Yiddish language in dictionary form and make permanent all the richness and subtlety of the language, so meticulously that (almost) all its speakers would have died by the time the task was complete.

Again it is hard for gentiles to enter into the lost world of the Jewish past: Vilna, the "Jerusalem of Lithuania," where the shopkeepers were so pious that they sold their wares in Hebrew and memories of the great Yeshivas in Lemberg and Grodno that taught the rabbis who taught the rabbis of America and Canada. The Jewish Museum of New York put on an exhibit in 1980 of treasures from Dantzig. The congregation of that Baltic city knew they were doomed, and in early 1939 they sold the land of their synagogue and grave-yard for whatever it would bring and packed up all their ceremonial objects (including a memorial to the loyal soldiers who had given their lives in 1914–1918 for the Fatherland) and shipped them to Jewish Theological Seminary in New York for safe-keeping, with picture books of shtetl life, the annual forest picnic of the Sons of Zion, and Rabbi Meyersohn's new academy in Bialystok whose thirteen-year-olds have the faces of boys and girls I taught.

It still lives. "You're right; we take it very seriously," the young people assure and reassure their grandparents, and take them to Temple Youth's performance of "Fiddler on the Roof," but there is heartbreak in trying to find this vanished world.

It is hard for gentiles to evaluate the Jewish school, but for a minority wishing to prevent its own values from being swallowed up in the great American pudding (which fears the end, perhaps within three generations, of Jewish identity through intermarriage and family limitation) a separate school system is critical. For many children in the soft suburbs, the Hebrew school they attend in the afternoon is their only exposure to intellectual rigor.

Bais Yaakov School for Girls, Baltimore, Maryland, 1963—$15,000. The only Jewish education project we received that was directed to female needs. Let's face it, traditional Judaism considers women as second-class citizens.

Hebrew Academy of San Francisco, 1979—$20,000 for a child-care program for the growing number of single-parent families as well as scholarships for the children of recent emigré families from Russia. Such a school would strengthen their Jewish identity as the public schools would not, though one result was that the poor kids were forced to learn two brand new languages at the same time. The Russians I knew were a difficult group to deal with, for the newcomers were suspicious of authority and yet had lived all their lives in a totally structured society (the KGB, after all, did care about what they did) and could not cope with loss of status where the engineer in Leningrad found himself—for how long?—a repairman in Boston.

The Merrill Trust made many grants, detailed elsewhere, to the needs of the Jewish elderly, to troubled families and adolescents, and over $1 million to Jewish hospitals, which were sometimes put in the medical, sometimes in the Jewish category. Through Dr. Melvin Krant of Brookline, Massachusetts, three grants went in different channels for university, temple, and hospice projects involved with the needs of bereaved and dying persons, wherein the traditional Jewish acceptance of death offered something to American culture, which pretends it doesn't exist.

The Trust also involved itself in trying to rebuild the alliance between Jews and Negroes. As outsiders Jews had traditionally been sensitive to mainstream America's mistreatment of blacks. Every institution of black progress had always received major Jewish support. When a black man was accused of a crime, it was a Jewish lawyer who defended him. It was the progressive northern schools and colleges with a strong Jewish influence, like my own, that went out of their way to welcome Negro students. The liberal wing of the Democratic party of Roosevelt, Truman, Stevenson, and Humphrey was built on the alliance of Jew and Negro.

Our Foundation gave sustained support to such alliance institutions: $270,000 to the *National Urban League;* $175,000 to the *United Negro College Fund;* $45,000 to the *Herbert Lehman Fund* within the NAACP to train black lawyers from the South, as well as to an endless number of minority scholarship programs at schools ranging from Francis Parker in Chicago ($65,000) to Manhattan Country School ($40,000). In the 1960s, we made many small grants designed to maintain that alliance, a force for civility and responsibility in American life worth supporting by a foundation neither black nor Jewish.

Temple Beth Jacob, Redwood City, California, 1979—$10,000 to rebuild the temple in a suburb south of San Francisco, burnt down by vandals. Back to the most traditional need of Jewish charity.

CONCLUSIONS

One evening around 1960, at an M.I.T. fraternity house in Boston, I listened to a badly worn pastor of the Bohemian Brethren speak on what it was like to lead a Christian congregation in a communist country. The big church in Prague had always been filled during the bourgeois 1930s: employees nodded respectfully to their employers, young men to the parents of their fiancees, and housewives worried about the Sunday roast. Now times were different. Christianity was written off though officially tolerated if it acted carefully, and the building was rarely a quarter full. But the congregation knew why it came. As the pastor stated: "We try to speak honestly about serious things."

In discussing religion that's where one begins—as the pastor, the member of the congregation, and the rich man with the checkbook, who all have experienced enough of life to respect the misfortunes that may allow one to think more clearly than in fat times.

Preserving the Future

The simplest use of money, "in dread of leaving an illiterate ministry to the churches when our present ministry shall be in the dust," is to train new leadership. Seminarians have always been poor, but in our times tuitions have risen so high, any form of government support has been so sorely cut that they must work long hours to pay their bills and are so burdened by debt that they must often ask whether all of this is worth it. An extra one or two thousand in financial aid makes a lot of difference.

And the church needs new sorts of leaders who demand more and offer more: women who are no longer accepting their historical status as faithful subordinates, blacks, Hispanics who insist that Christianity should help change an unjust society, and older men and women who have rethought their values and chosen new careers. Dulled ministers and rabbis in the middle of their work lives desperately need resharpening.

The Sharing of Pain

Reaganite Christians begin each day with their favorite Gospel verse: "To them that have shall be given, from them that have not shall be taken even that which they have" (Matthew 13:12). Other Christians are less upbeat about that.

The traditional message to the poor of just about all religions has been to emphasize the spiritual essence of existence. This may be interpreted to mean that if salvation is the only thing that matters, it is distracting to ask for higher wages. Or it may also be interpreted that the soul cannot be twisted and jeopardized by hopeless injustice: "Where there is no bread there is no Torah" (Pirke Aboth 3:21). The good shepherd helps his flock endure life's unavoidable pain. He helps them attain greater autonomy and dignity within the framework of their lives, but he has the duty also of showing them ways of changing that framework, which can include the demand for higher wages. And he helps his affluent sheep understand the social framework of their own lives and points out practical things they can do to make existence more bearable for other people.

It's a terrible thing to be poor in our country. Poor Americans do not sleep on the sidewalks as in Calcutta, but they suffer a particular pain of invisibility. Their own misery is measured against the comforts taken for granted in the hours of television they watch. Their lives do not really exist.

Apartheid is not a word used to describe class relations in the United States, but it has a reality in Chicago as well as Johannesburg. One duty of the pastor is, from personal awareness, to point this out to his comfortable parishioners and then to demand the resources with which to do something about it.

Speaking Truth to Power

Life in Poland may be more humanly bearable than in other communist countries because the strength of the Catholic church allows a means of standing up to the sheer mass of state authority. It offers both discipline and hope as well as a means for reaching out to others. One does not exist in atomized, impotent despair. Even in East Germany, a strait-jacketed land, the government wishes to enjoy minimal good relations with the Lutheran church, and under church protection a fragile peace movement whispers, very carefully, that perhaps both sides are to blame.

In Latin America, there is the power of the police and the state, the army (behind them mountain ranges of wealth, starting with local landowners and businessmen), and then the international banks and corporations. At the end, there is the ultimate reality of American military force, which includes the contra terrorists in Honduras who attack Nicaraguan schools and health centers. One Christian response to this sequence of power is Liberation Theology. It is the duty of the church to join the struggle against injustice even, when no other means exist, if that involves supporting armed revolution. It is only by being ready to join the revolution that the church has any hope of retaining its authority.

Predictably, the papacy condemns this reasoning. To fight against suffering only within the framework of class war leads to one more Marxist dictatorship. Better neighborhood clinics may be bought at too high a price.

American Christians have had their own experience in speaking truth to power. Fifteen and twenty years ago the braver of them gave leadership to the civil rights and antiwar struggles. Some are involved now in the Sanctuary movement, trying to protect Central American refugees against the police of the Immigration and Naturalization Service, in the process risking serious jail sentences. They aren't amateurs.

Liberation Theology has to mean what it says. If the only tyranny it fights is that represented by the capitalist system, fascist police, and everywhere of course American imperialism, then where do the Christians of Poland and

East Germany fit in? We fight the enemy closest to hand. The desperate young man in Soweto throwing rocks at the South African police isn't expected to be a political philosopher.

Nevertheless, we are trying to build a new generation of Christian leadership; we respect the simplicity of moral conviction; but we must demand an intellectual depth that just doesn't operate at the two-dimensional level of political thought today, whether left or right.

Network television, a nuclear waste dump, a transnational corporation that moves its plant from Cleveland to Sao Paulo without a thought to those left behind, or a new Pentagon weapons system represents power that a Christian must be able to recognize and know how to combat. So do the bureaucratic controls, police authority, betrayal, and lies of a communist state.

The foundation executive, accordingly, sits down and tries to work out a series of summer programs where the earnest young pastor works in a clinic in El Salvador, a branch office of Merrill Lynch and Company, and hitchhikes from Gdansk to Budapest.

Reconciliation

The "official" Christian has often not even understood what this word means. In the city of Belfast, for example, the most creative religious gesture one might perform would be to burn every Catholic and Protestant church to the ground. But if we are to escape the bondage of good guys and bad guys, the laws that state who are our brethren and who are not really even human beings, I suppose we have to begin with the church.

"In Jesus Christ there is neither Greek nor Jew." In Nazi Germany there were Catholic and Protestant pastors who interpreted that statement by St. Paul to mean that a baptised Jew remained a member of the congregation. No matter what the Nuremberg Laws stated, he could not be asked to leave. It was a narrow line. It said nothing about the rights of unbaptised Jews. But it was a doctrine of the church, if one had the courage to say so, and hundreds of priests and ministers—no bishops—suffered imprisonment, even death, to uphold it.

Who else? In how many services is one asked to say prayers for our brothers and sisters the Arabs, the Russians, the Afrikaners and the blacks who strike back at them, no better or worse than ourselves? For our brothers in bondage to drugs, in bondage with AIDS, or in bondage to violence as the terrorist who plants a bomb or the terrorist who sweeps in with his fighter plane and wipes out a whole village? For our sisters on welfare who sit at home with their fatherless children?

What I am trying to say is that if Jewish or Christian belief means the willingness to speak honestly about serious things, then one tries to strengthen this honesty and seriousness in any way that comes to hand. Sometimes it means by way of the institution: the school, the church, the agency, or the program. There are good ones. They can be found—sometimes through the individual woman and man of courage and selflessness, and sometimes a whole congregation turn themselves, for a moment, into saints. But it isn't necessary to be satisfied with the ordinary.

CHAPTER FIVE

Reaching to the Outsider

Those who accomplish the greatest results are always calm, self-possessed, patient, and polite. [Booker T. Washington]

White folk eat de apple, Black folk eat de co'. [Langston Hughes]

If we can't sit at the table of democracy, we'll knock the fucking legs off. [James Forman]

The dream is in the process and not the outcome. [Mel King]

Look, we've done enough for those guys. If they can make it, fine. If they can't, that's their problem." [Nashville publisher quoted by Richard Reeves in *American Journey* 1979 (p. 133).]

BLACK AND WHITE

The Merrill Trust's major commitment to black needs was in the field of education: to give school kids, graduate students, businessmen, and artists special support, whether in black, mixed, or largely white institutions, so that they could make something of their lives, train themselves to serve their people, and be useful citizens of our country. The trustees had their preferences and prejudices, but essentially our policy was to supply the tools. How those tools were used was the responsibility of the users.

We sought to build black institutions not only to serve individuals but to be sources of pride, strength, cohesion, and leadership within the black community. Here the main commitment was the $1.4 million to the federation of six institutions of the Atlanta University Center. In one way, this was sizable, with the largest single grant being $500,000 to establish a chair of economics at Morehouse College; in another way it should have been doubled if we were really committed to building a center of leadership quality. No matter how high a black may rise within a white institution, to become head of the Ford Foundation or a dean at Harvard, star at the Metropolitan Opera or ambassador, he is dependent on the decisions made ultimately by whites. Whether one believes in integrated or separate versions of society, blacks must have the option of working within institutions that they themselves control.

Our third goal was to relieve some of the misery of black life in America: medical services and food for poor families in Washington, support for women coming out of the Florida prison system, and working capital for a ceramics company in Mississippi so that small-town blacks could support themselves and not flee to the northern cities.

Our grants came out of the contradictory mix of feelings that all Americans have towards blacks. The man who supplied our Foundation's resources was moved in these same contradictory ways. All his life Charles E. Merrill retained the prejudices of his Florida and Mississippi background, though the prejudices of the North were not all that different. His image of a democratic society was the crowd that sat on the bleachers of the West Palm Beach ballpark. A lot of folk were excluded from that group. But he was proud of his grandfather, Riley Merrill, who had fought under Grant and Sherman, the only white Republican in Green Cove Springs (a carpetbagger?—my father would have been shocked by the word), who followed another definition of democracy by teaching at two black churches each Sunday morning. Free men ought to know how to read and write.

My father respected Amherst College's commitment to its black students. As an old man his closest friend was his Negro valet, and on their Atlantic crossings Leroy, called Mr. Ali from Pakistan, sat next to him at table. His last few winters were spent in Barbados, and when Samuel Levine (the great heart specialist from Boston) came to visit, my father invited every doctor on the island, half of them black, to the dinner in his honor.

Our grants were motivated partly by fear—a fear of black anger as expressed by crime, by riots, or even just by words. The riots of the 1960s probably brought whatever movement toward racial justice there was in American society. It made whites ask what price they would be willing to pay to keep them from recurring. Generosity was also motivated by better reasons. If white Americans have made even the most purely verbal commitment to democracy and Christianity, they cannot retain self-respect if they do not treat black people with fairness—the reasoning of Martin Luther King. And if the ideals of democracy and Christianity were carried out with any creativity during the 1960s and 1970s, that came to a large extent not only out of the force of black demands but also out of the example of black leadership.

America's commitment to racial equality and social change as a policy of the federal government has ended. The unimportant philanthropic foundation I am writing about is also ended. In the large and small framework one asks what has been accomplished. Were individuals, families, institutions, and communities helped to achieve a tangible, sustained step up? In some cases, yes. And yet the black community is so fragile, so vulnerable to outside pressures and to strains within that the combination of hard times and an unsympathetic national government brings greater misery in the 1980s than at almost any time in American history.

Does the consensus become that government—and perhaps philanthropy—should stop trying to serve the losers and join the winners? I try to measure what this particular foundation tried to accomplish against all the new disheartening facts. For example, by the 1980s there had come a sizable drop in black enrollment in both black and white colleges, an even greater drop in graduate schools, from thinner financial aid from families and colleges and government programs, from steadily poorer public secondary education, and from lack of hope. The support the Merrill Trust and others had given black colleges—and it was never much—had leached away.

A black politician like Mel King, who had been elected to the Massachusetts state house out of his long-term reputation as an honest, clear-minded social worker and who twice ran unsuccessfully for mayor of Boston, was left with the conclusion that the one piece of capital that blacks had permanently accumulated in the last twenty years was political skill. They had a better idea of how the system worked and how to get what they wanted.

Statistical Accuracy

"How much money did the Merrill Trust give to black causes and institutions? What was the percentage of such gifts to your overall total? How did those figures compare with what you gave Hispanics (broken down further between Puerto Ricans and Mexican Americans)?" These are relevant questions, and just about impossible to answer.[1]

The problem begins simply: add up the grants to Morehouse and Meharry, UNCF and NAACP, Martin Luther King scholarships at Scarborough Valley School, and the grant to encourage black geologists. If you're careful, these are the figures you are looking for. The large gifts from the Trust for endowment to my school, Commonwealth, gave us the resources to stick our neck

---

1. Statistical logic is hard to attain. If one gives $25,000 to the collection of Judaica at York University, Toronto, should this be placed within the Jewish category, the Canadian, or the one for libraries?

out, and for fifteen years or so half of our financial aid was allotted to our 9 to 11 percent black students. I can't think, however, of what percentage to put from these endowment funds into the black category.

Or from the hundreds of thousands of dollars given to settlement houses in New York City, job placement and drug programs, prison education, and the institutions that serve the nonwhite urban poor, including Jewish hospitals like Michael Reese in Chicago and Mount Sinai in New York. East Harlem Protestant Parish served both Puerto Ricans and blacks, as did New York Theological Seminary.

In 1971 we gave $40,000 to Boston City Hospital to support cardiovascular research by John Norman, a black thoracic surgeon. Along with our grants to the health care schools at Meharry, Morehouse, and Howard, this would make a tidy addition to our record of investment in black medical leadership. For Dr. Norman, however, the only social relevance of that grant, besides its use to him personally, was to strengthen the research component of City Hospital so that it did not become a sort of medical McDonald's offering fast grade-B service to the poor. To call support of his work part of the Trust's commitment to blacks would have seemed to him irrelevant or demeaning.

I don't want to belabor this point of statistical ambiguity. Comprehensive, accurate figures would be a useful way to measure the Trust's priorities and provide a base point for other foundations. The projects discussed in this chapter do add up to $5.3 million.

The Black College

"By almost any standards these 100 colleges are academic disaster areas." This statement by Christopher Jencks and David Riesman in an article, "The American Negro College," written in 1967 for the *Harvard Education Review*, was probably the most damning single criticism that these colleges had to face. Jencks and Riesman were neither amateurs nor bigots. The facts that they cited—authoritarian, often reactionary leadership, an often poorly educated faculty, limited physical resources, and a badly prepared student body from whom little was expected—were all ones that any individual who had had extended contact with such institutions recognized as true. Strengthened by the prestige of its Harvard platform, this attack by two well-known sociologists on the basic institutions of black education (and there weren't many) added up to a discouraging picture that the drive for black equality was being opposed not only by its traditional enemies—"you teach a nigger to read and you spoil a good cotton picker"—but by the liberals who were supposed to be its allies.

It is too easy for whites to walk away from any serious involvement in black problems. By the 1980s the most tangible spending by the Reagan administration that connected government and blacks was the program to build new prisons. Therefore it is worthwhile to review the grants made by a medium-sized and often amateurish foundation like our own: what did we try to accomplish, and how did our goals work out in reality?

The black educator who had the greatest impact upon my own ideas was Benjamin Mays, president of Morehouse College for twenty-six years. When he started school in the most backward part of South Carolina, his teacher marveled at the way he could, at the age of six, already read a bit and write and spell and announced publicly in church that Bennie was smart and would do great things someday. "I realized that God had called me to do something worthwhile in the world," he repeated over and over. "This birthright of equality is given by God. No society had the right to smother ambition, to destroy incentive, to stifle growth, to curb motivation, and to circumscribe the mind."[2] That fierce belief in equality and opportunity he tried to share with every student whom he met represented the ideal of every black educator at his best.

The issue for black colleges was not the admissions standards required of entering freshmen. They hardly existed. The standards of importance were those expected of graduating seniors. The best had to be prepared to enter the best white graduate schools anywhere, and they would prove the quality of their education and the potential of their race by the Ph.D.'s and M.D.'s that they earned.

The Merrill Trust gave $2.3 million to black colleges (including $175,000 to the United Negro College Fund).

Morehouse College, Atlanta, Georgia, 1958–1980—$865,000 (+ $55,000 to the Medical School). Morehouse was passed only by Harvard, Amherst, Hampshire, and Penn (if one excludes business schools) in the colleges we supported. I was chairman of its board of trustees for sixteen years, chosen by Dr. Mays partly because I had money and was committed to education and to racial equality, but also because I lived in Boston, a safe distance. Unlike an Atlanta businessman, I wouldn't get in the way.

The Morehouse of the 1950s was a college vastly different from mainstream places. It had a formal society. American institutions run, by and large, on a first-name basis, but at Morehouse I still said "Dr. Jones" to the man I had known for twenty years, and I never became used to addressing a sixteen-year-old freshman as "Mr. Williams." It was an island within the old South where every human being in it, from dean of faculty to youngest student and assistant janitor, was treated with dignity. The faculty was mixed, and though some fields like biology, chemistry, religion, and French were covered by

2. Charles Willie and Ronald Edmonds, *Black Colleges in America* (New York: Columbia University, Teachers College Press, 1978), p. 24.

blacks, physics and math were staffed by Indians, whose educational system turned out more theoretical scientists than the economy of Bombay could employ. There were Jewish refugees, Chinese who could not get jobs elsewhere, and northern whites in sociology or psychology who saw teaching at Morehouse as a way of fighting the American system and who could be stimulating and destructive as they worked out their personal problems in that role. Some faculty couples on that isolated campus were of mixed marriages. A few white southerners, often remarkable individuals, taught there out of Christian conviction.

In an institution proud of balancing its budget every year but doing so on a shoestring, the process of financial control bordered on the grotesque. Money assigned for roof repairs went for office equipment if that bill came first. When money was obtained for the typewriters, it might be lent instead to a desperate student who had to hand the registrar $300 by sundown. The business manager, who kept all these wheels more or less turning and who more or less could find, if he had to, the right papers in the mess on his desk, was an infuriating sort of person. When he eventually was fired, it was hard to find out what the college actually owed and what were its assets, yet it was only by such sleight of hand that an institution always so short of cash could survive.

The first Merrill Trust grant was $100,000 in 1959 to be spent on faculty salaries over five years. Dr. Thomas, the Trust's administrator, had felt that the faculty under Dr. Mays' leadership was adequate but badly needed leadership from professors with strong abilities in research and writing. There was a need for lighter teaching loads and a formal pattern of raises to allow the teachers some economic hope.

$20,000 in 1965 went for financial aid. The new welcome for blacks on almost every American campus meant that the resources of colleges far richer than Morehouse were being used to recruit black students. The Negro colleges, Mays said, were fighting for their lives to attract and hold on to their most talented students.

By 1970, when the Trust gave $50,000 for scholarships and faculty raises, conditions had become worse. Both private gifts and government funding had been reduced. Liberal white institutions were threatening Morehouse's existence not simply by attracting the good students but by hiring away their ablest faculty. Every white college needed black professors to get government and foundation support, to reassure students of their social commitment, and to beat out competition in this new status race. The Atlanta University Center was turned into a game preserve.

With a new president, Hugh Gloster, who had formerly been dean of faculty at Hampton Institute, a man with Dr. Mays' moral strengths and social convictions but with a more pragmatic style, the new problem of black nationalism had arisen. Knowledge existed and had relevance only as it applied directly to black needs. The thrust of a Morehouse education at its best had been to expose its students, no matter how poor or how poorly prepared, to the whole range of world culture, from Boyle's law to Keynesian economics, to which they had the right of entrance. Dr. Mays gave religious value to the Ph.D. as the symbol of attainment and authority, and more graduates of Morehouse had earned it than those of any other black college in the country. The new militants, however, stated that Boyle and Keynes were honkies, and that anything they said, as far as blacks were concerned, was bullshit. Morehouse was simply a representative of the Colonial Office of the power center on Wall Street, keeping the natives in line.

By the fall of 1968 the campus was under siege, not by its traditional white enemies but by these new black warriors. All that year Dr. Gloster worked eighteen-hour days, keeping in touch with real or rhetorical complaints, trying to respond to each new crisis, answering 2 A.M. phone calls that he'd better quit or Afrika was going to get him. In our meeting of April 1969 black power collided with the board of trustees. The young blacks in blue and white striped robes, led by an instructor of sociology at Spelman who was calling himself Brother Abdul, carrying a chicken claw as a sign of authority, strode into the boardroom and ordered us to appropriate one million dollars to establish a Martin Luther King, Jr. University of Black Culture and then resign. With control of Morehouse they could go on to control every other college in the Atlanta Center and convert the combined endowments, $20 million or more, to leadership of the black revolution in Amerikkka.

Along with the concern of elderly trustees for access to the toilet, our fear of the potential hysteria of the Spelman women who were the spear-carriers of the takeover and carried pressure-cans of hair spray and black paint in their belts (to use against our eyes, I learned later, in case of violence) and the urgent whispers to persuade hard-line trustees not to call the Atlanta police who would have had to fight their way into the building, torn the college apart, and put Brother Abdul on the front page of the *New York Times*, there were also serious conversations between the two parties about our role as trustees and our concepts of education and American democracy. Behind their rhetoric, a majority of our captors were young men and women who for the first time in their lives had forced authority—rich white authority usually walled off and distant—to speak directly with them.

After twenty-nine hours of wrangling, we released an agreement to bring faculty, students, and community representatives onto the board. The student trustees elected as spokesmen of revolutionary change came to interest themselves in details like more parking space for student cars and the right to entertain Spelman girls in their bedrooms.

I resigned from the chairmanship in 1973. The college and its fund-raising had become larger than I could deal with, and more emphasis was being placed on expansion, I felt, than on upgrading quality. I seemed to have lost touch with the part of Morehouse, faculty and students, most important to me.

In 1972, however, the Trust gave $500,000 to endow a chair in economics. This would strengthen the faculty and allow graduates to enter the American mainstream. At the same time I hoped that the college might avoid the homogenized orthodoxy of Samuelson Keynesianism and that the professor might show analytical toughness in examining the exploitiveness of American capitalism. Sometimes insecurity forces blacks to be all too conservative.

$100,000 went in 1977 to help complete the construction of a multipurpose administration building connected to a chapel named for Martin Luther King, Jr., the sort of financial dead weight year after year that sends college presidents to a blessedly final stroke.

$40,000 in 1980 to financial aid. Hard times were devastating the families— skilled auto workers in Detroit, black businessmen in Atlanta—who traditionally sent their sons to Morehouse. More help was now coming from the white business community in Atlanta, less and less from the federal government. As the 1980s were proving to be such a dangerous decade for all private black colleges, with falling enrollments and operating deficits met out of endowment, Morehouse's ability to survive became that much more important. Under Gloster, as under Mays, there was the same toughness, pride, and resourcefulness. The students shared the same historical arrogance that not only was a Morehouse Man a boon to all womankind but someone with the skill and determination to make it and, to varying extents, with some sense of obligation to those who hadn't made it. The Merrill Trust's somewhat grudging commitment to this college had involved us in the never-ending struggle for black survival in this strange land.

Spelman College, Atlanta, Georgia, 1963–1980—$147,000. Spelman, named after John D. Rockefeller's mother and always backed by the Rockefeller family, was Morehouse's sister institution across the street. The colleges shared courses—education, drama, Spanish at Spelman; sciences, economics, French at Morehouse—and a fair number of administrative functions. Their graduates traditionally married each other. There was a petty side to Spelman life: the light-skin-color in-fighting to be chosen Miss Maroon and White, a heavy gentility, and the cold-blooded careerism to marry an up-and-coming doctor and land a suburban home in Atlanta or Durham. On the other hand, out of Spelman came the YWCA directors, teachers, librarians, and nurses of black America when that was as high as a black woman could aspire and later on doctors, lawyers, government officials, and business executives.

The Trust's first $25,000 was to improve physical facilities, enrich the curriculum, strengthen the faculty, and enlarge financial aid. Only 8 percent of the graduates then went into graduate school as against 50 percent at Morehouse. The college's growing reputation was enlarging its drawing power and yet that did not allow the opportunity to improve student quality, reasoned the president, Albert Manley, because except for the top 5 or 10 percent, the great majority who came out of the black public schools were so uniformly poorly prepared. (The 1965 SAT average was verbal 363, math 325, and Spelman was America's leading college for black women.) In 1966 Dr. Manley applied for another $25,000 to introduce black elementary and secondary students in the general region to the arts. He wanted to reduce the cultural hardships of the average student who entered a college like Spelman, a lag that came from poor facilities and inadequate teachers, but Merrill trustees thought that the arts were unimportant to blacks, and the money was given for general purposes. $10,000 was awarded in 1972, however, for the purchase of work by black artists.

$40,000 in 1971 and $30,000 in 1975 went for financial aid, the latter in the social sciences. Spelman was suffering in the same way as Morehouse while talent scouts, not only from Smith and Barnard but from Emory and Duke, were trying to recruit bright black girls. But with affirmative action policies opening up all sorts of interesting jobs in government agencies and private institutions, there was a great need for black women with good training in economics and sociology. In 1976 Dr. Manley was replaced by Donald Stewart, an able, thoughtful young man from Chicago. (Why not a black woman? some faculty demanded. Five years ahead there would be all sorts of qualified women available, but not, it seemed, then.) Our last grant of $15,000 in 1980 went for endowment. In a way this was to sharpen the leadership thrust of one of the very few black colleges in the United States with financial resources (in 1982 with $21 million Spelman had the second largest endowment of any black private college) and a sense of confidence; yet with the special vulnerability of blacks at the slightest downturn in the American economy, this grant was also to reach out to girls too quick to abandon their hopes of a good education.

During the mid-1980s I put in three teaching stints at Spelman, which allowed somewhat of an insider's point of view of the black college. Compare *Cherry Orchard* and *Doll's House*. How do the same messages of resignation and defiance come out in Lorraine Hansberry's *Raisin in the Sun*, read last month? How does Socrates needle the good people of Athens? How would he needle the assumptions of Reagan's America, of Spelman College? Define *heresy*, define *treason*. Under what conditions would the same troublemaker be guilty of both?

At its worst, teaching there can be like pouring glue. All their lives most of these students have sat passively in large classrooms. They have no feelings for themselves as intelligent beings. They were never given this kind of dignity and lack the nerve to lay claim to it. A crippling pragmatism deadens intellectual curiosity. Will this topic be on the test? Will it help me get a job? Their basic education is television, and they have little factual knowledge at all of the outside world. In fact, how many teachers bother to check how accurately they can read or whether they can use a dictionary?

And yet if a teacher listens when a sparkling student makes contact after class, the best of these young women are wonderful, with a hunger—joyful and aching—for learning despite family deprivation, lack of money, poor preparations, and the disapproval of their friends. Someone had always pushed them on: there's nothing you can't do! Aim for the best. Don't make compromises.

This is the sort of student that a Spelman is created for, and asks money for: an elite education for the nonelite. I was interested, too, by the number of girls previously successful at mixed or white schools who had deliberately chosen a black institution: "I wanted to learn more about my own people." Or, unvoiced, to have less contact with the tensions that whites impose?

Clark College, Atlanta, Georgia, 1973—$25,000. Clark was looked down upon by Morehouse as a jock school, and if they won the football and basketball matches, it was because their athletes were not hampered by studies. Nevertheless, under an energetic, not overly refined president named Vivian Henderson, Clark built a strong, community-involved local science department, established in 1967 a Center for Studies in Public Policy that served as a service center for elected black officials in Georgia, maintained a Washington intern program, and studied practical problems like the impact of expressways upon black neighborhoods.

Interdenominational Theological School (ITS), Atlanta, Georgia, 1961– 1975—$80,000. ITS was a great opportunity to build an interdenominational school in a region plagued by rigid sectarianism. The school was planned and overplanned during the 1960s with, in typical Atlanta University Center style, more attention paid to what would happen if it failed than if it succeeded. A forgotten detail, however, was the mediocrity of its president. He was primarily interested, it seemed, in the size of the conference table in the always-locked boardroom, the grandeur of the safe when there was nothing to put inside it, and the number of books in the hodge-podge library of castoffs from every sort of northern donor. During the ferment of the civil rights and antiwar movement, ITS played about a zero role.

Atlanta University, Atlanta, Georgia, 1960–1966—$125,000. For a long time Atlanta University, founded 1865 in a boxcar, was the leading institution of the AUC. A weaker part of Dr. Mays' makeup was fear that he was looked down upon by Rufus Clement, and the two elderly presidents wrangled with each other at board meetings (one argument was over whose institution controlled a janitorial closet in the common administration building) like dinosaurs. Dr. Clement was the first black elected to a city school board in the South and became so much a part of the establishment that for three years he blocked the election of M. L. King, Jr. to the Morehouse board as "a slap in the face of white Atlanta."

During 1960 to 1963, the Trust made a grant of $70,800 for a three-year program of graduate training of high school teachers in the humanities and social sciences, the sort of support to the public schools that our Trust should have involved itself in at a much higher level but didn't.

$30,000 in 1960 went to back Dean Westerfield of the School of Business in his effort to recruit and train African administrators in the fundamentals of production, marketing, statistics, analysis, and public policy, a program that included supervised internships with Atlanta business firms. Americans are always convinced that teaching natives useful skills will free them from their addiction to rhetoric. It seemed a well-thought-out project at the (brief) time when African needs were taken seriously.

$25,000 was given in 1966 to strengthen the Department of Economics to raise salaries and reduce the impact of raiding by white universities. As management training positions become available to blacks, companies found it hard to locate candidates with the capacity and education for such work.

When Clement resigned around 1967 he was replaced by a weak successor, and the strength of AU's graduate training in education, business, social work, and science was undercut by Georgia State, offering the same courses to an integrated student body at a fraction of AU's cost. To meet annual deficits the university, as did Fisk and too many other black institutions, had to draw down its endowment (which dropped by 1981 from eight million to one million), and the future for this valuable university is in doubt.

Atlanta University Center Corporation, Atlanta, Georgia, 1972, 1977—$125,000. In the effort to weld the separate units of the center into a federal structure, like the Claremont colleges in California or Toronto University, the AUCC received major support from Ford, Rockefeller, and the federal government. The Center had its own power plant, library, cultural and academic programs (courses in Ibo and Swahili), student services (psychological counseling, job placement), relations with nonmember schools like Georgia Tech, central purchasing, and security. Institutional foot dragging, presidential egomania, and unequal standards produced a glue-slow willingness to respond to Ford's possible offer of $10 million. There was a chance to make the AUC a leader in black, Southern, and American education, and yet one could understand local resentment at the condescending authoritarianism of the Ford Foundation, which disregarded the fierce independence of which the students and alumni were so proud while graciously deciding to build up the AUCC and letting lesser colleges wither away. The major resource of the Center would be the new library to which the Merrill Trust gave $50,000 in 1972 for land purchase and $75,000 in 1977 for construction, next to Howard's the richest black library in the United States.

Tougaloo College, Jackson, Mississippi, 1964–1980—$70,000. Despite its poverty, intellectual as much as financial, and its isolation, Tougaloo had been a bastion of black independence within the dangerous world of white Mississippi. During Freedom Summer of 1964 it became a fortress for blacks and their white allies who were fighting for change. To strengthen the college's resources, a radical transfusion program was organized for that summer: Tougaloo staff members went to northern universities for intensive schooling while white volunteers, professors and graduate students, mainly from Brown and Harvard, came south to replace them. The Merrill Foundation put up $20,000 to help meet costs of both groups.

The Negro reaction was a human one, not gratitude but raging resentment at this colonial status. The qualities that had given dignity and value to Tougaloo under white pressure—its biracial faculty and the independence and universality of its intellectual concerns—became targets of the new breed of nationalists. Soul values denied the concept of universal values. Malcolm X and Eldridge Cleaver were the writers to study and above all, Franz Fanon, the Martinique-born psychiatrist who saw the white liberal intellectual as far more dangerous to the black soul than the most brutal colonialist. History became a fantasy Africa of peaceful villages, warrior queens, and the circles of wise old men until destroyed by the whites.

Brown, "bleeding from the ears" as its chaplain stated, quit the partnership. But even after the adolescent rage of black nationalism began to ebb, the college's needs remained, and the Merrill Trust appropriated a total of $50,000 more for scholarships in 1976 and 1980. There were new opportunities for blacks in business, even in Mississippi, and 40 percent of the black doctors, dentists, and lawyers in that state were Tougaloo graduates. Nevertheless, little support for such black colleges came from the federal government and white corporations.[3] With 62 percent of Tougaloo families earning less than $5,000 in the mid-1970s, the first priority, as always, was survival. The stated tuition figure was fantasy, and financial aid (to 96 percent of the students) was subsidized by low faculty salaries and the deadly habit of de-

3. UNCF figures for 1971–1972: of $223 million given by corporations to all colleges, the black ones received $4 million. Of federal aid of $4.9 billion, only $170 million went to black institutions.

ferred maintenance. And yet corporate support rose from $42,000 in 1975 to $305,000 in 1980, and alumni support rose from $5,000 and 6 percent to $100,000 and 31 percent. Between 1965 and 1975, 50 percent of the graduates were completing an advanced degree with a new interest in business administration, communications, engineering, and politics. But when the black economy within a state as poor as Mississippi turned down even further in the 1980s, Tougaloo saw all its advances jeopardized, and enrollment had fallen to 775 in 1982 and 600 in 1983. Other foundations had become tired, as the Merrill Trust had, of these never-ending appeals.

Rust College, Holly Springs, Mississippi, 1971–1977—$50,000. Rust is a tangible step below Tougaloo, and the philosopher kings at Ford and Rockefeller wondered whether the Rust Colleges should not simply be allowed to die. In 1967 it acquired a driving president, William McMillan, however, who in four years increased the value of the physical plant from two to eight million, the operating budget from $840,000 to $2.2 million, and the enrollment from 490 to 720. The SAT average stayed around 300 (388 at Spelman) and the Otis IQ at 101, details which did not occupy Dr. McMillan in his struggle to finish the library, put up a fine arts center, improve the quality of teaching by workshops, seminars, and better salaries, and expand programs in nursing, engineering, and computer science.

Mississippi Industrial College, Holly Springs, Mississippi, 1979—$5,000. Even weaker than Rust, founded in 1905 by a local man using his own resources and those from farmers, teachers, ministers, and storekeepers, Mississippi Industrial was the only entirely black founded and operating college in Mississippi. Its dean of faculty was a Commonwealth and Brandeis graduate, the son of a local garage mechanic, who wanted to train skilled factory- and office-workers for jobs in Memphis, where openings were beginning to come for young blacks who had the qualifications.

Miles College, Birmingham, Alabama, 1964, 1971—$55,000. Miles had been a nothing institution, a low-cost, open-door commuter college in a shabby collection of buildings in the ghetto of Birmingham that had lost its accreditation in 1958 because its library, faculty, and science facilities were below standard. Nevertheless, it provided 40 percent of the teachers serving 225,000 blacks in the metropolitan area. Its students tried to supply the same leadership of the civil rights struggle in that brutal and dangerous city that Morehouse and Spelman students had in Atlanta. Miles was given distinction when John Monro, the dean of Harvard College and a man of great moral strength, went and stayed for a dozen years to teach composition there to freshmen for whom formal English was a foreign language.

As Monro wrote in the late 1970s: "Our freshmen are invisible to the selective colleges, yet they can be taught to think straight, to deal with reasonably complicated information, and to write out their thoughts in clear, comprehensive, standard English prose. Fifteen to twenty percent of these invisible students are clearly able to do demanding college work, and the good colleges lose out because they don't know how to find or to handle them. There is a need for a close, professional scrutiny of the students' resources, a program of teaching that deals with their needs, and a competent, dedicated faculty. What we should emulate is the way that Malcolm X in a prison cell in Massachusetts started to educate himself by copying out one page a day from the dictionary. Liberal white colleges in the North aren't willing to do this for the badly trained Negro students they admit and then flunk out."[4]

The Merrill Trust gave $25,000 toward construction of a science building, needed for Miles to regain accreditation, and $30,000 for operating expenses. The experience of Miles College and the contribution of John Monro in the education of ghetto blacks—demanding results, not simply going through the motions and then retreating into despair—are worth more national attention than they have received.

Talladega College, Talladega, Alabama, 1969, 1979—$55,000. This college, 50 miles east of Birmingham, was always respected for its academic standards despite its small size (700 students in 1979; 500 in 1983), small endowment, isolation, and the poverty of its students (including an SAT average of 319). In 1960 it ranked 18 among the first 100 American colleges and universities in percentage of graduates awarded the M.D. and first among Negro colleges in the M.D. and the Ph.D. in science. In five years in the 1970s new library purchases had gone from $1,700 to $22,000, the surest sign of intellectual ambition. Talladega had a long reputation of good leadership but seems dangerously vulnerable in the 1980s.

Fisk University, Nashville, Tennessee, 1967, 1974—$37,000. With Howard and Morehouse, Fisk was traditionally one of the three leaders of black higher education in America. It was the first Negro college to be fully accredited by the Southern Association of Colleges and Schools, the first to acquire a chapter of Phi Beta Kappa, and was the institution closest to W. E. B. DuBois, this country's first black intellectual. Totally out of place, his bronze, German-trained figure with goatee, high collar, pile of books in his outstretched arms, glares angrily over the campus, frustrated by all these easy-going young men and women who don't take their studies seriously. There has been a rewarding academic partnership with Vanderbilt and strong financial support

4. Charles Willie and Ronald Edmonds, *Black Colleges in America* (New York: Columbia University, Teachers College Press, 1978), p. 235-6.

for a while from Ford, Rockefeller, and the federal government. Nevertheless, improvident leadership and bad times meant by the late 1970s the same habit as at Atlanta University and weaker institutions of paying for annual deficits out of endowment. In 1983 a cry for help went out just to meet an $80,000 fuel bill and allow the buildings to be heated again.

Knoxville College, Knoxville, Tennessee, 1972—$25,000. Knoxville, the only private Negro college in eastern Tennessee, was a weak institution with 90 percent of its 1,050 students receiving financial aid even though total cost ran less than $2,200, and with 70 percent of entering freshmen needing remedial work in math, reading, and writing. It had been hurt in the late 1960s by black nationalism and a foolish president who had overbuilt and wrecked the financial structure. The college already seemed terminal when its desperate fund-raiser begged me for a grant in 1972, but there was a good new president from Atlanta, the college supplied jobs and schooling to people who otherwise would have had neither, and perhaps our money might allow some stability to help turn the place around. It didn't.

Hampton Institute, Hampton, Virginia, 1972—$40,000 to establish a small business development center within the Institute's Business Division. President Nixon in 1969 had shifted the emphasis of government support from the social and political needs of minorities to economic self-help. This center stressed practical aspects of business, engaged guest lecturers from the business world and government, brought in 380 minority businessmen, from janitorial services to major building construction, and encouraged student participation in cooperative work projects. This project fitted the Trust's involvement in trying to upgrade managerial skills among blacks wherever a reasonable program seemed to present itself.

Several years later, however, I ran into a discouraged trustee of Hampton who wondered not only whether the college, like Fisk or Knoxville, would survive but whether it had any right to survive. With its grade-C students creamed off by the community colleges, its grade-B students by the state university system, and its grade-A students by the University of Virginia at Charlottesville or by private institutions further north, whom could it expect to show up? A lot of cash might keep the place afloat for a while, but who could be expected to give cash that wouldn't be better expended somewhere else? There wasn't the sense of purpose to aim for a higher reason for survival than the fact that Hampton Institute had been around a long time.

The position paper from the Ford Foundation, which argued that it might be better for the long-term status of black education if half of those substandard colleges were allowed to die, obviously applied to Hampton. For a stu-

dent to attend such an artificially protected institution and be convinced that
he was receiving an education of any value was self-delusion. That form of
Social Darwinism, however, that god-like assumption of the power of life and
death over black institutions by comfortable white philanthropists used to
infuriate Benjamin Mays. They did not recognize how close to hopeless poverty American racism had historically pushed and still pushed all black institutions. They did not understand black pride in these schools of theirs.
Blacks remembered what a great man old Professor Somebody had been
when he couldn't have gotten a job at any other college except a Hampton.
They remembered how the college choir sounded and the fact that Willie
Jones had found a start there when he lacked the money or the grades for
any place else, and out of Hampton he had gone on to become ambassador
to Liberia.

Howard University, Washington, D.C., 1972, 1978—$70,000 (plus $25,000
to College of Dentistry). Howard is the leading black educational institution
in the United States and, with its federal funding, the richest. In 1970 more
than half of U.S. black lawyers, physicians, engineers, and architects were
Howard graduates. Our major grant, however, $50,000 in 1972, was re-
quested by the local vice-president of Safeway Stores for a Technical Assistance Project to increase black ownership of radio and television outlet broadcasting stations. There has been a rapid rise in minority interest in the media,
and this money, with the university a conduit, was to help community organizations desiring to involve themselves in media and to improve minority
employment in the field.

$20,000 in 1978 went to the School of Urban Ecology for training in fields
of community service education, human development, employment in United
Nations agencies, macroenvironmental population studies, and microenvi-
ronmental job placement in clothing design. The school seemed to be doing
useful things, but its self-presentation was lost in such involuted, turgid cant
that the Merrill trustees lopped off $5,000 for bad writing. As I tried to explain
the reasons for our penalty, I felt that the project formulator did not understand a word I said.

United Negro College Fund, New York City, 1963, 1978—$175,000. The
UNCF is the most important funding source for black institutions, started in
1944 to coordinate and monitor the appeals by separate colleges. It has always
had strong corporate backing. Bob Magowan helped raise $600,000 for it one
year in San Francisco, and he presented the appeal to us its first time. The
weaker colleges would never have survived without these annual gifts. "A
mind is a terrible thing to waste" is their current slogan, an argument worth
respect.

Graduate and Professional Programs (Except Medical): $300,000

American Geological Institute, Washington, D.C., 1972—$25,000 to retool superfluous black-college agricultural scientists (at a time when only 4 percent of the U.S. population was actively engaged in agriculture) as geologists.

University of Mississippi, School of Law, Oxford, Mississippi, 1969— $25,000 for Negro scholarships. In 1966 there were three black lawyers practicing in Mississippi with a black population of 900,000 and no black students at the University's law school. In July 1965 the Ford Foundation established a five-year program for funding active recruitment, and the numbers went from three in 1965 to twenty-two in 1968. Officially, they did well, aided by strong support by the assistant dean; in actuality, from poor preparation and low morale, they were in bad shape. This grant was to help replace Ford money as that phased out, though the Merrill trustees were nervous about scrutiny by the state legislature that might involve Merrill Lynch.

I put my own money into the program and into support of individual students, a process inspiring and disheartening. The students were often of weak quality, so isolated, vulnerable, and even foolish—one graduate running up a $1,100 phone bill while looking for help in establishing her office.

Earl Warren Legal Training Program, New York, New York, 1979— $10,000. The Earl Warren Program started in 1972 out of the Ford project in Mississippi and the program of legal education begun by the NAACP. It is the only national, privately supported organization devoted exclusively to raising the number and quality of black lawyers. From 1972 to 1979, 2,500 scholarships were given to 1,121 students in seventy-one accredited law schools. From 1978 to 1979, 218 students were being supported, half of them female. Seventy-five percent of Earl Warren graduates work in the South. More than fifty Earl Warren scholars now belong to the Mississippi bar, another fifty in Arkansas.

National Board YWCA, New York, New York, 1972—$40,000 to train black women executives. The Y had traditionally been the first American organization outside of the church where an ambitious black woman could attain a position of any authority, and this project was to upgrade skills in modern management.

Scholarship Education and Defense Fund for Racial Equality, New York, New York, 1972, 1976—$45,000. SEDFRE, whose first appeal to the Merrill Trust was rejected from fear that it might be involved with the Black Panthers, had the purpose of training new black officials in the South and helping public officials and community groups reach funding appropriate to their needs. $346,000 from SEDFRE in 1969–1972 released $8.6 million federal and private grants to Jefferson County, Mississippi, alone. In dealings with the poorest sections of the South it sought to give administrative skills to a new leadership class, both pragmatic and responsible.

There were 120 counties in the rural South where in 1970 blacks constituted the majority of the population. Within the next few years these might go from white to black political control. The newly elected county commissioners would need help to revitalize impoverished governments and create jobs, to stem the pattern of out-migration, and to provide better community services and give hope. There were already a few black congressmen and state representatives, but the most telling elections are at the local level: school board members, sheriffs, police chiefs, and probate judges. SEDFRE set up training programs for new officials: identifying problems; setting priorities; planning budgets; and learning how to obtain government, foundation, and church funds.

The Merrill Trust made a second grant, $20,000 in 1976. By then SEDFRE was beginning to include northern areas, for example, helping community action agencies make successful transitions from total government support to economic self reliance. In Newark, when 60 percent of minority youth was unemployed, this grant was to help the Youth Development Institute in building a business careers program in development of skills and discipline.

Massachusetts Institute of Technology, Community Fellows Program, Cambridge, Massachusetts, 1979—$10,000 to a program started in 1971 as a way to allow community leaders, black and Hispanic, to take time out to reflect, acquire new skills or theoretical backgrounds, and recharge themselves. These organizers, city planners, attorneys, ministers, and agency executives suffer a burn-out rate higher than whites because the tasks are harder, clients more fractious, competition more bitter, and support personnel (the secretaries and bookkeepers who actually run most enterprises) less well trained. This program was high-cost since the fellows did not have the personal resources to support themselves, and for that reason the program was hard to sell.

Interracial Council for Business Opportunity, New York, New York, 1972, 1976—$20,000. ICBO was founded in 1963 by the National Urban League and the American Jewish Congress to help the development of minority business through management education, consultation by volunteers, and various forms of financing. Given our national value system, it is only by increasing their economic strength that minority groups in the United States can achieve equality. Black and Hispanics make up almost 25 percent of the U.S. population, but minority businesses represent only 1 percent of total sales. Resident business ownership reduces crime, raises pride, and creates role models. The present depression has been devastating to minority businesses, and ICBO operates a loan guarantee fund to help such beleaguered enterprises raise capital.

Black Urban Education Programs

National Scholarship Service and Fund for Negro Students, New York, New York, 1963—$25,000. NSSFNS was started in 1950 by an educator named Richard Plaut to recruit and fund bright students to go on to college and stop the terrible waste of Negro intelligence. Increasingly, however, the program turned to recruiting students for private secondary schools. The bright slum kid becomes less able as he grows older, and though 25 percent of all suburban kids have an IQ score of 125 or above (whatever that may mean), only 6 percent of poor city kids do. Under Plaut, NSSFNS had placed 275 black students between 1950 and 1962, but by 1963 the program had ground to a halt from tired leadership and lack of funds.

A committee of heads from Andover, Northfield, Emma Willard, Choate, and Commonwealth met to consider how NSSFNS could be reinvigorated, pushed by Dartmouth's offer of its campus for a summer preparatory program. Plaut and his colleagues felt threatened rather than challenged by the spirit, scope, and budget of this new program (with funding by Rockefeller, the Merrill Trust, and $1 per pupil membership fees from a rapidly increasing number of schools). The elite executive committee was not to be frustrated by this obstructionism when a firm contract had to be signed with Dartmouth right away. In March of 1964, the remaining funds of the Merrill grant were transferred to Choate, and NSSFNS and Richard Plaut disappeared.

Independent Schools Talent Search Program, Boston, Massachusetts, 1968—$25,000. ISTSP replaced the old NSSFNS and became the vehicle by which member schools could feel that they shared in the changes of the Great Society. Between 1963 and 1968, 934 students were placed in 110 private schools; the first graduates had been accepted at 45 colleges; and by 1968, 750 youngsters were currently enrolled. Of these, 72 percent were Negro, 16 percent were white, 5 percent were Puerto Rican, and 4 percent were American Indian (a group almost impossible to retain). Each student received a six-week experience at Dartmouth learning reading, writing, math skills, and skills of intellectual problemsolving, middle-class sports like soccer and swimming, and some exposure to the white institutional life they would have to endure. At a boarding school, three years would cost $10,000, and ISTSP helped meet this cost with, in 1968, $2.7 million in funds received from foundations, corporations, individuals, and the federal government's Office of Economic Opportunity. There was an exciting enthusiasm at first, but after the 1967 riots and an increasing militancy among blacks, both in the ghettos and in these nice private schools, funding became harder.

A Better Chance, Boston, Massachusetts, 1976, 1979—$50,000 (plus $5,000 in 1981 for the San Francisco Bay Area chapter). Under a driving, personable young black director, William Boyd, with a B.A. from Williams and a Ph.D. from Berkeley, ABC (ISTSP's next name) sought to develop a pool of secondary school graduates capable of going on to the best colleges and eventually increasing the number of professionally trained minority men and women in the United States. By 1976, 4,000 had participated in these programs, with 400 entering in September 1976. In 1979 Andover graduated its three hundredth ABC student. ABC was even more important by the mid-1970s as public schools became less adequate for talented youngsters. OEO support had ended as had the early optimism on how well nonwhite, working-class kids could fit into private schools. They were not always cooperative and successful, and yet there were impressive successes.

Student Christian Movement in New England, Cambridge, Massachusetts, 1963—$5,000 and *Northern Student Movement, Boston, Massachusetts, 1964—$10,000,* two names for the same organization. I became acquainted with its work in Boston's South End, where the dropout and delinquency rates were near the highest in New England. Boston was to be a pilot program ($2,000 of the 1964 grant went for expansion to New York) in trying to work out the way a middle-class student could teach a deprived child, how to use human, personal, nonabstract methods, and replace talk with action and through action replace white guilt with self-respect. Two developments were an increasing radicalization of the white student volunteers who came to see the problem not as bad schooling but as a brutally racist society, and increasing resentment by blacks who did not want any whites to come into their community and help them. The Northern Student Movement, which soon disappeared, was a catalyst of the radicalism of the 1960s.

Boston

For a ten-year period I became involved in a wide variety of biracial endeavors in the Boston area, out of which came this plethora of small grants amounting to $285,000. In some cases the outfit could not have managed a larger amount of money, but it was sad to see how the impetus had waned by the mid-1970s.

Commonwealth School, Urban School, Boston, 1967—$6,000. Urban School was Commonwealth's wholly owned subsidary, a summer school where 105 students (70 percent black) studied English, mathematics, science, and politics. We had a brilliant professional for reading, the major vehicle for intellectual growth. The aim was to improve study skills; to provide a friendly, reasonable environment; and to give some idea of the problems of Boston and the world. It was to be a radical, democratic school instead of an elite, liberal one. Tuition was $20, and many kids paid less.

The next summer we wangled a contract from OEO. A staff was hired and paid with promises as the office in Washington delayed and delayed in mailing its check. The day before closing a $5,000 check arrived, and the director raced out to cash it and paid off the staff in $10.00 bills. The next day came a telegram stating that the check had been sent in error—please return. But the money had been spent! That's what it means to work in partnership with the U.S. government. Urban School lasted two more years as part of Commonwealth's regular budget, but the enthusiasm of Freedom Summer had died.

Education Enrichment Program, Boston, Massachusetts, 1967—$10,000. This summer program, sponsored by the National Association of Independent Schools, sought to reach bright poor kids in the public schools; offer them stimulating courses in English, lab science, and history; and at the same time teach them to use imagination and self-reliance instead of rote obedience. The Boston public school system is a closed, defensive one suspicious of outside contacts and any criticism or comparison. Six private schools were involved. One unstated hope was that this program might widen their channels into the black community and attract more applicants, which did not really occur, but the program was well run, lasted eight or nine years, and benefited both sides.

Bridge Fund, Boston, Massachusetts, 1969–1977—$55,000 in four grants. Bridge was funded in 1966 by a committee of black social workers and white educators to place black students in white private and parochial schools. That program faded, to be replaced by a much larger one called Metco where innercity youngsters were bussed out to suburban high schools. Enough numbers were involved so that even if bright city kids benefited as individuals and the white suburban schools benefited, not always gladly, by this exposure to reality, the city schools were stripped of their natural leaders. Bridge's director, an experienced, unillusioned man named Alan Clarke, stated that he had never seen black classrooms so spiritless as they became as a result of this "creaming" policy. And much as he loathed Boston's public schools for their low standards and their contempt for black pupils, Clarke wasn't convinced of the long-range benefits of the placement programs. In his words: "The best definition of a good white school is one that as quickly and painlessly as possible makes each black student totally ashamed of his entire inheritance."

Wentworth Institute of Technology, Boston, Massachusetts, 1975–1978—$30,000. This traditional technical school had been started in 1904 to teach theoretical analysis and practical application. A new president was also concerned at the lack of black interest in technological fields, where jobs were available if a young person had the necessary skills. We helped bankroll a Summer Technical Internship Program for tenth and eleventh graders in two nine-week sessions involving mathematics and the basic theoretical aspects of engineering technology.

Commonwealth of Massachusetts, Department of Public Health—Family Health Services, Boston, Massachusetts, 1969—$25,000. Here we gave money to a public agency to establish a demonstration project for training minority women for careers in child care. This was then a growth field, newly important to the federal government: recognition of the value of early education for poor children, day care that would allow welfare mothers to get jobs, and job training for young women. Its director, Dr. Mary Worth, was trying to raise private funds to launch the project, which would then attract federal and state funding. Private money would also be flexible enough to send state employees to study at the Albert Schweitzer Hospital in Haiti in order to broaden their ideas.

Roxbury Medical Technical Institute, Boston, Massachusetts, 1972—$25,000. An appealing project, the Institute sought to open the whole health services field as a possible career for black youth, not just for the brightest who might become doctors and nurses but for youngsters wherever they happened to be. This involved extensive visits to hospitals (including a talk with the black chef at Massachusetts General); medical schools (as far away as Howard); and meetings, tutoring, and summer projects in biology with impressive black role models, male and female. The director had received sizable funding from a number of Boston physicians but was not a good administrator and paid overgenerous consulting fees to his friends, so the project faded away.

Catholic Charitable Bureau of Boston, 1969—$25,000 to train teaching interns to work in innercity schools. The Association of Urban Sisters was started in 1966 to improve parochial schools in the Roxbury/South End ghetto through enrichment programs, counseling services, and teacher workshops. Then it began to stress the recruitment and training of teachers out of these same communities and to build family involvement so that the schools could eventually be transferred from church to community control. This program was launched with generous support from the diocese and local foundations and corporations, but when that interest faded, the black community lacked the resources and skills to maintain them.

Central School, Cambridge, Massachusetts, 1973—$10,000. We funded this multiracial, parent-controlled place that sought to provide not only an alternative to the authoritarian, chaotic Cambridge school patterns and a model that some of these schools might emulate but also an example of neighborhood unity and initiative. Blacks, Hispanics, blue-collar whites, and mothers of single-parent families learned to work together and develop some sense that they might control their lives and not just passively endure what the system handed out to them.

Roxbury Community School, Boston, Massachusetts, 1979—$10,000. By 1979 this was one of the few alternative schools still functioning, out of a federation of Community schools that we and other foundations (Ford gave $550,000) had launched in 1970 as an alternative to the Boston public schools' rigidity, racial tension, political rivalries, and the sheer mass of budgets, buildings, and staff that paralyzed change. Roxbury survived because of the desperate efforts of its principal, Livaughn Chapman, who would sometimes phone me on Friday morning for a thousand dollars so that he could pay his staff something before they went home. Apprentices and mothers usually gave their services free, and the school was well enough run so that the per child annual cost—$1,465—was appreciably lower than the public-school figure. There was less tension, crowding, fear, and authoritarianism; children learned, but the black parents lacked the money to pay the bills and white Boston didn't care.

Black Precollege Education Programs—$140,000

Westside Preparatory School, Chicago, Illinois, 1980—$15,000. Marva Collins is an ex public schoolteacher who started Westside Prep in 1975 because she could no longer tolerate the low standards of public schools. She took eighteen neighborhood children already labeled as failures, and by a blend of no-nonsense discipline and abundant praise, tremendous energy, and a heavily structured class work of drills, memorization, interdisciplinary learning, and reading from the classics (Plato, Dante, Dickens) was able to improve reading skills and all-around academic attainment.

This produces an intensely American problem. On the one hand, her attack on red tape and apathetic public school teachers, her success, their failures, have her denounced as destructive and fraudulent. On the other hand, Marva Collins is made into a media star, called a "miracle teacher who works blackboard magic" by the national press, featured on CBS with a six-figure fee (channeled into a new building for her 200 students), asked to become Los Angeles' superintendent of public schools, and rumored to have been considered by President Reagan as Secretary of Education. Mrs. Collins does not bother to respond to critics and tells her children not to feel sorry for themselves but to go out and win.

Harlem Preparatory School, New York, New York, 1971—$30,000. Harlem Prep was started in 1967 to serve intelligent but unmotivated boys and girls and reached the size of 400 by 1971. It showed a tough-minded demand for results and a belligerent race pride so that ex dropouts stayed there and stayed on at college—only 10 out of 214 graduates dropped out of college. Fundamentally, of course, it was a creation of the vacillating interest of white checkwriters who gave generously at first and then went on to other topics. By the time the Merrill Trust involved itself, the school was crying out for help. Standard Oil made an emergency gift of $100,000, and Ford and Chase Manhattan helped too; but these gifts were not plugged into any organic funding source, the Harlem community could not pay even a portion of its heavy costs, and the school folded within a year.

Boys' Club of New York, New York, New York, 1968—$15,000 to help finance Project Broad Jump whose purpose was to accelerate the progress of students in grades 5 to 8 of the most crowded and culturally deprived public schools, first by intensive work in basic skills and study habits and second by placement in private schools. This meant dealing with an earlier age group than ABC concerned itself with, crucial when by eighth grade, as I saw too often with black applicants to Commonwealth, even a bright kid has been dulled out of competition in reading skill and the ability to deal with numbers. Boys' Club was trying to meet in particular the needs of Caribbean migrants, showing them how to make use of existing facilities in their area.

Innovative Learning and Training Center, Tallahassee, Florida, 1980—$15,000. ILTC was started in Boston in 1973 by a black Commonwealth graduate, Bahati McClain, for community and education service, which would include tutoring and workshops on community leadership, the changing status of women, the needs of the elderly. By the end of the 1970s many young blacks saw their future in the South rather than the North. Tallahassee could be considered a part of the new South, but with the students at Florida A&M

concerned mainly about clothes and parties, with fathers in the housing projects unemployed, mothers caring about sheer physical survival, and children
receiving no education or guidance for their future to be any better than their
present, it was as if all the promises of the 1960s had never existed.

Ms. McClain worked with black children in the housing projects: in English
and math, discussions on the reason for education, the purpose of life, ways
to build a neighborhood, and reasons to be proud of one's own race. She made
efforts to involve adults in concern for Haitian refugees and black women
prisoners (at the absolute bottom of the ladder); to establish contact with a
church (a traditional source of black strength that the new generation was
losing touch with); and to start a Community Coalition to break the cycle of
delinquency, crime, police violence, jail, unemployment, and then jail again.
A great black bitterness and frustration built up after the Miami riots. Violence and crime should not be the only ways to attract attention.

Black Scholarship Aid Within White Schools: $300,000

Francis W. Parker, Chicago, Illinois, 1960–1981—$80,000. Our sustained
support of Francis Parker came partly because it had been Mary Merrill's
school, which she credited for bringing her socially aware and intellectually
alive. Started in 1901, it expressed early on the ideals of the whole progressive
movement in American education. As Colonel Parker paraphrased the Battle
Hymn of the Republic: "As He died to make men holy let us live to make
men free." Parker vowed to experiment with new academic and social ideas,
to serve as a model for the public schools, and to make a point of representing
every facet of its community. It had 510 students age four to eighteen, a small
endowment, low salaries, and a handsome new plant. Parker prided itself on
catching reading difficulties early. It was one of the first private schools to
accept blacks, then included Hispanics and orientals as its neighborhood
changed, reaching a 19 percent minority average in the mid-1970s.

Choate-Rosemary Hall, Wallingford, Connecticut, 1978—$10,000. There
is no more establishment institution in the world than Choate-Rosemary Hall.
Its success-oriented preppies pad complacently between the Mellon Library
and the million-dollar gym and limit their outside reading, I suppose, to the
Wall Street Journal. Nevertheless, its headmaster, Charles Dey, who had
been one of the founders of the ISTSP/ABC program while at Dartmouth,
was belligerently committed to making the school pull its weight in relation
to the outside world and to exposing its homogeneous in-group to American
realities. He had hired a bright, lively black woman to make the process of
integration more bearable for minority students and was trying to accumulate
a war chest of gifts like ours to expand their numbers.

Scarborough School, Scarborough-on-Hudson, New York, 1969—$20,000 to support an effort to bring in more black students, starting with three per year entering first grade. There were already 18 black students out of 245, but the new headmaster, who had come from Bowdoin College admissions and felt that the black students there were the one in a hundred survivors, wanted to reach out to the children of the large black population in the towns near Scarborough before they became crippled by cultural lag.

St. Ann's Episcopal Church School, Brooklyn, New York, 1972–1976—$25,000. An elementary and secondary school (like *Brooklyn Friends,* 1973—$25,000) of 650 students with about a 15 percent black and Puerto Rican proportion. It attracted bright, high-powered kids and put them in advanced courses. There were fifty-three minority students among the 22 percent receiving financial aid, but forty-seven such families were paying full tuition, a source of pride to the administration. St. Ann's was a force for stabilization as well as opportunity, a school for the white and nonwhite, middle-class families of Brooklyn Heights, as well as for children out of Bedford-Stuyvesant only a few blocks away. The school aimed to help maintain the livability and cohesion of New York City life, offering good education and serious neighborhood involvement.

Manhattan Country School, New York, New York, 1970–1978—$40,000. Gus Trowbridge, the headmaster, had made a radical commitment to racial and economic diversity at the student, staff, and trustee level, which expressed itself in a student body about 40 percent black and Hispanic and also of varied intellectual levels, which he was convinced could be educated together with good teaching and without the need for tracking. He retained an old-fashioned belief in the public mission of private education and the need to combine physical and mental skills (one requirement was to learn how to milk a cow dry on the school farm). The result was a lively, creative environment that gave any visitor a sense of how beautiful children of all races are before they become turned off. Another result was an almost zero endowment and Trowbridge tied into frantic fund-raising all year long.

Advent School, Boston, Massachusetts, 1977—$10,000. Located in the Back Bay/Beacon Hill section of Boston, Advent is a small (110) primary school that draws students from all over the city because of its solid academic standards, its willingness to work with children with physical and learning disabilities, and its commitment to racial integration—30 percent are nonwhite. The headmaster, an Episcopal priest named Robert Day, saw Advent as a source of stability in a transient community of young business and professional families, and he found himself working almost harder as a marriage counselor than as a teacher.

Antioch College, Yellow Springs, Ohio, 1968—$25,000. For decades mid-western colleges like Oberlin and Carleton had had a noticeable Negro minority, but these were really black white people, the children of academics and doctors mostly, who, except for skin color, differed little from their white classmates. A sort of maverick with its alternating semesters of campus study and real-world work, Antioch made another experiment in the mid-1960s, reaching out not simply for brown-skinned middle-class students, the sort that every college was trying to recruit, but working-class students from the ghettoes of Chicago, Gary, and the industrial cities of Ohio. They were admitted with generous scholarships, but there was no real commitment either to showing them how to do the work of this quite academic institution or to insisting that it be performed. This meant a resentful minority contemptuous of a college unwilling to discipline or to help them and of their white peers and teachers who played up to them and were both afraid and condescending. It would be a shame not to take advantage of such a setup, and the campus became poorly disciplined, run-down, dirty, drug-filled, dangerous, and demoralized.

Institutions and Issues of Black Culture: $260,000

Elma Lewis School of Fine Arts, Boston, Massachusetts, 1969–1980— $55,000 in four grants. The Elma Lewis School first opened in 1950, but its great expansion came in 1968 when it purchased the abandoned Mishkan Tefila Temple for $1 and called itself the National Center of Afro-American Artists. There came great dreams of a 1,400-seat theatre, an Afro-American Museum of Art, an experimental theatre, a black symphony orchestra, a resident dance group, and a center for both national and local artistic life. As Ms. Lewis stated, "Black artists don't have any place to display their work except as an exotic piece in the white community. But the black artist isn't exotic. He's the stuff of life." Strong initial support came from Boston Gas and the *Globe*, the Ford Foundation, Senator Brooke, and Senator Kennedy. When I asked my fellow trustees for $40,000 in 1969, I was told that such a place wasn't important and given $5,000.

Hopes that the School like the Franklin Park Zoo nearby, also built on promises, would attract white as well as black visitors and thereby integrate and dignify the Dorchester community did not pan out, and all these dreams existed with a school always on the edge of collapse. There was a bad fire (probably arson), and the school went into receivership and almost folded in 1977. Nevertheless, Elma Lewis, a huge, sensitive, ferociously energetic woman, kept the place going in its cavernous ex synagogue year after year, paying the roof repairs with the heating money in all the maddening irrationality of black administration (I suppose the director of a black institution who faced facts objectively would simply slit his throat), accepting the eager child whether its parents could pay or not, and offering impressively high-quality courses in dance, music, theatre, and arts while all the passersby prophesied doom.

I remember going around the corner of a back stairway and running across a man teaching a little girl to play the flute. It was the only private space he could find, but he was a skilled and patient teacher and the girl was a good pupil.

Harlem School of the Arts, New York, New York, 1979—$15,000. This school was founded in 1964 by Dorothy Maynor, a distinguished black concert singer. It received strong support from Ford and $300,000 from the Columbia Broadcasting System Foundation and enjoyed less chaotic management than Elma Lewis' school. By 1979 about 1,100 students were enrolled in afterschool and private classes and summer activities, and we helped meet a last effort to pay off the $1 million mortgage.

Studio Watts Workshop, Los Angeles, California, 1970–1976—$70,000. Here was another approach to making the arts an integral part of the life of a depressed community by building artists' studios into a new housing project for the poor and elderly. Under another charismatic leader, James Woods, the Workshop, which had started out in two storefronts, aimed to go beyond polarization and anger and to allow the individual to express himself and the black artist to relate to the community. It also aimed at creating plays of high artistic value on the ghetto experience, opening up communication between closed groups, and building confidence, awareness, and change. It had the sheer pride of being able to say that its housing project had artists' studios built into it, which one can visit (at times) and whose production one can share.

Studio Museum in Harlem, New York, New York, 1981—$10,000. An article in *Art News* led me to three nonelitist New York ethnic museums (also *Bronx Museum of the Arts* and *Museo del Barrio*). This one offers studio space for artists, a photographic archive, and education programs. Our money went toward a program to document Afro-American art history.

Parting Ways: the Museum of Afro-American Ethnohistory, Plymouth, Massachusetts, 1979—$5,000. In 1792, ex slaves had been given a corner of the original Plimoth Plantation in recognition of their role as soldiers in the Revolutionary War. The Merrill Trust's small grant went to excavate and study that site and start a small museum as a way to make blacks (and whites) aware of their distant past and perhaps bring a few into the field of archeology.

Concerts in Black and White, Boston, Massachusetts, 1978, 1981—$20,000. This organization had been started in 1974 to provide minority classical musicians with the performance experience necessary for artistic growth and career building, a sort of bush-league team where the black violinist could get a start. In a music-saturated city like Boston, it sought new audiences for Beethoven's Ninth and for black composers. By 1981 the orchestra was close to collapse, the director, who took no salary, was barely meeting his payrolls. The last Merrill gift was to pay wages for a few more weeks when, after the orchestra folded, there were no other jobs.

North Carolina Cultural Arts Coalition, Raleigh, North Carolina, 1981—$10,000 to fund the Wake County Cultural Arts Coalition. In the so-called Golden Triangle of Raleigh, Durham, and Chapel Hill is to be found a collection of corporations, university research centers, and federal agencies giving employment to a strong black professional and middle class without the poverty, pollution, and crime of most urban centers. Dr. Charles Finch, a Commonwealth and Yale graduate, felt it important to build a program upon black strength instead of always upon black weakness. This grant helped fund a year-long series of events emphasizing the black community's contributions and needs: symposia on the church, family, and history; lectures by black scientists, engineers, and doctors at the biracial public schools; and a jazz-mobile for mixed concerts—a way to show both races how much black people had to give.

Center for Southern Folklore, Memphis, Tennessee, 1977—$5,000. This center aimed to acquire and store films, records, documents, and books of the rapidly disappearing folklore traditions of the South: blues and folktales, folk arts and crafts, the religious experience of black churches in Mississippi and in New Haven, and to awaken respect among young people of what old-time country folk had to contribute.

Boston University, Afro-American Studies Center, Boston, Massachusetts, 1972—$25,000. When pressure from black and radical white students pushed many universities into starting a course or even a department of black studies in the late 1960s, results were apt to vary from mediocre to fraudulent. A black professor was hastily hired away from Morehouse or Fisk, and a superficial curriculum and library were slapped together: an instant department. If its standards didn't measure up to those of the regular departments, they weren't expected to.

A professional like Adelaide Hill (A.B., Smith; Ph.D., Harvard), who had helped set up a center of African studies at Boston University as early as 1952, resented this condescension, and since 1969 had run a demanding M.A.

program of Afro-American studies. The twelve students of both races studied Afro-American and African history and sociology and did fieldwork in the agencies, jails, housing projects, and schools involved with the black community.

Berea College, Berea, Kentucky, 1981—$25,000 to strengthen the Afro-American Studies Program. This Appalachian college, founded in 1855, had accepted black students after the Civil War until forbidden by the state of Kentucky around 1910. It integrated its student body again in the 1950s. President Weatherford wanted this grant not to set up an independent department but to strengthen black studies within the whole relevant academic range: in English, music, sociology, and history; to expand the library; to invite visiting professors; and to set up a summer workshop for high school teachers on the black contribution to American society.

Black Urban Projects and Agencies: $1,510,000

National Urban League, 1962–1980—$270,000. The Urban League was the agency we backed most consistently because it was most directly involved in the desperate problem of jobs creation and social stability and because the two directors we dealt with, Whitney Young and Vernon Jordan, were outstanding men.

Our first $25,000 in 1962 was to the Friends and Neighbors program. From 1950 to 1960, the black population had increased by 50 percent in twenty northern cities. In the chaos that followed as bewildered immigrants from the rural South tried to adjust to their urban homes, the NUL tried to work for a certain stability by getting an established family to adopt a new family and serve as their guardian—helping them with job and school placement, groceries and clothing, leisure time, and church membership. We put up another $25,000 in 1967 to help a job-training program.

In March of 1968 came King's murder and the whole force of fear, guilt, concern, and loss felt by white Americans who had not supported King when he was alive now pressed them to see what they could do to give black Americans a sense of membership in this society. In our September meeting the trustees discussed how they could help black businessmen, the group they felt closest to. The Urban Coalition had been recently started, with publicity, promises, and capital, as a sign of commitment by the white business community to black economic progress. Many blacks felt this Urban Coalition was too obviously white-dominated, however, and so we backed the Urban League instead. Whitney Young had launched a New Thrust program in April 1968, trying to involve the black middle class into the problems of the ghetto and the reality of black poverty. Another component of New Thrust, however, was to upgrade the skills of black businessmen. Any new capital would be wasted unless well used: to manage inventory and cash flow, train reliable bookkeepers and accountants, help black contractors find new contacts and resources, and even to supply collateral to obtain Small Business Administration loans. This sounded sensible to Magowan and Regan, and we voted $100,000 in 1969 as a Martin Luther King Memorial Grant to aid black businessmen on the West Coast.

In 1971 $50,000 went to support the League's Veterans Affairs Program in Los Angeles, the Trust's sole grant to meet the needs of Vietnam's ex soldiers. Whitney Young, exhausted, attacked as a dangerous radical and as an Uncle Tom, was disheartened about the job picture for young black men, now running at 20 percent from the cutbacks in federal training and employment programs at a time of economic downturn. This situation was acute for black veterans—unskilled, resentful, and bewildered. Los Angeles was the city where conditions were worst. It was a huge area that attracted newcomers, and the problems of job placement, training, and education were so awful that the Los Angeles Urban League had desperate needs.

We voted $50,000 again in 1977, Vernon Jordan now president, to ameliorate the crisis in unemployment and social services delivery in New York City, and to keep open the lines of communication between classes and races by helping to deliver tangible services.

As times became even worse—the depression of the 1980s started years earlier in the black cities—our foundation, like most others, showed less interest in black needs, and our $20,000 in 1980 was a tag on. The black industrial and office worker seemed firmly established (no longer true by mid-1980s), but it was impossible to grasp even the facts of young male unemployment. Did it stand at 25 percent, at 60 percent, less because so many men worked at part-time, semilegal, cash-paid jobs they didn't report; more because so many blacks were too discouraged to look for jobs or enroll at unemployment offices? Was it true that a whole generation of black males was irretrievably lost to society from the cumulative effects of illiteracy and years of unemployment? And what, besides putting them in prison, did American society propose to do with them?

San Francisco Council of Churches, San Francisco, California, 1969— $20,000 to restore the Neighborhood Co-op, a grocery store in the Hunters Point-Bayview ghetto. This store had been started in 1965 and was underfinanced, underpatronized, and poorly managed, with debts of $90,000 and a $5,000 monthly loss, low shelf inventory, pilferage, and even armed robbery. A Safeway representative invited in by local businessmen felt, however, that the Co-op had potential. The neighborhood was poor, with high unemployment, but neat, without the hopelessness of Watts or Harlem. The Safeway conclusion was that management lacked knowledge and experience. Prices were high, perishables wilted, and naive buying had allowed a $4,000 inventory in French vermouth. Safeway loaned a store manager who had a good record as a teacher, offered a line of credit to restock the shelves, weeded out slow items and increased shelf space, improved security, helped recruit new members, and persuaded creditors to accept 25 cents cash on the dollar.

This sort of rational approach, avoiding high-priced artificial services and the lingo of professional management that delude the amateur, appealed to Bob Magowan and led to our $1 million project in 1970.

Roxbury Institute of Business Management, Boston, Massachusetts, 1970—$400,000
Harvard University Graduate School of Business, Boston, Massachusetts, 1970—$100,000
Stanford University Graduate School of Business, Stanford, California, 1970, 1971—$500,000

This collection of grants for the strengthening of minority management and entrepreneurial skills (at Stanford Mexican-Americans were also included) was the most imaginative and most frustrating decision that the Trust ever made. As Bob Magowan and Don Regan looked back on our earlier investments, they agreed with President Nixon that expenditure on welfare services just encouraged dependency. The goal of sympathetic whites should be to help blacks help themselves and encourage energetic businessmen to work their way up within the system, acquire profits that they would then reinvest within the black community, and generate jobs that led to independence.

This is what the Urban Coalition had set out to do in 1968, but we distrusted their self-congratulatory rhetoric. Our $100,000 to the National Urban League in 1969 and the capital and hard-boiled professional advice to the Hunters Point Co-op made better sense to Magowan. We were also influenced by the reasoning of a black administrator at Stanford named Henry Organ who had protested to me that the ablest minority students boxed themselves into marginal careers by majoring in political science and sociology whereas rigorous study in mathematics and economics would prepare them for jobs with a future that were actually going begging. Accordingly, Magowan proposed that we commit a million dollars to this purpose, a figure large enough to accomplish something, and work through the business schools of Stanford and Harvard.

Stanford had begun its first explicit recruitment of minority business students in 1965 and graduated four black MBAs in 1968. That was not our concern, Magowan felt. It was the self-interest of the school and of the corporations that supported it to produce as many visible junior executives as fast as possible as well as to tone down the spirit of black revolution by a colonial policy of co-opting its potential leadership.

Merrill money should be used instead to change the general way that the school served the black community. This led to a program with three objectives: (1) summer and part-time internships for students to participate in minority business and development activities (as in the bedraggled community of East Palo Alto, later Nairobi, across the highway), to hold administrative and teaching positions in black and Hispanic colleges, and to work in government agencies concerned with minority economic programs; (2) fellowships for minority businessmen in ongoing executive training courses, modeled on MIT's Sloan program in the tools of modern management; and (3) relevant curriculum development work. Between 1970 and 1974, 119 interns were recruited, most of them minority students. Such an intern could quickly become a pillar of strength in the typical black business; could get involved in serious decisionmaking, often over his head; and needed fast, often detailed faculty support. And of course there was a permanent problem that any black businessman who received such training would leave the ghetto as fast as possible, get a less-pressured, better-paid job as token executive in a white corporation, and buy a nice house in a white suburb.

Nevertheless, the investment was large enough to give a different slant to the school's long-range approach to its minority students. Once in Cambridge I met a strong, outgoing black man of about forty who had success written all over him, and when he found out who I was said that the Merrill program at Stanford had been the big first step in his career.

The $100,000 to Harvard was to support black students in their role as consultants to ghetto businesses in greater Boston. It is hard to measure how effectively this was done or whether Merrill money became simply an add-on to their regular scholarship budget. The $400,000, however, was a grant to the Roxbury Institute of Business Management, which had a symbiotic relationship to the school and seemed exactly the sort of place we were seeking.

It was an outgrowth of the New England Community Development Corporation, which had been funded by the Small Business Administration, Washington's commitment to the flourishing of black capitalism. I was impressed by the two personable, bright, seemingly experienced black business school professors who were its part-time directors. Should the Trust have given stricter guidelines? It was a field no one knew much about. Should we have doled out the capital in carefully monitored slices? Philanthropic colonialism was a fighting slogan at that time. Blacks were insisting on autonomy. The sacred word was *impact*. The hopes encouraged by LBJ's Great Society were already fading. This grant, its size, its freedom, was proof that the white establishment trusted and respected blacks. That was too important to flaw with mean-spirited cautions. I also suffered the unvoiced fear that if we didn't pay out all the money at once, our trustees might change their minds.

On my first visit the secretary showed off her exciting purple-red-orange furnishings and stated that our gift had been a shot in the arm to the entire community. What the white visitor did not notice was that RIBM was being fought over by the century-old feud between Booker T. Washington and W. E. B. DuBois. One of the directors followed the pragmatic Tuskegee ideology and was quite willing to set up small classes on accounting, taxes, and cash-flow management. The other was an intellectual who saw black Boston duplicating the colonial economy he had studied in Kenya. It was necessary to set priorities for the whole infrastructure, not waste energy on a handful of bookkeepers.

Neither director could give more than part-time involvement. The office manager used his new profile to snag a firmer job. The white businessmen on State Street five miles away—it might have been a hundred—who had volunteered their help did not show up. There seemed no sign of activity to show up for. The anguished secretary kept the office functioning, while the working capital leached away in monthly bills. By 1971 the economic downturn had already hit the black community. It was not a time for entrepreneurial dynamism but for holding on to what one still had. Dr. Thomas and I visited the place. We engaged a distinguished black economist from Cornell to offer suggestions. The discussions about structural reorganization, future plans, and Nixon's economic policies were always interesting, but nothing was happening. An infusion of more capital would help, it was suggested— and double the cost. We should have made demands, deadlines, and decisions, but there was also the fear that should one come too close to this tarbaby, one would never get loose. I had my school to run. The Roxbury Institute of Business Management faded away.

Why? How? The formless quality of the failure was maddening. The two directors were honest, intelligent, but not experienced in daily business. They did not love the mechanics of business as did Magowan and Regan. As RIBM's daily life became more frustrating, it became ever more tempting for the two to burrow ever more deeply into their offices at Harvard. Despite all the accounts of dynamic entrepreneurs written up in *Ebony*, perhaps the black world has had too much experience with failure to turn down a job at IBM or First National Bank for the risky loneliness of running one's own business. There may be lacking the fierce, family-disciplined energy that inspires the Chinese and Greek immigrant, that in the 1980s blanketed Manhattan with Korean produce stores?

1971 was a time burdened by anger. Any black businessman trying to succeed had to face every day, from his children, his brother-in-law, and his old buddies, the scorn that he had sold out to Whitey. The black world wanted to see him win, wanted to see him fail. And the white world? The Merrill trustees seldom discussed the RIBM case and never tried anything like that again.

Greater Washington Area Unitarian-Universalists, Washington, D.C., 1970—$25,000 to expand the activities of Unity House. This project came from Peter Magowan when he was head of the Washington branch of Safeway. Through a black executive who had worked for Safeway in San Francisco, there was an effort to restore Unity House, Frederick Douglass' old home in Cedar Hill, to put on a television play about the life of Douglass, establish a channel for recruiting black franchise executives for McDonald's, build a talent bank of white expertise that could be called upon to help inner-city residents, and upgrade the college and career counseling of black high school students and the teaching of black history in Unitarian-Universalist churches. The program would work through local leadership and tell them not what but how. Mr. Wright advised Safeway to lower its prices on the days that welfare checks were given out so that black mothers could obtain more food for their children. That was practical. Simply to recount the mishmash of Unity House activity shows the well-meaning chaos of that era's betterment ideas.

Tremont Methodist Church, Boston, Massachusetts, 1967, 1968—$34,000 to help finance a self-help program for the South End under the direction of a black social worker and politician named Mel King, then director of Boston's Urban League. The South End was an area of about 30,000 from forty-two ethnic backgrounds, although largely black. It was the poorest of Boston's neighborhoods; 30 percent of the adult population had not reached eighth grade, and middle-class whites were moving in to renovate large old houses (crime was to drive most of them out again)—gentrification that limited and made more costly the housing available to blacks. King felt that dependency-producing services provided by outsiders did more harm than good, and he sought to build up male role models to end the negative self-image and low expectations of blacks who saw themselves separated from people who accomplished things.

Roxbury Multi-Service Center, Boston, Massachusetts, 1975, 1979—$25,000. The Center has a large staff of social workers, mental health professionals, and business consultants to deal with multiproblem individuals and families. It is involved in rehabilitation of abandoned buildings and playgrounds, crime prevention (escort service for frightened old people and better street lighting), tutoring at a time when bussing confrontation had just about destroyed the Boston school system, a rehabilitative center for ex convicts, and tenant advocacy to help tenants and homeowners deal with landlords and city services.

What struck me as I read the appeals and met the representatives of so many of these black agencies was that the best of them had a better grasp of the theories and practical operations of a democratic society than most better-educated, better-financed whites. We whites have so much to learn if we could realize this.

Boston Housing Authority, United Community Planning Corporation, Boston, Massachusetts, 1981—$10,000. Boston public housing is known for mismanagement, corruption, run-down maintenance, fear, and irresponsible tenants. Hundreds of millions have been spent to replace old slums with new slums. In February 1980 Judge Garrity placed the entire BHA in receivership, with a young Harvard-educated lawyer, Harry Spence, and an able, nonpolitical, biracial staff put as receiver. Spence sought not merely to clean up the disorder but also to build a strong series of tenant committees to express their needs (working plumbing, cleaner hallways, and police protection) and monitor the way the system works. The tenants must also learn to take responsibility and monitor each other in order to learn a concept of active citizenship: learning communal action instead of passive suffering, complaining, and sabotage. A two-year budget of $750,000 had been set (financed mainly by Boston foundations) to create and train tenant teams and to upgrade the effectiveness of the bottom rung of American society that lives in these projects.

Southern Rural Projects: $80,000

Any money invested in rural projects had a dual purpose. The obvious one was to give some opportunity and stability to that world. The second, of concern to establishment northerners like our foundation's trustees, was to give some reason for southern blacks on farms and in the small towns to stay where they were born and not feel compelled to flee to Chicago and New York. It is a worldwide problem: to keep the villager in Anatolia from feeling his only escape is in Ankara or Frankfort, or the villager in Sicily, in the Altiplano of Peru, in Egypt, or in Mexico. The most effective use of development capital, whether state, private, or international, at this stage of history, should be to persuade villagers that they can find jobs, education, and a future for their children, interesting things to do on Sundays in the village where they grew up and not be driven to the slums of Cairo and Lima.

That is not an impossible task. One can invest capital and teach marketing and management skills to members of village cooperatives, set up small labor-intensive factories for manufacturing component parts, teach effective methods of gardening and animal husbandry (avoiding, if possible, the raising of beef cattle that, as in Costa Rica, destroys both land and jobs), experiment with local sources of energy from the wind and sun, improve schools and give instruction in contraception, set up village radio and perhaps even television centers so that there is something to occupy the evenings, encourage traveling theatre groups that give the villager a cultural expression within his frame of reference, and do not deculturalize him with a program fabricated in Miami.

This can sound ridiculous. It is too easy to see these projects as the Christian Socialist cottage crafts of pre-Raphaelite long-haired men and short-haired women of the 1880s, German poets wearing peasant blouses, and earnest vegetarians. Peasants dislike do-good intellectuals. They also dislike the party boss from Moscow or Cairo. The giant dams that seemed to provide a magic answer in the 1950s have had a higher price than ever expected. The giant reclamation projects usually foundered in corruption, inadequate planning, bad management, and authoritarian control. A large number of diversified rural projects, involving as much autonomy as possible, could have cumulative impact. Not many people who control the funds are interested.

Board of National Missions of the United Presbyterian Church in the USA, New York, New York, 1958—$31,000. The Presbyterian Church involved itself in a number of imaginative ideas in the 1960s, which I was led to through my friendship with George Todd, a founder of East Harlem Protestant Parish.

Through the mechanization of cotton production, work that had formerly required fourteen days of labor per acre could now be done in three. There was a population surplus of fifty families per 1,000 acres that meant increasing misery in the South and constant migration to the North. Mississippi Action for Community Education was organized in 1967 in Greenville and in turn set up Delta Enterprises, Incorporated, as the corporation for establishing new farms and nonfarm enterprises, centered in Holmes County, which was very poor but possessed a substantial number of blacks owning or leasing land. Projects included development of corn and grass pasture to raise and process pork, raising of hothouse tomatoes and cucumbers, highway and Christmas plants, and establishment of a casket factory, a labor-intensive industry with a protected market. We put $20,000 into the casket factory and $11,000 into the Lowndes County Co-op near Montgomery, Alabama, to help build and capitalize a black-owned general store, gas station, and beauty parlor.

National Council of the Churches of Christ in the USA, Delta Ministry, Greenville, Mississippi, 1969—$20,000 to finance a ceramics project spon-

sored by the Delta Opportunities Corporation, which had been established
in 1965 with help of the Ford Foundation, OEO, and the Presbyterian Church.
The Corporation owned 400 acres of land that was to serve as a new town
site and for workshops for displaced farm laborers. This particular factory
would manufacture ceramic products—black women handled the design and
moulding well—on contract for Shell Oil Company, which manufactures a
weed killer that does away with the need for cotton choppers. Capital was
needed to train skilled workers and to buy a new kiln.

Penn Community Services, Frogmore, South Carolina, 1973—$30,000. The
Penn Center had been founded in 1862 in coastal South Carolina as a school
and community center to educate and care for the freed slaves. An administrator I knew at the Rockefeller Brothers Fund had asked the Merrill Trust
to cooperate with them in backing this self-help co-op as a way of stabilizing
economic life of the rural South. Within the past ten years, 600,000 persons
had migrated out of South Carolina to the northeastern cities. The Center's
first black director was trying to organize co-ops of vegetable farmers and
fishermen, supply credit and advice to contractors and store owners, and
above all help black farmers hold on to their land when all the pressure of
southern business and government was involved in trying to push them off.
The center included a small museum devoted to local history to give pride
to the black cultural heritage.

Conclusions

What did the Merrill Trust accomplish through its investments in black
America? What lessons, what suggestions come out of the experience? What
are priorities for the next fifteen years?

We did show responsibility for the institutions, particularly the black college. If a presidential candidate has won two smashing victories despite the
opposition of 95 percent of all black voters, the Republicans may feel they
owe black Americans nothing. Therefore it will be crucial for blacks to control
their own institutions and not be too dependent on white sufferance. At a
total figure for the places covered in this chapter—$5.3 million—we backed
leaders, Morehouse and Spelman, and also Rust College and Miles. We
should have done more. The chair of economics at Morehouse in 1972 was
our last major grant, and like most foundations we followed other interests
in the 1970s. A number of grade-B white institutions with which we had closer
personal contacts got money instead. The most serious issues of the time are
the cumulative decay of the black family and the growing subcaste of unemployed, unemployable, illiterate, and totally alienated black males.

If I were director of a new foundation that had a million per year to spend
on black needs, what would I do?

1. *Nourishment, health, family.* After an election won with the slogan of Make America Great Again, no one in authority is wasting time on the needs of the poor. I would start with a $50,000 check to the Children's Defense Fund in Washington. It is the most effective group I know for collecting, publicizing, and lobbying the facts of child and maternal suffering—for pushing people to get things done. Find the church, agency, or clinic that involves itself with diet supplements and medical care for pregnant women and little children, counseling on sex education and contraceptives, and monitoring for high blood pressure, venereal disease, and diabetes. Have lunch with the chief of pediatrics at Boston City Hospital, Mount Sinai, or Michael Reese.

2. *Organization.* People are respected and respect themselves if they have Power, as Jesse Jackson has repeated over and over. The first step up for a distraught mother is to register and vote. Organization and leadership start at a low level. The organization of a food co-op where families trust each other enough to pool their funds and buy bulk staples cheaply, avoids junk food and the middleman. A black and a white or Hispanic mother working together as classroom representatives at their children's school or as neighborhood representatives can work to stop their teenage sons from fighting and getting arrested. It is possible to find a church or a school committed to that simplest level of democracy.

3. *Housing (harder to search out).* However malnourished it may be, there is apt to exist in any city some groups involved in rehabilitation and construction. Start with what exists, such as the East Harlem Urban Center. Learn the rules, the pitfalls. Start small until you find a hard-working, effective, honest group, then make a major investment. Here is the best vehicle for jobs.

4. *Economic Survival.* Write out a check for $50,000 to the National Urban League. I was impressed by the quality of the few southern cooperatives that our trust funded. Do similar ones still exist? The National Council of Churches, the Board of National Missions of the United Presbyterian Church, or the National Sharecroppers Fund could supply contacts. A revolving fund for low-cost loans plus consultation services to black businesses could be useful at the $150/200,000 level if you have the acumen to trust your judgment.

5. *Education.* $50,000 to the UNCF, basic channel for keeping the black college alive. Concentrate on two or three institutions, as we did with Morehouse, for a five to ten year commitment. Ditto for minority scholarships at your favorite white college. Even Harvard and Wesleyan match their grants with such a proportion of loans that hard-up students are scared away by fear of debt. Within black institutions fund sabbaticals and travel fellowships to allow faculty to upgrade themselves and recharge their batteries. With the greater number of far better paid openings in business available, the best black students are no longer going into teaching. Where will the black input into American intellectual life come from, the role models for young people?

This is a silent crisis that government and foundations are ignoring and that demands generous fellowship programs at both the college and graduate school level.

At the nonelite level, locate the innercity high schools recommended to you by a local university's dean of admissions (the best path for seeking out quality) for leadership and well-prepared students and gradually open the door for yourself with $1,000, $5,000, and then $20,000 gifts for lab and library supplies, book awards, summer projects for teachers as well as kids, and college scholarships. Put up a few thousand extra for repainting the walls and buying new furniture and new washroom fixtures. Public schools are usually such dreary looking places, and their students feel that nobody cares about them.

At the bottom, try to locate schools and programs that deal with the problem of adult illiteracy. La Guardia Community College in Manhattan is one such, with free courses for welfare mothers and a waiting list of eight months' duration. The federal government puts up about $1.65 a year to reach each illiterate adult in our society, and President Reagan's budget is trying to reduce even that.

6. *International Participation*. This is not a luxury. For thirty years I backed such a policy at Morehouse and Spelman that sent almost 300 students to Europe and (through Crossroads) to Africa. Looking for the ablest, most resourceful and ambitious men and women, exposing them to a year at the Sorbonne or the University of Vienna or Madrid, to wonderful new experiences and to loneliness and despair ("I'm nobody. I don't know anything."), and to almost the same trauma on reentry, when they know how much they've changed and no one else cares. Don't bother funding new courses in computer technology. Others will do that. Try to change the way a young person looks at the world. And fight the destructive pragmatism of black education: what isn't immediately practical is bullshit—the one-way street to life-long mediocrity.

Send a black teenager on a Crossroads work camp in Jamaica. Or on one of the church-sponsored volunteer groups doing sanitary and education work in Central America, for exposure to real poverty and to the way that the United States looks through its neighbors' eyes. Church channels in both this country and England could help you organize an exchange program for intelligent, responsible black women between Birmingham, Alabama, and Birmingham, England. America puts such a pressure of conformity, timidity, and narrowness upon its people—break the chains.

7. *The Arts*. Write a check of $20,000 to Harlem School of the Arts and to Elma Lewis in Boston. Buy $5,000 to $20,000 worth of canvasses, prints, and sculpture by black artists every year and give them away to any place where people have eyes. You'll enjoy yourself. Give the same amount to a black

college for a concert series of minority musicians or dancers. Stay away from big names.

8. *The Church.* Give scholarship aid for seminarians (the best black students are no longer headed toward the church), a sabbatical for a tired minister, a program of outreach to troubled people, a Christian fight against war and imperialism.

Know when to stay out of the way. During M. L. King's great bus boycott of 1956 in Montgomery, Alabama, juvenile delinquency just about disappeared. Life had purpose and was too exciting. The pride and anger coming out of Jesse Jackson's 1984 campaign gave a sharper sense of black self-worth than would a thousand well-run agencies.

THE SPANISH SPEAKING

In its first two years of operation the Merrill Trust became involved with the world of the Spanish speaking: with Puerto Ricans through the East Harlem Protestant Parish and with Mexican-Americans through the National Catholic Rural Life Conference in Des Moines. It is hard to choose the rational common denominator or know the limits of this chapter. Should the needs of Puertoriqueños in New York be placed with the needs of the same individuals in San Juan? Are the needs of East Los Angeles more relevantly discussed in the chapter on Mexico? Should American Indians be included here? The critical fact is that Hispanics are the fastest growing and by now largest ethnic minority in the United States. They have a special importance in their link to the desperately poor, revolutionary world to our south. If through decent education, jobs, housing and if through respect and a sharing of power they can be brought into the Rainbow Coalition of American pluralism, then we have a wholesome contact with a dangerously resentful world. If we continue to show our traditional Anglo contempt, then we are in trouble. Immigration laws that will have a Mexican-American halted a dozen times a day to check his papers, as in Johannesburg, will not help.

The Merrill Trust responded to this issue in often imaginative ways, sometimes grudgingly, better than the competition, but not as generously as the needs demanded.

Our first outreach to the Puerto Ricans was through the East Harlem Protestant Parish (which received $185,000 between 1958 and 1964 and is discussed in Chapter IV under *The Church and The City*).

The idea and the leaders who came out of EHPP had a strong impact upon the urban church, both Protestant and Catholic, during the 1960s and early 1970s, in training mainstream clergy to be sensitive to innercity, black, and

Spanish-speaking needs, and in giving theologically thorough, socially effec-
tive training to their indigenous ministers. The Metropolitan Urban Service
Training facility of the *Board of Missions of the Methodist Church*, New York
City ($30,000 in 1968) was one such offshoot. The *New York Theological
Seminary* ($130,000, 1969–1981), run by one of the founders of EHPP, George
Webber, set itself the mission of training the Puerto Rican and black ministers
of storefront churches who had usually an intense experience with their community's needs, a strong religious conviction, and an inadequate formal
education.

Aspira of America, New York, New York, 1972, 1980—$45,000. This is the
main private counseling and placement agency for bringing students into
mainstream colleges and should receive far stronger foundation support than
it does. In 1972 it had offices in Newark, Philadelphia, Chicago, and San Juan
as well as New York. It had counseled 7,000 students and parents and found
places for 1,500 Puerto Rican and other Hispanic students in 125 colleges and
universities with one million dollars in scholarship aid. Yet of 1.8 million
Puerto Ricans on the mainland in 1970 there were fewer than sixty doctors,
few lawyers and other professionals, and only a handful of elected representatives. Few go on to college, and half of these drop out. This is a young
population, and education is crucial to them.

At my own school we hired a young Puertoriqueña in 1973 to teach Spanish.
She was just out of Radcliffe, the *first* from her background to have gone
there. Education had been a devastating process for Aida. Because she aimed
so high, she had been ostracized by her high school classmates; because she
came out of the chaos of barrio life, she felt absolutely alienated from Radcliffe
assumptions.

*Cooperative Metropolitan Ministries, Boston, Massachusetts, 1973—
$25,000.* This had been started under an Office of Economic Opportunity
contract in 1970 to develop El Movimiento, the principal self-help agency for
50,000 Puerto Ricans in the Boston area: job training and placement, education, legal aid, and housing. Puerto Ricans were vulnerable to curtailment
of government services, unreasonable rent increases, and eviction proceed-
ings. El Movimiento sought to build a chain of self-help services that would
lead to independence: how to organize a legal rent strike, obtain lead screen-
ing for one's building or one's children, join bilingual programs, and how to
see blacks as allies rather than as enemies.

*Hispanic Theatre Company of Boston, Boston, Massachusetts, 1981—
$5,000* for El Pueblo Nuevo. By this date there were about 80,000 Hispanics
in Boston, twice as many as ten years before, with Puerto Ricans about 75

percent, still the most looked down upon in Boston's ethnic sandwich (though they ganged up to attack Indo-Chinese, the newest group). With less and less government and foundation interest in the needs of innercity people, this project was important both culturally (jazz, theatre, films), and socially, as a way for Latins, blacks, Haitians, and even Sicilians and Vietnamese to work together.

El Museo del Barrio, New York, New York, 1981—$10,000—a showcase for Puerto Rican culture including an art school and a gallery for contemporary and traditional art and film.

It was important for Safeway Stores to have good relations with the Chicano community of the western states, but our first commitment, *National Catholic Rural Life Conference, Des Moines, Iowa, 1960–1963—$80,000*, caused an unexpected backlash. Under the rubric "to help Americans of Mexican descent become more useful citizens," it was directed towards strengthening family services to migrant workers in the Midwest and Pacific Coast, the same people that were the targets of the organizing efforts of Cesar Chavez's United Farm Workers. This angered farmers who supplied fruits and vegetables to Safeway Stores, and they complained to Robert Magowan that the stores that bought their produce should not support a foundation that supported their enemies.

Presbyterian Church, New York, New York, 1966—$25,000 to improve the workings of the Community Services Unit of the San Diego Parish Ministry.

Roman Catholic Diocese of San Diego, San Diego, California, 1967–1968—$45,000, for language disability and psychological services to Spanish-speaking children.

These San Diego projects were our gesture towards a city undergoing serious racial trouble. By 1970, however, a new head of public relations at Safeway, Calvin Pond, was trying, at Magowan's initiative, to involve both the firm and the Foundation in a more constructive general policy, illustrated by the next three projects.

Mexican-American Community Programs Foundation, East Los Angeles, California, 1971—$20,000, for community marketing services. In the great ghetto of East Los Angeles, unemployment is twice the Anglo average, the high school dropout rate is ten times the rate of surrounding schools, and the reading averages are among the lowest in the nation. The 1970 figures showed that the average Mexican-American completes eighth grade, the average black eleventh, and the average white one and one-half years of college.

Blacks rioted in Watts in 1965; Mexican-Americans did not. As a result federal development funds went to the black community. The first major Chicano riot came in 1970.

Spanish-Speaking Unity Council of Alameda County, Oakland, California, 1971—$20,000. Started in 1964 to improve the socioeconomic condition of La Raza in Oakland and to preserve its cultural values, the council was a coalition of eighteen organizations, both militant and traditionalist, serving all classes and all ages and involving itself in basic education and on-the-job training programs. There is a tremendous need for special services for Chicano youth, and only recently have Mexican-Americans been involved in establishment charity like the United Bay Area Crusade.

Mexican-American Legal Defense and Education Fund, San Francisco, California, 1972—$15,000. This was for recruitment and financial aid in order to increase the number of Chicano lawyers. Of 350,000 lawyers in the United States fewer than 700 at that time were Chicano; in California the ratio was 1:16,000, while the Anglo society had 1:680.

The Trust's major investment in Mexican-American needs, however, in the Texan region as well as California, was in education. By the end of the century half of the state's primary school population is expected to be Hispanic.

Pomona College, Claremont, California, 1969—$25,000 for scholarships for Mexican-Americans. This was a difficult minority to bring in and retain. Their academic preparation was poor, their rote approach to learning ill-fitted them for the give and take and self-responsibility at a good school, and the social atmosphere of an Anglo college seemed so alien that a Chicano freshman became homesick and too often stayed home after Christmas vacation. The dropout ratio was even higher for girls, who were put off by the independence of Anglo girls and the exposure to career and sexual values hostile to those of the barrio.

In the late 1960s there was serious discussion among Claremont's six institutions about starting a seventh college oriented to Chicano needs. This, of course, raised the issue of whether education should stress integration into a single, pluralistic, multiracial society or whether the only feasible approach for a minority as insecure as Mexican-Americans was separate and bilingual education. For example, before a Chicano can learn English, should he first read and write Spanish well? Does an insistence upon English cause these uneasy students simply to quit? Jews, Greeks, and Poles became a part of American life by studying English in the public schools, not by protecting themselves in the isolation of bilingualism. Does this hold true in East Los Angeles, more like a European than an American city, unassimilable because of such a concentrated population so close to the homeland? We discussed this issue in meeting after meeting trying to decide what our own policy was, but the plan of a Mexican-American college at Claremont died.

The $650,000 we gave in 1968 to the *University of Santa Cruz* to establish a jointly (private and public) funded college saw the creation of Merrill College directed to the study of poverty and third world problems. By the early 1970s there was a deliberate effort to bring black and Hispanic students into Merrill. The Trust strengthened this program in 1980 by a $30,000 grant to endow financial aid to Hispanic students in the surrounding area who would otherwise concentrate on the limited goals of education at a community college. *Stanford University* received in 1969 a grant of $25,000 similar to Pomona's for financial aid earmarked for Mexican-Americans and Indians. A dozen years later President Donald Kennedy was generous enough to state that this gift established their recruitment campaign. By the mid-1970s enough Chicano high school seniors were directing themselves to Stanford that special efforts were no longer needed.

Community Foundation of Santa Clara County, San Jose, California, 1981—$25,000. In the education of Chicanos, the worst slippage comes between the end of the community college and successful transfer to a four-year institution. The cheap and practical community colleges serve that community well up to a point, allowing an easy transition from high school and a chance to catch up and find a sense of direction. For a student with any ability or ambition community colleges can be a dead end, but to transfer to an institution like San Jose State means extra costs. Even the few hundred dollars needed for rent, furniture, books, and the problems of getting a job and planning courses may be too much for a fragile individual. Extra resources are needed to maintain momentum. Santa Clara County, with a large Chicano population, a dozen community colleges, and the important institution at San Jose, was a place to begin.

Southern California School of Theology, Claremont, California, 1980—$25,000 for scholarships for Hispanic students to offer leadership in Los Angeles thirty-five miles away. In the United Methodist Church alone one hundred new Hispanic ministers are needed in the 1980s. These students may be recent college graduates, but there will also be women and older men changing their careers. There is a need almost as important to expose other seminary students to the richness of Spanish theology and culture.

Colegio de la Tierra, Goshen, California, 1978—$10,000. This is a little private two-year college in the San Joaquin Valley, started in 1970 as a service institution to Chicanos, offering practical courses in self-help skills, community leadership, teaching how to buy and manage property, how to deal with legal papers and obtain government aid, and even, for many adult students, how to read and write.

El Centro Campesino Cultural, San Juan Bautista, California, 1977— $10,000. The Center was designed to present theatre, film, concerts, radio and television programs, books, posters, and puppet shows and to become a focus for the surrounding Mexican-American community. Over a three-year period its only nonlocal support has been $17,500 from the National Endowment for the Arts. The Centro and the Colegio had both been referred to me by the provost of Merrill College at Santa Cruz, examples of tiny, important, starving Chicano institutions totally ignored by the Anglo establishment. It is possible to find places like this if one wants to and give them sustained support—which they lack the aggressiveness to push for.

Menaul School, Albuquerque, New Mexico, 1980—$10,000 for scholarship aid at a formerly Presbyterian Mission school (founded 1881) whose alumni comprise a large proportion of the Hispanic school administrators and Protestant ministers in New Mexico and southern Colorado. The majority of these students are not Mexican-Americans, however, but descendents of the Spanish settlers of the upper Rio Grande Valley.

University of New Mexico, Albuquerque, New Mexico, 1974—$7,000 for purchase of contemporary arts and crafts, a center chosen for its importance to the Indian and Mexican-American world.

University of Texas Medical School, San Antonio, Texas, 1970—$25,000 to counsel economically deprived high school students about careers in the medical and health sciences.

St. Mary's University, San Antonio, Texas, 1975—$20,000. This was an effort to interest Mexican-American high school students in the health professions and then to give them financial and educational support while they were in this university, the most important school for the Spanish-speaking population of central Texas.

Philbrook Art Center, Tulsa, Oklahoma, 1975—$10,000 for ethnic studies programs directed towards the Indian and Mexican communities.

Our first contact with Cubans came in 1961 when we gave $10,000 to the Centro Hispano Católico of the *Roman Catholic Diocese of Miami* to provide food, clothing, and shelter, and we gave $25,000 again in 1969. $20,000 was given in 1963 to the *International Rescue Committee*, New York, to help resettle Cuban refugees. $40,000 in 1969, 1972 to *Biscayne College*, Miami, for Catholic scholarships was primarily earmarked for poor Cubans, and also $20,000 in 1972 to *Cardinal Newman High School* in West Palm Beach. By then the Cuban newcomers were on their way, rather contemptuous of other groups who kept expecting help.

The Merrill Trust made a few grants to Indians.

Oklahomans for Indian Opportunity, Norman, Oklahoma, 1969—$20,000 for education, an appeal to Don Regan through an important political contact.

Roman Catholic Diocese of Portland, Bangor, Maine, 1970—$25,000 to help establish a binational secondary school in New Brunswick in an effort to cut dropout rates, alcoholism, and the self-destructiveness of Indian adolescents by teaching them in both their own language and English in a tribal-oriented school.

Navajo Community College, Chinle, Arizona, April–June, 1971, 1972— $55,000. Chinle opened in 1969, the first college located on an Indian reservation and the first controlled by an Indian board of regents. Two-thirds of its curriculum was devoted to vocational-technical subjects like agriculture and forestry, auto repairs and operation of heavy equipment, nursing, and office training; and one-third was devoted to liberal arts courses that would enable a student to transfer to a four-year college.

St. Jude's Roman Catholic Church, Tuba City, Arizona, January, 1972— $15,000 to establish a teen center. The American world seemed a hopeless one for these Hopi and Navajo adolescents, and they expressed their despair by lethargy, alcoholism, and suicide. Our contact, a young Jewish psychiatrist performing his alternative military service at this post, was trying to build a center where boys could find a better recreation than drinking, get themselves involved in job-training classes, be encouraged to speak about what they wanted, what they feared, and not just be lost in wordless misery.

Brigham Young University, Provo, Utah, 1970—$50,000 to help fund the American Indian Assistance Program in Agriculture and Home Management. In Mormon theology American Indians are descendents of the twelve lost tribes of Israel scattered by the Assyrian invasion of 712 B.C. Mormon missionaries may, accordingly, overstress that point until they wipe out, some critics claim, Indian identity. Service to improve Indian farming and home-making seemed practical, however.

I am unsure what to suggest to any other foundation as an Indian commitment. Indian projects have a high failure rate. They are bedeviled by the ideological conflict between wanting to help Indians succeed as individuals within the mainstream or respecting Indian society as a separate entity. A sense of justice does obligate our concern when the project has a ray of hope like that binational school in New Brunswick. If we respect the pluralism that is a root of the American way of life at its best, then we must try to nourish this unusual part of our heritage.

CHAPTER SIX

Picking Up the Pieces

He has sent me to announce good news to the poor, to proclaim release for prisoners and recovery of sight for the blind, to let the broken victims go free.   [Luke 4:18]

The path to a clean city starts with sweeping the sidewalk in front of your house.   [Gandhi]

We're depraved 'cause we're deprived.   [Bernstein, *West Side Story*]

One August morning a handsome young black couple came to my office trying to enter their not overly academic son into Commonwealth. She was a poodle groomer (a lucrative skill, even in hard times: a well-groomed poodle is part of your credit rating); he was a youth probation officer. His client group were twenty males from fourteen to nineteen convicted of violent crimes: assault, murder, and rape. Eighteen of the twenty were illiterate, or to use Mr. Shropshire's image: "If you gave each one of them a million dollars, only two could recognize their own names on the check and then endorse it on the other side." On their school records many of these illiterates had received A's and B's on the way up through the eighth grade, showing the ability to survive classroom life even if they didn't learn anything.

It was a hopeless job. Mr. Shropshire tried to protect himself by not getting too closely involved, but the one boy he did care about—George—was a fifteen-year-old who had participated in the killing of a heating oil delivery man during the great 1978 Boston snow fall. He just couldn't be torn up and thrown away. One possibility was a special three-year program at the Menninger Clinic in Kansas. The cost of this would have been $60,000 for the first year and $18,000 apiece for the remaining two. That $96,000 tab was more than the government of Massachusetts was willing to pick up, but the alternative was life imprisonment without parole. Since a year of prison at Walpole or Norfolk runs, by a fascinatingly precise rule of thumb, at twice the cost of a year at Harvard (and Harvard's costs were then over $10,000), if that boy lived fifty more years, as well he might if not wiped out in a fight or suicide, the bill paid by the taxpayers of Massachusetts, up each year as Harvard keeps raising its tuition, would come to over a million.

At every decision level involving this sort of individual and his family, until the last one—health care or housing, jobs or schooling, truancy or delinquency—the criterion most respected by whatever agency that signed the check was economy. A service or procedure that cost $180 was better than one costing $200. A procedure at $172.50 was better still. At the last line, however, when he is locked away in the correctional institute at $20,000, $30,000, and up per year for as long as he lives, all the hardliners are overjoyed and for those services willingly pay the taxes required.

Another case. In the early 1970s my school was offered a sixteen-year-old black girl, described as brilliant and beautiful—Doreen—who was a caricature of the ambitions and approaches of the Great Society. Her father, not in the picture, was vaguely European; her mother was cold, excitable, and shrewd—not caring enough to show responsibility but tenacious in seeing that Doreen received all the services promised her. I was not impressed by the self-consciously vivacious girl trying so hard to make a good impression—"Yes, I want to be a gynecologist"—but she *was* intelligent, and the contact who had recommended her, an experienced man, said I could risk this gamble with Doreen because she had the backing of an integrated support system.

We found out what an ISS was. Doreen immediately got into trouble with our classes, but her academic advisor lined up a Spanish tutor (a volunteer from Phillips Brooks House at Harvard) and a geometry tutor (a graduate student at M.I.T.) who set weekly appointments, which she usually forgot. Doreen, who suffered vague complaints, saw a doctor every other week and also a dentist. A family counselor met with the girl and mother to try and straighten out their legal and financial problems and used these meetings as a way to mediate between the two, who got along badly. Doreen also had a psychiatric social worker with whom she would talk about her dreams (fallout from a traumatic childhood), sexual problems, and worries about popularity. Somewhere, in some ultimate Cambridge agency as remote as Kafka's Castle, was someone who watched over this kingdom, but we never made contact.

Doreen's advisor at the school, a sensible woman, got her to sit down one afternoon and make up a week's schedule of the what and when of all her obligations, but she suddenly sprang out of her chair—"I'm late for my dentist!"—and ran out of the room. Both sides began to get angry. Her teachers ceased to enjoy the game of trying to pin her down. The mother felt we weren't doing right by her girl. Doreen resented being ordered about. June came and we told her there was no point in returning.

The story isn't ended. Five years later I was watching a television program, "Children of the Great Society," and there was Doreen. She and some other young people who had been processed by progress were being interviewed about their lives then and now. My school hadn't been Doreen's only good experience. We were followed by an outfit that had tried to improve disadvantaged youngsters through the arts, and she had endured operas, ballets, and symphony concerts. They were okay, but the whole thing got boring after a while, and she and a pal of hers used to rip up the backs of the seats in front of them during the operas to see what sort of stuffing they had.

Doreen laughed at what a foolish kid she had been but also at the presumptions of all those agencies and people who had tried so hard to make her into something she didn't want to be. Now she had a small child, who had been wandering around her mother during the show, held a steady job at a department store, and was taking courses at night so she could get an equivalency certificate that in turn would qualify her for another school where she could learn to be a secretary.

A third case. Through one of our parents, Commonwealth made contact with a white boy—Henry—a ward of the state's Child Welfare Agency, bright and strong enough to need a demanding school like ours. The agency would pay half his tuition, our school the other half—that was why, after all, we ran a scholarship drive. He was an appealing boy and willing to talk about his life. He had never had a father. His mother, a distraught alcoholic who had given birth in her teens, abandoned him, and Henry had been brought up by a poor, lonely, elderly Italian. They lived in cheap hotels in a variety of cities, a situation that no responsible agency should have permitted, but the old man liked to talk about all the interesting things he had done and thought about in his life, which awakened the little boy's intelligence, and he obviously loved his charge—"and that taught me to love." That phrase meant a lot to Henry. I heard it many times. Perhaps he knew it made an impression on adults. Henry had had a lot of experience with strangers.

Eventually the old man faded out of the picture, and Henry boarded with foster families and now at a small, state-funded home or commune (it was that period of history) for teenage boys run by a black graduate student and his wife. Mr. Williams was a fine man, respected by Henry, and he called on me to talk about the boy, who often substituted charm for effort. Nevertheless, Henry was elected student leader of the commune, graduated with decent grades (he worked hard senior year), won a large scholarship from

Pomona (he had lived in California with the elderly Italian), graduated from there (with semesters off when he ran out of money or out of steam), and moved to San Francisco and got a part-time office job while he put himself through law school. He wants to work for a corporation and make money, but he insists that he also wants to make sure, all his life, that he'll give a hand to boys like the one he was.

Back to the Charles E. Merrill Trust. How could our foundation have been effectively involved with the different schools, agencies, and programs that tried to deal with the lives of young people like those three?

In the first case, Mr. Shropshire's murderer, we could have put up the money for the Menninger Clinic's salvage job. We made a lot of mistakes; that wasn't one of them. It wasn't simply the expense involved but the hopelessness, and yet Mr. Shropshire, who was no amateur, felt that George was a salvageable boy, and the alternative, life imprisonment without parole, would be more costly to everyone in the long run. But it was American ghetto society that had created George and his pals who had killed the oil delivery man, and unless that society is fundamentally changed, no miracles at any price by the Menninger Clinic will do much good if the graduate returns to the same society.

The conclusion to Doreen's story, as foreshadowed on the television program, is probably reassuring. She appeared to be a resilient, good-natured, shrewd young woman, showing the Negro ability to survive: to survive poverty and neglect and to survive the frantic (short-lived) efforts of a foolish liberal society to make her into something special. Eventually she was finishing school. She probably had the determination to turn herself from a salesgirl into a secretary. She might avoid another illegitimate child. She would probably do reasonably well.

And lastly, Henry. He had the good fortune to run into Commonwealth, which, thanks to the Charles E. Merrill Trust, had the money (as did Pomona) to award him a scholarship and not quit when the state was six months late (as it usually was) in paying its share. Our school supplied stimulation, discipline, patience, and concern—all of which he needed. Ten years ago the state was willing to fund such a commune and hire a man like Mr. Williams to run it—Henry today wouldn't have that good fortune. But what saved Henry was the lonely old Italian who picked up the little boy and traveled around with him in the seedy hotels they shared in New England and California, stimulated his mind with his conversation, and gave him a soul with his love. How does that fit into a budget?

The 1980s are a pessimistic decade, and the cynicism and selfishness that go along with pessimism can be as destructive as the foolishness that accompanied the optimism of other times. We see only our failures, or the failures we blame on others, and the interconnected pathology of twentieth-century urban life appears so overwhelming that we have no idea of where to begin.

And with a national government cynical about social improvement and callous about the sufferings of the poor, those still concerned about making life bearable for people in trouble are worn out simply trying to get to the end of the week.

We are left with conclusions more sober than we would have settled for twenty years ago. Our resources are limited. Human values and human skills cannot be changed for the better in any short period of time by a single program, no matter how costly. Any serious problem has such a multiplicity of causes that any solution plausible enough to be politically appealing is sure to be inadequate. "You can't make problems go away by throwing money at them" is the all-purpose slogan of the conservatives now in authority. This slogan is used as an excuse for doing nothing at all, except when we are dealing with the problem of military security, which is solved by throwing in hundreds of billions of dollars.

So, as an agency executive with a specific responsibility to face, as a foundation trustee or a politician who votes yes or no, or as an individual who writes a check to charity, one tries to understand what makes sense and decides what price is worth paying. Most general solutions don't work, and one usually has to settle for a partial approach to an isolated problem, trying not to fall prey to cynicism when the solution simply causes a new problem. The process of struggle in itself may be more rewarding than the victory one first imagines, the sharing of a goal that is the release from loneliness and the sense of futility.

CHILDREN AND TROUBLE

For my children I will stand with my head bowed and my hand out.   [Boston Welfare Mother]

Where does one start in turning the long, usually one-way road to prison? Where does trouble first present itself, and what can a check-writing foundation do about it? The surest way is to work with the family unit and strengthen parents' resources in dealing with their own inadequacies and coping with the inadequacies of society. In America the temptation is to deal with the isolated problem and evade the general issue: family violence has increased in the late 1970s because more fathers are unemployed and, with time on their hands, they drink and then beat their wives and children. A family agency in Detroit cannot offset the decline of the auto industry.

Ramapo Anchorage Camp, Rhinebeck, New York, 1960–1979—$70,000. This Jewish-run camp serving children of every background was a favorite cause of Dr. Erdmann, the Magowan family physician. It specialized in experimental and therapeutic aid to severely disturbed children and had such an outstanding record that the State Department regularly included Ramapo on the itinerary of foreign educators, doctors, and camp directors. Our money, in five separate grants, went toward operating costs, winterizing to allow year-round operation, and a new program for preschool children. As times got worse by the late 1970s, funding was harder to obtain while the number of disturbed children needing help grew ever larger, and as social legislation helped families handle simpler problems, private agencies found themselves saddled with increasingly complex ones requiring a costly teamwork of case-workers, psychologists, psychiatrists, and pediatricians.

Citizen's Committee for Children of New York, 1965–1979—$70,000. Started during World War II when women war-workers needed help with their children, the Committee sought to monitor the daycare centers that mushroomed in dubious forms and to improve standards of day nurseries and children's services, with ignorance more often the problem than cruelty. By 1965 New York City spent twenty times as much on children's services than in 1945, and yet the problems were greater than ever. The education budget rose by 400 percent in the same period, and yet more children remained poorly educated than ever before. Merrill Trust grants went to strengthen a Division of Education Services to improve the newly decentralized city public school system, including the schooling of children in psychiatric hospitals, in detention schools, and in welfare hotels.

Children's Defense Fund (CDF), Washington, D.C., 1977—$15,000. Here was an interestingly difficult decision. The Fund—whose logo was a child's scrawl, "Dear Lord be good to me; the sea is so wide and my boat is so small"—started in 1972 as the Washington Research Project to help minority and poor people investigate federal programs designed to serve them. Vast numbers of children do not receive the services that a loving parent or a practical country should provide. In 1971 ten million received no medical care whatsoever, and six million were not fully immunized. Thousands under six stay at home alone all day because both parents work and there is no child care. Two million children were out of school in 1970, over one million were suspended, often for long periods. Children are denied fundamental rights and need the services that will enable them to grow up as healthy adults. Minority, poor, and handicapped children suffer disproportionately from such burdens, but a middle-class white child who crosses the line, that is, as a runaway, rapidly finds out how precarious are his rights too.

CDF has five priorities. First, *the right to education* should include all children, and those outside the average cannot be considered expendable. In Alabama, for example, both white and black retarded children must receive services of equal dollar value. Second, *due process* must be followed in school discipline. An unpleasant child just can't be told to beat it. Third, *privacy and human experimentation*. Poor and nonwhite children must be protected from electroshock mental treatments, behavior modification drugs, psycho-surgery, and other brutal short-cuts. Fourth, *children's health*. Those in most need of public health services are the least likely to receive them. A little money to serve a troubled child at home will spare a great deal of money in a custodial institution, a simple rule hard to put across to budget-cutters. Fifth, *juvenile justice*—how to protect children from savage jails, where a runaway boy is raped by adult cellmates, not because the jailors are brutes but because they have no other facilities to offer. Advocacy in all these areas should be specific and practical, not rhetorical and confrontational, pinpoint-ing the problems with careful homework, flexible approaches, and support from local groups.

I was particularly involved in this appeal and proposed it for $30,000 be-cause the problem was so serious (and would become more so as the Reagan Administration cut back on one social program after another) and because I had a great regard for the director, Marian Wright Edelman, the first black woman admitted to the Mississippi bar, whom I had known since she was a student at Spelman College. CDF, however, became confused in my col-leagues' eyes as an advocacy group defending muggers in the jungle of the juvenile court system and received only half the support I felt it deserved.

In the 1980s CDF was waging a holy war with the Reagan administration. Under the argument of safeguarding our future by expanding our military strength, federal budgets have cut deeper and deeper into services to mothers and children that might also be considered the safeguard of our future. By 1985, thirteen million children—one in five—were estimated by CDF to live in poverty, but the services that might allow such children to obtain better health, emotional balance, living environment, and education in order to—perhaps—climb out of poverty have been cut and cut again. These included cuts in Medicaid, the most important federal health program for mothers and children, cuts in nutrition programs that used to provide lunches for children in schools and day care centers, cuts in supplemental food programs for low-income pregnant women and infants, and cuts in immunization programs for preschool children.

Any amateur can imagine the relative cost/benefit ratio of such preventive maintenance now versus the health, delinquency, and unemployment costs of the same ex-child ten, twenty, or thirty years from now. Sometimes the figures are quite specific: $600 under the Education of the Disadvantaged program to supply reading and math services will hold a substandard child to grade level, and $2,400 is the public school average cost if he must repeat a grade.

By the 1980s Marian Edelman was concentrating her efforts in trying to slow down the plague of teenage pregnancy, the most important cause, she reasoned, of lifelong poverty, particularly for blacks.[1] The heart of the struggle was not simply sex education but of giving young people a future, a stake in the future, by giving them decent schools, decent jobs, prenatal care so they can have healthy babies, and child care so that they can work and gain the self-respect that keeps them from slipping back into a second and a third illegitimate birth. Mrs. Edelman sought to enlist the black churches as allies, a change often hard for them, and to set up family planning centers in the high schools.

The Merrill trustees had always interested themselves in problems of pregnancy and population, ranging from the individual teenager to the rates of worldwide population growth. Our first involvement was *Medical Research Foundation of Boston, 1959—$25,000* for research by Dr. S. Charles Kasdon, Medical Director of Booth Memorial Hospital, on the psychological causes of illegitimacy. A poor self-image, the girls' inability to communicate with their parents, and a passive attitude towards life seemed far more the cause than smiling strangers or simple ignorance that a good ninth grade biology course with appropriate diagrams could remedy. By the 1980s the percentage of unmarried women having babies had doubled since the end of World War II.

The National Alliance Concerned with School Age Parents, Washington, D.C., 1978—$10,000. The Alliance is a black-run group trying to make sense of the panicky statistics and trying to offer realistic approaches to a problem out of control. For example, one reason for the growth in illegitimacy has been simply the large number of females born in the 1950s and 1960s. As in Mexico or Algeria, a lot more young women of prime reproductive age happen to be available. And since young black males of the 1980s suffer an unemployment rate of about 50 percent, they cannot afford to marry their pregnant girlfriends. The proportion of all black teens becoming mothers was falling, but the proportion of unmarried black girls having babies was going up. Illegitimacy is a national disease, not just a black one. In 1969 the birthrates for single black mothers was eleven times the white rate; in 1975, only eight times.

The most important fact, however, is that by the mid-1980s, 55 percent of all black births (11 percent of whites) were to single women, and this progressive destruction of the black family is offsetting all the social and educational gains won since the 1960s. Black leadership was slow to face this crisis. White leadership was even slower to face the crisis that by 1985 almost half of America's black children and over half of its Hispanic children lived

1. Of the 3,680,000 babies born in the United States in 1982, 14 percent were born to adolescents. In 1984 CDF located in Chicago a twenty-four-year-old grandmother.

below the poverty line. In Senator Daniel Patrick Moynihan's figures, children make up only 27 percent of the nation but 40 percent of the people in poverty.

For girls of fourteen, the U.S. pregnancy rate is four times that of Canada, the second highest western country. Why? The lack of any governmental or social emphasis upon practical preventive measures is one reason. Concepts of traditional morality that prevent an accurate assessment of what actually exists is another. In the world of poverty, the girl involved has low self-esteem. It is better to be a mother with a baby to love than to be a nothing. There is also the need for a girl to accept her own sexuality, both in feelings and actions, of seeing her life as something she must actively take responsibility for and then act upon instead of relying passively on fate.

In the CDF's lobbying for practical responses to the crisis of adolescent pregnancy and to the whole general crisis of child and family poverty, what Marian Edelman found the hardest to deal with was the American preference to blame the victim. The moral character of the poor and the complicated details of their lack of motivation are examined obsessively. The neat coincidence that reduction in welfare benefits makes the poor more desperate and therefore more willing to work for lower wages is overlooked. Practical details like a higher minimum wage, greater availability of low-cost housing, better education and child health care, and the guaranteed maternity and child benefits that most European countries take for granted are ignored as much as the relationship between poverty and illegitimacy. Her unexpected adversary turned out to be old Reverend Malthus, that pioneer pessimist on population. If only the poor showed greater moral restraint they'd have fewer babies and happier homes. Mrs. Edelman argued otherwise. Hope and opportunity are the best contraceptives.

Catholic Alternatives, New York, New York, 1977–1980—$30,000 for sex education and counseling, often by other teenagers, with a special stress upon reaching the city's Hispanic population. A problem for this group was physical attack against their clinics by right-to-life militants: "You're no Catholic if you teach such things!"

Dorchester House Multi-Service Center, Boston, Massachusetts, 1980—$15,000 to the Early Childbearing Program. One-quarter of all births in North Dorchester were to girls under nineteen. There was a need to make contact with the pregnant girl, to break through loneliness and shame, and to give advice on health and on the process of childbearing. It also sought to aid a girl in trouble in raising a healthy baby, finish her education, get a job, stay off welfare, and build a stable life for herself.

Salvation Army Booth Memorial Hospital, Philadelphia, Pennsylvania, 1972—$25,000 (Booth Maternity Center). A young militant director, John

Franklin, was trying to reorganize the hospital and policies of patient care. He encouraged participation of all members of the health management team, including patients and former patients, in the running of the hospital and encouraged the adolescent parents to participate in health care planning. The Salvation Army policy was a single class of family-centered care, regardless of age, education, or family status. Husband or friend was encouraged to share in planning and to attend the delivery. Too many traditional medical practices disrupt normal relations between mother and child. The usual hospital hierarchy should be abandoned, and the management team should represent all groups, accepting a new approach to medical ideas and to a new type of patient, adolescent, often unmarried, oversensitive to being ordered around, with an increased percentage of single mothers keeping their babies, and with a pregnancy that represents defiance of authority. The medical staff need to be cured of the habit of saying, "Do as I tell you and don't make no trouble!" which simply reinforces behavior patterns of sullen alienation or random aggression. What seemed revolutionary in 1972 was beginning to be mainstream in 1982.

St. Anne's Maternity Hospital, Los Angeles, California, 1969—$25,000. This is a hospital run, since 1941, by Franciscan Sisters of the Sacred Heart, for unwed mothers eleven to seventeen (twenty years ago the age span was fourteen to twenty-eight), most of the younger cases from incest. Eight hundred girls had been turned away in 1968 from lack of room. Care includes psychological and social therapy, including the problem of should the girl keep the child or give it up for adoption. An education center was included in the hospital to allow girls to continue high school work or take training as beauticians, cashiers, or office workers.

Two girls, both black, at my school became mothers while ninth graders. One put the child out for adoption; the other kept hers. One mother was aggressive and foolish; the other sad and withdrawn. In each case I felt that an abortion would have reduced the long-range personal and social cost of the experience, but no one was prepared to make that choice in time.

Sex education, adolescent illegitimacy, abortion, and population control turn into ugly topics. There is racism, as (male) black militants insist, in liberals' concern to help black and Hispanic girls not have babies: fewer of Them. Even worse is the self-righteous anger of middle-aged white men who consider themselves agents of God's will in making sure that pregnant females be forced to give birth. When the babies arrive, those Christians have no interest at all in voting funds for their health and nurture. Their right to life has come to an end.

Spence Chapin Adoption Services, New York, New York, 1959–1979—

$95,000. Almost the oldest and best known private adoption agency, it is nonsectarian, interracial, and presses for adoption rather than institutional care. Two Trust grants went for the special needs of handicapped children, and $25,000 was given in 1969 to establish a branch agency in Harlem, which has the highest rate in the city for illegitimate births. Sophisticated teamwork is needed in dealing with mother, child, and adoptive parents, involving social work, pediatrics, psychology, anthropology, law, and genetics.

Spence Chapin's Children's House, New York, New York, 1977–1978— $25,000. This was set up in the mid-1970s as a diagnosis and treatment center for children under six with emotional or developmental problems—a therapeutic nursery, the only one for children of that age: learning disabilities, stuttering, autism, and schizophrenia. To help one child in 1977 cost $4,000 per year versus $12,000 in a hospital. Family instability, improper nutrition and health care, and lack of environmental stimulation lead to a rate of over 12 percent mental disability among children in many parts of Manhattan.

Task Force on Children Out of School (through the Massachusetts Advocacy Center) Boston, Massachusetts, 1979—$10,000. The Task Force was organized in 1969 to secure educational opportunities for Boston children, particularly those with special needs and foreign language. Its first aim was to gather accurate statistics on the number of such children and also on the problems they faced (the inability of a child in a wheelchair to climb stairs, for example) and then to push an unresourceful city school system into action. The thrust of this movement was embodied in the Chapter 766 Special Education Act, with one result being that school districts, even in the affluent suburbs, paid for the new services for handicapped children by cutting academic classes like advanced math or French for another minority. In the Task Force's thinking, such children can look after themselves, whereas accurate support for the handicapped will save millions in later costs for illness and unemployment. Money was also needed to push the schools to supply free lunches and lead poisoning testing for poor children, the latter a problem that middle-class people do not hear about.

Contact Care Center, Lafayette, California, 1981—$10,000. Is there more child abuse or is society now more sensitive and parents more free to talk openly about the despair that has driven them this far? Parents who beat their children are apt to be socially and emotionally isolated. They distrust traditional community services but will utilize an approach that preserves their anonymity, particularly in this initial cry for help. Contact Care runs a twenty-four-hour crisis hotline, a listening ministry for parents at the end of their rope who have struck their child or see themselves about to do so. Merrill

Trust money went to set up other stress centers in nearby low-income communities in the outer suburbs of San Francisco where mental health services were minimal.

ADDICTION AND SALVAGE

Drug Programs

My sister and I became involved in projects concerning runaways and drug addicts in the period between 1969 and 1975 when that seemed such an overwhelming problem for America. As a headmaster I had been agonizingly frustrated by the impact of drugs on my own students, for whom attempts at face-to-face counseling by teachers or education from outside experts had little effect. Some of them got in over their heads. To find drugs was like, for an earlier generation, finding God, as one graduate put it, or like Ahab's search for the Truth behind the white whale. The secrecy and deceit, the youngest ninth grader knowing more about what went on at Commonwealth School than I did, and the closeness to criminality with the police on one side and the pushers on the other, badly hurt the school. Later on I was surprised at the resiliency of those gamblers; they went on to college, got involved in other things, made useful careers, and were amusedly sympathetic at how upset I had been. A few were arrested. A black teacher went to jail for importing hashish from India in the false bottoms of crates containing musical instruments.

The Trust put money into a wide variety of treatment centers. It is hard to judge how effective these were and where one approach was better than another and where the addicts cleansed themselves instead of drifting back again. Addicts are losers. Should one put one's money (there's never very much) into backing winners? Sometimes I loathed even more the righteous who had no idea of the agony of that world, where drugs were in truth the symptom and the disease was a brutal society, accepting napalm upon Vietnamese villages, as the militants repeated, while condemning pot and long hair.

Youth Projects, Incorporated, San Francisco, California, 1969—$25,000. This money was to support the Haight-Ashbury Medical Clinic. Haight-Ashbury became a magnet of the hippie youth world in the mid-1960s for pilgrims looking for an immediate answer to life's problems, with psychedelic drugs an integral part of their existence. This neighborhood turned into a disaster area with inadequate housing, food, and health care. The Youth Projects' clinic was inundated as soon as it opened in 1967. In two years it had served

50,000 patients, expanding from drug problems to general medical needs. Marijuana and LSD were being replaced by methamphetamine or speed, which burns out its users. Money was needed to keep the drug treatment program going until expected federal funds might arrive.

Ecumenical Ministry in the Haight-Ashbury, San Francisco, California, 1970—$10,000. Speed, barbiturates, and heroin were making the drug scene even more dangerous. Detoxification and psychiatric counseling were needed first, then the effort to reunite young people with their families. There came a conviction that the patients had to be removed from the chaotic, desperate subculture, which meant a far more involved and costly residential program.

Jewish Family and Children's Service of Metropolitan Toronto, Canada, 1970—$25,000 to finance services of Trailer House, a day center for drug-scarred youths. This started as a Jewish project but soon turned to serving all who came. The Yorkville neighborhood was the focus of the youth world since the mid-1960s, with an influx of depressed and agitated runaways, paranoid about the police and the Royal Canadian Mounted Police Narcotics Squad. Local hospitals were unfamiliar with treatment of drug problems and their staff were hostile: "These young people deserve to be punished!" Trailer House became trusted and served 1,200 patients aged thirteen to twenty-five its first summer and by its second was winning police sympathy and hospital help in trying to deal with the new plague of speed. One function of Trailer House was to educate other service agencies to the realities of drug use, for which their previous experience had left them completely unprepared.

Association of Boston Urban Priests, Boston, Massachusetts, 1970— $32,000 to establish a pilot center for addicts and runaways. This project was run by Paul Shanley, a charismatic priest who had left a comfortable suburban parish because he could not push his congregation into taking any action against either racism or the war in Vietnam. With a prescience that proved frightening, he foretold the waves of runaways (one million in 1969 and three in 1970) who were on the road or headed for Boston and San Francisco, which enjoyed an interesting drug and rock scene and were romanticized as tolerant and supportive communities. At first these were fugitives from homes scarred with alcoholism and violence, then homes that seemed all right on the surface, but were in reality cold, hypocritical, prejudiced, and then homes that actually were warm and upright but whose children were just overwhelmed by the destructiveness of the society around them and the rootless despair of their age group. Shanley also foretold the shift in drug styles from marijuana to heroin (a reality in Harlem in 1961 when the Trust was funding the East

Harlem Protestant Parish but something else again when it struck at white middle-class kids) plus the coming of the irrational mystery cults to replace a lifeless Christianity and a bankrupt secularism. Shanley set his first priority as simple survival (to keep runaways from prostitution, crime, disease, and starvation), and his second was reconciliation. All too often child and parents were just beginning to talk when the father would cry out, "But first of all, get a haircut!" and the boy would run away again in fury. The Trust's project was a failure because the youth center was too near a police station, which frightened away the kids. After a while Shanley left the street scene, started a retreat center in New Hampshire for youth workers as burnt out as he was, and then a center for homosexuals where they could share their problems and help build a positive sense of themselves.

Massachusetts General Hospital, Boston, Massachusetts, 1971—$10,000 to support an evening van at Harvard Square and other hangouts. Drugs, hepatitis, venereal disease, and psychiatric counseling were the priorities for the staff, who dressed and talked like hippies so as not to frighten off the street people. A serious need came also in periodontia, for poor hygiene and malnutrition ravaged their mouths.

Cambridgeport Problem Center, Cambridge, Massachusetts, 1971–1975—$30,000. This project started as a free clinic to dropouts and runaways, soon became swamped with demands, and the Problem Center opened to deal with nonmedical problems. Psychiatrists, lawyers, social workers, and clinical psychologists made up the staff, but a formal rule was that whoever first saw a client would carry the case: there would be no bureaucratic shunting from one department to another. The first goal was to build trust by offering practical help in a nonjudgmental way to people who had fallen through the cracks, who wanted to reconstruct their lives but did not know where to begin, and who were usually in trouble with the law and did not know their rights.

The $10,000 in 1975 was to support a shift of focus to meeting the needs of the entire community: the poor, elderly, blacks, Puerto Ricans, and Portuguese. The Center had become a licensed drug treatment center (stressing prevention rather than rehabilitation), still stressing its conviction that drug-taking was the symptom, not the problem.

Interseminarian, Boston, Massachusetts, 1972–1978—$40,000. Interseminarian supplied the legal structure and formal direction to Place, an advice center and crash pad in Boston's South End. It was a hostel for runaways under seventeen, originally suburban and now increasingly working-class, nonwhite, and urban. There was a hot line with 1,000 calls a week and an emergency van and, on the longer term, a sophisticated research program to measure the effectiveness of agencies and methods in dealing with young people. The drug scene seemed less of a crisis situation than in 1970, and the main stress of Interseminarian's staff was training street volunteers, for whom there was a tremendous need.

Place monitored the pulse of the Boston area and warned of coming problems and of gaps in the social service network. It provided an emergency ambulance service, training program for emergency medical technicians, and referral files of 3,000 utilizable agencies. As government and foundation money dried up, the staff of agencies like this quit and enrolled at business schools.

Daytop Village, New York, New York, 1969—$25,000. Daytop was founded in 1963 under the auspices of the New York State judiciary system with help from the National Institute of Mental Health. It had a $1.2 million annual budget with room at three centers for 500 patients. The daily patient cost was $10.50 as against $20 in jail and $50 in the hospital. Neither jail nor sympathy has any rehabilitative value: 90 percent of the addicts released from the centers in Lexington, Kentucky or Fort Worth, Texas relapse within a year. The addict sees nothing as his fault. He simply lacks the weapons that others possess for their battle with life. Heroin helps him escape, and in pursuit of heroin he can muster extraordinary cunning.

Since the heroin addict is untouched by the approaches of normal psychotherapy, Daytop's staff adopted a brutally hard-nosed approach. An applicant is told to phone for an appointment at 2:30 P.M. sharp. If he is five minutes late he is dropped to the bottom of the list. He must prove that he wants help. Every detail of Daytop life is designed to shock. He won't be treated like a spoiled child. The staff are former junkies; they know the game. He cleans tables and mops floors. In withdrawal agony he is ignored. In group therapy there is insistence on 100 percent honesty, relieving tensions by violent shouting at each other to speed up personality alteration, a fierce attack therapy. After three months there is a 75 percent chance of finishing the eighteen-month program. Job training is offered in auto mechanics, plumbing, and electrical work. The road back starts with the search for an autocratic tribal father figure.

Odyssey House, New York, New York, 1970—$35,000. The first Odyssey House started in 1966 with addicts who wanted to cure themselves without using other drugs. By 1970 it had eight inpatient centers and five storefront facilities all across the United States. The motto of founder Julianne Denser-Gerber was "I never turn a child away." The drug program is everywhere, from Harlem to Palm Beach. By the end of 1970 there were 100,000 young people on heroin in New York City. Lawyers see this as crime, but Dr. Densen-

Gerber sees it as an illness. A law may be passed, but the child by then will be dead. You can't cure people retroactively. The suffering kids are also, of course, the pushers.

Odyssey House's approach is that addicts can function without drugs. They can be treated through psychiatric intervention and then can carry responsibility to prevent others from being hooked. Treatment begins with an intensive in-resident phase. Residents enforce their own rules and check con men and game players, assuming that each person has the innate capacity to function positively when properly challenged, and they try to combat dependency, loneliness, and low self-esteem. After ten or twelve months at Odyssey, the patient starts moving out part-time in school, job, speaking engagements, and family.

Lower East Side Information and Service Center for Narcotics Addiction, New York, New York, 1972—$15,000. This is a comprehensive clinic with extensive use of methadone. There is an open-ended hopelessness about methadone therapy. The state supplies its addicts with this drug to avoid the violence that heroin-users must employ for their purchases. The methadone people don't get any better but they don't cause much trouble and gradually they rot away. Black militants see the policy as an establishment plot to emasculate ghetto resistance.

In Iran, after the Moslem revolution of the Ayatollah Khomeini, addicts and pushers were arrested and shot. The human suffering of that approach may be no worse. A former student of mine, an apprentice lawyer in a Boston housing court, disagrees. In the ghetto world that he saw, street corner drug selling may in hard times be literally the only job available and drug consumption the only relief to anticipate. An agile fourteen-year-old runner can earn $100/200 a day.

Marathon House, Gaylordsville, Connecticut, 1972—$10,000. In this self-help drug rehabilitation center in a family environment, eighteen young men and women, mostly from the middle class, facing jail sentences of two to five years each for drug possession, were offered two years at Marathon as an alternative. The program is described as psychologically intense, with only 2 percent considered incurable, and is funded by public agencies and private gifts.

Reflections: Middle-class society treats middle-class deviants more generously than it does working class ones. What is the unit cost of one of those pilgrim's two-year stay in that charming New England village? How lonely will the real world seem afterwards? How nostalgic will they feel for those intense group discussions around the dining room table?

Reality House West, San Francisco, California, 1973—$20,000 for operating costs and a country retreat for retraining ex addicts and alcoholics. The goals are to help addicts avoid self-destruction through self- and group awareness and to become resourceful through realistic behavior and concern for themselves and others. In 1973 the cost to the federal government for the treatment of drug addiction was estimated at $350 million, a billion by the 1980s—half in treatment programs, half in enforcement. How can we deal with the complexity of human nature? How can we also provide training and job placement for these ex addicts, 75 percent of whom are minority, uneducated, poorly motivated, and have no marketable skills.

Greenwich House, New York, New York, 1960–1978—$100,000. Greenwich was started in 1902 to strengthen family life and to promote better relations between different ethnic groups in Manhattan's Lower West Side. There are theatre and music groups, classes in ceramics, and classes in learning foreign languages and English. By the 1960s, with an increasingly Puerto Rican clientele, the House became involved in narcotics prevention and treatment. In 1968 two hundred addicts a month were being treated through group therapy and individual counseling. The Merrill Trust's five grants went for preventive programs for teenagers considered narcotics-prone: to employ a psychiatric social worker for counseling, to establish a coffee house to get them off the street corners where LSD was for sale at $5 a cube, and to pay a young street worker who hung out at teenage haunts and tried to involve their people in wholesome activities or in drug counseling. In 1978, $10,000 was given to support an evening recreation program to bring together racially mixed and alienated teens.

The Trust gave about $440,000 to sixteen different agencies, mainly between 1969 and 1972 when the drug scene seemed so newly threatening. A few projects were followed up, but we became interested in other topics or persuaded ourselves that drug addiction had become endemic, like malaria, rather than epidemic. What we accomplished with our grants, what any of those agencies accomplished, I don't know. Emptying the sea with teacups.

By the mid-1980s the drug scene worldwide is far worse. The production and merchandising have become an indispensable part of the economics and politics of one nation after another: opium in Pakistan, Burma, and Indonesia; marijuana in Mexico, Belize, and Jamaica; cocaine in Colombia, Bolivia, Peru, and Ecuador—the ultimate third world revenge upon the consumerist nations of the West. Cocaine seems an appropriate scourge: the indulgence of Beautiful People, the tool for ambitious businessmen to maintain aggressiveness, the short cut to sexiness and charm (priced so cheaply by now that all classes can share), followed by a landslide of self-loathing.

My last year at Commonwealth rumor fingered one foolish senior as a snorter, but by then I was too tired and angry to drive myself to one more confrontation.

Addiction Research Foundation, Palo Alto, California, 1978, 1981— $50,000. Stop Now, San Francisco, California, 1981—$10,000. Peter Magowan had us back these two groups, the $50,000 to Addiction Research being to examine ways of motivating smokers to give up cigarettes. To me this seemed a futile way of spending a large amount of money. If smoking does have a significant role in the death rates of cancer of the lung (also of the bladder, mouth, lip, voicebox, and pancreas, particularly when combined with alcohol), emphysema, heart attacks, and strokes in the United States and other industrialized countries, then nicotine addiction is a disease worth fighting. Nevertheless, the methods used by the American Cancer Society and the agencies funded by the Merrill Trust appear innocuous.

Anti-smoking outfits duck the primary fact that smoking is the product of a billion-dollar industry. The half a dozen corporations that control that industry are not going to tolerate any serious threat to their authority. Hundreds of millions of dollars are spent to ensure that *You* want to be like those narrow-eyed, lean, hard cowhands, those elegant ladies and gentlemen, and those laughing sexy kids whose vibrancy is enhanced by a cigarette. That advertising will be withdrawn from any newspaper or magazine too critical of the tobacco culture. Few of the women's magazines were willing to run articles on the impact of smoking upon female health. The political power of the two states controlled by the tobacco industry, Virginia and North Carolina, keeps the federal government from much beyond cosmetic action.

Accordingly, any campaign to attack smoking must start by attacking corporate investment in the habit, which is not the American way of doing things. To get people to fight a powerful force outside or inside themselves, frustration must be converted into anger: "You have been bamboozled—get back at them!" Strike at the jugular. Have addicts fight withdrawal pains by picketing corporate headquarters: "[Name deleted] makes millions from lung cancer." (In a way it does.) (Make sure there is a good lawyer on the staff. It is safer to attack the CIA.) Picket retail stores that make such profits from selling cigarettes, like Safeway. Print up thousands of ugly little stickers—"Cigarettes cause bladder cancer," "Smoking means earlier menopause and birth defects," photographs of terminal emphysema victims—and have the freedom fighters paste them on all those ads of lean, hard cowhands and elegant ladies. Make the fight against smoking exciting like driving racing cars.[2]

2. Caution: Heavy smokers die, on the average, three to four years earlier than do non-smokers. If they quit smoking and lived longer, that extra cost would bankrupt Social Security. And yet at this date the lung cancer death rate for white males has begun to turn down, an example of what propaganda can accomplish.

National Council on Alcoholism, New York, New York, 1961—$20,000. Alcoholics Rehabilitation Association of San Francisco, 1963—$2,500. Pacific Medical Center, San Francisco, California, 1972, 1975—$25,000 for support of the Alcoholism Clinic.

Alcoholism, of course, is a far more destructive scourge than smoking and burdens Russia and Finland, Ireland and France, and Mexico and Chile even worse than it does our own country. It is a worldwide disease.

Again we ignore the therapy of anger. The alcoholic is already weakened by a wide range of flaws going back to childhood and reinforced each day by his frustrations at work and at home, but he is also the victim of a powerful industry involved in production and merchandising. The alcoholic trying to recover his freedom and self-respect might be encouraged to strike back against those lying advertisements. Rocks thrown through the windows of bars and liquor stores? A number of states have increased their controls and penalties for drunken driving, which might include compulsory service in hospitals for alcoholism along with jail sentences and loss of license. Those who exploit society should pay a greater share of the costs.

HOUSES AND HOMES

It were better for mankind that the millions of the rich were thrown into the sea than so spent as to encourage the slothful, the drunken, the unworthy. [Andrew Carnegie]

When [the poor] see the delay and caution with which relief is given, it does not appear to them a conscientious scruple, but as the cold and calculating action of a selfish man. [Jane Addams]

Neighborhood houses and mission societies, boys' and girls' clubs, homes and help for orphans and delinquents have always been a traditional concern for philanthropy; the Merrill Trust gave about $350,000 to the first group, $270,000 to the second, and $510,000 to the third (plus $50,000 for job training), mainly in the vicinity of New York City.

New York City Mission Society, 1960–1979—$72,000. New York City's oldest community service organization served over 500,000 persons ranging from the south Bronx to the Lower East Side. There were programs for children, youth, parents, and the aged. One stress was upon teaching the fundamentals of child rearing; another was work projects for teens in high delinquency areas. It sponsored the only all-Spanish old-age club in Manhattan. It was proud also of its work in leadership training such as for lay leaders for Harlem churches. The Society saw one young man through the Manhattan School of Music, and he became the first Puerto Rican to win a Fulbright to Rome. Its scholarship helped enable an Hispanic dishwasher to become a Presbyterian pastor. Merrill Trust money went for a new building in central Harlem and support of summer camps.

Grosvenor Neighborhood House, 1961–1978—$100,000.

Henry Street Settlement, 1972–1977—$50,000. Thirty thousand in 1972 was given to help fund a remedial program for children aged eight through twelve certified as uneducable in regular public school systems—similar to the First Presbyterian project of 1970 in Chicago. There has been a change of emphasis, from trying to absorb immigrant groups—which used to be Jewish, Irish, Italian and are now black, Puerto Rican, and Chinese—that used to stress assimilation and social reform into a new policy of offering to the poorest increased options for survival, with the slogan being participation rather than elite leadership. People must make their own choices and learn to confront social structure rather than institutions defining for minority groups what the 'good life' should be.[3] The children, unable to master the public schools, come from the most culturally and economically impoverished sections of the city. The Settlement House is organizing an educational experiment for fifty children now out on the streets with the hope to return them to the regular system within a year. There are efforts to involve parents in collaboration with a special child center of Teacher's College within New York City's decentralized school system. If foundation funding for this program could be found now, later funds might arrive from New York State.

Bowery Mission and Young Men's Home, 1981—$5,000. Founded in 1879 to meet the needs of alcoholic and homeless men: meals, fresh clothing, and showers. This sort of institution is scorned as garbage-can charity, but as times get bad, its clientele broadens.

JOBS TRAINING

We are in a race between the ability of a lumbering, perplexed, imperfect society to move fast enough—and catastrophe.   [William Bender, Director of Boston's Permanent Charity Fund, 1969.]

Dynamy, Wilmington, Delaware, 1973–1976—$15,000. Dynamy was founded in 1968 to give experience to young people ages sixteen to twenty in the daily realities of city living, to allow them to test vocational and career

---

3. This trendy conclusion might be more appealing to the college-educated social worker and the self-styled militant than to the harassed mother who might actually want practical rules on how to run her home and keep her children healthy and get them through school.

possibilities, and to awaken and develop community resources. Interns work with sponsors in medicine, education, government, law, arts, and business, and in a city like Worcester, Massachusetts, high school seniors became involved with Dynamy instead of enrolling in school. The apprenticeship concept, where young people would learn a trade by working with individual masters, just like in the eighteenth century, became fashionable for a while in the mid-1970s: obtaining a practical education through performing interesting jobs, not through reading dumb old books. Since the eager apprentice usually had too short an attention span to carry out the endlessly repetitive tasks that are the essence of such a learning method, a heavy demand was placed upon the altruism of the master. Just the same, it was a protest against the mediocrity of the average high school where work was apt to be neither intellectually stimulating nor practically useful.

Jobs for Youth, New York, New York, 1969–1977—$42,500. Jobs for Youth was a citywide agency that processed 6,000 applications in 1968 and placed 60 percent in jobs. It worked with students having problems in reading and arithmetic and also with young prisoners being considered for parole. Once a client was placed as a delivery boy, shelf stocker, or floor sweeper, the agency sought to maintain contact, showing him how to qualify for a training program that would supply a higher skill. The job situation for minority youth became worse during the 1970s, with a large percentage so illiterate that they could not fill out a job form or read the names of subway stations. The agency gave useful training in details like how to survive an interview and how to understand what is meant by a workday or by courtesy to an employer, but when it applied to the Merrill Trust for a fourth grant, I was turned off by the unit cost of about $1,100 per job. At sixteen and eighteen years of age these young men were already unemployable, to be written off, which we are apt to do at younger and younger ages.

How do we deal with illiteracy, a problem worldwide as city life and state concern decays? We Americans might show some humility in looking for help. *World Education* (New York City), to which the Trust had given $10,000 in 1980 for its work with adolescents in Mexico City, started in Lucknow when India was still under British rule as a service to teach illiterate adults how to read and write and manage their lives. World Education has tried to replicate the skills it learned there in other Asian countries and in Mexico and New York.

What proportion of adolescent and adult Americans can read and write? Jonathan Kozol, who has spent a lifetime fighting the linkage between ignorance and poverty, gives the shocking figures that 44 percent of blacks, 56 percent of Hispanics are functional or marginal illiterates (*Illiterate America* [*Garden City, N.Y.: Anchor/Doubleday, 1985*]). Not much sustained investment, public or private, has been allotted to the problem—illiterates are un-attractive people and use up a lot of effort with marginal results. The problem in motivation may be that even if illiteracy stops the black New Yorkers or the black and white teenager in Liverpool from getting a job, the job that literacy might offer and the life that such a job might offer don't seem worth much. There isn't enough difference between before and after. The historical successes of literacy campaigns—in Cuba in the early years of Castro's rev-olution and in Nicaragua after the Sandinista revolution—came when an existing society was turned upside down and the old rules of exclusion and contempt towards those at the bottom seemed to have been broken.

The Sandinistas put a tremendous effort into that second crusade to follow the military crusade against the Somoza dictatorship. The exguerrilleros were converted into teachers. Middle-class adolescents were recruited in Managua to spend half a year in a village, in the hut of a campesino family. Generous aid came from Europe: pencils from the government of Finland, notebooks and teaching manuals from the Swiss labor unions, and financial support from the German Social-Democrats, and within sixteen or eighteen months, the illiteracy rate had been lowered from 52 percent to 12 percent, a precision hard to accept but repeated to me in 1982 at the American embassy in Man-agua, clearly not a friendly source.

But along with the enthusiastic teachers and the help from abroad, the reason given for this victory was the new attitude of the students being taught. They saw themselves as free, respected citizens asked to play a new role in a new society. If they possessed this new dignity it was only proper that they should learn how to read and write. And if such an attitude is lacking, hiring new reading teachers, no matter how skilled, in New York and Liverpool is not going to clear up the problem.

Washington County Vocational and Technical Institute, Calais, Maine, 1976—$20,000 to serve unemployed and educationally disadvantaged adults and out-of-school youths by improving literacy and numerical skills and by offering job counseling and placement services. The northern Maine coast is as depressed as Mississippi. Traditional skills have deteriorated. A new fed-erally funded Marine Center had been set up in nearby Eastport to teach skills in fishing, in boat building and maintenance, and private funds were needed to help the state match the federal grant.

Union Settlement Association, New York, New York, 1972—$25,000 to fund the College Readiness Program to assist young people in preparing for and applying to college. This was started by trustees, faculty, and students of Union Theological and serves Upper East Side students, 80 percent of whom are black and Puerto Rican and working in cooperation with Benjamin

Franklin High, the only academic high school in Harlem. Four hundred students have been helped to a college education by means of summer workshops, intensive counseling on college choices and applications as well as follow-up of students in college.

Herald Tribune Fresh Air Fund, New York, New York, 1959–1962—$60,000. My father sent an annual check to this favorite charity of his in the name of his three children, a way to get us into the habit of giving. Both able and handicapped children were involved in the same programs and the same cabins, to motivate the handicapped to try harder and to teach the able to be less cruel. There is only so much one can do physically for a handicapped child—the rest is psychological and social.

Girl Scout Council of Greater New York, 1974—$20,000. To support a community leadership program called Take Stock in New York and to develop an awareness of concern, commitment, and cooperation as vital to survival of city dwellers: how Girl Scouts can make a difference. Service to society includes antilitter projects, care for miniplaygrounds and parks, service as tutors to slow learners, care for children, and running workshops.

One is touched by this effort to teach young people to serve, to think of other needs than just their own, and yet when service is interpreted as picking up trash (a part of this program), with the obvious scorn of the girls' peers for such labor, there comes a moment when the teenage St. Francis is pushed into being a normal adolescent and says to hell with it.

Homes for Girls and Boys—Juvenile Delinquency

George Junior Republic, Freeville, New York, 1959—$25,000 for a new building. This is one of the oldest boys' homes, stressing self-government by its citizens. It prints its own money and runs its own bank to stress an immediate connection between productivity and reward.

Boy's Home Association, Jacksonville, Florida, 1959–1970—$55,000. Florida Sheriffs' Boys' Ranch, Live Oak, Florida, 1964–1968—$37,500. These were two charities dear to the heart of my father's old friend, Sam Marks. The ranch served abandoned or neglected boys referred by juvenile courts and child care authorities. It was patterned after Father Flanagan's Boys' Town in Nebraska. Boys were admitted between ages eight and twelve and stayed until the end of high school and performed all the necessary farm and maintenance chores.

Yellowstone Boys Ranch, Billings, Montana, 1976—$10,000. This ranch was started in 1956 to avoid incarceration for boys in trouble. The boys do farming, gardening, and livestock care. The usual age has been nine to twelve, but increasingly boys are referred at younger ages and extra resources are needed for these new changes.

Massachusetts Protestant Social Services, Baldwinsville, Massachusetts, 1972–1976—$25,000 to support a home for emotionally disturbed girls twelve to eighteen, a total of forty living in small units. The reading level of troubled adolescents has dropped throughout the state; whereas one-half of these girls used to function adequately in a local high school, now it is only one or two out of the entire group.

Rehabilitation is expensive, supports a large, often self-serving bureaucracy of public and private welfare workers, and does not enjoy an overly high success rate; but as it becomes federal policy to scorn and cut aid to all such services, small problems become big problems at far higher costs up to the ultimate cost of building one more maximum security jail.

Goddard-Riverside Community Center, New York, New York, 1968– 1976—$90,000. This program made a strong impression upon our foundation, and when a Merrill Lynch vice president presented the first check of $25,000 in 1968 he was deeply moved by what he saw. The fatal shooting by police of two Puerto Ricans in 1965 led to a riot and demonstration but also led to a serious reversal of police policy in Precinct 24. Under Operation Friend all officers took instruction in Spanish language and Puerto Rican culture. The precinct's Community Council met regularly with local people to discuss community problems; a training program was established to encourage black and Puerto Rican enlistment as well as another program to train young men to drive large trucks. Kite-flying contests and holiday parties were organized for children, and a group of 24th Precinct officers made a trip to Lajos, Puerto Rico, and then invited children from there to visit them in New York.

As the changes brought about by school decentralization in New York increased tensions, the Community Center, with $25,000 by the Merrill Trust in 1969, financed a confrontation weekend of school personnel, police, community leaders, and militant students to discuss the whole philosophy of authority and discipline, law and order. In 1972, $25,000 went to replicate this program in adjacent neighborhoods; in 1976, $15,000 to help maintain two youth workers in the staff. As more young people became involved than ever before, budget cuts meant fewer officers and fewer projects.

If extra cash and imagination existed, here would be the project to which to invite visitors from Liverpool and Frankfort, where the same problems exist between police and West Indian and Turkish teenagers with exactly the same mismanagement. Americans do have some hard-won skills to share.

Boston Foundation, Summerthing, Boston, Massachusetts, 1973—$25,000. Summerthing was started in 1968 to involve young city folk, white and black, in a neighborhood arts festival to counter the patterns of boredom, frustration, and anger that built up to violence, what militants of that period dismissed as counterinsurgency. The policy changed from entertainment (free rock concerts, which caused more harm than benefit) to year-round service and educational programs, such as the Curiosity Caravan, a big yellow bus with language and math games that provided fun for children and experience for its middle-class volunteers. This Caravan was turned for a while into a mobile tutoring center with professional teachers attached to public schools in the winter, to community centers and housing projects, teaching basic academic skills.

Thompson Academy, Boston, Massachusetts, 1977—$10,000. Thompson was a long-established boys' home set on an island in Boston Harbor, but as its traditional farm facilities had less to offer contemporary teenagers it gained a new role as neutral turf for meetings between whites and blacks close to the bitter racial frontiers of South Boston and Dorchester. The stress is not upon friendship between the two groups but upon a realistic awareness of common needs.

Outward Bound, Greenwich, Connecticut, 1970–1976—$35,000 and in *1975–1978—$15,000* to *Hurricane Island Outward Bound School, Rockport, Maine.* It is hard to know in what precise category to place Outward Bound because it has diverse programs—off the Maine Coast, in Oregon's Cascades, and in the Great Smokies—used by high school and college students, teachers, prison workers, businessmen, Peace Corps volunteers, Harlem blacks, and Florida delinquents. The program was started in 1941 by Kurt Hahn, a refugee German educator living in England, who was distressed by the high death rate among young seamen in their lifeboats after their ships had been torpedoed. They died not from exposure or from lack of supplies but from lack of the will to live. Hahn tried to teach survival skills and the spirit of tenacity. The seamen who went through his school, first started in the bleak Welsh port of Aberdovey, stayed alive as others didn't.

Josh Miner, an American who had taught under Hahn, began the first American program in 1962 in Colorado. He argued that youngsters want adventure and excitement but live in an age that denies them challenge. The programs widened, including sea, mountain, wilderness, and females, and taught participants to fight fear and exhaustion, to learn to trust each other, confronting people with anxiety, and challenging their intellectual, physical, and spiritual capacities, ending with a forty-eight- or seventy-two-hour period where the individual is left totally alone to find his food and his inner support as best he may. In the process the youngster discovers a greater inventory of strengths and skills than ever imagined.

A number of my students became involved in these programs and highly respected what they gained. In some cases it came too close to a religious experience, and they were left always trying to find their way back. At the other end, a Harlem boy whose daily life was wrapped up in street survival might feel he was being asked to play games with these artificial challenges that middle-class whites admired too readily.

CRIME AND PUNISHMENT

I was in prison and you visited me.   [St. Matthew]

If a person is clearly guilty, do not allow the technical difficulties of the law to keep you from arresting and punishing him.   [Adolph Hitler]

As a case goes further and further, the technical innocence of the defendant becomes less and less important.   [F. Lee Bailey]

People involved in the police, courts, and prison system are so overwhelmed getting from one end of the day to the next that it is hard for them to reflect on any imaginative changes that might be considered. In imprisonment the British have tried the weekend lockup. A rowdy but nondangerous individual may stay home Monday through Friday so that he can keep his job and support his family, but on Friday evening he reports to jail, a process that punishes him inconveniently and keeps him out of the pubs and away from his buddies during these two tempting nights. For youth offenders, the British have also experimented with shorter and far more strenuous terms. A delinquent gets a three-month rather than three-year sentence, but the demands of discipline, work, and all-out exertion resemble a Marine boot camp. He has avoided rotting away in a long term in jail, and surviving the rigor of those three months may give him some pride and a realistic fear of exposing himself to that again. The concept of a criminal paying compensation to the victim or his family is an idea expanding in our country. There is also a New York City experiment in socially useful workcamps for chronic petty offenders.

Above all, with the paralysis of American courts caused by social pathology, slow-moving procedures, and the national disease of litigation, there is a need for any approaches that bypass the formal legal system. The Merrill Trust backed three such projects:

Home Advisory Council of New York, 1968—$15,000. The Council was formed in 1946 by a group of professional people at the request of the New York City Family Court to ameliorate conflict and help parents live together. The Family Court received 15,000 cases a year, often charges of assault and disorderly conduct, with quite inadequate resources: a small probation staff, a few caseworkers, and an alcohol clinic. One way the Council sought to relieve the Family Court was to train volunteer counselors from among mature, talented women—the class in 1968 numbering ten. The Merrill grant went to match a Ford Foundation $550,000 challenge to establish similar units in four upstate New York cities with the hope then of expanding nationally.

American Friends Service Committee, Philadelphia, Pennsylvania, 1978—$5,000 for the Grassroots Citizen Dispute Resolution Clearinghouse. In line with Chief Justice Burger's concern that overcrowded courts be relieved of disputes that could be handled at a lower level, there has been some Department of Justice funding of Neighborhood Justice Centers. The Friends, however, have been experimenting with wholly community-based dispute resolution trying to involve neighborhood people known by their judgment and fairness to be natural settlers of disputes. This avoids the expense, delay, and acrimony of a trial and encourages the belief that people can take care of their own problems.

Crime and Justice Foundation, Boston, 1978—$15,000. Though newly named and reorganized in 1975, this group has a long involvement in correctional reform, crime prevention, and public education in criminal justice. Our grant went to support of Neighborhood Justice Centers to train community volunteers to mediate both civil and criminal complaints between people who know each other.

Central Massachusetts Legal Services, Worcester, Massachusetts, 1979—$10,000. This agency was designed to help persons who do not have ready access to legal aid or other social services, and most of its $400,000 budget came from the Federal Legal Services Corporation, now drastically cut under the Reagan administration. Because government funding is always intricate, rigid, and slow, private funding is needed. Merrill money went to support community-based legal projects in the Worcester area, primarily among the elderly. Of the 110,000 elderly in central Massachusetts, 35 percent live below the poverty level. They are easily confused and do not understand their rights with landlords, utilities, merchants, doctors, and government agencies. This advocacy project aimed to meet these problems and let the aged feel that they still have some control over their environment, for example, to show an isolated, low-income woman where to turn when a new washing machine proves defective or a landlord fails to keep an apartment up to contract levels.

In addition to the previous project we invested about $350,000 in various projects centered around jails and rehabilitation.

Father Dismas Clark Foundation, St. Louis, Missouri, 1961—$20,000. Father Dismas Clark, a former math teacher at St. Louis University High, had dedicated his life to helping ex convicts find employment and a meaningful way of life. He would gamble on men whom he considered good risks and who seemed eager to get jobs and find a normal place in the world. All too often his office was a phone booth, but in 1959 he found an abandoned elementary school building and turned it, freshly painted and cleaned, into a shelter. Dismas is the crucified thief who asked Jesus to forgive him. The shelter saved the State of Missouri $800,000 its first year by allowing men, up to 1,500 the second year, to be paroled to an institution that would guarantee a job.

Father Clark's most painful fact was that federal, state, and local penal institutions cost American taxpayers $24 billion in 1958, and yet when the convicts were released, little was done to protect the public against new crime and new jailing. Clark received a lot of criticism in St. Louis for coddling ex cons. His was the Trust's first project involved with penal issues.

National Endowment for the Humanities, Washington, 1969—$15,000 to fund the Student Tutor Education Project (STEP), a liberal arts training program at Walpole, a maximum security prison outside Boston. STEP's organizer was an inspired social worker named Babette Spiegel who felt that prison education programs failed because they gave so little and asked so little. Her aim was to identify prisoners of above-average intellectual, artistic, and leadership qualities who, if properly reached, could lead useful lives upon release. For the twenty-week course on *Identity* they read Margaret Mead, Malcolm X, and Machiavelli, among other writers, and this Merrill grant went to meet operating costs, plans for expansion to other jails, and set up a structure to place the graduates into interested colleges.

I myself taught a few classes at Walpole on American history. The most interesting student was an arrogant, brilliant young man named Stanley Bond who had held up twenty different Western Union offices in order to raise capital to open a coffee house. He quoted Sartre and Kirkegaard and made any teacher feel second-rate. His pal was an older, courteous man named Lefty Gilday who used to ask my advice about how to raise his teenage children.

Mrs. Spiegel got Stanley paroled into a special program at Brandeis. He called upon her once with a nice but homely girlfriend, and Mrs. Spiegal felt that for a man so handsome that girls simply melted at his feet to choose this companion for her intellectual qualities was a sign of his regeneration. Well, Stanley broke loose from college with a different sort of Brandeis girl and with Lefty's help robbed a bank and killed the guard. Both of them went back to Walpole. Stanley, always the intellectual, accumulated a sophisticated collection of chemicals in order to get out of jail by other means and blew himself up. Mrs. Spiegel lost heart and the project died.

Osborne Association, New York, New York, 1971–1980—$70,000. The Trust made four grants to Osborne, mainly for endowment and operating costs. This is one of the oldest, most respected groups involved in prison reform. "We will turn the prison from a scrap heap into a repair shop," Thomas Osborne said in 1916. Its stated goals are to prepare prisoners for a successful life in society, to do away with destructive conditions and provide constructive ones (specifically to work for educational and vocational training, medical and psychiatric services, and firm but fair discipline), and to provide on-the-spot surveys of state and federal institutions. In sixty years about 50,000 individuals have been served by Osborne with aid to men still in jail as well as their families. With the job market so tight, there is a much greater demand for counseling.

The last two Merrill grants went to support the Work Experience and Social Restitution projects in partnership with New York state and county probation departments, helping the ex offender acquire job skills and work habit formation and placing him in a heterogeneous setting where he associates with regular people.

Religious Society of Friends of Philadelphia and Vicinity, 1972—$15,000 to the Prison Service Committee of Southern New Jersey with programs such as Friendly Visitors, Volunteer Probation Counselors, Community Sponsor, as well as the Cell Block Theatre giving plays and poetry readings throughout New Jersey. Quakers have always been involved with problems of incarceration and rehabilitation, though some of the reforms they sponsored in nineteenth century Pennsylvania are blood chilling: years of solitary confinement in silence for prisoners to reflect on their guilt, with food and the materials of wholesome employment handed into the cell through a swinging door so that they would not even see a guard.

Windsor County Mental Health Services, Springfield, Vermont, 1972—$25,000. A reward of foundation work is the sort of people you run across every so often. Christopher and Maida St. John, he a Yale Law student, she a psychiatric social worker, came to my office to ask for help in organizing a program for prisoners and their families at the Vermont State Prison in Windsor. Built in 1830, the prison was a granite pile with few education or rehabilitation services, and the state was considering a huge, super-costly, max-imum security replacement. The St. Johns felt that better results at lower cost could be obtained by channeling through the Vermont Bar Association volunteer efforts into the existing prison, helping families stay in contact, helping them with the simplest services (transportation, child care), and stim-ulating state agencies to meet the needs of both groups. The goal was to allow the families and even the prisoners to feel that they can acquire more au-tonomy and that there are alternatives to incarceration. The skeleton of a Prisoner Community Relations Center already existed, and the St. Johns' work there gave them credibility with prisoners and staff. They figured that Vermont was a good state in which to begin, with a total prison population of less than 1,000, where one could look at different ways of approaching the problem, something not possible with the sheer mass of the system in New York or Massachusetts.[4]

Strengthened by a stubborn idealism (people in trouble, even criminals, should be treated decently) and a pretty shrewd awareness of human be-havior and institutional behavior, these two young people seemed to know how to get results.

Massachusetts Council of Churches, Boston, Massachusetts, 1973— *$40,000* to fund an Omni-Crime Prevention Center in Roxbury-Dorchester. John Boone had been appointed Commissioner of Corrections in 1972, partly due to the lobbying of the Massachusetts Council on Crime and Correction, and as a black man (a Morehouse alumnus) and a reformer willing to do battle with the guards' union and any number of statehouse politicians, he immediately became a controversial figure. He argued that the prisons run in America today dehumanize rather than rehabilitate prisoners. He worked for innovations like furloughs (of 250 prisoners let out Christmas week, 248 returned) and prerelease work programs to cut down on the violence, recid-ivism, and overwhelming cost of the prison system. This was the time when Governor Rockefeller was making headlines by his "lock'em up for life" prom-ise for drug pushers in New York, which Boone saw as bankrupting the state,

---

4. How do we measure that new gimmick—the expansion of private prisons? Corrections Corporation of America, a newly formed company based in Nashville, has been financed by the Massey Burch Investment Group, the same investors who started the now-booming Hospital Corporation of America. Corrections Corporation's founder, Thomas Beasley, a real estate and insurance businessman, plans to run the company's prisons much as the Hospital Corporation runs its nearly 150 hospitals. He will use large purchase orders and centralized accounting and management and will hire experienced wardens from the public agencies. The company's first venture is a $4 million, 300-bed detention facility for illegal aliens in Houston. (*Christian Science Monitor*, 11 April 1984)

Why stop there? Since private administration is automatically more efficient than public, the next step is to privatize the military establishment. For example, Merrill Lynch might contract to raise, equip and maintain the Major Donald Regan Marine Battalion, which it would rent out to the Pentagon. The well-paid marines would be proud of their ML shoulder patch, and acts of gallantry would be encouraged by generous cash bonuses.

not only in maintaining the prisoners but in having to supply welfare to their families.

He wanted to replace the archaic prison system with a widespread network of community programs: a prerelease center in Shirley for men with drug-related crimes, another in Mattapan (a biracial suburb of Boston) where they could seek jobs and housing, and the Crime Prevention network of home security, safe streets, and public education, involving both victims and ex offenders, with ombudsmen to link the Center with the Department of Corrections. As Boone saw it, the crisis was not simply the lack of money for new ideas but the cynicism and apathy that keep people from even hoping that something could be done.

Boone was already in a fragile position by 1973, and one purpose of a large grant like this was to strengthen his hand. He lasted one more year. Not much came of the Crime Prevention Center, and Roxbury-Dorchester remained dangerous and demoralized communities.

Northampton County Area Community College, Bethlehem, Pennsylvania, 1973—$15,000 for a director and development costs of a proposed para-teacher program in eight Pennsylvania state jails. These had a total population of 6,000, of whom 60 percent were black. There was an overwhelming need for basic and vocational education (the average grade equivalency was 5.6), but 15 to 20 percent of the prisoners were ready for postsecondary education. Every institution had some program, financed mostly by the federal government, and these were now being administered by the Pennsylvania Department of Education rather than the Bureau of Corrections.

This particular program had a double purpose: to improve the education of and gain college credit for prisoners and to give accomplishment to prisoner teachers and tutors. The aim was to train fifteen parateachers from each institution. The Northampton County Area Community College had shown an interest in prison education, and Merrill money would keep the program going until federal funds arrived.

South Forty Corporation, New York, New York, 1978–1979—$25,000. The South Forty project is located at the Bedford Hills Correctional Facility in Westchester County, the largest total confinement institution for women in New York State. Women's prisons, of smaller size, have limited education programs in comparison with men's. Along with counseling and postrelease services, South Forty stresses accredited correspondence courses available in up to seventy colleges. A professional teacher with local volunteers helps students in difficult subjects like math, science, and writing and coordinates the coursework and leads the discussions that let the women feel they are participating in a group endeavor. The New York prison system was shifting to a strict enforcement of all its rules that related to security. This might be useful to discipline but was rough on morale. Therefore it seemed more important than ever to expand an educational program that concerned itself with the possibility of any individual, even in prison, to grow intellectually and creatively.

Southern Coalition of Jails and Prisons, Nashville, Tennessee, 1981— $10,000 to fund the Florida Clearinghouse on Criminal Justice in Tallahassee. The Southern Coalition was led by a committee of Protestant ministers in six southern states to monitor prison conditions, to improve medical and educational services, and to help ex prisoners get jobs and, if possible, not return. The Coalition and its subsidiary, the Clearinghouse, served as conduits to a program launched by a black ex student of mine, called Aid to Incarcerated Mothers. Florida's female prison population has doubled in the last decade, from 1,800 to 3,500 in 1980, with 60 percent of the prisoners black, jailed mainly for nonviolent crimes like shoplifting and passing bad checks. Inadequate medical care, poor diet, and no exercise leave them less healthy when they leave than when they enter. About the only work program is sewing underwear for male prisoners, and education services, even to illiterates, stop for any woman over twenty-one. Seventy percent of these black female prisoners were heads of their households; their absence meant even worse disruption of their children's lives. Aid to Incarcerated Mothers' purpose was to serve as a transition house in Tallahassee for these women coming out of prison: offering personal, medical, legal, and spiritual counseling and training in household management and child care, with peer support on survival by former prisoners. Selection of applicants would be according to greatest need as opposed to the traditional one of most likely to succeed.

Street Theatre, White Plains, New York, 1974–1981—$45,000. This is the creation of a tenacious, driven leader, Gray Smith, a graduate of Yale Drama School, who has tried to reach the nonwhite prison and street population of Westchester County with dramatic productions that tell the reality of the life they know. The company started as community theatre presenting plays from a portable stage in the streets of Ossining and other poor towns of Westchester, then in Sing Sing and Bedford Hills prisons. The first play was about the sufferings of a family on welfare. There was an intense interaction with the audience, who saw their own lives acted out on the stage and their repressed emotions articulated and clarified. The first Merrill grant went to expand the workshop program within Sing Sing, the first of its kind, to respond to the needs of men behind bars. It included a training program, for regular actors and directors to learn how to play in jails, and for ex inmate directors to learn how to mount productions both in jail and outside. By 1978 some thirty prison productions had been put on, all by inmates.

In 1981 Smith felt that his priority had shifted to the needs of young people in Westchester's high crime areas. Nice suburbs like White Plains, New Rochelle, Port Chester, and Pelham had all developed their own ghetto neighborhoods with the city diseases of crime, vandalism, and drugs. There was a marked rise in rates of truancy, police involvement, drug and alcohol abuse, teenage pregnancy, and suicide. One play that Street Theatre's new *Project Youth* (to which the Trust gave $20,000) put on was "Wanna Job?," showing how to acquire job getting and keeping skills like promptness, discipline, middle-class grooming, courtesy, and showing sensitivity also to the question of "If I learn all these things, will I forget who I am?" with the response of "No, you'll just add another dimension to your personality." If kids can earn money on a job, they'll keep out of trouble and gain self-confidence and skill for other jobs.

"Crime Don't Pay No Wages" was a second play directed for performance in high school gymnasiums, enthusiastically received by students and school staff, a paradoxical source of pain for Smith, whose company was on the edge of bankruptcy and who saw only the rapid increases of unemployment in every town he brought his play to. There were few private jobs for unskilled young people and training programs like CETA, the Comprehensive Employment and Training Act, were being dismantled. It was clear to the dumbest kid that his problems were not considered important to general American society, and it was hard to work out an argument that crime did *not* pay if one was clever enough.

Karen Horney Clinic, New York, New York, 1977—$10,000. This clinic, named after one of Freud's colleagues, provides low-cost mental-health treatment for residents in east midtown Manhattan, but our grant was in response to a proposal for psychiatric first aid for victims of senseless violence. A lot of money is spent on understanding, justice, and rehabilitation for the criminal, but the plight of the victim of an assault is ignored. How to prevent the development of lasting trauma? Given the American legal style, a woman is raped not once but three times—the second time being questioned by the police and the third being cross examined by the defense attorney.

Conclusions

This is an interesting list of projects having to do with Crime and Punishment funded by the Charles E. Merrill Trust at a total of $405,000—not very much. The topic brings up a number of conclusions. The first two are simple.

Any project in this field will be controversial and probably unsuccessful. If your foundation involves itself here, expect scorn and ridicule. There is too high a failure rate. Nevertheless, with all the money you invest in DNA research, Stanford Business School, and chamber groups that play Scarlatti, give some thought to the needs of black women prisoners at the absolute bottom of society who grope for something better out of life for themselves and their children.

Second, how easy it is to get money for incarceration, how hard for prevention. Only do-gooders and pointy-headed bureaucrats concern themselves with ways to give direction to a child's life or stability to a family under pressure. The pillars of society vote taxes for the steel and concrete warehouses that lock up the failures.

Third, how differently do white and black Americans look at crime and punishment. Foundation executives and trustees lead sheltered lives. They have few black friends who talk freely about the subject. The purpose of the state is to protect the rich against the poor (a conclusion I reached on a trip to Brazil where reality is more sharply expressed than in our country and there was an armed cop on every street corner); the first line of defense is the police, courts, and prison system. Prisons are built to put away, primarily, black and Spanish-speaking people who cause trouble, a detail you notice the first time you ever enter a jail. It was Leroy Jones who said that given the realities of race oppression in America, black prisoners should be treated as POWs. No matter what the Nixons and Reagans say about black crime, they welcome it as a way of disciplining the white lower classes to vote conservative, against their objective economic interests, expressing racial fears by a vote for law and order.

Because there is not a revolutionary tradition among American blacks, unbearable resentment, until it explodes as a riot, is expressed by crime. When the Moslems and Black Panthers in the years between 1964 and 1974 tried to change individual resentment and violence into a revolutionary attitude based on race and class, the white establishment responded with every variety of police terror. This might be by informers and agents setting the poorly disciplined black leaders against each other, or by outright killing, whether the murder of Malcolm X or the shoot-out in Chicago in 1971 that eliminated the Panther leadership. My own black students back in the early 1970s told me of a plan called *King Arthur* which was known to the President, the FBI, and the mayors of all the larger cities. On a certain day, when blacks had caused just too much bother, *King Arthur* would be proclaimed on the telex machines and all black people, even professors and NAACP executives, would be gathered together in certain areas of the cities and then shipped to great camps, already prepared, in places like West Virginia and Montana. Whitey had done that already with the Nisei in 1942. He knew how.

Experienced social workers used to say that if you got the standard inarticulate working class male—white, black, brown—past the dangerous years of fifteen through twenty-three he would marry, fit himself into a regular job, settle down, and more or less accept the constraints of life. The vicissitudes of going from one job to another were in themselves educational and taught him how to get along with circumstance and other people. But if we are seeing a whole generation of black and Puerto Rican males who have never known the discipline of any job or the self-respect of any paycheck, then it is foolish to expect automatic stability when they turn the magic age. Joblessness and contempt equal genocide, whether by random violence, alcohol and drugs, suicide, or just by death of the soul.

CHAPTER SEVEN

Medicine

In medical care the United States has gone from an economy of add-on to one of trade-off. Americans have traditionally assumed that any new medical procedure could be automatically absorbed within our total health care budget. Now we are painfully beginning to realize that our resources are limited. The sources given to one group of patients may not be available for another.   [Howard Hiatt]

In 1967 I wrote the directors of three Boston hospitals—John Knowles at Massachusetts General, Howard Hiatt at Beth Israel, and Charles Janeway at Children's—to ask how a foundation our size could serve medicine most effectively. Dr. Knowles suggested investment in the better utilization of scarce resources of equipment, space, and trained manpower and in ways by which hospitals could reach out to community problems or disease before and after the patient appears at the clinic. Dr. Hiatt felt that there were sufficient government finances for the social involvement of medicine not to make this our concern, but that with wartime pressure for immediate results in every field, federal readiness to help in any basic studies was being seriously curtailed. Accordingly we should provide funds for undramatic but needed contact with chemistry, biology, and physics so that the individual researcher has the theoretical background of knowledge against which to fit his specific facts. Dr. Janeway saw the need of foundations to help match the government grants for new hospital construction so that hospitals could stay ahead of the crunch that comes when every single facility is overused to the point of paralysis.

Each of those three careful statements made good sense, but how was our committee of intelligent amateurs, we five trustees, to judge between them? Sometimes, almost by chance we supported an idea, an ideal, that the reader

263

of this book may respond to with our same excitement, and he will envy that freedom of ours to do something fine with all those dollars we spent. At other times our gifts were an expression of loyalty to the institution that served our community—the Southampton Hospital or Children's in San Francisco, an old friend, a doctor, or perhaps just a fund-raiser. We decided yes or no, but asked few questions. Suppose we hadn't been nagged at by all the salesmen who remorselessly bugged us? Suppose we had sat down in a quiet room with wise old men who would have given us expert, disinterested advice? What would we have done differently? I don't know.

Nevertheless, at the end of this foundation's life and the expenditure of almost $20 million in all the fields of health care, one is still surprised at how little direction we exercised and how few policies we established and sustained. If few periods of medical history surpassed our twenty-three-year lifetime in its technological changes and research findings, the reader will be hard put to find a coherent picture of progress. The $485,000 doled out, grant by grant, to Southampton Hospital between 1959 and 1981 reveal some picture of an average hospital's changing needs. The $300,000 in 1974 to Harvard School of Public Health was employed by Dean Hiatt to examine the priorities of that decade. Otherwise any awareness of change comes in details scattered among the different headings: the expansion of chemotherapy at Memorial Sloan-Kettering, changing attitudes in obstetrics and terminal care, the arrival of a new diagnostic tool like the computerized axial tomograph (CAT) scanner. Although we five trustees were amateurs, we had a wide acquaintanceship with the different facets of medicine. Nevertheless, I look in vain through our records or my memory for efforts to understand where medicine was heading.

Perhaps the two major changes over the course of those twenty-three years were the tremendous rise in total costs and the beginning of a new attitude toward the profession as a whole. Less than 6 percent of the gross national product went for general health needs when we started and almost 10 percent when we closed shop. And by the 1980s was there coming a slippage in America's respect for and trust in the medical profession? It was not simply that medical care got too costly and doctors got too rich. The doubts did not touch one's own personal doctor, of course, but had medical care become an industry, an uncontrollable force, and was medically preserved life no longer an unalloyed boon?

EDUCATION—MEDICAL SCHOOLS

It is hard to measure the allocation of funds for education, research, and patient care in neat categories when every medical school, like every major hospital, is involved in all three. The relevant categories in American medical education during the Trust's active life, if one could delimit them accurately, might be the changes in emphasis. In the 1960s the stress was upon science and research, and the breakthroughs were coming from a new partnership between research in the basic sciences, especially biochemistry, and medicine's utilization of this new knowledge. Harvard represented the epitome of this type of training, and critics felt that not enough concern was given to the human needs of the patient.

By the late 1960s anger at the war in Vietnam had broadened to anger at every organ of the Establishment that tolerated such a war, and the unjust society out of which it came. This included the medical establishment and the code of values, including educational and financial values, of the American Medical Association (AMA). There was a new interest in family and community medicine, new voices heard from the blacks and women entering the profession, in some ways a consideration of female values of human caring with less emphasis on competition and hierarchy, and a demand for greater democracy within hospital administration. As the medical schools made some concession to these demands, there were doctors who feared that the rigorously intellectual and scientific training that alone would produce the research of the future was being watered down.

The third, perhaps most destructive trend in medical education was the popular conviction that in bad times an M.D. and an M.B.A. were the only secure degrees. It wasn't simply that the humanities and social sciences had lost value. Even a Ph.D. in physics from Cal Tech offered insufficient protection. Bio-Chem I had become not a premed course for teaching biochemistry but a means of weeding out the marginals: B+ is failure. The grade alone counts. If one's colleagues' experiments are sabotaged, the crucial textbooks stolen from the shelves so that no one else can cram for the exam, if no course can be risked (no matter how intellectually rewarding) that won't guarantee an A—what a generation of doctors are we training! If they can deal only with success, to be obtained only through intense, narrow, supremely self-centered approaches, how will they deal with failure? The patient dies: the doctor has flunked the exam. The family sues.

Building new medical schools is not the answer when their graduates fight for ever more limited and financially rewarding specialties. The disease becomes international. American rejects study at Guadalajara, Bologna, and Grenada while American hospitals hire their residents from Iran, Pakistan, and Colombia. The schools become unsure where to turn. Shorten the course of study, as Boston University has done, with a combined B.S.-M.D. at the end of six years? Insist on the full four years to allow greater involvement with the social side of medicine, as with the fourth-year Cornell students sent to the International Rescue Committee's camps in Thailand? Accept a proportion of candidates at sophomore year in college in order to reduce the pathology of competition?

The medical school disease is the dual one of the over-loaded curriculum and the burnt-out student. There is a need to employ teaching methods that emphasize problem solving and the mastery of basic principles rather than the mind-killing memorization of detail. There is a need to teach sensitivity to costs: is this test necessary, can a cheaper one give just as useful information? Human disease is not a purely scientific phenomenon.

Have the medical schools bred a callousness that corrupts both undergraduate education and medical practice? Have the doctors they turn out (and there may be too many of them now) been the reason for the loss of confidence in the medical system that we suffer in the 1980s?[1]

Harvard Medical School, Boston, Massachusetts, 1959–1980—$60,000. Our first two grants went to support beds for teaching and science of the Departments of Medicine and Surgery at the Peter Bent Brigham Hospital. In 1980, $10,000 was a gift in memory of John Erdman, a brilliant researcher at Massachusetts General Hospital who had died young.

Boston University School of Medicine, Boston, Massachusetts, 1966— $25,000 toward construction of a new building. Boston University followed both an eight-year and a six-year program, starting medical studies in the third year of the university with accordingly less expense and less competitive trauma. The school was strong in medicine, psychiatry, and radiology; weak in preventive medicine and obstetrics; and relatively weak in basic sciences and library resources. Its Law Medicine Research Institute was the first of its kind in the United States. Money was needed to reconstruct the awkward, inefficient, and aging physical plant.

Tufts University School of Medicine, Massachusetts, 1976—$40,000 for scholarship endowment. Of 9,000 applicants, 146 were accepted(!). One third of these received financial aid as a way to encourage minority and low-income students. Federal aid to medical schools and students was declining, and Dean Cavazos felt strongly that loan funds were not the answer. A large medical school debt (on top of an undergraduate debt) carried through the residency years forces the doctor into the type of high-priced medicine that, in specialty and region, allows him to pay it off. Students must be treated generously if society is going to expect them to act generously later on—a simple statement that should be engraved on doors of bronze.

Tufts' students took their clinical work at *New England Medical Center Hospital,* to which the Trust gave $35,000 in 1969 towards its $72 million,

1. In his President's report to the Harvard Board of Overseers released in April 1984, Derek Bok gives the estimate of 25,000 to 50,000 surplus doctors by 1990.

ten-year development program. One of its research projects was to provide computerized diagnostic assistance to physicians in small towns. A doctor in western Massachusetts needs to know the proper saline content of the blood of a patient of a given age, weight, and sex. The computer types out the required answer but also knows what further questions to present, and on the basis of the doctor's replies will present follow-up suggestions of further testing, diagnosis, and treatment. This project was seen as an important way to upgrade the professional resources of doctors far from a tertiary hospital. Later on it was criticized as part of the whole American trend of overtesting[2] and overtreatment, not always helpful to the patient and a cause for the steady rise in hospital costs.

Tufts/New England had a strong commitment to the social needs of medicine and became exposed more than it had ever expected to black suspicion of any form of white help. In the early 1960s, it helped start, in cooperation with Tougaloo College, a Tufts Delta Health Center to serve patients, upgrade doctors, and train paraprofessionals at the Mound Bayou Community Hospital in Bolivar County, a desperately poor, black area of northwestern Mississippi. A fair amount of federal funds were available if matched, and the Merrill Trust gave $30,000 in 1971 as a catalyst to get the project established. With the rise of black nationalism in the Deep South, Tufts found itself attacked for colonialism and was glad to turn over its sponsorship to Meharry.

In 1971 the Medical Center, with major federal funding, used staff from Tufts' medical and dental schools to launch the Columbia Point Health Center in Boston. Columbia Point was an isolated, demoralized housing project, stuck out into Boston Harbor and largely black and Puerto Rican. The Health Center was an optimistic effort to break the poverty cycle by upgrading health care, using two approaches: the first was an experiment with a public school to give comprehensive care to all children, including those with physical, mental, and emotional handicaps. The other was to train local leadership (mothers in the thirties and forties with signs of character and status) as health aides. The Merrill Trust gave $20,000 in 1972 for the latter program, which shortly fell apart in community resentment, including violence, toward any intervention.

Doris Bennett, the pediatrician who had started the program and had seen it destroyed, concluded: "The children had all had their immunization records up to date, and two of my first patients were old enough to be in jail for homicide."

Dartmouth College Medical School, Hanover, New Hampshire, 1962– 1976—$90,000. Dartmouth had had a two-year medical school since 1914. In the late 1950s its trustees decided that its most effective contribution in meet-

2. In his 1984 report, Derek Bok gives a figure of $20 billion for the annual cost of diagnostic tests in the United States.

ing the nationwide shortage of doctors—with the rise in population and the new demands for medical services, the nation's supply of doctors would have to be doubled over the next twenty years—would be to expand faculty, reorganize curriculum, and build a new plant for its existing program (less costly and more effective than going on to the standard four years). Nine hundred vacancies existed in 1962 in the third and fourth year classes of medical schools that could absorb extra students by placing most of them in their affiliated hospitals. Dartmouth saw itself as the nation's prototype two-year school; the Trust gave $25,000 in 1962 to this policy of upgrading.

By mid-1960s the policy had changed, and the Trust gave $25,000 in 1967 to support expansion to a four-year school. This new development gave Dartmouth (as also *Brown University, Providence, Rhode Island, 1967—$25,000*) an opportunity to work out a fresh approach to the teaching of medicine, and reexamine premedical, preclinical, and clinical training from the college level to internship. The issue is not merely the explosion in medical knowledge but also new ways by which a school can plan for a better total system of health.

In 1976 $40,000 went to modernize medical education and improve health care in rural New England: to supply students with rural clinical practice while helping communities solve their pressing health problems with preventive, diagnostic, and therapeutic care. Communities, the medical school, and government cooperated in setting up a regional system with well-children clinics, a consultation clinic for high-risk infants and pregnant women, screening and follow-up for children with learning disabilities, and consultation (particularly for patients with mental health problems) via closed-circuit television.

City College of City University of New York—Sophie Davis Center for Biomedical Education, New York, New York, 1977—$40,000. Started in 1973, the Center set itself three goals. The first was to educate primary care practitioners in preventive and therapeutic care in underserved urban communities as well as to bring in lay community leaders to share in these programs. The second was to organize a six-year B.S./M.D. training program, eliminating redundant undergraduate courses but emphasizing nonscience courses in literature, languages, comparative religion, ethics, and philosophy. The aim was to develop a sophisticated understanding of the physical and social environment factors that contribute to good and bad health. Twenty percent of each student's time is devoted to actual service in the needy areas of New York City leading to real life involvement with the problems of deprived communities. Final clinical training was supplied by cooperating medical schools like Howard and Meharry, Mt. Sinai, N.Y.U., and the University of Puerto Rico. And third, the Center sought by an early admission program to eliminate the destructive competition suffered by premed students.

Hahnemann Medical College and Hospital, Philadelphia, Pennsylvania, 1960–1975—$120,000 for construction and program support. Hahnemann used to rate high among U.S. medical schools, but then its financial position became weak and its reputation slipped. In the mid-1950s came the start of a real effort to reorganize and revitalize the school. The struggle to rebuild quality in an institution that had once been first-rate was a process that Don Regan found fascinating and provided the reason for a number of the Trust's long-range commitments like Hahnemann. The faculty was strengthened with a new core of full-time clinicians. New research programs, from cancer to vagrancy, were started up with large-scale federal support. Hahnemann faculty joined "What's New in Medicine" teams that the State Department sponsored in Greece, Yugoslavia, Spain, Israel, and Pakistan. A program of refresher courses for doctors in twenty community hospitals begun in the mid-1960s had within ten years grown to a continuing education program serving 2,500 doctors a year.

Women's Medical College of Pennsylvania, Philadelphia, 1970, 1976—$55,000. The college opened in 1850 when women were denied admission to medical schools. Although women are now able to go anywhere, in 1970 only 7 percent of current doctors and 9 percent of medical students (over 25 percent by 1980) were female. In 1970, W.M.C. graduated twice as many female students (236) as any other medical school. (S.U.N.Y. was next with 100; University of Michigan at 76.) Flexible scheduling with a part-time residency program is tolerated to meet the needs of married staff. The college became coed in 1969 and changed its name to Medical College of Pennsylvania but was still committed to enhancing the status of women in medicine. It has a strong retraining program to return inactive doctors, especially women, to medicine. There is a comprehensive daycare and child development center for children of faculty, staff, and students, and because it is located near the intersection of main highways, it has a major accident service.

Wake Forest University, Gray School of Medicine, Winston-Salem, North Carolina, 1977—$50,000 to help solve problems of underserved rural communities, reduce professional isolation, strengthen local medical resources. Money was needed to develop the Model Family Practice Clinic for teaching and for expansion of overextended support services. Large support came to the school from Duke Endowment and Reynolds funds. Would that affect any campaign to prevent lung cancer by propaganda against smoking?

A *New York Times* article in 1964 by the secretary of the AMA, Walter Wiggins, launched an interesting program by the Trust. Dr. Wiggins was protesting the widening gap between well and poorly financed medical schools. From 1940 to 1961 the average annual budgets of medical schools

had risen from $500,000 to $5,100,000. In funds spent for research and training programs, with the federal government the major donor, the average
expenditure at the top was $11,300,000 and at the bottom, $1,700,000. Rising
costs and this widening gap in support threatened now the very existence of
many good schools, mainly in the South and West. When I wrote Dr. Wiggins
for names, he suggested the following as well-run institutions with good potential, which each received a grant of $25,000: *Medical College of South
Carolina, Charleston, S.C.; Loma Linda School of Medicine, Loma Linda,
California; University of Arkansas School of Medicine, Little Rock, Arkansas*
(the only medical school in the state); *University of New Mexico School of
Medicine, Albuquerque, New Mexico, 1965—$25,000; University of Ken-
tucky College of Medicine, Lexington, Kentucky, 1965—$25,000.*

*Columbia University, College of Physicians and Surgeons, New York, New
York, 1980—$50,000* for scholarships (along with similar gifts at that meeting
to *Johns Hopkins* and *Cornell*)—a part of Doris Magowan's concern for the
increasing pressures that the 1980s were bringing to both schools and
students.

Cornell University Medical College, New York, New York, 1980—$50,000
for scholarships for students interested in academic medicine and clinical
research since government assistance (and public opinion) is now focused on
students preparing for primary care in areas of acute physician shortage like
the inner city and the rural south. Academic leadership is needed for the
training of future physicians, but lower salaries are offered and longer training
required. New doctors spend five to seven years of fellowship training when
they are starting their families as well as trying to pay off their debts, in
contrast to colleagues with a lucrative specialty practice or the benefits of a
government scholarship program.
      In 1981 a grant of $20,000 went to the International Rescue Committee to
establish a joint medical program in their Thailand centers in cooperation
with New York Hospital–Cornell Medical Center. This would serve Cambodian refugees as well as provide American students training in crisis medicine: without the back-up of modern labs and skilled staff.

Aid to Minorities

Meharry Medical College, Nashville, Tennessee, 1959–1981—$335,000 in
five grants. Meharry received more money from the Merrill Trust than did
any other medical school and next to Morehouse was our major commitment
to a black institution. Founded in 1876, Meharry has schools of medicine,
dentistry, nursing, and medical technology. With the exception of Howard
and later Morehouse, it is the only AMA-accredited Negro medical college

in the United States. The most important fact is that even in 1980, over half of all the practicing black physicians and dentists in the United States were Meharry and Howard graduates.

Our first grant, $25,000 in 1959, went for salaries. The average salary for a full professor at Meharry was then $9,000; the average at nearby Vanderbilt was $18,000.

In 1969 $50,000 went toward the $88 million capital drive (with $34 million coming from the federal government) to construct a new hospital, neighborhood health center, outpatient clinic, dormitories, computer center, and basic medical science building. The push was to expand enrollment as fast as resources and faculty will allow in order to increase the number of blacks in medicine and to develop better health care for the poor. Thirty thousand black doctors are needed to reach the white average of 157 per 100,000. The situation is even worse for black dentists, a diminishing group numbering 4 percent of the total American supply in 1940 and 2 percent in 1980.

In 1972 $200,000 went for construction and implementation of the new Comprehensive Health Services Center that seeks not only to train practitioners but to develop an idea of what is community medicine, where prevention is more important than cure. Meharry served a community of 93,000 and through its ambulatory programs sought to establish a model for others in both care and education. The crucial point was not to shunt these low-income patients to a different doctor each time they came in but to refer them to the same health care team. Efforts were made to combine social and mental health, to refer time-consuming procedures to paramedics, which would also be a new source of jobs.

In 1978 $40,000 went to support two faculty members in the basic sciences. Enrollment was now 1,060, up from 409 ten years earlier. Black enrollment in all types of medical schools has recently turned down, a result of hard times, reduced federal support, less hope, and Meharry itself is in financial difficulties.

National Medical Fellowships, New York, New York, 1971—$40,000 to help increase the number of Negro, Puerto Rican, Mexican American, and Native American physicians. Medical schools were beginning to open their doors to the black graduates admitted to colleges in the mid-1960s, and there was, for a while, a new black interest in medicine to replace the earlier short-term interest in political science and sociology. Money was badly needed, however, to maintain this momentum, which soon flagged, and this program was clearly one that the Merrill Trust should have supported more than it did.

Morehouse School of Medicine, Atlanta, Georgia, 1980, 1981—$50,000: $40,000 as matching funds for the Basic Medical Sciences building and

$10,000 for scholarships. The School of Medicine opened in 1978 with twenty-four freshmen, nineteen of them black, first as a two-year school whose graduates would go on to Emory, Howard, Meharry, and the Medical College of Georgia. Its aim was to remedy the terrible discrepancy between white and black medical resources: in Georgia there is one white physician for every 926 white people and one black physician for every 9,652 black people, a situation that is not improving.[3] In 1974, 10 percent of medical students in the United States were minority; by 1978, 8 percent were minority, 6 percent black. Morehouse directed its students towards poor rural and innercity practice. Even at Howard, only 40 percent of its graduates choose these areas.

Forty-five million dollars over five years were needed for start-up costs, plus $10 million for faculty endowment, for a school whose four-year peak size would be less than 200 students. Wouldn't it be cheaper, I asked Dr. Louis Sullivan, the Boston University-educated dean, to pay the costs of those students at established medical schools? He felt that that approach had not worked. The intense medical school competition and the system of in-group information-sharing have meant a high failure rate in the minority out-group. With intensive tutoring and close supervision, Morehouse would stress cooperation rather than rivalry. Almost immediately, the medical school began repaying part of its costs by its contribution to the science resources of the Atlanta University Center.

By the mid-1980s Morehouse seemed in solid shape, graduating twenty-one M.D.s a year and aiming for sixty-four a year by the 1990s. Dr. Sullivan insisted that the greatest financial need was for scholarship endowment. In 1978 nineteen out of twenty-four entering freshmen were on federal scholarships, and in 1984 only four out of the school's total of 122 students were on federal scholarships. Morehouse's tuition of $9,000 (and a student must add on about $8,000 in living expenses) is near the bottom for all private medical schools, but when student family income averages less than $20,000, financial pressures begin to destroy the academic environment. Too much thought is going simply into worry about the monthly bills, and a graduation debt of $30,000 (plus the debt from college years) precludes the practice in low-pay, public-health medicine that Morehouse was founded to provide. What sort of national social policy does this crisis express?

The 1980s nevertheless did provide two further reasons for Morehouse's existence. The first was as an articulate, respected voice for the needs of poor people. Among all the other priorities of American medicine, these will be ignored, as usual, unless a voice with status keeps raising the issue. Second, with all the catastrophic messages about the collapse of the black family, it

3. The average life expectancy of black males in some Georgia rural counties is fifty years, ten to nineteen years less than the average for white males in the same counties, and below the average even for Kenya. (Louis Sullivan, *New England Journal of Medicine*, September 29, 1983.)

is the obligation of the black physician not simply to care for the health of individual patients but to be encouraged to do whatever he can to bolster the health and confidence of the family.

Some Conclusions

In 1963 the awareness that America's supply of doctors would have to be doubled over the next twenty years to keep pace with the rise in population and the new demands for medical services led to a major effort, largely funded by the federal government, to increase the number and size of medical schools. Twenty years later the solution has, as usual, become part of the problem. The number of new doctors has increased, but despite the government's efforts to get them to practice in the rural South and in the inner cities, these doctors prefer to practice in the suburbs and nicer parts of town and to practice as high-cost specialists. Moreover, the expenses of medical school, with its debts to be paid off, and the competition within the suburbs and within the specialties mean that the doctors must practice an aggressive form of medicine with enough procedures, consultations, and operations to pay their bills.

Sometimes an example can be exposed. For example, in two contiguous Vermont counties in the 1970s, one of them had five times as many tonsillectomies as the other, as revealed by a computer operated by the Harvard School of Public Health. The explanation came because the busier county had a new private health center whose capital costs had to be amortized.[1]

Dental Schools, $225,000 for education and $250,000 for dental/facial area research.

Forsyth Dental Infirmary for Children, Boston, Massachusetts, 1967– 1979—$105,000. Forsyth was founded in 1914 as an effort to raise the level of dental education from providing skilled mechanical care to discovering the causes and prevention of oral disease. By 1955 its emphasis was on the research training of graduate dentists: oral bacteriology, use of topical fluoride to control tooth decay in children, occlusal deformity (why more common in advanced countries?), growth and resumption of bone, design of dental equipment. The Merrill Trust gave $50,000 in 1967 and 1969 for construction and debt reduction, after rejecting an appeal in 1966 because Don Regan thought their 3.25 percent return on endowment a sign of weak management. $30,000 in 1973 went to improve library facilities, $25,000 in 1979 for modernization

4. In the *New York Times* (25 March 1986) Joseph Califano, Secretary of Health, Education, and Welfare from 1977 to 1979, states that the rate of major cardiovascular surgery for patients with the same symptoms is twice as high in Des Moines as in Iowa City.

of training clinics for dental hygienists. Graduates are badly needed, and it is an attractive career for minority students.

Dr. John Hein, director of what is perhaps the major dental school in the country, saw the profession threatened by two quite different problems: lack of research funds in a field so necessary and so unglamorous, and the insufficient numbers of new personnel coming into the profession, whether as dentists or technicians, when dentistry is no longer seen as a ladder for advancement.

University of Kentucky, College of Dentistry, Lexington, Kentucky, 1974— $25,000 for scholarships. There is a need to reach the ablest Appalachian students who otherwise attend out-of-state institutions and leave the region—the mountain areas that suffer almost the worst health care in the nation. The College's reputation is shown by the fact that seven deans of dental schools have come out of it since 1961.

Howard University, College of Dentistry, Washington, D.C., 1974— $25,000. Dental care is one of the most serious black medical deficits. From neglect, poor diet, and poor hygiene, blacks in the southeastern states have five times the U.S. rate of dental disease, and a 1:12,500 rate versus the national rate of 1:2,000. Black enrollment in dental schools is dropping because of competition with better jobs in industry, government, and management. More black dentists have graduated from Howard than from all other dental schools combined. Seventy-five percent of the current dental students, however, must hold other jobs in order to survive, and since they are already academically behind, this means poor results and relegation to low-paid, low-grade ghetto practice. Merrill money went towards a loan fund, grants to students to allow practical apprenticeship and community service in the Washington ghetto, and funds to establish a neighborhood health services training center. Here is a field, and also at Meharry's School of Dentistry, that should receive foundation support.

Boston University Medical Center, School of Graduate Dentistry, Boston, Massachusetts, 1977—$30,000. This is a school connected with the whole range of health and disease in the mouth. With neglected people, it is the mouth—from poor diet and hygiene—that goes first. A dentist should become scientifically oriented as a basis for his clinical practice and understand the part played by science in improving management of the most practical clinical problems—the underlying philosophy of the school's new course: biology of disease. Dentists are apt to be all too narrowly pragmatic.

Tufts University, School of Dental Medicine, 1978—$5,000 to help develop an artificial saliva chewing gum. When a patient undergoes any sustained x-ray or radium treatment for cancer in the facial area, one by-product is destruction of the salivary glands. A dry mouth leads to gum disorders and brittle, easily broken teeth. The idea of an artificial saliva through special chewing gum was a project worked out by a young Greek-American, female dental researcher, a graduate of Commonwealth School. Here small, precise grants can not only be of value for research but for encouraging the career of the researcher.

Medical Research Foundation of Boston, Boston, Massachusetts, 1963–1971—$85,000. Here was a series of grants to support research on maxillofacial prosthetics by Dr. Joseph Barron. Dr. Barron, whose artistic skill as a sculptor fitted his career as a dental surgeon, found himself increasingly involved in working on prosthetic devices for patients whose faces had been torn apart by accidents or cancer surgery. After such surgery the natural impulse is to lock oneself in a closet for the rest of one's life, but with skillful repair surgery and prosthetics, the individual can go back out into the world. The financial problems were serious because usually the patient had used up all his savings for the initial operation and insurance companies were reluctant to pay for prosthetic devices. The Medical Research Foundation was a no-cost channel that relayed our money to Dr. Barron, without deducting the usual 15 percent for administration as a regular hospital or university would have. Dr. Barron involved himself in teaching younger colleagues but also in teaching welfare agencies so they would see these facial appliances worth paying for like an artificial limb.

Society for the Rehabilitation of the Facially Disfigured, New York, New York, 1967–1980—$125,000 for teaching, research, and patient care at the Center for Craniofacial Anomalies. The Society, led by Dr. John Converse, sponsors the activities of the Institute of Reconstructive Plastic Surgery at New York University Medical Center, which maintains clinics at Manhattan Eye, Ear, and Throat, New York University, and at Bellevue. It provides clinical care, professional training, and research in the areas of facial disfigurement caused by auto accidents, wounds, burns, tumors, and congenital defects.

Nursing Education

A severe shortage of nurses in the United States occurred in the mid-1960s. Although numbers increased, the demands did even more so: with a rising and aging population growth, there were more hospitals and health agencies, advances in medical sciences, increased demands for medical services, and increased use of nurses in doctors' offices. Federal efforts tried to meet this need by grants for physical facilities, expansion of nursing school programs, and student loans. Nursing was a neglected area of philanthropic investment, and the Merrill Trust was no exception, giving only $385,000 to sixteen institutions. One reason is establishment sexism: no profession primarily staffed by women is taken seriously. Another reason is that organized nursing—the American Nurses' Association and the National League for Nursing—has been a successful lobbyist in Congress for maintaining federal support for nursing education and has not built a strong constituency within private philanthropy. And with the opening of new job horizons by the late 1970s, a young woman with any gumption began to feel she could aim higher than the traditional careers of nursing and teaching.

Frontier Nursing School, Hyden, Kentucky, 1980—$15,000. This is a colorful, long-established, and highly regarded service offering family-centered primary health care to the people of Leslie, Clay, Perry, and Harlan Counties, in the poorest region of Appalachia, whose midwives and nurse practitioners went by horseback and now by jeep into the most remote and primitive areas. The Merrill grant went to support the continuing education fund to allow nurses to attend courses in distant centers.

We also backed *New England Deaconess Hospital, Boston, Massachusetts, 1975—$20,000,* to finance the new School Nursing building and *Case Western Reserve, Cleveland, Ohio, 1979—$25,000,* to aid its nursing students' work for bachelor's and advanced degrees. Most of our interest in nursing education was a by-product, however, of Don Regan's policy of aiding Catholic institutions, usually ignored by non-Catholic foundations.

Grey Nuns of the Sacred Heart, Philadelphia, Pennsylvania, 1977–1981—$15,000. This order was funded in Canada to serve the poor, foundlings, aged, young, and needy. As social demands increased, the numbers of new sisters diminished, and to meet accreditation standards the sisters needed to be better prepared and often retrained.

College of St. Teresa, Winona, Minnesota, 1971—$25,000. This college was started in 1907 by the Franciscan Sisters at a time when few midwestern women were educated beyond the eighth grade. Courses are given in social work, nursing, physical therapy, dietetics, and medical technology with recent expansion into the training of teachers for retarded and learning-disabled children. St. Teresa has more graduates in health service majors than any other college in Minnesota.

Government loans are oppressive for these women going into low-income careers; therefore, there was a need for reasonable grants to allow competition with the state schools in attracting transfer students as well as freshmen from rural high schools. Nevertheless, even though anyone who has ever been hospitalized knows how dependent he is upon the professional and human quality of his nurses, the fact remains that philanthropy does not give much attention to the profession.

In 1982 I was asked by the director of Beth Israel, one of Boston's leading hospitals and proud of the high reputation of its nursing staff, to make a series of visits to examine the hospital's training program, and in the course of those twenty-three visits I learned a lot about the needs of nurses. The more technologically and competitively educated are the bright young doctors who come out of American medical schools, the less they seem to respond to a patient's suffering. A doctor taught to conquer disease is devastated when the system doesn't work. At such a time the nurse becomes all-important. How can she retain gentleness and concern as overwork builds up and up? How can she be rewarded with added education and authority and still not be removed from patient care into administration? What are useful things a foundation might do to improve the lives of nurses?

Help prevent burnout. No other profession gives its members so much responsibility so early. At twenty-two they may be making a midnight life and death decision together with some junior resident, and this pressure increases their isolation from society until they can take no more. Overwork is one cause of burnout. A grant that allows a hospital to cut down on its nurses' workload may be the most tangible way to improve patient care. In the Merrill Trust's twenty-three years no one ever presented such a proposal.

Allow the overburdened nurse to stand back a bit from her job and renew her resources. A fund that pays two-thirds or three-fourths of graduate tuition will upgrade her skills, prestige, self-image, and be a way of showing that the hospital takes its staff seriously. Six months, even six weeks of sabbatical study every few years will be fully worth the expense. How many hospitals do you know that even consider this? How about sending an intellectually curious nurse on an exchange with a British hospital to examine the different approaches of a socialized system?

Help free the young nurse from debt. Many women go into their first job still owing $7,000 to $10,000 on their undergraduate costs, and, unlike doctors, they don't earn the salaries to retire these debts readily. Make an annual bonus to young nurses specifically earmarked to debt reduction.

If you have come to know a specific hospital well, ask what can be done in daily administration to improve the status of nurses. Are they included in all medical conferences? Is it standard procedure for doctors to ask their opinions? Is it understood that they don't fetch coffee? Is the physician known for his arrogance to nurses (there are plenty in every hospital) cautioned by the director?

Major changes in the rewards offered to nurses must be made rapidly if that profession, like teaching, is still to attract and retain first-rate members.

MOTHERS AND CHILDREN

The needs of women in childbirth and of sick and injured children are so obvious that if you are asked to support a place trying to serve these two groups, the only decent thing to do is to write out a check. The first person to suffer when anything goes wrong is the child. When Beirut is fought over, when Coventry or Hamburg is bombed, there is the same silent bandaged child staring out at you: "Why did you do this to me? I wasn't being bad." In Ethiopia, Somalia, India, and Cambodia, the child with swollen belly and shriveled limbs and sunken eyes is always the same. Our first response is anger—these little creatures have done nothing to deserve this—and then remorse and guilt when we think of our own children.

Playing with a healthy, happy two-year old grandchild, we are struck by how early the basic cards are dealt: loving, responsible, united parents, a secure neighborhood, food and care and stimulus that lead to a strong body, an alert mind, the ability to give and accept love, and above all, a sense of trust. At its simplest, when the child is thirsty, someone will give him a drink of water. And the child with an absent or angry father, a dulled or distraught mother, surroundings of noise and chaos, poor food, not simply in Ethiopia but in the United States because it is no longer part of our national priorities to insure that poor children are properly nourished, is already at two and three on its own one-way street.

Well, the Foundation met the appeals that were presented to it for children's and mothers' needs with probably less conscious design than in other fields like research or hospital administration. In the 1980s, however, first priority for private philanthropy might be nutrition (the sort of project the Merrill Trust funded at the refugee camps at the International Rescue Committee) including the organization of innercity co-ops to sell wholesome food (not TV junk) at low prices and to show mothers how to learn from each other and share their resources. Aid to nutrition starts with encouraging poor women—poverty is female—to register and vote and learn to fight for their needs.[5]

How can we help women in childbirth? The kindly trustee writes out a check to the maternity hospital—for the new wing, the new perinatal center, or the new fetal monitoring unit described in the glossy pamphlet. He is glad

---

5. It is unfair to criticize only capitalist medicine. In Czechoslovakia all care is free of course but if your child needs a serious operation, who does it, senior surgeon or resident? A sealed envelope with a month's wages affects that decision. Your boy slices his thumb with a rusty knife. There is no penicillin until one hands the right person a bottle of Johnny Walker.

to be a part of scientific progress and community caring. He is shocked when this modest philanthropy is attacked by some female militant. That overrated institution he has just patronized is an example of everything wrong with maternal care in America today! With its stress on expensive, unnecessary, and often harmful procedures, with its routines adapted to the convenience and profit of its obstetricians, with procedures almost consciously designed to make childbirth as unnatural and depersonalized as possible, that hospital does more harm than good!

With less thorough clinical training of young doctors, they rely on a $200 ultrasound test to ascertain the baby's position rather than a 1¢ glove worn by an obstetrician who can give a proper pelvic examination. The expensive new fetal monitoring system reinforces the doctor's hunch that the delivery may have complications, but because these warnings are on the monitor's printout as a matter of record, if anything does go wrong the patient can sue. The doctor decides on a caesarean, not because that is the wisest procedure medically but to protect himself legally.

It is only fair of course to insist on the realities of obstetrical progress over the past twenty to thirty years. Ultrasound scanning has replaced the overuse of x-rays. The whole process of pregnancy is treated far more humanely. Both parents are brought into the preparations from early on. Father is invited to attend the birth, and it is into his arms that the strange little animal is placed. Nursing is taken for granted instead of being discouraged as a bother for the staff. The siblings are allowed to visit. Infant mortality rates fell 38 percent from 1960 to 1975 and maternal mortality by 71 percent, with credit given to the expansion of neighborhood health centers, better nutrition as a result of the food stamp program, even pollution controls, as well as to better hospital procedures.[6]

Perhaps a midwife or female obstetrician may be willing to take on a smaller, less lucrative patient load and make use of this dramatic event in a woman's life as an opportunity to help her re-evaluate her role as wife, mother, worker, human being. Can the mother examine her priorities and the way she looks at herself, and use this process of childbirth as the beginning of taking an active part in her life instead of being passive, ignorant, frightened, scorned because she is making a nuisance of herself, wiped out with anesthesia, her need to be with her child subordinated to the hospital's routine, and the whole birth experience just one more proof that she is a second-class human being?

To the established obstetrician, target of this change of values, the natural childbirth rhetoric can seem dangerous as well as sentimental. What have we accomplished in medical care if racing back to home delivery is touted as progress? Those who praise natural ways forget that Mother Nature always

6. Paul Starr, *The Social Transformation of American Medicine* (New York: Basic Books, 1982), p. 410.

accepted a high failure rate. The mother of tradition had eight pregnancies because three or four children were sure to die. My grandmother, whose husband was the doctor of Green Cove Springs, Florida, had four children. One died in infancy and one at four. She was unlucky but not unusually so. The young people of today want traditional methods and a modern survival rate. If things go wrong, they sue. This means that obstetricians pay up to $80,000 per year in malpractice premiums and are quitting the field.

Pregnancy

University of Chicago, Division of Biological Sciences, Pritzker School of Medicine, Chicago, 1976—$25,000 to support the Perinatal Center Program. The complex has 665 beds and serves 21,000 inpatients, 200,000 outpatients, and 100,000 emergency patients per year. Pressures facing such a hospital are rising costs, changing patterns of financial support, ever-increasing needs for health care, and—what is often overlooked—ever-rising public expectations of care, at a time when the number of doctors serving the innercity is declining. Seventy percent of infant deaths occur in the first month and are related to prematurity and low birth weight. Improved care in pregnancy and at birth can be costly because a miscarriage is often nature's way of getting rid of a defective fetus. The better care that now allows diabetic mothers to carry a child to term is one reason for the spread of that genetic disease. To keep a premature infant alive may mean a lifetime of heartache for the parents of that defective child and staggering costs for family and society.

And yet it is unacceptable to write off innercity mothers and infants whose special suffering is caused by their social class or by changes in political policy. Cutbacks in food stamps and medical aid to the poor, in vaccine programs (which mean more measles, rubella, and mumps) have ended the long steady fall in the infant mortality rate. When Milton Friedman monetarism dominates national fiscal policy, in Chile or Brazil, United States or Britain, children die.

Providence Lying-In Hospital, Providence, Rhode Island, 1976—$15,000. Before 1970 Providence Lying-In was considered a good, active maternity hospital, and it is now a regional center providing total care for women and infants, as well as a tertiary care center for exceptionally high-risk patients, offering on-going care and education. It is a teaching affiliate of Brown with a gynecology service that is one of the largest in the country. A Special Care Unit for Distressed Infants: "An incredibly tiny infant struggles for life aided by the best that modern medicine and technology can provide." The heroic rhetoric is disturbing; perhaps everyone might be better off if that incredibly tiny infant were allowed to die.

Two paradoxes present themselves at any maternity hospital. In one wing abortions are being performed to kill an unborn child who may be as old as twenty weeks. In another wing every possible effort is spent to keep alive a newborn who may be as young as twenty-four weeks. The contrast between these two tasks may be devastating for the nurses involved. A multiproblem premature is treated with the most sophisticated care imaginable. No one counts the costs. But there might not be enough money in the public health budget—perhaps no more than to pay bus transportation and sitter's fees— that would allow an ignorant, unhealthy mother to come for check-ups that might have prevented such a traumatic delivery. Or, there might not be money to ensure sustained check-ups on the scarred child when it returns home. Americans prefer dramatic sentimentality to practical compassion. Prevention of trouble is not an important part of the public budget, no matter how high the costs that might be avoided. Some English maternity hospitals have a policy of pairing a new mother with a nearby woman of similar background whose baby arrived three to six months earlier. Such a mentor can answer simple questions, offer encouragement, and relieve the frightening isolation that a new mother suddenly finds herself in.

Five Colleges, Incorporated, Amherst, Massachusetts, 1970—$20,000 to finance biological research by Dr. Oscar Schotte on the effects of ionizing radiation on embryo development: *teratology*—the causation of monsters. Women are vulnerable in early pregnancy to any form of radiation, which worries women but not generals. Agent Orange, the defoliant used in Vietnam to uncover the Ho Chi Minh Trail, which caused birth defects among Vietnamese children, then among the children of American soldiers who got too close, is not a subject the Pentagon cares to discuss.

Tulane Medical Center, New Orleans, Louisiana, 1979—$50,000. No modern perinatal care exists in many areas of Louisiana and Southern Mississippi, and Tulane supplies both out- and inpatient care, as well as education to local medical personnel in advanced obstetrical and intensive infant care. The hospital policy is that every distressed infant receive specialized care until its condition is stabilized. There is need for both fetal and maternal care from conception on, with perinatal screening to identify early the pregnancy risk. It is a region where traditionally men are more sensitive to repairing their cars than their wives.

Children's Medicine—$905,000

Children's Hospital, San Francisco, 1959–1979—$310,000. Children's in San Francisco received the Trust's largest support of any hospital outside New

York and Boston. It was started in 1875 when eight women doctors opened the first clinic for needy women and children. Later it became a general hospital, one of 363 teaching hospitals in the United States and affiliated with the University of California and Stanford, but with its major emphasis still on children. Research programs have specialized in hematology, pulmonary and cardiac diseases, muscular dystrophy, cerebral palsy, peripheral vascular diseases, and morphogenesis of cardiac anomalies. It was one of the first institutions to use an eye coagulation machine to treat retinal detachment other than by surgery.

Of the Merrill Trust money, $110,000 went toward new equipment ranging from an x-ray film developer to a CAT scanner; $100,000 toward construction and renovation. Piecemeal growth had led to dysfunctional and uneconomical buildings. New construction allowed economy and integration as well as expansion. In 1968 $100,000 went to establish the Perinatal Health Center, still a major new department in pediatrics, in a new $2 million building, with facilities for premature infants, special treatment to prevent birth defects and brain damage, and care of high-risk mothers—the first of its kind in the United States. Two interesting approaches were a mobile intensive care unit for transferring sick infants from home or other hospitals; and a Perinatal Special Procedures Unit, with a specialized team that would work either at Children's or transfer itself to a lesser hospital for a procedure like catheterization of the arterial system, mechanical ventilation of the infant, or measurement of blood gas tension. Before the Sabine vaccine, this was the major hospital in California for care of polio patients. It is also one of two breast-milk banks.

Children's Hospital at Stanford, Palo Alto, California, 1979—$25,000 to support construction of a specialized treatment room in the planned Fay Hospital. This is a useful new approach going beyond the usual out-patient practice and taking pressure off facilities, cutting costs for families by bringing the child into the hospital only for an active service and then letting it return home at night, which in pediatrics may become customary. The hospital had started in 1919 as a convalescent home for children suffering from long-term diseases like rheumatic fever, polio, and tuberculosis. It is now a center for childhood cancer, cystic fibrosis, hemophilia, and complicated orthopedic problems.

Children's Hospital Medical Center, Boston, Massachusetts, 1967—$50,000 to continue its development campaign, such as a new pressure chamber for heart surgery on children too ill to survive surgery in a normal operative environment. A world leader in education and research linked with

Harvard Medical School faculty, Children's considers itself a hospital first and takes selected referrals from all over New England and in fact takes seriously ill children from all over the United States and the world. Long-distance consultation is well employed but the facilities are crowded, and there is a need to expand the clinics to cut down the increasingly long waiting time. In this hospital was the first successful surgery on the great vessels of the heart, the isolation of the polio virus, the first breakthroughs in leukemia and cystic fibrosis, the first measles vaccine, and team research in mental retardation.

Children's Hospital, Washington, 1969–1973—$50,000 to the new Children's Hospital Medical Center affiliated with George Washington, Georgetown, and Howard medical schools. This was an ambitious project with planning costs alone running at $67,000 per month. One of its goals was to establish a Comprehensive Health Care Program to reach beyond the walls of the Hospital and send teams of doctors, nurses, psychiatrists, and community health workers to bring total health care to innercity children not receiving medical attention. Our 1969 grant was $30,000 toward a ghetto nutrition clinic. As one looks back at this rhetoric from the 1980s, at a time when innercity children are wasting away from simple old-fashioned malnutrition, one doesn't know whether to laugh or cry.

Greater Baltimore Medical Center, Baltimore, Maryland, 1967—$25,000 for support of Baltimore Community Pediatric Program where pediatricians and interns rotate their location assignments and accordingly gain experience at a large university hospital; at a city hospital with indigent patients, tuberculosis, and every sort of contagious disease; and at a community hospital specializing in family care.

Children's Orthopedic Hospital and Medical Center, Seattle, Washington, 1971, 1975—$50,000. (It was a challenge to Charlie Cole to think up every possible excuse for directing Merrill Trust money to Seattle during the early 1970s as we, single-handed, pulled the disaster-struck city back from the brink.) Our two grants went to the Department of Rehabilitative Medicine to meet the needs of children with multiple handicaps by hiring a nurse specialist to assume primary nursing responsibilities. Most of the work can be done on an outpatient basis, creating the need for comprehensive evaluation and treatment for the child and training for his parents. A valuable new approach with inpatients is parent care teams, under supervision of a ward nurse, for feeding and dressing children not acutely ill.

THE HANDICAPPED

Mental Health and Mental Illness—$640,000

James Jackson Putnam Children's Center, Boston, Massachusetts, 1970—$10,000. This community-oriented psychiatric clinic in predominately black Roxbury treats disturbed preschool children and their families and trains psychiatrists, social workers, and nursery school teachers. Treatment is slow and expensive, and heavy staffing is needed for the 100 children and their parents. One has to be convinced that serious intervention in early childhood will prevent worse and costlier suffering later, which is hard if the society to which the child returns is itself sick.

Preventive medicine is not rewarding. It brings limited fees for doctors, its costs are not reimbursable by the insurance agencies, and federal funding is set up to pay for expensive diseases of the poor and not for low-cost prevention.

Mount Sinai Hospital, New York, New York, 1969—$30,000 to help finance a comprehensive mental health program for the 1966 first-grade class at Public School 198 on 3rd Avenue and 96th Street. The personality differences leading to dropping out, delinquency, violence, and narcotics come from within the individual and also from social forces. The disadvantaged child falls behind and feels defeated and inadequate, and the need becomes, therefore, to mobilize the team resources of preventive psychiatry. What can be done when a full-scale psychiatric program is made available to such a school of mixed ethnic groups (sixty-nine Puerto Ricans, fifty-six whites, thirty-three blacks) and many poor families? This group and an untreated control group were going to be assessed and evaluated at the end of four years, after work with family and teachers, speech therapy, and remedial reading.

This appeal left a strange aftertaste. The estimated cost was over $500,000. If the program didn't amount to much, here was one more research effort designed to serve researchers. If it did really help those children find better resources with which to grow up in New York, think of all the other public school classes who do not and never will receive any such aid.

Pacific Psychotherapy Associates, San Francisco, California, 1976–1978—$20,000. A full-service, community-based clinic, taking referrals from the Greater Bay Area and specializing in mental health care to the disadvantaged, underserved, alienated, and subdelinquent minorities, all too often in jail because there is no appropriate treatment facility. San Francisco has a staggering juvenile crime problem, and PPA was trying to establish a community residence to modify destructive behavior.

Almost the first decision made by the Trust in the field of mental illness was to reject an appeal by the Menninger Foundation. It described itself, probably with justification, as the most important research and treatment center in the United States, but we were turned off by the glossiness of the sales pitch—and the vastness of Menninger's finances.

A question comes of whether our society is going forward (research and better treatment) or backward (greater stress) in the field of mental illness as well as in retardation. Can medical treatment remedy the cumulative impact of unemployment, poor housing, malnutrition, and fear of war? How does one explain to a child even the faintest reality of what is meant by nuclear war ("Do you mean to say that everyone everywhere will be killed: you and Mom and me and the baby and kitty? What's the purpose of it? Why doesn't someone do something about it?") and expect it to grow up sane and be willing to accept rational rules and rational goals? What are children's nightmares about war—we don't want to know—which are closer to reality than the June 1982 words of Secretary of Defense Caspar Weinberger that the United States must be prepared to fight and win a sustained nuclear war.

McLean Hospital, Belmont, Massachusetts, 1974—$20,000. This mental hospital opened in 1818, an affiliate of Massachusetts General, had received a matching grant for construction of a new laboratory facility for the study of schizophrenia. There are two million sufferers from the disease in the United States, and the amazing statistic is that one out of four hospital beds is occupied by a schizophrenic.

In its appeal, McLean's stressed the difficulty in obtaining funds for treatment and research in mental illness. Ex patients and their families lack loyalty toward a mental hospital.

Psychiatric Research Foundation, New York, New York, 1968—$15,000 served as a channel (as did the *Gralnick Foundation, 1969—$25,000*) to finance a statistical research project by Dr. Jonathan Slocum, director of Craig House, a private psychiatric hospital in Beacon, New York. Since case histories are classified as confidential by hospitals and psychiatrists, this blockage of information flow hinders any attempt to make surveys of psychiatric patients. Dr. Slocum had developed a code to preserve patient anonymity while establishing a system of information assembly that permitted storage of significant data on computer tape. Our two grants went to support a program for coding information on patients in 150 hospitals: what treatments prove best, what characteristics certain patients are apt to have, and ways to ease paperwork loads by providing computer printouts of statistical data needed on discharge forms.

Phillips Brooks House, Harvard University, Cambridge, Massachusetts,

1962—$25,000 to meet the deficit of the Wellmet Project. This was an ambitious project to utilize Harvard-Radcliffe volunteers in helping to rehabilitate mental patients. It included a ward visit program by student teams to engage patients and combat their isolation and withdrawal; case aid of one student attached to one patient to remotivate a patient to involve himself in his own cure and try to provide a place for him in the outside community; and the Wellmet Halfway House to allow mental patients to live with students and share the running of the house. Patients lacked families and vocations to return to, and previously they had to stay in the hospital since no channel existed for transition. This program was successful enough (and received a further $15,000 in 1965 directly to Wellmet) that its student leaders served as consultants for similar programs at other universities and in Denmark, England, and Brazil in an effort to break the hopelessness of long-term stay. The need for practical and caring human response can often make this service of benefit also for the volunteers.

The Bridge, New York, New York, 1972, 1980—$30,000 to maintain services at this halfway house. The usual rehospitalization rate for mental patients is 60 percent. The Bridge has kept its rate below 30 percent. The policy of deinstitutionalization meant in 1972 a doubling of services demand in just one year. The second $15,000 in 1980 went to place mentally disabled adults into decent apartments on Manhattan's West Side. Modern psychiatric approaches and the use of powerful new drugs shorten hospitalization, often to a matter of months, but patients are still left with major problems before they can become functioning and self-supporting, if they ever do. The theory of dehospitalizing patients to the community meant, in actuality, dumping these miserable people into wretched hotels or, a cut below, letting them sleep in doorways and bus terminals.

College Mental Health Center of Boston, Boston, Massachusetts, 1973—$25,000 to set up an evaluation program and computerized retrieval system. Dr. John Sturrock, an Australian-born psychiatrist, had helped organize a cooperative, multicollege mental health center for small institutions (not Harvard or MIT, large and rich enough to have their own facilities) with twenty-two now affiliated. The population is heterogeneous (a business student from Northeastern University or a drama major at Emerson College), and though problems may be similar—angry confrontation with authority, politicization of the campus, harder economic climate, and ever-changing styles of drug use—the reactions of different types of students (an eighteen-year-old from a small town or from the inner city) will be different. Therefore, a sophisticated data retrieval system to put 10,000 cases (at $5.00 per case) on file was needed.

For example, what are the rules of presuicidal behavior? Suicides are apt to occur on sunny days or after exciting football victories: the weather is fine and everyone else feels swell, I can't blame other circumstances—it's me! Does the expression of homosexuality (rejection of American aggression in Vietnam leading to rejection of the John Wayne machismo that motivates it?) or bisexuality (anything goes, there are no rules for anything) follow social trends, or are these conditions innate?

Somerville Mental Health Association, Somerville, Massachusetts, 1973—$20,000. Dr. Patricia Papernow, who had had a long experience of working with runaways and youthful drug users, had organized a group called Committee for Training Resources to help mature, responsible lay people—cops, nurses, teachers, daycare aides, and bartenders—be better prepared to help others. She felt that a Freudian psychiatrist is socially of little value. His training is too long, costly, and theoretical, but it is possible to provide training that will allow the pillar of the community, however limited that community may be, to give helpful support to an unhappy person with an aggressive child, a divorce, a dying parent, or an alcoholic spouse. When children or even adults are too inarticulate to use words for their problem, how can role-playing games reach them?

Ossining Open Door Associates, Ossining, New York, 1976—$20,000 for the Tappan Zee Mental Health Clinic, established "to comfort the elderly, counsel the young, listen to the lonely" in a very poor area.

Retardation—$365,000

A hopeless field. In Poland the care of retarded children and also of the insane is left to the church (aided by small subsidies) since a socialist state sees no rational reason to waste its limited resources on such a no-win problem. Mental retardation might be called an illness of sophisticated societies because, traditionally, defective children died more easily and also fitted more easily into a community of large families where low-skilled jobs were available and where people were not so hung up on classification. There is greater retardation among black families and yet a more humane acceptance.

The Merrill Trust invested a lot of money into institutions serving the retarded, both children and adults. It is a problem the average person tries to avoid unless he has been forced to have personal contact with it. Then it becomes devastating. Is retardation increasing because modern medicine is more skilled in keeping alive defective, multiproblem children? Will pauperization of welfare families mean an increase? Or does our greater knowledge of causation and treatment allow us to make headway? In England, where more limited resources have sometimes forced greater clarity on social problems, a majority of physicians answered a 1981 questionnaire stating that they were in favor of letting a severely handicapped child die at birth. In the United States, however, the recent trend has been towards tighter, state-enforced controls upon hospitals that might in the past have allowed a hopeless child to slip away.

Graham Home for Children, New York, New York, 1969—$25,000 to expand facilities. This home was originally for orphans for whom no foster care was available and is now for children emotionally and mentally disturbed, most of whom are severely retarded in school work and are from backgrounds of great deprivation. The 160 boys and girls live in a suburban cottage system unsegregated by age to retain the hierarchy of family living. An aftercare center in New York City tries to look after youngsters who return to the city as strangers.

Elwyn Institute, Elwyn, Pennsylvania, 1969, 1973—$35,000 towards construction of a new center for brain damaged children. Elwyn has 1,250 patients—children and young adults with learning difficulties—750 of whom are in training programs. Serious attention is paid to brain-damaged children to increase social competence, academic skill, and emotional maturity. A private institution like Elwyn will develop new methods and techniques that other places can share, making a new effort to escape the old tradition of total isolation with locked doors, even to the fire escapes. New workshops contract for jobs with local industries. In 1973 the annual costs of $6,000 for residents and $3,000 for day pupils were half that of other schools.

National Association for Retarded Citizens, Arlington, Texas, 1979—$25,000 to prepare guidelines for teachers designing curricula on the prevention of mental retardation. Six million Americans are affected, 3 percent of all newborns (120,000 infants a year). Retardation is the third leading chronic illness in the United States. The etiology is often undetermined, but causes include genetic disease, accidents, physical neglect, malnutrition, mistreatment, and psychosocial deprivation. The Merrill grant went to design a junior and senior high school curriculum on the problem and an accompanying movie. With welfare cutbacks, mental retardation will increase. A more sensible use for this money might have been to upgrade school lunch and breakfast programs in our poorest areas. One comes back to the question of economic class. Middle-class people prefer to rely on middle-class concepts—movies and curriculum—and on approaches that mean jobs for middle-class people. Working-class people approach issues more concretely: better food for poor kids.

New Hope-New Horizons, Keene, New Hampshire, 1974—$10,000. In the pretty, tree-shaded towns of southern New Hampshire there is an endless range of social problems made worse by weak state support. This agency runs a seven-week summer camp to help retarded children survive at home and at school rather than in an institution. It also runs a Home Bound Workers Program (making birdhouse assembly kits, for example) that can almost be self-supporting.

New Hampshire Association for Retarded Citizens, Concord, 1979—$5,000. Again, New Hampshire's low taxes are fine for its citizens as taxpayers but not if they need any services. The state ranks down with Mississippi in the money it spends on the retarded in helping them to lead adequate personal lives and to function as self-supporting citizens. There are well-meaning laws on the books, but funds and energy are needed to turn these legal resources into tangible action: for research and education (England has advanced legislation in this field), publicity, and upgrading of a facility like the Laconia State School.

Clausen House, Oakland, California, 1976, 1981—$50,000. Clausen House is an Episcopalian-sponsored residential facility for eighty adults, for training toward maximum self-sufficiency and community participation. In custodial situations the retarded receive no challenge and vegetate into helplessness. Clausen House clients, in their six different houses and one apartment building, receive training in home management, kitchen skills, personal and clothing care, health and safety, financial management, and phone use and even act in a drama group that gives shows to retirement homes and community agencies. In most cases a retarded adult leaves a training school at eighteen or twenty-one bound back to his parents' home, a board-and-care home, or a state hospital. Clausen is an alternative.

Handicapped—$935,000

Scottish Rite Hospital for Crippled Children, Atlanta, Georgia, 1980—$10,000 for endowment at the first purely orthopedic hospital for children in the United States. "No child will ever be turned away for lack of money."

Crotched Mountain Foundation, Franceston, New Hampshire, 1966—$15,000. The Center was started in 1953 for children disabled by disease (muscular dystrophy, polio, and cerebral palsy), birth defects, or accident. In the 1960s deaf children were included and then adults, a strong medical and technical library was built, and a new stress was placed on research programs and clinical training for nurses, teachers, therapists, and social workers. With

New Hampshire's low resources, there was a need for a private institution to do what in other states would be taken over by public ones. By the end of the 1960s, however, this long-term, isolated treatment seemed old fashioned and became less respected.

Philadelphia Home for Incurables, Philadelphia, Pennsylvania, 1975— $10,000 (what a terrible name!) for facilities and programs relevant to the young adult. This home addressed how to face problems, starting with self-acceptance of those handicapped from birth or by an accident that made a paraplegic overnight.

Clarke School for the Deaf, Northampton, Massachusetts, 1959–1979— $420,000. This school for the deaf, the oldest and best known of the oral schools (in contrast to *Gallaudet College in Washington, 1962—$15,000,* where students are taught to communicate through sign language) in the country, received this large total of grants through the personal commitment of Charles Cole. He was always interested in the problems of handicapped persons, and his respect for Clarke led to sustained support. The money went to every sort of purpose: salaries, property purchase (to increase enrollment facilities after the great rubella epidemic of 1964 left so many hearing-impaired infants), classroom equipment, construction costs for a new dormitory, scholarships, and endowment.

From its beginning in 1867 Clarke has been committed to mainstreaming deaf children, which has meant refusing to accept sign language that locks the deaf into a rigid subculture where only those who know the code can communicate with each other. When Clarke began, not one deaf child was being taught to speak. Alexander Graham Bell, whose wife was deaf, was much involved with the early technology of hearing aids that the school experimented with.

The school's major statement has been that deafness is an educational rather than a medical problem. People with normal hearing do not realize how the blanking out of sound limits and confuses the comprehension from eyes alone. Even when they have graduated from high school, most deaf youngsters read at only a third- or fourth-grade level. Clarke therefore sets itself to the task of trying to upgrade the standards expected from handicapped children. This is difficult because deaf children become shrewd little diplomats and learn to smile and nod at the right times and fool amateurs into thinking they understand.

The school tries to intervene in the hearing-learning process as early as possible with a parent-infant program for children as young as four to six months, with a preschool where deaf and normal children are mixed together, and with a residential program that may begin at four and one-half years of age. This seems disturbingly young, and yet it is seen as a way to adapt a child to his hearing aid in order to stimulate whatever residual hearing he possesses at a time when most children are learning language as naturally as they breathe. The school is beginning the long, complex process of teaching oral education. This includes work with siblings and grandparents as well as parents, and it involves psychological as well as technical counseling, starting with that terrible question: "Why did God do this to me?"

Clarke sees its main functions as that of teaching teachers, conducting research in every detail of hearing and speech, and serving as a national resource center. In its work with deaf children, however, the place is oddly frustrated. By the 1980s the annual charge for a residential pupil came to $11,000, the cost to $17,000, and if a child needed the services and could not pay, he usually found his way in. This meant an annual operating deficit of $800,000, met through some endowment plus tireless fund-raising. The Commonwealth of Massachusetts and other states used to be willing to put up the total cost per pupil. This is no longer true. Under the theme of mainstreaming, to keep the child at home and in his local school, the Commonwealth now hires its own special teachers, at less cost and at much less effectiveness. Accordingly, one result is unused facilities, empty dormitory rooms, and a rising unit cost at what is actually a highly professional resource.

St. Mary's Hospital and Medical Center, San Francisco, California, 1978— $50,000 to establish a Speech and Hearing Center. Established in 1857, the oldest children's hospital in the West is a large general hospital equipped for just about any illness, though it carries on little research. Merrill Trust money went to help screen 43,000 parochial school children so that early detection, diagnosis, and therapy could be provided to avert the behavioral problems often developed by children with speech and hearing handicaps. Hearing loss is the United States' major handicapping disability, affecting 14.5 million people, including 3 million schoolchildren.

Blindness—Care and Research—$272,500

Eye Research Institute of the Retina Foundation, Boston, Massachusetts, 1973–1977—$60,000 for research in retinoblastomy, the second most common cancer of the eye, affecting children under five, and with obvious hereditary origin. For unknown reasons, its frequency has doubled over the past twenty years. With injection of a live human virus, Dr. Charles Schepens, the Belgian-born director, has been able to induce retinoblastomy in the eye of a lab rat and notice similarities of the same virus causation in cancers of the brain and spinal cord. Although the Retina Foundation, the largest independent eye research institute in the world, prided itself on its lean budget, it had been hurt by the recent drop in research funding. Eye research is the poor relation in the general field of medical research. In its surgical treatment for detached retinas, the Foundation's doctors have raised the success rate from 40 to 85 percent.

In 1977 $25,000 went for research in causes of abnormal blood vessel growth in diabetic retinopathy, the leading cause (15 percent) of new blindness in the United States and which causes blindness in 2 percent of all diabetics. Forty percent of diabetics suffer some form of retinopathy, increasing geometrically as this genetic disease is disseminated throughout the population. There is no understanding of the basic cause of this process.

Massachusetts Eye and Ear Hospital, Boston, 1975—$20,000. This hospital has been a leader in advanced research: retrolental fibropasia from expansion and then decay of blood vessels from too much oxygen (formerly given to premature babies), glaucoma, surgical and then laser repair of detached retinas, and use of ultracold in surgery.

Research to Prevent Blindness, New York, New York, 1975, 1979— $45,000. This institute is the creation of Dr. Jules Stein, who left medicine to pursue a career in the entertainment industry. After becoming wealthy within the Music Corporation of America, he returned to his former profession and started up this institute to meet funding needs of eye research by serving as a catalyst between the research scientist and the sources of money. The annual cost for caring for the visually disabled in America is over $5 billion, and yet research receives little support. Dr. Stein sought to provide the departments of ophthalmology at almost fifty medical schools with money to strengthen and stimulate those areas of research where they have most interest and competence—in unrestricted funds as opposed to the narrow government research contracts.

RESEARCH

General

It is hard for the intelligent amateur in charge of foundation funds to chart policy in regard to medical research. If a member of your family has been touched by meningitis, if you have read an interesting article in the *Times* about gonorrhea, if you have just had a long talk with a charismatic fundraiser, it is easy to turn chance experience into policy. Perhaps the wisest approach is to see where all the noise is heading and then go in the opposite direction.

For the first ten years of the Merrill Trust we put little money into medical research, feeling that federal support was meeting that need. As government aid shrank we became more involved, reaching a total of about $2.2 million. As the government became ever more finicky in the procedures demanded, we chose the institution or individual we respected and then trusted them to follow their own directions. In some cases, where government agencies and private foundations were demanding immediate results, we were willing to fund basic scientific research from which, in the long run, medical progress will come. As the usual givers become mean and narrow, one is under obligation, even with limited funds, to become imaginative and generous.[7]

Medical Research Foundation, Boston, Massachusetts, 1967—$10,000 to aid Dr. Stanley Cortell's research on kidney function. Dr. Cortell, with a B.S. from MIT and an M.D. from Tufts, was then only thirty-one, too young to have an established record. Moreover, he wanted only a modest sum of money. For both reasons the check writers at the National Institute of Health were turned off. A doctor I respected said that Cortell was an honest, imaginative man and that the work he was doing (testing kidney function under varying levels of CO_2 and sodium, as in asthma and coronary trouble) was potentially important.

Case Western Reserve, Institute of Pathology, School of Medicine, Cleveland, Ohio, 1969—$25,000 to help finance research in structure and function relations in biomembranes, particularly as they relate to cancer. Dr. Robert Cook had his application to National Institute of Health (NIH) rejected because they were supporting only researchers who had already proved their productivity by the number of papers they had written, which Dr. Cook was too young to have done. The director of the Institute of Pathology appealed to Charles Cole, who presented the project as another example of what a private foundation should be willing to risk.

Boston Biomedical Research Institute, Boston, Massachusetts, 1972– 1981—$65,000. This institute was founded in 1950 to do basic research in life sciences—cell physiology, bioorganic chemistry, and metabolic regulation, with broad laboratory programs in biology and medicine and specialized programs for young scientists. Research was also done on the mechanism of muscle contraction, the function of joints and their malfunction in arthritis,

7. A radical comment was made by E. Richard Brown (*Rockefeller Medicine Men*) as quoted: "The Rockefeller philanthropies favored scientific medicine because it helped 'legitimize' the inequalities of capitalism by diverting attention from the social causes of disease . . ." (Paul Starr, *The Social Transformation of American Medicine* (New York: Basic Books, 1982), p. 227.

the body's regulatory mechanisms from before birth to old age, and defects in cell development that lead to cancer. These are studied at the molecular level with the use of all scientific disciplines. The Institute worked with Massachusetts General, Harvard, and MIT in postdoctoral research and yet had an interest in attracting and training bright high school students. Boston Biomedical was one of the top ten research institutes in the country when measured by the level of federal funding and the quality of its multidisciplinary publications, one of few such institutes not limited to the study of a single disease. Ninety percent of the $4.5 million budget was met from Washington, and since this source is restricted and diminishing, there came an almost desperate effort to look for private funding, which was harder and harder to obtain by the 1980s.

Worcester Foundation of Experimental Biology, Worcester, Massachusetts, 1973, 1978—$45,000. The researchers at the Harvard School of Public Health, on whose visiting committee I served for twelve years, suffered low morale not only from the reductions in federal support but also from the rigidly detailed contracts that left no room for following up new ideas. Applied research was funded towards very specific goals, basic long-range research dried up, and the work teams were cut back or disbanded while applied cancer research had more funds poured into it than there were qualified programs to handle them.

The Worcester Foundation was begun in 1944 for interdisciplinary research in regulatory biology and basic research into life functions upon which applied research has to be based if it will have any chance to grow: cell biology, endocrinology, neurobiology (how the brain and nervous system regulate bodily processes). Out of this knowledge came an understanding of schizophrenia in terms of altered biochemistry, the processes by which maternal diet limitation leads to mental retardation, and the relation between pituitary function and ovulation, the study of which produced the contraceptive pill.

In 1978 $10,000 went towards the Science Apprenticeship Scholarship Program of support for college students given actual work experience in ongoing professional research programs under individualized supervision, clearly an idea that deserved richer funding.

Bio-Research Institute, Cambridge, Massachusetts, 1966—$28,000. The first $10,000 went to finance construction of a small building for a special type of Syrian golden hamster particularly susceptible to myopathic heart disease. With every nook and cranny of the Institute crowded with animal cages, more space was needed for genetic research. The Institute was too small, and its Swiss-born director, Freddy Homburger, was too stubborn to lure government funding. It seemed rational that a small amount of money here might gain more tangible results than a large amount to a huge institution.

The Merrill Lynch vice-president asked to deliver the check reported that Dr. Homburger was suing the firm. He had a reputation as an aggressive operator, and as I hunted for references I received the ultimate statement: "He is not the sort of man Charles E. Merrill would have liked." On the other side: "In research, support the creative bastard rather than the socially responsible, nice second rater."

In 1970 $18,000 went towards research on a newly discovered blood component in mice related in an unknown way to cancer of the breast. The mouse susceptible to breast cancer shows blood characteristics, even at an early age, missing in other mice. Is this transmitted through male mice or through lactation? Can one take mass blood samples from different categories of women to search for the same relations?

A lot of interesting work was being done in a small area with small amounts of money. Then one day some local kids broke into the lab, let all the cute little animals out of their cages, and after a few hours of random play, all the genetic precision of the program was ruined.

Allergies

When Charles Cole became president of Amherst College in the late 1940s and proceeded to hobble the fraternities, double the Jewish quota, and intellectualize the curriculum, one result of this greater sophistication was a much higher proportion of students coming to the infirmary with allergic disorders than had been true with the coonskin-coat and hip-flask folk of former administrations.

Samuel Merritt Hospital, Oakland, California, 1961–1980—$142,000 in six grants. In 1965–1969 $100,000 of this support went to Dr. Albert Rowe's research program in food allergy, the only one in the world. Dr. Rowe, then in his seventies, had devoted most of his professional life to this study. One-third of the population, he had discovered, are allergic to wheat, eggs, corn, chocolate, beef, or milk, and he employed food elimination diets to test what causes trouble like asthma, migraine, colitis, eczema, gastro-intestinal illness, toxemia, and sinus. Skin tests are not reliable for food allergies, too many doctors are insensitive to diet causation, and food labels on commercial bakery products are often inaccurate and throw off allergic patients trying to measure their diets. With his advanced age, Dr. Rowe was looking for funds to accelerate his research and provide permanent funding for his lab.

International Psychiatric Research Foundation, New York, New York, 1972—$50,000 for research and educational projects on the use of hypnosis as a way to avoid overmedication and unnecessary surgery, conducted by Dr. Herbert Spiegel of Columbia's College of Physicians and Surgeons. In case of illness, there is an overwhelming pressure to do something, even when not useful. Our country suffers from the saturation of drugs, from overprescription by doctors, overadvertising, the lack of discipline by patients who will not change their lifestyles and cannot cope with pain, drugs given in oversupply, at the wrong time, and which conflict with other drugs until one has the figure (stated in the late 1960s by Howard Hiatt when he was chief of medicine at Beth Israel) that 16 percent of his hospital's admissions were for iatrogenic ailments (those caused by doctors). Dr. Spiegel was conducting research on the range of ailments where hypnosis had a potential for relief, comfort, and even cure; on the capacity for concentration that allowed some patients to gain relief and others not; and on the use of hypnosis for control of smoking and overeating.

Tucson Hospitals Medical Education Program, Tucson, Arizona, 1977— $20,000 for research on headaches. Twenty-five million Americans suffer from migraine headaches. Though such a headache results wholly or in part from reaction to emotional stress, it is a physical not a psychological disease. One cannot will away a migraine attack any more than can an epileptic decide not to have a seizure. Migraines can be controlled, however, and the attacks can be reduced in number or eliminated by avoiding or learning to control some of the causes, whether allergies or causes like bright light, heat or cold, motion or noise, or oral contraceptives.

Venereal Disease

American Social Health Association, New York, New York, 1972, 1975— $50,000. The Social Health Association is the only nongovernment agency devoted to venereal disease prevention and control. Despite the appalling rise in frequency: from 500 cases per 100,000 in San Francisco in 1966 to 2,000 cases per 100,000 in 1971, with gonorrhea the single most frequently reported communicable disease in the United States and with $50 million in public funds per year for the institutional care of advanced syphilitics, public opposition has made federal research support erratic and tentative. And now there come the incurable diseases of genital herpes and AIDS. Merrill Trust funds went for publicity and start-up funds for the National Foundation for Venereal Disease Research, to provide technical support, and to set research priorities.

University of Washington, School of Medicine, Seattle, Washington, 1977—$20,000 for research on the increasing resistance of gonococci to penicillin and other antibiotics. This is a rapidly increasing phenomenon in the Far East as well as in the United States and Europe, an example of a relatively common infectious agent becoming difficult to treat. I was led to this project through a *New York Times* article on Dr. Stanley Falkow's effort to conduct research on the spread of resistance genes, for its own value and as a rosetta stone to study the genetic spread of resistance. Merrill funds went to support research associates from foreign countries and the purchase of new lab equipment.

Funding, public and private, goes for research on diseases with aggressive money-raising leadership, particularly if it can produce pictures of appealing little children whom Your Dollar can cure, or on diseases like coronary and cancer suffered by older people with money and influence. Tropical diseases—schistosomiasis, which affects a quarter of a billion people; trachoma, perhaps half a billion—seem distant. Dental and mental health research is unglamorous; oddly enough, so is eye research. The trifling $70,000 appropriated for research in venereal disease by a foundation, in medical fields as progressive as ours, is typical of American limitations. As the spreading resistance to poorly used antibiotics makes control much more difficult than it was thirty years ago, the problem could have been solved with education, social discipline, and a government willing to face the issue and pay the price. Venereal disease was rampant throughout China when the Communists took power in 1949. With a great publicity campaign, with priority given to widespread treatment centers, thorough follow-up, harsh sanctions against slackers, and a massive drive with cheap antibiotics, the disease was largely eradicated before bacterial resistance could take hold. But VD mainly affects marginal people, the young and poor, and Americans would rather evade the issue.

Blood

Children's Blood Foundation, New York, New York, 1960–1981— *$105,000. Community Blood Council of Greater New York, New York, 1965—* *$10,000* to help construct a national center for the study of blood transfusion problems. There are chaotic conditions of procurement, processing, distribution, and agency coordination in the blood business. With 150 blood banks in the city, one hospital sees an oversupply of one type going to waste that a nearby hospital is crying for. With professional donors there is an increasing danger of hepatitis—and now AIDS—spread and therefore the need to keep recruiting volunteers. Also needed is electronic data control to keep down costs through centralized administration. (By the late 1970s a commercial company was importing plasma from Haiti, a country so desperately poor that Haitians were selling their blood to wealthy Americans.)

Beth Israel Hospital, Boston, Massachusetts, 1964–1981—($206,000 in five grants); $25,000 in 1981 for research in autotransfusion procedures. When a patient will require massive blood transfusion in the course of major surgery, there is the dual problem of drawing down bloodbank supplies and the danger of infection from unknown donors. If his own blood is withdrawn, cleaned, and then returned in the course of the operation (a logical process) both problems are avoided.

Coronary Disease—$387,000

Mt. Zion Hospital and Medical Center, San Francisco, California, 1971— $75,000 for research in the role of behavior patterns and emotional stress as well as diet, smoking, and lack of exercise in causing heart trouble. It is possible to produce in lab animals a human type of behavior pattern leading to disease. What are intermediate mechanisms by which a personality upset can lead to elevation of blood cholesterol and therefore a heart attack?

New York Hospital-Cornell Medical Center, New York, New York, 1967– *1981—$132,000* in six grants to the Cardiovascular Center. This center stresses the development of new ways to prevent stroke and heart attack and to identify early on those who are prone to such. Our first $27,000 went to purchase an ultrasonic scanning device, a noninvasive method (allowing for more detailed pictures than by x-ray and with far less shock than catheterization) for measuring strain upon a patient's heart. By placing a sound probe over the chest the doctor can discover not only the degree to which the heart muscle has thickened but also how it is performing. Three grants went to study the relation between hypertension and cardiovascular disease, hypertension now seen as a multiform problem with a special need to examine how it expresses itself in pregnancy.

Providence Medical Center, Seattle, Washington, 1977, 1979—$50,000 for the Reconstructive Cardiovascular Research Center. Cardiovascular disease causes more deaths in western culture than all other diseases combined, but most patients can be aided by reconstructive surgery. Coronary artery bypass operation is the most frequently performed clinical cardiac surgery in the world.[8] The first $25,000 went towards establishing a $5 million endowment to make the Center self-sustaining and independent of federal funding. In 1979 $25,000 went towards a $550,000 electron microscope system to help

8. In 1982, 159,000 people underwent such surgery with a total cost of $2.5 to $3 billion, roughly 1 percent of the total U.S. health expenditures. The British rate, largely from budget constraints, is 10 percent of the U.S. rate. (Henry Aaron and William Schwartz, *The Painful Prescription—Rationing Hospital Care* (Washington, D.C.: Brookings Institute, 1984), pp. 63–92.)

understand questions about subcellular events important in cardiovascular disease and treatment. The Center involved itself in repairing the failing heart, preventing strokes, repairing and replacing damaged arteries and heart valves, salvaging limbs and preventing amputations, and improving artificial devices.

Cancer—$685,000

Medical Research Foundation of Boston, Boston, Massachusetts, 1964— $40,000 to help finance a cancer detection clinic designed to offer private patients of moderate means a thorough examination directed towards the detection of cancer in its early stages, a program of Charles Kasdon, an ob-stetrician, gynecologist, and oncologist interested in the social as well as sci-entific side of medical research.

Regional Tumor Treatment Center, San Francisco, California, 1971— $35,000 for construction. Few cancer patients can obtain all the services they require (surgery, chemotherapy, and radiation) at one location. Even at big centers in such a complex field, there is a need for full-time physicians to coordinate patient care with integrated therapy.

Cold Spring Harbor Laboratory of Quantitative Biology, Long Island City, New York, 1971, 1977—$35,000. Thirty thousand dollars was given to win-terize the laboratory's facilities to allow cold weather meetings and $5,000 to subsidize its three-volume report on the 1976 conference on the origins of human cancer.

A central focus of the 1976 conference was on cancer as an environmental disease. Recent research has shown the following developments: (1) an in-creasing awareness of the cultural, geographic, and environmental differ-ences of various forms of cancer; (2) breakthroughs in certain chemical and x-ray treatment programs but acceptance of the fact that most common can-cers still show little change in survival rates; (3) a new sensitivity to the increasing number of chemicals in the environment that are mutagenic and potentially carcinogenic; and (4) marked advances in our understanding of mammalian cell function and its transformation of viruses. Cancer is increas-ingly being considered an environmental disease—you pay twenty years later for the mistakes of your own lifestyle or of your society's—but prevention receives less attention than it deserves.

The Cold Spring Harbor facility was highly respected by Howard Hiatt, Dean of Harvard's School of Public Health, for the seriousness of its research in the basic sciences on which all applied cancer study is based and for its willingness to consider new approaches.

Dr. Hiatt emphasized the computer as the major research tool. The basic American statistical unit is the county. If one puts the morbidity rates of these 10,000 counties into the memory bank and then starts hunting for anomalies and common denominators, one can ask why some counties with a special ethnic group, a special industry, or a special diet habit will have an unusual rate of cancer of the colon and a county one hundred miles away will suffer from cancer of the esophagus. Why do women of Japanese origin born in America have five times the rate of breast cancer as women born in Japan? To put these statistics into the hands of public health officials, the public schools, or the public media and then to go from information to action seem easier in a country with a far less-developed medical system but a far more-developed system of social control like the People's Republic of China. (And yet the Chinese government shows no concern for the mass addiction to smoking that will present a whopping bill in twenty years.) You decide what you want, and you pay the price.

Harvard School of Public Health, Boston, Massachusetts, 1980, $25,000 to hire Dr. John Cairns. The Australian-born director of the Mill Hill Laboratories of the Imperial Cancer Research Fund in London (since 1972), and a world-renowned molecular biologist, had been appointed professor at Harvard. His work in the 1960s on the replication of DNA was considered a milestone in that field, and this had gone on to later research on mutagenic (DNA-damaging) agents in the role of certain chemicals in cancer production. Dr. Cairns had shown that the bacterium *escherichia coli* was capable of adapting to the presence of a particular class of chemical mutagens. He demonstrated that this response was a consequence of induced appearance of an extremely efficient system that repaired DNA damage caused by these mutagens. A similar phenomenon had been found in some strains of laboratory animals and might be the mechanism by which those animals become protected against the cancer-inducing properties of such chemicals.

Dean Hiatt saw the struggle against cancer as based upon three major approaches: medical, environmental, and basic scientific. Medical involves both treatment and diagnosis, with more ambiguities in both than the layman may recognize. Conventional approaches to breast cancer were, in his eyes, an example of such confusion. Until recently American surgeons preferred to employ radical mastectomy as the most reliable treatment, despite its physical and psychological maiming, and despite the fact that British doctors performed far fewer radical operations and yet had a death rate no higher than ours. American doctors have sometimes used surgery as a result of very subtle traces that do show up on laboratory tests but do not appear clinically and that never really turn into cancer—an example of American readiness to overtreat. Accordingly, a basic theme of cancer research (and all research) must always be to examine procedures that should not be done.

This Merrill Trust grant allowed the School of Public Health to put Dr. Cairns on the payroll for a couple of years; after that he was picked as a MacArthur Foundation Scholar.

Memorial Sloan-Kettering Cancer Center, New York, New York, 1959–1984 (one of the residuary grantees). The Trust gave $410,000 in eight grants—our major support to any research center. The history of cancer treatment is a recent one. Some procedures in radiology and surgery had been effective, but until 1945, in the words of Dr. Richard Rifkind, the approach was primarily an analytical one: "Give it a name, give it a classification—and watch the patient die." Memorial Sloan-Kettering was the first major hospital to specialize in the development and use of chemotherapy. Its researchers were willing to accept the fact that in some cases, as with aspirin and penicillin, practical service may come first and scientific comprehension after. Memorial Sloan-Kettering was known for its aggressive approach to treatment and for its stress on both basic and applied research and their interactions in the great American tradition of landing an army in Normandy or a man on the moon. Again to quote Dr. Rifkind: "Science—medicine—humanity, there are no boundaries between them. Solve a problem with every tool you possess, bring the research breakthrough as fast as possible to the bedside—or don't waste our time!"[9]

The Trust's long-range involvement with this great hospital was essentially an involvement with the careers of two remarkable doctors, Marguerite Sykes and George Cotzias. Dr. Sykes was almost thirty when she entered medical school. She became interested in cancer, particularly the new field of chemotherapy that was opening up in the late 1950s and became an alternative to radiation and surgery. The Trust gave $100,000 in 1959–1961 to support the clinical evaluation of new chemotherapeutic compounds against lymphomas and various forms of metastatic cancer. In 1959 Dr. Sykes had tested twenty-one new chemical agents or combinations on adult patients in 232 separate clinical trials. Each testing continued until the tolerated dosages and toxic manifestations were clearly understood and any evidence of therapeutic activity was noted. If appropriate, a large-scale clinical program was undertaken to determine the magnitude of response in various forms of cancer and to compare the new agent's effectiveness with that of other drugs. Next came

9. In their study of British medical policy, Aaron and Schwartz, *The Painful Prescription—Rationing Hospital Care*, p. 49, describe the British as less driven than Americans by the "don't just stand there, do something" attitude toward disease. Medical intervention is limited not only by budget constraints upon the National Health Service but by the basic attitudes of both doctors and patients. The authors appear sympathetic to skeptical oncologists who hold that the United States is squandering large sums of money on ineffective treatment even if, apart from certain rare tumors, there is little hard evidence that the duration of life of a good quality is usefully extended through chemotherapy. American physicians confuse activity with progress.

the efforts to improve accuracy of interpretation and to accelerate appraisal and administration of new drugs.

A third grant of $50,000 was made in 1971 to provide furnishings and equipment for the Sloan-Kettering Chemotherapy Clinical Research Facility to be located in the eighth floor of the new hospital building. Higher five-year survival rates were being seen in 85 percent of cases in localized breast, colon, and uterine cancers. Dr. Hiatt had earlier characterized chemotherapy as an approach to a hopeless case that a doctor would try in order to convince the family and himself that at least he was doing something. No longer true.

In 1973 the Trust gave $150,000 at Dr. Sykes' suggestion toward construction of a Protected Environment Unit as part of the Clinical Cancer Research Center. Responding to the need for patients undergoing bone marrow transplantation after intensive immuno-chemotherapy to be protected from infection, eight laminar flow rooms were built to supply a bacteriologically sterile atmosphere.

In 1975 Dr. George Cotzias transferred to Sloan-Kettering from the Associated Universities-Brookhaven National Laboratory on Long Island to which the Trust had given $25,000 in 1970 and again in 1973 to support his research on Parkinson's disease. The death from Parkinson's of Win Smith, former head of Merrill Lynch and the Trust's first chairman, had prompted a grant of $115,000 to the Neurological Institute of Columbia-Presbyterian in 1959–1960 and another $15,000 in 1960 for similar research at Massachusetts General Hospital, but progress at that time was painfully slow. At Brookhaven, however, Dr. Cotzias had persisted in treating Parkinson's with L-dopa after other scientists had discarded it. This treatment had greatly benefited 75 percent of his patients and helped other diseases of the brain and nervous system, which led him further to the study of drug impacts upon schizophrenia. Cotzias distrusted all drugs as potential poisons and tried to see the medical, emotional, and social needs of his patients rather than rely too far on the short cuts of drug treatment. How do we allow people to live with themselves and with others when illness strikes? How do we develop collaboration with people who have nonmedical and nonscientific skills: "Activating people to use their own resources appears to me far superior to increasing the dollars spent per patient, which our society is more willing to do."

Dr. Cotzias developed cancer shortly after transferring to Sloan-Kettering, allowed himself to be used as a guinea pig with the powerful new drug, interferon, and worked almost up to the day of his death in 1977. He was deeply concerned that he would not be able to finish his work but had the gratification of knowing that he had succeeded in opening up a whole new field of research at the Center in linkages between the central nervous system and cancer. His first inquiry into the effects of L-dopa in alleviating the pain of cancer had led him further to ask whether the extraordinary effect of L-dopa on longevity was associated with protection against spontaneous cancer in animals.

In his honor the Trust gave $50,000 through Sloan-Kettering in 1977 and $25,000 in 1980 through Cornell University Medical College to establish a joint George C. Cotzias Chair in Neuroscience. In 1979 another $50,000 was given in his name for costs of the Clinical Chemotherapy Service. The service was engaged in drug development, a field in such a period of growth and creativity that there had been a tenfold increase in patient entry into treatment programs, with tangible improvement in most mortality rates except for lung cancer. Dr. Sykes stressed the flexibility that private funding allowed to initiate a new program and carry it far enough until it could compete for funding from the National Cancer Institute or American Cancer Society.

HOSPITALS

To assure better health to Americans by building hospitals has been compared to ending crime by building jails or assuring national defense by building nuclear weapons. There are no limits. In regard to hospitals the Merrill Trust again followed no general policy. Our money went for expansion and modernization, research, new equipment, new approaches in administration, treatment methods, and community outreach. As with schools and colleges, if we decided to back an institution we accepted its statement of its own priorities, which I think makes sense. The overspecialized foundation too proud to deal with bricks and mortar, or the collapsing heating plant, or cumulative debt crisis, and that will support only imaginative programs, can end up crippling the institution it claims to help. Its generous gift simply expands the budget, and when the foundation withdraws—"That was seed money. We're leaving you on your own now"—the poor administrator is left with a whole new level of obligations to meet. Foundations can get wrapped up in caring only about their own prestige.

The Merrill Trust spent about $6 million in hospitals and clinics including $2,525,000 that was assigned to the four named beneficiaries.

Midwest

Woodlawn Hospital, Chicago, Illinois, 1972—$25,000 for new construction and expansion. In Chicago (as elsewhere) old private hospitals, small and large, are dying off or relocating, leaving entire communities without medical services. Woodlawn serves a largely black community of almost 600,000. Three hospitals in this area have left; four are planning to leave. Woodlawn plans to stay and respond to the needs put upon it. South Chicago is a poor area in health needs with a high ratio of infant mortality, childhood tuberculosis, and upper respiratory disease. And, what the general public does not realize is that Chicago has half as many doctors per capita now as in the nineteenth and early twentieth centuries, especially on the South Side. The Woodlawn medical staff had an average of sixty-three doctors in 1972, the oldest doctors supplying the bulk of admissions. The hospital had a close relation with Saul Alinsky's Woodlawn Association, an example of a broadly based and stable black association.

Michael Reese Health and Medical Center, Chicago, Illinois, 1972—$50,000. This is Chicago's leading Jewish hospital, founded in 1881 and named after a German immigrant who made the first gift. As the near South Side became a slum, the hospital in 1946 decided, like Woodlawn, not to move, but to try instead to supply leadership in restoring its blighted neighborhood. It is the family doctor for 42,000 patients. It has the largest nonpublic psychiatric clinic in Illinois and has a unique program for deaf and blind children.

Reese is so heavily involved in patient care that it has little financial flexibility and accordingly has little ability to plan ahead or evaluate capital needs. Because the Trust's Jewish category was always less pressured than the medical, we sought out Reese and asked it to present an appeal as an example of a Jewish institution that has made itself a fundamental part of America's urban life.

Jewish Hospital of Louisville, Kentucky, 1972—$36,000 to establish a cadaver kidney transplantation unit as a way to avoid perpetual dialysis. There is a need for more hemodialysis machines to take advantage of improved technology and increase the patient load, as one machine can accommodate only four patients per week. (Is hemodialysis a right? Can a patient's widow sue a hospital for homicide if dialysis was denied? If dialysis service is now subsidized by the U.S. government at an annual cost of $1.4 billion, with an estimate of $2 billion before 1990, can sufferers of other diseases sue because their needs are unrecognized?) The situation becomes further complicated when dialysis becomes a profitable major industry. Such a service at a clinic, run by a corporation like National Medical Care Incorporated, receives 100 percent reimbursement from the government even if the costs are three times as high as if performed at home, where reimbursement would be only 80 percent.[10]

10. Paul Starr, *The Social Transformation of American Medicine* (New York: Basic Books, 1982), pp. 442–43.

New York City

Maimonides Medical Center, Brooklyn, New York, 1965–1973—$75,000.
More and more low-income patients are moving into this part of Brooklyn,
and by 1965 this care for the poor had led to a $600,000 accumulated deficit.
The main building, opened in 1922, needed replacement for costly and inconvenient use of space. One grant was to aid technological improvization in
the labs, such as an electronic bladder stimulator for paraplegics. The last
grant of $35,000 was to support the new emergency center. There is a serious
shortage of medical services in Brooklyn, since 40 percent of Brooklyn physicians had died, retired, or relocated to the suburbs during the 1960s, making
quick medical attention, especially on weekends, hard to find. A greater responsibility is placed on the emergency ward, and there is greater need for
a new one-day surgery center, offering financial relief to both patient and
hospital in the treatment of skin cancers, fractures, benign tumors, and even
some hernias.

*Yeshiva University, Albert Einstein College of Medicine, Bronx, New York,
1960, 1971—$100,000.* In 1960 $40,000 was given for medical services to the
poor. The New York City subsidy covers only a portion of the medical costs
even if building costs are covered by the city.
  In 1971 $50,000 was given to develop an outpatient dialysis center freeing
vitally needed hospital beds and allowing patients with kidney failure to lead
almost normal lives. There is a great need for new facilities in that poor Bronx
area. Einstein is a new medical school unfettered by tradition with already
a strong reputation in urban health delivery.

*Columbia University, College of Physicians and Surgeons/Presbyterian
Hospital, New York, New York, 1959–1980—$582,000* in twelve grants. The
College of Physicians and Surgeons joined with Presbyterian Hospital in 1928
to form the world's first complete medical center with thirteen specialty hospitals, clinics, and teaching institutions. The Trust gave our largest cumulative
medical support to this center.
  Of this, $242,000 went for various research projects. (1) In 1959 $25,000
was given for clinical research with experimental surgical techniques tried
on patients at Bellevue Hospital. With the decrease in wards and the number
of semiprivate patients increased through Blue Cross and other insurance,
research becomes more difficult. (2) In 1959 $115,000 was given for research
in the Neurological Institute on Parkinson's disease. (3) In 1969 $32,000 was
given to orthopedic research labs studying the rate and pattern of bone formation from first to thirty-sixth week following a reproducible injury through
dog experimentation: producing a standard break in its forelimb. (4) In 1972,

1980 $70,000 was given to further Dr. Herbert Spiegel's research in developing various pain control strategies utilizing hypnosis. Doris Magowan, who had suffered from severe headaches throughout her life, was interested in this project as a way of seeking relief without the use of drugs.

Another $200,000 was given for improved services. In 1971 $100,000 went toward upgrading care of emergency trauma patients in the new Martin Luther King Pavilion of Harlem Hospital. This is one of the largest municipal hospitals in a ghetto long deprived of decent medical care, with research needed on methods of treatment with this increasing problem of urban violence. In 1972 $100,000 was given to Presbyterian Hospital to upgrade the badly overcrowded emergency unit. Presbyterian was opened in 1868 to serve the poor of New York. It was a teaching hospital since its beginning and was termed by *Fortune* magazine among the nation's ten best. The outpatient clinic built in 1927 to serve 600 patients now serves 2,250 on a peak day. The emergency unit has become the family doctor for its Washington Heights community, and there must be effective triage between the acutely injured, seriously ill, and minor ailing. In 1979 $50,000 was given to pay for a surgical conference room. Today's surgical patients are ambulatory sooner than ever, a value perhaps of America's high hospital costs: everyone wants to get the patient home as soon as possible; in Sweden, where charges are carried by national insurance, people are more relaxed. Finally, $50,000 in 1980 was given for scholarships for medical students, out of Doris Magowan's concern for a responsibility the Trust should meet as financial aid continued to diminish.

Roosevelt Hospital, New York, New York, 1960–1970—$105,000 in five grants. Fifty thousand dollars went for expansion and modernization in 1960 and 1962, part of a $12.5 million campaign for new beds, operating rooms, a complete new area for obstetrics, new research labs, and enlarged facilities for nurses' training. Roosevelt supplies 2.5 percent of the hospital services available in New York City. Its psychiatric unit for short-term emergency care was one of the first in a general hospital.

In 1970 $35,000 went toward expansion of computerized equipment to monitor critically ill patients. In 1975 $20,000 was used to purchase an ultrasound machine vital to diagnostic procedures. A combination of delays in third-party reimbursement procedures, unionization of the hospital's 2,400 employees, doubling of heat and electricity costs within 18 months, and general inflation all added up to crisis.

Boston and Middle Atlantic States

Massachusetts General Hospital (MGH), Boston, Massachusetts, 1959–1981—$525,000 in eight grants for the "world's greatest hospital." Its size (in 1976 figures: 16,000 operations; 400,000 clinical blood tests; 70,000 bio-culture exams; 25,000 blood transfusions; 90,000 x-ray exams; and 1,000 beds); its history since 1811 (first use of ether in surgery, first social service department of any American hospital, new treatment of mass burns after the Coconut Grove fire of 1941, and first replacement of a severed arm); its awesome record for quality with its interns—the top students from the best U.S. medical schools; its stress on the interdependency of medicine and biology, chemistry, and physics, aided by nearness to the basic science resources of Harvard and M.I.T. (which have enormously increased the cost of medical research); its ongoing research projects in cancer, bone structure, the relation between chemical balance and growth, and the use of radioactive chemicals to pinpoint brain tumors—all combine to earn MGH that title. Research continues in constructive surgery: replacement and reconstruction of blood vessels, kidney transplant, hip resections, and open heart surgery, which require huge operating rooms and large teams of doctors, nurses, and technicians with extraordinary means to prevent contamination.

The complexity of trying to describe what is MGH, what it has done, and what it is trying to accomplish underlines the complexity of running such a hospital. These complexities include (1) how to keep these administrative details in some sort of order; (2) how to maintain the high quality of research and patient care, keeping all these prima donnas in a disciplined interrelationship and yet not having administrative control turned into bureaucratic dullness; (3) staying alert to social needs and political realities; and (4) maintaining a constant level of fund-raising to meet deficits, finance research, and construction. One compares the job with running the Pentagon, and yet the job is harder because the ultimate goal is the professional but also humane treatment of the suffering individual, whether an aged Italian immigrant with congestive heart failure, a burned child, or a teenager suffering from an overdose. Over the course of twenty years I came close enough to the hospital to see the ability and commitment of the people there, and despite the flypaper of administration, there is a high level of imagination and concern.

In 1965 $30,000 went toward construction of the new surgical building, at a time when the new developments in surgery were rendering obsolete all previous arrangements. And yet new developments included ideas as well as techniques, such as the concept of hospital groups that cut across specialist lines so that eye surgeons consult psychiatrists on postoperative results that determine the drugs to use.

Research: In 1959–1960, $65,000 went toward Parkinson's disease, which went along with the $115,000 at the same time to Columbia Physicians and Surgeons. "The gains are pitifully small—no signs of a breakthrough" was the MGH report, which had to wait till the discovery of L-dopa by Dr. George Cotzias at Sloan Kettering. In 1975 $25,000 went for research on fluid and protein exchange across the myocardium of unaesthetized sheep, a project by a brilliant young surgeon, John Erdmann, as a base for further study of heart transplants.

Public Health and Hospital Administration: $385,000, 1972–1981. This commitment came through the initiative of Mary Merrill, who had been a volunteer for thirteen years in the emergency ward and had learned a good deal about the relationship between institution and individual. In 1972 $50,000 went to defray costs of a black resident and of a female resident-not-in-pediatrics as a way to obtain visibility for those two easily overlooked minorities.

A large sum, $335,000 went towards strengthening the system of satellite clinics mainly centered in Charlestown and Chelsea as a way of meeting American anomalies of cost, manpower, and access. In 1970 eastern Massachusetts possessed more neurosurgeons than all of Great Britain, while only 2 percent of current medical school graduates were then entering family medicine. In Boston and Brookline, 90 percent of doctors and pediatricians serve the upper-40-percent income bracket while 10 percent take care of 60 percent. A well-baby clinic in England is run by nurses; in the United States it is run by doctors. The issue in American medicine is not how to increase the total numbers of MDs, but how to make more effective use of what there are.

Accordingly, the hospital director, John Knowles, and the director of the Bunker Hill Health Center, John Connelly, reorganized two neighborhood health centers into formal subsidiaries of MGH where decentralized care could be faster and more in touch with local needs, cheaper than at the hospital, and a source of pride and identity for those worn-down communities. One was in Charlestown (an isolated, poor, Irish community originally made up of longshoremen, proud of its patriotism, accustomed to alcoholism, unprepared for the heroin addiction its veterans brought back from Vietnam, and brutal in its treatment of black and oriental outsiders); the other was in Chelsea (Irish, Polish, Jewish, Italian, and increasingly Hispanic). The program had been originally backed by HEW, the city, and MGH, but the Merrill grants helped to establish a health team approach in which social and psychiatric workers, nutritionists, health educators, and speech therapists in preventive medicine would collaborate. In 1972 $20,000 went to fund two fragile clinics at Uphams Park and Fields Corner in Dorchester. In 1971 $10,000 went for a program in adolescent medicine—a van at Harvard Square with a staff in hippie garb trying to attract suspicious teenagers for VD, hepatitis, respiratory, and periodontal treatment.

The $10,000 in 1977 and $55,000 in 1981 went to initiate programs with families of abused or severely neglected children in Chelsea, and new varieties of care for old people.

Beth Israel Hospital, Boston, Massachusetts, 1964–1981—$206,000 in five grants. Beth Israel was opened in 1916 as a way to serve Boston's Jewish patients and, more importantly, to supply hospital facilities to Boston's Jewish physicians at a time when anti-Semitic quotas were a fact of life in American medical and academic society. It is one of the country's 200 major teaching hospitals, with a strong tradition in medical research, of adaptability to changing social needs, and also of sensitivity to human needs. The Trust grants went for new approaches in postgraduate education; a partnership with a small hospital in an industrial suburb to expand a program of community medicine; setting up a model of psychiatric triage at a time when deinstitutionalization was changing all the rules of mental health treatment; strengthening the ambulatory care center in order to cut down overnight admissions; and research in reuse of the patient's own blood in lengthy operations.

As a former educator, I had been asked by the director, Dr. Mitchell Rabkin, to evaluate its teaching programs, and as a result made twenty-three visits in the early months of 1982. This amateur had three suggestions. One: to what extent can one trust the clinical and medical judgment of a resident on duty thirty-four hours straight? "That's what we had to endure! He should get used to it, too," the older physicians retort. Nevertheless. Two: every departing resident should have one of his recommendations written by a nurse. That might lead him to show respect for the female staff closest to patients and whom the overworked, insecure residents treat like servants. Three: I was observing a heart bypass operation, watching the surgeon knit away at the blood vessels surrounding that strange pink fluttering organ, but when I moved around to the anesthetist's post I noticed by the skull-like face of the patient that she must have been close to eighty. Should such an operation be inflicted upon someone that old?

Another time, when a nineteen-year-old exotic dancer with interesting joint and dermatological problems had been wheeled in front of a conference and the detail in her write-up was pointed out that she was consuming a fifth of liquor a day, I blew up, after she left, that no one had asked, "Honey, why are you trying to kill yourself?"

Nevertheless, though my visits hardly benefited anyone beyond myself, it was interesting to learn about the workings of a major hospital and bit by bit to understand what is meant by good medicine. I joined Dr. L's team of residents and observed a pattern of diagnostic inquiry that was intellectually demanding without being personally threatening. The team worked together figuring out the details of evidence, and no one received a debit point for saying, "I don't know." I watched a beautiful example of pedagogy where an apprentice surgeon was being guided through a gall bladder excision by a professor who let his younger colleague do whatever he could perform readily, taking over the difficult parts, explaining why as well as how. I traveled with a team under a female senior resident who was deft, clear, and kept her peers on the topic, always kind: "You run from room to room, but when you greet the patient, you act as if you had all the time in the world." Another resident said he often worked a hundred hours a week—destructive, but it's the only way to learn. He liked the combative excitement of surgery. I was with him when the parents of an accident victim with a lacerated liver came up and said, "Doctor, you saved our girl!"—his reward.

I spent much time with the nursing staff (predominately Catholic, whereas the doctors are predominately Jewish), of which Beth Israel is very proud under a system of primary care whereby one nurse is directly responsible for all services to a specific patient: all records, all procedures, baths and bed pans included, relations with family, and relations with and even against the hospital machinery. Even on days off, the primary care nurse keeps in touch with how the patient is progressing. This means a fearsome responsibility— "I become the mother, the daughter, the sister they never had"—and over and over the head nurses and supervisors I spoke with brought up the subject of burnout and the need to retain kindness as well as competence, stamina, and thoroughness.

Despite my cynicism about technology, I was impressed by the effectiveness of the retrieval system. A doctor types the patient's name into a terminal and receives a display of all the current lab test results. The patient is suffering from an odd disease, and a specialist has recommended a procedure the resident doesn't know; he types out the key word, and the computer gives the latest journal and textbook bibliography.

Nevertheless, there seemed less emphasis upon beautiful technology for its own sake, for example, in cases of hypertension a sense of trying relaxation therapy before the overuse of drugs or an effort to avoid the infinitely costly hip and knee replacement operations by encouraging better habits of daily self-care. The patient takes as much responsibility as possible for his own health, is shown as much as he can comprehend of what is going on inside and around him, and is led to believe that his dignity and autonomy are respected.

Albert Einstein Medical Center, Philadelphia, Pennsylvania, 1973— $35,000 for the transition of present ambulatory outpatient clinics to a system of hospital-based, private-group-practice appointments. The twenty-nine outpatient clinics in the hospital have no relationship with each other, and therefore care is fragmented, with no control of often incompatible medicines. The clinics are free, but the lack of coordination and lack of knowledge of the patient mean inferior care. Under a new plan a group of primary physicians will see all ambulatory patients regardless of their ability to pay, with appointments made as with private patients, and through computerization there is an effective retrieval of patient records. Money was needed to improve office facilities and develop training programs for primary physicians in an effort to bring dignity and quality to charity care.

George Washington University Hospital, Washington, D.C., 1981— $10,000 to the Trauma Department in respect for its treatment of President Reagan after he had been shot.

Western Hospitals

University of Utah, Medical Center, Salt Lake City, Utah, 1976—$30,000 for the expansion fund. This Center, completed in 1965, was the major supplier of health manpower and referral services for nearly 20 percent of the geographical area of the United States. Among its specialized services were a newborn intensive care unit, a poison control center, an organ bank for donors and recipients with 200 kidney transplants in ten years, a home dialysis training center, a burn and trauma center, and within its pediatrics division a special in-depth instruction service to diabetic children.

Pacific Medical Center, San Francisco, California, 1969–1980—$155,000 in seven grants. Founded in 1858 as the Presbyterian Hospital Medical Center, it conducts intensive specialty and refresher courses for American and foreign physicians. Its Institute of Medical Sciences has involved itself in the problems of infant brain damage and human organ transplant, the effects of outer space radiation on brain capillaries, a new cardiopulmonary intensive care unit whose programmed computer can predict complications hours before clinical signs begin to show, the substitution of silicone joints in hands of arthritic patients, and a screening method to test newborn infants for deafness when an operation readily restores hearing.

The Center's facilities become obsolete as hospital services become increasingly technical. The Trust's first grant of $50,000 in 1969 went for new construction, with clusters of patient rooms around a central station that can be readily converted from one use to another. Two grants went to fund research on amyotrophic lateral sclerosis, a rapidly progressive fatal disease caused by damage to motor nerve cells in the spinal cord. Three grants went to the alcoholism clinic, an effort to meet this problem through outpatient services far less costly than hospitalization. In 1980 $25,000 went for renovation of the health science library, a clearinghouse where the public can go for medical information and a way of encouraging individuals to take more responsibility for their own health.

University of California, San Francisco, California, 1979—$50,000 for the modernization of Moffitt Hospital. The development of gross deficiencies leading to functional obsolescence, severe lack of patient amenities, and conflicts with current standards for bacterial environmental control (as well as with current seismic control standards) mean a need for major renovation of a building completed in 1955. If a building that new is already that obsolete, how adequate was the original design and how costly are these continual changes in standards?

Community Hospital of the Monterey Peninsula, Carmel, California, 1976—$20,000. This appeal was toward the purchase of a computerized axial tomographic (CAT) scanner, described as a fundamental new diagnostic tool to produce cross-sectional pictures of areas of the brain and body shadowy or invisible when viewed with conventional x-ray techniques: for brain tumors, blood clots, strokes, and some birth defects. By passing a beam of x-rays through the body and using a computer to detect minute alterations in the rates at which various body structures alternate the rays, it is possible to distinguish between normal and changed structures.

In 1976 the Trust received three such appeals for Monterey Community, Children's in San Francisco, and Good Samaritan in Palm Beach, and Bob Magowan and I sought the advice of Howard Hiatt at Harvard's School of Public Health. Harvey Fineberg, a professor at the School's Center for the Analysis of Health Practices who had been examining the issue of computerized tomography (analyzing in slices), replied that such analysis was safe and painless (unlike other diagnostic procedures like injecting radio-opaque substances into a blood vessel to allow a brain x-ray) and did reveal interesting information but that such resulting information (about, for example, a brain tumor) had almost no clinical impact on survival rates. Dr. Fineberg argued that the $500/600,000 purchase price and approximately $500,000 annual upkeep plus rapid obsolescence, along with the relatively few occasions when the scanners were employed as useful diagnostic tools in most major hospitals, made the investment questionable. This was one of the few times when the Trust attempted to influence institutional policy, with ambiguous results.

Local Hospitals and Health Centers

A friend of mine who worked in the medical section of the Ford Foundation said that once in 1955 their leadership became nervous at all the money they had and therefore authorized a grant of $20,000 apiece to almost every accredited hospital in the United States (including at least one in every congressional district), a means to hold off populist criticism that was beginning to seem threatening. And, according to Paul Ylvisacker, an executive of the Ford Foundation at that time, they also included a brothel in Cleveland called Lying In. Such scattering is condemned by every rational philanthropist, yet for my friend, whose job it was to read all the thank-you letters, the intensity of gratitude for this random generosity disturbed his theories: "Your check arrived just in time for us to make a major repair on our furnace, which was about to collapse." "We gave raises to all our nonmedical staff, who had been underpaid for so long they were ready to quit. You should see the change in morale this has meant." "This allowed us to buy a modern x-ray machine and saved our accreditation."

No matter how disciplined a foundation may be, it must have some proportion of its grants distributed at random. The institutions at the bottom must receive some help, not because they are outstanding but because they are so needy. It is certainly true that the best thing to do for many hospitals, schools, orphan asylums, and welfare agencies would be to burn them to the ground, preferably with the chief administrator locked in his office. Nevertheless, a lot of useful standard service is delivered by acceptable standard staff to needy standard people, and if the institution is run by reasonable human beings they have, probably, sensible ways to employ $10,000 or $50,000. Foundation heads should not get so uptight about excellence. If the wife of a Merrill Lynch vice-president wants a check for a Catholic hospital where she is head of the Ladies' Guild, $20,000 is just as well spent there as in the search for the Holy Grail of Cancer Cure at some super center with an annual budget of a hundred million dollars.

Southampton Hospital, Southampton, New York, 1959–1981—$485,000 in ten grants. Charles E. Merrill bought a house in Southampton in 1926. Robert and Doris Magowan bought their own house in 1948. It was a community that meant a great deal to that side of the family, and the center of that community was the hospital, which served summer people and vacationers as well as a year-round population of town and retired people, farmers and fishermen—a rapidly growing population and one that relied increasingly on hospital care until the patient occupancy was often over 100 percent.

Our grants, spread over twenty-two years, form a summary of standard hospital needs: purchase and installation of an intercom system—$15,000; building expansion—$50,000; cardiac monitoring equipment—$30,000; emergency suite—$50,000; physical therapy suite—$50,000; intensive care and coronary units—$250,000; support to help offset deficits, reimbursement delays, and mortgage payments—$25,000; support of the ophthalmological laboratory in developing electronic instruments for diagnosis and surgery—$65,000; new and replacement equipment—$25,000; and support of the costs of indigent ladies and gentlemen—$25,000. The change in the hospital's status, from an adequate local institution to the major hospital in eastern Long Island, reflected partly the sustained and string-free quality of the Trust's support.

St. Mary's Hospital, West Palm Beach, Florida, 1981—$10,000 to support an $18 million renovation project. St. Mary's states that it stresses the spiritual in health care and, unlike its misnamed neighbor, Good Samaritan, will accept Medicaid patients. Both hospitals received $252,000 apiece between 1957 and 1981 as named beneficiaries of Mr. Merrill's estate.

Appalachian Regional Hospitals, Harlan, Kentucky, 1967—$25,000. These hospitals were built in the mid-1950s by the United Mine Workers through its Welfare and Retirement Fund at a cost of $30 million to provide care for a region with a shortage of hospitals and medical services. By the early 1960s, the smaller mining companies had to stop paying the levy, and the hospitals were going broke. The United Presbyterian Church picked up the responsibility as the hospitals were about to close. (The Merrill Trust gave $25,000 to that project in 1964). The Appalachian Regional Hospitals evolved as an umbrella association to take over from the church and organize a national fundraising campaign. The region cannot support its own needs, and the hospitals not only meet medical needs (respiratory diseases or effects of malnutrition) but also train job skills and supply employment.

Health Center of the Mendocino Coast, Mendocino, California, 1973—$25,000. The northern Pacific Coast is as beautiful and as depressed as Appalachia. With a lack of steady jobs from the dying fishing and lumbering industries, 20 percent of Mendocino County is on welfare. Industrial accidents, respiratory disease, and arthritis from the climate; hepatitis and dysentery from contaminated water; venereal disease (California has the highest rate in the nation); and malnutrition (from high costs, low income, and poor education) all add up to miserable health conditions, and the $27 minimum charge at the Fort Bragg Hospital emergency ward means that a local person won't look for medical help until his case becomes serious. Merrill money went for start-up costs at the Mendocino Center (which had two nurses, a social worker, and a doctor three mornings a week) with the hope that fees and government support would keep it going.

My daughter lived for some years in Mendocino, and when she phoned the pediatrician that her two-year-old had a high fever and complained that her neck hurt when she turned her head, the doctor guessed meningitis, had her rushed to Fort Bragg, and saved her life. One is grateful for such pockets of medical skill.

Mountainview Memorial Hospital, White Sulphur Springs, Montana, 1975—$10,000. Charlie Cole's second wife had lived in this isolated mountain area where Memorial was Meagher County's only medical facility. Logging, sawmills, and ranching meant serious accidents, and snow blocked the roads in winter.

Monadnock Community Hospital, Peterborough, New Hampshire, 1976—
$10,000. In the early 1960s this was a mediocre, underequipped, and un-
derstaffed small town hospital with a dwindling number of doctors on call.
There was sufficient community impetus, however, to hire a well-trained,
energetic director, bring together a reinvigorated board of trustees, pay the
price of serious local support (plus small grants from the federal government
and a few foundations like ours), and within ten years build an institution
that was a credit to the region. Staff, space, and equipment were upgraded;
specialties were set up in physical and respiratory therapy; a small but well-
equipped coronary care unit was started; new labs and x-ray equipment were
purchased; new changes were made in the maternity service to make it more
humane; and a full-time social service department was begun (needed in a
community poorer and far more troubled than seems true on the surface).
Major surgery is practiced that used to be sent to Hanover or Boston, and
the quality of the hospital has attracted a sizable number of general and
specialty physicians to the area.

The moral of the story is that this region of south-central New Hampshire
finds itself served by a good hospital but has also given itself a new self-respect
by sharing the effort to put together that good hospital.

Mound Bayou Community Hospital, Mound Bayou, Mississippi, 1971,
1976—$45,000. Mound Bayou is a small, all-black community northwest of
Jackson, which has always had its own city officials, its own black bank and
businesses, where freedmen could own property in the 1880s and civil rights
workers could seek refuge in the 1960s. It was a place where black men and
women learned administrative skills and habits of independence. Around
1960 Tufts University helped to open the Delta Health Center in cooperation
with Tougaloo College. Despite the physical shabbiness, I had been impressed by the spirit of the place on a visit in 1966, and the Trust's $30,000
in 1971 to the North Bolivar County Health and Civic Improvement Council
supplied matching funds for a federal grant to their outpatient facility. In
1976 $15,000 went to construction costs for a modern forty-four-bed hospital.
The four counties of northern Mississippi served by this hospital have a population of 200,000, 60 percent of whom are black. In Sunflower the median
white income in 1975 was $7,715, and the median black income was $2,525.
The mechanization of cotton culture has meant high rural unemployment.
Such a hospital helps stabilize the community and stop, a bit, all of black
Mississippi from moving to Chicago and St. Louis.

Somerville Women's Health Project, Somerville, Massachusetts, 1975,
1977—$30,000. Of all the medical groups that the Trust supported, Somer-
ville Women's Health Project made the greatest appeal to me, and one of
my bitterest regrets is that we did not give enough support to keep it alive.

It had been started in 1971 by a group of Cambridge women who shared a common interest in women's health care and wanted to translate their ideas into the reality of a working-class city. No community within greater Boston was poorer, by any index, than Somerville, with its 16 percent unemployment, 20 percent alcoholism, and 40 percent high school dropout rates. Bars and auto repair shops seem the only two going businesses. At the bottom of this society, no matter of what ethnic origin (Irish, Portuguese, Greek, Italian, or West Indian), are the women, worse off than ever by the late 1970s because their unemployed menfolk had nothing to do except drink and then return home and beat their wives.

The women doctors and staff at the Project followed a set of strong principles. The first was that care is free because health care in a good society is a right, not a privilege that must be paid for. Preventive medicine (checkups, well-baby exams, Pap smears) must become a routine part of life. Somerville's women, constantly under pressure to provide their families with the necessities of life, seemed to feel that it was a sign of weakness to seek medical care for themselves except in dire emergency, but when they brought their children they could be led to talk about themselves. Despite cramped quarters and limited facilities, medical service was courteous as well as competent. In the efforts to help these badly educated, discouraged women and girls understand how their bodies worked, what their ailments were, and what the doctor or nurse was going to do, the staff sought to help them see the world as a rational (if often unfair) place to which they could respond in a rational way. Girls can learn how to avoid pregnancy and venereal disease. They don't have to accept suffering as fate.

At the time of my first visit there was a sign in the staff room of "no checks this month." Cutbacks by HEW were matched by cutbacks from private sources, and lack of staff meant a three months' wait for anything save emergency needs. The Project was accustomed to working within a very tight budget, but when I returned to plan towards a third grant, it was too late and the doors were closed.

PROBLEM SOLVING

Massachusetts Institute of Technology (MIT), Cambridge, Massachusetts, 1973—$100,000 for the development of a program in health care and management under MIT's Division of Health Sciences and Technology. In its interdisciplinary research on the interface of medicine and engineering, MIT has one of the most comprehensive programs in the world, relating engineering and physical sciences, planning and management technology. One-third of MIT's research bears somehow on the medical and life sciences, 12 percent of its graduates go into medicine, and it was one of the first National Cancer Centers under Nixon's cancer program. J. R. Killian, Chairman of the Corporation Development Committee, had asked for $1 million. We were turned off by the rhetorical pretentiousness. Does the liberal world indulge itself in such megalomania that simple folk are frightened back into angry nostalgia?

And yet the Program in Health Care Planning and Management that the Institute was trying to fund seemed reasonable. In the past decade the supply of health workers has doubled, yet the gap between demand for and availability of quality health care is just as acute. There is a need to develop a realistic set of goals and recruit a core group of pre- and postdoctoral fellows to work this out.

Harvard School of Public Health, Boston, Massachusetts, 1959–1981— $485,000 in eight grants. From its beginning the Merrill Trust had been interested in the School of Public Health. Dr. Frederic Stare had advised the Magowans helpfully on a rare potassium deficiency ailment suffered by their youngest son, and out of respect for this we had made three grants totaling $100,000 for construction and research in the Department of Nutrition. In 1965 $25,000 was given to its Center for Population Studies to provide a training program for physicians, nurses, and social workers to improve contraceptive care for low-income married women. The school had established a joint faculty appointment with Harvard Divinity School to examine ethical and social issues involved with population control, a dimension that militants ignored. Our commitment came, however, after the appointment in 1972 of Howard Hiatt as dean, one of Derek Bok's first decisions after taking over the presidency from Nathan Pusey. The next year we backed with $25,000 Dr. Hiatt's first innovation, a Center for Analysis of Health Practices—why do doctors do what they do and is it worth it?

Dr. Hiatt had been a cancer researcher at the Institute Pasteur in Paris and chief of medicine at Beth Israel Hospital. Over the many years I had known him, I respected his imaginativeness, breadth of interests, clarity about priorities, and his iconoclasm about what he saw as an all-too-often self-serving profession. He wanted to broaden the ways of looking at medical problems, insisting upon basic scientific understanding through biochemistry and biophysics of cell structure as the foundation for any medical research as well as social science tools like the computer for quantitative analysis. In fact, one of his aims was to break the bottleneck of the M.D. in health programs. People had to be reminded, for example, that deaths in England and Wales from streptococcal disease fell from 25,000 per million children per year to 25 before the first antibacterial drug was discovered, from improvement in hygiene and living standards.

Dr. Hiatt also insisted, as few doctors did at that time, that our medical resources were limited. No matter who signed the check, the cost was paid by society. The resources that went for coronary artery bypass operations or a computerized axial tomograph might not be available for unglamorous needs such as immunization against childhood diseases or hospice care for the dying.

He had turned down offers to head the medical schools at Yale, Johns Hopkins and Stanford because he felt that medical schools had such rigid curricula that little change in either procedures or goals would be possible.[11] The School of Public Health was not Harvard's strongest, but it did allow a flexibility to concentrate on major societal needs.

In 1976 the Merrill Trust made a grant of $300,000 to be used, over three years, for the hiring of special staff for education, research, and implementation of new approaches in the field of public health. If philanthropy is to accomplish anything useful, it will do this by trusting an individual or an institution of quality and then putting up a sizable slice of capital.

The School's main thrust had been in occupational and environmental health, particularly involving respiratory disease; epidemiology, focussing on cancer; and tropical ailments, mainly schistosomiasis, a parasitical disease spread in stagnant water, as in the Nile Delta, and that affects perhaps 200 million. Some departments were widely respected, others humdrum. Dr. Hiatt had raised almost $10 million, but all of this money had been for specific programs. What he was looking for now were unrestricted funds that might be used to bring in brilliant specialists to help change major approaches and set up new priorities.

This new staff would look at three general fields. The first was problems of structure and function in American medicine. Our medicine is clumsy (try to call a doctor at midnight), unfair according to who gets served and who doesn't, and unbelievably expensive. The profession kept demanding more resources, and laymen kept complaining that they were poorly served. Perhaps a better approach was to examine the unnecessary operation (most tonsillectomies); procedure (intensive care units for patients, perhaps with pulmonary edema, who could be just as well treated in a conventional setting); facility (duplicate units for transplants and heart surgery in the same city); and staffing (use of doctors when nurses would be just as effective). In summary, to make better use of what one already had instead of demanding more and more.

A second need was to face the health impact of environmental changes. Dr. Hiatt felt that much of the $2.5 billion spent since 1970 on the moonshot-style cancer crash program had been wasted. The knowledge base was

11. "It's easier to move a cemetery than to change the curriculum of a medical school," a dean's remark quoted by Paul Starr, *The Social Transformation of American Medicine*, p. 355.

inadequate. Money was committed to costly experimental drug treatment programs for solid tumors that were of limited promise, and little was committed to research in basic science and on prevention. Despite huge expenditures, the cure rates of some of the most common cancers—lung, stomach, breast, and colon—were little better than they had been thirty years ago. Probably 90 percent of cancers are dependent upon the environment, on diet (Icelanders dying of stomach cancer because they eat smoked fish), smoking, and pollutants. An aim of medicine, therefore, at a period of high costs and limited resources, should be to draw back from constructing one more multi-million-dollar treatment center and to concentrate on less exciting but more promising (and more controversial) efforts to identify and control the responsible environmental factors. A further aim should be to combine these with new research approaches in genetics: why does sustained smoking cause lung cancer in some individuals and not in others? There are the paths, with the computer as a research tool, where resources should be invested.

A third need was in health problems of developing countries, where the American approach may be irrelevant or even harmful, stripping young doctors from the Philippines or Colombia to work as residents in New Jersey community hospitals or with great self-praise erecting a mammoth structure in Monrovia or Addis Ababa whose operating rooms set up for cardiac surgery gather dust while children die in the streets outside of measles, dysentery, and malnutrition. The need is rather to stress the priorities of preventive medicine and primary care within the framework of these countries' needs and resources and to look at population control not as a search for the perfect contraceptive but in its relation to nutrition, overall health, and the role of old people in the family.

Accordingly, the sort of new approaches that the School of Public Health might consider with the aid of such a grant as ours would first be to emphasize combined approaches to medical programs. Representatives of basic and behavioral sciences, economics, engineering, statistics, business administration, and ethics are needed to help make decisions from every different point of view. We have looked for too many magic gimmicks like DDT against a specific insect that then destroyed its natural predators and created a new generation of insects immune to DDT and left the situation worse than at the beginning. Three hundred thousand dollars is not much money, but it could allow the hiring of two or three brilliant researchers in mid-career as well as the younger assistants they would attract. There could be a chance to experiment and free the school from budget constraints so tight, at a time of failing federal funding of public health services, that it could barely afford a new janitor.

Towards the end of his deanship Hiatt had come to the conclusion that the most lethal epidemic of all was nuclear war, and in 1981 the Trust invested

$10,000 to expand his secretarial resources for more effective propaganda against it.

CONCLUSIONS

He who becomes wealthy on the misery of others cannot be trusted.   [Proverb of the Mono people of Liberia.]

The cheerful confidence during the 1960s and 1970s in the wisdom and good will of the American medical profession that Merrill trustees showed was duplicated by most other charitable foundations, organs of government, and generous individuals. That profession was more or less given a blank check, best illustrated by the rising percentage of the gross national product allotted to health needs: from 4.5 percent in 1950 to 9.4 percent in 1980.

Accordingly, as the climate of opinion toward the medical establishment darkened in the latter part of the 1970s, there came a feeling even among people as iatrophilic (friendly to doctors) as Merrill trustees that perhaps we had been taken. No limit existed to the relentless demand for new resources. Medical costs were high but not entirely because new buildings, new procedures, and new demands for new services kept going up in price. They were high because insurance companies and government agencies, foundations and philanthropists, and ultimately patients and taxpayers were willing to put up whatever was charged. Sometimes the costs were financial: unnecessary testing or services delivered by a doctor that could just as well be provided by a nurse or a paramedic. Sometimes the costs were intensely human: unnecessary operations and hospital stays and the torture of keeping alive hopeless old people and defective children. A conclusion still shocking for Americans is that we are victims of medicine. No other nation in history has been as obsessed by the search for health, and the money we have paid to indulge this obsession has turned us into a nation of hypochondriacs. Cancer is not our primary disease—it is fear of cancer.

One can spend all the money now being invested in the MX missile and still not accomplish much. Therefore, what are the ideas that a responsible foundation might consider?

First, consider new approaches in administration. The upgrading of the outpatient services and clinics or the concept of the day hospital at Palo Alto Children's that allows the patient to go home at night means a great saving in hospital construction costs, in patient costs, and, for children, in the trauma of being away from home. Review the practices of overcredentialization. Where can jobs be performed adequately by lower-skilled, lower-paid staff?

There are a number of radical changes coming down the road in American medicine for which philanthropists as well as doctors are unprepared. One is the rapid spread of the for-profit hospital chain. The Hospital Corporation of America, for example, owned or managed 300 hospitals with 43,000 beds in 1981, and the trend goes on down to emergency centers in shopping malls to which one can drive with a sudden pain in the night, get a fast response, and pay with the Visa card. Is the individual doctor hired by the corporation left with divided loyalties? Should he acquire a marketing personality and prescribe a lot of tests, procedures, and spare parts like a go-getting garage mechanic? If he doesn't, if he thinks patients need less medicine and more exercise, if he treats too many patients who can't pay the fee, then he may not get his contract renewed. (The concluding chapter of Paul Starr's *The Social Transformation of American Medicine* gives an excellent study of this issue.)

The second change, caused by that unstoppable rise in the health care percentage of the GNP, is increasingly strict federal and state rules on costs and procedures. The freedom of both doctor and hospital to charge what they think best—if they expect to obtain third party reimbursement—is being rapidly eroded. The fee that may be charged for a tonsillectomy, the number of hospital days allowed for a gall bladder excision, even the decision to make an operation without peer review, all are being set by rule. And this change will affect the American assumption that each new medical procedure is an add-on. We can afford artificial hearts and liver transplants as we could afford by-pass operations. Progress! New technological changes, an aging population, and the ever-rising demands for health care mean that the costs are being pushed out of reach. We have gone from automatic add-ons to the beginning of a policy, like Britain's, of either-or. Neither the government nor the insurance companies nor the employers paying for Blue Cross-Blue Shield coverage of their work force are as uncritical as they used to be, which can also mean patients sent home sooner than their health situations warranted and hospitals with empty beds, even closed wings—one more new financial crisis. Coming our way is the word no one wants to use, and not simply for the poor: rationing.[12]

Second, specialize in the community health center serving poor people, whether inner-city (Somerville Women's Health Center in Boston) or rural (Mendocino, California; Mound Bayou, Mississippi). Learn enough about them, acquire some expertise so that you, even as an amateur, can judge their contribution, the influence they carry in the life of the community, and the impact they have upon the dignity and confidence of their patients. Ten thousand dollars can go a long way in such an organization. Say you'll be back in a year to see how it was spent.

12. Henry Aaron and William Schwartz, *The Painful Prescription—Rationing Hospital Care* (Washington, D.C.: Brookings Institute, 1984) is a thought-provoking source on this topic.

Third, a dangerous, long-term trend for American medicine is the deteriorating quality of scientific education. Both America and England are following the same short-sighted policy of cutting government support for students and institutions at every level. There has been in our country since the early 1970s a frantic drive towards medical school as guarantee of future income and status, but high quality scholarship in the basic sciences that lays the foundation of all progress is not being encouraged. One of the costs of defense and computer technology is the lure of their lavish salaries for serious students in more important, less well-paid fields.[13]

A foundation can operate creatively in this field in all sorts of different ways, most obviously in offering graduate fellowships, particularly to students of diverse interests—biology and economics, physics and philosophy—rather than to intense specialists. At the undergraduate level: an endowed scholarship program for science and premed majors as the Trust did at Maryville College in Tennessee; scholarship and equipment support at a Goucher, a women's college proud of the rigor of its science courses, or at a Morehouse or Talladega, with reputations for educating black physicians; or money and counseling for the brightest science-oriented Hispanic students in the second year of California community colleges so they will go on to San Jose or Berkeley. At the younger level, send an annual check of $1,000 to the science department of every public high school in your city to be used as it sees best, award summer study fellowships for faculty, give a prize of $500 or $1,000 (and add on second and third prizes to broaden the competition) toward college expenses for the best boy and best girl (make your money accomplish two purposes) in science.

You can spend $10,000 a year on such a program, or $500,000. After a while you will begin to accomplish something.

Fourth, help your favorite college or university, sponsor a conference on life, medicine and death, or nature and humanity. The election landslide of 1984 revealed that Americans prefer simple, upbeat answers to complicated questions. The ability to face up to crucial problems is hampered because no one is willing to discuss them honestly, broadly, or in depth. One particular issue like abortion is worked over by both sides, with one detail, such as when does a fertilized ovum become a citizen with constitutional rights, argued out to mind-destroying lengths. But the whole range of issues must be examined—to what extent should a problem pregnancy or a severely defective child be maintained, the reproductive rights of the retarded, and the values of life. What resources go to the rich old man versus the inner-city child? Go further: what are the changing relations between resources and population, city and village; job creation and job destruction; or ideology and technology?

13. A Commonwealth student, a gifted computer entrepreneur, was offered a starting salary of $25,000 while still in twelfth grade.

What is happening within our lifetime and our children's, using moral, scientific, and economic criteria with arguments invited from adolescents and wise old men, social workers and black militants. One million dollars would fund a university chair on the topic; $5,000 would fund a series of speakers.

Fifth, there are lots of imaginative ways to spend money in the field of medicine, but where the need is greatest, money by itself is least effective. In *Man Adapting*, the Nobel Prize winning author Rene Dubos has a chapter called "The Mirage of Health" where he describes the thinking, as World War II was coming to an end, of the Labour Party planners of the National Health Insurance program. They reasoned that if comprehensive and free health care were offered to every man, woman, and child in Great Britain, there would be a great demand on these services at first for what might be called capital goods—a hernia operation, a set of false teeth—to compensate for the cumulative lacks of the war years and also of the prewar years when medical care was dependent on whether the patient could pay. Once capital needs had been taken care of, the demand for and cost of ordinary health maintenance would slacken off and would indeed slacken progressively as better nutrition, housing, and education continued to raise the general level of British health.

Wrong. The costs of the program started high and continued to go up. Once the average citizen came to accept the fact that he and his children were entitled to free health care, he realized how much of it he wanted. The aches and fevers that had previously been accepted as part of life's unavoidable suffering were now seen as hardships that a doctor could cure and a socialist state pay for. National Health money went not only for false teeth but for wigs. The results were positive, in a way that conservative American critics ignore, in the falling rate of infant mortality, of the rates of childhood diseases, and in the rise of average life expectancy.

There were a couple of defects. One was the immensely larger cost not only to pay for doctors, nurses, and clinics but for the structure that regulated the system. When tighter budgets cut back on all state expenditures, services were cut, not administrative costs. The other was that the British, like Americans, came to take for granted that there was a medical solution to every problem. If you had a hangover you took a pill or, if more sophisticated, a shot of vitamin B12 instead of resolving not to drink so stupidly. With the threat of a heart attack, you saw the doctor instead of changing your weight, diet, and habits of exercise.

Medical care, whether in a socialist or capitalist country, must begin with the assumption that health and disease are part of the total way the individual exists. They are not outside forces that outside intervention must be called upon to set right. The food one eats every day—the balance of it, the additives, and substitutes put in to improve shelf life or color or flavor; the stress upon sweet, salt, and fat; and the overprocessing of junk food—all these processes determine our health. What can be done to cut tooth decay and obesity, diseases of working class Americans? What is the health impact of the thousands of items put up for sale at our supermarkets, including those whose profits funded the Merrill Trust?

And to go beyond the purely physical side of life: Does the job you do seem interesting and useful or is it boring and futile? (Unfair to ask when the question for too many Americans is, "Do I have, will I have a job, any job?") Do you deal with other people at a basic level of equality and mutual respect or is your daily life marked by animosity, resentment, and fear? Do you play an active part in your own world or do you sit passively before television and know that They are running things? What sort of moral convictions do you possess that take you outside of yourself? Do you have some idea of the workings of your own body and of how those change according to age? What thinking have you given to the idea of your own death and to your wife's or husband's?

Sixth, equality. Perhaps it is a mistake, however, to look at medical values too abstractly. If good health care is increasingly seen as the privilege of those who can pay, one more fragment of our marketplace society, foundation money might therefore be invested in very old-fashioned ways—in support of the few remaining hospitals that pledge themselves to serve the sick and injured as best they can—and find out later what the patients can afford.

CHAPTER EIGHT

Growing Old and Dying

What have we come to when people are shoveled away, as if that whole life of hard work, dignity, self-respect, could be discarded at the end like an old beer can. [May Sarton, *Journal of A Solitude*]

O rage! O désespoir! O vieillesse enemie! [Corneille, *Le Cid*]

Growing old and dying are democratic activities. You don't need credentials. Accordingly, any discussion of the topic starts with our own lives, what we have observed with our grandparents, our parents, and eventually with ourselves. It is against personal reality that we measure every fact, every theory.

My father died at seventy. He had the resources to command every form of medical treatment, but the intensive medication for heart collapse caused his kidneys to fail and the medication for his kidneys helped bring on an agonizing form of shingles. I remember a sense of sadness at how alone he seemed despite all the people around him, a sense of anger at all the procedures when what the poor man needed was a priest to help him and us to say goodbye, which wasn't part of our family tradition.

My father-in-law died at eighty-five. He had been taken from his retirement home to an excellent suburban hospital. His life had been such misery to himself the last year that what my wife and I were hoping for was pneumonia, to end things rapidly, and our major efforts were directed toward blocking the activity of this well-run hospital and its well-trained, well-meaning staff to halt that process of dying. The staff knew so many procedures to employ, and none of these procedures by now had any meaning. The final confrontation came over our refusal to allow either antibiotics or tube feeding. I remember the tears of an exhausted young nurse to whom our actions seemed a denial of everything she had been trained to do or to believe. Well, if we did not authorize the tube feeding, there was no point in the patient remaining in the hospital. He went back to the home and died a day or two later.

My mother died at ninety-two. When I had been summoned because she was in a coma and might go fast, the doctor who looked after her asked me if he should just try to make her comfortable, or did my sister and I want him to place her in a hospital where heroic measures might keep her alive two or three months more. In God's name, no! Were we sure about that? We wouldn't change our minds later, he asked in a way that disturbed me. Many middle-aged children suddenly realize that they have ignored their parents for many years and are going to set things right by demanding the costliest treatment that the insurance company will pay for.

In the nineteenth century the most dreaded institution was the workhouse. It was the end of the road for life's losers and was kept deliberately brutal, in a way only Charles Dickens could describe, so that these losers would do everything conceivable to avoid burdening the tax rolls by workhouse charity. Our time's equivalent of the workhouse is the nursing home. There is probably no man or woman over sixty, no matter what his income, who doesn't have a dread at the back of his mind of ending his days in a nursing home. Accordingly, foundation philanthropy in regards to growing old and dying begins with trying to ameliorate the conditions of nursing home existence or to work out alternatives. How can old people be helped to lead lives that include a workable minimum of independence, dignity, security, and comfort? There are ingenious social and technological approaches worth funding.

In a paradoxical way, as medical science becomes more and more complicated so that the intelligent amateur has less and less understanding of what is going on and the costs of a hospital stay or an operation balloon irrationally, there may be need for simplicity. "Is this what you/we/he/she really want? Is it worth the cost?" And at a certain moment, the foundation trustee, disregarding the experts, picks up his checkbook and goes home.

Residences

St. Barnabas Hospital for Chronic Diseases, New York, New York, 1964— $25,000. There has been a change from custodial care of incurables to rehabilitation in this hospital of 412 beds opened in 1866. About a quarter of the patients are indigent. The hospital has a strong neurosurgical program with six operations each day on patients suffering from Parkinson's disease and other motor disorders. There is a great national need for beds for chronic disease, second only to beds for mental disease, and in both cases not a concern that attracts philanthropy. Another detail noticed at St. Barnabas is that technology increases rather than diminishes the need for manpower. In 1959, 156 employees were needed for 100 patients; five years later, 224.

Carmelite Sisters of the Aged and Infirm of South Florida, West Palm Beach, Florida, 1973—$45,000.

Little Sisters of the Poor, Minneapolis, Minnesota, 1976—$10,000. This order, which was founded in France in 1839 and arrived in this country in 1868, is dedicated to providing geriatric care. The average age of patients is eighty-five, and most are on welfare. Buildings are old and no longer agree with the fire code.

Federation of Protestant Welfare Agencies, New York, New York, 1973—$25,000 to help establish resident councils for the elderly, enabling residents of the fifty-seven-member nursing homes to participate in the day-to-day administrative decisions that affect their lives. The aim was to draw these residents into responsible activity and therefore maintain their ability to perform their own functions so that they are not simply shifted about like pieces of furniture.

Edward Everett Hale House, Boston, Massachusetts, 1975—$8,000 for physical renovation. Hale House was a small (fifty beds), well-run residence, stressing identity and dignity, with a cheerful, congenial atmosphere, for older people not requiring bed care. In Boston's Back Bay, it avoided the isolation of all too many retirement homes and offered easy access to churches, transportation, and cultural life. It had a civilizing impact upon a student-saturated area of the city. The chorus from Commonwealth School gave one or two concerts there a year, and because young people are generous as well as selfish, they found the experience a rewarding one.

Presbyterian Home of the District of Columbia, Washington, D.C., 1979—$5,000. Under the Life Care Plan, an entering guest turns over all present and future assets to the Home and then receives all support for the rest of his life plus payment of funeral expenses. There is economic logic to the plan, but its pauperized dependency is chilling.

How to Help Old People Cope

Hudson Guild, New York, New York, 1966, 1972—$65,000. Serving the Chelsea area of the lower West Side. It addresses how to help the elderly live more independently through crafts, games, recreation, and excursions and provides low-cost hot meals to combat undernourishment, isolation, and the fear of senility.

United Jewish Welfare Fund of Toronto, 1972—$25,000. The Fund's Coordinated Services of the Jewish Elderly assumed a dual responsibility—to look after the personal needs of individual old people and to encourage them through their clubs to look after their own needs: a community Passover Seder for isolated older persons; kosher meals on wheels; a sheltered workshop; an outpatient clinic; and clubs for meeting health, housing, and family and legal problems—essentially all the ways of holding onto lives of independence and purpose. It is possible to recruit intelligent volunteer help, but money is needed to hire a professional staff to coordinate and sustain their efforts.

New York Board of Rabbis, New York, New York, 1960—$10,000 to print religious literature for the old, infirm, and mentally ill.

Combined Jewish Philanthropies of Greater Boston, Boston, Massachusetts, 1970, 1978—$50,000. The first grant was to build a centralized responsibility for the elderly, a place where older people could turn for assistance. The second was to help start up a shared residence program, where six aged people would share two adjoining apartments. In this alternative to the lonely apartment and the nursing home, a social worker would come around once a week to help with shopping, handle problems, and mediate disputes.

Federation of Jewish Philanthropies, New York, New York, 1976–1978—$40,000. Despite its other obligations, the Federation in mid-1970s was putting a major emphasis on ameliorating the desperate condition of the elderly. Project Sustain sought to provide relationships, support, protection, and transportation for isolated, fearful residents in high-crime Brooklyn neighborhoods: a lifeline to essential services and the larger society. It also helped relocate elderly folk left behind in decaying, violent neighborhoods.

In 1978 $15,000 was given to prevent such decay and violence by showing a specific community how to stabilize itself: by better maintenance (painting, repair, and trash collection); security; and counseling to encourage shopkeepers and the retired to stay, keep their community alive, and learn how to deal with outsiders.

Jewish Federation of Cincinnati, Cincinnati, Ohio, 1972—$40,000 towards a central service program for the elderly: kosher meals for home delivery or at a central lounge; and the establishment of a central contact and referral system in order to reach out to isolated individuals, allow the aged to stay in their own homes, and delay the need for institutionalization.

As the Merrill Trust became involved with one such Jewish program after another, not because we chose to but because Charles E. Merrill's will said that we had to, we acquired a great respect for the Jewish tradition of care for the elderly, from which other Americans have a lot to learn.

On Lok Development Corporation, San Francisco, California, 1977— $10,000. This group is dedicated to serving the Chinese and other foreign-born frail elderly, often with little English.

Church of the Covenant, Boston, Massachusetts, 1978—$20,000. Larry Hill, pastor of this Back Bay church, was trying to serve two beleaguered groups at the same time—musicians and elderly. He had organized a chamber orchestra, one of Boston's many, but his innovation, which we helped fund, was an evening bus service that brought old people to the concerts, followed by a cheese and wine get-together afterwards, and then took them back to protected drop-off areas. Music and socializing were offered to the elderly, and their presence in the audience was a reward to the young musicians.

Diocese of Long Island, Garden City, New York, 1979—$10,000 to the Aged and Infirm Clergy Fund to allow the security of a livable income and to provide for emergencies. The clergy are often not eligible for Social Security, they possess inadequate pensions, and their sober life styles allow them and their wives to live a long time. From this fund no individual may receive more than $600 per year. Again one needs a Dickens to describe that level of genteel penury.

Visiting Nurse Association of Palm Beach County, Florida, 1978—$10,000. In the Western countries, we are now coming to a time when a death age in the eighties, at least for women, becomes common. Due to the victories of modern medicine, the elderly have become a two-generation community. The VNA in this particular town sees itself playing a frontline role in trying to diminish the costs of hospitalization by offering physical and psychological support at home.

National Association of Independent Schools, Boston, Massachusetts, 1977—$10,000 for Elderhostel. This program seeks to develop a regional network of schools and colleges to be used as low-cost summer hostels that will allow old folk a sense of adventure while they take minicourses on T. S. Eliot, astronomy, the natural history of the Connecticut Valley, or new fields of biological research.

Jamaica Service Program for Older Adults, Jamaica, New York, 1980—

$10,000 for Project Lifeline to allow the elderly to remain in the community as long as possible. Old people have two basic fears. One is to be taken away to a nursing home where they are ordered about like retarded children. The other is of being stricken by a heart attack or stroke or broken hip and having to lie, unable to reach the phone and call for help, on the floor in their own filth. Lifeline is a 24-hour emergency response system where the old person phones in to a central switchboard once or twice a day. If a call is not made, the monitor initiates the call, and if he or she receives no answer, dispatches a messenger, who has a key to each member's apartment, to check on what's up. The annual cost (device and maintenance) runs $300 to $600, funded by the individual or a welfare agency, and pays for itself (these senior citizens are monitored in their movements much like grizzly bears in Yellowstone Park with subcutaneous electronic devices) almost immediately in lower nursing home costs.

Massachusetts General Hospital, Boston, Massachusetts, 1981—$50,000 for three grants to meet the needs of the elderly:
(1) *Restorative Care Facility* reduces and postpones institutionalization of the elderly and disabled in order to avoid the destructiveness of the nursing home;
(2) *Chelsea Health Center* collects data in examination of families prone to child and elder abuse and tries to match this group with control families of similar degree of instability and stress and yet where violence does not occur; and
(3) *Family Care* places the elderly, after a period of acute hospitalization, in foster homes. The caregivers receive payment, usually much less than a nursing home would require, but in many cases they also welcome this human responsibility they have assumed.

Work

Worthwhile people are fast smart rich thin young. Less worthwhile people are slow dumb poor fat old. To grow old in a youth-centered country like our own is to be the racist who sees himself turn into a nigger.

Age Center of New England, Boston, Massachusetts, 1961—$40,000 for research and operations. The Center was started in 1954 to try to understand the real facts about old people. By 1961 about 1,000 people aged fifty to ninety had shared in the Center's research on personal and social problems including employment, housing, recreation, finance and health. Ninety-nine percent of people interviewed did not wish to move to special housing projects. They had an intense need to feel useful, to play a role in their communities, and to use their skills in volunteer work. The Center wished, therefore, to search out and classify work opportunities suitable for old people such as being consultants for small businesses.

Civic Center and Clearing House, Boston, Massachusetts, 1964–1979— $50,000. The Trust made five small grants to the Civic Center, which grew out of the Age Center and, under a particularly able director, Herta Loeser, broadened its range of concern in an everwidening approach to the world of work: middle-aged women whose children have left home and will use volunteer jobs as a way to gain confidence, expertise, and credentials for landing paid jobs; female liberal arts graduates who realize that their expensive degrees lead no place; middle-aged men in early retirement at sixty or between forty and fifty whose corporations have collapsed under them or who feel passed over in promotion and are looking for a career transition.

Elder Craftsmen Shop, New York, New York, 1977—$15,000 to meet the needs of the newly and often unhappily retired, the fastest growing group in our country. The Shop operates a training program for representatives from senior centers, retirement homes, and churches who will go back and teach their skills, and also serves as a retail outlet for crafts.

9-to-5 Organization for Women Office Workers, Boston, Massachusetts, 1981—$15,000. 9-to-5 was a sort of labor union, a consciousness raising organization, the name of a jazzy movie starring Jane Fonda. It began as an effort to improve career opportunities for Boston's 250,000 female clerical workers and then gave increasing attention to the needs of workers over forty. A poor national economy, a rising divorce rate, and rapidly changing sex roles have caused dramatic upheavals in the work lives of older women who often lack practical knowledge and self-confidence. 9-to-5 wished to organize a Career Awareness Program for older women to improve their status and skills.

The new office machines mean a desperate need for unions to protect women workers in their isolated cubicles. The flickering letters on the word processor screen will wreck their eyesight. All material is retrievable by computer—no longer even an excuse to walk over to the filing cabinet. Some machines have a device to monitor how many key strokes the employee taps per hour. She is tied to her machine like a cow to its stanchion.

Working Women Education Fund, Cleveland, Ohio, 1981—$15,000 The Fund is a national organization of women office workers, patterned after 9-to-5, to win better pay, promotion opportunities, respect, and a say over their work lives. Twenty to twenty-five percent of the members are black or Hispanic, and 25 percent are over forty. No matter how other statistics change, the average female worker still earns 59 percent of what the average male worker gets at the same job.[1] The Fund has concrete goals to push for pay upgrading and for changes in hiring practices that will employ older women. Merrill money went for an Older Women Workers' Project to scrutinize unfair employment practices and strengthen enforcement of existing laws, vital at a time when the Equal Rights Amendment was going down to defeat.

Industrial States Policy Center—Ohio State Council for Senior Citizens, Youngstown, Ohio, 1981—$10,000. The Council recruits members from hard-hit cities of northern Ohio in its fight against inflation, high utility rates, and inadequate health care. Its director is a seventy-five-year-old former nurse concerned about the problems of older women: the widow in her mid-fifties too young for Social Security and who can't qualify for her husband's disability payments, whose children can't or won't help, and who can't even find a part-time job. One project was a 24-hour hot-line, OWL (Older Women's Line), as part of a support network sensitive to their needs.

Midwest Academy, Chicago, Illinois, 1981—$10,000. The Academy began in 1973 as an adult education school involved in training labor and community organizers, developing civil leadership and pride, teaching practical skills like public speaking, chairing a meeting, and fund raising. A current program is to train housewives with grown children to become active in school, church, and civil organizations. Women have organized their lives and their families' lives, yet are shy about putting themselves forward in community projects.

When Donald Regan resigned from the Trust to become Secretary of the Treasury, Mary Merrill replaced him for our final agenda. Her concern for the needs of older women meant a change in the sort of institution we supported. Old people should not be too refined in looking for help. What they need is political organizations (Gray Panthers) and labor unions. Foundations might channel more money in those directions than they do.

Medical Care—$243,000

I think you should prolong life, but you should not prolong dying.   [Henry Aaron and William Schwartz, *The Painful Prescription*]

My father died in 1956 at seventy. At that age today, given all our medical advances, he might expect another ten years of life. What suffering he would be put through!

1. This is because women work at 59 percent of men's productivity, claims George Gildner, President Reagan's favorite economist, in his book *Wealth and Poverty*. "The cure for both unemployment and low productivity is for women to quit their jobs and go home, and for their husbands to work very hard to support them."

An elderly American must face the paradox of not knowing whether the medical profession is a friend or her most dangerous enemy. The miracles of modern science have raised American life expectancy at birth from forty-eight in 1900 to seventy-four for white men and seventy-eight for white women in 1984. Bypass surgery has lowered the death rate from coronary disease, some types of cancers have begun to show decline, and dialysis has cut mortality from kidney failure. New drugs for suppressing tissue rejections have improved the odds for successful organ transplants, at least for wealthy patients. Two Stanford University medical professors, Donald Fries and Lawrence Crapo, spoke at the American Association for the Advancement of Science at Washington in 1981 on the fact that there was no real reason for not hoping to raise the average age of death to eighty-five. After that there is a rapid organ deterioration that seems unmodifiable.

In 1980 11 percent of Americans were over sixty-five, more than double the number in 1950, but they ran up 30 percent of the country's health bills. Can we afford this new medicine? Can we afford the increasing costs of supporting an ageing population? The newest solution to this whole question are rigid rules of third party reimbursement for the care of each medical problem. If Medicare sets five days as the maximum for which it will reimburse hospital treatment of an elderly widow with pneumonia, on the sixth day she is sent home, whether she is cured or not. If, a few days later, she must return in even worse shape, that's that.

The Reagan administration's anger at high Social Security costs, its efforts to reduce those benefits plus others such as food stamps and legal and housing aid, show that old folks are as expendable as Negro mothers. Although not officially encouraged, the most rational and patriotic act that the underfinanced oldster can perform is to commit suicide.

During the life of the Merrill Trust, I suggested the idea of funding a research program to develop a vaccine that, when taken by an individual over sixty-five, would render him immune to antibiotic therapy. This would allow pneumonia to come back as the fastest, most merciful form of death to the aged. One could do worse.

> In its commitment to the preservation of life, medical care ironically has come to symbolize a prototypically modern form of torture, combining benevolence, indifference and technical wizardry.   [Paul Starr, *The Social Transformation of American Medicine*]

Washington University Medical School, Seattle, Washington, 1971— $35,000. This grant financed Medic One, a specially equipped ambulance, Seattle's Mobile Intensive Coronary Care Unit, which would race through traffic to the side of someone who had just keeled over and supply equipment and trained staff to keep him or her alive as the vehicle raced back to the hospital. The miracles accomplished by this vehicle appealed to Charlie Cole, who had one heart attack in 1972 and died of a second in 1978.

Here, however, science blurs with religion. Howard Hiatt, dean of Harvard's School of Public Health, who made a career specialty of attacking superfluous procedures, raised the issue that a patient brought back to life by such a miracle is apt to suffer major personality changes and usually dies anyway of a subsequent attack within the year. After a certain age—65? 75?—should not a lethal heart attack be seen as a sign of God's grace? Is a gimmick like that superambulance worth funding?

Communications Foundation, Washington, D.C., 1981—$10,000 to the Fund for Integrative Bio-Medical Research. This program seeks to measure and modify the process of ageing in animals and man and to measure effects of antiageing agents on immune responses. It is part of a comprehensive program launched in 1981 to initiate in human subjects valid studies of drugs that will increase median survival in order to improve the quality of life in later years. This is interesting, perhaps valuable, and raises the question of who, and with the bill paid by whom, receives these services.

St. Barnabas Medical Center Research Foundation, Livingston, New Jersey, 1974–1976—$33,000 to study the incidence of brain degeneration in the elderly. Even with the middle-aged, there is loss of memory, impairment of judgment, inability to learn new material, and apathy. A little too much of this and the patient is written off and dumped into a nursing home. Cerebral degeneration comes from infection, cancer, lack of oxygen from atherosclerosis, Huntington's and Parkinson's diseases, malnutrition, and boredom. Dr. Jonathan Slocum, medical director of a mental hospital on the Hudson and director of this program, felt strongly that senile patients receive inferior treatment in this country because it is assumed that nothing can be done for them. Specific research can lead to specific treatment that can partly prevent and even partly reverse this process.

Dr. Robert Rowe, chief of geriatrics at Beth Israel Hospital (Boston) and professor at Harvard Medical School, sees the primary need not to treat sick old people (geriatrics) but to study the process of ageing (gerontology) and to compare normal old people with normal young people. In reality, only 5 percent of people over sixty-five are in nursing homes. Today a woman of sixty-five has an average life expectancy of eighteen years (that means half will be living over eighty-three), and a man has fourteen years. Rowe feels that gerontologists are readier not to plug the failing oldster into Intensive Care procedure than are the general practitioners because they are closer to that reality and more willing to accept the limitations of life. He sees the need of attracting bright young people into his training program where they would take courses in decision theory, biostatistics, economics, and clinical epidemiology, aiming to become professors of gerontology at the medical schools and not wasting their time looking after poor old folks with congestive heart failure.

We can no longer afford the resources to keep dysfunctional people alive, but we can learn better ways of treating reversible disease. For example, the most destructive ailment among old men is incontinence. Daughter or daughter-in-law gives up in despair and sends Dad away because he wets the bed every night. At Beth Israel Hospital, however, they have learned to cure 50 percent of the cases of geriatric incontinence.

American society follows three contradictory policies: medical research steadily advances the level of average life expectancy; taxpayers love Grandma but begrudge any extra dollar going into Social Security; and the solution of last resort, the nursing home, is the most expensive of all.

Facing the End

A story in a December 1983 *New York Times*, discussing the financial problems of Medicare, told of an eighty-year-old stroke victim who had run up a bill of $40,000 in his two-and-a-half-day hospital stay. The incident was presented by a government official to explain why Medicare costs ran so high. With the desire to give the best care and to prolong life whenever possible, costs like this were not unusual. As in most discussions, no one raised the basic issues.

The primary one is the ghastly set of medical priorities where a poor old man who needs some practical kindness his last day or two before he slips away is made to suffer an assault of useless technological torture.

The second issue is economics. Two days of practical kindness could be purchased for $400—1 percent.

The third issue is morality. Every culture has feared death, but twentieth-century America has turned this fear into disease. That old man is to be kept alive, at any cost, for each extra hour that can be forced out of him. A young woman in California, a quadriplegic since childhood who feels that life has no savor or hope, must be forced fed by court order so that she cannot starve herself to death. Why?

Because we are a consumerist society? We can afford a heart bypass operation as we can afford an Apple computer. Dead men don't drink Chivas Regal! Physicians who fight for Miracles of Modern Medicine do so not simply out of greed, but because the statement "Unto Thy hands I commend my spirit" threatens their rank in society, their whole picture of themselves?

Cancer Care, Incorporated, National Cancer Foundation, New York, New

York, 1975, 1978—$15,000 to aid patients and their families. This institution provides counseling to help prevent family breakdown in the face of tragedy and financial aid to supplement a family's depleted funds and special services to children devastated by a parent's suffering, personality changes, and deterioration, and who express their own misery in jealousy, anger, and delinquency. It also addresses how to avoid shunting the child to a foster home when the family breaks up.

National Society for Cancer Relief, London, England, 1971—$15,000 toward aid in developing terminal care homes.

Texas Medical Center, Houston, Texas, 1972—$25,000 for fellowships at the Institute of Religious and Human Development. The Center is the largest integrated medical center in the world. This institute is concerned with the relationship between ethics and medicine and provides clinical pastoral education for students of five southwestern seminaries. It has an ecumenical faculty in a state famous for rigid sectarian loyalties and tries to face new ethical issues like genetic engineering and behavior control, turning off the machines to let a patient die, and changes in values concerning family, property, and behavior. Its Center for Ecumenical Celebration is the Rothko Chapel, lined with large abstract paintings, meditative areas of pure color, and aiming to provide a genuine worship center.

Beth-el Temple, Belmont, Massachusetts, 1971—$25,000 to finance the understanding of dying, death, and bereavement. The leader of this program was an oncologist, Melvin Krant, who became concerned about the undignified manner with which these problems were faced in American society. The emphasis on technology in health care has replaced reason and compassion. The breakdown of traditional family structures means that people end their lives in institutions where the staffs are frightened of the dying and do not know how to deal with them. A dying person is more alone today than ever before in history. To help a man die well is a positive experience: it cannot simply be seen as a failure of medicine.

Tufts University, School of Medicine, Boston, Massachusetts, 1973—$40,000 for the Program of Human Values. I have been struck by the almost groping effort to search for values in the whole field of medical care. The costly new hospital wing and piece of new equipment, the miracle drug, and the bravura operation no longer seem as important. We may be seeing a change of values: to get adequate medical care to people at a reasonable price, to use simple procedures by nonovertrained personnel, to question standard procedures when these just beef up costs. Perhaps this is a new realism of medical economics: we don't have infinite resources, and what is given the moribund patient of eighty does not reach the patient of ten or thirty. The great heart transplants are vaudeville acts. Death cannot be seen as the supreme enemy when in actuality it may be a sober friend of both individual and society.

This Program of Human Values at Tufts Medical School was an effort, again involving Dr. Krant, to consider issues like abortion, suicide, permanent dialysis, and the legal rights of the retarded and senile. The staff involved was mixed—from academic, administrative (including the football coach), and medical backgrounds. Merrill Trust money gave structure to the program, supplying a core that might receive further funding from elsewhere.

Temple Sinai, Brookline, Massachusetts, 1981—$20,000 for the Hospice of Brookline. The hospice movement is a community effort to integrate medical, nursing, psychological, and ministerial professionals with a cadre of volunteers to bring a program of compassionate caring to the dying. Care at home allows patients and families, who are fugitives from the medical system, to experience a sense of control over events. The hospice is a revolt against medicine and is therefore resented by many doctors. A chronic debilitating disease can exhaust the physical and psychic resources of any person afflicted and of the most loving family members, and there is need for community support to give strength for living, or for dying.

Brookline, one of Boston's inner suburbs, is second only to St. Petersburg, Florida, in its proportions of the aged. It is well served by Boston's teaching hospitals for acute care, less well for integrated home care. This project was not a success. The directors of the community hospital involved with the hospice worried that their patients would fear that cancer from these dying people would be catching. They kept raising more objections till the project fell apart.

Hospice of Marin, San Rafael, California, 1979—$10,000. Directed mainly toward terminal cancer patients and their families, this is the second hospice organized in the United States. It seeks to keep patients comfortable, active, informed, involved, and at home as long as possible. Money was not needed for daily costs since the Hospice has many sources of financial support but for program expansion and establishment of standards for the rapidly proliferating programs starting up across the country.

Hospice of the Monterey Peninsula, Carmel, California, 1980—$10,000 to provide the care for six patients in an environment that allows dignity and companionship if cure is not possible. This means honest, open communication between family and medical professionals, realistic information about treatment, help with pain, and aid to home patients.

Center for Attitudinal Healing, Tiburon, California, 1980—$5,000. This Center organizes a peer counseling program by letter and phone (the annual phone bill comes to $12,000) for children suffering from terminal or critical illness: cancer, leukemia, muscular dystrophy, cystic fibrosis, or catastrophic accidents, where children can support each other and in so doing endure or transcend their own illnesses. The director, Dr. Gerald Jampolski, communicates in Californese—good vibes, nonjudgmentalism—and has a sharp eye for media exposure, but he makes sense. Americans are unable to deal with the realities of fatal illness: get-well cards, the big smile, and phrases like "feeling better today?" while all the time doctor, family, and child silently know the opposite is true. Terminal illness is endured in an isolation of fear, guilt, and anger suffered silently with everyone hypermedicated. The training that doctors receive does not equip them to deal with death, seen as personal failure, and they take out their frustration on the patients and the nurses.

CHAPTER NINE

Culture

I must study Politicks and War that my son may have the liberty to study Mathematicks & Philosophy. My sons ought to study Mathematics & Philosophy, Geography, natural History, Naval Architecture, navigation, Commerce and Agriculture, in order to give their Children a right to study Painting, Poetry, Musick, Architecture, Statuary, Tapestry & Porcelaine.   [John Adams to Abigail, Paris, 1780]

MONEY AND ART

In the beginning was the checkbook.

That isn't exactly true. Mozart made music because he couldn't help making music. He was urged on by his father Leopold, who knew a good investment when he saw one. But eventually he needed men with checkbooks—the Archbishop of Salzburg, the nobility of Vienna, the merchants of Prague, and Emperor Josef II—to make him a fair payment for what he did. His three last greatest symphonies were composed in a vacuum: he worked them out on his piano because no one would pay to hear them. From a kidney ailment that could have been cleared up with antibiotics, from exhaustion and frantic despair that three months at the MacDowell Colony with regular hours and a good diet would have spared him, he died a failure at thirty-six.

Count Esterhazy. Lorenzo di Medici. Isabella d'Este. Peggy Guggenheim. The National Endowment for the Arts. The Ministry of Culture. Louis XIV. The Manchester City Council. The Charles E. Merrill Trust.

"The only thing I want is privacy and a little leisure and comfort in which to work," was the request of the Austrian poet Rainer Maria Rilke. It sounds simple. It is almost impossible.

As in every activity one can act wisely or stupidly, but it has always been

339

possible to give intelligent support to creative artists without going broke, overwhelming them, or falling victim to a swollen ego. One starts off with a large check to the MacDowell Colony in Peterboro, in southern New Hampshire, the dream of artists through the ages. Or one gives $10,000 apiece to the art departments of twenty colleges for them to spend within a year on the work of current artists. Write a check to the Architectural League of New York for a mural to be painted on a building wall. The Ingram Merrill Foundation, funded by my brother, awards fellowships to artists who are beginning to establish themselves. They are no longer promising, charming youngsters, and they aren't established successes: they do need backing while they work on their third book. When the stakes get high, corruption sets in. If the checkbook belongs to the ministry of culture, the artist may be well fed and very anxious. Music critics in Zürich and Cambridge faulted Shostakovich for his unwillingness to experiment with atonality, the new music set in motion by Schoenberg in the 1920s: Shostakovich, whose job, whose freedom, whose life itself were dependent on Stalin's ability to whistle a tune from his symphonies.

The great painters of the Mexican Revolution—Rivera, Orozco, Siquieros—were patronized by a state less repressive than Stalin's or where, for a while, revolution, state, and artists were going in the same direction. A lot of American painters envied the central place in society occupied by their Mexican peers. In *The Captive Mind*, written around 1950 on the role of the intellectual within the communist world, Czeslaw Milosz examines the paradox of artists and revolution: The artist in socialist society must fight for the integrity of each canvas or poem he produces. When he flees to the West, he has the freedom to do whatever he wants, and nobody cares.

During the depression of the 1930s the American government, for the first time in our history, did patronize artists on a large scale through the WPA and paid them for post office murals, guidebooks, and histories, and popular theatre including a Harlem production of *Macbeth* set in Haiti. Some of this was not far from Mexico in spirit, and there was a lot of criticism. The reply of the WPA's director, Harry Hopkins, was simple: "Artists have to eat."

A long-term, securely funded relationship between government and art waited, however, until 1965 when Congress passed the National Foundation on the Arts and Humanities Act. This established a framework for the National Endowment for the Arts, which finally started doing something in 1969 under its first director, Nancy Hanks, appointed by President Nixon. The Endowment, patterned on similar ventures in Britain, Canada, and New York State, became heavily committed to the support of both institutions and individuals, and to meet its matching grants (as well as those made by the Ford Foundation, a government in its own right), smaller foundations like the Charles E. Merrill Trust got involved.

In *Twigs for an Eagle's Nest*, Michael Straight, deputy director of the National Endowment from 1969 to 1978, describes the theory and practice of this giant system of patronage.[1] The Endowment did many valuable things, from the support of radio broadcasts and museum exhibits to art classes in old people's homes, veterans' hospitals, and prisons. The tone that comes across in Straight's report, however, is of defeat and fear. There was fear that Senator Helms would stand on the Senate floor and recite the dirty words in Erica Jong's *Fear of Flying*, subsidized by and dedicated to the Foundation; fear that Senator Proxmire would call a grant trivial; fear that other congressmen would find signs of communism; and fear of being called censors like the Philistines who had hooted at Stravinsky and called Ibsen obscene.

The foundation like ours that has a concern for the transmission and the survival of art plays the role of Good Citizen. One starts with support of those institutions of world class that set the standards of what is an outstanding museum or opera company. The combinations of patronage, competition, and freedom to be found in this country mean that a large proportion of such institutions are now American. One could give all one's money every year to the Metropolitan Museum of Art in New York and strengthen a leadership that enriches a far wider community than New York City or even the United States.

One probably wouldn't. Millionaires and foundation trustees are pressed so hard to assume responsibility for the needs of their home towns that they are forced to support the local or regional institution: the De Young Museum in San Francisco, Ballet West in Salt Lake City, or the Nelson Gallery in Kansas City. Within every millionaire's heart there is a dream that he will help turn Kansas City not into Paris or Athens but perhaps Bruges. Poets will dedicate sonnets to him, and pretty girls will hand him bouquets.

At the next level down are the struggling little groups—Monadnock Music, the Attic Theatre, the Studio Museum in Harlem—which may be obscure but first-rate, or obscure and second-rate, and which provide jobs for the participants, a channel for playwrights and composers, and a chance for an audience to sit within arm's length of the cellist or Ophelia. Perhaps your patronage will allow it to prosper and become firm, or perhaps it will die, but a rich culture of active local institutions is the garden out of which artists come.

What standards, then, do exist? If one is trying to examine the economics of art, what sort of value theory to employ? The man who painted a cavalry charge of 1870 had to put down all those sabers, boots, and flashing nostrils and was held therefore to some labor theory of value. But what makes a Jackson Pollock worth $500,000 to the Melbourne City Museum? "We've got to have a Pollock!" What policy does any museum have toward Picasso, our

1. New York/Berkeley: Devon Press, 1979, pp. 167-68.

century's superartist, who left an estate of a billion dollars and who turned to gold whatever his pencil touched, like Midas?

There aren't many rules to follow. Don't bid against other millionaires for the same few masterpieces auctioned off at Sotheby's or Parke Bernet, which turns art into a game for "beautiful people," and thieves. Monitor your institution, and if the performances are inept and slovenly, heavy, cute, or joyless, take your checkbook and go home.

Lastly, there is the care for the audience: financing the art center of Grand Rapids, the Harlem School of the Arts, or a cultural forum for West Point cadets. The Merrill Trust, like American society in general, put big money into such enterprises. Why?

One can have too much art or have it too passively. Think of being able to carry a machine around in your pocket and press a button and out comes Beethoven's *Eroica*. Even Jules Verne couldn't imagine that. Sometimes I question those fine public broadcasting stations that our Trust supported in San Francisco, New York, and Boston where one has music, all day long, as a background for ironing and doing homework and eating till Mozart becomes Muzak. *Sesame Street*, even the *Narnia* series, helps turn children into life-long consumers. Whether it's *Fidelio* by the Vienna Opera or *All in the Family*—you sit on the couch with a can of beer and punch a button to switch channels. Consuming culture by walking in and out of galleries enjoys the same relationship to art as watching a political convention does to being a citizen or watching X-rated movies does to making love.

Perhaps the rule about creating and responding to art is that it cannot be too easy. Both craftsmanship and intensity are needed. There is no American writer with a more lyric appreciation of music than Willa Cather. Her characters hunger for it with all their souls when they are first exposed to an opera or a recital. Cather grew up in Red Cloud, Nebraska. She knew what she hungered for and what a life without music meant on those farms and in those desolate towns.

In 1952 on a visit to Belgrade, not yet fully rebuilt since the war, I happened upon an exhibit, in a complex of wooden barracks, of reproductions of great paintings presented by UNESCO. The pictures were adequately lighted and hung, nothing special. A few thousand dollars was the probable cost, but the barracks were jammed. The only ingredients were the works themselves and the hungry spectators.

Another example came from a week in Warsaw in 1957, a city even more devastated than Belgrade and just emerging from a Stalinist constraint worse than anything Tito had imposed. The sold-out work all spring was a production of Beckett's *Waiting for Godot*. It is a play that never meant anything to me: pretentious, empty, boring. For its Polish audience it was overwhelming. After the sufferings they had endured, after the deprivation from genuine reality through the simplistic socialist realism forced upon them, Beckett's picture of life, the three lost tramps on a barren stage waiting for someone who will never come, was a totally honest picture of the world they knew, and the audiences sat through the performances in tears.

Likewise in Poland and other Stalinist countries, as Milosz writes in *The Captive Mind,* people crowded into any performance of the classics—Shakespeare, Chekhov, Molière, Schiller—because the saturation of their lives by the shopworn jargon of official socialism made them long for language that was rich and complicated, for characters that wrestled with honesty in intense ways, and where the slightest gesture or change in voice to emphasize an allusion to freedom or ambiguity that the censor was too dull-witted to catch reminded them that other values did still exist. The audience was worthy of the artist.

Is it only in Warsaw or Red Cloud that people understand art? That's sentimental cynicism. But how do we retain the sensitivity of response that is the opposite of consumerism? By smallness of scale? Once at Commonwealth School a chamber group performed a Brahms sextet in the middle of our gym with the student body crowded around the players. The room had good acoustics. The walls rang with the sound, and touching each other, almost touching the musicians, the students—at most times pretty ordinary teenagers—were carried away by the music. Can we retain a sensitive response by broadening performance so that as many actors as possible, not simply the stars, share the captivity of Anne Frank, and by insisting on what is first-rate? Or, is this achieved by the enemies you choose to attack? Elsinore and Warsaw are not the only places where Hamlet would experience betrayal.

There aren't easy answers to the question of how best to support the creative artist and the theatres and museums that carry his or her work. Are equality and culture deadly enemies, as T. S. Eliot insists? Great cultures have all been elite affairs, centered in small upper-class communities alongside the folk culture of the poor.[2] Only a self-consciously aristocratic culture can resist the mediocrity of America's authoritarian democracy, expressed in our day even more forcefully than in Eliot's in—to use Michael Straight's words—the condescension of mass advertising and the fevered banality of mass entertainment.

The elite stick with Bartok and Schoenberg, the masses have Loretta Lynn and the Rolling Stones, and the uninteresting people in the middle have— what?—Luciano Pavarotti singing Verdi? I am still enough of a Marxist, or had too many arguments with blacks, or taught too many children of Harvard professors to buy all the claims of elite culture. The language is culture, the reality is privilege. The highly cultured become a Mandarinate, like the Aca-

2. Dwight MacDonald in *Against the Grain,* quoted by Michael Straight in *Twigs for an Eagle's Nest* (New York/Berkeley: Devon Press, 1979), p. 61.

démie Française in their silly costumes who spend an afternoon on condemnation of a franglais adverb that has tried to sneak into the dictionary, and then quit for aperitifs. Scholarship becomes so refined in its desire to escape practicality that it turns from the abstract into the silly.

The taxpayer is at the bottom of everything, not simply the federal government. The economy he supports also supports Safeway Stores and, a bit more abstractly, Merrill Lynch & Company and the grants the Merrill Foundation made, and the $10,000 annual fees its trustees received. The man with the hoe doesn't understand Plato or Schoenberg, but somewhere along the line there has to be some concern to create a society that respects Schoenberg and his atonal music and also the man with the hoe. Otherwise both of them are despised, whether by the network executives on Madison Avenue or the Stalins who decide what are the limits of socialist realism.

The Merrill Trust spent about $10.5 million for all the variety that culture might represent from museums to orchestras to libraries, television, and the fight against pornography. The majority of these grants were made during the last decade of the Trust's life. The level of patronage by the government and other foundations was dropping. Our new policy of many more small grants ($5,000/$20,000) widened our range. As Magowan and Merrill children grew older we were affected by their interests. With more experience as trustees we became aware of what role in the field of culture a foundation like ours could play. We had endless doubts about the value of whatever we tried to do, but spending money to clean up a river or help artists create something of beauty, that seemed real.

MUSEUMS

A pretty girl naked is worth all the statues in the world.   [Warren G. Harding]

The most lavish new museum building in our country is the I. M. Pei addition to the National Gallery in Washington. Pei left the neoclassic style of the building the Mellons financed and took exciting adventures in the handling of space. There are walkways at different levels, tremendous transverse steel beams, cascades of greenery from the planting, and great windows that fill the central opening with light. There are special exhibits to see—when I was there, a precious collection of Persian miniatures—of high value and elegant presentation. But it isn't until one walks out of the building and tries to evaluate what one has observed that the surprised conclusion comes of how unimportant were any of the actual exhibits. The museum was not designed to serve as a display case for painting and sculpture, as were the old National Gallery at its flank or the Hirschhorn across the Mall. The building

itself is the work of art. The visitor enters to pay respect to, be awed by—
what? The grandeur of Pei's architectural design? The grandeur of Mellon's
generosity? The grandeur of our nation's capitalist system?

The nearest analogy I can think of, from illustrations out of schoolbooks,
is the temple of the Capitoline Jupiter from Augustinian Rome. There is the
same enclosure of great space (vaster—the Romans lacked steel), the awe-
inspiring and expensive use of polished marble, the dwarfing of the individual, the emptiness, and the worship within the temple of the power and
wealth of Rome. There wasn't much mysticism in Roman worship. Personal
religion was a matter of the little shrine in the corner of a home. Official
religion was a worship of the republic and then the empire and its emperor
with the individual god as expression of the nation's will—the system.

In his love of the monumental and contempt for cost, Pei is a Roman architect. And, in his accumulation of wealth and his sense of obligation to the
commonwealth, Mellon was a Roman figure. The museum becomes temple,
and in America as in Rome the visitor gives homage and is encouraged to
give loyalty to the system that brought it forth.

The National Gallery is a temple too, as are the Metropolitan and the
Louvre. The great period of museum building that started in the late nineteenth century, through the generosity of bankers, merchant princes, and
industrialists, came at a time of waning religious faith. The museum replaced
the cathedral as a symbol of the city's desire to worship something beyond
itself. Everyone was welcome. Even members of the working classes might
come to receive a vision of beauty and be uplifted from their daily cares.
Would they gain the faith to keep on struggling and receive a sense of the
system's concern for beauty so they wouldn't join labor unions? But even in
the most ornate museum the ultimate emphasis is upon the art works themselves, as in the Bruegel room in the Vienna Kunstgeschichte and the Velaz-
quez, Goya, and Bosch canvasses in the Prado. The Pei building is troubling
because the works of art have almost disappeared. We are left with the vast
pile of marble, glass, and steel that demands some act of worship from the
visitors within the combination of wealth and space.

What are the functions of the great museum? To assemble in one tasteful
and secure palace the treasures of its culture—the Mona Lisa? To give the
citizen a sense of his indebtedness to the past—Keats' *Ode to a Grecian Urn:*
"Still unravished bride of quietness/Foster-child of silence and slow time?"
Despite his tired feet the watcher is freed from himself. See what man can
create! Don't accept the mean and ordinary!

I never see one of the little herds of children being led through a museum
without a sense of poignancy. They are both excited and bored, and the
teacher is good or less good at trying to get them to concentrate (boys enjoy
naked ladies). As a boy I was fascinated by Homer's *Gulf Stream*, the Negro

on the broken and drifting boat surrounded by sharks, at the Metropolitan Museum. Essentially the aim is to plug them into an appreciation and also a responsibility for art. No matter what education tries to accomplish, the barbarian always remains near by, the man with the hoe who cannot understand and will destroy, the Goth, and the revolutionary: Mrs. X who smashed the Portland Vase at the British Museum to draw attention to women's rights; the unhappy young man who burned down the Golden Temple at Kyoto because its ever-praised beauty seemed inhuman; the Hitler Jugend leader Baldur von Schirach ("When I hear the word culture I reach for my gun"); and the brainless German, British, and American bomber pilots. The forces of destruction are always very close.

Art is exposed to variations of temperature and humidity, bright lights (which most paintings were not made to withstand), carbon dioxide from the visitors themselves, and the increasing pollution of fast-growing cities that strikes buildings and their contents (e.g., the Parthenon and Canterbury Cathedral). If art is given religious value, the most appropriate form of blasphemy is to destroy it, by the individual without a place in society or the anarchist who used to assassinate princes.

The great show has allowed the creation of the worldwide museum—the treasures of King Tutankhamen, of Vienna, Dresden, and the Kremlin. This allows a first exposure to the greatest works despite the distractions of numbers. The pilgrims shuffle through the great Picasso show as they would have to the altar of the Black Madonna at Czestechowa. Publicity is raised to such a level that the impresario's ego becomes the object of display. Art is known by its cost (e.g., Van Gogh's *Paysage au Soleil Levant,* which went for $9.9 million in 1984 at Sotheby's). It competes with the Olympics or races up Mount Everest as a symbol of national pride. Contributions come from all across England to retain a Van Dyck from being carried off by an American or an Arab.

And, with the increase of price and the publicity of price, when purchasing a million-dollar painting puts the museum onto the varsity, comes the linkage between art and crime. If the criminals want something badly, the shabby guards of some Italian museum aren't going to stop them. They learn the skills to break into the most modern building and slash the canvas from its frame, roll it up, and escape. The distraught director issues pleas in the press as to how the fragile loot should be treated as the mother of the stolen baby pleads with its kidnappers to give her child its medicine. The art historian becomes the criminal with the theft of a smoky madonna from some dark little Romanesque church in Catalonia that only the parishioners see. Not only may he make a good thing for himself, he has been a servant of the people, allowing thousands of art lovers in New York to enjoy a work that only a few hundred yokels used to. The museum director encourages sensitive intellectuals like Andre Malraux to steal heads of Buddha in Cambodia or steles from the jungles of Guatemala. Crime now but praised in Schliemann's and Lord Elgin's day.

When Perry Rathbone was director of the Museum of Fine Arts in Boston there came a newspaper story that the museum had knowingly bought gold objects stolen from Turkey. The objects were displayed with vague cards about place (Near East) and date, but the protests of the Turkish government were loud and specific, and the museum was embarrassed. Shortly after the scandal, a vandal scratched one of the museum's classic paintings. It was the first such act of vandalism that it had suffered, a trustee bitterly stated when he and I met at one of the institution's festivals, and the museum's involvement with theft and the cynical vandalism were not coincidental.

And finally there is the overstress on display as art form and the exaggeration of professionalism until the director becomes more important than the artist. Paradoxically, the first such bravura display was made for negative reasons, in the exhibit of degenerate art (Nolde, Kirchner, Beckman, and others) culled from the Reich's museums and presented in Munich in 1937 with care so that the color schemes of juxtaposed paintings clashed with each other and the lighting was angled to shine in the viewer's eyes.

In museum support one starts with money for acquisitions. One seeks to produce a well-balanced collection ("We need one eighteenth century English landscape") or to concentrate. An acquisitions campaign can be creative, attracting forgotten canvasses out of attics and basements and bringing attention to an ignored period as the Karolik collection at Boston's Museum of Fine Arts did to American paintings from 1820 to 1860.

It is competitive bidding by museums that has sent prices to astronomical levels. Some areas, such as large abstract canvasses of the New York school of the 1950s and 1960s, are overvalued, and if collectors would refuse to buy, instead of panicking that a rival might pick up a Pollock, prices would come down. On the other hand, some people are excited by price and buy a Pollock or a year's tuition at Sarah Lawrence just because it costs a lot. There are always new millionaires. My father was wrong when he thought the class was dying out, and a Bronfmann or Hunt will be challenged by a million-dollar tag and the chance to beat out a rival.

The Getty Museum outside Los Angeles threatens the world market today. After the death of J. Paul Getty in 1976 the museum was established with an endowment of $1.6 billion, and to avoid losing its tax-exempt status, it was obliged by federal law to spend $65 million a year. When its endowment rises again from sale of its shares in Getty Oil worth about $1.1 billion, it will then have to spend $90 million a year: more money than all the museums in Europe and the United States put together![3] What wonderful things an endowment like that might accomplish around the world! There could be arts centers in

3. As reported in the *Manchester Guardian Weekly,* 25 March 1984.

drab cities, classes and exhibitions, fellowships for study in New York and Paris, murals commissioned for great blank walls, or resources offered to artists in Turkey and Italy instead of stripping these countries for the bottomless appetite of American museums. Not a chance! Getty distrusted anything to do with education. Young people are carried away by socialist ideas hostile to the values of the philanthropists who help them. Accordingly, all prices, all collections, every piece of art in any gallery, in any church, any stately home, anywhere, is at risk to this endowment in Malibu.

Money is needed for modernization: a new roof, new lighting, or climate control. The new American galleries of the De Young Museum that the Merrill Trust helped furnish attracted the tremendous gift in 1978 of more than a hundred paintings from the collection of Mr. and Mrs. John D. Rockefeller, III.

The Billy Rose Foundation made a large grant that allowed the Metropolitan Museum to stay open free to the public on Tuesday evenings. There was a generous act directed to make urban life more enjoyable.

Money is needed to support the museum as educator. We are running a race between the destructive and creative forces of society, fought out at every level, and one area is the minds and hearts of young people. Does art become a part of their lives? The Fogg Museum is located 300 yards away from Cambridge's largest public high school, yet there is little effort to make that path a two-way street.

M. H. De Young Memorial Museum, San Francisco, California, 1961–1980—$787,500. From 1958 to 1981 the Merrill Trust awarded about $4 million to more than eighty-five different museums. The largest figure came in these eleven grants to the De Young, with which Doris Magowan was closely involved, and was our major commitment as good citizens to the life of San Francisco. It was a concentration of resources upon a single institution that balanced our predilection elsewhere to go in so many different directions.

The De Young was founded in 1894 as a part of the California International Exposition. It had always possessed a rich and varied collection ranging from Dutch and Flemish to Roman, Egyptian, and American art. The wing called the Asian Art Museum, which displayed work from Turkey to Japan, was greatly enriched by the gift of the Avery Brundage collection, valued in 1960 at $20 million. In 1973 another expansion was made with new galleries concentrating upon art from West Africa, New Guinea, and pre-Columbian America. And in 1972 the De Young merged with the Museum of the Legion of Honor, a museum devoted to the history of French art and culture, in order to avoid duplication of collections and services. By the 1980s the two combined museums ranked third in the nation in annual attendance.

The first Merrill gift established a bookstore, which was making an annual profit of $80,000 by 1979. In 1966–1967 $100,000 went towards strengthening the collection of American impressionists by the purchase of canvasses by Maurice Prendergast, John Henry Twachtman, and Childe Hassam. A matching grant of $400,000 was appropriated in 1972, half for administrative needs (offices, conservation labs, storage rooms, art school facilities, a restaurant—meat and potatoes services always hard to fund), and half was to establish a new wing of American art. The most elegant single item was a panoramic wallpaper of Captain James Cook's exploration of the South Seas printed by Joseph Dufour. A further $150,000 went toward the purchase of antique furniture to furnish three English period rooms of Georgian, Adam, and Regency style.

The importance of the new galleries was underscored when Mr. and Mrs. John D. Rockefeller announced in 1978 their donation to the De Young. That collection of American art had been formed slowly and carefully, ranging from the seventeenth century to the midtwentieth, and was considered by connoisseurs to be the finest privately held collection of paintings in this country. Before the bequest, the Rockefellers had been besieged by the leading art museums, but they felt that such a collection of American art should be established on the West Coast and had been impressed by the De Young's efforts to build an American wing of quality.

San Francisco has always been proud of a tradition of civic responsibility by its leading families. The individual who spends only on himself does not win respect. The series of grants to a museum of the De Young's quality was a way for the Magowans and the other trustees to share that honorable tradition.

Smithsonian Institution, Washington, D.C., 1972–1980—$365,000. The Smithsonian Institution, founded in 1846 under the guardianship of the United States Congress, is dedicated to promoting public education, basic research, and natural science in the arts, science, and industry. It has grown into a complex of museums exhibiting over 75 million items to the general public. At the same time it sponsors museums of art and design, centers of astrophysical and ecological research and bird preservation, and an international center and quarterly for scholars. The Merrill Trust became involved with the Smithsonian while S. Dillon Ripley was secretary, and his tremendous range of intellectual interest and administrative skill was one reason for our sustained commitment. Doris Magowan was a trustee during the 1970s.

National Collection of Fine Arts, Washington, D.C., 1972–1980—$194,000. Our major project here was $85,000 for installation, remodeling, and acquisitions of the Doris M. Magowan Gallery of Portrait Miniatures. The Institution has the largest and most comprehensive collection of American miniatures of its kind, and the gallery was built expressly suited to their scale and intimate nature.

In 1972 the Trust gave $25,000 to support the Smithsonian's traveling Exhibition Services, which send exhibits on topics ranging from theatre arts and women's history to archaeology and anthropology to schools and museums throughout the United States and Canada. A further $59,000 was also given to develop sets of 35 mm color slides with accompanying cassettes to be sold in the museum shops, a project then expanded into full audio-visual programs for schools. In 1977 $25,000 funded two fellowships for research in American art, which were useful at a time when graduate fellowships were being cut back all across the country.

Cooper-Hewitt Museum, New York, New York, 1973–1979—$90,000. The Cooper-Hewitt Museum of Decorative Arts and Design, established in 1897, was absorbed into the Smithsonian complex. With its rich treasury of drawings and prints, textiles and wallpaper, jewelry, fashions, architecture, and every form of interior and industrial design, it is comparable to the Victoria and Albert Museum in London and the Musée des Arts Décoratifs in Paris. The Museum's new home in the former Andrew Carnegie property on Fifth Avenue and Ninetieth needed a good deal of work, and our grants went for renovation, indexing, and storage, and the costs of producing a series of catalogs.

Metropolitan Museum of Art, New York, New York, 1972, 1980—$125,000. In 1972 $100,000 went to support the $63.6-million goal for building projects, endowed curatorships, and education programs arising out of the 1970 Centennial. The stress is no longer upon size and scope but on the new range of uses to which the museum can be put once the collection is suitably housed and interpreted to an increasingly broad constituency. Since 1926 no new structures for exhibit galleries had been built, attendance had quadrupled, and the museum was called on for services unheard of at that time. New star exhibits included the Temple of Dendur given by the Egyptian government; the Michael Rockefeller collection from Oceania, Africa, and the Americas; the Western European Arts galleries; and a vastly expanded American wing. Money was also earmarked for education programs for children and university scholars, book purchases, an effective computerized system of museum accession and catalog records, and traveling exhibits to New York public schools.

By 1972 the Metropolitan had become New York's premier tourist attraction with splashy shows, headline-catching acquisitions, and continuous capital expansion. One million dollars went for a Greek vase, and $5,554,000 went for a Velazquez portrait, the costliest painting yet sold at public auction.

Thomas Hoving, curator from 1967 to 1977, represented the extravagant style of the new museum directors with their exciting rises and often sickening falls.

Museum of Fine Arts, Boston, Massachusetts, 1964–1979—$120,000 in four grants, most for conservation and education purposes. Funds were needed for restoring, repairing, cleaning, and conserving the art works, the hidden museum: to remove a Flemish woodcut print from a panel so brittle that it would crumble at a touch and piece by piece remount it on a sheet of handmade paper that matched the color and texture of the fifteenth-century original.

In 1970 $50,000 went for a centennial capital campaign whose main objective was a new Asiatic wing. Only 3 percent of the Chinese acquisitions and 1 percent of the Japanese could be placed on display at one time. The campaign sought to make the museum and its programs more accessible to the public.

In the field of education close to 75,000 students a year were reached through lectures and classes. Television programs were sent out to eighty public broadcasting stations. Four hundred exhibits were circulated to 3,000 different schools, groups, and clubs in New England.

Museum of Modern Art, New York, New York, 1961, 1978—$50,000. The first grant was to enlarge facilities and strengthen the museum program; the second formed part of a $36 million capital campaign. It was the first museum in the country to specialize in modern art, joined later by the Guggenheim and Whitney. It was also the first museum to make major use of film. The last grant went toward the complex expansion program to double the gallery space along with construction of a forty-two-story apartment tower atop a new West wing, allowing substantial annual support and capital, the only way to keep this once outstanding museum from running downhill.

Albright-Knox Art Gallery, Buffalo, New York, 1967, 1980—$35,000. In this classic Greek marble structure there is, next to the museums in New York City, the best collection of abstract art in the United States, with at least one work of every major artist, both American and European.

Denver Art Museum, Denver, Colorado, 1967—$25,000. Walters Art Gallery, Baltimore, Maryland, 1967—$25,000. Los Angeles County Museum of Art, Los Angeles, California, 1968, 1972—$75,000. Museum of Fine Arts, Houston, Texas, 1971—$25,000. Walker Art Center, Minneapolis, Minnesota, 1972—$25,000 toward equipment and technical services for a comprehensive audiovisual program. The Center has been affiliated with the

Guthrie Theatre next door since 1963, carries on strong educational activities in music, dance, poetry, and hopes to become a regional center for study of film.

Worcester Art Museum, Worcester, Massachusetts, 1965, 1972—$70,000 to install a humidity control system. It is a modest-sized museum in a dull city but is nationally respected for its quality and innovativeness: free art classes for children since 1911, free public concerts since 1919, a film program since 1933, and a three-year professional school. Pollution from auto and industrial fumes forced the need for a sophisticated system to filter and wash incoming air.

Brooklyn Museum, Brooklyn, New York, 1972–1978—$105,000. An excellent museum in a shabby, out-of-the-way location with inadequate funds for maintenance and display. It carries on a strong tradition of fostering community activity with exhibitions of every sort: Afro-American artisans, Haitians and Puerto Ricans, and old people and children. One grant went to provide a weekly program on cable television, and another went to improve videotaped interpretation of collections and special exhibits. "In America only a small percentage of the visiting public possesses the visual literacy to fully comprehend and enjoy great works of art," the appeal explained. Despite the condescension of that statement, the Brooklyn Museum, so heavily used, so widely ranging in its collections, and so un-chic, is the sort of institution that deserves foundation support.

Munson-Williams-Proctor Institute, Utica, New York, 1973—$20,000. This is an important local museum with a strong American collection but needs funds to add a Thomas Eakins and a Winslow Homer.

Seattle Art Museum, Seattle, Washington, 1966–1978—$70,000, Art Institute of Chicago, Chicago, Illinois, 1973—$50,000, Philbrook Art Center, Tulsa, Oklahoma, 1975, 1980—$30,000. One grant went to support ethnic studies programs for disadvantaged and minority children, with a special exhibit of textiles and jewelry from the Niger Delta to complement the permanent collection of African masks, bronzes, and musical instruments and games, along with African student speakers from the University of Tulsa. There were also efforts to build up the offerings directed toward Indian children.

Pennsylvania Academy of the Fine Arts, Philadelphia, Pennsylvania, 1976—$20,000 to help purchase works of living American artists. It is of value to compare historic and contemporary art, and this is particularly useful for students at an art school. The Academy was the oldest art school (1791) in the United States, and Thomas Eakins, Mary Cassatt, and John Marin studied there. Deficits and a heavy mortgage weighed upon its budget, and money was needed for everything. Could the new president raise enough cash to save the place?

Philadelphia Museum of Art, Philadelphia, Pennsylvania, 1966—$25,000 to strengthen the library. *Guggenheim Museum, New York, New York, 1979—$15,000* for the fellowship program, offering intensive on-the-job training in research and curatorial skills to specially qualified students of art history, the next generation of museum professionals.

San Francisco Museum of Art, San Francisco, California, 1966–1981— $115,000. Unlike the De Young, this museum emphasized contemporary art from Matisse and Picasso to current American and Bay Area artists. The museum was one of the favorite concerns of the old Jewish families of San Francisco—Haas, Strauss, and Fleischhacker—and their sense of civic responsibility. Merrill Trust money went for acquisitions, mainly through the annual awards to promising, undiscovered regional artists.

Museum of the City of New York, New York, 1971, 1981—$75,000 mainly for educational services. The museum has a wonderful costume exhibit, as well as ones in Currier and Ives, theater, furniture, toys, decorative arts, photographs.

City Art Museum of St. Louis, Missouri, 1965—$25,000. Any family trip to the big town included the City Art Museum along with the zoo and a Cardinals' game at Busch Stadium. The museum was at first overstocked by panoramic western landscapes of Bierstadt and Company given by wealthy German families, but Perry Rathbone, who started his curatorial career here before moving on to Boston, upgraded the quality and style of exhibits after the war and built a well-balanced collection.

The Merrill trustees made lists of such regional museums, symphony orchestras, zoos, hospitals, and universities, and at each meeting checked off one from each category.

Parrish Art Museum, Southampton, New York, 1971–1980—$85,000. The museum dwelt in an elegant Italian Renaissance building and was originally a boneyard of classical casts. Around the 1960s, however, there came a push to set up interesting exhibits, broaden its collections, and extend its services to the community with films, concerts, and children's art classes. Our money went to pay for new storage space, temperature and humidity control, and two exhibits: photographs by Alfred Stieglitz and Fifty Years of Long Island Art.

Palm Beach Art Institute, Palm Beach, Florida, 1973–1981—$75,000 for the Norton Gallery and School of Art, partly to establish a print room and an adult art school.

Society of the Four Arts, Palm Beach, Florida, 1969–1980—$80,000. This institution sought to encourage art, music, drama, and literature through exhibitions, concerts, lectures, films, and a public library. We helped fund a new wing, with proper temperature and humidity control and completely fireproofed, to encourage exhibits, and also supplied extra money to support a major exhibit of paintings from the Royal Academy in London: Reynolds, Gainsborough, Constable, and Turner.

Oakland Museum, Oakland, California, 1970–1981—$70,000. Here was a perfect example, along with the Oakland Symphony, of a cultural institution as center of community pride. It is a strongly ranging museum, focused on California, with scientific and historical as well as artistic exhibits, in a run-down section of a rundown city. A morning at the place leaves a visitor with all sorts of thoughts as to what a museum like this does to supply a common bond to that kaleidoscopic California mix of black, Hispanic, Asian, and Anglo backgrounds and to offer all those noisy straggles of school children some sense that here is a culture worth sharing.

Harvard University, Fogg Museum, Cambridge, Massachusetts, 1981—$10,000 to mount the Jacob Van Ruisdael exhibition at this elitist nursery of curators and art historians.

Katonah Gallery, Katonah, New York, 1972–1981—$125,000. Both Magowans were impressed by the artistic and intellectual contribution that the Katonah Gallery offered its Westchester County and Connecticut community, and it was through them that the Trust made its eight grants. The Gallery had no collection of its own but served as the locus for special exhibits as well as concerts, lectures, movies, and art fairs. Because it did imaginative things, it was able to attract a large volunteer staff. It acquired a reputation for using its resources carefully, and it built a long-term relationship with the important museums of the Northeast as well as with private collectors and galleries in New York City who respected its professionalism. The Trust's first $25,000 in 1972 helped broaden the Gallery's confidence, and its next step was to begin the annual Charles E. Merrill lecture series, which brought in speakers like Buckminster Fuller, Jan Fonteyn (director of Boston's Museum of Fine

Arts), Barbara Tuchman, and anthropologists, curators, and art historians. In turn these speakers widened the Gallery's professional contacts and made it easier to ask for advice or the loan of a special work for an exhibition.

The Katonah Gallery made itself a model for other small museums of how to rely upon imagination to do important things, not just size and cash. For Doris Magowan this was proof of the value of the small, well-run institution and the need for a responsible foundation to seek this out and then give sustained support.

ART PURCHASE PROJECT

One of our most enjoyable programs was administered during 1972–1974 and cost $170,000 for the purchase of contemporary crafts, painting, graphics, and sculpture.

We had given $10,000 to the Atlanta Art Museum for the purchase of one drawing and one print, which raised the question of the economics of esthetics. Why does one work of art that looks very much like another have a value ten times as high—quality, age, or fashion? To what extent does a purchase of expensive art represent the self-esteem of the purchaser, the business acumen of the Madison Avenue middleman, the megalomania of the museum director, and the greed of a Picasso? Purchase of art should have two priorities: the pleasure and re-creation of those who consume it and the encouragement, support, and growth of the artists who produce it.

By 1972 the downturn of the economy was hurting artists, a class that had benefited during the fat 1960s. How would it be possible to put as much money as possible into the hands of practicing artists with a minimum used up in administration? Great prize competitions do more harm than good in their support of winning, the whole Richard Nixon ethic, as well as subservience to high-priced experts and selection committees. Instead, we should find people with some judgment who enjoy the process of choosing art with someone else's money and therefore need not be paid, and spend enough money as widely—and as fast—as possible so that a lot of practicing artists get decent checks (not all that common in 1972) and have their works put on walls and not in museum basements.

Accordingly, we chose ten colleges and universities whose art departments or museums had repute and which represented the geographical and political variety our trustees respected and sent them checks for $10,000 for purchases from working artists, the full amount to be spent within a year, no single item costing more than $1,000.

University of Wisconsin, Madison, Wisconsin. The Elvehjem Art Center is among the two or three largest university art museums in America with a program of service to the academic community, the city, and the state.

Goucher College, Towson, Maryland. Goucher, a women's college of about 1,000 in the outer suburbs of Baltimore, was a financially pressed school whose obvious priorities had to be salaries and scholarships but which enjoyed the distinction of an excellent art department that served visiting students from Johns Hopkins University as well as its own young women. On the college visits I used to make, I had always been impressed by the variety and quality of Goucher's exhibits. The money went to buy prints by artists in the Baltimore and Washington areas.

Grinnell College, Grinnell, Iowa. Grinnell was the first college I thought of, remembering the activity and richness of its art center from a visit in 1963. In a rural state like Iowa, the artistic involvements of Grinnell and the state universities have an importance not true in New York or Massachusetts.

University of Oklahoma, Norman, Oklahoma. The university's museum had a surprisingly large Oriental collection, a fair variety of European art, over two hundred paintings by American Indians, and a good collection of contemporary American art, but had only a small acquisition budget.

Spelman College, Atlanta, Georgia. Spelman had a small but well-equipped, Rockefeller-funded art center with a good faculty, both permanent and visiting, and tangible student interest. It owned a broad collection of African and Jamaican objects plus painting and sculpture by Negro artists that were displayed throughout the campus and loaned to museums and other colleges. Our gift would expand an existing program of acquiring work from young black artists and would reach exactly the sort of people who needed encouragement most.

Pomona College, Claremont, California. When I asked advice from museum directors or art department heads, Pomona's name usually came up. Their gallery was rich in early Italian painters and Expressionist prints, and a gift like ours allowed expansion into California art of astounding variety, much of it ephemeral but some very good.

Colby College, Waterville, Maine. The college's museum is one of the best in New England. The remoteness of Waterville in those long winters gives Colby's art and music resources a special value to the region. Its collection is devoted mainly to American art from the early eighteenth century on, and it sponsored an outstanding exhibit, *Maine and its Artists, 1710–1963*, which went off on tour to Portland, Boston, and New York.

Vassar College, Poughkeepsie, New York. Vassar's art gallery has a sophisticated collection of graphics, paintings, and sculpture supported by an art library of 27,000 volumes. The art department is a high-powered one in its historical, esthetic, and studio courses but constrained by finances in any purchases.

McGill University, Montreal, Canada. McGill does not have a formal art museum, but its collection hung throughout the campus is so extensive that no study of any Canadian artist omits references to work owned by that university.

University of British Columbia, Vancouver, Canada. The Fine Arts Gallery at the University had been active for many years and had mounted many interesting exhibitions but was never in a position to buy works of art. Likewise, the department of fine arts had increasingly felt the lack of an adequate teaching collection. In an area where art prices are modest, our grant allowed a great step forward in the purchase of graphics.

The joy of these underfed museum directors encouraged us to repeat the program. The stock market's plunge in 1974 cut us back to seven colleges at $7,000 each, but harder times made the luxury of these gifts even more appreciated. (In our usual fear of repeating ourselves we did not continue this delightful project.)

Fisk University, Nashville, Tennessee. Fisk's art department is known among black institutions for its Alfred Stieglitz collection of twentieth-century American and European painting given by his widow Georgia O'Keefe (and largely kept in storage from lack of space and security) as well as a prize collection of his photography. The University has a fine collection of African and black American art but needed money to expand its holding of contemporary graphics and sculpture.

Maryville College, Maryville, Tennessee. The college had a small but lively art department so tightly budgeted that the director begged that $2,000 of our gift be set aside for book and slide purchases and for summer fellowships. The Appalachian area enjoys a rich crafts tradition, and much of this money went to purchase quilts, weaving, furniture, and ceramics. As the director wrote: "To be able to pay a student $200 for a quilt allows her suddenly to give a different name to herself. She is not simply a hobbyist, she has become a professional craftsman, and out of that comes a new seriousness towards her work."

University of Nebraska, Omaha, Nebraska. The Sheldon Art Gallery has specialized in twentieth-century American art in all media and has a strong regional reputation. The director purchased ceramics, glass, tapestry, wood, and metal with our money in order to build a collection of crafts.

Carleton College, Northfield, Minnesota. The money went toward purchases in the field of twentieth-century prints as well as the construction of a Japanese sculpture garden.

University of New Mexico, Albuquerque, New Mexico. This money given bought arts and crafts out of the rich Latino and Indian tradition.

Laval University, Quebec, Canada. This university has a large school of visual arts, specializing in graphics, and our grant meant support to French-speaking artists who exert a disproportionate influence on Canada's art scene.

Outside of this program but in similar style was a grant in 1974 of $10,000 to the *Confederation Centre and Gallery in Charlottestown, Prince Edward Island.* PEI is the smallest of the Canadian provinces and, except for July and August when it fills up with vacationers, is almost the most isolated. In an effort to maintain some sort of cultural life, particularly in wintertime, so that restless young people don't simply leave for Toronto and Montreal, the Centre was trying to build a collection of cultural machinery—videotape cameras for use in the creative drama classes enabling students to watch and criticize their performances, tape recorders for dance recitals, and cameras and basic lighting equipment so that young people could make their own movies. The abandoned one-room school houses are now being turned into art and community centers in some of the isolated towns and are responsive to workshop programs able to employ such big-city equipment.

FINDING THE PAST

A foundation does not have to be practical. Along with giving money to hospitals and nursery schools, it can follow lonely impulses of delight. In the second half of its life, the Merrill Trust gave $905,000 to thirty-eight projects in archaeology, historical reconstruction, and crafts preservation both in this country and abroad. Doris Magowan loved beautiful old things: buildings, furniture, and gardens, and felt that if these could be preserved and shared, people today might appreciate what they had received from yesterday and develop a sense of responsibility in handing it on to tomorrow. The pleasure they find in looking at an eighteenth-century drawing room or walking along the garden paths at Williamsburg or Giverny frees them from the hasty surroundings of their daily lives, brings them silence or thoughtfulness, and may also offer a certain discipline. You aren't just a tourist in life. If you have education, money, and some leisure, you have obligations.

Charles Cole was a professional historian. The past should have a role in teaching the present. It was also a constant intellectual challenge to find out what really happened and to work out new interpretations that allow a different light on a problem or a sequence of events. The past was not simply writing on a blackboard that people in authority could erase and rewrite as it suited them. Mary Merrill saw reconstructions like Plimoth Plantation as a way to learn how people actually managed their lives. What sort of social institutions did they build? In particular, what lives were led by women, who were ignored in standard history?

Honest history and archaeology are threatened by the ideologues and the sentimentalists. Do white scholars insist that the great ruins at Zimbabwe were built by Phoenicians because they cannot accept the fact that they might have been built by blacks? Were the earliest city-dwellers in Poland Slavic or German? If the archaeologist discovers material that does not agree with his hypothesis, he or she takes care to destroy it. On the other side are the mythmakers, leading their millons of Disneyland pilgrims to a saccharine version of the 1890s, some variant of Freedomland with virtues of independence and neighborliness presented in a way that hides ugly details and leaves troubling questions unraised. Disneyland history becomes political: it is through invocation of a sentimentalized past that we escape complicated questions about our cities, our classes, and our race relationships, the contradictions of the outside world, and remain satisfied with a simplistic Norman Rockwell patriotism. Everyone knew his place and Mom was happy to stay in the kitchen.

Can one go in the other direction and try to learn the facts as accurately as possible from a handful of pottery fragments, an estate inventory, or an analysis of bones in a rubbish bin, using modern tools like the computer to keep track of detail and asking modern questions about women and blacks in a never-ending search for what it was like, not freezing the past into a predetermined mold? The pace was slower than today's, but the past did move; it was laden with contradictions and confrontations as well as smells and flies and the moans of women who died in childbirth.

Colonial Williamsburg, 1978, 1981—$25,000. Williamsburg, launched by John D. Rockefeller in the late 1920s, was the first such restoration complex that gave Americans a sense of pride in their colonial history. The governor's palace, the smell of boxwood, the inns and craft shops, and the countless souvenirs that people took home made an impact upon American design, even in paint colors, wallpaper patterns, pewter, and glass.

At the same time the conflict came between those who wanted to stress the style, dignity, and grandeur of the past and those who searched for accuracy and would make the compromises that accuracy demanded. At Williamsburg the historians seized control and by the late 1970s were in the process of dismantling the elegant draperies and chandeliers in a bitter atmosphere—destruction of beauty by small-minded academics!

We gave $15,000 in 1978 to support the education program. Charles Longsworth had left the presidency of Hampshire College with the directive to strengthen the educational as opposed to the purely tourist qualities of Williamsburg. In a large-scale, carefully accurate way, the institution tried to give the countless visitors a picture of an eighteenth-century town and kept alive American crafts traditions. Eighty thousand children passed through the place per year. It is history on a scale that they can understand, and it aims to present new ways of looking at their own time. How do craftsman, curator, and archaeologist tie together the eighteenth and the twentieth centuries? What can such a reconstruction offer to a black schoolchild other than the fact that his ancestors were slaves, pieces of property like furniture? Colonial Williamsburg also organizes in-depth study packages, lasting from one to eight weeks for an intense study of eighteenth-century civilization. The base questions were fundamentally what is history, what is a community, and how do those questions pose other questions about the world around us?

In 1981 $10,000 went toward a Decorative Arts Museum due to open in 1983 that would display the antique textiles attracting scholars from as far away as the Victoria and Albert in London and the Palace Museum in Beijing. The Trust grant went to preparing fragile exhibits at the sophisticated in-house laboratory.

Plimoth Plantation, Plymouth, Massachusetts, 1973–1981—$40,000. Plimoth Plantation was chartered in 1947 to foster public knowledge of the Pilgrims and their role in colonial America. Most of the houses and public buildings were erected in the 1950s, and a reconstructed Mayflower II was sailed over from England. By 1970, however, the same fight broke out as at Williamsburg between Disneylanders and historians looking for the grubby reality of 1627, and there were hard words and tears as gardens and floors were torn up and pretty furniture banished. Plimoth was a medieval village, more brightly colored, noisy, varied, and litigious than the schoolbooks ever represented. Mary Merrill, herself a skilled handweaver, served as liaison with the Boston Weavers Guild, who made period clothing and coverlets for interpreters and houses.

Our first gift went for costume materials, facsimile copies of the three hundred books mentioned in estate inventories, and school study kits for better teacher preparation. During the winter school groups were invited to spend weekends at the Plantation, with sleeping bags, no running water, and only the fireplace for heat, which gave a different side of seventeenth-century life. The second gift went toward construction of a barn, an imposing tourist attraction while it was being put up. By 1980 a new approach was to have the interpreters assume specific personalities: Charity Clamworth who came from Gloucester (and spoke with its accent and vocabulary) and whose world view reached no further than 1627. Visiting children were fascinated by the rules and tried all sorts of ways to trip the placid seventeenth-century individual into an anachronism. History is constantly reinterpreted. I remember one French exchange student at Commonwealth who compared the Pilgrims who had come on the Mayflower with the boat people who had fled Vietnam in even worse vessels—but there was a place for the Pilgrims to settle then.

Old Sturbridge, Massachusetts, 1966–1978—$30,000. Old Sturbridge opened to the public in 1948, with farmhouses, animal pens, forges, and mills from another period—1790–1840—to depict agricultural, crafts, and early industrial life in New England. Over 80,000 students come to Sturbridge every year. Our 1978 grant supported the teacher training program to bring more imaginative teaching back in the classrooms.

Shaker Community, Hancock, Massachusetts, 1972, 1975—$30,000. The Shakers were doomed to extinction by celibacy, but their traditions of group living and simple craftsmanship and of housing and design had a strong effect on American culture. Our money went for restoration of a school house and privy (which meant involving architectural students in restoration research) and helping the institution become a popular tourist center, which gave employment to young guides.

Historic Harrisville, New Hampshire, 1974—$10,000. Harrisville is a small textile village in southern New Hampshire, its huge granite mill and brick houses around the mill pond unchanged since the 1820s and 1830s. The woolen mill went bankrupt in 1970 when so many others in New England were collapsing, but the owner brought in other industries, established a handweaving loom workshop, and sought to preserve jobs and an organic community as well as the historic buildings.

National Trust for Historic Preservation in the United States, Washington, D.C., 1971–1980—$70,000. This trust, similar to the National Trust in Great Britain, was started in 1949 to preserve buildings, sites, and objects significant in American history and culture. It runs a revolving loan fund for private, nonprofit conservation groups employed in Annapolis, Charleston, and Savannah as well as offering matching grants and mortgage guaranty funds. It seeks to preserve the historical building in a meaningful relationship to its surrounding, often threatened by possible sale of adjacent lands. Most of the Merrill money was given to establish a National Historical Preservation Fund and purchase nearby lands.

Henry Francis DuPont Winterthur Museum, Winterthur, Delaware, 1972–1980—$40,000. This museum was opened in 1927 to exhibit collections of mid-nineteenth-century domestic architecture, textiles, pewter, ceramics, paintings, and prints in period rooms. Later a Winterthur program in Early American Culture was organized to train students for museum work, teaching, and gardening. Merrill funds went to catalogue material on English furniture and American silver, to purchase seventeenth- and eighteenth-century English glass and ceramic objects, and to establish a new conservation training program.

Flagler Museum, Palm Beach, Florida, 1975—$5,000 to meet expenses at Whitehall, built in 1901 as a wedding present to Henry Flagler's third wife, and a monument to this great entrepreneur, a part of the Standard Oil and Rockefeller world of hotel and railroad. The *Historical Society of Palm Beach County*, headquartered in the Flagler Museum, received $15,000 in 1975 to fund a history of the local area and publish historical manuscripts of pioneer life in central Florida.

Foundation for San Francisco's Architectural Heritage, 1976, 1978—$15,000 to protect unique Victorian buildings against progress and decay. Preservation and rehabilitation can make economic as well as esthetic sense: buying and then reselling to responsible buyers and helping low-income families learn the necessary skills of restoration.

City of San Francisco, 1981—$10,000 toward restoration of the cable car system, last in the world, the symbol of San Francisco. The total cost will be $58 million, of which $10 million must be raised privately. This was the pet project of Mayor Dianne Feinstein, and Peter Magowan felt it politic for us to participate.

Tor House, Carmel, California, 1980—$15,000 for restoration of Robinson Jeffers' house at Big Sur. Set within a walled garden, the house was built by hand with stone from the Pacific beach and contains his personal library. Purchase, restoration, and operating costs were set at $400,000. Jeffers loved hawks and pretty much despised human beings and might be amused to see his house and himself turned into a monument.

Rugby Restoration Association, Rugby, Tennessee, 1977—$10,000. In one of the poorest sections of Appalachia, an effort to restore some impressive Victorian wooden buildings, combining two interesting theories that historic restoration can be a vehicle for community development and education and that libraries (and there are none in this area) can encourage a consciousness of cultural identity that helps people resist forces overwhelming their lives. Of this $10,000, half went for reconstruction purposes and half went to libraries in Rugby, Del Rio, and Cabbagetown.

Doris Magowan and Donald Regan felt committed to the Trust's obligation to maintain our national buildings around Washington. *White House Historical Association, 1971—$100,000* to fund current refurbishing, particularly of the central hall on the second floor. *Department of State, 1976, 1980—$30,000* toward the acquisition of outstanding Americana for use in the diplomatic reception rooms. *Commandant's House, 1976—$25,000* to acquire period pieces of historical significance to the Marine Corps. *Mount Vernon Ladies Association of the Union, Mount Vernon, Virginia, 1981—$50,000* to construct and endow a new research center for Washington memorabilia, part of a $10-million capital campaign that involved Regan as he became secretary of the treasury.

Archaeology

Foundation for Illinois Archaeology, Evanston, Illinois, 1974, 1975—$30,000. Stuart Struever, a professor of archaeology at Northwestern University and a specialist in the culture of the Mississippi Valley, had located at the Koster farm in Kampsville, Illinois, in a small, sheltered, fertile valley above the Illinois River, a settlement where Indians had lived for over 7,500 years. Every so often mudslides would cover the settlement, drive away the current settlers, and provide a sterile foundation for the next group, which produced a delineated layer cake of thirteen periods. Each community was a separate entity. The inhabitants were not a brutish, short-lived tribe of hunters but were orderly, settled agriculturalists and traders, and Struever sought to examine their life using the most sophisticated modern methods. This meant interdisciplinary cooperation between statisticians, chemists (tracing traffic origins in metal traces from soil samples), biologists and nutritionists (pollen samples tell the vegetables grown, bones tell the animals eaten, the protein this implies, and the resulting health), pathologists (what disease traces are left in human bones), computer engineers to keep track of quantitative relations between artifacts, and social scientists to make generalizations out of these data. Mary Merrill, who came from Illinois and was interested in archaeology, read of Struever's work in a *New York Times* article, made contact with him, and had me present these two appeals, along with similar ones in technology and textiles, to the Foundation.

Struever turned the dig into a major education center, using student volunteers from graduate school to junior high. He was particularly proud of his youngest kids: out of hard work twelve- and thirteen-year-olds acquired a commitment to learning and a respect for the past.

Lowie Museum of Anthropology, University of California, Berkeley, California, 1981—$10,000 for the conservation program of over 3,000 ancient Peruvian textiles excavated between 1899 and 1905. Their specific provenance is known so they can be dated and studied in relation to accompanying materials, and at least half need conservation attention.

Peabody Museum, Harvard University, Cambridge, Massachusetts, 1980, 1981—$20,000 to finance photography, cataloguing, and preservation of the collection of pre-Columbian textiles. The frantic pace of collecting from the mid-nineteenth century on left few resources for the care of collections already assembled. When by the mid-twentieth century countries in Latin America tried to stop this looting, the Peabody turned its eyes to the irreplaceable treasures in its basement, so poorly stored that they were unavailable for teaching purposes as well as deteriorating further with each year. This was especially true of Peruvian textiles preserved in the dry coastal deserts for almost 5,000 years, records of societies that left no written accounts.

Crafts, Technology, and Textiles

Handweavers Guild of America, West Hartford, Connecticut, 1980, 1981—$20,000. Half the grant went for library development, and half went for exhibit and catalogue of the 1982 conference at Seattle. The Guild, the largest single craft organization with 22,000 members, publishes *Shuttle, Spindle & Dyepot,* the major bulletin for handweavers, offers study scholarships for isolated, poor, and handicapped weavers and runs an accreditation program for weavers in order to establish objective standards of quality.

Fashion Institute of Technology, New York, New York, 1981—$10,000. The Institute was started in 1944 to provide the fashion industry with new talent and offer gifted students a new choice of careers in fashion and related fields. Merrill funds went to the Industrial Design Production Laboratory in the Textile Design Department, acquainting students with technological advances in looms and dyes.

Pioneer Craft House, Salt Lake City, Utah, 1972, 1976—$10,000. This is a center for young craftsmen, writers, musicians, and architects and includes a children's arboretum, a puppet theatre, and a rehabilitation program serving the handicapped and prisoners.

American Crafts Council, New York, New York, 1976—$10,000. This is the largest visual arts organization in the United States concerned with the needs of the artist who works in clay, metals, wood fibers, plastics, and glass. The Council supports the Museum of Contemporary Crafts, an excellent journal (*Craft Horizons*), a large library, and exhibit touring program. Practical help is given through group insurance, a collection service for bad debts, tax and customs information, and leadership programs to Indians and Appalachian folk.

Eastern Illinois University Foundation, Chicago, Illinois, 1976, 1978— $20,000. The university's new School of Fine Arts under an aggressive dean named Vaughn Jaenicke sought to avoid being one more fourth-rate copy of the Fogg Museum and instead built on a living tradition of folk crafts. Our money funded in their first arts festival a series of prizes and purchase awards in painting, sculpture and glass, metalcraft, woodworking, furniture, ceramics, spinning, weaving, needlepoint, and quiltmaking. It was hard to evade Mr. Jaenicke's enthusiasm for a second festival—this time with the addition of bookbinding, marionettes, and country music. Such awards meant that craftsmen who had actually sold something now regarded themselves as professional, and as people worth taking seriously.

PERFORMING ARTS

Big and Small Music

The basic symbol of twentieth-century performing arts is the symphony orchestra. This presents big music to society, and on television, radio, and records at an even more important level than through its concerts. In many cities, whether you are talking of Philadelphia or Oakland, it is the center of community pride: as a bank of artists for chamber groups and operas and conservatory faculties, as a training ground for young musicians, as a channel of culture into the public schools, and as ambassadors of that community to nearby towns or to the Soviet Union. Each orchestra offers a vehicle of service, often quite humble in pretensions, to hundreds of volunteers. A symphony orchestra is also big business and involves financial dealings of a staggering size and complexity. We invested in twenty different orchestras for a total over $1 million, San Francisco receiving the most.

San Francisco Symphony, 1966–1981—$185,000. Since its origins in 1854, this orchestra was traditionally financed by box office receipts and annual campaigns, with an endowment fund started in 1954. After a period of decline, the arrival in 1963 of Josef Krips from Vienna brought a strong rise in quality with a longer season and better musicians. The orchestra offered a core of musicians to all other musical groups of the city as well as being the major cultural asset in northern California, serving approximately 500,000 listeners. There was a strong emphasis on twentieth-century music and overseas touring, a natural destination being Japan. Seiji Ozawa was its best known conductor, a symptom of our time's celebrity disease as he frantically commuted between San Francisco and Boston, trying to direct both orchestras at the same time.

The symphony's tangible improvement brought it a Ford Foundation $2.5-million challenge grant in 1966, but large grants just fueled, as in other orchestras, musicians' demands for higher salaries. In 1969–1970 (when the Trust gave $30,000) the orchestra broke even, but the 1976–1977 deficit reached $800,000, worsened by illnesses of guest artists and a strike of city employees that shut down the Opera House. The Trust gave $25,000 in 1977 and $50,000 in 1979, when the deficit reached $1.5 million. Proposition 13 cut local funding and there was no compensatory support from the state. The National Endowment for the Arts made a $750,000 challenge grant on a 1 to 3 basis to encourage search for other sources of funding. With the opening in 1981 of Louise Davies Symphony Hall (financed through the *San Francisco Performing Arts Center* to which the Trust gave $135,000 between 1976 and 1981), the symphony for the first time had its own hall.

Philadelphia Orchestra Association, 1969–1977—$115,000. The Philadelphia Orchestra was founded in 1900, was the first to broadcast on network radio, to tour Europe, to be televised, to have a fifty-two-week season, and was famous for its direction by Leopold Stokowski and Eugene Ormandy. When we made our first gift of $50,000, however, Philadelphia represented the financial crisis that all the major American orchestras were suffering. The combined annual operating loss of the top five—New York, Boston, Philadelphia, Cleveland, and Chicago—had gone from $2.9 million in 1964 to $5.7 in 1968. New income—Ford's matching grants of $80 million in 1966 to sixty orchestras—just encouraged new salary costs, and famous orchestras found themselves living off their endowments, merging, or (like Detroit) having to endure a thirty-four-week musicians' strike. A large foundation like Andrew W. Mellon might offset this spiral process (though musicians so traditionally underpaid had the right to demand more money) by putting up challenge grants for endowment, with incentive rewards offered to orchestras that could stay in the black for five years. Small foundations like ours ran in with their emergency gifts that merely postponed the crises.

In retrospect 1969 looks more prosperous than our own time, but it was a year when state and federal governments, corporations and foundations were switching their support from cultural institutions to ghetto projects, and the pillar-of-society philanthropists who had kept the orchestras going had to share their resources with museums, hospitals, and universities. It was easy to envy the Vienna Staatsoper or the Berlin Philharmonic with their guaranteed subsidies for reasons of tradition, prestige, and tourist revenues.

Musical Arts Association of Cleveland, Ohio, 1970–1977—$115,000 for support of the Cleveland Orchestra, another prestigious group directed by a famous personality, George Szell, out of the old music world of Budapest, Vienna, and Prague. Szell was described as a musical autocrat, a compulsive pedagogue, a fire-eating tyrant, an inhuman perfectionist, and his orchestra was described as performing like an exquisite string quartet, combining an American orchestra's technical perfection, beauty of mind, and adaptability with warm-hearted, spontaneous musicmaking in the best European tradition. The orchestra went on important State-Department-sponsored tours to Moscow and Warsaw in 1965 and to Japan in 1970, gave 210 concerts a year, carried on a strong education tradition with music appreciation classes in the public schools and special concerts that attracted 80,000 school children annually, and during the 1970s, like its host city, ran up such huge deficits that its endowment had almost been extinguished. (1979 joke: "What is the difference between Cleveland and the *Titanic*?" "Cleveland has a better orchestra.")

Boston Symphony Orchestra, 1970–1979—$100,000. Half of this went in 1970 to meet operating expenses; two grants in 1971 and 1979 were for support of the Berkshire Music Center at Tanglewood. Symphony Hall, built in 1900, has the finest acoustics in the United States. The orchestra has been known for its directors, particularly Serge Koussevitzky, and for its willingness to launch new composers. It has taken on ambitious international tours: in 1956 it was the first Western orchestra to visit the Soviet Union, and under Ozawa in 1977 made a remarkable tour of China with efforts to bring Chinese musicians, so long cut off from Western music, into its concerts as fellow players. The BSO was famous also for its Pops and Esplanade concerts under Arthur Fiedler, a way to reach a new audience and to keep that team of musicians at performance pitch during spring and summer. Thirty-five million records by the BSO were sold between 1917 and 1970. It has probably the largest endowment of any orchestra in the world.

National Symphony Orchestra, Washington, D.C., 1970–1978—$110,000 for endowment, salaries, and general operations in its home, the *John F. Kennedy Center for the Performing Arts* (which received $135,000 from the

Trust 1963–1979). The cost for this center had originally been estimated at $30 million. By 1970 that had risen to $66 million with a 1,200-seat theatre; a 2,750-seat symphony hall, a 2,500-seat hall for opera, musical comedy, and ballet; and by 1979 a 500-seat Terrace Theater given by the Japanese for the bicentennial. One special cost was soundproofing against jet aircraft; another, of course, was megalomania as the nation's artistic center even if not much money came from the federal government.

Oakland Symphony Association, Oakland, California, 1969–1979—$45,000. Our first gift of $30,000 was to help match a Ford matching grant of $1 million. This orchestra was founded in 1937 as an amateur organization and turned professional in 1960; by 1968 it gave fifty concerts a year, and by 1978, it gave 150 concerts to an audience of 150,000. It is not only in the wide spread of services to its rather deprived community—concerts in 90 elementary schools in the Bay Area reaching 21,000 children; specially low-priced tickets for handicapped, aged, and young listeners; a special 150-voice chorus; sponsorship of the Youth Symphony; and recruitment of young blacks for summer employment—that this orchestra serves Oakland. In the volunteer support it recruits, the enthusiasm for culture it creates, and, even more important, the pride it creates in its city's major accomplishment, the symphony builds a link between community and orchestra one would never find in any state-financed and taken-for-granted European institution.

We made a number of grants to such local orchestras, where a modest gift would have impact upon a limited budget and where a gift from a national foundation, obtained perhaps through some Merrill Lynch branch manager, strengthened pride.

American Symphony Orchestra, New York, New York, 1971—$35,000. Founded in 1962 by Leopold Stokowski as an opportunity for young musicians right out of conservatories to develop artistry in New York City, this orchestra won discriminating audiences and reviewers in a demanding and varied repertory and had soloists of the highest caliber, 40 percent of whom were women. In six years free concerts had been given to over 300,000 public school children.

Atlanta Symphony, 1971—$30,000.

Denver Symphony, 1972—$30,000 for on-campus rehearsals, symposia, workshops, and concerts at the University of Colorado and Denver University, where the universities themselves were in such bad financial shape they could do little to bring serious music to their students. Besides extensive concerts for all ages of school children, the symphony performs at two state penitentiaries and a mental hospital. The orchestra also puts a strong emphasis upon music by American composers, so hard, once one has played *Appalachian Spring* and *American in Paris,* to hear.

Utah Symphony, Salt Lake City, 1968, 1973—$50,000. The first $25,000 went to match a $1.5 million Ford grant; the second was to encourage participation by high school students in formal concerts. As many as ninety young people were so involved, with the instrumentalists playing alongside the regular members. This orchestra served the mountain West from Nevada to Montana, supplied musicians for the ballet and opera, and gave concerts at the huge (5,000 seats) Mormon Tabernacle, but local giving went to meet expanding services and operating costs, and there were no financial reserves to meet this Ford grant.

Buffalo Philharmonic, Buffalo, New York, 1973, 1976—$25,000. An archetypal Merrill Lynch vice-president was chairman of the board and obtained these two grants. The Philharmonic became a permanent orchestra in 1932 and though it often led a precarious existence, it attracted good young conductors like William Steinberg, Josef Krips, and Michael Tilson Thomas, who later went on to make their names with major groups.

Small Music—$195,000

The staggering problem of keeping a symphony orchestra alive from one end of a year to the next, of dealing with unions, inflated conductors, and bravura soloists, fund drives, foundations and government agencies, school performances and student workshops, may well make the performance of good music way down on the list of priorities. Accordingly, the rewarding groups to listen to and to support may be the ones small enough to express the creativity and skill of their artists as their first priority. During the 1970s we gave $220,000 to further different groups—some that we knew well, others presented at random.

Monadnock Music, Peterborough, New Hampshire, 1974–1980—$57,000. Since 1966 Monadnock Music has been giving free concerts in the churches and town halls of southern New Hampshire. Under an unusual director, James Bolle, the orchestra specializes in Baroque and modern music. It has performed fifty different Haydn symphonies, with an orchestra and concert halls the size of which Haydn wrote for, with an audience in shirt sleeves and children sleeping on the benches, and with a bowl at the doorway for people to put their contributions. The players work for peanut salaries (plus room and board) because of the music seldom heard elsewhere and the rewards of Bolle's leadership. The audience has the readiness to listen to the most advanced composers (if the concert is free, there is less fear that Rzewski's *Instrumental Studies* will scare away customers), concert versions of *Don Giovanni* or Gluck's *Orfeo*, and a performance of Beethoven's *Eroica* given by an orchestra of two dozen players with every sinew of the music standing out instead of being blanketed by big-band sonority with a herd of cellists stretching to the horizon like bison on the Great Plains. People don't come to the concerts to pay homage to a public-relationized personality: they come to hear good music played by good musicians. There's a world of difference between these two concepts.

Center for Chamber Music at Apple Hill, Nelson, New Hampshire, 1974–1981—$33,000. This is a mixed group that is a summer camp for serious students ranging from adolescence to middle age with a chamber orchestra of professional quality and a service facility for musical education to gifted pupils of New Hampshire public schools. Its first director, Eugene Rosov, was an interesting theoretician in the economics of small music and also its value in rebuilding an active response toward music, toward art, and toward life itself rather than the passivity that large-scale concert consumption encourages. Rosov also attacked what he termed Heifetzian "God, mustn't miss a note" precision that destroyed passion and spontaneity. "To feel that you may dare—this should be the object of perfect teaching."

Marlboro School of Music, Marlboro, Vermont, 1970—$20,000. Marlboro Music, under the leadership of Rudolph Serkin, is both a high-class summer festival of chamber music in southern Vermont and also a school for advanced young musicians.

Pro Musicis Foundation, New York, New York, 1976–1979—$10,000. Pro Musicis was originally organized in France in 1965 by a Franciscan brother and was later expanded to this country in 1969 to link professional careers in music to social service. It finances concerts by young musicians who then agree to give their next concert free, in a prison, a hospital, or a nursing home. The second gift was to open a new branch in San Francisco involving concerts at San Quentin.

Ballet—$430,000

San Francisco Ballet, 1962–1979—$122,500 in six grants. The San Francisco Ballet Company started in 1933 to supply the San Francisco Opera with dancers and early on evolved a ballet school to assure the new company a permanent source of well-trained talent. The Ballet Company made a name for itself from the beginning, staging the evening-long classics—*Coppelia, Swan Lake*, and *Nutcracker*—in their entirety. By the mid-1950s it had won a national reputation to rank with the New York City Ballet, and ten years later was the most traveled classical ballet in the world.

In 1964 the Ford Foundation made a complex of grants amounting to $7,750,000 to encourage the long-range professional development of ballet, to strengthen the companies with strong artistic direction, and to improve the generally inadequate standards that prevailed in the teaching of professional ballet. It was the best thing far and away that ever happened to dance in this country. San Francisco received a $650,000 matching grant out of this largesse, to which the Merrill Trust contributed $20,000. Our foundation gave another $20,000 in 1969 to support the company's collaboration with California schools and colleges, and to support an experimental summer season with untrained choreographers, designers, and composers. Dance is the growth industry of the arts: ticket sales increased 500 percent between 1969 and 1979, and more people go to the ballet than to football games. It is an expensive product, however, and ticket sales generally cover only 55 percent of needed income. Dancers' salaries are low, and yet ticket prices must be kept down in order to attract young audiences.

The San Francisco Ballet had good leadership at the time of this revolutionary change in American dance, in which Ford played such a role. Could the annual battles to raise the extra funds necessary for solvency, stability, and decent wages keep pace with the creativity of the company? Dance has become an integral part of American cultural life since the 1950s, but would art lovers in Boise and Atlanta put up the money, beyond what they paid for tickets, to pay for this quality of performance? Except for the two Roosevelts and John F. Kennedy, all twentieth-century presidents have come from small towns and do not understand the city and its cultural responsibilities.

Stern Grove Festival, San Francisco, California, 1971–1981—$23,500. Stern Grove is a beautiful natural amphitheater surrounded by eucalyptus, redwood, and fir trees near the heart of San Francisco where free performances of music and dance (funded traditionally by the city's Jewish community) are offered in warm weather.

Ballet West, Salt Lake City, Utah, 1969–1979—$95,000. Ballet West is probably the leading cultural organization of the six-state Rocky Mountain region that it serves. Founded in 1964 with Ford help, it plays an important role in the decentralization of the dance and in the decentralization of American culture in general as something beyond half a dozen cities on the two coasts. It is well known enough to make extensive European and national tours and yet invests heavily in lecture-demonstration performances for public schoolchildren. In one 1969 performance in Vernal, Utah, 2,000 out of the town's 5,000 inhabitants attended. Our two last grants went to help improve salaries that were low enough to put the company at risk from its better-paying competitors.

American Ballet Theatre, New York, New York, 1977—$25,000 to help in mounting and rehearsing new productions. This is the oldest classical ballet company in America and one of the major training centers for dance companies everywhere. It has made fifteen international tours, often sponsored by the State Department, including two to the Soviet Union. In the 1970s, New York had become the ballet center of the world, exercising the same drawing power upon dancers of the Kirov and Bolshoi companies as upon every desperate teenager in every town in this country.

New York City Ballet, 1974, 1977—$35,000. In operation since 1948, the New York City Ballet is one of the foremost dance companies in the world. Composers such as Stravinsky, Bernstein, Copland, Hindemith, and Menotti wrote for this company; artists like Noguchi, Chagall, Roualt, and Rauschenberg created the sets. At the time of the Merrill Trust's first grant, its landlord, the City Center of Music and Dance, was in such thin shape that only salaries and taxes were being paid. At our second grant the company was suffering a $2.8 million operating deficit that threatened to shut it down.

Boston Ballet, Boston, Massachusetts, 1972–1981—$60,000. This is the only professional ballet company in New England and had grown from an audience of 6,000 in 1963 to one of 170,000 at the time of our first grant. It takes its educational responsibilities seriously in performances for public schoolchildren and in the variety of training programs that start with children recruited for the Christmas *Nutcracker Suite.* Under Virginia Williams, it became one of the two leading schools for young dancers in the United States. It tours extensively in New England and has made trips to Israel and China. By 1981, 83 percent of the budget was covered by earned income, the highest percentage in the United States. There is of course the same hand-to-mouth existence depending on many small gifts, and the 1974 gift from Ford was matched fifteen minutes before the deadline.

Opera and Performing Arts Centers—$610,000

Support for opera splits into two categories. One, at tremendous cost, is to maintain the great companies that supply the nation's leadership and attract the international stars and the prize-winning students. The second category is help to all the odd little workshops and ephemeral groups that consider nonestablishment composers and approaches and unknown conductors and singers and that spark the American musical scene.

San Francisco Opera, San Francisco, California, 1965–1980—$148,000 (plus $25,000 to its Opera's education and touring subsidiary, *Western Opera Theatre*). Until 1938 San Francisco was an offshoot of the Metropolitan, importing both conductors and singers from New York. Now it is independent, and though the season is relatively short (eight weeks plus the annual tour to Southern California, Sacramento, Portland, and Seattle), its repertory is equal to the Met's and often more adventurous. It has given the American premiers of works by Strauss, Poulenc, Ravel, Britten, Orff, and Cherubini and the American debuts of stars like George London, Tito Gobbi, Elizabeth Schwartzkopf, and Leontyne Price. Up to 160,000 students per year from two hundred Bay Area schools have been brought to special-price performances. The Merrill Trust put up $43,000 in 1969 for a new production of *La Traviata* and $55,000 in 1972 for a new *Tosca*. In 1980 $25,000 went toward purchase of new instruments: a contrabassoon, for example, costs $15,000.

Metropolitan Opera, New York, New York, 1967–1981—$140,000. The Merrill Trust first became involved with the Met after the calamitous 1966–1967 season that ended with a $6.6 million deficit. The move to Lincoln Center had been costly, and there were construction delays that shortened the season, labor difficulties, greater operating expenses, and lower income. And yet that year there had been 214 performances, the largest repertory of any opera company anywhere, with virtually every Lincoln Center performance sold out, plus the successful Texaco Saturday afternoon broadcasts and an ambitious program for training young singers. No matter what the success, the costs and deficits rose. By 1974 the thirty-one-week, 300-performance New York season, the national tour, and the education and audience development programs all meant new big losses from wage increases; a decline in contributions and the New York City subsidy; higher costs for heating, air conditioning, and maintenance; along with a need of raising seed money to expand into television.

Bob Magowan's only image for our five grants was pouring money down a rathole. But the Vienna Staatsoper receives 70 percent of its costs from the government, and La Scala receives 80 percent. The Met doesn't, which means fundraising without end among foundations, philanthropists, and music-lovers who listen to the Saturday broadcasts. We put up $65,000 in 1974–1976 to meet challenge grants from the National Endowment of the Arts and $50,000 in 1979–1981 for training of young artists.

Opera Company of Boston, Boston, Massachusetts, 1965–1981—$76,000.
This company is one person, Sarah Caldwell, a gifted impresario in her ability
to experiment with or bring back to life great works like Berlioz's *Trojans*,
Prokofief's *War and Peace*, plus Bellinis and Donizettis and Verdis, to help
restore an entire art form like bel canto singing, to launch new artists like
Beverly Sills, and make Boston an operatic center whether it really wanted
to be one or not. If you learn too much about the company, you get turned
off by the personality cult around its director as well as her spasms of bad
taste and financial foolishness. Reality (unpaid bills and wages and the shabby
existing facilities) did not limit fantasy (extravagant performances and dreams
of a gala new theatre). In 1982 Sarah Caldwell signed a contract with another
fantasy team, Ferdinand and Imelda Marcos, to bring opera to the Philippines. A reasonable person might never have had the reckless spark to launch
an opera company that at its best offers a wonderful imaginativeness.

*Associate Artists' Opera Company of New England, Boston, Massachu-
setts, 1974—$5,000.* An ephemeral group, but it gave jobs to musicians and
enjoyment to listeners.

New York City Opera, New York, 1978—$25,000.

Santa Fe Opera, New Mexico, 1972, 1976—$50,000.

Chicago Opera Theatre, Illinois, 1979, 1981—$30,000. This company was
organized in 1970 to provide opportunities and experience for Illinois singers
and musicians in performance of professional operas. It has a resident house
but also gives performances in Chicago and in Illinois schools, universities,
churches, gyms, and suburban auditoriums.

Lyric Opera of Chicago, 1980—$10,000.

*City of Grand Rapids Performing Arts Center, Grand Rapids, Michigan,
1978—$15,000.* Started in the 1960s as a major project to rebuild the down-
town business district, this center by 1978 had become the biggest civic re-
development project the city had ever undertaken, with a $20-million con-
vention and arts center financed by the federal government and city hotel
tax and parking fees. Another $900,000 was sought privately for furnishings,
art works, and landscaping.

Boise State University, Boise, Idaho, 1981—$10,000 to be used toward
construction of a new music department facility in conjunction with the Mor-
rison Center for Fine and Performing Arts, at a total cost of $13 million.

One is reminded of the small French cities of the thirteenth century that bankrupted themselves seeking to build the biggest and tallest cathedral in the land. Beauvais seemed as if it were going to win the prize, but the roof kept falling in and only the apse and transept were ever finished.

Association of Graduates of the United States Military Academy, West Point, New York, 1973—*$10,000* to support the Fine Arts Forum. At a time when a military career was so unpopular that first-rate young men no longer wished to become officers, the Association thought that such a forum would broaden West Point's appeal. Any cadet, however, was well advised not to be seen too often at the Forum. The Air Force Academy in Colorado Springs had developed exams that appealed to—but also excluded—sensitive applicants: "*Emperor* is the name of (1) a racing car; (2) a symphony; (3) a concerto; or (4) a quartet?" The correct answer, of course, is Beethoven's *Emperor* Concerto. Any potential cadet knowledgeable enough to put down Haydn's *Emperor* Quartet would not be correct U.S. officer material.

Theatre

The reaction to overpriced and second-rate commercial entertainment, which includes the run-of-the-mill movie out of Hollywood and the run-of-the-mill play out of Broadway, is subsidized, noncommercial theatre. This can be on a grandiose scale at Lincoln Center or on a peanut scale at the San Francisco Attic. It can be worse than commercial theatre since it does not have to meet the discipline of the box office. But there is a courageous as well as crack-brained quality to the independent theatre movement of the last twenty years. One has to admire the irrationality of actors who make do on $80.00 a week. This movement, which our Foundation strongly supported— $900,000 to thirty-five groups—in the second half of its duration, gives a counterargument to the shopworn criticism of American cultural conformity, capitalist control, and popular passivity.

New York City

Theatre in Education, 1968—*$15,000*. A group that sought to bring Shakespeare into secondary schools from Connecticut to Delaware, in fifty-minute versions with a stress upon sensitivity to language. It was primarily funded by the American Theatre Association and fees by participating schools, but there is wide discrepancy between fees and costs, especially among schools in poor neighborhoods.

New Phoenix Repertory Company, through *Theatre Incorporated, 1973–*

1977—$25,000. The Phoenix Theatre is the oldest repertory group in New York, having offered 136 productions from 1945 through 1973. It gives tours with workshops, demonstrations, and seminars. In 1977 $5,000 went to back the effort to search out and upgrade to Broadway standards new plays as well as to revive classics.

South Street Theatre Company, 1974–1980—$20,000. This company was originally attached to the *South Street Seaport Museum* (1972—$10,000 to restore docks, buildings, and sailing ships) presenting American plays to local people and tourists at the time of the Bicentennial. By 1980 it had moved to 42nd Street, a force for revitalization of that shabby area. It was the only Broadway theatre with a modular stage and flexible audience positions and by then was stressing American premiers of foreign plays.

Circle in the Square, 1975—$5,000. The year 1951 marked the beginning of off-Broadway theatre, which nurtured (or revived) a new generation of actors, playwrights, and directors: Tennessee Williams, Truman Capote, Dylan Thomas, Eugene O'Neill, and Saul Bellow. Circle in the Square was a leader here, a haven for high-quality, serious theatre, seeking to develop a new audience through moderately priced subscription tickets. The Merrill grant went towards maintaining the cash reserve project launched by the Ford Foundation.

Westside Community Repertory Theatre, 1981—$5,000. This is a tiny, family-run theatre, started by two Cuban refugees, that put on four classic plays a year: Schnitzler, Shaw, Molière, Goldoni, all historically costumed, finely detailed, and with accurate sets: "A shoestring operation, it has nevertheless kept itself in shoes." A chance for young professionals to attempt the classics free of ethnic stereotyping that too often limits them to First Prisoner and Taxi Driver. Small grants were needed for improvement and expansion outside the merciless tensions of commercial theatre.

Repertory Theatre of Lincoln Center, 1963, 1973. A group much heralded at its start ("just as good as Europe"), the Repertory Theatre received funds from the Trust for costs and deficits. When it folded in 1973, our second grant was passed to the New York Shakespeare Festival, which took over the theatre at Lincoln Center under the much publicized Joseph Papp. It never really got off the ground in any way that compared with the Lincoln Center's musical offerings.

Lincoln Center for the Performing Arts, 1977, 1979—$45,000. This money went toward operating costs and support of a three-year project to develop new approaches to teacher training and curriculum development.

Great centers like Lincoln and Kennedy elicit two contradictory responses. They do present the starred performers and groups in a showcase that attracts a mass audience and sets a standard as well as inflating institutional, civic, and national prestige. On the other hand, the super-publicity and super-cost of these extravaganzas, like the blockbuster shows at prestige museums, may have a harmful effect in persuading the average ticket-buyer and screen-viewer that only in such gaudy trappings can first-rate art be found. To launch and maintain these centers demands so much money that funding for just as valuable, less noisy groups is dried up.

New England/Boston

Eugene O'Neill Memorial Theatre, Waterford, Connecticut, 1972–1980— *$35,000.* The O'Neill Theatre was an interesting conglomerate involving an actors' school, a playwrights' workshop, a center for international conferences on the theatre (including one on Africa), a showboat that gave musical comedies in different harbors of Manhattan, and a theatre for the deaf. The legitimate theatre has always been a mission in which society can read and study itself. In recent years, however, rising costs and expansion of other media have hurt this function of theatre in America. The O'Neill Theatre has sought to upgrade and broaden the standards of the American theatre, serving as a working laboratory as well as a showcase.

Trinity Personna Company, Providence, Rhode Island, 1975–1979— *$15,000.* Trinity sought to be a force for life and renewal in blighted downtown Providence, offering a wide variety of classic and modern plays and mounting an ambitious program to thousands of public school students as well as to several colleges within a fifty-mile radius.

Marlboro College, Marlboro, Vermont, 1974—$75,000 for construction of a theatre. This isolated and financially precarious college in southern Vermont was very dependent on the quality of the intellectual and artistic life that went on within it. There were more practical needs than for this handsome building, but its real class strengthened the pride of the college.

People's Theatre, Cambridge, Massachusetts, 1973–1981—$35,000. This was a serious little group still believing in class and racial brotherhood within its casting and organization while bringing good, free performances to a new audience in community centers, housing projects, playgrounds, and hospitals. It was the only noncollege theatre in the Boston area to present original scripts by both white and black playwrights, the only opening for new writers and directors and for black actors and technical workers, and, in fact, one of the few biracial groups still alive when the radical movement died. It presented plays on fighting with the expressway or the housing authority, on problems of the Vietnam veteran as well as Chekhov and Dylan Thomas. Despite careful budgeting and miniscule salaries, People's closed by 1982.

Boston Shakespeare Company, Massachusetts, 1978–1981—$50,000. Here was a major commitment to one small company, helping it reach stability and grow from a shoestring team of actors supporting themselves as taxi-drivers and waiters to becoming, for a moment, Boston's oldest and largest resident theatre, and one of the few in the entire country performing a full September–June season of Shakespeare. Young people were involved in special student matinees, in van trips to city suburban schools (i.e., a special fifty-minute *Macbeth* as a study in character), or in an imaginative idea like a free Halloween show for children of a high-crime and multiracial neighborhood. One could observe the actors grow (the Lear and Hamlet had started out as an insurance claims adjustor); pick up professional skills of movement, timing, and diction; and acquire the skills to tackle new roles.

After a while, sadly, the competent performance of repertory classics may not seem challenging enough to directors, trustees, and media critics. They are tempted by imaginative presentations—for example, *Hamlet* performed on bicycles. Some flashy personality like Peter Sellars is hired to put on a couple of headline shows, runs up staggering debts, and then quits to sign on with a more exciting company. Nevertheless, perhaps the struggle showed to keep such little arts groups, schools, and social agencies alive; this maintenance of noncommercial values is, for some people, our time's equivalent of a religious commitment.

Boston Center for the Arts, Massachusetts, 1975–1980—$45,000. This institution was a rational effort, despite the miserable economic climate, to develop an arts center (out of a former battle of Gettysburg cyclorama) that would also upgrade the discouraged South End and serve as a means for blacks and whites to share work and recreation. In a way it was pretentious, but Mozart opera and Caribbean dance were put on in the auditorium, and an experimental theatre was burrowed into the basement. One room was rented by the Boston Ballet for rehearsals, there were painting studies and exhibit rooms, a Neighborhood Art Center attracting both adults and children, and the sponsorship of a Chinese festival and a Puerto Rican Three Kings night—a lot of light and movement that helped cut down local crime and encouraged the start of small business activity. After the megalomania of Kennedy and Lincoln, it was refreshing to observe the modest scale and democratic operation of this outfit.

Grand Monadnock Arts Council, Keene, New Hampshire, 1980—$10,000.
The Council had been organized to administer government funds helping
communities in southern New Hampshire celebrate the Bicentennial. It went
on to sponsor local programs: a concert series at the Keene synagogue, bus
trips to museums in Boston and New York, and a conference on business and
the arts. Then, as times got worse, outside funding dried up, and every school
district sought to save money by dropping its arts classes as frills, the Council
channeled expertise and funding to seventy-five area primary and secondary
schools (public and private) with a student population of 19,000. Minigrants
were made on a matching basis (though the poorest communities received
service free) for visiting musicians, folk dancers, puppet and mime groups,
and weaving and pottery classes. In its per capita public expenditure for the
arts in 1980 (13¢), New Hampshire ranked fifty-fifth in the nation, after
Guam.

The Rest of the Country

Children's Theatre Company and School, Minneapolis, Minnesota, 1977—
$25,000.

American Repertory Theatre Company, Tulsa, Oklahoma, 1980—$20,000.

University of Pittsburgh, Pittsburgh, Pennsylvania, 1972, 1979—$45,000.

Arts Assembly of Jacksonville, Jacksonville, Florida, 1981—$25,000.

San Francisco Actor's Workshop, San Francisco, California, 1964—
$15,000. One of the best-known theatrical ventures in the United States, the
Workshop was struggling to survive. The public is willing to subsidize museums, orchestras, and dance companies but not theatre, although Ford and
even the city had made some recent modest grants. On tour the Workshop
had gone from Los Angeles to Seattle and in the previous two years had given
performances to over 30,000 schoolchildren in northern California.
    Some interesting remarks by its director, Herbert Blair: "The path of the
American theatre lies as far from Broadway as possible, in the repertory
theatres dedicated to the idea of working as a team. . . . Stamina resembling
folly is indispensable. Such work may also be fun for the proud, the diso-
riented, the single-minded, and the strong. In such enterprises, the normally
easy going and practically well adjusted are most often the 'rats' who abandon
ship."

American Conservatory Theatre, San Francisco, California, 1967–1980—

$75,000. This theatre started in 1961 in New York to stage off-Broadway productions and conduct an actors' school. In 1966 it moved west and for a while divided its time between San Francisco and Chicago with plays like *Tartuffe, Under Milkwood, Endgame,* and *Six Characters in Search for an Author.* Ford gave $245,000 to reduce its deficit. In the mid-1960s $200,000 came from San Francisco individuals, with $200,000 still needed, part of it supplied by the first Merrill grant. There was also a black actor's workshop, a young conservatory for actors ages nine to eighteen, and an evening extension program. It was the nation's largest and most active repertory company, with overseas tours to Russia and Japan.

Free Public Theatre Foundation, Los Angeles, California, 1976—$5,000 for free performances of Shakespeare (*Romeo and Juliet* had reached an audience of 40,000 in 1975) to try to build a new audience for the older and Spanish-speaking, for the less educated and poorer, and for people afraid to leave their neighborhoods.

San Francisco Attic Theatre, California, 1979–1981—$15,000. The theatre started to provide training and performing experience, with emphasis on children and young adults. Fifty to ninety such artists aged eight to eighteen enrolled each year, with high quality performances and tickets cheap enough for the whole family to attend. There was a tradition of careful budgetry, yet a large portion of expenses (for utilities, rental scenery supplies, and advertising) were out of control in an era of inflation, and salaries were too low for morale.

Seattle Repertory Theatre, Washington, 1971–1980—$65,000. Operating out of a 1962 World's Fair theatre, this group became the largest repertory company west of Minneapolis and north of San Francisco. It made guest trips as far away as Norway, helped launch repertory companies in Alaska and Montana, brought in large numbers of students and old people through cut-rate tickets, and started an experimental theatre in downtown Seattle. Our first grant, during Seattle's blackest period, was to help allow the United Arts Council to concentrate on other, more desperately situated organizations.

SUPPORT TO ARTISTS—$200,000

MacDowell Colony, Peterborough, New Hampshire, 1966, 1978—$40,000. MacDowell Colony is the most perfect facility to help artists create that the human mind has ever thought up. After the composer Edward MacDowell died in 1906, his widow employed the $30,000 sent by the Mendelssohn Glee

Club of New York for his care to fund a colony where artists, writers, and musicians could come for concentration and work. "On fire with a campaign to free the human spirit," Mrs. MacDowell gave concerts and lectures to raise money. She was a firm disbeliever in the Mozart myth that talent flourishes in adversity: "Who can say what he would have achieved if he had had a happier life?" She was afraid that the best poem might be the one that just escaped being written. "It's what I've dedicated my life to prevent—the non-writing of the great poem."

Rising from an early and celibate bedtime after a carefree evening of croquet and poetry reading, the artists go to work in their silent cottages, with pianos for composers, easels and large windows for painters, and typewriters for authors. A basket lunch is delivered silently at noon, but winter heat is from stoves, not fireplaces, so that dilatory artists will not waste time staring at crackling flames. Twenty-three Pulitzer Prizes have been won by Mac-Dowell alumni, including E. A. Robinson, Willa Cather, Thornton Wilder, Aaron Copland, and Alice Walker. Affluent artists pay a reasonable figure for board; thin artists receive generous scholarships. This policy meant growing deficits, and the two Merrill grants went for endowment.

Thorne Music Fund, New York, New York, 1967, 1973—$45,000 to provide stipends for career American composers. Many people like to supply scholarships and commissions to young musicians starting their careers. When the composer comes into his mature and productive (and just as nonremunerative) middle years, he is less appealing. Even well-known composers are surprisingly unsuccessful in obtaining any form of financial stability. The Fund provides fellowships of $300 to $400 per month and payments for serious medical needs and pensions.

"The mass media and instant communication put a lot of pressure on the artist to be *with it*, and we are anxious to help the ones who are strongly committed to their own personal artistic vision and have the guts to go their own way."

Ragdale, Lake Forest, Illinois, 1981—$10,000. Ragdale is a mini-MacDowell Colony set in a rambling old house overlooking a last stretch of virgin prairie north of Chicago. There is room for seven artists or writers, who pay fifty dollars per week.

PEN American Center, New York, New York, 1975, 1976—$25,000. PEN is an international lobby or professional association for writers, more important abroad than within the United States, and involves itself in issues of copyrights and translations as well as intellectual freedom. Our two grants went to encourage the training of young translators, particularly needed for third-world authors working in languages like Vietnamese, Turkish, or Swahili.

University of California, Santa Cruz, California, 1977—$15,000 for the selection and production of artistically serious plays written by students throughout the University of California system. Playback to the Trust was an angry letter denouncing the selection committee as sexist and a counterletter by a committee member threatening to sue the complainer.

Our foundation's trustees had proposed an award in honor of James Merrill, who had made himself a major figure in contemporary poetry. James, an elitist disturbed by the lack of relationship between quality and quantity in the verse industry, proposed using the money to ascertain which university graduated the largest number of poets, inviting them to stand in a long line, and then shooting every other one. Nothing came of the idea.

American Institute for Performing and Fine Arts Management, New York, New York, 1981—$10,000. The Institute is involved in workshops, seminars, and writings on all facets of music publishing, copyright, and education through that channel. Gunther Schuller of the New England Conservatory used our grant to publish works by forgotten nineteenth- and early-twentieth-century composers belonging to the Boston School, such as John Knowles Paine, Frederick Converse, and Arthur Bird, whose music is in oblivion because it is difficult to obtain. If well published, such works would supply a better idea of America's musical heritage.

ARTS EDUCATION—$920,000

Juilliard School of Music, New York, New York, 1969–1980—$115,000 for scholarships, endowment, and general purposes. Founded in 1905, Juilliard entered its new building at Lincoln Center in 1969, the most complete facility in the world for training in the performing arts. In the academic division there is a concurrent program in the liberal arts, the Institute of Special Studies to encourage laymen to take a broader interest in musical literature and performance, and a precollege division for talented children. There is also a new program in opera and another to develop American conductors. (Most of the conductors of the United States' seventy-five major symphony orchestras are European.) Fifty percent of the students receive financial aid. The Ford Foundation gave $7 million in the early 1970s, and Mrs. DeWitt Wallace gave $5 million to build an endowment to try and reduce the pressures of annual deficits.

Only Moscow and Leningrad have conservatories that can match Juilliard.

Manhattan School of Music, New York, New York, 1962–1975—$120,000.
Our first grant of $25,000 went toward the purchase of the Juilliard properties
in upper Manhattan as the latter prepared to move to Lincoln Center. The
Manhattan facilities were limited and rundown, but construction costs were
so high that it seemed wise to buy out Juilliard, increase enrollment from 625
to 1,000, and take over intact the Juilliard preparatory school of 700 students.
By 1967, this enrollment target was raised to 2,000 as Juilliard went on to cut
its size in order to concentrate on the absolute elite. Other Merrill grants
went for scholarships and salaries. Manhattan is one of the few independent
conservatories to survive and grow.

*University of Rochester/Eastman School of Music, Rochester, New York,
1970—$35,000.* The University of Rochester had such a high endowment
($415 million) with its well-managed investments of Kodak and Xerox that
the Merrill Trust kept evading its appeals. The Eastman School, however,
which had its own endowment of $56 million, did deserve serious support for
the high quality of its graduates as players and conductors. The school is the
site of an annual festival of American music, and its Philharmonic has been
sponsored by the State Department.

*New England Conservatory of Music, Boston, Massachusetts, 1967–
1977—$65,000.* The New England Conservatory, just as good as Eastman but
with an entirely different sort of financial underpinning, is a disturbing example of how an old (1867), famous, large, high-quality, important music school
can exist year after year close to collapse. In 1967 it had 368 undergraduate
and 144 graduate full-time students, with 350 adults and 1,300 children in
the extension programs. Half of the graduates become teachers, and half
become professional performers, employed by most of the symphonies in the
United States, with thirty-three in the Boston Symphony Orchestra alone.
Only a very large gift, however, from Mrs. John D. Rockefeller, Jr., an alumna,
and the energy of the director, Gunther Schuller, had kept the school going.
    In 1971 the finances seemed even worse, with a $1.1 million deficit and
survival purchased by cannibalizing the endowment. Our $20,000 was sup-
posed to maintain impetus and bring in even larger gifts from Ford, Mrs.
Rockefeller again, Mellon, and Firestone. A 137 percent salary increase over
the past five years had been one cause of trouble, and the building was deteriorating. Management promised effective new cost control methods. And
yet the 250 annual student and faculty concerts, free or at modest cost, to
the Boston community were a valuable part of that city's cultural life.

*San Francisco Conservatory of Music, San Francisco, California, 1970–
1977—$40,000* for scholarships and endowment. The Conservatory sees itself
as the only first-quality, independent conservatory west of Oberlin in Ohio.

There was a marked improvement in both size and quality of the student body during this period. One Merrill grant went to endow a violin scholarship. The shortage of outstanding string players is a nationwide problem, and many western students lack the money with which to study with outstanding teachers in the East.

The Conservatory was proud of its tradition of social responsibility, its concerts given in jails, hospitals, and nursing homes, its Foster Student Program of one-to-one teaching at ghetto schools, and its program with Chinese children at the elementary school level. It has recently started a course in Asian music and a chamber music program for high school students.

Seattle Youth Symphony, Seattle, Washington, 1979—$25,000.

Shenandoah College, Conservatory of Music, Winchester, Virginia, 1972, 1976—$30,000.

Ithaca Community Music School, Ithaca, New York, 1974—$5,000. As public schools' budgets cut out classes in the arts, the subject has become expendable. Accordingly, the responsibility is put on private institutions to teach the children whose parents can pay. Because of its policy of open access by any child, this school had serious deficits.

Kodaly Center of America, West Newton, Massachusetts, 1977–1980— $20,000. Two grants were given for teacher and student stipends in the teaching of music according to the system developed by Zoltan Kodaly. Based upon multiethnic folk music, this is a rigid system run by true believers, but their standards for teacher training are high, and the combination of imaginativeness and discipline has helped hold attention and build learning skills among children in devastated communities like the South Bronx. The American artistic establishment is a pretty homogeneous one, and the Kodaly activists with their Hungarian accents bring diversity and intensity.

Society of the Third Street Music School Settlement, New York, New York, 1968, 1981—$20,000. This combination of school and settlement house— teaching the whole child and the whole community—was started in 1894 by a Goucher College graduate who began teaching at 10¢ per lesson in order to bring the joy of music into the lives of the poor. It was supported by old-fashioned philanthropists (Lewisohn, Morgan, and Baruch) and by musicians (Paderewski and Schumann-Heink) who gave concerts in its behalf. Eight-hundred-fifty pupils were involved, both pre-professionals and amateurs, at the time of our first grant. In 1981 $5,000 was given to sustain a program of bringing public school classes into the settlement house for art and music instruction during regular school hours.

Young Audiences, New York, New York, 1962–1981—$45,000. Young Audiences was launched around 1950 to offer musical concerts in the public, parochial, and private schools of New York City. For many children this was their first exposure to live music—a string quartet or brass ensemble, later on ethnic music, folk and modern dance, and theatre—and the closeness to the artists, with music being made by musicians near enough to touch, made an often intense impact. Although the New York City Board of Education tried to cover all 586 elementary schools, the major commitment was to see what could be done for children with emotional and behavioral problems in twenty-seven schools in particularly poor neighborhoods. Our first two grants in 1962 and 1963 went for concerts, instruments, and lessons for those scarred children. By 1981 there were thirty-eight chapters of Young Audiences nationwide, a cumulative audience perhaps of 35 million. Because of decreased government funding for the arts, fund-raising from private sources became frantically competitive, and the last Merrill grant went to increase public awareness through news releases, spot announcements, videotapes, and artists' appearances.

Young Audiences of Massachusetts, Boston, Massachusetts, 1973–1981—$50,000. By the early 1970s public and foundation support for the arts all over the country was falling. Our grants to the Massachusetts branch of Young Audiences were given to build a sounder financial position and to train classroom teachers so they could follow up the impact of these concerts in Boston and even more-deprived small towns of Massachusetts and New Hampshire, as well as to supply jobs for musicians and dancers. In 1981 $10,000 went to build a cash flow reserve. Musicians must be paid promptly, but the City of Boston pays its bill months later, and the money that fills the space in between had to be borrowed at high interest.

Skowhegan School of Painting and Sculpture, Skowhegan, Maine, 1972–1979—$55,000. Skowhegan accepts seventy advanced students for an intensive nine-week course. The atmosphere is one of no-nonsense practicality: painting students grind their own colors, make their own sizing glue, and stretch their own canvasses. There is a strong spirit of criticism and self-criticism and an effort to teach qualities of resilience, honesty, and self-discipline. Art institutes were having a rough time in the early 1970s, borrowing money for operations from endowment. Times became worse, and our last two grants went for salaries, scholarships, a new sewage system, and other efforts to reduce the mortgage and increase the endowment.

Rhode Island School of Design, Providence, Rhode Island, 1972—$50,000 for partial scholarships. With 1,275 students, RISD is the largest fully accredited, independent college of art in the country, with the largest number of applicants and the lowest student-to-faculty ratio (11:1). It has three major departments: the divisions of fine arts, communications design, and architectural studies. Financial aid in 1972 stood at $367,000, with one-half allotted to sixty artistically talented minority students and one-half to 125 middle-income students, priced out of the market.

READING AND WRITING

In *The Book of Laughter and Forgetting,* Milan Kundera writes that Dr. Housak, president of Czechoslovakia, turns his country into a nation of children because they have no sense of the past. There is a socialist present that came out of a cloudy fascist—bourgeois—feudal past, but the Czech Communist party puts into practical effect the theories that George Orwell expressed in *1984:* the party in power can control the future if it is able to exercise control of the past. Accordingly, a Czech librarian must never get too far from his scissors and paste pot as the standards of what is right and wrong, progressive and reactionary, change and rechange not only for the present but for the past.

An American librarian must be prepared for guerrilla raids by moral militants who clean out his shelves of dirty and unpatriotic books. Otherwise he doesn't suffer the dangers of his Czech counterparts. His problem is being ignored. Reading books is not an important part of American culture, and when budgets are cut, libraries are the place to begin. If Americans do not respect the sources of an accurate, objective knowledge of their own past and of the world outside their borders, they become as ignorant as Dr. Housak's subjects.

The Merrill Trust put a total of $2.5 million into libraries: $1,920,000 into school, college, seminary, museum, and scholarly libraries; $300,000 into public libraries, ranging from New York City's to the one at Centerville, Massachusetts; and $275,000 for libraries abroad. The grants went for acquisitions, construction and modernization, endowment, cataloguing, and microfilming. Each trustee was equally interested: here was an obvious way of upgrading our society's levels of civilization along with all the pleasures of a vicarious browse through a bookstore.

A check for $1,000 for new books will be appreciated by any institution you know, but the problems come as much from surfeit as from hunger.

"We're drowning in information and starving for knowledge. The old sausage grinder is going to turn out more sausage than you can eat," stated Rutherford Rogers (*New York Times,* 25 February 1985), former university librarian at Yale, referring to the 800,000 books and 400,000 periodicals published each year around the globe. The whole library system is suffering from overload: too many books, too little money and space, and the problems of unassimilated technological changes. The Research Libraries, a consortium founded in 1974, now links three dozen major research libraries through a computer at Stanford University, which includes catalogues in Chinese, Japanese, Korean, and Arabic. This group has also tried to apportion specialization among its members (Cornell University, for example, collects material on Southeast Asia) and encourages wider use of interlibrary loans. Too few librarians possess sufficient funds or time to plan ahead or work out a philosophy of what they really need. Here is a field for foundation investment, or perhaps one allots that $1,000 check to hire an intelligent clerk to walk along the shelves and pitch out the junk. Yale adds four to five miles of books each year.

New York Public Library, New York, 1972–1980—$250,000. In our role as good citizen we made sizable grants to the New York Public Library as we did to Central Park. Both were institutions that civilized city life. The central building is the core of one of the largest and most used library systems in the world, ranking with the Library of Congress, the British Museum, and the Bibliothèque Nationale in Paris. There are eighty-three branches for service to all New York State residents and even out-of-staters. Over two million readers use the research resources every year. Our first $100,000 went for acquisition and preservation of books and documents in the economics division. Different New York corporations make great use of that division with its one million volumes. These materials are costly, and money is needed to purchase new materials and to microfilm deteriorating books, pamphlets, and periodicals. In 1978 $50,000 went to support the branch library system. These libraries operate free of charge to the public, but budget cuts have recently limited their services.

San Francisco Public Library, San Francisco, California, 1972–1980—$20,000.

Pierpont Morgan Library, New York, New York, 1961–1980—$70,000. J. P. Morgan and his son were great collectors of books as well as of art. The building was completed in 1906, holding a rich collection of first editions and rare volumes. The library became increasingly important during the 1960s and 1970s not only in sharing its facilities with universities but in its research activity with European libraries and its educational work in conservation and restoration, training students to handle any problem in leather or paper. The double pressure of inflation and increased demands burdened even the Morgan's endowment, and our last two grants went for operating support.

Boston Public Library, Boston, Massachusetts, 1979—$20,000 to help supply a permanent base for programs, courses, publications, exhibits, and special events. The New York Public Library has a larger endowment but receives little (and diminishing) support from the city for maintenance. In Boston the city used to handle upkeep well, but the library needed private support for the special intellectual programs that it took seriously and that had been stimulated by a challenge grant from the National Education Association. By 1981 urban decay was seen in cutback of both services and hours in central and branch libraries, and the need by then was for private funds for the simplest level of maintenance.

Boston Athenaeum, Boston, Massachusetts, 1976–1981—$30,000. The Athenaeum is almost the oldest (1807) private library in the country, owned and maintained by 1,050 shareholders with nearly 500,000 volumes plus archives. The generosity of its friends allowed a gentlemanly attitude toward money, but inflation (particularly in book prices), the need for renovation, and a higher endowment for staff pensions and operating costs forced the Athenaeum into the world of fund raising, which included selling its portraits of George and Martha Washington to the National Gallery. Our second grant, $10,000, was to establish a book fund in the field of decorative arts and design.

Newberry Library, Chicago, Illinois, 1981—$10,000. The Newberry Library occupies a handsome old building, enjoys a $19-million endowment, and spends $300,000 per year on new books. Its collections of United States, Latin American, and Renaissance history are among the best in the world. Our grant went for a fund to purchase modern books in history, made through Mary Merrill in honor of her father, Philip Klohr, a lifelong reader of history.

Folger Shakespeare Library, Washington, D.C., 1975–1981—$75,000. This library is administered by the trustees of Amherst College but is entirely independent and must raise its own funds. It has the world's largest collection of books, manuscripts, artworks, and costumes about Shakespeare and the history and production of his plays and, in fact, on the heritage of the English and continental Renaissance. Increased costs for climate control, precautions for water and fire damage, and security raised the costs, and by the late 1970s this library was also monitoring traveling exhibits on Shakespeare's world.

Harvard University, Widener Library, Cambridge, Massachusetts, 1960–1981—$150,000. After the Library of Congress and New York Public Library, Widener is the largest library in the United States and probably the leading university library in the world. The Merrill Trust made six grants, for book repair, endowment, the Robert A. Magowan Fund to strengthen English literature (at 135,000 volumes the largest identifiable collection within the library), and for modernization. This latter need included microform (a process for reproducing printed matter in a much-reduced size), microfiche (a sheet or slide of microfilm containing rows of microimages of pages of printed matter), and the conversion of card catalogues to machine-readable form. The Magowans' youngest son Mark, who worked for a leading publisher of art books, served on the alumni visiting committee to Widener and was particularly interested in these projects.

Bancroft Library, University of California, Berkeley, California, 1977, 1980—$20,000. Bancroft is the rare books collection of the University at Berkeley. One of its major resources is the Mark Twain papers, and both our grants went to this project.

American Antiquarian Society, Worcester, Massachusetts, 1972—$35,000 to improve the society's bindery.

Charles Cole was particularly concerned about the scholarly presses, dying as inexorably as Yiddish. These supplied books that weren't dependent on best-seller lists—works of criticism and history that would be lost while commercial publishers dream of finding another *Jaws.* In 1972 we put up $35,000 to support *Columbia University's* press and $25,000 to the *Cooperative Council of Literary Magazines* in New York; $35,000 went to the *Woodrow Wilson International Center for Scholars* in Washington for the establishment and expansion of the *Wilson Quarterly.*

MEDIA AND PORNOGRAPHY—$500,000

Woe unto them that call evil good.   [Isaiah 5:20]

If one has to watch a lot of television programs, perhaps at the side of an aged parent, one makes all sorts of melancholy conclusions about the state of American culture, with its combination of unbelievably costly technology and intellectual mediocrity. T. S. Eliot, not a reliable critic in this field, looked on television as the equivalent of gonorrhea: a loathsome communicable disease.[4]

Support of public television was a field we tried to stay clear of until the last years of the Trust—when we spent, as well as for radio, $370,000—because the costs were astronomical and because any interest would have had us exposed to every friend, partner, and customer who wanted us to back his favorite station. The Corporation for Public Broadcasting, Exxon and Mobil in search of respectability, and the Ford Foundation are the institutions that

4. Michael Straight, *Twigs for an Eagle's Nest* (New York/Berkeley: Devon Press, 1979), p. 60.

can support individual stations and individual programs, but just because these dinosaurs dominate the field, there is a need for modest creatures like Merrill to fill in the gaps. The furor in 1980 of whether showing "Death of a Princess" on public television would imperil our relations with Saudi Arabia and our supply of oil reveals the danger of too close a dependence upon any major source of financing.

National Gallery of Art, Washington, D.C., 1970—$10,000 to meet production costs of Kenneth Clark's series *Civilization* for showing in schools and on television, the perfect example of what the medium can accomplish and so rarely does.

KQED, San Francisco, California, 1978–1980—$25,000. KQED ranges among the top five audience ratings of the 260 public television stations across the country and is at the very top in terms of public support in relation to community size. One grant went to support "Agenda for a Small Planet," a series of programs on issues of global significance in relation to the interdependence of developed and developing nations.

Educational Broadcasting Corporation (Channel 13/WNET), New York, New York, 1978, 1981—$35,000. WNET is the principal producer of prime-time programs for public television and is the nation's largest public station. At the present time over four hundred schools (public, private, and parochial) turn to Channel 13/WNET for programing during the school day. Over five hundred special teachers use its facilities in their work with home-bound children.

WGBH Educational Foundation, Boston, Massachusetts, 1975–1980—$220,000. WGBH is important for the production and distribution of its own programs as well as transmission of programs by the BBC. It is outstanding for variety and quality. A question: does educational TV reach only its own cult audience, except for spectaculars like its ballet programs? Does it have any influence on either the producers or consumers of commercial television?

In 1975 $5,000 was given for a series on three American Jewish families to show divergence of Jewish background and opinion. Even such small support from a non-Jewish foundation like ours was considered important. This followed a fine program that WGBH distributed on Israeli and Egyptian families who had both lost sons in the war against each other.

In 1977 $200,000 was given for the production of *World*, a series on world problems: labor conflict in Communist Poland, the impact of mass tourism on third-world countries, and the crisis of the textile industry. This grant preceded a Merrill Lynch investment of $250,000 in 1979 on the *Enterprise* series.

In 1980 $15,000 was given for the production of a series on the war in Vietnam, using French, Swedish, North Vietnamese, and American footage on all sides of that agony, trying to put together an integrated, objective presentation of a story that Americans until recently preferred to forget.

WBAI, through the Pacifica Foundation, New York, New York, 1981—$10,000. A small, nonprofit, listener-sponsored station meeting programing needs (women's and community issues, current events, and live arts programs) not furnished by others.

WBUR, Boston, Massachusetts, 1981—$15,000. Sponsored by Boston University, WBUR presents good jazz and classical music, and though more conservative than formerly (the programs of the gay community and from Norfolk Prison have been dropped) it did win a United Press International award in 1980 for the best local news coverage in New England.

Episcopal Radio-TV Foundation, Incorporated, Atlanta, Georgia, 1966–1979—$70,000. From 1966 to 1972 $40,000 was given for programing and running expenses; $30,000 was given in 1978–1979 for the production of C. S. Lewis's *The Chronicles of Narnia.* These books by Lewis have sold over six million copies in this country alone. Costs of film production were estimated at $1.5 million, with additional network air time and promotion amounting to $3 million more. Kraft committed $3 million to the *Narnia* project, but contract negotiations in London and New York, production consultants, executive meetings, and travel costs added up to an additional $140,000, and these costs we helped meet.

I read the whole *Narnia* series twice to my own children and agree that there is a theological seriousness as well as imaginative fantasy to Lewis's writing that can be effectively translated into television. Nevertheless, I found the project disturbing. Can good television (I mean good as opposed to either unbelievably excellent or second-rate) be produced at a reasonable price? Is the search for perfection, at the cost of megabudget technology and administration and therefore financing, worth it? The higher the cost, the greater the need to play things safe with mediocrity of committee aesthetics and subservience to sources of capital. Even good television leads to passivity in children, as passive in refined *Masterpiece Theatre* families as in vulgar *Hogan's Heroes* families, exposed to such quantity that everything runs together and A simply = B = C to the end of time. Educational television brings enrichment expertise into the classroom; too much of it turns the teacher into a technician. The exposure to massive television, whether good or bad (it's usually bad), prepares children for a lifetime of consumption of opinion, reality, and sensation prepared for them by distant centers at great cost, which the viewers pay for one way or another.

What should be foundation policy? *Narnia* is better than Woody Woodpecker. Perhaps the expansion of cable television will allow decentralized programing, which will allow a wider range of people to get into the act. Or so much more quantity that standards drop even further? The Markle Foundation of New York City, which studies and supports the field of mass communications, is just about the only foundation, along with Ford, to look critically at the technology, democratic responsiveness, and educational possibilities of this medium.

Morality in Media, New York, New York, 1976—$10,000. This is a national, multidenominational organization working to stop traffic in pornography, involving a newsletter, radio spots, cooperation with law enforcement groups, and encouraging dialogue on obscenity laws.

Here was a complex issue. The 1970s saw the expansion of two dangerous movements in American society. One was the metastasis of big-business pornography that the Supreme Court's first amendment rulings made impossible to limit. The other was the radical right action groups trying to defend traditional values by bringing prayer into public school classrooms, fighting abortion (which included assaults on abortion clinics), stopping sex education classes in the public schools, censoring libraries for *Huckleberry Finn* and *Catcher in the Rye,* and frightening the easily frightened media executives into tightening up the range of subjects that could be presented on television.

On the one hand, censorship is a step towards the closed society whether we are talking about South Africa, pre-1960 Mississippi, or Czechoslovakia. On the other, an anything-goes climate of pornography, violence, and crime frightens ordinary citizens so that they will choose security, moral and physical, over what they see as license. The fundamentalist liberalism of the American Civil Liberties Union, which feels compelled to defend Nazi demonstrations and hard-core porn, fosters the very backlash—"Is there no way by which we can protect ourselves!"—that considers many aspects of freedom as expendable.

Maybe it is wrong to limit pornography only to explicit sex. There is the pornography of violence on our movie and television screens, the pornography of luxury and total selfishness, and the wonderful things we can buy and play with if we have enough money. There is the pornography of mountains of surplus food while children go hungry in Detroit and in Manila and Port-au-Prince. There is the pornography of a worldwide obsession with war. Maybe those examples are more obscene.

Women Against Pornography, through the Women's Liberation Writing Collective, New York, New York, 1980—$20,000. The Collective, started in 1970 by a $10,000 grant from the *Ladies Home Journal,* launched Women Against Pornography in 1979. It was a militant group whose stand differed from other morality groups in three important ways.

First, it stressed the big-business quality of pornography. According to *Forbes Magazine*, organized pornography is a $4-billion (!?) industry per annum, equal to the combined gross of the record and movie business. *Penthouse, Playboy*, and *Hustler* alone have a combined readership of ten million. The spectacular success of films like *Deep Throat* makes pornography acceptable in suburban shopping malls. Produced for $25,000, it grossed millions. Child pornography is now estimated as having involved 300,000 children under sixteen, some as young as three. The newest market is home video cassettes.

Second, pornography is to be seen as brutality, not as erotica. The June 1978 cover of *Hustler* showed a naked woman being fed head first into a grinder and coming out as chopped meat. Degrading images of women condone an attitude of violence and shape a society in which rape, wife-battering, and child molestation steadily increase. Wife-battering is now considered the most frequently occurring crime in the country. The Department of Justice reported 154,000 cases of rape in 1977, but the FBI estimated that ten times that number went unreported. Rapes are now more violent and humiliating, and one-half of all rape victims are under eighteen. In 1978 three thousand cases of gonorrhea from intercourse were reported in children under nine; nine thousand cases were reported in children ages ten to fourteen.

Third, the fight against pornography must be political. By tours of the world of Times Square; slide show presentations at women's groups, colleges, and high schools (including material on how pornography influences advertising to make violence chic); and media program conferences, the aim is to develop grassroots leadership among women: "You can do something!" The Merrill grant was the first large one that Women Against Pornography received, a proof of respectability.

The president of *Playboy*: "a fascist hate group."

CHAPTER TEN

International

And who is my neighbor?   [Luke 11:29]

Because Merrill Lynch had several offices north of the border and Safeway owned about five hundred stores there, Canada was a natural area for sustained commitment. As individuals the trustees had enjoyed enriching contacts with England, France, and Italy, and it was a pleasure to show our appreciation. If one is interested in music or architecture or wildlife, national frontiers are irrelevant. Charles Cole had worked for the Rockefeller Foundation on Mexican agriculture and had been ambassador to Chile. It was logical for him to see Latin America as a cold war battlefield where our contributions had a role to play. Jewish contacts led us to Israel, and Don Regan's concern for Merrill Lynch involvements plus his quirky pleasure in doing the opposite of everyone else led us to the Arabs.

To go beyond this, however, was difficult. Charles E. Merrill had not been interested. To argue for justice and compassion or, over the long run, for enlightened self-interest, took pushing.

A total of $2.7 million went for Canada and Europe, about $1.14 million for the Caribbean and Latin America (not counting $1 million or more for Hispanics in this country), $1.06 million for the Near East and Asia, $475,000 for black Africa for a total nearing $5.4 million plus $1.3 million for general international service and for American schools and institutes of international studies.

This reaches close to $6.7 million, over 6 percent of our total expenditures, more than we had ever set out to spend. The small scale of the projects, the fact that we often had a factual knowledge of the individuals and agencies involved meant that the money was pretty accurately employed. But given

395

the sad times of our interdependent world, it was not as much as should be spent by Americans, who are so well off and so vulnerable.[1]

CANADA

Relations between Canada and the United States have always been ambiguous. Or at least they have been so from the Canadian point of view, since from the American, the neighboring country exists as a half dozen stereotypes not much more sophisticated than the smiling Mountie on a travel poster. A real question comes of whether Canada, in reality, is a colony, culturally and economically, of the United States: subservient to American movies, television programs, and publishing companies, the major units of its economy the branch offices of American corporations. American friendship is expressed in sentimental terms—the unguarded frontier and gratitude for smuggling the State Department employees out of Teheran—but the neglect and ignorance are real.

Canadian resentment appears in criticism of American philanthropic practices. American foundations give little support to Canadian cultural institutions. American corporations with Canadian branches give primarily to charities chosen by headquarters. The local office feels that it is off the hook with a check to the community chest. Americans take Canadian goodwill for granted and are surprised and a bit hurt when our neighbors complain.

Universities

In 1964 the Foundation started a policy of support ($342,000) to Canadian universities. At that time only 5 percent of the college age group went on to higher education (as against 15 percent in the United States), although enrollment was expected to double within the next decade. The general picture, with one or two exceptions like McGill, was of mediocrity and provincialism. Salaries were so low that an American appointment was much more appealing. Plant and equipment were inadequate and libraries were weak: not one of the thirty-five leading North American university libraries was in Canada. Graduate education, especially in science and technology, had been neglected, and those who studied abroad were apt not to return. Over all, Canadian academic standards were sober, unstimulating, and uncreative, with an interest only in European culture.

1. In Waldemar Nielsen's *The Golden Donors*, only Ford, Rockefeller, and Carnegie among the large foundations concern themselves with any major international giving. Even a huge new foundation as imaginative as Robert Wood Johnson limits itself to concern for American health needs only.

University of British Columbia, Vancouver, 1964—$25,000. This was the second largest English-speaking university in Canada. It was dependent on provincial funding, and the effort to launch satellite institutions meant less money to the university. In 1972 the Trust made a second grant of $10,000 for the purchase of contemporary art, used to expand the graphics collection.

University of Montreal, 1964—$25,000. This is the major French-speaking university in Canada.

University of Manitoba, Winnipeg, 1964—$25,000. The University began as a degree-granting body in 1877, but instruction was given by affiliated Catholic, Presbyterian, and Church of England colleges (and now a Ukrainian one). The University began to offer courses itself in 1900, and a new campus outside town was built in 1929. In 1965 it had 6,000 students. Graduate departments at the larger Canadian universities must be strengthened so that students won't go off to the United States for advanced study. Even in the mid-1960s only 60 percent of university professors in Canada were of Canadian birth.

McGill University, Montreal, 1965—$55,000. McGill was founded in 1821. Its affiliated Royal Victoria College at the end of the nineteenth century was the first college for women in Canada. Fifteen percent of its students are non-Canadian from Hong Kong, the Caribbean, and Africa, giving a strong international atmosphere. Cheaper than an American university of similar quality, it is not sure of its policy of encouraging American students, who sometimes can be economically useful.

University of Saskatchewan, Saskatoon, 1965—$25,000 to strengthen the humanities. In the effort to double the university student population, the federal and provincial governments were starting an average of two universities a year with all the resulting problems imaginable: construction, staffing, and the desperate effort to maintain quality. Upon a university like Saskatchewan there is such pressure of growth that a real question exists of how to achieve excellence. Enrollment went from 5,765 in 1959 to 11,500 in 1964, and the library budget went from $200,000 to $750,000. It had a new institute of northern studies, but since the province's priority is agriculture and engineering, private funds were needed for the humanities.

Memorial University of Newfoundland, St. Johns, 1966—$25,000. Newfoundland, which was an independent dominion, then a British colony 1934–49, then a Canadian province, has the lowest per capita income and the worst sense of isolation of the nation. Operating costs of the first ten years of the University's existence were paid in part by annual grants from the Carnegie

Corporation. There are hopes for a $1-million marine sciences lab. Tuition is only $400, but the province is so poor that the Merrill grant went for scholarships. Only 6 percent of the class of 1965 entered graduate school.

Toronto University, 1966, 1977—$45,000. Founded in 1827, the Toronto University has 100 buildings on the central campus and many others scattered through metropolitan Toronto in subsidiary campuses, including 6,000 students in one meandering building at Scarborough, twenty miles outside of town, and a total enrollment of 23,000. In the 1960s a special effort was made to expand graduate studies, particularly in non-Western fields: China, Japan, Russia, and Islam. In 1977, $20,000 went toward a capital drive to strengthen the graduate schools which enrolled 25 percent of all Canadian graduate students, supply better equipment and facilities for teaching, initiate new programs, and build a more esthetically pleasing physical environment.

Queen's University, Kingston, Ontario, 1967—$25,000.

University of Alberta, Edmonton, 1967—$25,000.

York University, Toronto, 1969, 1973—$50,000. York was started in 1959 as an affiliate of the University of Toronto, became independent in 1965, and is a private university with some federal and provincial support. Students are involved in curriculum and planning, and there is more flexibility and experimentation than at other Canadian universities. It has a Center for Research in Exploratory Space Sciences and plans one in environmental studies. By 1969, with the massive expansion and upgrading of Canadian universities, the much-criticized brain-drain to the south had slowed down. The new complaint against Americans then became that they dominated certain fields, especially in the social sciences; used American texts, analogies, and prejudices; and hired American graduate students as their assistants.

In 1973 $25,000 was given to strengthen the library in Judaica. Recent expansion of courses in Jewish studies across North America has found most institutions with inadequate library resources, particularly in Canada where no university had such a program before ten years ago. When almost half of Canadian Jewry immigrated after 1945, there has been neither time nor resources to develop major nonuniversity collections. With book costs skyrocketing, the faculty must rely on their private libraries and have to lend books to their students. There is a need to buy standard reference works, classical texts, and also archival material in Hebrew Canadiana before it is lost.

University of Prince Edward Island, Charlottetown, 1975—$10,000. In 1964 only one of twelve islanders going to college enrolled in local colleges. The others went off, mainly to Toronto and Montreal, and a large proportion stayed away. The university in such a thinly populated, isolated island is seen not only as a source of jobs, a balance to summer tourist industry, but as a way to make the island livable and stabilize its population.

King's College, Halifax, 1980—$20,000. This college, almost an adjunct of larger, better-known Dalhousie, was founded by Loyalist refugees from King's College, which then became Columbia. Concerned about the provincialism of his institution, King's new president wanted this grant to endow an annual scholarship for a student from New England, even more provincial as far as knowledge of Canada is concerned.

We aided three hospitals in Montreal:

Royal Victoria, 1967—$25,000 to construct laboratory facilities for the division of hematology. One-third of its medical staff are Americans. More emphasis on research than at any other teaching hospital in Canada.

Montreal Children's, 1979—$25,000 for a program to coordinate the scheduling and follow-up of children's immunization through centralized computer control. Little Evan got into the memory bank when he had his diphtheria shot; now the computer will tell the clinic to remind his mother to bring him in for a measles vaccine. By 1979 clinical research had been frozen. Financial constraints impair practical application like this of new knowledge, even for a hospital with Children's prestige that sets standards for institutions ranging from the Arctic to Kenya.

St. Luke, 1980—$20,000. This hospital is proud of its specialty in all forms of liver ailments, but as the major hospital for the French-speaking majority of Montreal it is responsible for clinics and health programs for schools, work centers, and communities among the 300,000 residents of its catchment area. Most funding is from the Province of Quebec, which concerns itself with the maintenance of current services only. The Trust's money went to improve the occupational therapy program. For the year when the citizens of Quebec would vote on whether to negotiate a new constitutional relationship with the rest of Canada, it seemed of value to deliberately choose a French institution.

And the following, mainly in Toronto:

Metropolitan Toronto Zoological Society, 1971—$40,000.

Jewish Family and Child Service of Metropolitan, Toronto, 1970—$25,000 to finance the Trailer House Drug Rehabilitation Program at a time when the American drug plague was spreading across the border.

United Jewish Welfare Fund, 1972—$25,000 to develop services for the noninstitutionalized elderly.

Sir William Campbell Foundation, Campbell House, 1978—$10,000 for furnishings of the Georgian period to a historical center that interested Peter Magowan while he was head of Safeway Stores' international division.

Winnipeg Symphony, 1972—$20,000, called the best orchestra west of Toronto, to improve its string section.

Confederation Center Gallery, Charlottetown, Prince Edward Island, 1974—$10,000. In the smallest and almost the poorest and most isolated of the provinces, the gallery wanted funds to bring theatre, dance, and art out to country schools during the winter months.

There are few binational institutions shared with the United States as there are very few bilingual institutions within Canada.

American Historical Association, Washington, D.C., 1966—$8,000 toward the American share of a $25,000 endowment to award a biannual prize for the best book published on Canadian-American relations, a project that appealed to Charlie Cole.

Roman Catholic Diocese of Portland, Maine, 1970—$25,000 to establish a secondary school for Indians from both Maine and New Brunswick, an effort to cut dropout rates, alcoholism, and the self-destructiveness of American Indian adolescents by teaching them in both their own language and English in a tribal-oriented school.

National Theatre School, Montreal, 1971—$30,000 to commission bilingual plays and put on bilingual productions in high schools. For my part this was one of the best grants the Trust ever made. The efforts to hold Canada together politically have a frighteningly limited cultural foundation to build upon. An institution is French-speaking (if one likes statistics, there are more theatres, mainly French, in Montreal than in all the rest of Canada combined) or English-speaking. With the exception of the National Ballet Company in Ottawa and this school, they don't include both. When the two peoples are angry at each other there are not even places where they can argue face to face. In the Theatre School a class on Racine would be held, of course, in French and one on Shakespeare in English, but those in fencing or stage design or voice control would alternate randomly, and the groups that performed at a high school in Moose Jaw or Trois Rivières were mixed.

In all the routine that work for this Trust entailed, there were some great rewards. One of them was to listen to the fervor of this director as he spoke of trying to convince his countrymen that to possess two languages and two cultures might be taken as a sign of richness and strength, not just division and weakness. An American foundation could share in this effort, for benefit not simply to Canadians.

ENGLAND

For American philanthropists concerned with England, there is the temptation to see an England of the past—the old towns and timeless countryside, the cathedrals and aristocratic homes, and our favorite streets of London—not the present. The English people we see, as we read about them and meet them on the screen, are out of the past—the fresh-cheeked schoolchildren, the honest, slow-moving policemen, tradesmen and sturdy widows, craftsmen and scholars, kindly country folks in worn tweeds. Which is our privilege, of course. If American money goes for repairing cathedrals, British money can be invested in supersonic technology or the needs of Pakistani teenagers in Birmingham. But Americans should have some awareness of what the present is.

In fact, this might be worded more strongly. One subject, still new to most Europeans, where we Americans have experience, is facing the problems of a multiracial society. The resentment, fear, and hatred on both sides in Birmingham, Bradford, Bristol, and Liverpool; the outbreaks of violence; the crisis in jobs and housing; police brutality; the total alienation of the young, nonwhite male—all this we have known over a much longer time and in some cases we have worked out approaches worth emulating. As a beginning, foundations can write checks to English church groups dealing with racial discrimination as well as with cathedral repair. At a more ambitious level, how about fellowships, in both directions, for university students, social workers, community leaders, and police officers? Don't get hung up on credentials. The housewife, white or black, who has learned how to deal with mothers of the other race in keeping their sons from fighting and getting arrested in South Boston has a lot to offer mothers like herself in Leeds or Notting Hill Gate. A two-week visit to England (she could lodge with neighborhood people, and air fare plus a day of sightseeing and shopping in London would be the only major cost) would have her come home with greater status, confidence, and breadth of vision, and she would be ready to welcome her English hostess.

Dealing with the outsider—the Turkish and Sicilian *Gastarbeiter* in Germany, the Algerian and Portuguese in France, the Vietnamese in Czechoslovakia—is a problem that no country is handling well.

(An interesting fact: out of the $1,122,000 the Trust gave to U.K. institutions, all of it went to English institutions, a point raised by Welsh and Scots and ignored by Americans and English.)

Association for Rescue at Sea, New York, New York, 1977—$5,000. The English charity: for the Royal National Lifeboat Institution to purchase a new boat.

Ambiance Inter-Action, New York and London, 1980—$15,000. This was almost our one grant for today's needs. Inter-Action is an interestingly complicated group in Camden, North London, founded by an American, to encourage popular culture and mutual help projects in city neighborhoods. One aim is to reclaim disused urban sites and turn them into gardens. It has helped twenty groups to utilize urban wasteland, to give local groups confidence in dealing with government, and to reduce vandalism by giving young people interesting, useful things to do. Inter-Action sponsors adult and children's plays, a lunch-hour practice theatre for beginning actors, and a community playmobile. Merrill money went toward a rural center for handicapped people and low-cost temporary housing for U.S. and third-world trainees.

Education

London School of Economics, 1973–1977—$50,000 toward moving and rehousing the British Library of Political and Economic Science, the world's largest in this field.

St. Catherine's College, Oxford University, 1975–1981—$80,000. Peter Magowan, who had taken a year of graduate study at St. Catherine's, was concerned that, despite Britain's entrance into the European Economic Community, there was little serious intellectual contact with Europe. In 1975 $30,000 went to support fellowships in European studies. A brilliant economist in the first group of fellows wrote a book on the pros and cons of Greek entrance into the Common Market that had a strong impact on Greek public opinion. In 1981 $50,000 went to fund visits by European scholars.

Churchill College, Cambridge University, 1979—$30,000 to fund two junior research fellowships. Churchill was a deliberate postwar effort to remedy the traditional British weakness in the sciences, and the College was handsomely endowed in laboratories and living facilities. As times became worse, however, both government and private funds became increasingly tied to applied research. There was a little unattached money for long-range theoretical research by bright young scholars at the beginning of their careers. This grant, to which I was led by a friend on the Churchill faculty, and which supported one fellow in mathematics and another in zoology, generated more response than one might have imagined.

American School in London, 1970—$15,000 for operating expenses. Charlie Cole and Doris Magowan were always sympathetic to the needs of children of foreign service personnel, even more true at a school like this oriented toward well-heeled families of executives in the oil and multinational corporations.

Gilman School, Baltimore, 1979—$15,000 to fund a teacher exchange in Eton, where the falling pound and high English costs wear upon teachers going in both directions. Here is a field where a little cash has a tangible impact.

Nature Conservation

Leeds Castle Foundation, Kent, 1978–1980—$15,000. This is a mixed institution, a garden of roses and box, espaliered fruit trees, and rare birds around a castle dating back to 857, at the same time a center for international conferences on medicine and the arts.

Wildfowl Trust, Slimbridge, Gloucestershire, 1977–1980—$70,000 under Sir Peter Scott, famous painter and naturalist, to establish sanctuaries in England and Northern Ireland to illustrate the beauty and diversity of nature and the complexity of the environment. What are the threats to the environment, and how can one combat them? How can wildfowl be used for teaching principles of biology, ecology, and conservation? How can children be reached to give them a lasting commitment to protecting this resource?

Wildlife Preservation Trust International, Philadelphia, 1977–1980—$25,000. An institute on the Island of Jersey, off the coast of Normandy, set up by the author Gerald Durrell to establish and maintain breeding colonies of endangered species like the Mauritius kestrel, the pink pigeon, and flying foxes. One grant went to develop a facility for small predators.

Culture

London Sinfonietta, 1973—$5,000. This is a chamber orchestra specializing in modern music—it had just finished a major Schoenberg series—and needed funds not only to be independent of popular taste (and Arts Council support) but also to give the ample rehearsal time that difficult modern music demands.

American Friends of Covent Garden and the Royal Ballet, 1980–1981— $30,000, for the $16.4 million capital campaign of the Royal Opera House. The British government had promised £650,000 but then withdrew its offer. The opera house is in critical physical condition and badly needs funds for modernizing and upgrading. Since American visitors have shared the beauty of its ballet and opera, it is clearly an obligation for an American foundation.

Halcyon Foundation, New York, New York, 1977–1980—$45,000 for the American Museum in Britain, Bath. The Museum had been founded in 1961 to increase Anglo-American understanding by interpreting the history and arts of the United States. It was the first American museum to be established outside the United States and contained a large research library and historically furnished rooms from the Colonial Period until the Civil War.

Victoria and Albert Museum, South Kensington, London, 1976–1981— $40,000. This Museum, whose cornerstone was laid by Queen Victoria in 1899, puts its accent on the applied arts with a practical objective of improving contemporary design. The severe cutbacks by the mid-1970s in all government support must be offset by private contributions, both for its own exhibits (a need to house its great Oriental collection) and for its services to hundreds of museums and galleries, its programs of conservation and research, and its role as a show window. Handweavers like Mary Merrill see the Textile Department as *the* resource center of the world, with no other place having as great a range of outstanding textiles. Its study room is a mecca, and accordingly there is need for improved storage facilities and conservation. In 1981 $15,000 went to the Department of Textiles and Dress as a reserve fund to purchase valuable textiles as they come on the market. As art prices go up, people sell objects rather than give them to the Victoria and Albert, and the purchase budget cannot keep pace.

Textile Conservation Centre, Hampton Court Palace, Surrey, 1978— $10,000 to support the educational program. The Centre seeks to unite the training of an art historian with that of a technical conservator, in a three-year course whose graduates will head museum conservation departments. Articles in need of repair come from as far as Iran, South Africa, and Japan.

Wyre Forest District Council, 1979—$5,000 to the Bewdley Museum, Worcester, for the purchase and installation of a brass foundry. Bewdley is a small river town between Worcester and Birmingham, and this historical museum tried to show the crafts background of the Midlands and the reality of preindustrial daily life. In hard times the Council authorities cut ever deeper into nonessential services. A modest American grant might not only allow the Museum to expand but might also help draw official attention to itself.

Cathedrals and Other Architectural Programs ($202,000)

Both my sister and I were committed to a program supporting the reconstruction of English cathedrals as a way of preserving that glorious tradition of architecture.

St. Paul's, London, 1972—$50,000. St. Paul's was designed by Sir Christopher Wren after the fire of London in 1666. It incurred direct bomb damage by the Germans during World War II, and there were increasingly serious cracks in foundations and walls caused by traffic movement. The massive twin towers were moving apart, and the great dome itself would soon be in jeopardy. Seven and a half million dollars was needed for emergency repair, of which $1 million would come from the United States.

Westminster Abbey, London, 1975–1981—$90,000, directly and through the Historic Churches Preservation Fund with its office in New York City. The Abbey's first structure was begun under Edward the Confessor, but the existing church dates from Henry III in 1272.

Ely, 1975–1978—$15,000. Ely, started by the Benedictines around 1080, is the noblest and largest of the Norman cathedrals, rising above the fens of Cambridgeshire. Ely is a small town off the beaten track and does not suffer the pollution corroding Canterbury nor the traffic shaking St. Paul's, but sheer age has affected major parts of both surface and structure. Stainless steel rods and concrete grouting were needed to reinforce the great Norman tower and belfry. Our second grant went to restoration of the north side of the Lady Chapel and repair of the pinnacles strengthening the buttresses that keep the walls from buckling.

Canterbury, 1975–1978—$17,000, for urgent repairs against effects of airborne chemical pollution. The problems of deterioration in a modern industrial environment have suddenly become acute, and there is a need to repair stained glass; to clean, repair, support, and replace stone fabric; and to perform basic work on bearing walls and bell towers close to collapse. Also needed are funds to hire craftsmen and train apprentices in masonry and stained glass work.

Wells, 1979–1980—$30,000, to the oldest completely Gothic cathedral in Europe. Its 700-year-old West Front of 300 statues, the greatest gallery of medieval stone sculpture in existence, badly needs restoration. In 1338, cracks in the masonry supporting the great central tower forced addition of inverted arches inside, England's earliest example of architectural conservation. There is a need to clean limestone statues with hot quick-lime poultices and puttying crevices to keep out water and stop freezing and cracking. Stone is used from the original quarry of 1200.

National Trust, London, 1971–1981—$250,000 in ten grants. The National Trust was founded in 1894 by an act of Parliament for promoting the permanent preservation of lands and tenements of beauty or historic interest. These came to include sites of England's earliest history from Hadrian's Wall to Runnymede; homes of rare birds, beasts, and flowers; and historic mansions and their parks, crucial in a country as crowded and urban as England. Lands, houses, and chattels could be accepted in payment of death duties. Next to the Crown and the Forestry Commission, the National Trust, with its 400,000 acres including whole villages, islands, abbeys, and water mills, is the largest landowner in the United Kingdom.

This preservation of the past for the benefit of the living, and for their children, meant a great deal to Doris Magowan. And the aristocratic gardens of these National Trust properties have assumed a new importance in the current destruction of the British landscape. Mixed forests are being replaced by fast-growing pine plantations. Ever larger fields separated by wire fencing replace the sprawling brush fences that sheltered wild flowers, small animals, and insect-eating birds, whose job must be taken by insecticides. The infinite variety of English apples is replaced by two, Delicious and Mackintosh, the only ones acceptable by the European Economic Community, and the old orchards are being bulldozed. All the mistakes ever made by the Americans that we are gradually learning to undo are being frantically copied by the English. The stately gardens funded by American millionaires where colonels' widows exclaim at the rows of delphiniums are closer to scientific reality than the rationalized nonsense of university agronomists.

In 1971–1976, $100,000 was given for the purchases of furniture and paintings at Uppark, Sussex. In *A Writer's Britain* (New York: Knopf, 1979) Margaret Drabble mentions that H. G. Wells's mother was a housekeeper at Uppark, where the servants' quarters were landscaped out of sight underground because their intrusive presence would spoil the view. In *The Time Machine* Wells projected a future where the laboring classes lived in tunnels and caves beneath the earth, emerging at night to prey upon the pretty, helpless, useless upper classes.

In 1973–1975, $40,000 was given to the National Trust to purchase furnishings in Trust houses that would otherwise be sold or dispersed.

In 1977, $25,000 was given for renovation and preservation of Mompesson, an eighteenth-century townhouse in the cathedral close at Salisbury: to keep the house open, repair flooring, restore woodwork, and buy a chandelier, carpets, and curtains.

In 1978, $20,000 went for restoration of the state bedroom, library, and parlor of Hanbury Hall, completed in 1701.

In 1979, $30,000 helped furnish two rooms in Claydon House in Buckinghamshire.

In 1981, $15,000 went for restoration of Baddesley Clinton, a Tudor house with beautiful gardens near Birmingham.

EUROPE

American Services

The schools, libraries, hospitals, and churches founded for Americans or shared, like the Protestant cemeteries, with the English were designed for a more leisurely style of travel than today's, but even if they are not noticed by the tourist six hours from home, they still serve the student, artist, businessman, government official, or wanderer who make their sojourn abroad, and often they serve the foreigner whose culture doesn't enjoy the institutions that Americans take for granted.

American Library in Paris, 1977—$10,000. A convenient, well-organized, courteously run facility that is more patronized by the French than the Americans for it is one of the few libraries in France where it is easy to use a book or find reference material.

American Hospital in Paris, 1972—$50,000. This is the place of last resort for traveler and exile.

International Institute for Girls in Spain, Madrid, 1971—$25,000. This was started in the late nineteenth century by Smith, Mount Holyoke, and Wellesley graduates as a Protestant school for girls but, though retaining its original name, gradually turned itself into the American Library. During the Franco period it contained a variety of books that the average Spanish library could not risk, and in democratic Spain it became a valuable example of what is meant by a comprehensive modern library. With inflation and the costs of new benefits to its staff, the Institute, like so many cultural institutions everywhere, is close to extinction.

American Academy in Rome, 1976–1979—$65,000. Other nations also have academies in Rome, but the American is the only one financed solely by private gifts and endowment. It provides wonderful facilities and living quarters for artists and scholars who can work at leisure, with freedom and a lack of pressure hard to find in American universities.

Villa I Tatti, Florence, 1977—$20,000, for the Center for Italian Renaissance Studies. This beautiful villa, originally the home of Bernard Berenson, the art historian, is administered, but not supported by Harvard University, and supplies library facilities for scholars, particularly in their critical early years, to develop their talents.

St. James Protestant Episcopal Church, Florence, 1965—$10,000. This institution was attended by a niece of the Magowans while she studied music.

Education

Catholic University of Lublin, through the Catholic Relief Services, *New York City, 1959—$25,000.* The Polish government was less totalitarian than most communist states, and one of the exceptions it tolerated was this autonomous university in southeastern Poland. It possessed schools of theology, law, teacher training, and humanities, and although its facilities were much poorer than those of the Marie Sklodowska Curie University in the same city, its integrity made it a valuable part of Poland's limited independence. Our gift supplied hard currency for student and faculty study in the West and for the purchase of books and scientific equipment.

Polish Institute of Arts and Sciences in America, New York, New York, 1959, 1962—$20,000. When the relatively liberal Wradislaw Gomulka replaced the previous Stalinist regime in 1956, the Ford Foundation exploited this thaw by funding a generous program of foreign study fellowships in Western Europe as well as the United States. Although afraid of heretical ideas, the Polish government needed non-Soviet training for students in medicine, science, and technology. Ford agreed under the condition that for every two fellowships granted in these fields, a third would be in the humanities. The long-range imagination of this program made it one of the finest examples of American foundation administration.

By 1959 the Polish thaw had hardened again and the Merrill Trust possessed a tiny fraction of Ford's resources, but through the Institute of Arts and Sciences we sent money to *Kultura*, an emigré magazine in a working class suburb of Paris that also ran a cultural and documentation center. Polish students, writers, and artists who found themselves in Paris were always sure of receiving whatever help the magazine could afford, and our money went to augment its resources and aid these fragile contacts between East and West.

College of Europe, Belgium, 1975—$15,000. The College of Europe had been started shortly after the end of World War II to supply graduate education in the social sciences, mainly to students from Belgium, Holland, Germany, Italy, and France. Its director since the mid-1960s, a former professor at the Catholic University of Lublin named Jerzy Lukaszewski, was concerned about the need for scholarship support to students from countries outside the European Economic Community: from newly democratic Spain and Portugal and from Poland, Romania, Egypt, and Turkey, not only because they had so much to learn, but because their hunger for new ideas meant they had so much to give students who took for granted the freedom and efficiency of Western Europe.

American-Scandinavian Foundation, New York, New York, 1977—$5,000, for Icelandic-American cultural exchange.

Salzburg Seminar in American Studies, Cambridge, Massachusetts, 1972– 1979—$65,000. This summer institute was started in the 1950s as a way of sharing American economic and intellectual concerns with European students and perhaps more important, ways of looking at those concerns. It had much the same goals in mind as my father in launching the Merrill Institute for economists, businessmen, and government officials in Southampton, Long Island. With the passage of time both funding and leadership became increasingly European, but the Salzburg Seminar remains an important part of American-European intellectual exchange. The Seminar sent European students to study and teach at American universities and brought Americans to Salzburg.

Thessalonica Agricultural and Industrial Institute, New York, New York, 1971–1981—$70,000. This was a large school, 1,000 students from grade nine through junior college, for small-town Greek boys training to be more efficient farmers, carpenters, electricians, machinists, and business managers, going against the grain of the usual Greek lycée whose students want to enter the professions and live in Athens. Girls are now admitted with training in child care, home economics, family planning, and village skills.

Anatolia College, Thessalonica, Greece, 1972—$25,000. The College took its name from the Greek refugees coming out of Turkey in the 1920s who desperately needed an education to make a new start for themselves. It was part of the great American Protestant contribution in the Balkans and Near

East. The Merrill grant came during the Papadopoulos dictatorship and was used for management education needed in that time of economic expansion.

St. Gerard's School, Bray, County Wicklow, Ireland, 1978, 1980—$20,000. This school south of Dublin would be considered conservative and authoritarian by American standards, yet it was a strong effort to modernize Irish education through coeducation, foreign exchange programs (including one with my own school), respect for science, skilled attention to the needs of slow learners, and less emphasis on sectarian religion. Ireland has a new industrial structure and a newly rich business class, and St. Gerard's headmaster was trying to build a school that would meet their needs.

Virgilian Society of America, South Norwalk, Connecticut, 1964–1976— $15,000. This Society was committed to improving the teaching of Latin in American schools, and one phase of this was a small summer school at Cumae on the Bay of Naples where teachers could study classical literature and culture.

American Hungarian Foundation, New Brunswick, New Jersey, 1976– 1978—$40,000. An old friend of Bob Magowan's had brought our attention to this foundation, which encouraged student exchange over a wide age level.

Culture and Society

Irish Georgian Society, New York, New York, 1978—$5,000, for the restoration of eighteenth-century buildings.

National Museum of Ireland, Dublin, 1981—$15,000, for the Art and Industrial Division to hire a full-time cabinetmaker and restorer.

Versailles Foundation, New York, New York, 1973–1981—$105,000. This was primarily the creation of a brilliant curator, Gerald van der Kamp, who was trying to restore and maintain the Palace of Versailles as an international monument. Most of our money went for the restoration of the great Salon des Glaces and also the Petit Trianon, and repairs of the Napoleonic rooms after a Breton nationalist exploded a bomb in the palace. Van der Kamp became interested in restoring Monet's house and gardens at Giverny where as an old man Monet painted his bridge and lily ponds over and over again. Our four grants toward that project made one of our favorite decisions.

Committee for the Rescue of Italian Art, Florence, 1966—$10,000. This committee started up for emergency aid in the Florence flood and then broadened to include Venice.

Giorgio Cini Foundation, Venice, 1976—$20,000.

International Fund for Monuments, Venice Committee, New York, New York, 1970–1977—$30,000. In the tremendous effort needed to protect the city of Venice from tidal flooding, decay of its ancient foundations, and corrosion of the building's stone work, one problem was to find an organization more committed to serving the city than its own executives. My sister respected this organization as well as the art and architecture of the city.

Groton School, Groton, Massachusetts, 1965–1974—$47,500. We made four grants to support the archaeological dig at Lefkandi (a major early settlement area of Greece, 3000–700 B.C.) on the island of Euboea by Hugh Sackett, one of Groton's teachers and a friend of Peter Magowan.

American School of Classical Studies at Athens, Boston, Massachusetts, 1971–1976—$60,000, for endowment to support book acquisitions of the famous Gennadius Library of Byzantine, Renaissance, and modern studies and for publications of the School's excavations at Isthmia.

Claremont Graduate School, Claremont, California, 1971—$30,000, to support the Institute for Antiquity and Christianity's sponsorship of cataloging, microfilming, and repair of manuscripts and books in the library of St. John the Theologian on Patmos. Patmos had not suffered the burning and looting of the other Aegean islands, and its library offers a fine documentary source on the economic, political, and cultural life of the Balkans.

Modern Greek Studies Association, Cambridge, Massachusetts, 1981— $10,000. As the Greek immigrant community becomes more established and confident, it feels the need to examine its cultural traditions and share them with outsiders. Our gift went to maintain the Association's quarterly on Byzantine and modern studies.

Hellenic Society for the Protection of Nature, Athens, 1972—$10,000. To Greeks, beaches are made to build hotels on, and animals are made to be shot. The Society is the sole conservation group in Greece, as usual the creation of one bad-tempered eccentric who pressures the government to enforce existing laws on nature preserves, pressures strip miners to replant trees and the power company to erect nesting platforms on top of electricity pylons, and pressures fishermen to complain about fertilizer and pesticide run-offs. Local mayors are beginning to be concerned about pollution, but there is little interest in conservation in the Mediterranean area, which the Aswan Dam is turning into a dead sea. An activist seeks refuge in the ultimate argument: if sea and beaches become hopelessly polluted, this will turn away tourists.

Friends of Danilo Dolci through the Congregational Board of Missions, *New York, New York, 1963—$10,000*. Dolci was a Sicilian social worker who involved himself in teaching the poor to organize themselves against exploitation by landowners, terrorism by the Mafia, and neglect by the state, using Gandhian methods of vivid direct action. This small, early grant caused a hot dispute within the Trust. Wasn't support of such an undertaking the responsibility of all those wealthy Milanese? For the wealthy Milanese concerned with smuggling their capital into Swiss banks, cheating on their taxes, and avoiding being kidnapped, the poor of Sicily are further away than the moon. Who is one's neighbor?

LATIN AMERICA—$1,141,500

Mexico—$184,500

Poor Mexico—so far from God, so close to the United States.   [Octavio Paz]

The relationship between Mexico and the United States is a hopeless one. Both sides are caught by history, myth, and tomorrow's newspaper. One country is so poor, with such unemployment and inflation, and so tortured by the out-of-control birthrate. The Yanquis grabbed Texas and California and captured the capital, their marines storming the cliffs of Chapultepec, and the last cadet wraps himself in the tricolor and hurls himself to death. The Yanquis grabbed the oil, mines, railroads, were pushed away after the 1911 revolution, and came back to own the banks and businesses. They hint that they might be willing to import the great vegetable surpluses of Sonora, then change their minds, slap on a quota or a new set of specifications, and give not a thought to the tomatoes rotting in the fields.

The statistics are simple. The 1940 census gave Mexico a population of 19.5 million, the 1980 estimate is 65 million. In 1940 Mexico City was less than 1.5 million, today it is around 12 million. The estimate for 2000 runs about 20 million, though it is hard to believe there will be water or oxygen for that number. Inflation, made worse by the oil revenues, made worse again by the collapse of the peso, runs over 30 percent, unemployment over 20 percent, disguised by traditional styles of underemployment, whether by peddling plastic combs or sitting at a government desk. The only escape route is emigration, temporary or permanent, legal or illegal.

From the U.S. point of view, the problem is so staggering that we do not know how to react. In its twenty-three years the Charles E. Merrill trust appropriated less than $200,000 to projects directly connected with Mexico. Although the projects were useful, our insensitivity to the scale of Mexican needs is typical of American neglect. On the other hand, the tangle of rival political authorities, irresponsible personalities, rhetoric, and violence and corruption leads to a paralysis difficult for any private institution to function within.

El Colegio de Mexico, 1966—$10,000. This is a small, high-class graduate school, mainly of scholars in the social sciences, in Mexico City. Our money went toward stipends for visiting professors.

Universidad Autonoma de Guadalajara, 1976—$7,000. This university is a wealthy, fast-growing, conservative private university oriented toward problems of economic development and technology rather than politics, with a medical school popular among Americans. Since Mexico has been famous for its artists, this gift for paintings to hang in the new buildings seemed a logical sign of our foundation's respect.

University of Arizona, 1968, 1972—$35,000, Department of Agricultural Economics, to establish a research program in that field at the University of Sonora, Hermosillo. Northern Sonora has become an important producer of cattle, tomatoes, cotton, wheat, and rice. With genetic research, intensive irrigation, and fertilizer use, the yield per acre and the costs have increased markedly, but the university offers no training in the business aspects of agriculture. A cooperative program has been established between the two universities with students and faculty going in both directions.

A grant of $10,000 was given in 1972 to support research on nontariff and quantitative restrictions on U.S. Common Market trade in agricultural products. Such study, if turned to practical use, is crucial for Mexican exporters.

Catholic Relief Services, New York, New York, 1974–1976—$30,000. Ten thousand dollars was divided between water supply projects for Indian farmers in the southern state of Chiapas and scholarships in basic agricultural skills of farmers in the Socio-Cultural Institute of Nacajuca, Tabasco; $20,000 went for a development program in Yucatan. The theory was sensible, to strengthen the economic and social resources of the villages so that refugees would not flock to Mexico City or the U.S. border, but the scale was inadequate.

Acción International, Cambridge, Massachusetts, 1979—$15,000. Acción is a community self-help and economic development agency started in Caracas in the early 1960s. Its first aim was to show the newcomers from the villages how to survive in the city; how to work together to obtain services like water, sewerage, electricity, bus transportation, and schooling from the authorities; and how to find housing and in the process break out of the atomization of city life, learn to trust and rely on others as well as on oneself, and develop leadership with stress on pragmatic methods rather than ideology. Acción then went on to economic objectives. It sought to combat the universal Latin American disease of unemployment by encouraging small-scale, entrepreneurial activity as opposed to overcentralized, overadministered government projects or the bringing in of foreign industry based upon low wages and, in the long run, exportation of capital. The third objective was for the Americans to back out of the process, leaving both administration and funding of the projects in local hands. I was much impressed by what I saw of Acción staff in Peru, Brazil, and Costa Rica as well as in Cambridge, and by their pragmatic, humane approach to social problems, and persuaded the Trust to make six grants amounting to $141,000 between 1967 and 1981.

The Mexican project was in the northern city of Monterrey (population two million), which had a large industrial base but few social services and little attempt to remedy unemployment though only one-third of the heads of families have fixed jobs. With business, university, and government cooperation, the Acción branch in Monterrey might become the catalyst for a project to provide technical assistance and guarantee loans to microbusinesses from local banks. The Trust grant helped supply start-up capital, but there was enough Mexican interest in the project for it to become self-sufficient within three years.

American Friends Service Committee, Philadelphia, Pennsylvania, 1965— $12,000 to support a family planning program in Mexico City.

Pathfinder Fund, Chestnut Hill, Massachusetts, 1978—$25,000, for an injectable contraceptive demonstration project in Mexico. Any direct U.S. involvement, private or public, in Latin America stirs up such a visceral response that a clinical program like this, which can be replicated anywhere, has better chances for success if the presentation center is in Mexico.

Population Institute, Washington, D.C., 1977–1980—$25,000. The Institute put its emphasis on the direct spreading by every means possible of the message of birth control. On one hand an aim was to bring together leaders from all Latin American national broadcasting systems for a conference in Mexico City on the relation between the media and population control, on the other to sponsor pop songs that reached the teenager, transistor in hand, standing on a street corner in Vera Cruz or East Los Angeles, about what is meant by sexual responsibility. The Institute set up its major Latin American office in Costa Rica, whose population growth rate—once higher than Mexico's—had been brought down from 3.6 percent to 2.8 percent within ten years as a result of an intensive family planning program broadcast over all the radio stations. In Mexico, enthusiastic government support from President

Lopez Portillo reversed a long pro-natalist policy and helped lower a 3.4 percent growth rate in 1960–1970 to 2.5 percent by 1982.

The Population Institute, run by a go-getter named Rodney Shaw, felt that this turnaround in two countries as different as Mexico and Costa Rica showed what could be accomplished through sustained media propaganda, by winning over the national leadership (including the Mexican Council of Bishops, which does not see eye-to-eye with the Vatican), and by establishing a wide network of family planning clinics in cities and towns. One can speak to young women who would like education and jobs for themselves and young men who are not condemned to prove their macho self-worth by the number of children they father.

Puerto Rico and the Caribbean—$225,000

The difficulty of knowing where to place Puerto Rico in this book reflects the ambiguity of its status, neither a state nor a colony, to be included after Mexico as part of Latin America, part of the Caribbean (or adjunct of New York City?).

Catholic University of Puerto Rico, Ponce, 1969–1979—$50,000. This university was founded in 1948 in the island's second largest city. Our first grant went to support student loan funds as a way to augment the low financial aid supplied by the U.S. and Puerto Rican governments. In 1975, $10,000 was given for the College of Sciences. Better prepared students from private schools went to the state university; weaker students to the more expensive Catholic University. A special need was to train more women in science so they might better participate in the Puerto Rican economy. In 1978, $15,000 went to the new School of Medicine to train primary care doctors.

College of the Sacred Heart, Santurce, 1970—$25,000, to expand library holdings. The College sets itself to educate women for positions of leadership in affairs of the island and to serve as mothers of future citizens.

University of Puerto Rico, Rio Piedras, San Juan, 1968—$30,000 to help establish a graduate school of library science. In its central and satellite campuses the university at the end of the 1960s enrolled 28,000 students. With the rapid increase of the island's gross national product in the 1960s came an increasing demand for college-trained personnel, and the Commonwealth government had stated its determination to pay for the higher education of all qualified students who wanted it. There was a need for professional librarians, desperately short in the entire Caribbean area, and therefore of a crash program to train Puerto Ricans in U.S. graduate schools and bring them back to train local staff.

College Entrance Examination Board, New York, New York, 1964— *$20,000,* to train counselors of high school students in Puerto Rico in order to allow the graduates to fit more readily into mainland colleges.

Caribbean Economic Development Corporation, San Juan, 1971—$30,000, to finance the activities of the North-South Center, an organization of importance to Dr. Cole as a channel of Latin-United States dialogue and a sign of Puerto Rican importance in hemisphere economic, cultural, and scientific life.

By the 1980s the combination of hard times, ever-increasing pressures of population with escape routes to England and the United States now closed, nationalism, and a growing spirit of revolution had made the whole Caribbean an explosive area. The easy solution of just more tourism forced a terrible contrast with local poverty that perhaps did more harm than good. The Caribbean Basin Initiative of the Reagan administration sought to face unemployment by encouraging the growth of light industry, based on the region's one surplus, cheap labor, yet this was a doubtful solution when it simply encouraged American employers to shut down plants in the United States in order to start up one more low-cost export platform. The need to invade Grenada was blamed on the Cubans and of course the Russians. This Falklands-style "victory" showed how easy it is to win popular support for any nationalist adventure.

University College of the West Indies, Kingston, Jamaica, 1964—$10,000. When the former British islands became independent, there was a fleeting hope that they might bind together in a working confederation whose symbol would be this university. Economic competition and the fierce rivalry between the islands' politicians kept this from working out.

St. Croix Country Day School, Virgin Islands, 1979—$5,000, a recent school that aims to supply good academic education and serve as a source of unity (the enrollment is half-and-half black and white) in an intensely divided society. There is also a need to train skilled local labor (a contractor will pay an M.B.A. $12,000 and a concrete finisher $40,000) and instill a respect for work on an island with too many unemployed blacks and idle whites.

Inter-American Improvement Association, Richmond, California, 1968— *$10,000,* to start a comprehensive boarding school in Saint Ann, Jamaica, in an effort to raise standards of living and economic productivity. Before independence few children went beyond primary school, and there is a need for every level of practical skill.

Acción International, Cambridge, Massachusetts, 1981—$10,000, to help start up a microcredit program among the street hawkers of Santo Domingo. The tiny entrepreneurs of the informal economy have the energetic self-interest to look after themselves if they can be aided to borrow $50 to $500 capital at 15 percent, as opposed to 30–35 percent, in order to purchase a *triciclo* or a set of shoe repair tools. They can learn to work together through a cooperative that disciplines its members on repayment (and keeps the interest down) and encourages confidence and self-awareness.

Haiti is the poorest, most densely populated country in the western hemisphere. The aim of most Haitians is to escape to the United States, but where Americans are sympathetic to white, middle-class Cubans fleeing communism, they aren't to black Haitians fleeing poverty and a noncommunist dictatorship. In the promised land they are apt to be held in concentration camps run by the Justice Department or recruited by labor contractors in Florida in a system of almost debt peonage.

Holy Trinity School, Port-au-Prince, 1970—$15,000, for scholarship aid to Episcopalian students. This is a large (1,000) primary school for boys and girls run by forty nuns. Funds, staff, and facilities are inadequate, and the tuition of $2.00 to $4.00 per month can be paid by only a few families. The school provides a noon meal and medical and dental work and has begun a head start program for orphans.

*Friends of École la Providence, Newton Centre, Massachusetts, 1979—$5,000.*This school, whose funding center is in a Boston suburb, trains Haitians in agricultural and vocational skills (dressmaking, tailoring, house building) so that they can make a living in the villages. The usual government lycée is city-oriented and motivates its graduates to go to New York. The Haitian government claims to be concerned about rural development, and what happens at La Providence can serve as a model elsewhere.

Central America ($250,000)

Central America shows U.S. policy at perhaps its worst. We have exploited it through giant companies, United Fruit the best known, approved of oppressive land-owning and business oligarchies, and supported the worst type of military dictators (as F.D.R. said of Anastasio Somoza during World War II: "He's a son-of-a-bitch, but he's *our* son-of-a-bitch"). When the Arbenz administration sought to nationalize the large estates in Guatemala, the CIA helped to overthrow him. We are left now with the savage civil war in El Salvador, the growing civil war in Nicaragua, and the instinctive policy of the Reagan administration to come down in favor of the Right. An unavoidable conclusion is that Central America is as locked into U.S. control as Eastern Europe is to Russian—"It's *our* turf!" No serious change in power relationships will be tolerated for any reason. There is little that a private foundation can do besides backing isolated, decently run projects.

Guatemala

Catholic Relief Services, 1972—$10,000, for an Indian education program. Sixty-five percent of children die before age five. A 3 percent growth rate means that 50 percent of the population is under eighteen. Two percent own 72 percent of the land. Malnutrition kills children through pneumonia and tuberculosis and leaves survivors stunted. Catholic Relief Services wanted to hire an American and a German woman to design film strips for teachers to show Indian women better techniques of food selection and preparation. Many common fruits and plants have good vitamins and mineral content to augment the staple corn and beans. These simple goals would show women how to gain more control of their lives and play a more self-directed role in society.

In 1976, $20,000 was given for the relief of victims of the February earthquake that left 22,000 dead, 75,000 injured, and 1,000,000 homeless. Within hours Catholic Relief Services acted and started shipping tremendous quantities of vaccines, antibiotics, blankets, tools, and shelter materials. A question: does the very massiveness of American aid deculturalize the people who receive it?

Oxfam America, Boston, Massachusetts, 1979—$7,500. Oxfam's main goal is to build economic and social life in rural communities and avoid the cancerous growth of a Mexico City. After the 1976 earthquake, it set up Program Kuchubal to help villagers rebuild their homes with cheap and locally available antiseismic materials. The physical side of disaster relief, moreover, must always be subordinate to the social, training villagers in working together and acquiring leadership skills. The tragic result of this policy, however, is that to train natural leaders to positions of authority marks them for assassination by the hit squads of the dictatorship, whose purpose is to liquidate exactly such troublemakers.

Honduras—$175,000

Because of trustee Charles Cole's State Department contacts, Honduras received more money than any other Latin American country except Mexico.

Escuela Agricultural Panamericana, Boston, Massachusetts, 1978–1979—$35,000, a technical school offering training in livestock raising, use of modern machinery, the basic agricultural sciences. Its 260 students come from fourteen countries.

Catholic Relief Services, New York, New York, 1966–1975—$130,000. Through the United States Ambassador, Joseph Jova, $20,000 was given in 1966 to encourage farmers to emerge from misery and poverty, change their thinking and values, gain a sense of hope and initiative, and avoid the violence growing in Guatemala. Of this first grant, $10,000 went to train local monitors who would interpret and utilize the National Radio Schools that present material on literacy and home economics as well as music. The other $10,000 went to train community leaders in consumer, production, and credit co-ops. Rural people have so little initiative, Ambassador Jova stated, and need honest, intelligent, and unemotional leadership.

In 1968, $35,000 went to the *Honduran-American Binational Cultural Institute* in Tegucigalpa and San Pedro Sulá for new construction. The latter town is a fast-growing agriculture center with a large concentration of American firms and therefore has the need for English-speaking employees. Dr. Cole supported the appeal by writing: "These Binational Centers are institutions where local nationals overtly identify themselves with the United States and further objectives which it approves and supports. They are living and visible examples of the private, democratic organizations so characteristic of the United States—and play a significant role in destroying myths about the imperialism and materialism of the United States."

In 1969, $20,000 was given to finance a leadership training program conducted by Caritas in the areas affected by Marxist guerillas infiltrating across the Guatemalan border. Again Ambassador Jova stressed the need for honest unemotional leadership. Probably he was right. Any emotional demand for justice might well result in the death of that leader. The Trust grant would be directly supervised by the ambassador's office to ensure higher productivity in this country that, despite its position as the third most important banana-growing nation in the world, suffers from 50 percent illiteracy, high child mortality, 3.4 percent annual population growth, and the worst living conditions of any Latin American country except Bolivia.

In 1971, $25,000 was given to encourage Farmers Housewives' Clubs. In Honduras the most exploited are the women, who live a life of drudgery, fatalism, distrust, and loneliness. They rise at four to grind corn for tortillas, haul water from contaminated streams, and bear up to ten children of whom half will die by age five. These housewives' clubs began in 1967, partly as a result of new ideas spread by the radio schools and partly from a co-op started to distribute United States food supplies. This experiment in democratic self-organization provoked a flood of new interests, skills, and demands among women. An interest in family planning will rise out of these new ideas, not from foreign propaganda.

Acción International, Cambridge, Massachusetts, $10,000, to encourage fruit and vegetable co-ops on the Costa Rican model.

These projects leave one with troubled thoughts. Honduras is so poor that any money that may alleviate misery and encourage new leadership, offer some spark and hope to women, or build new housing is worth voting. On the other hand, given the power of United Fruit, the most useful thing a foundation might do would be to encourage labor unions among the banana workers so they demanded something as simple as higher wages; but the American weapons in the hands of the police and the military are sold and bought expressly to prevent this. Food given by the U.S. government in crisis times keeps starvation from becoming apocalyptic. Merrill grants help teach English through the Binational Cultural Institutes so that American corporations can hire more useful employees and train rural leadership unemotional enough to know the limits of what it is wise to ask for. In this colonial situation the Merrill Trust plays a cosmetic role designed to fool the natives or, more likely, Americans as to what reality is.

And if by the mid-1980s Honduras is being converted into a massive, long-term staging area for potential U.S. military action against Nicaragua, and anywhere else, civilian needs become less and less relevant.

Nicaragua

Catholic Relief Services, 1973—$20,000, for earthquake rehabilitation. The international aid for this catastrophe was largely made use of, as was most else in Nicaragua, for the profit of the Somoza family. But by the late 1970s guerrilla opposition turned into civil war, and despite the military resources earlier supplied by the Americans, Somoza was overthrown. The question arose of how pluralistic, how Marxist was the more-or-less democratic coalition that replaced the military dictatorship. Like Russians, Americans are made nervous by democratic socialism—Sandinismo and Solidarity, Allende's in Chile and Dubček's in Czechoslovakia: it cannot be fitted into the naive political education they have received. Russians blame the CIA. Americans prefer to imagine any socialist movement as simply a front for the string-pullers in Havana and Moscow, and by their hostility they then obtain the totalitarian reality they have proclaimed.

The Catholic church has outgrown this simplistic desire for purity, and, in 1979, $15,000 from the Trust was sent through Catholic Relief Services toward a program of employment creation in San Judas, a working class barrio in Managua where 500 homes were destroyed in the civil war and which by then was suffering 50 percent unemployment. A local group was trying to organize a cooperative clothing factory that would produce shirts, jobs, practice in cooperative administration, and set an example of American and Catholic concerns.

Should one help a Marxist government? Should one help a military dictatorship? Precise philanthropy may more effectively reach the people who need it in Nicaragua than in Honduras and Guatemala. If Americans free themselves from their paranoia about socialism, they might find, in the long run, the Sandinista pattern a more hopeful one in Latin America than control by foreign banks and corporations and domestic police and military until, when the revolution of despair does come, everything blows apart.

Costa Rica

University of Costa Rica, San Jose, 1971—$30,000, to finance a teachers' conference to implement academic reform, ranging from kindergarten to graduate school, which could be a pilot program for all Latin America. Charlie Cole had a great respect for Costa Rica: a long-time tradition of democracy, no army, and with 35 percent of the national budget directed to education. Nevertheless, high oil and other import costs, bills due for foolish spending in fat times, and high fixed costs of a welfare system that falling commodity prices could no longer pay for (as with Uruguay) meant inflation and unemployment and the collapse of the currency—problems that a traditional leadership, whether liberal or conservative, did not know how to handle. When asked for American help, Jeane Kirkpatrick replied by offering new weapons and training to the gendarmerie.

Acción, 1981—$10,000 for rural projects like reforestation, development of production and marketing co-ops in fruit and vegetables, and experiment in new products like honey, milk, cheese. Large-scale American capital was coming in for cattle ranching and commodity farming (Dole pineapples), which led to deforestation and the dislocation of farmers who, as everywhere else, took refuge in the capital city. Can one reverse the process through better management of subsistence farming?

South America—$380,000

A toast to the brave people of Bolivia. [Ronald Reagan at a state dinner in Brasilia, 1984]

Chile—$145,000

Dr. Cole retired as president of Amherst in 1960, went to work for the Rockefeller Foundation in their program of Mexican agricultural development, and was appointed ambassador to Chile by President Kennedy. He took his job seriously, acquired respect for the leadership of the Christian Democrat presidents Alessandri and Frei, admired the honesty and concern for constitutional procedure of its army and gendarmerie, and feared the radicalism of its socialist and communist unions under the leadership of Allende. For these reasons he encouraged us to support cooperatives under Catholic direction that might meet the desperate needs of the poor, undercut the claims of the Marxists that they alone had a message to offer, and allow useful patronage from the American embassy.

Cole had retired before Allende took power, but he was so affronted by what he considered the excesses of that regime that he could not form an objective judgment on what the Pinochet dictatorship wreaked upon Chile.

Catholic Relief Services, 1962–1966—$105,000 in eight grants. Forty thousand dollars went to a cultural center and garden co-op for the Mapuche Indians in the southern village of Chol Chol under Father James Mundell, a priest whom Dr. Cole admired.

In 1962, $15,000 was given to finance a clothes-making co-op in the slums of Santiago under the auspices of Techo (which means *roof*). Cole felt that the Communists exploited the anger of the poor but did nothing to help them make any real improvement in their lives nor did they allow any other group to help.

In 1963, $10,000 more was given to help a waste paper co-op increase its reclamation capacity, providing capital to buy a second truck, a wire bailer, a mechanical press, and a sanitary washroom. This loan, whose repayment by the Papeleros to Techo would serve as a revolving fund for other co-ops, to a rather sophisticated board of former garbage pickers, had value in showing that people of any background can raise themselves by their own efforts.

Another $20,000 in 1963 went to the *Institute of Rural Education* in Santiago, a private Catholic foundation, to build a training center in Chillan, Nuble province, for fruit and vegetable gardening, pig and poultry raising, reforestation, home economics, and hygiene. Forty Peace Corps volunteers were working at this project.

There was no common language in this social action. The liberal Catholics within the Christian Democrats wanted to change the attitudes of rural and city workers, showing them how to act together, gain technical skills and small amounts of working capital, and out of that would come, in time, a basic change in society. The Communists and even more stridently nationalistic Socialists saw their first goal to break foreign (U.S.) control of the Chilean economy, and their next goal was to end the bourgeois-landowner domination of a very unequal society. They dismissed these co-ops as the self-indulgence of do-good liberals, trivial, indeed harmful in dividing the working classes, confusing them as to their real interests, and cynically disguising the reality of who had power in Chile and for what purpose. If they had cared to be generous, and there was no reason why they should, the Left could have pointed out how confused was Ambassador Cole, an honorable man. He had an intense respect for these courageous Catholic reformers, but his basic charge as United States ambassador was to protect the interests of Anaconda Copper, ITT, and the other American corporations in Chile. When the military dictatorship seized power in 1973, to the relief of just about the entire middle class, it proceeded to outlaw the Christian Democrats, abolish their do-good projects, and imprison their leaders almost as thoroughly as it did the Communists and Socialists.

In 1964 the Trust gave $10,000 to *Ictus,* an independent theatre group. Culture in Latin America, like academia, was apt to be Marxist or extreme right-wing. There was an urgent need to build a liberal center, whether as in Chile, Catholic supported, or as in the cultural institution the Trust funded in Uruguay, secular. One wing of the CIA backed this fragile liberalism; the other wing concentrated on strengthening its traditional contacts with the military.

International Rescue Committee, New York, New York, 1976—$5,000 for resettlement expenses of Chilean refugees, the fall-out from the military takeover. Communist refugees could find shelter in Cuba or Romania; noncommunists had a rougher time, partly because there was no existing Chilean community in the United States to help absorb them.

American Friends Service Committee, Philadelphia, Pennsylvania, 1980– 1981—$15,500. Half of this amount ($7,500) was for child feeding centers in the shanty towns (*callampas*) surrounding Santiago in which there is strong parish leadership as well as community initiative. The other half ($8,000) was for family projects in cooperation with the Netherlands Interchurch Coordinating Committee. One approach was to combat malnutrition by encouraging breast feeding, not the custom in Chile. By stimulating discussion groups on health problems, including how to pressure the state to carry out in practice the public health laws that existed on paper, these two foreign organizations sought to develop a sense of shared community interest and responsibility. The drawback (as in Guatemala) was that if one encouraged community initiative beyond a minimum, one simply marked out those leaders for the police.

For a while the Pinochet government was a showcase for Milton Friedman economics. By devaluating the currency to limit imports and encourage exports, by cutting all social services in order to reduce state costs, by breaking the labor movement and therefore opposition to low wages, and by censoring

any media description of the misery this caused, these Chicago-school mone-
tarists were able to bring down inflation and work supply-side miracles that
the Reagan administration might envy. High fuel costs to be paid in dollars,
high international interest rates, and a luxury import binge had not been
figured into the equation, however. Pinochet did not have the control he
thought he had, and by the 1980s the middle class was as devastated as the
proletariat.

Peru—$95,500

*American Friends Service Committee, Philadelphia, Pennsylvania, 1965—
$12,000,* for an urban community development program in Lima. After a
disastrous fire in 1963 destroyed one of the worst barriadas, 300 families were
relocated in a desert area, Pamplona Alta, outside the city. This became the
Friends' first South American program: supplying food, temporary housing,
and a survey of working skills and then setting up training courses and workshops to make children's overalls and metal beds and helping these former
peasants acquire attitudes of cooperation.

Acción International, Cambridge, Massachusetts, 1968–1971—$45,000. In
1968, $15,000 was given to finance expansion into Peru with help of trained
Brazilian and Venezuelan staff, with courses given to Peace Corps volunteers,
police, city officials, and private groups, an example of international cooperation among professionals in supernationalistic South America.

In 1971, $30,000 was granted for development of neighborhood organi-
zations and job programs in Lima. Like every other third-world nation, Peru
has the problem of rural people leaving their villages for the big city, looking
for jobs, a better chance for the children, or the excitement of city life (television in the bars), and Lima had grown from 500,000 in 1940 to 2,000,000
in 1970, the new settlers settling into squatter colonies around the city's outskirts. The Acción director (a Peruvian with a Yale degree and an American
wife) was able to see beyond the poverty of these barriadas (the official term,
Pueblos Jovenes, young towns) to the resourcefulness of their settlers. They
were people with the drive to make something of themselves, and if they first
lived in huts made out of tarpaper and packing cases, the next step was a
corrugated tin roof, then brick walls, windows, a second story, and finally a
balcony, in chaos that affronted city planners but expressing a tremendous
desire to get ahead. It was a dynamic, intelligent community. Acción supplied
some capital and skill for a couple of miniscule production co-ops (leather
and rug working) but essentially aid in dealing with government, how to press
a well-meaning but paralyzed bureaucracy to supply water and electricity,

buses and schools, and how to tap skills and money from the international community.

Catholic Relief Services, 1970—$30,000. In early 1970 came the earthquake that destroyed so much of north-central Peru. Ten thousand dollars from the Merrill Trust went to support a German *Herz Jesu* project in Huaras (a badly damaged commercial city in the north) to help hold its population by rebuilding a technical school. If young men and women learn a skill—in car and electrical motors, metal and carpentry trades, or home economics—then they can make use of whatever economic reconstruction that arrives. They aren't lured to become street peddlers in Lima. German charity is less impulsive than American (120 large boxes of vanilla-flavored Metrecal sent at great expense after the earthquake, gathering dust in a Lima warehouse because it could not fit into any local diet), more effective because its financing stability (every German is expected to put down on his tax form a 1 percent contribution to the church of his choice) allows the ability to work for long-range goals. I liked the idea of partnership with what seemed a well-run German project.

Twenty thousand dollars went to the Archbishopric of Cuzco, $10,000 for a five-day boarding school to allow Indian adolescents to gain a secondary education. The village schools went only through sixth grade. Although the left-wing dictatorship of that period was nominally anticlerical, it was pragmatic enough to accept church aid in schooling (the state pays the salaries and the church pays for construction and supplies) and in radio programs directed toward the mountain villages about child care, nutrition, and hygiene. "Would this include material about family planning?" I asked the Spanish-born Jesuit secretary of the archbishop. "If the people are interested in that topic, we'll eventually get to it."

Ten thousand dollars went to economic development. American projects are usually too huge—highways and dams hard to adapt to a poor country with a weak administrative structure. Peruvian projects lose themselves in thickets of overcentralization and conflicting regulations, a lack of disciplined cost/return planning that brought the country close to bankruptcy by the late 1970s (e.g., Turkey, Poland, Zaire). But if a local group can raise half the capital for a specific need, it can borrow the remaining half at low interest from a state bank. The archbishop's secretary, Alejandro Repulles, wanted to use this $10,000 as down payment on a small canning plant in Cuzco that would cut waste and expand food resources and on a sawmill and training school in Urcos, on the edge of the rain forest. This would be an example of responsible capitalism, not just low wages and quick profits.

Total state control is the enemy in every Latin American country. A healthy church involved in social action is a way to keep alive the ideas of a pluralistic society.

Brazil—$106,000

When I give food to the poor they call me a saint. When I ask why the poor have no food they call me a communist.   [Dom Helder Camara, Archbishop of Recife and Olinda]

With a military dictatorship as brutal and for a while as successful as Brazil's, there was an even greater moral question than with Guatemala. The overspending and tremendous foreign debt that accompanied O Milagro Brasileiro brought an acute demand for hard currency, which we helped meet. The justification is human need, which should not be fenced off for ideological reasons. A nation and its people remain regardless of political administration. What encourages people to take care of their own affairs in the long run encourages democracy.

Acción International, $41,000. In 1967, $11,000 was given to encourage community organization and job training in São Paulo, an even faster growing megapolis than Mexico City, which was receiving 1,000 fugitives a day from the Northeast, stricken by drought, overpopulation, and the dispossession of squatters by huge agricorporations. In 1976, $30,000 was given for aid to small business in Bahia and Recife, two coastal cities of the Northeast, with a desperate need for industry to take up unemployment. The typical Brazilian approach, desk-pounding "leadership" colliding with foot-dragging bureaucracy, was to launch a brand new, capital-intensive factory, a branch of some international firm, which required disciplines that local people did not possess. The workers, therefore, would be trucked in from São Paulo, a thousand miles away, with half a dozen local people hired to sweep the floors and clean the lavatories.

Acción's approach instead was to identify perhaps 200 aggressive, able heads of small business (micro-*empresas*: a sandal-making workshop, a printing press, and a shop making beer mugs out of old bottles), help them obtain a commercial loan at 18 rather than 40 percent interest, help with accounting and taxes and planning of cash flow, and with such aid allow these 200 mini-capitalists to go from three employees to five, which means 400 new jobs— far more jobs, with a miniscule investment of capital, than from a new factory. If the twentieth is the century of deadly words, with all sorts of atrocities perpetuated in the name of socialism and democracy and nationalism, it is of value to stress a modest pragmatism. A by-product of our grant was jobs for students, collecting statistics on actual conditions, and in the process freeing themselves from the sterile (and in Brazil, very dangerous) abstractions of university socialism.

Catholic Relief Services, 1977—$20,000, for welfare services of the bishoprics of Bahia-Salvador, Feira da Santana, and Recife. The church in Brazil has been a liberal force, in revulsion against the brutality of the regime and the terrible differences between rich and poor, and also out of a caution that when the regime eventually falls, the church should not be carried down with it. The small grants given to these bishops' offices I had visited during my two weeks' stay in 1976 went for a job training program in the black city of Bahia and a housing co-op in the new market city of Feira da Santana to build machinery for making bricks of compressed earth. Recife is the home of Cardinal Helder Camara, the most famous opponent of the regime. Though he had been attacked as a Communist and his name forbidden in the media, he could not be arrested or murdered because he was internationally famous. French intellectuals would complain. He shows the value of courage in saying obvious things and dealing with the poorest people, such as in trying to organize house servants for minimum rights. Also to hire lawyers to supply papers for squatters in the interior, who are being pushed out by the great land corporations like Volkswagen. Without papers they are given $200, enough to get drunk on; with papers they receive $2,000, capital for a new life.

Oxfam, Oxford, England, 1977—$15,000, for helping poor people in Amazonian towns start cooperative farms for raising vegetables and fruit, also for a tile-making co-op in a leper colony. William Yates, the Englishman in charge of Oxfam's Recife headquarters, had become cynical about the value of much international charity. He saw it as a bandaid, deflecting attention from injustice and inequality that were the real issue, or in disaster relief turning people into welfare cases. His justification of outside help was to encourage people to work together for what the community itself wanted. Even if it is a soccer field or a chapel, the outside expert keeps his mouth shut. When the villagers ask him questions—how to rent a truck, how to lay a gradient—he should give factual answers, not proffer advice. Then when the village has built its soccer field, the citizens see that they need more practical items like a new well. By then they will have acquired skills of working together and the welfare project will be theirs, not something forced upon them by the Ministry of Development or the all-wise foreigner.

Yates had lived in the Nordeste for eight years and had learned so much that I asked him how come he hadn't been killed—in Brazil too much knowledge is lethal. He replied that he kept a low profile and put nothing in the mail. When he needed to send a report, he went to the Recife airport for the weekly plane to London, looked for a properly dressed, middle-aged person reading a Dorothy Sayers mystery in the waiting room and gave him the letter to post from home. It was foolproof.

Pathfinder Fund, Inc., 1978—$25,000, to train physicians in family planning in Minas Gerais. The Brazilians are intensely sensitive about North American efforts to limit Brazil's population. A hundred million inhabitants— irrespective of whether they have jobs, schools, transportation, or even food— is a symbol of national pride. There is beginning to occur concern, even within government circles, about cutting back this rise, with the projection that São Paulo may reach 20 million people by the year 2000, but it is such a lurid topic that any facing up to it has to be carried out on tiptoes. The value therefore of a private institution like Pathfinder that utilizes money from private sources for medical training (the Charles E. Merrill Trust, not AID— are there accountants who actually check on this?).

By the 1980s, of course, Brazil became the world's basket case. Its international debt stood at $90–$95 billion. Payments on the interest of this debt represented 79 percent of its 1982 export sales. To evade the nightmare of default, as also with Mexico, Argentina, Peru, Poland, Romania, Turkey, Philippines, and other debtors American banks (at high fees) were rolling over loans, lending more money with which to pay themselves interest. The International Monetary Fund was trying to pressure Brazil to put its house in order by imposing austerity: curbing inflation and deficits by forcing down imports, wages, and government services. "Cuts in public spending" is a euphemism for saying that health, education, and welfare budgets are slashed, and improved balance of payments today will be paid for with higher rates of infant mortality, illiteracy, and malnutrition tomorrow. Neither Brazil nor any other country cuts its military budget. In 1984 President Belaunde Terry of Peru purchased 26 Mirage fighters from France at a cost of $600 million.

This deflationary wring-out is creating massive unemployment, bankruptcies, and a misery among all classes worse than that of the 1930s. It is an end to all the false promises of the 1950s and 1960s not only to Brazilians but to most Latin Americans, Africans, and Asians—a process of demodernization. These unhappy people might be better off if they could return to the traditional ways of life they had abandoned. The fugitives who came to São Paulo, however, are not going to return to the drought-stricken backlands (*sertãos*) of the Nordeste any more than unemployed blacks in South Chicago are going to return to the cotton fields of Mississippi.

If, in pursuit of O Milagro Brasileiro, government borrowed foolishly and the international banks lent foolishly, they were saloons selling drinks on credit to alcoholics. No government can risk provoking a revolution out of its people's despair. A major difference between the 1980s and the 1930s is that demographic changes mean a far higher proportion of young people in every third-world country, young men unemployed, angry, restless, and often armed. Those IMF austerities can be characterized as designed primarily to save the great banks of New York. A point may come when it may seem no worse to default on that $90 billion debt than to condemn Brazil until eternity to simply paying the interest.

One approach must be to have the governments of the industrial nations assume a proportion of these debts from the private banks while at the same time forcing those banks to write down and restructure them. The cost of such a reorganization would come nowhere near the costs of one default on Brazil's scale, but that solution requires speed, generosity, forethought, and cooperation—not easy to find at this time.

Another approach is return to a policy of low-interest development loans and even outright gifts. Despite their own problems, United States, Canada, Britain, West Germany, Switzerland, and Japan are still wealthy nations. A broken Southern world will not buy their exports. Those millions of angry young men with cheap guns will be expensive. The real danger, hard for comfortable people to comprehend, is not Sandinista socialism but the nihilism of despair.

Private philanthropy, even at the miniscule level of the Merrill Trust, can keep open the channels that large-scale government aid will utilize, train technicians and administrators, maintain contacts, offer a little hope, and buy a little time. It can propose binational projects in order to modify the selfishness of nationalism and demand matching funds to awaken some faint concepts of civic responsibility. It can put pressure on politicians and public opinion in the comfortable countries, as Oxfam and Catholic Relief Services try to do, about the realities of hunger. But there is little time, and the most generous help is wiped out by one 0.5 percent raise in the prime lending rate.

Uruguay

Congress for Cultural Freedom, Paris, 1965—$25,000, to support a non-Marxist cultural center in Montevideo. (See CIA.)

Bolivia

Oxfam America, Boston, Massachusetts, 1979—$7,500. Cochabamba Potato Producers' Association was given this money to provide technical aid to Quechua and Aymara-speaking persons on their tiny Altiplano farms. The year was the beginning of the great cocaine boom in Bolivia, and not much attention was being paid to potato raising.

NEAR EAST

Israel—$248,000

The Charles E. Merrill Trust did not back any Israeli project until 1971. This came from our prejudice against almost any foreign grants except to Latin America, partly from our feeling that Israel was the responsibility of Jewish charity. Merrill Lynch had offices in Dhahran and Abu Dabi, Beirut and Teheran, and we respected Don Regan's concern that the firm not be known as pro-Zionist. By the 1970s our policy became more flexible, although we tried to restrict ourselves to cultural and scientific institutions or to ones that served Arabs as well.

Israeli-American relations, beneath the rhetoric, have a miserable quality. Israel is "America's staunchest democratic ally in the Mideast." It is a costly legacy, a damn nuisance, a brutal theocracy, and a textbook example of a client state (like Taiwan) that manipulates its protector's foreign policy. If Israelis believe that American support is automatic, that can be harmful for both countries. At any rate, if most Israeli resources go into military needs, then its civil budget for health, education, and welfare has partly to be met by American philanthropy. With so many Israeli institutions financed by the United Jewish Appeal, then it is true that one gains a tax credit for supporting a foreign government, as Arab critics point out.

Israelis resent the American need for gratitude: "This paper towel dispenser given in memory of Goldie Weintraub, Morristown, New Jersey." They resent control this money gives. They resent the blank-check support by Americans of the most hawkish elements in Israel's body politic. They resent being perpetual teenagers. They resent Israel's 100 percent inflation that stems partly from the constant inflow of dollars.

A non-Jewish foundation can be useful. Intelligent and sustained American support of Arab institutions keeps open communications between Americans and Arabs from which Jewish-Americans and even Israelis benefit. Any dialogue, no matter how limited, that allows enemies to see each other as human beings benefits everyone. Where government is slow-moving, heavy-handed, and suspicious, it is crucial to encourage small and flexible programs that may be dependent on a personal friendship or the good will built up by some institution like the American University in Beirut that has been around for a long time.

United Jewish Appeal, New York, New York, 1972—$25,000, to the Israel Education Fund for construction of an Arab–Jewish sports facility in Haifa. The IEF is a capital fund to build high schools and award high school scholarships to all Israeli citizens, meaning Arab and Druse, seeking to win Arab loyalty to the state, if not the nation. Haifa is the only city where Jews and

Arabs live in proximity, and its mixed community center (Beit-ha-gefen, 'House of the Vine') is the only one of its kind. Operation funds came from the Israeli government and the Haifa municipality, but there is no money for construction.

American Friends of the Israel Museum, Jerusalem, 1975—$25,000. It takes time for a foreigner visiting this and any other institution in Israel to get used to being frisked by a guard when he enters. The Museum is second only to the Western Wall as a place to visit for all Israelis and foreigners: "A force for cultural values and the nurturance of democratic ideals, a force to develop humane values by strengthening the lives and interrelationships of Christian, Jewish, and Moslem families through the creative arts." The Youth Wing involves 12,000 child members, one-half from underprivileged homes. One educational aim of this wing, with participating Moslem families, is to reevaluate the role of girls in modern society. Merrill funds went to train art teachers and guides and encourage traveling art exhibits.

American Friends of the Hebrew University, New York and Jerusalem, 1976–1979—$50,000. Our first grant went for the import of American books, increasingly limited with rising book costs and the devaluation of the Israeli pound. Nevertheless, it is crucial for Israeli students to keep up with developments in all fields of human knowledge. The second grant went for subscriptions to 100 U.S. science periodicals to the joint national and university library, serving every institution in the whole country, increasingly isolated from the outside world by lack of foreign currency.

American Friends of the Haifa University, 1978—$5,000, to the Institute of Evolution. American foundations like Ford and Rockefeller finance science projects only if they promise immediate results. There is, here as in other countries, a crying need for support of long-range research, for example, the effects of marine pollution on barnacles. The genetic changes within the barnacle from organic, industrial, and thermal pollutants are a useful way to monitor ecological damage.

American Committee of the Weizmann Institute of Science, New York and Rehovat, 1978—$15,000. The Institute was founded in 1934 by Dr. Chaim Weizmann, the first president of Israel, to serve Palestine's agricultural industry and the world's scientific community. It carries through an advanced program in cancer research and another in upgrading the protein content of wheat that can be grown in arid climates. The Trust's grant went toward working out an up-to-date mathematics curriculum, translated from Hebrew into Arabic, with training courses for Arabic-speaking teachers.

Fellowship in Israel for Arab-Jewish Youth, Cambridge, Massachusetts, 1979—$10,000. This group was started by Unitarians during World War II to rebuild the lives of Jewish children who survived the Holocaust. Even then, however, there was a concern for Arab–Jewish relations. Most of its funds go to supply scholarships for Arabs in Israeli secondary schools and universities, but money is needed for summer camps for teenagers, an Arab–Jewish folklore group (the first in Israel), and a students' club in Haifa. It is a low-profile, small-budget, nonpolitical group trying to build a sense of continuity and trust.

American Friends' Service Committee, Philadelphia, Pennsylvania, 1978– 1981—$13,000. The 1978 grant to the Arab–Israeli Assistance Fund went for preschool activities' centers in the Gaza Strip, legal assistance to Arab residents of East Jerusalem (a project that cost the Friends considerable American support), and the needs of retarded Sephardic children in the Negev. (The UJA doesn't want to hear about retarded children or battered women, as if such problems don't exist in Israel.)

The 1981 grant went to Middle East Peace Workers' Team. The absence of formal war has not changed the level of antipathy between Israelis and Palestinians. PLO and Likud leadership shout at the same level of confrontation, but there are also moderate voices on both sides, anxious to talk reasonably if channels can be opened. Friends' sponsorship allows a neutral turf for private talks and also projects where Arabs and Jews can do physical work together.

Jerusalem Foundation, New York, New York, 1980—$10,000. Teddy Kollek, mayor of Jerusalem, is a man who believes that Arabs are human beings and, therefore, opposed the Begin government run by hardliners closer to the American establishment. Through this private foundation he tried to fund social services toward the poor Arab (and Armenian and Jewish) inhabitants of the city. Sample projects have been an imaginative park on the border between the Arab and Jewish sectors to attract children and parents of both groups, bookmobiles with Arab books printed in Cairo, Amman, and even Damascus. Merrill money went to equip a playground and an old people's club in the poorest Moslem center of the city.

Tel Aviv University, 1980–1981—$50,000, to the Center for Strategic Studies for the development of security planning. Peter Magowan, through his friendship with General Aharon Yariv, formerly head of Israeli intelligence and negotiator with Egypt on the disengagement of forces in the Sinai, was attracted to this think-tank. He had been much impressed by the intellectual quality of Israeli military and political analysts and felt the need to support an organization as independent as this to monitor government policy. I thought these two decisions broke our rules by coming too close to the mechanics of the Israeli state.

Arabs—$225,000

Americans of our generation share a new and complicated set of relations with the Arabs (and for a while the Iranians) that brings out the worst qualities of both groups. (Some) Arabs are so rich and so newly rich that they are stereotyped, flattered, exploited, and despised by Americans as we, a few decades back, were treated by Europeans. At one extreme are the Saudis, whose gigantic, instant projects attract foreign adventurers as dead meat does flies. Then there are the Palestinians who are dehumanized as killers, or made into martyrs by every crowd that wants to get back at the Israelis or Americans or, as always, the Jews. And then there are the Egyptians, where the alliance with Sadat was paid for by billions of dollars poured into the bottomless pit of Cairo—to improve the transportation and communications systems, drinking water and sewage disposal, and government administration and industrial production, until, as usual, the remedy becomes part of the disease.

In an area with problems as vast as these, perhaps the only thing that private philanthropy can do is to act precisely to support those institutions and individuals who have been there long enough to have made themselves trusted (giving a microfilm edition of the *New York Times* to the library of the American University of Cairo, for example).

American Middle East Rehabilitation, Incorporated, New York, New York, 1967—$15,000, toward vocational training of Arab refugees.

American University of Beirut, 1972—$30,000, for the modernization of Blair Hall. The University was first chartered in 1863 as Syrian Protestant College. In 1972 it had 4,300 students representing sixty countries, with 75 percent from Arab countries. It represented the American missionary and educational commitment at its best; supplied doctors, educators, engineers, and scientists throughout the Moslem world; and built up a capital of good will that later generations overdrew. The University and, particularly the medical school hospital, tried to remain neutral and serve both sides in the terrible wars that destroyed Lebanon and Beirut, and it will be a channel for reconstruction if anything can.

American Schools of Oriental Research, Cambridge, Massachusetts, 1969–1978—$60,000, to expand scholarly activities within the Arab world. This institution was founded in 1900 in Jerusalem, with its major branch in Baghdad in 1921. As directors, William Albright and Nelson Glueck brought it a worldwide reputation in the 1930s and 1940s. Then later, when American–Arab relations eroded, the American Schools of Oriental Research became desperately important as a way of maintaining scholarly contacts, including those between Jews and Arabs, in politically neutral areas of study. Sometimes American government support would be embarrassingly lavish; then, after 1970, flood was replaced by drought, and programs had to be curtailed, trained staff fired, and the library allowed to run down. Private funds, even our Trust's small grants, were needed to allow continuity in the training of American scholars and in maintaining a nonpolitical American presence in the Mideast where Arabs would trust an institution and individuals who just don't come and go. Our money went to fund the centers in both Jerusalem and Amman.

University of Chicago, Oriental Institute, 1980—$5,000, for study in Sumerian excavations at Nippur in southern Iraq. Nippur lasted from 5000 B.C. to 800 A.D., and with new scientific methods of study it is possible to learn more about the lives of the common people including their climate and diet. During the late 1960s and early 1970s, the Institute was almost the only American presence in Iraq—not all contacts had been broken.

Institute for International Education Programs, Boston, Massachusetts, 1978–1979—$15,000. The Institute was the creation of an Israeli-born educator named Shimon Chasdi, an old-fashioned Zionist who believed in brotherhood: individuals can free themselves from prejudice and work together for common goals. Even before Sadat's trip to Jerusalem opened a dialogue, Chasdi had organized a seminar at Harvard of American, Turkish, Iranian, Israeli, and Egyptian educators to discuss common problems of urban adolescents. "I could give you an accurate breakdown of the Turkish army, but I haven't the faintest idea of what is taught in their schools," as one member stated. The conference started icily, but within a few days, an Israeli deputy minister was talking face-to-face with the head of a teacher-training institute in Teheran or the director of Cairo University high school. The Trust's next grant was to fund a second seminar in 1980, this time in Cairo, on the education of science teachers with the dream of producing a textbook on the Red Sea, written by Israeli, Jordanian, Egyptian, and Saudi biologists, to be used in the schools of all four countries. Politics intervened.

Tulane Medical Center, School of Public Health and Tropical Medicine, New Orleans, Louisiana, 1979—$30,000, for support of a Qalyub schistosomiasis project in Egypt. Little American money is invested in tropical disease research, prevention, and treatment. Although perhaps 250 million people suffer from schistosomiasis (a parasitical disease affecting intestines and bladder), it was not known to American doctors until thousands of soldiers became infected with it following the invasion of Leyte in the Philippines. It is spreading fast in Africa today as new irrigation schemes bring the freshwater snails that are its vector into virgin areas. In Egypt, half the population is infected, particularly in the Delta and the Aswan Dam flood area. Research and control work in Egypt can be financed by counterpart currency used to repay loans, but dollars are needed for the expenses of Egyptians studying at U.S. institutions and for the purchase of equipment. Qalyub is a major field research effort in the south Nile Delta of eight villages involving 40,000 people, and work is needed to test new immunological procedures, the use of a promising new drug, Praziquantel, and biological ways of interrupting the parasite's life cycle.

Turkey—$234,500

Roberts College, Istanbul, 1960—$20,000, for the development of the new School of Business Administration and Economics. Roberts dates back to 1863. It is America's oldest and most important contribution to education in Turkey, and although the schools were turned over to the government in 1971, English has always been the language of instruction. Smaller size and better facilities and administration meant that Roberts never became the proletarian jungle of the regular universities and was not racked by the same violence. The 1960 grant was a part of the Foundation's long-term policy of supporting business schools.

Bogazici University, 1980—$20,000, through the Harvard Graduate School of Education. Bogazici was Roberts' name after nationalization, and Merrill money went for a program in adult education. There has been a tremendous expansion of Turkish university facilities in the last twenty years to meet the needs of a rapidly growing population. The cure becomes the disease, and the university system churns out ten times as many graduates as there are openings in the state bureaucracy, the professions, and business, so unemployed ex-students become gunmen for Left or Right. Bogazici, aided by Harvard, is trying to develop a more practical, job-oriented style of education, plus adult evening courses (for small-town mayors in the Istanbul area, for example). With Turkey close to collapse and U.S. aid funds earmarked for Israel and Egypt, it was valuable to have private resources available.

Development Foundation of Turkey, Ankara, 1968–1979—$97,000. The Foundation was led by an American-educated Turk named Altan Unver and was an effort to meet the problems of rural Turkey. In a country where the state seeks to exercise almost total control, this independent organization was an anomaly, for a while the only private agency of its kind in the entire country.

In 1968, $22,000 was given for rural development projects around Tarsus, St. Paul's city on the southeastern coast. There are agricultural banks in Turkey directed to give low-interest loans to farmers, but higher collateral is required than most can supply. By providing such collateral to teachable farmers, the Foundation was able to unlock large quantities of government money. Tarsus is one of the many small industrial cities near the coast, and the Foundation was trying to encourage industrial chicken-raising to meet their needs. The farmers would have liked to expand from 20 chickens to 100. The goal was to show them how to expand to 5,000, with all the disciplines necessary to receive a batch of 1,000 day-old chicks by plane from England, run hygienic raising sheds, kill and dress the birds, and if they had made a contract to supply 500 dressed birds for a truck at 5:00 A.M. on Thursday, those 500 would be there on the dot, ready to go—none of which is the Turkish way of doing things.

In 1971, $25,000 was given for the expansion of family-planning activities. Any national policy of population control is attacked from Right and Left. Right insists that Turkish security must be based upon a nation of 100 million, every man a soldier, while Left dismisses the issue as an imperialist plot. Istanbul, Izmir, and Ankara have growth rates at the European level. The villages of Anatolia have double that. Yet where modernization occurs, it is possible to persuade families that a family of three or four children, as opposed to six or eight, means better education plus money for a new tractor. The Foundation's approach was the bulk import of condoms from Germany and Sweden with Merrill money (the government would not allocate foreign currency), their testing and packaging (a labor-intensive task to perform in Turkey), and sale through regular stores in villages and towns.

In 1975, $20,000 was given for program development, the raising of dairy cattle in Diyarbakir on the Syrian frontier, and beekeeping in villages near Ankara. The East is to Turkey what the South is to Italy, a backward area of impacted poverty, in both countries attracting a sizable amount of government concern without much to show for it.

In 1979, $30,000 went for a crafts program that would offer jobs in mountain villages of the Caucasus devastated by earthquakes. In Turkey, like Brazil, a small amount of money precisely and promptly employed has the value of sums five or ten times larger handled through state channels.

Environmental Problems Foundation of Turkey, Ankara, 1981—$10,000, to a new, weak organization, the only one in Turkey. Its first objective is education. The Turks are so bedeviled by inflation, unemployment, terrorism,

and incipient civil war that it is hard to attract attention to problems of deforestation and land erosion, the pellmell urbanization of the whole Istanbul-
Bosphorus area. The Foundation tries to accomplish tangible tasks like maintaining an up-to-date library on environmental legislation of other countries
that the Turks may make use of, encouraging children's literature on nature
that can be distributed to school libraries, as well as making an inventory of
environmental issues facing Turkey and raising a consciousness of the threats
these imply and how alternative technologies may be less destructive. As
a result of the Foundation's lobbying, a basic land-use law was enacted in
1983.

There is little interest by American philanthropy in such an organization,
and the two small Greek and Turkish grants we made are, I think, unusual.
Such aid has a double impact, not only to meet a budget but to allow a director
to point to this international concern as a way of attracting local attention.
Greeks and Turks, Italians and Arabs don't have the interest or resources to
care about their deteriorating environment. To search out the fragile agencies
that do exist is crucial.

Long Island University, Greenvale, New York, 1971—$25,000, for heavy
equipment needed to furnish excavation of the temple of Aphrodite in Knidos.
Knidos is one of the last great unexcavated Greek cities, on the southwest
coast of Turkey, active from pre-Cycladic and Mycenaean times to Rome and
Byzantium, badly ravaged by Arabs and archaeologists but still a useful training ground for young scholars.

*Fogg Art Museum, Harvard University, Cambridge, Massachusetts,
1973—$25,000,* to support the excavation at Sardis, north of Izmir. At this
spot where European and Near Eastern Civilization met, the major trading
center of King Croesus, there was also the largest of all early synagogues,
dating from around 200 A.D. The dig at Sardis has been praised by the State
Department as a valuable example of Turkish–American cooperation as students, professors, experts, and laborers work together.

Armenian and Greek influence in the West gives Turkey a bad press and
inhibits philanthropic concern. It is, and always has been, a brutal country.
The sad part of the international terrorism by Armenians is that this violence
not only seeks to avenge the terrible massacres of 1915, the first systematic
genocide, which Hitler found educational, but has a pedagogical purpose, to
force the Turkish authorities to admit the fact in their high school textbooks
and to say that they are sorry—which, for the Turks, is intolerable.

And at a time when Turkey was inching its way out from disaster and
trying to repay its astronomical debts and relate its investments to what it
most needed, President Kenan Evren announced in November 1983 that the

nation would start construction of three nuclear power plants and finalize plans for a $4.3 billion aircraft industry to manufacture F-16s.

ASIA—$353,500

International Rescue Committee, New York, New York, 1968–1981—$57,500. Twenty-five thousand dollars was given in 1968 to finance a day-care center at the refugee village of Ap Doi Moi in Vietnam. The IRC was trying to set up handicraft schools, supply tools for processing lumber as a source of income, supply better soybean and rice seed, and establish a grass-weaving co-op. Few men were available for employment, as they were drafted into one or another of the fighting forces; a day-care center would free women for gardening and also teach them something about hygiene. In all the bottomless tragedy of Vietnam, this was the Trust's only project.

In 1971, $15,000 was given to help Bengali refugee doctors and teachers who had fled across the Indian border near Calcutta to escape terror by Pakistani soldiers and Moslem militants. In 1980, $7,500 was given for housing and medical needs of 70,000 Afghan refugees fleeing across the Pakistan border from Russian terror.

A grant of $10,000 was made in 1981 for support of a joint program with the New York Hospital–Cornell Medical Center to supply medical help to Cambodian refugees in Thai camps. One purpose of this project was to give young American doctors experience in practicing crisis medicine under primitive conditions.

U.S. Committee for UNICEF, New York, New York, 1973—$20,000, to expand family health services in Bangkok and fund wards for undernourished children in Philippine provincial hospitals. UNICEF had the resources to buy relief items at rates far lower than market prices, and each dollar of what it supplied was augmented by $2.50 from the recipient country. UNICEF is confused with UNESCO, and American prejudice against the United Nations made this a hard project to sell.

Massachusetts Institute of Technology, Cambridge, 1973—$25,000, for All-India Institute of Medical Sciences, New Delhi. This major hospital was established in 1953 with help from the World Health Organization, Rockefeller Foundation, New Zealand, Australia, France, and East Germany and helps set the standard of medical education throughout India. Through the Harvard School of Public Health, I had met the director of its Department of Gastroenterology, Dr. B. N. Tandon, a remarkable man trying to combat what he saw as the harmful impact of American medical priorities upon Indian doctors. They returned home from their expensive foreign training excited about cancer therapy and open-heart surgery when the needs of India were in diarrhea, malnutrition, and family planning. How could Dr. Tandon persuade his ambitious students that village practice was intellectually as well as socially rewarding? Good medicine does not have to be expensive or complicated, and ignorant people are as intelligent as the educated when approached the right way. Tandon sought to train paramedics in habits of thoroughness (to vaccinate all children, chlorinate all wells, and screen for TB), train women to find vitamins and protein sources in local plants (not through expensive Swedish drugs), and train doctors in ways of discussing family planning. All medical budgets had recently been cut, India putting its money into defense and industry, and Merrill funds went into the village programs and a drawing account at MIT for American chemicals, laboratory equipment, and library materials.

St. Elizabeth's Hospital, Boston, Massachusetts, 1981—$15,000, a channel employed to support Dr. Tandon's research in hepatitis. This is India's fastest growing disease as well as almost the hardest to prevent and cure, increasing by 500 percent since 1970 in the Indian cities as the British water and sewage systems wear out and population builds up. In 1979 Tandon had founded the Digestive Diseases Foundation to aid his work on hepatitis, publish a quarterly on Afro-Asian health problems, establish fellowships for medical students in village work, and fund the continuing education of paramedics. Because so little American money goes into tropical diseases, even small grants have impact.

Council on International and Public Affairs, New York, New York, 1980—$10,000, to support B. R. Deolalikar's student apprentice program in Ahmedabad. Deolaliker, who had been civil affairs officer of the Sadubhai Trust, one of India's largest corporations in pharmaceuticals and textiles, and a consultant for UNICEF and the World Bank, saw two major failings in most development programs: First, agencies like Acción and the Development Foundation of Turkey help energetic, capable people already on their way up the ladder, but many people are passed over. There is a need to train villagers in artisanal skills, help slum-dwellers put in a public water system, and show demoralized refugees how to work together. Second, most projects are too large and too remotely administered. The "socialists" who come out of the universities to administer them often have little idea of who and what they are talking about. There is a need to recruit student volunteers for village and urban work to keep alive the dying Gandhian tradition of service, and just as important, to give realistic education to the elite. Merrill Trust money helped pay volunteer stipends in this nonstate program, which could readily be replicated in Bombay or Delhi.

Philippines—$24,000. A short visit to Manila in 1973 as part of a lifelong friendship with a Catholic lawyer named Alejandro Lichauco, a Harvard graduate who was for a while imprisoned as an enemy of the Marcos dictatorship, led me to these three small grants. The aim was not only to help the poor and to defend some form of independent social action but also to rebuild credit for Americans, who had acquired a reputation for exploitation and control of the Philippine economy.

Isabella Cultural Corporation, Manila, 1973—$14,000, to help Father Ben Villote establish job-training programs for young men and women in the farming town of Tipas, south of Manila. With little industry and a rate of population increase over 3 percent per year, the Philippines have a terrible problem of underemployment: one store clerk sells you a package of envelopes, a second wraps it, a third rings up the purchase, and a fourth opens the door and wishes you a good day. Villote, a belligerent Jesuit priest, was trying to set up crafts schools for car and electronic machine repair, hairdressing, that would allow small-town adolescents to learn marketable skills and in the process learn how to discuss their personal and social problems together.

Catholic Relief Services, New York, New York, 1978—$5,000 through the Archbishopric of Manila for a vocational training project in the parish of Santa Ana. Father Villote had by then moved to one of the poorest slums of Manila and was trying to organize his parishioners to work together to set their own goals and approaches in the fight against poverty. I offered more money than this, but he turned it down as hurting their self-reliance.

Archdiocese of Lingayen-Dagupan, Pangasinan Province, 1980—$5,000, to establish a two-year school for adolescent dropouts in English, math, and history to prepare them for better jobs. Lichauco faulted the minimalist goals of most training programs. Young people are not simply would-be car mechanics but are also citizens and human beings.

Maryknoll Sisters, Maryknoll, New York, 1960—$50,000, for medical work among the poor in Korea, Hong Kong, and Taiwan.

United Board for Christian Higher Education in Asia, New York, New York, 1963—$35,000, to support Christian colleges in South Korea, Taiwan, and the Philippines. It is fashionable to disparage missionary activity as cultural imperialism. The developing countries should set their own goals. Westerners should abstain from value judgments. When most of Asian education, however, is controlled by the state, with national security (total control) as the only priority, or by student terrorists, it is important to have some reasonably independent institutions that can follow educational and social goals not completely political.

Goshen College, Goshen, Indiana, 1980—$20,000, for starting an exchange program with Sichuan University in the western city of Chengdu. Eight professors from Sichuan teach Chinese and study American education methods at the Mennonite College of Goshen, while twenty American undergraduates and two teachers go in the opposite direction. Goshen's president, Lawrence Burkholder, had been a missionary in China during World War II and was proud that his exchange program had been negotiated directly without any State Department involvement. Goshen already enjoyed a high reputation for its work programs in Poland, Haiti, Central America, and Korea.

Guilford College, Greensboro, North Carolina, 1980—$15,000, to start up a faculty exchange with a private university in Tokyo. At a small-town college like Guilford or Goshen, exchange programs have a striking impact upon the way that their students regard the world.

Johns Hopkins University, School of Public Health, Baltimore, Maryland, 1971–1976—$50,000, for research on influence of maternal diet on embryo and lactating offspring, a study conducted on animals in Baltimore and humans in Taiwan. Rats suffering from malnutrition have a low survival rate, stunted growth, low intelligence, and suffer from excitability and indecision. A diet supplement of good-quality protein, a mix of amino acids, can be supplied expectant mothers at the cost of two cents per person per day. The second grant was to run a controlled experiment in Taiwan where some mothers received protein additives and others did not. A conclusion was that children whose mothers had been poorly nourished before their birth could not overcome these deficiencies through a good postnatal diet, and when they suffered a later diet crisis were more apt to succumb. Cutbacks by the Reagan administration in family welfare have seen, by mid-1980s, American children with kwashiorkor and marasmus, third-world diseases of advanced malnutrition, beginning to show up at hospitals in Washington, Detroit, and Boston.

AFRICA—$476,000

We had more controversy about African grants than in any single category. It is hard for Americans and Africans to feel that they are speaking the same language. What a Westerner calls corruption, an African calls respect for family and tribal tradition. Western concern for the environment is racist because white Americans are more concerned about elephants than they are about human beings.

It is also hard to be sure of any single fact, much less the interpretations of the facts, because each fact must be judged against the motivation of the person telling it. It has no objective existence in itself. The Republic of South Africa has the most complicated pattern of racial oppression known to history. Does the participation of American corporations in the South African economy encourage a flexibility in the hiring of blacks that a national corporation could not risk? It does. Does the participation give a form of international approval that an insecure government badly needs? It does. The oppression of apartheid has caused misery and humiliation and thousands of deaths through police brutality. The killing of (black) opponents of Idi Amin in Uganda was estimated by Amnesty International and the International Rescue Committee as running between 200,000 and 500,000, but American blacks will not tolerate the comparison. People are not interested in the truth. They just want to win arguments.

By the mid-1980s, no other land mass in the world was undergoing the suffering of Africa.

Education

Perhaps the simplest need has been the education of new leadership. American and European education can be grossly misused, or in some cases may be unusable, but that's where one has to begin. Aid to African education was popular during the Kennedy years, and then Americans—and the Merrill Trust—lost interest.

In America

Atlanta University, 1961—$30,000. The dean of the business school in this black graduate university made a trip to Africa to recruit students, and we paid for his travel costs and some scholarship aid.

Yale University Law School, 1962—$30,000, part of an ambitious program to educate African law professors. If the new nations were to escape becoming dictatorships, there was a need to strengthen the tradition of law, and the American legal experience is important to this.

World University Service, Cambridge, Massachusetts, 1963, 1966—$15,000, two small grants to help destitute, unsponsored African students. So many of these had come with high hopes and such limited resources, often made up of all the little gifts from siblings, godparents, cousins, uncles, and nephews to whom they would be indebted for the rest of their lives, but even in poverty African students were almost always well groomed, spirited, optimistic.

African American Institute, New York, New York, 1967—$15,000, for graduate students. Dr. Cole's reasoning was that there would be less emotional dislocation and a better chance to readjust back in Africa if students came when they were older. And in our search for the practical, $10,000 was granted to African Student Aid Fund, for students in agriculture.

In Africa

Phillips Brooks House, Cambridge, Massachusetts, 1963, 1966—$15,000, an old-fashioned social service agency attached to Harvard University that became a funding channel for volunteer student teachers in Tanganyika and then as Volunteers for Africa in the southern half of the continent. It was a small, highly principled, well-run group, hampered in actuality by its success, since President Nyerere thought it unhealthy for young Africans to be exposed to whites who did things too well.

African-American Institute, New York, New York, 1963—$2,000, to the Highfield Community, a desperately poor school of 1,200 students in what was then Rhodesia. It was one of the few opportunities for blacks then to obtain a secondary education.

Fairfield Foundation, New York, New York, 1961—$20,000 to the Institute of Congolese Studies in Brazzaville, Equatorial Congo. The appeal had come to me through a friend at the Congress for Cultural Freedom in Paris. As the French-speaking African colonies achieved their independence at top speed, the fear arose that the lack of trained civil servants and of any state structure would cause repetition of the chaos and bloodshed of the Belgian Congo. This Institute, which received funding from the CIA, gave two-month intensive courses in how to run a government: theories of accounting and budget making, office procedure, a smattering of economics and French administrative law, and current affairs. No matter how frantic the process, it was better than nothing and allowed the future officials of these new nations to meet each other. In the colonial world it had been easier to go from the Ivory Coast to Paris than to Dahomey, not to mention Nigeria.

Strathmore College, Nairobi, 1963–1979—$95,000. Strathmore had been started in 1960, funded at first by Ford as a symbol of continued Western concern for and service to newly independent Kenya. Its head was a young, strongly Catholic, Yale-Harvard American named David Sperling, one of the finest men I came to know through the Foundation. The college's educational function was to fill the gap between the secondary schools and the university. Every African nation had to have its national university, airline, sports stadium, and hydroelectric dam, whether there was a basis for one of these symbols or not.

Strathmore offered a two-year course for Europeans, Syrians, Indians and Pakistanis, Kikuyu, Luo, and Masai—all the ethnic units that made up the new country—and tried to offer them some ideas and skills, some way to know and respect each other, and some concept of service. As the spirit of nationalism became stronger and narrower, Asians were driven out of Kenya as well as Greeks and Italians. From year to year Sperling had no idea of how much longer an independent Strathmore would be tolerated. He became a Kenyan citizen to show his allegiance and strengthen the college, and then found himself trying to protect not merely the right of Indians and Pakistanis to attend but also non-Kikuyu Kenyans. No matter what the official rhetoric, tribalism held stronger loyalties than nationalism, a Western concept, and Sperling had to show a stubborn diplomacy not to have the college be turned into a Kikuyu training school.

Oddly enough, after the death of Kenyatta in 1978, an event feared by everyone as the beginning of Kenya's disruption, things became better. The examples of dictatorship, revolution, and civil war all around the borders—Strathmore was admitting refugees from Uganda, Ethiopia, Somalia, and Zimbabwe—made the Kenya establishment feel that their country's constitutionalism was not to be taken for granted and that Strathmore College under its expatriate American president was a source of unity and nonpolitical independence worth preserving.

Strathmore has received support from Irish and German agencies as well as from a few American foundations like Phelps Stokes and our own. It is an example of what modest but sustained private philanthropy can achieve.

American Friends of Maru a Pula School, New York, New York, 1979— $25,000. Maru a Pula was founded in Botswana in 1975 to educate future leaders, both male and female, for this desperately poor country, which used to be Bechuanaland, plus black children from South Africa unable to tolerate apartheid and whites who wanted a humane education. Maru a Pula had no hired employees other than a couple of cooks, and everyone, from the headmaster on down, shared in the labor around the place from sweeping out classrooms to building the swimming pool. The school was determined that its graduates would not become an elite, and therefore on two days a week students and faculty worked in nearby villages to make bricks, teach, or tend the sick. Modest funding had come from American sources for scholarships and salaries for the 280 students and 15 teachers, and there is an affiliation with Groton in Massachusetts. Then in 1979 came a grant of $195,000 from AID for equipment and library books, the sort of flood-drought financing that makes American involvement in the Third World seem simple-minded.

Operation Crossroads Africa, New York, New York, 1962–1980—$62,000. Crossroads is the oldest and most important institution for building human relations between the United States and Africa. It was founded in 1958 by a black minister named James Robinson who believed in the value of young people working side by side as the simplest path to international understanding. It has sent more than 5,000 Africans to this country on professional internships. The Americans build schools, community centers, and clinics, together with African students, in the process learning about another set of values, the realities of third-world development and poverty, and turning themselves into ambassadors for Africa. University departments of African studies, the World Bank, Peace Corps, and foreign service are staffed with Crossroads alumni, as are the international departments of such companies as Union Carbide, ITT, Ford, and Chemical Bank.

The Crossroads administration was always imaginative in the tasks it took on. There was special recruitment in Quebec to attract French-speaking volunteers for West Africa. Another time it accepted a contract to train secretaries in Kenya, since often a colony became a nation with fewer than a dozen women able to do office work. In recent years it has been expanding in Moslem countries (Sudan, Egypt, Tunisia), into southern Africa (Botswana, Angola, Mozambique), and has been building contact with left-wing countries like Tanzania, Algeria, and Guinea.

Other Issues

In 1972–1974, through MIT and Berkeley, $25,000 was granted by the Trust for ocean fisheries development on the Biafran coast of Nigeria. This seemed a practical, well-planned project to fund boat purchase, processing, and marketing facilities and help with jobs and food production. An Ibo graduate student in philosophy and physics whom I knew named Uriah Chinwah would be the link between these funding channels and the Nigerian government, and this flexible American capital would then release major amounts of state and private funds. Chinwah picked fights with all his university contacts. "Mr. Chinwah does not seem to understand American administrative procedure" was a protest he dismissed as racist, and I have no idea what happened to the money as it reached southeastern Nigeria. The moral is never to undertake any business dealings with a Nigerian unless you control each stage of the process.

American Friends Service Committee, Philadelphia, Pennsylvania, 1972, 1980—$32,500. In 1980, $7,500 was given to help postwar Zimbabwe become economically self-supporting and in the process establish a weaving and vegetable-raising center for refugee women, set up a school for refugee children near Salisbury, and fund church efforts to meet emergency needs of refugees. In 1972, $25,000 was given for birth control centers in West Africa.

Union Artists, Johannesburg, 1972—$12,000 to set up a Bantu art center. One of my former students, a resourceful young woman, had decided to postpone college and, through Jewish contacts in Johannesburg, try to start a theatre and an art center, a place where blacks and whites could work together. With the police enforcing rules of apartheid on one side and the new spirit of black power ("We're not interested in accepting your condescension any longer!") on the other, the project was not a success.

This list of international grants shows the fields that the Merrill trustees drifted into, most of them valuable, some not. Another foundation might begin by choosing a general agency with a good track record—CARE, Oxfam, Catholic Relief Services, American Friends Service Committee—and back it with annual gifts, concentrating perhaps on an important region like Mexico or a specific goal like development of leadership skills among village women. A common emphasis of these agencies is upon small-scale projects that teach community self-reliance and cooperation—alternatives to this century's diseases of the desperate migration from village to city and the giant state project; the super dam or highway or housing project that will solve all problems, a symbol of the megalomania, waste, social destruction, and bankruptcy that corrupts the nation not simply from all the bribes and rake-offs involved but from the contrast between rhetorical promise and daily shoddiness. "Think globally, act locally," is the Oxfam motto.

Or, one can gradually search out one's own channels. I became interested in Turkey because it is a fascinating, important country fighting for survival but also because Turkish society is so totally dominated by the state that the handful of private agencies that do exist play a far more influential role than their limited budgets would have you think. Fifty thousand dollars from abroad exerts a lot of leverage, not the least because it illustrates to an insecure leadership class the importance that the wealthy, values-setting West assigns to these village crafts centers or environmental programs.

The effectiveness of international philanthropy is bound up with this whole issue of leverage. The outsider has a distance, a set of comparisons the insider lacks. He can take risks. If he fails the heavens won't fall. If he succeeds he can let a local politician take the credit. If all national prestige is invested in high technology, he can experiment with low technology: techniques and cheap tools for turning waste banana fiber into paper and roofing material, for making pressed-earth building blocks, for creating energy from sun and wind, and for constructing cheap, sturdy man-propelled, load-carrying vehicles.

The person with the checkbook doesn't have to play ball with all the sacred assumptions of the home team. In the Kenya education project are Luo and Kikuyu women as well as men included in its leadership? In the big new hospital in Lima, do your fellowships include researchers from Chile and Ecuador? If the local people are affronted by your questions, put your checkbook back into your briefcase.

THE CIA

One morning in 1965 two heavy set, middle-aged men came into my office and introduced themselves as representatives of the CIA. It is hard not to feel a sense of fear in meeting agents of the secret police, but they looked as respectable as the president and vice-president of some wholesale lumber company. They wanted to talk about the Foundation. They had been impressed by the farsightedness of our gifts to African and, in this country, black projects. Perhaps we might cooperate. The Foundation could continue to make such grants or, if both sides were in agreement (the decision would always be ours) similar ones suggested by them could be made: they would put up $75,000 and we $25,000, we would gain the credit, and institutions that both sides respected but which could not be openly funded by a government agency would benefit. An interesting idea, I agreed, but impossible to implement given our meticulous bookkeeping. Such funds couldn't be disguised.

"It isn't all that difficult. We've had experience."

We talked around the project. They sympathized with my complaint, an obsession by now, of how difficult it was to persuade the conservative mind that communism must be fought by reform and change. We made jokes about the FBI, the agency, more than the KGB, that they feared. I promised to consult my colleagues.

"Who sups with the devil needs a long spoon." A German proverb. The secret police had wanted me to work with them—an exciting morning for a humble schoolteacher. The field I taught was American history, and it was clear that the means and goals of political authority are no longer what the textbooks say. Also clear, once these persuasive visitors had left, was that their proposal would change the way our Foundation did business.

Hypothesis turned into reality that summer with a proposal from a friend of mine, an executive at the Congress for Cultural Freedom in Paris, to back a cultural center in Montevideo. In 1961 we had given $20,000 to the Institute for Congolese Studies in Brazzaville, the training school for government officials in newly independent African nations. The Congress had sponsored this and the CIA had funded it, the friend stated, which I had not known but which did not surprise me. The Congress itself, which I had been acquainted with while living in Paris during the 1950s, was a CIA front, another new fact, with its magazines like *Encounter* in London, *Preuves* in Paris, *Die Monat* in West Berlin, its services to political refugees and its international conferences on political and intellectual issues.

Some of the well-known figures who wrote for the magazines and spoke at the conferences—Koestler, Isherwood, Silone, Milosz—may have had suspicions about where the ultimate funding came from, but they had not asked questions. During the 1950s the Congress had given crucial support to anti-Communist intellectuals when prestige—Sartre and Picasso are the first names to mind—was lined up on the side of the Russians and there was always money available for any pro-Soviet enterprise. During the 1960s the same battle was being fought in Latin America. University, journalistic, artistic life was even more firmly dominated by the Marxists, particularly after Castro's victory, than in Europe. Anti-Communist leadership could not be abandoned to the military, big business, the Catholic hierarchy in the brainless, brutal Right. There had to be a third force, and in Latin America no money existed for its support, hardly even the concept of what was meant by the independent liberal mind.

Despite its size, Uruguay in the 1960s was an important country. It was the oldest, most stable democracy on the continent, but with its society increasingly pressured by fascist violence on the Right and student terrorism on the Left, the Middle badly needed support. A cultural center like this one could be a rallying point. Financing from abroad by foundations like ours would give it some independence in the jungle of Uruguayan politics. A grant of $25,000 from us with $75,000 from the CIA, which took the project seriously, would make an impact.

The logic was inescapable. It was the reasoning I had employed myself, usually unsuccessfully, with my fellow trustees. When the Montevideo project came to a vote, however, at the September 1965 meeting we found ourselves, to our surprise, in agreement. We would put up our own money, the idea made sense, but turn down the matching funds. It wasn't the way we did business.

What should the policy of a foundation be toward the CIA? I am sure that the Catholic theatre group in Santiago, *Ictus,* that we funded in 1964 received CIA support. The agency invested a lot of money during the 1960s in welfare and cultural projects designed to strengthen the Christian Democrats against Allende's socialists and the Communists. In 1976 and 1980 we made two grants totaling $25,000 to keep *Encounter* alive. By then the Congress for Cultural Freedom, unmasked in 1966, had collapsed, and I don't know whether the British International Publishing Corporation and the American Open Court Publishing Company, which supported the *London Review*, were also CIA channels. It is a good magazine, pro-European, pro-American, and anti-Communist since its inception, one of the few journals in the English-speaking world "devoted to the transatlantic free marketplace of many-sided argument and analysis," as it describes itself. Did Crossroads Africa receive CIA support in the 1960s? It would have made sense.

It is hard to discuss the CIA intelligently, for the agency is the automatic whipping boy of liberals who do not want to know the realities of secret war with the Communists, and the automatic ideal of John Wayne conservatives who admire it not despite its illegality and brutality but because of those qualities. What is forgotten by both sides is that in its early years the most dangerous enemy of an effective, long-range American foreign policy as seen by the State Department was not the Soviet Union but Congress. The extreme Right in the Senate (McCarthy of Wisconsin, McCarran of Nevada, Knowland of California, Jenner of Indiana) and House (Nixon is the best-known name) had demoralized and just about destroyed any leadership in foreign policy trying to deal with the complexities of reality. If George Marshall was being called one of the traitors who had handed China to the Communists, no official less important could afford to stick his neck out.

There was a need for an agency whose actions and budget would not be under congressional scrutiny and could therefore deal with long-range problems that Cold War politicians did not understand. Support to the socialist labor unions in Norway and West Berlin (the caveman Right never grasped the difference between socialist and communist) was one CIA policy. Support to the Congress for Cultural Freedom in Paris was another: funding, for example, of its anthologies in French translation of Polish, Hungarian, and Romanian poetry, as respect for the cultural traditions of Eastern Europe countries under Soviet control, which if done openly would not have been tolerated by Congress or by European intellectuals.

The CIA helped organize the destruction of Mossadeq in Iran, Arbenz in Guatemala, Allende in Chile, and one attack after another on Cuba from the Bay of Pigs invasion to assassination attempts on Castro's life and the spreading of swine plague. The Agency involved itself in such complicated skullduggery in so many different places that it gave an automatic excuse for failure by any anti-American government. If anything went wrong in Iran or Algeria or Brazil, you can guess who was to blame.

There are two conclusions. One is the danger of allowing a police agency to operate without effective controls. Without responsible monitoring, it evolves into gangster ramifications that threaten the democracy it is supposed to protect and threaten the agency itself. The second conclusion is harder to deal with. If Americans are conditioned by their education and by what they are fed in the media to be unable to face the complexities of reality in all their conflicting shades of grey, if they insist on seeing everything as black and white, Good Guys and Bad Guys, with the demand for immediate results, then long-range policy will have to be carried out in secret. A nation gets the secret police it deserves.

SUPPORT SYSTEMS—$1.3 MILLION

Henceforth, every nation's foreign policy must be judged by one consideration: Does it lead us to a world of law and order or does it lead back towards chaos and death.   [Albert Einstein, 1946]

Peace—$25,000

Our grants to Arab–Jewish cooperation in Israel under the sponsorship of many different organizations were committed to relieving the blind prejudice that leads to war. All the different international exchange programs have that as an ultimate goal. For programs strictly concerned with peace, however, the Trust made three small grants.

World Veterans Fund, New York, New York, 1966—$10,000. This was an organization of veterans from fifty-one countries with an aim of promoting constructive relations among associations of war veterans. One concern was to work out policies on the best usage of United Nations' forces: training of such troops in the techniques and psychology of peace, procedures of handling spare parts for trucks, and special foods of different national diets.

World Conference of Religion for Peace, New York, New York, 1979—$5,000 for a conference in New York City to include representatives of all religions, similar to previous ones in Washington, New Delhi, Kyoto, and Louvain. Funding was needed for travel costs of third-world delegates to attend and break through the parochialism of western Christianity.

Harvard School of Public Health, Boston, Massachusetts, 1981—$10,000 to meet Dean Hiatt's secretarial costs in his effort to reach mainstream opinion-formers—the American Medical Association, President Reagan, the *Reader's Digest*—on the costs of nuclear war, the last epidemic. One example he employed was the $160,000 costs for treating one badly burned eleven-year-old boy who received eighty blood transfusions and still died. Suppose one were faced with 100,000 such cases, 10 million, or 50 million? The Pentagon has urged doctors and hospitals to stockpile plasma in order to treat victims of a nuclear attack. Hiatt's reply was that the only medicine needed in vast quantities is morphine, to help victims die as rapidly and painlessly as possible.

Exchange and Hospitality—$500,000

Eisenhower Exchange Fellowships, Philadelphia, Pennsylvania, 1977, 1979—$30,000, for men and women ages thirty to forty-five, irrespective of government, political, or academic affiliation, who have demonstrated achievement. Stress is upon broad experience and leadership status. Started originally with Europeans, these fellowships by mid-1970s represented eighty-six different countries.

Farmers and World Affairs, Camden, New Jersey, 1972, 1975—$40,000 to promote exchange of ideas among world farmers. In the 1970s, major programs were involved with India, Pakistan, Egypt, and Venezuela, with a new emphasis on farm leaders from developing countries.

Institute of International Education, New York, New York, 1959–1978—$55,000. The first grant of $20,000 in 1959 went to train graduate students from Caribbean countries. The Institute administers exchange programs for a variety of public and private agencies in the United States and abroad, the largest being the Fulbright program, and that of the Venezuelan government that sends thousands of students each year to the United States. Up to 120,000 individuals are given assistance or counseling per year. By the 1970s, there was interest in new fields like ecology and population, and with the Fulbright cutback, private agencies became more important.

American Friends Service Committee, Philadelphia, Pennsylvania, 1959, 1962—$53,000, for international work camps; seminars in Poland, West Germany, Japan, India, and Yugoslavia; affiliation service between American and foreign schools (Commonwealth School received a three-week visit from a Soviet teacher through this program); and Volunteer International Service program for recent college graduates.

League of Women Voters Education Fund, Washington, D.C., 1965–1971—$55,000, and the *LWV Overseas Education Fund, 1968, 1975—$30,000.* The Overseas Education Fund had been established in 1947 at the request of the State Department to bring women leaders from Germany and

Japan to learn how the democratic processes are employed in the United States. At the same time, there was an honest effort not to impose American values or methods on these visitors. The program was expanded into Latin America with a center in Bogotá. New areas of interest were the environment, leadership in volunteer agencies, and efforts to encourage inner-city political participation.

Center for Inter-American Relations, New York, New York, 1975, 1977—$50,000. The Center is committed to understanding through the performing and visual arts, literature and public affairs, particularly in the effort to present Latin American music and musicians to large audiences.

International Center in New York, 1961–1976—$65,000. This Center opened in 1959 in midtown Manhattan to offer facilities for the personal and social needs of foreign students, business trainees, and doctors and nurses. It was hardly able to respond both physically and financially to the ever-increasing demands on its service. We gave $95,000 to similar welcome centers in New York, Washington, and San Francisco.

Experiment in International Living, Putney, Vermont, 1965–1980—$95,000. The Experiment, started in 1932, is the oldest institution of its kind in the United States. It aims to develop mutual respect among the peoples of the world by providing an intensive cross-cultural experience for its participants. It started in Western Europe and now is involved everywhere including Africa and the Soviet Union. Participants live with a foreign family and share travel in groups of local and American young people. There has been a steady expansion of types of visitors going in both directions: medical and law students, teachers, and college students on independent study programs. A new School for International Training in nearby Brattleboro offers advanced degrees in language teaching and international administration.

There is the uncomfortable paradox that a great ease and cheapness of intercontinental travel are matched by increased American isolationism and a loss of interest in both foreign language and history. Accordingly, the Experiment, which involves over 35,000 individuals each year, becomes ever more important.

Nothing is easy. Most educated people believe fervently in international exchange, particularly among students, and criticize the meanness of nationalism. And yet the Americans, like the Russians, have been willing to exploit their students and volunteers for intelligence gathering and even recruitment. For a while both India and Brazil put severe limitations upon American scholars and Peace Corps workers, suspecting that they wanted to learn more about their host countries than the latter thought wise.

Education—$80,000

Franklin Book Programs, New York, New York, 1967, 1971—$50,000. This organization has tried to aid education in Asia, Africa, and Latin America by strengthening book publishing capacity, book distribution systems and libraries, and developing professionalism in the entire spectrum of publishing. Specific examples of concern: medical books in Spanish and Portuguese; one-volume encyclopedias in Arabic, Urdu, Bengali, Indonesian; low-priced paperbacks in Iranian, a model bookshop in Teheran.

World Press Freedom Committee, Omaha, Nebraska, 1981—$15,000. This committee was established in 1976 to offer aid to third-world media such as providing a clearinghouse for used newspaper and broadcasting equipment and providing money for fellowships, seminars, equipment, and training. Press freedom is a painful field: the Third World complains of American domination and misrepresentation; Americans complain that most of the nations talking about freedom mean simply the freedom of the government to impose its own point of view.

United Nations International School, New York, New York, 1967—$15,000 for scholarships, teacher training, and financial stability. It addresses how to present a cohesive curriculum for its 648 students of 74 nations and 30 languages without submerging the cultural yearnings of its nationalities and how to avoid a bland curriculum and confront the students with more than one version of the same facts (i.e., the revolutions of 1789 and 1917).

Refugees and Prisoners—$170,000

International Rescue Committee, New York, New York, 1960–1981—$165,000 in nine grants. The IRC is the major American organization serving the needs of refugees wherever they arise, and a history of the committee (or even of the Merrill Trust's involvement with it) gives a history of the whole melancholy topic, a topic resented by Americans, who like to be thought of as generous people but dislike the claims put to that quality by Jews, Haitians, Vietnamese, and one troublesome people after another.

$25,000, 1969, for resettlement of professionals, mainly Hungarians, and for money to allow refugees to leave the terrible camp Valka near Nuremberg and move into regular apartments.

$20,000, 1963, to resettle Cuban professionals.

$25,000, 1968, to finance a day-care center in Vietnam.

$20,000, 1970, to resettle Eastern European professionals in the United States, mainly Czechs and Jewish Poles. Older professionals in a declining labor market have trouble getting jobs and housing.

$15,000, 1971, to help save East Pakistan doctors and teachers in the Calcutta area. Probably 200,000 people were killed in the spring of 1971 by the Pakistani army and police, and 7 million refugees fled into India. IRC felt that its priority was to save the cultural leaders, particularly those who could then work in the refugee camps.

$10,000, 1976, for Chileans fleeing the Pinochet dictatorship, and Kurds fleeing Iraq.

$15,000, 1978, for resettling Czech dissidents in Austria, the 500,000 refugees from Angola now in Zaire (30 percent on the brink of starvation and therefore needing seeds and agricultural tools), and aid to Ugandan professionals in Kenya who have fled Idi Amin.

$15,000, 1980, for 700,000 Afghans who have fled across the border of Pakistan and 500,000 Ethiopians in the Sudan.

$20,000, 1981. By this time the Trustees were all tired of refugees and the IRC. Are Haitians fleeing a dictatorship or are they simply impoverished black people? Vietnamese have the resourcefulness, drive, and fierce family loyalties of immigrant groups of the past and have begun to make it as shrimp fishermen, restaurant owners, and gangsters. El Salvador. Somalia. My own school, Commonwealth, in Boston, ran summer sessions for children from Laos and Cambodia to serve these newcomers and to serve our American youngsters, who need to feel they are part of the world.

New York University, New York Institute for the Humanities, 1981— $15,000. This institute serves writers and scholars with modest sums until they can fit into the New York intellectual scene. Merrill grants went to a Russian filmmaker, a Lithuanian poet, and an Argentine teacher.

Amnesty International, New York, New York, 1977—$15,000, a group started in London to defend those imprisoned and tortured for their beliefs. Active publicity can embarrass some states and make them act more circumspectly and can also raise prisoner morale. Amnesty International tries to act neutrally, attacking the use of mental hospital incarceration for dissidents in the Soviet Union as well as torture in Uruguay, but the American government criticizes it as more sensitive to right wing cruelty than to left.

American Schools and Institutes of International Studies—$530,000

Johns Hopkins University, School of Advanced International Studies, Washington, D.C., 1962–1981—$190,000. During World War II businessmen, government officials, and educators gathered resources to establish a school (opened in 1944) to train men to serve both government and business for a time when the United States would be confronted with vastly increased international responsibilities. By 1950 the school became one of the regular academic divisions of Johns Hopkins University, and an overseas center was opened in Bologna.

In 1962 and 1966 the Trust gave $50,000 for fellowships in order to diversify and upgrade the student body. In 1972 and 1975, $65,000 was given to strengthen the Department of International Economics. Graduates now must have a sound knowledge of new developments in quantitative analysis made possible by the computer, of behavioral approaches used in decisionmaking, and of the realities of the new multinational corporation. In 1980 and 1981, $75,000 went to establish a Foreign Policy Institute to address issues of security, energy, and economic policy.

Monterey Institute of Foreign Studies, Monterey, California, 1971, 1976—$50,000. This school, with a 1970s enrollment of 350 students, offers a broad program of languages, area studies, social studies, and courses in translation and interpretation.

Tufts University, Fletcher School of Law and Diplomacy, Medford, Massachusetts, 1967–1979—$75,000. In 1967 and 1971, $50,000 was given to support a Latin American Teaching Fellowship Program. The student enrollment in Latin American universities has grown so fast that there is a critical shortage of professors. An imaginative approach was this fellowship program to send American graduate students (at the predissertation level) to fill junior faculty positions in those universities. They would teach for nine months and remain six months further for research in their dissertation topics. The Trust's second grant was used to encourage Latin American corporate funding of the reverse process in sending graduate students to Tufts.

Georgetown University, Washington, D.C., 1971–1980—$120,000. In 1971, $25,000 was given to the School of Foreign Service, to revise the master's program. The School, established in 1919, was the first program of its kind in any American college. It sought to meet the needs of both public and private institutions and supply the linkage between knowledge and practical operations. Advances in science, technology, economics, and knowledge of human behavior have made the world profoundly different in the last fifteen to twenty years, with the need, therefore, to synthesize this new material while still retaining a core knowledge of history, economics, and political science.

Between 1972 and 1980, the Trust gave $95,000 to the Center for Strategic and International Studies. The Center was opened in 1962 to study foreign affairs as affecting the interests of the United States and to further reasonable international policies. A strong interest is the economic issue of developing countries like the Philippines, Malaysia, and the Andean common market, with a new stress on food and energy. The Trust's last two grants were for a new program looking at the problems of the 1980s: the East-West power balance, population and migration, the aging Western economies, flash points for conflict, the future of business, and the international cultural revolution.

Columbia University, New York, New York, 1981—$25,000, for operating support of the Russian Institute.

The field of foreign policy was never a priority of the Trust, but the $530,000 to the eight institutions just listed represents a responsible commitment. What conclusions can one make about the preparation and working out of American foreign policy?

One is troubled by the paradoxes, the terrible costs of American mistakes, and the flaws of our decisionmaking policies. Our greatest success of the post-1945 period was the Marshall Plan in its contribution to the rebuilding and unification of Europe. That very success in Europe allowed us to overrate our capabilities, and in Asia, Africa, Latin America, where there were not the honest, skilled, and internationally oriented administrative cadres we had relied upon in Europe, we failed badly while trying to follow the same general policies.

In the late 1940s, it was hard for Americans to realize that we simply lacked the resources to force other countries to work out their destinies according to our way of looking at things. The Chiang Kai-Shek government, despite vast American aid, collapsed and was replaced by the Communists, for example. The right wing of the Republicans blamed the Democrats, from George Marshall and Dean Acheson on down to low-level officials and academics, as soft on communism, incompetent, or downright treasonous. One result of this attack was that when the Democrats returned to power in 1961, Kennedy and his advisors could not risk any criticism of their patriotism and forcefulness in dealing with the ever-worsening war in Vietnam. They could not risk any compromise, any withdrawal—Halberstam wrote in *The Best and the Brightest*. They had to fight for "victory" as singlemindedly as any California Republican. When the war was taken over by President Johnson, as Henry Kissinger reasons in *The Years of Power*, the liberal establishment and its institutions like the Foreign Policy Association and Johns Hopkins School of International Studies, paralyzed by guilt, abandoned responsibility for sharing its management, attacked the administration, and were in turn attacked by Left and Right.

No hint of these issues appeared in any of the appeals the Merrill Trust received. Money was requested to train second- and third-echelon staff, even if the real decisions were made by senators, some of them knowledgeable and responsible, some of them primitives, and the often ignorant and confused leaders in the White House. And young people who had felt themselves used, exploited, or thrown away in the Vietnam agony, retreated into slogans or simply apathy.

How should a democratic country conduct its foreign policy? We haven't learned yet.

CHAPTER ELEVEN

Environment and Conservation

All the great civilizations of the world began with the cutting down of the first tree. The majority of them disappeared with the cutting down of the last. [From the wall of an agricultural station in Guanacaste province, Costa Rica]

Approximately 80 percent of our air pollution stems from hydrocarbons released by vegetation. [Ronald Reagan]

In late 1965 a slight, middle-aged lady from New Zealand by way of London came into my office to persuade the Trust to support her project of planting trees around the edge of the Sahara Desert. The Sahara is expanding rapidly, eroding the fertile land at its borders, but Miss Campbell-Purdie believed that the planting of tree belts with roots reaching down to the subsoil moisture might reverse the process. She had chosen Morocco as the place to begin in 1960 because there the water for irrigation was nearest the surface. Also, the money she possessed would not take her further from London than Morocco. She rented a house and forty-five acres of land at Tiznit, on the edge of the Sahara. The Minister of Agriculture gave her 600 eucalyptus seedlings, and she hired ten men to plant the three-inch seedlings, which by 1964 had grown to twelve feet. Wheat and barley were sown within the circle of eucalyptus trees.

In 1962, with Algeria now independent she went to Algiers, but the new government had so many problems that it could find no time for trees. After a year of frustration Miss Campbell-Purdie took a house in Bou Saada, a desert village, and won the support of the Minister of Agriculture, who sent her 1,000 eucalyptus, acacia, and honey locust seedlings, which bear a nutritious bean with a high sugar content. As she had hoped, water was found less than ten feet under the surface. In December 1964, with the help of Algerian volunteers and some money from St. Martin-in-the-Fields in London, she planted 10,000 more trees. A year later 70 percent of these were still alive.

These pilot projects proved her hypothesis. Now she wanted to raise major funds to show governments and international organizations that the Sahara and all deserts can be reclaimed. Her first need was $33,185 to plant areas near Bou Saada with 336,000 trees and pay for tractors, a truck, irrigation equipment, and the labor of 100 men for 300 days. The project would stop the encroachment of the desert, provide work for the unemployed, and create a microclimate where these plantings would increase humidity, holding the passing clouds and causing the rainfall to double or triple in four to five years. Once the trees had begun to grow, grain crops could be introduced and the standard of living improved.

I fell in love with Wendy Campbell-Purdie and promised her $10,000. The Johnson government was beginning to worry about the sagging dollar and frowned on foundations that made foreign grants, but eventually we located War-on-Want in London, which agreed to serve as a conduit. She took the money and dropped out of my life.

But suppose we had shut down our humdrum commitments and given that visionary all the money we had? Vicariously we could have followed her across Libya to Egypt, or westward through Morocco to Mauritania, down to the desert borders of Mali, Senegal, Upper Volta, and Niger. The drought that devastated the Sahel (the savannah lands of the desert's southern edge) in the early 1970s and all middle Africa in the 1980s might have been prevented, and the Merrill Trust and Miss Campbell-Purdie would have planted concentric rings of eucalyptus and honey locust that would have halted, turned back, and in a few hundred years extinguished the Sahara.

Instead, Algeria spends 25 percent of its annual budget on arms bought from the Soviets, the Moroccans about the same on arms bought from the Americans, and the Arab involvement with forests is limited to the days immediately after independence when Moroccans and Libyans chopped down hundreds of thousands of trees planted by their French and Italian masters in order to show their emancipation from European values.

The Charles E. Merrill Trust spent well over $2 million on various environmental and conservation projects besides that tree-planting one. They brought us a sense of accomplishment, and the amounts we gave to the National Audubon and World Wildlife or to little outfits dedicated to cleaning up one river or holding on to one duck marsh have had some impact.

At first any wildlife project brings innocent pleasure to all: an osprey on its nest or a galloping zebra is proof of God's grace. Once one tries to attain some sort of critical mass, however, trouble begins. Ospreys are threatened with extinction because DDT residues in fish cause their eggs' shells to become so thin they break before hatching, but outlawing DDT stops a farmer from protecting his crops against insects. The United States is rich enough to tolerate a sentimental concern for ospreys by city-bred conservationists. A poor country cannot. The love of racing zebras is racism. Whites love African animals. They don't care two pins for African humans whose crop lands these animals destroy and whose children need the protein these animals supply. Salmon can be brought back to the Thames and the Connecticut by rigorous pollution controls, but the extra costs these controls mean upon some marginal factory may make the difference between whether it survives or goes under, taking with it all the jobs that support a town. When the price of oil or coal really takes off, to talk of environmental controls is to risk a lynch mob.

So, back to worrying about the breeding habits of loons. But if the rising price of wood makes it imperative to step up the clear-cut lumbering off of Maine and New Hampshire forests, a loon-lover in turn becomes an enemy of the people.

Nature lovers are kooks, scorned by wholesome, well-adjusted people. The conservation movement that began around 1900, led by men like Roosevelt, Pinchot, Muir, and Burroughs who were concerned about the precarious remnants of our wildlife and forests, was the creation of Easterners. For a Westerner, a bison or a bear was to shoot. A tree was to cut down. To worry about the future, to constrain men's natural love of hunting, the Paul Bunyan-John Wayne conviction that nature is there to conquer, to exploit as much as we want, right now, was to challenge everything that America stood for. Like abolition, prohibition, the United Nations, and concern for the rights of Indians, conservation was as unnatural as the metric system, a fixation of long-haired men and short-haired women to be despised as such.

Well-adjusted people and their governments must be kicked in the face by circumstance before they acquire any sense of urgency about the deforestation and desertification of the Third World and the cumulative pollution of the industrial world. It takes the explosion at the Union Carbide pesticide plant in Bhopal, the meltdown of the Soviet reactor in Chernobyl, or the plans to install a giant underground nuclear waste dump in Hillsboro, New Hampshire, whether its citizens agree or not, to awaken real fear for the future. Then people find other things to think about and forget.

MUSEUMS AND EDUCATION

Museums—$625,000

One starts with children. Two display cases of a section of ground, summer and winter, cut away to show what goes on beneath the surface: roots, insects, the communication tunnels of moles, and in winter the chipmunk curled up in his little seed cellar. We show the interrelated complexity of nature, answer questions, and encourage even more. The museums take us from the aesthetic—the gorgeous dioramas of Pacific birds and African mammals at the Museum of Natural History that entranced me as a boy on Sunday afternoons—to the scientific: this how a bird's wing works, this is the cycle of destruction and renewal of animal wastes. From the scientific to the social: the smiling green diorama shows the good farm in balance with nature, the one in blacks and yellows shows the chain of overuse, erosion, pollution, floods, and bankruptcy. All the fierce loyalties of children are awakened to defend birds and animals, forests and rivers. The ignorant and evil who think only about their immediate wants must be put down. This way of looking at nature and society, if properly awakened at age ten, will last a whole life long.

American Museum of Natural History, New York, New York, 1972— $100,000. The museum, a never-ending source of adventure in its limitless riches. A visitor sees himself in the child holding on to his parent's hand, pointing at the tiger who has just killed a peacock in the bamboo forest, or in the noisy convoy of schoolkids shoving each other in the hallway. There are always needs to display material better, add a contemporary dimension, and involve visitors in greater participation. We made one large grant for general administration.

Field Museum of Natural History, Chicago, Illinois, 1972—$50,000. The *other* museum. The Trust's grant was to support a program of public education: Man in His Environment.

Children's Museum, Boston, Massachusetts, 1972–1978—$30,000. Operating for years in an inaccessible suburban location, it nevertheless had lines of children waiting outside to enter on a Sunday, and later moved down to an abandoned warehouse on the waterfront. Under its director, Michael Spock, this museum runs under a fascinatingly integrated philosophy, directed more toward other cultures and other times than simply toward science and nature. It possesses the most complete collection of Indian material in New England, with exhibits on how Indians see the world around them today as well as in colonial times. A group of Indians protested, however, that a collection of masks was sacred and should be locked away and veiled, not stared at by outsiders. Accordingly, despite its motto of *Do Touch*, the Museum has made an important part of its educational message the fact that there are certain things we have no right to interfere with.

There is awareness of a child's sense of scale: a corner with a small padded bench, a bookcase built low to the floor with perhaps twenty volumes in it, behind an exhibit, allowing privacy where someone could sit quietly and read for half an hour without being bothered. There is a Japanese house where you remove your shoes before entering, with an interesting bathroom (children are fascinated by plumbing). In a complicated fashion people are integrated among the exhibits, with a special invitation to the retarded, children and adults, because there is nothing to break or be harmed by, and in the Museum's easy-going confusion they don't get in the way. The aides working in one project are delinquents paroled by the Youth Board: they can work and play with children and be paid for it, so long as they also go to regular school each morning.

A recent exhibit centered around death and the way that children experience loss. Some adults became indignant, and others wrote intense letters to say that at last a door had been opened for them to talk about this with their children.

Children's Museum of History, Natural History and Science, Utica, New York, 1981—$15,000 for operating expenses. By the 1980s the cutbacks in public funding were stripping the schools in this manufacturing city of upstate New York of science courses as well as art and music and other frills and at the same time causing classroom sizes to rise by 20 or 30 percent until the teachers were turned into cops simply trying to keep order. The responsibility for supplying an intellectual input into these children's education, therefore, in what was a very poor region, has become that of the Museum. The families are too poor to afford even a 50¢ admissions fee, and though one can get private grants for an exciting exhibit, no one gives money for meat-and-potato needs like fuel oil. In the past the director had gone to the appropriate National Endowment Office in Washington to look for backing and received it, or received less with at least an apology; under the present administration the response was to be laughed at: "We really don't give a damn. This is not one of our priorities."

(In the early 1970s there was a morbid introspection among charitable foundations as to what was their proper function when the state had taken responsibility for education, health, culture, and welfare. In the 1980s the answer becomes easy.)

The director, Alton Whitt, came to feel that the primary purpose of the Museum was to teach children how to think, but as he wrestled with the implications of that verb, what struck him was how early in life did class condition intelligence. The eight-year-old from an educated suburban family is fascinated by the computer game geared to awakening math reasoning— you run a used robot shop, the robots bought at one price and sold at another; lower your sales price and you'll have a smaller unit profit but will sell a larger quantity: what decision do you make? The kid goes excitedly from one game to the next. His parents are proud of his brightness and offer advice (discouraged). The lower-class white kid will finish one game. If encouraged by Museum staff he might start another. His parents don't care much one way or another. The inner-city black kid comes by himself. He finds nothing that interests him: "Don't you have a game where you blow up other planets?" and sort of drifts away.

Whitt worries at the earlier and earlier age at which American society writes off its young people. It isn't simply the illiterate black sixteen-year-old whose life is—let's face it—without a future. The average inner-city eight-year-old is already on a one-way street to nowhere. What can a museum do to break through this Calvinist predestination, at any level, by any means?

Museum of Science, Boston, 1959–1977—$170,000. Its long-time director, Bradford Washburn, was such an enthusiast, devoting his tremendous spirit to building and constantly expanding the Museum as the center for hands-on scientific education in New England, that it was impossible to escape being drawn into the circle of his energies. He set out to integrate natural history, science and industry, public health, and medicine into one single plant. He sought to relate the exhibits to what was taught in the public schools, to train teachers, and to train recent college graduates interested in science education and museum administration. Washburn showed great skill in cadging displays from corporations and government agencies—a space capsule, a giant beating heart, a racing car, a dinosaur—but the very richness of this smorgasbord disturbed me. The child excitedly and then frantically runs from one exhibit to the next, tugging at a lever, peering through a window, caught up in these unconnected sensations, and hard-put to fit together what he had seen.

On the child's second visit, however, he begins to concentrate on what he wants to learn. The museum is also close enough to educational reality to be commissioned by the adjoining city of Somerville to design its math and science curriculum as well as to run training classes for its teachers. Roger Nichols, its director of the 1980s, worried about the tiny numbers of girls seriously interested in science. His approach to this was to organize a series of science pyjama parties for junior high (and even younger) girls that combined all the excitement of an over-night in sleeping bags at the museum with talks and demonstrations given by young female scientists.

Palace of Arts and Sciences, San Francisco, California, 1970–1981—$90,000. This museum, whose building dated from the Panama Pacific Exposition of 1915, became the Exploratorium of scientific, technical, and human perception. Its director, Frank Oppenheimer, felt that both children and adults can become familiar with phenomena basic to the environment. The Exploratorium contained a mix of participatory exhibits and demonstrations that show the mechanisms of human sensory perceptions—a playful and a serious environment with three-dimensional exhibits made on the premises or supplied by industry, universities, and research labs. Like its Boston counterpart, the Exploratorium was closely involved with the San Francisco school system, most fruitfully so in its part-time student volunteers. As the schools are finding more problems with the basic processes of education, museums like the Exploratorium provide a missing experimental, integrative, and motivating function. The children who pack the building, climbing into and testing out machinery develop, without being aware of it, the conviction that there is nothing they cannot understand. Yet the museum always existed in a precarious financial position, starting each fiscal year assured of only half the required funds.

California Academy of Sciences, San Francisco, California, 1972–1980—$100,000. This was the West's oldest scientific institution, a leading natural history research and education center. Merrill money went for the usual complex of endowment, capital expansion, and operating funds, and specifically for a permanent exhibit of ecology and the construction of a new Hall of Man.

Pacific Science Center, Seattle, Washington, 1975—$40,000 to develop the Space Theatre portion of the Astronomy Education Laboratory, placing the viewer into the environment he is viewing, whether on a trip into the asteroid belt or into the fumaroles of an active volcano.

Environmental Education—$300,000

Institute for Environmental Education, Cleveland, Ohio, 1975—$5,000, to train teacher-student teams how to explore solutions: how to clean up the badly polluted Cuyahoga River or how by soil analysis to know where to put a town's proposed new sewage treatment plant. It wanted to serve as a model, in methods and curriculum, for other communities.

Sanibel–Captiva Conservation Foundation, 1981—$10,000. On Florida's Gulf Coast south of Tampa, this effort was the child of 'Ding' Darling, a cartoonist, later head of the U.S. Fish and Wildlife Agency and lifelong propagandist to protect the environment of these two islands. It wages a rear-guard action to expand its scrub and swamp land holdings and educate (warn) the visitors and residents about what used to be two beautiful islands of birds, raccoons, alligators, and sea shells before they are destroyed by motels and condominiums.

Harris Center for Conservation Education, Hancock, New Hampshire, 1981—$10,000. The Center was founded in 1970 to demonstrate the complex interconnectedness of man and nature in the Monadnock region of southern New Hampshire and sought to involve itself in environmental education in the public schools. The state's price in having no income tax is a thin budget for every public service, including the schools, and accordingly a great need for what a private agency can supply. The Center has always stressed wet-lands conservation but now is trying to make people sensitive to the future of New England agriculture and to the narrow agricultural base on which New Hampshire rests.

Izaak Walton League of America, Arlington, Virginia, 1972—$25,000. The League supports an Urban Environment Affairs Project in fifteen cities, set-ting itself two serious educational tasks. One is to awaken a concern for en-vironmental problems among inner-city dwellers, who suffer from air, water, and food pollution but consider such concern, as they do the antiwar move-ment, a liberal cop-out when first priority must always be the fight for equality in jobs, housing, and political clout. The other is to involve college students in a sustained commitment to conservation. That volatile group dumped the antiwar movement when they no longer felt threatened by the draft, picked up ecology and picturesque Earth Days, and then became tired of that. There is a need for traditional institutions like Izaak Walton and Audubon to reach these new enthusiasts and provide structure to their energy.

Fund for Animals, New York, New York, 1972—$10,000. For some time this sort of United Fund and Red Cross for animals was a one-man show under Cleveland Amory. It sponsored magazine ads against fur coats of seal and leopard and radio and television shows on whale killing and seal clubbing, nagging at governmental agencies and respectable groups like Audubon. Its priority now is the protection of ocean mammals—whales threatened by the Japanese and Russians, seals and sea otters threatened by Alaskans and Canadians.

The Merrill Trust backed five such education/propaganda groups in 1972. Is the conservation movement, like the population movement, benefited by this pluralistic leadership, or is there overlapping and overadministration?

Taft School, Watertown, Connecticut, 1972—$20,000 to support a program of outdoor leadership activities. John Esty, a headmaster sensitive to the changing demands placed on traditional schools like Taft, worried about the lot of the inarticulate, physically oriented boy who felt himself marginal, no matter what his economic class, in a society increasingly competitive, verbal, and dependent on academic credentials. Properly educated, such boys might find respected careers in the environmental movement, where outdoor leadership is valued and nature speaks for itself.

Millbrook School for Boys, Millbrook, New York, 1966—$15,000 towards a new building to house the zoo and aquarium. That zoo was Millbrook's heart, almost its reason for being. An intense, impressively integrated philosophy had been involved in its defense: a direct contact with animals would motivate the desire to go into more abstract science; training in responsible practicality—how to clean out a cage without being bitten. It was the equivalent of a chapel with its almost religious respect for the individuality and needs of animals, as important as we are but different.

Woodlands and Whitewater Institute, Cherry Grove, West Virginia, 1976– 1980—$10,000. Institute and director were interestingly complicated. Daniel Taylor-Ide had spent much of his boyhood in India, where his grandparents had been medical missionaries, and after an education at Commonwealth School, Johns Hopkins, and Harvard, he had become family planning consultant to the Nepalese government. He was an impassioned mountain-climber both in Alaska and the Himalayas but had adopted the Buddhist custom of turning back 200 yards from the summit: nature is to be respected, not conquered.

He built the Institute on the highest mountain in West Virginia, a way to expose families to a natural environment as arduous as it was beautiful, and through that shared experience he sought to strengthen the relations between fathers and sons, what he saw as the weakest link in the American family. The family program expanded to a course of study in the region's history, ecology, folklore, ethics, and geology that Taylor-Ide sought to make as rewarding to sophisticated college students as to small-town Appalachian youngsters. He also tried to combine his love for Appalachia and the Himalayas by organizing visits of medical students to Nepalese valleys to expose them to a different culture and alternate concepts of medical care: how does a doctor function without the support of high-tech resources? If a student showed up who really needed what the Institute offered, Taylor-Ide wasn't too interested in how much he could pay, and therefore the finances were always shaky, but it was a wonderfully spirited place.

SUNDAY AFTERNOON

Zoos and Aquariums—$625,000

For a while we made a specialty of zoos. Don Regan had always found them fascinating and pointed out that more people visited zoos each year than attended all football and baseball games. Doris Magowan was attracted to their new function as nurseries for endangered species. An emperor of the Chou Dynasty started the first zoo—the Garden of Intelligence—in 1100 B.C. with animals from all over China. The Egyptians, the Emperor Augustus, and Louis XIV kept zoos. The first modern zoo was started under Napoleon at Jardin des Plantes in Paris (1804).

New York Zoological Society, Bronx, 1965–1979—$180,000. This largest and most famous zoo dates from 1899 and has been concerned with endangered species since its beginning. At its entrance is a shocking graveyard with the names and termination dates of all the world's vanished species, starting slowly with the Near Eastern lion in Biblical times and the dodo in the eighteenth century and then moving to the flood of species wiped out in the last 100, the last 25 years. As early as 1905 the Bronx sent breeding stock of bison to the Wichita Game Preserve in Oklahoma. The 1970s were seen by Laurance Rockefeller, one of the Zoo's benefactors, as the crucial decade for trying to turn around the process of destruction, and a major priority was to establish a Wildlife Survival Center. The Bronx has always tried to acquire rarities (a contribution to their extinction?) like the gorilla, okapi, platypus, and king penguins among its 1,100 kinds of animals, 1,500 birds, and 692 reptiles.

Merrill grants went toward the World of Night (a house built for night creatures), the great open African and wild Asian areas, a shop to sell Asian handicrafts, printed material for the Zoo's education program, and the creation of a reserve fund to stabilize cash flow.

Zoological Society of San Diego, California, 1967–1980—$125,000. The "second" zoo is remarkable for its variety of species that can be exhibited outside all year long, its elegance of display, and the scientific sophistication of its breeding program. Small enclosures were being replaced by naturalistic and spacious ones to heighten breeding potential, particularly of the most vulnerable species. There were new multilevel viewing sites and walkways, a rain forest for hornbills and cockatoos, and another for orangutans, langurs, and gibbons, the largest primate collection in the world. The Trust also contributed to the famous Institute for Comparative Biology and its study of diseases like malaria in birds and leukemia in primates.

Lincoln Park Zoo, Chicago, Illinois, 1980—$25,000. This is the largest public attraction in Chicago with four million visitors a year, the fifth most heavily visited zoo in the world, and one of the last still free of charge. The Merrill grant was in response to a $17 million campaign for new facilities including a waterfowl lagoon and flamingo dome and new areas for large mammals and hoofed ones.

St. Louis Zoo, St. Louis, Missouri, 1966—$25,000. Every family visit to St. Louis centered on three attractions: the zoo, the art museum, and a Cardinals' game at Busch Stadium. After Hamburg's, this zoo was the first to build large moated areas that avoided bars and fitted together an integrated mix of animals plus the great screened cages of birds that visitors could walk through. It had a penguin house with air chilled, filtered, and passed before germicidal lamps to keep down airborne fungus. It also had a children's area where they could feed and pat the animals.

Zoological Society of Philadelphia, 1966—$25,000. Founded in 1859, the oldest in the United States, "for the instruction and recreation of the people," it has a popular children's zoo, was the first place where trumpeter swans bred in captivity, and is famous for its research laboratory that examines animal diets and conducts careful postmortems. Philadelphia's diets are copied throughout the world with the recognition that, as with humans, the main demise of sedentary animals is heart disease and no longer tuberculosis.

San Francisco Zoological Society, California, 1967–1981—$65,000. This zoo involved itself in children's education, teaching ecology, geography, elementary zoology, and also trying to teach, through physical contact with small animals, kindness and responsibility. One of our projects was to finance zoomobiles that visited camps and hospitals. We helped renovate the lion house. The zoo contains an elk meadow and California's only insect zoo.

Metropolitan Toronto Zoological Society, Canada, 1971—$40,000. Canada's first and part of Toronto's great success story, this zoo was to have the best of everything in science, education, and esthetics. Animals were encouraged to follow natural instincts in prowling, nesting, and wallowing, and this might help people be less remote from animal life. Our grant came at a time when Merrill Lynch was under rough competitive pressure from local investment firms and showed the corporation's sense of responsibility to its host city.

Boston Zoological Society, Boston, Massachusetts, 1972, 1975—$40,000. Franklin Park had once been the center of an Irish-Jewish residential area with its pleasant zoo a part of Sunday afternoon. Then that part of Boston became black, and the zoo was allowed to decay into a sort of Auschwitz of the animal world, with mangy animals, rats, and a decayed, slow, politically appointed staff. Then at the end of the 1960s came a much heralded program of rebirth: the zoo would stress the balanced habitat, centered on Africa, and its presence would attract white visitors and school children and help integrate the city. Work on the project has gone on and on, with completion dates postponed, and the zoo no longer seems important.

New England Aquarium Corporation, Boston, Massachusetts, 1966–1978—$40,000. Construction on this aquarium began in 1965 as part of the great Boston waterfront renewal and as a gesture toward the dying New England fishing industry. Because it was well designed and conveniently located, as Franklin Park was not, it rapidly became one of Boston's leading tourist attractions. Its most exciting detail is the multistory central tank of sharks and giant turtles.

Gardens and Parks—$815,000

As the quality of urban life deteriorates in every part of the globe at the end of the twentieth century, the importance of gardens and parks becomes ever greater. The building-up of banks and nurseries (as in zoos, of endangered species), the development of new tree varieties that will grow along the Los Angeles freeways or in the clay deserts that the Brazilians are making of Amazonia, and the planting of trees that supply shelter for birds and animals offer areas of peace and beauty for people to re-create themselves and to replace carbon dioxide with oxygen—there is a field for foundation energy that can reconcile the most argumentative opponents.

New York Botanical Garden, Bronx, New York, 1969–1981—$85,000. We became involved in the Garden's twenty-five-year, $40-million drive to turn around decades of neglect. Its main conservatory and research strength had been in microbiology, taxonomy, genetics, paleobiology, ecology, and biochemistry. Its library contained 370,000 volumes. By the 1980s the scientific atmosphere had changed. Knowledge is not enough. The scientific goals of the campaign were to (1) develop new botanical knowledge and techniques to expand food sources; (2) develop new control mechanisms for plant diseases; (3) conserve plant resources and educate people not to waste or pollute; and (4) make a complete inventory of the world's plants.

Our gifts went for maintenance and expansion, the Children's Garden, and an imaginative project called Grocery Store Biology, a new Institute of Urban Horticulture.

Brooklyn Botanic Garden, New York, 1976—$35,000 to support the garden's community education program. The garden was founded in 1900 on wasteland and though small has been meticulously kept up. The steady cutback in New York City support means cutback of education programs for both adults and children and of outreach to schools, housing projects, and the elderly.

Denver Botanic Gardens, Denver, Colorado, 1970—$25,000. These gardens have scientific importance for their concentration on plants of the mountains and plains, and they maintain satellite units outside of the city for specialized study. A strong school program is maintained, and 125 children each summer are invited to plant and care for their own ten-by-ten-foot plots, expanded to Denver's vacant lots in 1970.

National Arboretum, Washington, D.C., 1975, 1980—$20,000. With Washington's location in the intermediate climatic zone, the Arboretum contains a wide range of trees and shrubs. The staff conducts research on trees suitable for city planting as well as on plants important in medicine, forestry, and industry. Our second grant went to fund a trip to Japan to gather natural hybrids. Although the Arboretum is a strong institution, its budget is so tightly controlled that only private funds allow any expansion beyond the daily routine.

Strybing Arboretum Society of Golden Gate Park, San Francisco, California, 1972–1981—$80,000. This Arboretum is a series of botanic gardens, with sixty-four acres of specimens from all over the world. It includes a delightful little garden for the blind with braille tablets and a special program for handicapped and retarded children that tries to proceed from identifying plants to the confidence needed for identifying words. Although some Merrill funds went to develop Heidelberg Hill, a scrubby area adjacent to the Arboretum, most went for upkeep and expansion of the Helen Crocker Library.

Pacific Tropical Botanical Garden, New York, 1972–1978—$115,000. For almost ten years, Doris Magowan was a trustee of this Garden, established on three islands of Hawaii, and we gave sustained support to its work in conservation, medicine, and nutrition. Only 10 percent of all plant research is devoted to tropical botany, which concerns 90 percent of all plants. Population growth and modern technology threaten the fragile ecology of plant life in the Hawaiian islands, and the Botanical Garden found itself moving from conservation efforts there to a concern for the entire Pacific area. The Merrill Trust helped fund a survey of all Pacific botany along with a water control project and a palm collection as well as a training program to encourage young people to enter horticulture.

American Horticultural Society, Mt. Vernon, Virginia, 1976–1977—$40,000. Our first grant went to screening and greening the parking lot of its headquarters—parking lots don't have to be ugly—the second to its Plant Sciences Data Center of cultivated ornamental plants with 200,000 on record. For example, what trees, shrubs, and ground cover can best survive air pollution?

Church of Bethesda by the Sea, Palm Beach, Florida, 1967—$30,000 to beautify the grounds and garden, a place where the elderly like to sit and stroll.

Filoli Center, Woodside, California, 1979–1981—$45,000. Filoli is a 650-acre estate on the east side of the Coast range south of San Francisco with magnificent Italian-English formal gardens. Merrill money went toward a new greenhouse.

Old Sturbridge, Sturbridge, Massachusetts, 1970—$5,000, to save from extinction the older varieties of apples—Black Billyflower, Northern Spy, Cox, Orange Pippin—threatened by the ubiquitous Mackintosh and Delicious.

Connecticut Agricultural Experimental Station, New Haven, 1969–1976—$35,000, to finance research on a blight-resistant chestnut tree. There had been some success in developing such landscape chestnuts hybridized with Oriental trees, but efforts at quantity propagation had not worked out. Research is needed on better methods of pollination and on new types of fungicides. Genetic experiments on transferring hypovirulence to chestnut sprouts may be useful elsewhere, as in controlling the Dutch elm disease.

Parks, Recreation, and Cultural Affairs Administration, New York, New York, 1971—$50,000. A *Times* article on the decay of Central Park from overuse, vandalism, litter, and inadequate maintenance sparked this project. New Yorkers are so very dependent on Central Park as the place where they can breathe and feel themselves human again. A grant from our foundation would be an example of good citizenship. August Heckscher, Mayor Lindsay's Commissioner of Parks, came up with all sorts of ideas but finally settled on installing a sprinkler system in the Sheep Meadow in the heart of the park to save it from becoming a dust bowl and in emergencies to serve as crowd control.

Southampton Village Park Fund, Southampton, New York, 1969–1980— $35,000. Urbanization in metropolitan New York and its outlying areas means the loss of 2,000 acres a week to construction. Development sprawl in Southampton, 100 miles east of Manhattan, meant, even before the sixties, congestion, a network of unplanned roads and unzoned houses, a dropping water table, and the loss of open spaces, never missed till they were gone. The Village Park Fund was an effort to reverse the process: to establish a park as a recreation facility for the poor, to try and establish a few wildlife refuges, and to work for scenic easements: an agreement from an owner not to develop his property.

Fund for the Preservation of Wildlife and Natural Areas, Boston, Massachusetts, 1972–1979—$65,000. No town on earth is further from Southampton than Somerville, a congested (22,000 inhabitants per square mile) industrial suburb of Boston known for poor schools, alcoholism, unemployment, and family violence. This particular Fund had been established by the Boston Safe Deposit and Trust Company to attract gifts of land and money to towns too poor to meet matching grants from the federal government or private foundations. It was ugly cities exactly like Somerville that such funds were designed to serve. Fifty thousand dollars from the Merrill Trust was therefore matched by individual, business, foundation, and state funds that in turn released $100,000 from Washington. This $200,000 total was used to improve landscaping around the public buildings and to construct attractive passenger shelters at bus stops. The moral of the story is that the Somervilles of this country can be served by government money and not just the Scarsdales and Winnetkas, which know the ropes and have good connections.

Our second grant, $15,000 in 1979, went to help the Fund purchase remaining bits of wild areas—rocky hilltops, stretches of beach, patches of woodland and meadows, or a stream and its banks in an abandoned factory area—that still exist within metropolitan Boston. The land can still be saved from developers or from being converted into dumps, but a public-minded purchaser must act fast: in a few years nothing will be left. Then after purchase, the Fund can show a neighborhood how to obtain federal and state reimbursement (a slow process) and how to set up a community corporation to oversee and protect the property.

Friends of the Public Garden, Boston, Massachusetts, 1981—$20,000. The Public Garden and the Common comprise a beautiful and spacious area in the middle of Boston, but as Mayor Kevin White became less and less interested in the practicalities of administration—there was money available for luxuries, not for necessities—not simply capital improvements like new lighting or special planting but the simplest maintenance had to be taken over by a private group like the Friends. Our grant went toward replacement of trees infected by the Dutch elm blight, salaries for trash collectors, and renovation of the Robert Gould Shaw/54th Regiment monument, a memorial to the first black volunteers who fought for the Union, many of whom fell with their commander in the assault on Ft. Wagner, South Carolina, in 1863.

PRESERVATION

Land and Conservation Programs—$525,000

New England and New York—$355,000

University of Massachusetts, Amherst, 1969—$22,500, to finance a study of the Connecticut Valley. In March 1969 the trustees of our foundation were persuaded by Charlie Cole and Doris Magowan to put a special emphasis on institutions—local, national, and international—working for conservation of natural resources and the fight against pollution. The cumulative cutbacks in federal support meant that work had to be carried on with private funding or not at all. This study by a professor of government was an effort to make future plans for the Connecticut Valley area, which was threatened by a steady increase in urban pressures and by the random building spurred by the rapidly growing university (which went from 2,000 to 25,000 students in twenty-five years). What are the demographic trends, where are the road-blocks, and what is the best strategy for political action and public education?

Town of Amherst, Massachusetts, 1972—$15,000 to help buy twenty-seven acres of woods, wetland, open pasture, and a brook adjoining a conservation area for wildlife study, hiking, and bird watching.

Connecticut River Watershed Council, Easthampton, Massachusetts, 1970–1971—$95,000. The Council was established to encourage the wise use of the river's resources: conservation of water, land and forest, fish and wild-life, watershed protection, retention of scenic values, and flood-plain zoning. The second grant of $45,000 was earmarked to acquisition of shad and salmon spawning areas. By 1981, 140 salmon had been counted. It was also an effort to encourage high school and university students to involve themselves in scientific conservation as a career.

Nashua River Watershed Association, Ayer, Massachusetts, 1977—$5,000. In the 1960s the Nashua River was a sewer ditch, fouled and made lifeless by factory wastes and sewage run-offs from Groton, Fitchburg, and Ayer.

Through factual, precise work with factories, with technical assistance, threats of legal action, and monitoring of results by biologists, the Association has helped bring back fish and waterfowl, canoeing, and even swimming.

Land Conservation Trust, Beverly, Massachusetts, 1980—$15,000, for use of the Massachusetts Farm and Conservation Lands Trust. During the 1980s the constant loss of agricultural land may well occupy more national attention than any other land use issue. In Massachusetts, for example, there were 35,000 farms in 1940 occupying two million acres; in 1975 there were 4,700 farms on 630,000 acres. And yet with intensive management, these could supply a significant part of the state's food and fibre requirements, especially important with increasingly high transportation costs. In fact, by 1980 there has been a small but noticeable increase in family farms. Similar to what the Nature Conservancy does to catch woods or wetlands as they come on the market, the Farm and Conservation Lands Trust seeks working capital to purchase property for resale later as a working farm rather than as a shopping center or housing development.

Trustees of Reservations, Milton, Massachusetts, 1971—$25,000 to protect Bartholomew's Cobble, a natural rock garden in Ashley Falls, in southwestern Massachusetts, with adjacent marsh, meadow, rocks, and wildlife threatened by unzoned building. Trustees of Reservations, set up in 1891 to guard land of natural beauty and historic interest, is considered the model for Britain's National Trust.

Joshua's Tract Conservation and Historic Trust, Storrs, Connecticut, 1970–1973—$25,000, to help purchase and preserve woodlands and meadows, stone walls and treelined roads, historic houses, and outlook sites and hold off the devastation by superhighways and real estate developments.

Society for Protection of New Hampshire Forests, Concord, New Hampshire, 1977—$10,000. The Society's purpose is to interest state and federal agencies, private corporations, and individuals to protect forests as a long-range resource rather than to let them be destroyed for short-run profits. Almost nine million acres have been set aside in eighty-eight sites. The Society has an Environment Loan Fund to aid private and public groups to purchase endangered areas in time and also acts as a middleman with road and utility companies to show how necessary construction can be carried on with minimum damage. With skyrocketing land prices there is need for conservation advocacy against the lobbying of developers, and as wood becomes increasingly important for heat and construction, need for more scientific forest management. The Society tries to avoid a collision course between environmental and economic demands, and it opposes the hard-core conservationists who wish to leave forests untouched. That militancy is rejected as economically self-indulgent and scientifically harmful, for selective cutting benefits both trees and animals.

Nature Conservancy, Arlington, Virginia, 1977–1980—$80,000. The Conservancy was the original group that employed the land purchase loan fund to help a local community or conservation group pick up a crucial piece of property when it came on the market. Sometimes the canyon or marsh is offered by a sensitive seller at a give-away price, but the buyers, nevertheless, must act faster than their resources may allow. The Merrill Trust allotted $45,000 through the San Francisco office (1970–1977) for Pacific Coast projects and $80,000 through the Arlington office for the Adirondack Conservancy around the Lake Champlain-St. Lawrence area and for the purchase of Mashomack Forest on the eastern tip of Long Island. The 2,100 acres of that forest support the largest nesting osprey colony in New York State.

Group for America's South Fork, Bridgehampton, New York, 1975–1981— $20,000, to preserve the beauty of eastern Long Island by careful town planning; monitoring of water level and atmosphere; and concern for bird, fish, and shellfish habitats.

A look at these projects reveals some of the ethical ambiguities and class biases of the movement, highlighted by the Watt-Gorsuch counterattack during the Reagan administration. The conservationist's enemy is the developer, whose concept of progress is a Meadowbrook Acres of fifty identical little houses pouring their sewage run-off into that same brook. The conservationist speaks for the town family that would like a meadow or a brook for a picnic or a hike. He speaks for the gentry who will use any argument, democratic or aristocratic, to protect the privacy and beauty of their properties. A couple have two children and would like a home of their own. Where will they find one?

On a flight once from Frankfort to Munich, I was struck by the sharp borders between town and country of the German landscape. There was none of the sprawl that disfigures ours. The Germans achieve this result by authoritarian zoning, the ideal of American planners. A town allots just so much land for new construction. When that is used up, construction stops. The young husband makes an apartment out of his parents' attic.

Conservation of natural resources is based upon making a nuisance of oneself. The lake in Southampton on which the Magowans live has beautiful marshy edges where a couple of swan families breed each summer. A neighbor's teenager likes to water ski. Does one take out an injunction from the Village Conservation Commission to stop the teenager? That is possible, but at an obvious price. The swans have disappeared.

The West—$190,000

Nature Conservancy, San Francisco, California, 1970–1977—$45,000, for land acquisition: access land to Aravaipa canyon in Arizona's Sonora Desert, tidelands and marshes in San Francisco Bay, acreage on Santa Cruz Island off Santa Barbara and on the Big Sur Coast, an area used by big horn sheep in the Santa Rosa Mountains, and Elkhorn Slough, the only major undisturbed estuary on the California coast.

Point Reyes Bird Observatory, Bolinas, California, 1970—$30,000. This is an ornithological research facility in Marin County and on an off-coast island concerned with migration, home range, breeding territories, the impact of humans and pollution, and the ecology of estuaries and lagoons.

Audubon Canyon Ranch, San Francisco, California, 1971–1981—$65,000. The Ranch includes over 800 acres of rolling land and canyons in Marin County around the Bolinas Basin. The Basin is a feeding ground for nesting herons and egrets, a wintering area for waterfowl and migrant shorebirds and a link in the Pacific flyway. As other habitats elsewhere are destroyed, Bolinas becomes more important, and there is a need to restore logged-off and ravaged land, now threatened by development and superhighways. Through a strong involvement with the California Department of Education, it tries to expose city children to what a natural area means. The Ranch sees itself as a political as well as ecological catalyst, for the stakes are high and wild lands are so valuable that they will be gobbled up unless fought for aggressively.

Marine Ecological Institute, Redwood City, California, 1972—$25,000. This institute is a regional environmental center concerned with the conservation, development, and management of the San Francisco Bay through education and research. The Bay is an important estuary and a great natural harbor that is being rapidly destroyed. The environmental case must be presented to young people through field trips, student research projects, and vocational counseling.

Oceans and Fish—$170,000

University of Washington, Seattle, Washington, 1966—$20,000, to finance fish-breeding experiments with Chinook salmon. Experiments had begun in 1949 to determine whether a run of these fish could be established in an artificial environment and whether new types could be developed that would resist pollution and disease and would migrate young and mature early. Early maturation reduces exposure to natural risks at sea and increases the quantity of fish on the return run. Another project at the University was to cross rainbow trout with steelhead, expanding now into the Great Lakes to replace trout killed off by lampreys in the 1950s. Like all state institutions, the University is given a restricted budget and needs private funds for research.

Marine Biology Laboratory and Oceanographic Institution, Woods Hole, Massachusetts, 1970–1974—$90,000. Established in 1888, Woods Hole is one of the oldest marine laboratories in the world. We appropriated $15,000 in 1972 to publish a book on Ascidians (sea squirts), one of the smaller phyla but remarkable for their genetic polymorphism (variety of form and color in the same species) and important in the study of evolution. Seventy-five thousand dollars was given to finance the education activities of the Oceanographic Institution, the major independent marine research and education institution in the United States.

Federation of Fly Fishermen, El Segundo, California, 1976—$7,500, to provide water quality surveillance teams with the necessary scientific equipment to test streams and lakes for bacteria, oxygen, and acidity. The Federation is ready to report violations to government authorities and follow up until the conditions are changed.

Trout Unlimited, Denver, Colorado, 1972, 1978—$25,000. Our first grant was to publicize the issue of the devastating catches by Danish fishermen that were threatening to wipe out the Atlantic salmon. The second grant was a memorial to Charles Cole after his death in 1978.

Wildlife Conservation

Audubon Societies, 1964–1981—$197,500. If Paul Bunyan represents the exploitative American attitude towards nature, John James Audubon represents the other side of wonder, respect, and allegiance that come the nearest to a religious conviction that many Americans possess. And although Audubon bird-watchers are, in cartoon and story, the epitome of sweet, harmless marginals, the society, like the Sierra Club, has found itself from the beginning involved in controversial politics.

National Audubon Society, New York, 1964–1981—$92,500. This, the oldest and largest conservation organization, has 300 branches, established to advance public understanding of the need to protect soil, water, plants, and wildlife and the relation between the wise use of these resources and human welfare. The peregrine falcon, whooping crane, California condor, West Indian flamingo, roseate spoonbill, and one species after another come to the edge of extinction and force the need to combine scientific research, propaganda, and administrative skill to try and bring them back to safety. The Merrill Trust funded a golden eagle program in Texas. Twenty thousand golden eagles had been killed between 1945 and 1965, mainly from airplanes, theoretically to protect lambs, but essentially because it's fun to shoot an eagle from a plane. In 1972, $40,000 went toward a study of the California condor in its relation with man.

In 1982 I spent a week in Costa Rica and in San Jose's run-down zoo came face-to-face with a demoralized rose-breasted grosbeak, a long way from his cheerful breeding grounds in New Hampshire. Warning: the care that Audubon invests in New Hampshire is wasted if the same birds are lost when their tropical habitats are logged off and converted into pineapple plantations and cattle ranches.

Massachusetts Audubon Society, Lincoln, Massachusetts, 1967–1978— $85,000. It was in Massachusetts that the first Audubon Society was founded in 1896 to stop the carnage of wildfowl for food and of ornamental birds for skins and feathers. The Migratory Bird Treaty with Canada in 1916 and later with Mexico was one of National's earliest political victories. The first Merrill grant went for land acquisition in the Oxbow curve of the Connecticut River to stop encroachments on existing property from a private dump. The next three grants went for different approaches to public education: for teacher training in environmental studies, study of wetlands problems, production of a sophisticated slide show, and work on the technical aspects of air and water pollution control. The oil industry, construction companies, and labor unions are not composed of fools and monsters. If they can be helped to understand the goals of federal legislation like the Coastal Zone Management Act and shown how to meet its requirements and still do business, they can be treated as allies.

Florida Audubon Society, Palm Beach, Florida (including aid for the Pine Jog Environmental Sciences Center and Audubon Society of the Everglades), *1966–1978—$76,000*, for support of the Pine Jog Sanctuary and its educational programs.

Conservation Foundation, New York, New York, 1962—$22,500. The Merrill Trust's first conservation grant financed a study of the behavior and ecology of the mountain lion, including the need to educate the public on the value of predators in nature's system. In 1964, $10,000 went to produce comic books in Spanish to help Latin American peasants understand questions of land use, contour plowing, and forest and water conservation.

Sierra Club Foundation, San Francisco, California, 1972–1978—$60,000. The Sierra Club is the example of the politicalization of the environmental

movement. The Trust's first grant of $50,000 in 1972, for support of programs
in environmental science, came when the Club was mainly known for its
gorgeous books. Behind those photographs, however, was a hard-boiled research organization accumulating statistical and scientific information on the
impact of energy production, transportation, people, and livestock on park
and wilderness areas. It had the expertise to monitor the growing complexity
of environmental impact statements required by federal agencies. Its educational program began with traveling teams that made evening appearances
in different parts of San Francisco to discuss issues of transportation, energy,
and waste disposal from the community viewpoint, then brought the public
to examine the same issues within the framework of city, state, and nation.
Education included the involvement of high school seniors in research projects
that put equal stress on the scientific and social details and tried to involve
inner-city youth with nature through hikes and overnight hostel trips.

The goal was to build an awareness of how actions, by individual and
society, relate to the environment until this becomes natural to the thinking
of every citizen. This gave a religious quality to the Sierra Club's work that
made it intensely moving to young people and provoked attack by blacks as
a social cop-out and attacks by businessmen, union leaders, and politicians
who resented its opposition to progress. The issue of Alaska's mining, timber,
and oil exploitation at the expense of environment propelled the Club into
the middle of politics by the mid-1970s. To walk into a bar in Anchorage
wearing a Sierra Club button would risk having your face punched.

In 1978 the Merrill Trust's second grant was $10,000, a sign of diminishing
interest (and not just by our foundation) in the environment, limited to the
noncontroversial Service Trip Program. That sought to recruit young people
to work and learn in the wilderness, performing practical tasks like removing
trash and litter, maintaining trails, replanting: seeking to minimize human
destructiveness.

The issues became economic and political as well as scientific and religious.
By appointing James Watt as Secretary of the Interior and Ann Gorsuch as
Director of the Environmental Protection Agency, the Reagan administration
limited the power of environmentalists to put brakes on economic development. The Sierra Club, as described by Tim Peckenpaugh in a report for the
Republican Study Committee, was an elitist outfit trying to manipulate press
and courts to pursue its ever-expanding agenda, with the ultimate goal of
preserving the privileged status of affluent liberals. Sierra Club militants responded in 1981 by collecting 300,000 signatures for the recall of Watt. Watt,
by pointing to this persecution, made himself the most valuable fund-raiser
the Republicans possessed. In the same symbiotic way the Club exploited
Watt and Gorsuch to increase its membership.

A tax-exempt charity cannot legally be a lobbying agent, but to protect a
redwood tree other than by chaining yourself to it implies political activity,

either through the enforcement of existing laws (threatening to sue a government agency that does not enforce its charter), in the making of new laws
(when does education become propaganda?), or, in crucial elections, outright
support of candidates. To plant a tree or to cut one down are political acts.

*African Wildlife Leadership Foundation, New York, New York, 1967–
1981—$65,000.* The six grants here went to help Tanzania finance the de-
velopment of its national park system, to save the mountain gorillas of
Rwanda, to continue a nature education program in the Sudan, and to train
African students in the administration of nature preserves. With major support from Ford, Rockefeller, and the United Nations, this foundation seeks
to transfer responsibility for African wildlife from white to black hands, a
crucial objective, but the pressures of population will probably make these
efforts in vain. From 1970 to 1980 the elephant population of Uganda's huge
Kabalega National Park fell from 9,000 to 160.

*Smithsonian Institution, International Council for Bird Preservation,
Washington, D.C., 1977–1980—$25,000.* This Council, the oldest interna-
tional conservation organization charged with bird protection, has sixty-five
national sections around the world. We sponsored a project involved with
pheasants and cranes and another with endangered birds of Mauritius and
the Seychelles in the Indian Ocean.

World Wildlife, Washington, D.C., 1972–1980—$210,000. Here, out of
Doris Magowan's special concern, was our major investment in international
conservation. Our first $10,000 was to participate in Prince Bernhard of the
Netherlands' $10 million fund to save endangered species and natural en-
vironments anywhere in the world. Our second $10,000 went to support a
conservation bank that was distributing $17 million to 1,200 projects in eighty
nations, a catalyst to government action: to rescue the tiger, Javan rhino,
orangutan, monkey-eating eagle, vicuña, and to preserve a bird sanctuary in
Kenya and green turtle nesting beaches in Costa Rica. Fish, like children, do
not vote; the need, therefore, comes of a private agency like this with leaders
like Prince Bernhard and the Duke of Edinburgh, independent of political
budgets.

In 1977 we allotted $100,000 for research in the marine environment to
examine the whole question of farming the oceans to focus on critical marine
habitats, law of the seas legislation, and maritime pollution. The threat to
the seas is the most dangerous that we face today. Where should we establish
whale sanctuaries in Baja California or manatee habitats and marshes for
bird migrations, how should we bar dumping of radioactive wastes and protect Palau from becoming an international tanker port—in sum, to establish
priorities of what can be saved. Subsequent grants went to projects in Swa-

ziland and the Caribbean, even warden posts for wetland sanctuaries in Afghanistan, and $50,000 in 1980 went for the Global Marine Program.

In 1982 the Duke of Edinburgh made an American visit for World Wildlife, and by putting up $10,000 one could share with him either an intimate dinner party for 100 given in Malibu by Mrs. Getty or a Houston ranch safari with Anne Armstrong, former Ambassador to Great Britain.

Hellenic Society for the Protection of Nature, Athens, Greece, 1972— *$10,000.*

Environmental Problems Foundation of Turkey, Ankara, Turkey, 1981— *$10,000.*

National Parks and Wildlife Foundation, Sidney, Australia, 1970—$25,000, our one Australian grant.

The two small grants to the Greek and Turkish agencies were probably as important as the $210,000 to World Wildlife. A concern for the environment is rare in these countries. American aid strengthens a weak budget and brings status to a fragile concept.

CONCERN AND POLITICS—$115,000

No real problem will be solved rapidly no matter how much money is spent. [Jane Lee Eddy, Taconic Foundation]

The protection of wild things implies the protection of wild human societies, more vulnerable to progress than whooping cranes.

Anthropology Resource Center, Boston, Massachusetts, 1979—$5,000, to a shoestring outfit run out of a Harvard basement by a militant, Shelton Davis, who waged a one-man war against the Brazilian government for its genocidal campaign against the Indians of the Amazon Forests (perhaps 50,000 still remaining). By their highway into the interior, by the destruction of forests for cattle-raising (temporarily, until the topsoil leaches away), by disease, alcoholism, and sometimes by outright murder, despite impressive protective agencies, the government has tried to get rid of these hindrances. Davis tries to speak at international conferences, raise questions, cause trouble, and uncover the worst abuses to embarrass the Brazilians and slow down the process of extermination.

Cultural Survival, Cambridge, Massachusetts, 1976–1981—$15,000. Founded by another Harvard anthropologist, Maybury Lewis, who was concerned at the destruction of traditional society: agricultural expansion into grazing lands in Kenya, the wiping out of forests in Peru and Venezuela, and the corruption of culture in Nepal by large-scale tourism. One of Cultural Survival's targets is the philanthropy of unloading upon native peoples the contraceptive drugs and procedures (i.e., the Dalkon shield) outlawed for Americans and Western Europeans. Merrill money went partly to train Masai leadership to mediate between modern and traditional culture in Kenya.

Wunderman Foundation, New York, New York, 1979—$5,000. Hans Guggenheim, an MIT anthropologist, had lived for years among the Dogon, a grazing people in Mali at the southwestern edges of the Sahara. The heart of their culture was the intricately carved wooden doors of their granaries. As modern culture spreads and granaries are held shut by pieces of corrugated iron, the sense of identity fades. Guggenheim sought to fund a few elderly carvers who would show younger men how to create such doors not only to restore the spirit of village life but also to create examples of good art that could be sold in tourist shops, instead of the usual airport junk, to bring in revenue. This project was an example of the idiosyncratic imaginativeness that foundations should look for.

(Notice how few and small these grants are—more and larger appeals would have been rejected.)

Humane Society of the United States, Washington, D.C. (for Institute for the Study of Animal Problems), *1980 $15,000*, to another version of concern for living things. The Institute, founded in 1976 by an English scientist, Dr. Carl Rowan, sees itself as a bridge between the scientific community and the humane movement. The problems faced today are much more complex than a simple campaign against cruelty—the drunken cabdriver beating his horse, brutal Newfoundlanders clubbing baby seals. (Give some thought, perhaps, to the lot of the sealers and Inuit trappers rendered marginal by this new sensitivity—unemployment and alcoholism.)

The first problem is to humanize the modern intensive husbandry systems. Four billion meat- and egg-producing animals are slaughtered (the industry term is *disassembly process*) yearly, most of them kept in confinement systems preventing normal behavior. Calves are raised in narrow boxes because lack of movement means paler, softer veal. Hens are penned together like subway commuters. The crowding sometimes means that they go insane and peck out each other's eyes, to be stopped only by clipping their beaks. The efficient way to guarantee high milk production is to keep cows permanently fastened to their stanchions, and in New Zealand tails are often amputated to make it easier to clean their rear ends. The second problem is to cut down unnecessary cruelty to the 100 million laboratory animals killed each year in the United States for research and product testing: rabbits who have nail polish dropped into their eyes to test Pure Food and Drug specifications. When cats are not fed they become lethargic, and when given electric shocks they become excitable—university students carry out such imaginative experiments. Few scientists have the slightest interest in the question of cruelty.

Why is this important? Because workers in these animal Belsens and Dachaus then go home and beat their children? Because callousness to animals simply spreads, as with pornography, the acceptance of callousness as the base of our society? Because we are all—rabbits and General Motors executives—God's creatures and should have some concern for each other?

Pacific Legal Foundation, Sacramento, California, 1979—$25,000. Everyone likes Smoky the Bear. Nobody wants to destroy our forests. Few politicians want to copy Spiro Agnew's "If you've seen one tree you've seen 'em all!" But this country needs balanced implementation of priorities for its environmental laws. The most influential group lobbying for balance is the Pacific Legal Foundation, whose appeal was sent to the Merrill Trust by a Safeway executive.

The Foundation is an independent, public-interest law firm seeking to represent economic, social, and environmental interests in a balanced fashion. It monitors precedent-setting cases in frontier areas: land use, environment, and social welfare. It believes in competition, free enterprise, private property rights, and freedom from excessive regulation. To continue litigation now having a significant impact in helping assure a brighter future for business, industry, and the average tax-paying citizen, the Foundation employs ten full-time attorneys in Sacramento and five in Washington. Over the years 1976–1979 it received $325,000 from the Construction Industry Advance Fund.

Center for the Study of Public Policy, Somerville, Massachusetts, 1981—$10,000. This center is staffed by young militants and involves itself in study of the disposal of toxic wastes, of crucial importance to an industrial city like Somerville, whose air and water are flavored by pollutants. This threat was symbolized in March of 1980 by the derailment of a train carrying tank cars of poisonous chemicals, which caused the evacuation of a good part of the community. At a time when environmental standards are being relaxed at every level, it becomes crucial for such lobbying groups to keep fighting.

Natural Resources Defense Council, New York, New York, 1979–1981—$40,000. The Council is a legal advocacy group dedicated to protecting America's endangered natural resources and the quality of the human environment. Our first $20,000 went to support its Year of the Coast program to protect resources threatened by intense development pressures: waste disposal, the siting of refinery and shipping complexes, oil drilling at Georges

Bank, and foolish summer homes built far out into the reach of Massachusetts winter storms.

The second grant, on our foundation's last agenda, went to support the Council's Clean Air Project. The Clean Air Act of 1970, up for reauthorization by Congress, was under intense attack for requiring expensive controls in the construction of automobile exhaust systems and in air-scrubbing mechanisms of power-plant and factory chimneys. Such controls have hurt the price competitiveness of American autos and have put new burdens upon American industry. Popular rejection of such controls was one reason American voters elected (and re-elected) Ronald Reagan. Accordingly, Congress' reexamination of the Clean Air Act in 1981 could go either toward modification of the most costly and complicated rules or it could scrap all but the most cosmetic ones. As different corporations pressed for changes in the federal antipollution regulations, they were surprised by how little opposition they received.

The Council was pressing a counterattack stating that the relaxation of standards for suspended particulates and sulfur dioxide led to carcinogenic air pollutants and to the rapid build-up of acid rain. It sought to emphasize the lethal effects of that rain upon lakes, forests, and soil downwind from Youngstown and Cleveland and also through its expertise to make studies of alternate approaches: for example, a study to show government and private interests in California and the Pacific Northwest how energy needs could be met without new coal or nuclear power plants.

As our foundation's trustees were debating this appeal, the argument was raised that we would be exposed to serious criticism as opposing the free working-out of the president's economic recovery program. Nevertheless, the Republican senator from Vermont, a state hurt by acid rain, had become one of the Council's strongest supporters. In its pragmatic search for such allies, the Council follows an assumption that most Americans would prefer to safeguard the environment and protect their jobs. In bad times they can be frightened into shortsighted postures, but if they are offered honest facts citizens will by and large respect long-range values.

CONCLUSIONS

Perhaps the value of this undisciplined mix of grants that The Charles E. Merrill Trust made in the field of Environment and Conservation has been to illustrate the topic's dizzying complexity. We might have accomplished something of historic worth by bankrolling Wendy Campbell-Purdie's Sahara tree scheme with a million dollars or five million, but trying to civilize the Nashua River and Central Park, strengthen the breeding programs at the San

Diego Zoo, help the Town of Amherst buy recreation land, and sustain the school programs of Utica's children's museum—these were important too, and sometimes $5,000 was the relevant grant and sometimes $100,000.

If a philanthropic foundation seeks to play the role of good citizen, the simplest way to begin is by planting trees. It gives employment, a small-scale version of Roosevelt's Civilian Conservation Corps that took young men off street corners. It links the present with the future, a sign that someone still believes in the future and will try to ensure its security by planting a tree rather than by buying a gun.

As one looks over these hundred or so projects, one is struck too by the number that speak to children. Children don't get as good a deal in our society as Americans like to think. We put a lot of money into schools, and some are good and some aren't, but I'm not sure how much sensitivity is employed in trying to learn what are children's concepts of the world, their sense of time and scale, the way they interact with the objects around them, and what they look for out of their world.

The passivity imposed by an addiction to television, this age's equivalent of the gin that nineteenth-century working class mothers used to quiet their children, means hour after hour spent in watching violent, vulgar actings out whose ultimate goal is to have them wheedle their parents into buying a box of Frosty Flakes. This keeps the kids out of the way, and eventually they become teenagers and citizens of another fantasy land, and then they grow up.

Children like animals, they like to climb and experiment with things, and they like adults to listen to them and for moments at a time give them un-divided attention. It is true that along with the tribe of Frosty Flakes/Dis-neyland salesmen there is an opposition tribe who sometimes have made an equally profitable career out of selling the public the belief that they know the real language of childhood. It takes even more skill to tell the honest from the fake here because the specialists themselves are not apt to know. The poor foundation trustee groping for useful answers must try to look for what seems to originate from an individual on the spot, in a framework small enough so that policy is conditioned by what happened last week, not one set by headquarters. Above all, one should look for what encourages children to *do* rather than to accept.

Because the Merrill Trust gave money to the Pacific Legal Foundation and to the Sierra Club, we came down on both sides of the basic argument: does concern for nature impede economic progress? Are conservationists senti-mental hypocrites, protected usually by inherited incomes, who can afford to despise the entrepreneurs, engineers, contractors, and working men who sup-ply the oil that drives their cars, the coal that warms their homes, the profits that pay for their children's education, and the checks they write to Audubon?

A conservationist dreams of building his cabin in the Sierras. As soon as he has done so, he tries to make absolutely sure that no one else gets the right to do the same thing. Conservationists are liberals who want a broader distribution of wealth to ghetto dwellers, but they oppose the expansion of the economy that alone will allow any real improvement in ghetto jobs. In their support of zoning, land programs that keep vacationers away from forests and beaches, birth control programs for the poor, and education that teaches children to believe that zebras have more rights than black children, conservationists, at the bottom line, are thinking primarily of themselves. Those zebras are window-dressing.

Every executive of every conservation outfit should be required to answer the unpleasant questions raised in the preceding paragraph.

One answer, of course, is to ask what time frame is under consideration and how widespread the benefits and costs. This year's benefits and costs of exploitation of the Amazon forest, of deregulation of a coal-fired factory in Youngstown, Ohio, of dumping wastes from a nuclear power plant into the ocean, and of planting wheat on marginal land in Kansas for export to Russia are one thing. Those benefits and costs ten years from now, or twenty, are another. The hard-headed pragmatists so proud of their bottom-line realism who give no concern for what will exist in twenty years, when their cute little grandchildren, starting families of their own, will be apt to die from a wide variety of cancers encouraged by grandpa's actions, are the dwellers in Fantasyland who should be locked away in cages.

The conservationist is the steward of the future. We have not inherited the world from our parents; we have borrowed it from our children. Nevertheless, conservationists cannot evade questions about today. They probably will have to ally themselves with another marginal group, the antiwar crowd, for it is the senseless worldwide preoccupation with arms and war that is gutting our natural resources and spreading, more than by any other cause, poverty and inflation. When right-wingers attack the social programs of the welfare state as causing inflation, they don't mention the Vietnam War or our arms race with the Soviet Union, which have brought about infinitely greater economic damage. To protect the future, whether represented by redwoods or children, the first step is to do whatever one can to prevent a nuclear war, to cut down on the insane scale of arms purchases, and to see the Russians as human beings, good and bad like ourselves, rather than as abstract monsters.

And then, to protect the redwood, the loon, the zebra, and the child, conservationists must try to work out some other measure of society than the one we now take for granted. Human beings do not have the right to demand too much for themselves. We have to scale down, at every level, what we expect as our natural rights: the size of our car and our family, the amount of steak we eat, the number of times a day we flush the toilet, and the number of years we care to live. We need to learn a realistic modesty, hard for Americans, in the demands we make upon life. There are other ways of obtaining energy than from giant oil-tankers from Arabia. There are other ways of growing food than by stripping the topsoil off the prairies or by jamming a thousand hens into a single cage. There may be other ways of manufacturing well-made, low-cost goods than by giant assembly lines or by runaway factories in Sri Lanka with girls paid two dollars a day.

Practical people despise such ideas as fanciful but are willing to accept the concept of inevitable nuclear war. They are not bothered by the misery of other people's children so long as theirs are safe. Conservationists have a long-term economic and political struggle on their hands not simply through the candidates they vote for in November but in the options they expect those candidates to present. And perhaps it is a religious struggle, too.

In 1967 my wife and I took our two sons to Arizona, which included a couple of nights at Lake Powell where Glen Canyon Dam blocks the Colorado River just to the east of the Grand Canyon. One could have a drink in the air-conditioned bar of the Wawheep Marina and watch the waterskiers. With an outboard it was about an hour's trip up a branch of Glen Canyon to the great natural bridge that used to be inaccessible except by an arduous hike on foot or horseback.

Our brief stay at Lake Powell left me troubled. The silt coming down the Colorado will in twenty or thirty years turn the lake behind Glen Canyon Dam, like the lake behind Aswan Dam, into a swamp. The intricately sculptured sandstone cliffs of the canyon, still sharp and clear beneath the water, will be converted into mud within a far shorter time. We could rent a boat and speed up the lake to look at the great natural bridge, but did we have the right? A handsome woman works at the next desk in your office. Do you have the right to ask her to take off her clothes because it would please you to look at her naked? No, you don't. What is unusually beautiful perhaps should not be too accessible. Some care must be implied in finding it, or else one is like the customers at a strip-tease joint who leave the bar more disappointed than they expected.

The most educational exhibit at Boston Children's Museum may be the Indian ritual masks veiled and locked away. Ordinary people, including the museum director, don't have the right to look at them. They have the power, by unlocking the doors and taking off the veils—the Indian priests come only once a year and the museum "owns" the masks. But they don't have the *right*, which gets across into the minds of some of the children who read about the masks at the Indian exhibit. Why are the masks veiled? Couldn't the director come there at night when everyone else is gone and unlock the door? No, he can't.

CHAPTER TWELVE

How Things Work

Frank presentation of ominous facts was never more necessary
than it is today because we seem to have developed escapism into
a system of thought. [Joseph Schumpeter, *Capitalism—Socialism—Democracy*]

Seest thou a man diligent in his business? He shall stand before
kings. [17th century New England proverb]

If you so smart, boy, why ain't you rich? [Texan proverb]

It was only natural that a foundation set up with Charles E. Merrill's money
should place a major thrust in the fields of business and economics, and we
appropriated about $11 million to institutions involved there. Both Robert
Magowan and Donald Regan were fascinated by the question of how things
work in a complicated technological society, particularly in the world of business. It was a way they saw to repay the capitalist system that supplied our
personal wealth and the foundation's resources. On the whole, I feel that
Mr. Merrill would have been pleased by the projects they proposed.

He enjoyed making money. He enjoyed the tension, combat, the professional skill involved in making a deal, the relation between all the complicated
background facts and the simple fight to win, and the artistry of knowing
when to concede with a laugh and when to hold absolutely firm. At the same
time he was an intellectual sensitive to change and willing to try out new
ideas.

He had come to Wall Street in the days of the personal firm, in the crash
of 1907 had accepted the reality of failure as well as of success, and had been
caught up in the fever of the 1920s. Despite an objectivity that made him see
the cracks in the system and sell out most of his own investments in the spring
of 1929, the excitement of the last wild rise had him buy back into the market

before summer's end. He survived the crash and the endless depression that followed, and in the stagnation of the 1930s he thought about the basic questions of how to locate new supplies of capital and how to train new leadership. He thought about the relationship between underwriting houses like Merrill Lynch, the corporations they financed, and the investors whose accounts they serviced. He thought about the employment of new methods to incorporate rather than rely on the traditional partnership, to hunt for a large new market of small investors, to issue a public financial statement and put money into research and advertising, and to set up branches all across the country. And new values—to create a financial system that was honest, effective, understandable, that would not be a tool for insiders and gamblers, and that would have the rationality and usefulness to win public support. As he described his concepts of business: "I saw an opportunity to render a real public service and at the same time to make a great deal of money."

Charles E. Merrill's involvement with the financing of Safeway Stores on the West Coast offered a different field of concentration—a broader, more positive field than Wall Street—and allowed him another way to look at economic life. He became fascinated by the channels by which food went from farmer to processor to wholesaler to store shelf to market basket. How, at each step, could this be done most expeditiously, with a minimum of waste and delay? If he ever got to heaven, he liked to say, it was because his leadership in Safeway had reduced the price of milk in Los Angeles by a penny a quart.

The stores operated in a rough world. The labor scene in San Francisco in the 1930s was dominated by Harry Bridges and a hard-fighting collection of unions. Politicians in both Colorado and California threatened a punitive tax on all chain stores, with Safeway a primary target, and the company fought back with sophisticated public relations techniques that later became a standard part of politics. Merrill learned how to profit even in a high-cost state like Alaska, where the trucks rolled off the ships fully loaded as if they were coming ashore in Normandy. World War II saw a great expansion again of Wall Street and of Merrill Lynch, with sixty partners and jokes about "we the people" and "the thundering herd."

Even though a semi-invalid from his first heart attack in 1944 until his death in 1956, Merrill remained the boss, a source of new ideas and a catalyst in pushing his partners into new directions. He gave a lot of thought to postwar problems. He was not able to hire George Marshall to work for him (as earlier he had not been able to hire Calvin Coolidge), but he did become interested in new methods of executive recruitment and in 1946 worked out a program with Robert Magowan, the first director, to train young exofficers. Donald Regan, a major fresh out of the Marines, was one of the first students. He would have been intrigued by the computer revolution and, I think, by the development of the European Economic Community. And he was always excited, till the end of his life, to find an ambitious, energetic, intelligent young man and be able to give him generous backing.

This field of management and economics was one where the Trust concentrated its resources: seven of its grants were for half a million or more. We financed training programs for government as well as corporation managers, the executives of hospitals and cultural institutions, black entrepreneurs, and female vice-presidents. We tried to help business management come to terms with the tremendous expansions of current scale, range, and technology from the multinational corporation to the computer and the avalanches of government regulations. And, we tried to strengthen the schools for all the new students of the unillusioned 1970s who saw an M.B.A. as the only degree (besides the M.D.) with a hold on the future.

Here I was out of my depth. I was the only man on the foundation who had inherited rather than made his own money, which, as Plato was the first to state, conditions one's attitudes toward political economy. My thinking had been affected by listening to my father's business friends at the dinner table in Southampton. They seemed to have a narrow view of reality, as even a teenager might observe, and opposed the New Deal mainly because it threatened their incomes and freedom of action. My sole involvement in the management system was eighteen months as draughtsman in the G-2 section of Fifth Army Headquarters in Italy. That was useful, however, for the American army, unlike the caste army of the British, was the military expression of our civilian society, and Mark Clark's generals ran their jobs like corporation executives. I made two observations.

The first was that if effective leadership is based upon accurate information coming up from below, how does the boss define *accurate?* When the German counterattack on the Anzio beachhead had been stopped by Allied artillery, General Clark's need was to flatter the 15th Air Force into thinking that its frontline bombing had done the trick (so they would keep on lending us their planes). Accordingly, G-2 was ordered to keep on interrogating prisoners until some exhausted German confessed that yes, sir, it was those planes. . . . When General Marshall demanded from Washington why it was that the Americans and British never broke out of that beachhead even when they outnumbered the enemy, Clark ordered the draughtsmen of G-2 (Intelligence) and G-3 (Operations) to make a series of maps for the first ten days to show that breakout was impossible. When, to his horror, our maps revealed that the Allies had outnumbered the Germans for eight of those ten days, we were ordered at frantic speed to work up a new series with Allied units diminished and German units pulled down into the front to prove. . . .

Secondly, in military and corporate administration, how wide should be the scope of management's understanding? At its best, the efficiency of the

American war machine boggled the mind. To get 400 guns scattered up and down a valley to concentrate on a German counterattack within three minutes—no one in the world could beat us. To comprehend the political reality posed by some newly taken hill town was beyond the training of our officers. The Podestà invites the junior executives for drinks to celebrate San Vittore's liberation from barbarism. Some scruffy bystanders complain that the Podestà is a fascist who handed his opponents over to the Germans. "Communists," the Podestà snorts, and his charming wife refills the major's glass.

I dwell on these Fifth Army analogies because the same contradictions appeared, at far greater cost, in Vietnam. The outstanding figure in that war was Robert McNamara, who had taught at Harvard Business School, had developed the logistics of mass bombing against the Germans and Japanese, and had been president of Ford Motor Company when Kennedy named him secretary of defense. In his understanding of technology and industry, in his command of every tool of management, and in his leadership ability and force of character, McNamara represented the American system at its best. And yet against a small, primitive nation whose leaders said they would die before they surrendered, the United States was defeated. Our strengths as well as our weaknesses were turned against us. The computer programmers, electronic engineers, social psychologists, research chemists, and skilled machinists were as beaten as the generals and the ignorant, frightened nineteen-year-old infantrymen.

All of which is a digression in this chapter on the Merrill Trust's involvement with schools of business administration and departments of economics. Nevertheless, the example of Vietnam seems to show that the more serious the question—the inextricable linkage of inflation and unemployment, the increasing concentration of corporate control, the decline of America as an industrial nation, the erosion of natural resources and the pile-up of pollutants, the existence of an unassimilatable subproletariat, the aborted, desperate economies of most third-world nations—the less it can be answered by our well-trained economists and businessmen, or indeed, the less it is even faced. Energy is invested in exciting mergers and takeovers, finagling the tax system, and abstruse new approaches in accounting. If it is profitable to close the old plant in Cleveland and open a new one in São Paulo, what happens to the workers left behind is not the company's responsibility.

Even if Americans have come to accept Japan's industrial supremacy, they have not yet fully comprehended the enormous mass of Japanese investment in U.S. government and private securities. (In 1986 Merrill Lynch, if one uses the measurement of control of capital, was replaced by Nomura Securities as the world's largest investment firm.) If their financiers develop doubts about the long-range health of the dollar or of the American economy in general and decide to disinvest with all deliberate speed, as American bankers might disinvest in Brazil—then what? Does anyone worry? Has anyone really been minding the store?

New York University, Graduate School Business Administration, New York, New York, 1966–1971—$4,075,000. This grant to build a fourteen-story Charles E. Merrill Hall for study of banking, finance, and security markets was the largest one we made to any institution for any project. It was an appropriate gift of service to the Wall Street community where Charles E. Merrill and his firm had made their money and of service to a major university under strong leadership in a period of growth.

James Hester, a former Rhodes scholar, had been appointed president in 1962 at the age of thirty-eight, a man of great ability, energy, and charm who by 1964 had obtained a $25 million challenge grant from the Ford Foundation to aim toward a capital figure of $100 million. In 1966, at the time of our first grant, N.Y.U. was the largest private university in the country. President Hester wanted to create a national institution for students of varying degrees of good intellectual ability. The faculty was also of uneven quality, and this $100 million capital drive was to attract and hold first-rate professors, build a library, put up and renovate buildings, increase endowment, and develop educational research programs.

Founded in 1921, the Graduate School of Business Administration was the largest school of its kind with 300 day and 3,900 night students and was already distinguished in finance and economics. The library, filled to capacity all day long, would be hopelessly congested when day enrollment would increase, as planned, to 1,000. That first $25,000 in 1966 for architectural studies was seen as a gift in itself, not the first of many. We were wrong. By 1968 Hester had persuaded us to appropriate $3 million for construction of Charles E. Merrill Hall. Delays in utilization of the money led into rising costs, which meant re-evaluation of methods and goals, which led to worse costs—from $3 to $8 million—along with the decision to raise the height from six to fourteen stories. The Merrill Trust appropriated another million in April 1971. Salomon Brothers added $3 million to fund a center for the study of financial institutions housed within Merrill Hall. This helped the university attract what it saw as the best international business faculty in the country and move ahead in building top-rated units in marketing, accounting, and general management.

Stanford University, Graduate School of Business, Stanford, California, 1960–1980—$1,670,000. Stanford University, in all the variety of its undergraduate and graduate schools, meant a great deal to Robert Magowan as the West Coast's equivalent to Harvard's leadership in the East, and the Trust allotted it almost $2 million. Most of this went to the Graduate School of

Business in nine grants. The school had begun in 1925 as a result of Herbert Hoover's work in interesting Pacific Coast businessmen in the need for such an institution. By the 1960s it included a major program for retraining business executives funded by the Alfred Sloan Foundation and large-scale Ford Foundation support to train teachers of business administration from the Third World.

The Merrill Trust's first involvement was $50,000 in 1960 (with $110,000 more added between 1973 and 1980) as collateral for a student loan fund. Such financial aid was needed by Stanford in order to compete with other schools, but since an M.B.A. increases any person's lifetime earning capacity by so much, a loan rather than a grant was fairer. Our money served as a reserve collateral fund to release low-interest bank loans. The program was carefully monitored and suffered only a 0.3 percent delinquency rate.

Our project that invested $500,000 into the training of minority businessmen is described in Chapter 5. I was impressed by the commitment shown by the Business School for an enterprise so different from its usual concerns.

In November 1977 the Trust gave $1 million to fund the Robert A. Magowan Professorship in Marketing and to supply teaching and research in functional aspects of marketing (advertising, selling, distribution) including marketing for nonprofit organizations and application of mathematical models. Under the leadership of Arjay Miller, who had formerly been president of Ford Motors, Stanford had become just about number one in American business schools, and the first holder of this professorship, Dr. David Montgomery, was a pioneer in applying computerized methods of decision-making to marketing decisions.

University of Chicago, Graduate School of Business, Chicago, Illinois, 1972, 1980—$1,020,000. One day in the late 1960s, George Shultz, who was to become secretary of labor and then secretary of the treasury under Nixon and secretary of state under Reagan, asked me to see him in Cambridge and suggested that the Merrill Trust give the Graduate School of Business at the University of Chicago five million dollars. I answered that Chicago was a nice school but we had many commitments. How about a hundred thousand? Such a policy of scatteration was a sign of very ordinary minds, Mr. Shultz implied, and the only way to accomplish anything of value with our money was to give major support to a few outstanding institutions like his. Then we would be remembered and respected. The interview broke up without agreement.

Nevertheless, in 1972 the Graduate School of Business was among the three chosen by Donald Regan to receive grants of a million dollars apiece to encourage training in management for nonprofit organizations. He felt that many valuable institutions—hospitals, museums, orchestras, community agencies—were headed for collapse because their executives did not know how to handle new situations and new times. To understand cash flow and capital management, to decide where computerization was useful and where a waste, to plan ahead and distribute job responsibility—these were skills that could be learned.

The grant (plus about $250,000 in accumulated income) was used to start up the Center for the Management of Public and Nonprofit Enterprise: $600,000 for endowment, $400,000 for operations. A number of Merrill M.B.A. fellowships were granted within the Center, concentrating on core courses in accounting, statistics, management, behavioral science, and then elective courses like philanthropy or the economics of higher education. Among the Fellows was a Phi Beta Kappa graduate in classical archaeology from Wellesley, a graduate electrical engineer from New Delhi, and a B.A. in economics from Wesleyan University interested in theater management. The crossfertilization of these mixtures was useful for students who learn that work experience and institutional savvy are even more prized in the M.B.A. entering the nonprofit and public sectors than in the business world.

University of Pennsylvania, Wharton School of Finance and Commerce, Philadelphia, Pennsylvania, 1963–1972—$1,125,000. Donald Regan had a high respect for the University of Pennsylvania and was chairman of its board of trustees from 1974 to 1978. We gave $2,890,000 to the university as a whole, of which $1,125,000 went to the Wharton School. Founded in 1881 as a gift from Joseph Wharton, a Philadelphia industrialist and philanthropist, it was the world's first collegiate school of business and management.

Businessmen believe that politicians put in unbalanced budgets, government controls, and the welfare state because American voters are too ignorant of the laws of economics to see through their promises. If the voters have been taught anything at all, it is by left-wing professors trained in Samuelson, or worse. For a while Regan considered commissioning through Wharton a foolproof textbook to stop people from thinking irresponsible ideas. He changed his mind, however, and settled for three summer sessions, 1963–1965, to which we gave $125,000 for high school teachers to study economics. They were regular courses in theory, history, and social application that had about thirty teachers each summer and, after initial suspicion that we might be trying to impose Merrill Lynch values upon them, were enthusiastically received. For a while we discussed many such programs to improve the quality of economics teaching, like fellowships for graduate training of junior faculty in small colleges, but eventually agreed on the simpler policy of gifts to departments of economics and business in a wide variety of colleges that they could use as they saw fit. That summer program for public school-teachers was an excellent one, however, and should have been retained.

At Regan's request, we gave Wharton $1,000,000 in 1972 to encourage training in the management of public and nonprofit institutions. Seven hundred and fifty thousand dollars was used in the construction of Vance Hall, not what we had in mind, but which provided space to accommodate expansion of the Public Management Program.

Cornell University, Graduate School of Business and Public Administration, Ithaca, New York, 1960–1972—$1,070,000. This school, which did not achieve graduate status until 1955, is one of the youngest in the country. It quickly showed the university's commitment to international education and helped set up the Middle Eastern Technical University at Ankara; established a school for management at the University of the West Indies in Trinidad; and gave courses for AID staff as well as for middle management executives, agribusiness managers, and hospital, government, and university administrators. Our first two grants—$35,000 in 1960 and again in 1965—went for fellowships for students from Common Market countries and funds for summer research projects for young professors, a way to keep them from being enticed by the better-known schools. Its faculty policy, backed by another $35,000 in 1970, was to hire good young people and pay them well rather than bid away high-priced stars from other universities.

In 1972 Cornell was the third business school to receive $1,000,000. As David Thomas described his school (of which he became Dean in 1982), it was strong in accounting and finance, with an excellent teaching faculty, and pretty strong in research. The weakness that worried him was an imbalance of quantitative and qualitative course work. Those candidates taking the Ph.D. in business and who became professors all seemed to acquire strong quantitative backgrounds, and as a result, there was a serious shortage of high caliber qualitative people who could expose students to creative problemsolving, business policy, and work in human relations.

What the best business schools do not do well, Dr. Thomas went on, is to develop skills required to define the problems that need to be solved, to plan for achieving desired results, or to carry out decisions and plans. Instruction in problemsolving and decisionmaking takes place in a vacuum. There is not a real-world context in which decisions must be implemented, in which a rational analysis is undercut by emotional behavior of human beings. Some attention is given by business schools to problems of monopolistic competition, pollution, and the erosion of natural resources, but the attention is minimal. It is as though the main focus is centered on turning out efficient managers who will maximize corporate profits and therefore maximize human welfare through employment, payment of income taxes, and returns to owners—a classic reliance upon the magic workings of Adam Smith's invisible hand.

What should we teach the person who will be an executive twenty years from now? This is a question worth asking, but any set of answers radical enough to be relevant will disturb those involved in the planning. To start with, if we still aim for a relatively democratic society, using both political and economic standards, what price are we willing to pay?

Other Business Schools

Princeton University, Financial Research Center, Princeton, New Jersey, 1972, 1980—$300,000, for research and program support. When it received $250,000 in 1972, the Center was doing practical work in interest and money rates that could be of great value to Merrill Lynch in the corporate, municipal, and government bond areas, and for that reason had been proposed to the Trust by Winthrop Lenz, the firm's chairman of the board: "When it is considered that the Charles E. Merrill Trust owns over 1.6 million shares of Merrill Lynch stock, it is evident that the success or failure of the firm in the next few years will be an important determinant of the future size and scope of the Trust."

The analysis of financial markets is a field neglected by foundations, a problem because business firms are interested in application whereas the university interest is in theory. Merrill Lynch had always been a strong supporter of Princeton, as also of Chicago, partly because it saw the Center as a way to interest undergraduates in the field of finance. The business community is the greatest consumer of trained manpower and new knowledge and should be concerned about the sources of both.

Vanderbilt University, Graduate School of Management, Nashville, Tennessee, 1970, 1976—$75,000. Don Regan had a high regard for Vanderbilt as a regional leader, and we gave it $230,000 between 1964 and 1978. Its new school of management became particularly strong in areas of finance. It built close relations with the surrounding business community, and local businessmen lectured as adjunct faculty members.

Duke University, Graduate School of Business Administration, Durham, North Carolina, 1970—$35,000. Duke, with Vanderbilt, Emory, and Tulane, is one of the places undervalued by northeasterners. Its S.A.T. average for entering undergraduates ran about 630 during the 1970s, and its endowment of $130 million was well employed in academic programs and in efforts to make a place for its new black students. The archaic lifestyle of its fraternities, fueled by alcohol and prejudice, was probably the university's weakest side.

Southern Methodist University, School of Business Administration, Dallas, Texas, 1973—$65,000. S.M.U. is one of the largest private universities in the

Southwest (in 1977 we appropriated $50,000 for general scholarships at a time when the university was trying to raise its minority percentage—1 percent in 1966 and 5.5 percent in 1970) and is proud of its school of administration started in 1965 by a group of Dallas businessmen. Our grant went toward the ten-year development plan aiming to make it a national school. It stressed individualized learning and the concept of learning by doing and involvement in live business problems. One detail was a Life Planning Center to assist students in determining their personal objectives.

Rice University, Jesse H. Jones Graduate School of Administration, Houston, Texas, 1977—$50,000. The northeastern academic establishment just does not comprehend a university like Rice with an endowment of $225 million and S.A.T. averages of its 2,600 undergraduates at Verbal 630 and Math 686. It may accept the wealth, because that's Texas, but less so the intellectual distinction, particularly in science. The School of Administration was opened in 1977 with a $5-million grant from the Houston Endowment and aimed to train students for careers in public and nonprofit as well as business organizations.

Southeastern University, College of Business and Financial Administration, Washington, D.C., 1973—$15,000, to a totally different type of institution, predominately black, established by the YMCA in 1879, and with 37 percent of its students foreign (the majority from Nigeria, Liberia, and Sierra Leone). In the middle of urban Washington, the students have practical involvement in the world of business and government. Our grant went to upgrade the 13,000-volume library.

University of Detroit, Evening College of Business & Administration, Detroit, Michigan, 1975—$15,000, toward the rebuilding of downtown campus across the street from the $500-million Renaissance Center. There had been a massive investment of human and financial resources in the renewal of Detroit, and this evening college placed a bachelor's degree within reach of thousands who could not attend college during the day. Given the realities of industrial decay and black alienation, however, the input of money and rhetoric made less difference than optimists thought it might.

Temple University, School of Business Administration, Philadelphia, Pennsylvania, 1977—$35,000, for support of faculty and student development. The university has 35,000 students and a faculty of close to 3,000. The school of Business Administration is currently educating management trainees to enter government service as well as health and education administration, industrial relations, and performing arts institutions. As economic conditions become worse, there is a need for better management of resources in higher education rather than continuing a frantic search for more money for ever-increasing budgets.

How hard it must be to recruit good public employees when they receive such contempt, from their president on down, and must endure such maddeningly detailed regulations and erratic financing.

University of Miami, School of Business Administration, Miami, Florida, 1978—$15,000 for construction of buildings to house the school, part of the $129 million Mid-Century Campaign to improve programs and facilities, strengthen the faculty, and increase endowment and scholarships.

These monster campaigns serve the purpose of preventing a dangerous overaccumulation of capital among the rich. In a precapitalist society the richest man of the village was expected to bankroll a fiesta or invite everyone to the wedding of his oldest daughter. That entertained the community and cut him back down to size. Among the Kwakiutl on the Northwest Pacific coast, clan heads competed with each other in a potlache of blanket-burning. It was the cumulative quality of capitalism, of money breeding ever more money, that made it so feared in traditional society. But if Miami University is out for $129 million, its administration recruits the city's leadership to shake each other down—my $200,000 for the new gym challenged by your $300,000 computer program—and civic status becomes the tradeoff for loss in economic power. It is another variety of progressive income tax that is perhaps even more effective in checking capital accumulation. President Reagan has appealed to the rich to replace government welfare with private generosity, but the percentage of his own gross income given to charity—1.2 percent in 1980 after a mind-boggling 1.3 percent in 1979—shows that he does not understand the rules of the game.

Brigham Young University, Provo, Utah, 1978—$50,000, toward the new building of the Graduate School of Management. Brigham Young is the largest university in the Rocky Mountains region and perhaps the largest church-related university in the country. Although its endowment in 1964 was only $4 million (up to $20 million by 1978) and tuitions were low, the deficits were picked up by the Mormon church. The faculty paid the price of its style of financing and were overloaded by too many courses and too many students at a 21:1 ratio. The university's wealth, conservatism (Bob Hope: Provo is so conservative that people there get high on Ovaltine), and enthrallment to the bizarre theology of Mormonism had Charlie Cole and myself reluctant to help it. Nevertheless, the number of Mormons in Safeway's executive ranks made it politic to take the place seriously, and Bob Magowan respected the church's sense of obligation for social welfare and the high standards of honesty among Mormon employees.

Brunswick Junior College, Brunswick, Georgia, 1978—$10,000, to its Chair for the Study of Private Enterprise. The Chair, established by a group of local businessmen, sponsors an Economic Education Awards Program that rewards teachers who provide economic education in an effective manner. It also plans to expose teachers in other disciplines to private enterprise philosophy through seminars and workshops and to reach elementary and secondary teachers through audiovisual materials and in-service courses. It would be intriguing to see this program in action. The picture of music teacher and gym coach reporting for their weekly seminar in Private Enterprise Philosophy (the PEP Hour!) evokes comparisons with Maoist China.

Harvard Graduate School of Education, Cambridge, Massachusetts, 1963—$25,000, for fellowships to candidates for the M.A.T. degree with the suggestion that, where appropriate, such fellows should take at least one course in economics. Magowan was an alumnus visitor to the school and wasted no opportunity to encourage economic literacy.

Morehouse College, Atlanta, Georgia, 1972—$500,000, to fund a Chair in Economics.

In addition, one should add the grants (under Women's Education) to women's colleges to encourage the understanding of economics and skill in business highlighted by the $250,000 to Mount Holyoke on the administration of complex organizations. One should also add about $300,000 to both college and high schools to build technical competence in computers.

Can people be aided to think rationally and work skillfully? I suppose that was the basic purpose of our funding.

CHAPTER THIRTEEN

How It Adds Up

To loose the bands of wickedness, to undo the heavy burdens, and to let the oppressed go free—to deal thy bread to the hungry and bring the poor that are cast out to thy house—then shall thy light break forth as the morning.   [Isaiah 58:6–8]

The federal budget: 99 percent for defense—keeps America strong—and 1 percent for delivering mail. That's it. <u>Leave us alone</u>. [Terry Dolan, National Conservative Political Action Committee]

The last meeting has ended, the guests have said good-bye at the banquet of mutual appreciation, the staff's retirement benefits have been negotiated, and the final checks have been signed. Surrounded by overfilled wastebaskets, the chairman and administrator sit in their respective offices, cleaning out the files. The phone rings. An upbeat voice would like to talk about a wonderful new idea.

"You're too late. It's all over."

All the things we tried. All the mistakes we made. If we had only known.

If your favorite millionaire died tomorrow and his will appointed you administrator of a foundation to spend his money, your problems of choice, at least 90 percent of them, would not be arduous ones. With society as it exists today, in our country and across the globe, imagination and insight in the intelligent disbursement of philanthropic funds are, except at the margins, superfluous.

If that millionaire gave you a bank balance, write checks on it as fast as possible to CARE, Oxfam, or Catholic Relief Services to feed the starving in Africa, the almost starving in Latin American cities, and through local agencies the same in our own cities so that you have the right to sleep at night.

For extra motivation, leaf through the ads of the latest *New Yorker* and note the luxuries that Americans are encouraged to regard as necessities.

The great conceptual breakthrough of the 1980s is the soup kitchen. The federal government shrugs off the problem of suffering, and accordingly the safety net of public welfare for the truly needy becomes an assumption that allows conservatives an untroubled conscience—the same assumption trusted by the Pharisee and the Levite as they passed by the traveler set upon by robbers. Churches set up cots in their basements.

> Wasn't there a time
> When food was sacred?
> When a dead child
> starved naked
> among the oranges
> in the marketplace
> spoiled
> the appetite?

> [Alice Walker, *Horses make a landscape
> look more beautiful*]

No matter what concerns the millionaire selected as your responsibility, the priority for 90 percent of funding is simple maintenance. No special acumen is needed for decisionmaking, the choice of institution is almost irrelevant: Morehouse or N.Y.U. (Amherst and Deerfield have as much as they need) and almost any hospital, symphony, church, or conservation group. Aided by imaginative as well as unfair tax laws, our country has built up an ecology of interlocking private institutions that have created a society, at its best, diversified, compassionate, and inventive. Yet inflation, an uneven economy, an obsession with war, and an emphasis upon self-centered individualism at the expense of the community are eroding this capital. Too many of these institutions stay in operation by meeting deficits with funds from endowment and by deferring maintenance. Write checks to repair the roof, replace the heating plant, or repaint the hallways. Ignore the appeal for that grand new performing arts center.

Apply yourself to the deferred maintenance of human resources. In the field I know best, education, money is always needed for aid to maintain the American dream that good schooling is the right of any able, ambitious, disciplined girl and boy, not the privilege of rich kids, and also to maintain a reasonably open society and to bring new members into the governing classes. Study or travel fellowships for graduate students are needed to prevent academic training from being too narrow or too debt-ridden. Grants for hiring younger staff bring new life and new ideas into the school and bring new hope into a slowly dying profession.

In art and culture, so long as one does not give too much to the Metropolitan

Opera and the Metropolitan Museum, which can look after themselves, it does not make much difference where one begins. Write a check to the Architectural League of New York to commission murals on the sides of city buildings. Fund a dozen universities' purchase of work by practicing artists. Measure how each institution wrestles with the paradox of aristocratic quality and democratic access. The quartet that plays Beethoven and Schoenberg can be subsidized to give free concerts in a high school gymnasium or a prison.

In medicine, a believer in *USA Number 1* buys a lithotriptor ($1.3 million, from Munich) or a nuclear magnetic resonator ($2 to $3 million) for the Great Hospital, with his name engraved on it. A lithotriptor destroys kidney stones by underwater sound waves, is fast, nontraumatic, and relatively inexpensive to use, and if the stones reappear can be employed again and again since surgery cannot, due to the buildup of scar tissue. The nuclear magnetic resonator (NMR) is an even more sophisticated, comprehensive diagnostic tool than yesterday's computerized axial tomograph and is well worth (perhaps) the price tag.

Otherwise, medical needs are pretty humdrum. The popular ailments are probably receiving as much money as they can profitably employ, except for VD and the tropical diseases—schistosomiasis, chagras fever, malaria (it's coming back), and trachoma—that do not strike us or our friends. By now the United States has a surplus of white male doctors, but funding is needed for neighborhood clinics, like the Somerville Women's Health Center that slipped through the Merrill Trust's fingers, and for unglamorous, dying programs in prenatal and mental health, dental care for the poor, and immunization and nutrition. A few hundred dollars accurately spent today will save thousands in repair work ten or twenty years down the road.

There it is. A grade-B administrator with a deft secretary and a reliable bookkeeper and a few members of the millionaire's family and peer group to widen (or narrow) the radar screen can run a 90 percent adequate foundation. Forget the carping critics. If he possesses the slightest skill in picking out honest leadership from the pretentious and second rate, he'll turn in a useful job—however undistinguished—he can be proud of. Society, at home and abroad, suffers such obvious, worsening ills that a perverse brilliance is required *not* to spend money sensibly.

How about the remaining 10 percent?

Or suppose one was not satisfied with that meat-and-potatoes ideal of keeping the show on the road. Should the foundation administrator be Melville's Captain Ahab, obsessed by the pursuit of his White Whale of evil or salvation?

That's something else.

How does philanthropy respond to the needs of society? Well, what is American society? What does it see as its needs—or doesn't see? Answers have to start from the conclusions emerging out of the election of 1984.

Walter Mondale was a traditional liberal endeavoring to win with the traditional Democratic coalition that dated back to Roosevelt and Truman, a man with respect for pluralism, with compassion for the insulted and injured, who made an effort to present the complexity and seriousness of the major issues while being careful not to let his patriotism be doubted. He was a decent, intelligent, unexciting politician who revealed to his television viewers a sense of exhaustion: physical, from the terrible demands of a presidential campaign; and intellectual, as his opponents repeated, because the liberal ideas he was espousing had run their course. They no longer fitted the needs of the time nor the beliefs of American voters.

In 1940 a broken France changed its arrogant motto of 1789—*Liberté, Egalité, Fraternité*—to the cautious words—Family, Work, Nation—more suitable for Pétain's government at Vichy. Listening to the campaign speeches of both parties in 1984, one might conclude that most Americans were satisfied with the aged Maréchal's set of ideals.

Ronald Reagan calls himself a prophet, with Franklin D. Roosevelt the most important president of the twentieth century, one who understands the fundamental hopes and loyalties of the average American. He is absolutely right. Liberals have wasted a lot of energy ridiculing his preference for style over substance—the presidency as television commercial, his obsessions and his impatience with the inconvenient fact, and his confusion of history with myth. If these details bother intellectuals that shows how marginal those people are.[1]

The small town of our mythic past—Green Cove Springs and Amherst—which is America for Reagan, is the America our fellow citizens prefer to believe in. It was so for my father, no matter what conflicting facts he knew. Simple problems could be met by simple answers. In trouble one relied upon oneself, one's family and neighbors, and upon a caring, Protestant, American God. Government was alien, heavy-handed, and slovenly. Of course there were faults then as now, but America is to be loved and respected just as it is. For younger voters that conclusion came with the impact of revelation: freedom from guilt, introspection, and constant analysis. America was back and standing tall. Those left out were losers. Who wants to run with the losers?

Maybe there were no losers. Blacks claim to be hurt by this administration's policies. Not true. Only their self-serving leaders have been affronted. With earnest kindliness, the president goes on radio to ask all Americans to give generously to the United Negro College Fund.

If we ask what do the president and the voter looking at his television screen know about reality, how about the foundation executive? All the habits

1. The words of intellectuals roll off the minds of the German working class like drops of water off well-oiled leather. [Adolph Hitler, *Mein Kampf*]

of administration are arranged to protect his ignorance, beginning with the thirtieth-floor office on Madison Avenue and the receptionist with honey-colored hair and Radcliffe accent paid to screen out deadbeats. The foundation budget allots $25,000 for agricultural development in Central America. Is this to be spent in rightist Honduras or in leftist Nicaragua? In what country and under what system is there a better chance that those extra resources reach the campesinos who need them? How will the executive who signs the checks know? The newspaper will just confuse him. Does he travel to Central America? Does he possess a knowledgeable friend he can trust? Has he at least worked out a set of beliefs based to some extent on the suffering, failures, lies, and humiliations he has witnessed himself?

Does he know a friend who has had an abortion, has he sat beside the bed of someone dying of cancer, had a long conversation with a welfare mother, been knocked down by an out-of-control teenager, lain on a rubber sheet waiting for a dangerous operation in a strange hospital, or realized that he didn't have the right papers when an angry policeman starts to question him?

Pelted long enough by a pitiless storm, even mad old King Lear realizes that he should have given more care to the poor naked wretches who had to endure such suffering over and over.

"He that is ready to slip with his feet is as a lamp despised in the thought of him that is at ease" (Job 12:5). Job, so respected when he was successful, learns that misfortune means moral inferiority. "I am not inferior to you!" he cries out to his comfortable comforters. He is wrong.

Should we go beyond maintenance and search for new ideas? The road goes through generosity as well as through knowledge and imagination: the extra coins that the Good Samaritan gave to the innkeeper so that he would show a little more care than the minimum to the injured traveler.

In the 5,000 grants made by the Merrill Trust to 2,000 institutions, some were more imaginative and useful than others. Out of that experience, I might seek—if I were launching a new foundation at this time—to concentrate more on the following fields.

1. Poverty is female. The single-parent household is the suffering heart as well as the carrier of poverty. In partnership with a hospital or church, a foundation might establish a family center, perhaps in a border zone—black/white, black/Hispanic—as a vehicle for reconciliation. This would include gynecological and pediatric services, classes in sex education for adolescents, job counseling and training, classes in literacy and home economics, a voter registration center, child-care facilities, and perhaps temporary quarters for battered wives. Money would be spent for cheerful furnishings. Staff would be urged to show courtesy and kindness and to try and involve their clients in the decisionmaking. Sounds old fashioned, doesn't it? Back to Hull House. Life at the bottom hasn't changed all that much.

2. On East 53rd Street in New York there is a plot of land the size of a town house converted into a minipark. A canopy of locust trees supplies shade, and a thin curtain of water running down the side wall gives a restful murmur as in a Damascus courtyard. One can buy snacks or just sit. A man is hired to keep the place clean. An iron gate protects the park from vandals. This little luxury is not cheap, but it could be copied in Harlem as well as on other nice streets.

Wall Street corporations like Merrill Lynch and Salomon Brothers that are totally dependent upon subway transportation might sponsor individual cars, attractively designed with the firm's logo, meticulously clean, supervised by courteous attendants who hold a black belt in kung fu. Foundations must invest more than they do in breaking down apartheid in American cities. Forget Johannesburg. In New York one class is able to buy quite a nice daily life. The other is pushed to the wall for the amenities of existence. Almost their only contact with each other is in the subway.

3. The Merrill Trust never made a sustained commitment to low-cost housing. In New York exists the East Harlem Urban Coalition (led by a pastor named Norman Eddy who received his training in the 1950s and 1960s with the East Harlem Protestant Parish) that endeavors to rehabilitate abandoned tenements in order to supply housing, jobs, and job training. For about $100,000 (including $30,000 of federal money for a new boiler, $10,000 for new piping, and scrounged equipment and volunteered labor) the Coalition fixed up a building of twenty-eight apartments. If the task had been done by public agencies, the cost would have been $60,000 per apartment for a total of $1,680,000. In most communities little housing groups like this, often church-led, do exist and can be strengthened. Construction work demands both skilled and unskilled labor: one way to reach the young black male we don't know what to do with.

4. In conservation the priority is to save and rebuild the world's forests, supporting research on trees that will grow in the clay of newly cleared jungles as well as along urban freeways. Some third-world countries have effective programs but few trained staff. One to two hundred thousand dollars per year for fellowships at Yale School of Forestry would equip new leadership from Costa Rica, Ecuador, Indonesia, and India.

5. American society is, by and large, cautious about challenging the *sacred egoism* (Mussolini's term) of patriotism. It is only by living and working abroad that one gains some distance on what is taken for granted at home. When the Peace Corps began in the early 1960s, conservatives feared that the young volunteers would pick up dangerous socialist ideas. Many did.

Several organizations have built a reputation for long-term, well-run projects: American Field Service, the English Speaking Union, Eisenhower Exchange Fellowships, Crossroads Africa, and small-budget colleges like

Goshen, Kalamazoo, Guilford, and Macalester. Choose an institution your budget affords and back a program long enough to make a difference. One police precinct in New York sent its officers to Puerto Rico to help them learn Spanish and learn respect for Puerto Rican culture. A new field might be American-British exchanges of black and white women who have shown neighborhood leadership in dealing with racial conflict. This is not a luxury issue. All over the world a hardline nationalism is coming back, new re-workings of the old caution of "keep to your own kind."

6. In medicine one might go in two opposite directions. The first is to make sure that research at the highest intellectual level is maintained without de-mands for immediate applicability. Recruit a distinguished university or hos-pital committee and have them award fellowships to a selection of outstand-ing men and women in their early thirties for research in the structure and function of the cell, starting point for what works and what goes wrong in the human body.

Or, offer fellowships for a year or even a month of study in the relations between medicine and the social sciences: statistics and computer analysis, cost controls and public policy, pollution and epidemiology, or the study of British procedures where limited resources force stricter discipline—in effect, the politics and economics of medicine.

7. The Merrill Trust invested $500,000 in the field of population control. Growth, more or less stabilized in the West and Japan, is wild in Latin Amer-ica, Asia, and above all Africa. The world held about 1 billion people in 1850, 2 billion in 1920, 5 billion in 1985, and will perhaps hold 8 billion by 2020—that's the curve. And it's the basic fact for almost every ill we suffer, from the fall of the water table, erosion, deforestation, and accumulation of CO_2 in the atmosphere to war and massacre.

Foolish folk have confused the issues: black male militants of the early 1970s who called birth control honky genocide, Brazilian patriots for whom a hundred million citizens was defiance to Yanqui imperialism, old-fashioned Communists who inherited Marx's contempt for Malthus, popes, and Reagan-ites who claim that the solution is not contraception but the inculcation of entrepreneurial values.

As the Trust did, one can support International Planned Parenthood Fed-eration, the largest and most widely spread private institution; the Population Institute in Washington, which seeks to popularize the message with rock songs for teenagers in Vera Cruz and East Los Angeles and with television soap operas in India; and Pathfinder Fund in Boston, which is committed to medical (laparoscopic sterilization) and educational approaches. The eco-nomic devastation throughout the third world and the United States' over-reaction on the abortion issue have broken the movement's momentum, but the structures remain to be fleshed out again. In the long run any support of better education of females and of women's economic independence brings with it a lower birthrate.

8. At 90 percent of cost (never pay 100 percent of anything), offer the services of cold-blooded Republican accountants to check the books of a hundred different voluntary agencies. A major reason for the ineffectiveness of nonprofit institutions is incompetent bookkeeping.

These are suggestions, along with the ideas discussed earlier (like supporting public schools and the struggle against nuclear war). The Merrill Trust gave 1 percent of its resources to Latin American projects; nothing less than 10 percent is adequate proof of concern for this suffering hemisphere.

Nevertheless, these approaches do not answer the questions that have to be faced by anyone trying to examine the priorities of philanthropy. What is the role of the private foundation as the federal government step by step abandons responsibility for the "good society"? In America today what are the definitions of the good society and the "good citizen"? Organized charity kids itself when it claims to be uninterested in politics.

For a short period, from the early 1960s to the early 1970s, the government showed some commitment to the ideals of equality and justice and put a lot of money into programs often poorly run, although some were better run than today's conservatives admit. The present administration is dismantling what remains of those programs, as well as others dating back to the years of Truman and Roosevelt. Along with the cumulative threat from our deficit, military needs have priority. But perhaps those arguments are not the reasons for the new priorities. They may be simply excuses. The militarization of America, which ensures that there are no funds for social programs, is not a sacrifice to be apologized for but is considered a positive good.

In the cold clean austerity planned by lean hard conservatives like Charles Murray in *Losing Ground,* the bible of the second Reagan administration, the entire welfare and income-support structure would be scrapped. The unfortunate would have no recourse whatsoever except family and friends, public or private local services (the soup kitchen), and the job market. Teen-aged mothers would have to rely upon support from their parents or the father of the child and would perhaps have to work as well. Adolescents not job-ready would find they were job-ready after all. They could work for low wages and accept the discipline of the work place if the alternative were grim enough.

Under such austerity the American economy is no longer burdened by the costs of a parasitical welfare system, or artificially high wages, and becomes competitive again. The working poor who tried to play by the rules and worked hard and who took responsibility for their families and taught their children pride and discipline find themselves respected again. "Billions for equal opportunity, not one cent for equal outcome," Murray's most often quoted statement.

We are offered a second chance to accept the values of Herbert Hoover, which a foolish America rejected in 1932. There are appealing points (it won't be readers of this book who will suffer) in cleaning out the corruption of our welfare system. But there is a cynical mendacity of that vision of some ultimate starting line called Equal Opportunity where all seventeen-year-olds line up—graduates of housing projects, street corners, ghetto schools, and meals of soda pop and noodles—alongside graduates of Deerfield and nice homes in Scarsdale. That turns the stomach.

We are also offered a new role model: Singapore. That city-state has been made wealthy and respected by a generation of bustling entrepreneurs in their brand-new skyscrapers. An efficient education system has trained a technically competent, hard-working labor force, undistracted by labor unions. A strong police force limits dissent.

So, if America aims for the ideal of Singapore (where a citizen is either a businessman, a loyal employee, or a cop), where does philanthropy fit in? It pays for the soup kitchens. Children should not beg in the streets—New York is not Calcutta. I suppose committees keep on raising money for museums and whales. Because those who run society will be wealthier, they can give more money to charity if they want to. The rich and powerful deserve to be because they are stronger, which means better. American political thought enjoyed organic contact with Social Darwinism long before the term was invented. The jungle is run by tigers, not by committees of sloths and lemurs. And the tiger, when full, is encouraged to be generous: for example, the Charles E. Merrill Trust.

Nevertheless, cynicism warps the mind. Social Darwinism always had to compete with other doctrines. A system of constitutional law, no matter how often twisted by high-priced lawyers, insisted that all citizens had equal rights. A belief that all children should start life with somewhat equal chances built an almost religious respect for the ideal of the public school. The Connecticut Federalist back around 1805 who protested, "Why should I pay taxes to educate another man's child?" did not win out. And these two beliefs were gradually and unevenly extended into a set of assumptions that every human being should have the right of some minimum of health care, housing, job opportunity, old age security, political participation, and the pleasures of walking in the park and visiting the museum. The "good society" is not a market-basket of purchasable items. The millionaire makes his gifts not just out of charity, or buying his way into heaven, or even a conclusion that it's smarter to build hospitals and schools than simply more jails. In some groping way he may share an intimation of citizenship where to be equal has actually more dignity than to be superior. A collection of art, like a cathedral, lacks fundamental value unless it is free for all to enjoy. Even in a private room at the best hospital, one shares enough of the democracy of pain to insist, in some corner of one's mind, that every sufferer must have decent care.

A state structure exists to monitor and to extend these assumptions as honestly and effectively as possible. The role of the state is not simply to protect the rich against the poor or to hold off the mobs from pillaging our condominiums. It is the instrumentality of society, and as the latter's values change the state acquires and gives up various bits of authority.

The inertia and vested interests of the machinery lead to paralysis and parasitism, as Ronald Reagan insists. He has usefully challenged liberal orthodoxy on the values of the society it wants and the prices we all must pay to attain them. He would limit state authority to military needs plus a certain minimum of administrative and security functions. His ideal is intriguingly similar to Lenin's of the ultimate future of the communist state, once the end of class war allows it to wither away to a structure of bookkeepers and file clerks.

Lenin's dream of the minimal state never got off the ground. Threats of counterrevolution and capitalist attack demanded ever more vigilant countermeasures. Reagan's minimalism must also make compromises when new threats keep turning up from Moscow, Havana, or Managua. It's a neat symbiosis.

Twenty or forty years ago the leadership in America that had purpose and energy, pride and youth came from the Left. The elderly Republicans were locked away in memories of past significance, filled with self-pity, and apprehensive of some game plan where they were targeted for destruction. Today, in its worn tweeds and scuffed shoes, the Left is the team locked away in gloomy introspection. They sense a secret plan, remorseless as whatever Stalin set out for the People's Democracies of Eastern Europe, that step by step will, in the name of freedom, destroy the freedoms of all those who do not fit into Calvin Coolidge's noble concept that the business of America is business.

Conservative leadership, trying to force a balanced budget by the 1990s, does represent that plan by eliminating all the governmental services President Reagan dismisses as outmoded and wasteful. These priorities will mean even rougher times ahead for children of poverty who will receive no more hot lunches at school, for middle-class students relying upon subsidized loans to help them get through their higher education, and for long-range concerns in environment, public health, and urban transportation and housing.

The wealthy, who are not concerned about such questions, receive the benefits they voted and paid for. The top tax bracket has dropped from 70 to 50 to about 30 percent in five years. The state is the executive committee of the bourgeois class, as Lenin remarked, and delivers the goods.

Nobody owns the future, of course. Americans voted in these neoconservatives with their dark suits and logical ideas, and as the economy wears down they'll vote them out. The inspired part of this total plan, however, is how the system may be kept in operation for a long, long time.

If there really is no cash available for Congress to spend on social services, then it doesn't make much difference which party wins the elections. Even if the Democrats came back, they would lack the resources with which to make any significant changes. They might carry out ceremonial acts and make rhetorical noises, but why would intelligent voters elect politicians without authority?

Well, how about taking funds from the defense budget? In a militarized society that becomes unpatriotic. The fate of poor Fritz Mondale warns Democrats about having that tab laid on them. But suppose one argues that the money that should go for good things like nerve gas and nuclear missiles pays for an awful lot of waste, fraud, and mismanagement? That's the part to cut. But evidence to back up such accusations becomes increasingly hard to obtain as the executive branch closes down one channel of information after another. Even the 1917 Espionage Act is dusted off to warn investigators that it is not in the national interest to raise improper questions. No matter what efforts the Soviets might make to act peacefully, it will be very hard to dismantle the American military establishment.

At the same time, if the militants like Terry Dolan of the National Conservative Political Action Committee do win out, their extremist concepts of the minimal state—99 percent for defense, 1 percent for delivering mail—may simply not be worth defending. Better dead than red? Better red than dead? It's dumb to limit political argument that simplistically. Nevertheless, to be worth defending a society must be worth living in. The word is conservatism, the fact is greed. If the contributors to the NCPAC define freedom as the right to drive a Mercedes from corporation to condo to country club unconcerned by anything glimpsed through the side windows, what's in it for the rest of us? Do we threaten the grandchildren of the entire world into nuclear war to protect this?

> Poor naked wretches, wheresoe'er you are,
> That bide the pelting of this pitiless storm.
> How shall your houseless heads and unfed sides,
> Your looped and windowed raggedness, defend you
> From seasons such as these? O, I have ta'en
> Too little care of this!
>
> [Shakespeare, *King Lear*, act 3, scene 4]

Woe unto them who crush my people to pieces and grind the faces of the poor.   [Isaiah 3:15]

Those who have more share with those who have less. An image of charity has always been the knight, San Martin, who divides his cloak with the charming beggar, and the tableau was painted over and over by El Greco and other Spanish artists. It does not stand up to any mean-minded cost-benefit analysis.

Have you ever tried to slice a cloak in half on horseback with a sword, and how much benefit does either man gain from half a cloak? The saint should have given the beggar the whole cloak or at least enough money to buy himself a sweater. But we enjoy the spontaneity and grace and overlook the ineffectiveness typical of much philanthropy.

Sitting down with a bucket of money and setting out to do good—there's a scenario for all sorts of abstract reasoning, and one fits in somewhere Thoreau's statement that if anyone approached him with the intent of doing him good he would run in the opposite direction. Given the nature of man and his ability to destroy himself and to corrupt the environment that he inhabits, it is naive to expect too much from any list of improvements that a wealthy foundation or well-run liberal state can offer. The militant places his trust in a new environment with a new set of ground rules: the Puritan will leave old England and across the ocean set up a city on a hill; when the working class controls the means of production then vice and crime and envy and oppression will cease; when European colonialism will have been destroyed, then the traditional African respect for family, community, and the spirits of nature will create new nations built in harmony and justice. It is not simply American to view the nature of man as a series of solvable social problems.

Theory on the nature and needs of man is an intriguing topic to argue about, and given the American fear of abstract thinking, it is something to build a college course upon where students can read Plato, Job, St. Matthew, and Lenin. I wonder how relevant this sort of theory is to any discussion of philanthropy. As chairman of the Charles E. Merrill Trust I used to regret our lack of resources when the institutions or problems we were trying to face had such needs: Negro colleges, ugly cities, landless peasants, and polluted rivers. There is the other side to that coin, however. If your resources are limited, the results you can possibly expect are also limited. Out of that comes modesty and realism.

You can strengthen one institution rather than another for the services it offers to a special group (Morehouse College), help create a new place (a state university based on small residential units so that students are not turned into pebbles, e.g., Santa Cruz), or allow a leader to move in new directions (Stanford to recruit a new class of Mexican-Americans or Harvard to work out new approaches in the graduate education of women). Or write out medium-sized checks to a hundred different colleges to allow them to give—not loan—financial aid to a thousand students, pay better salaries to their teachers, buy new books for their libraries, and repair their heating systems. At least you don't create a solution worse than the original problem.

Those details put together add up to a theory of education and a theory of the nature of man as consistent as any offered by a minister of education in Moscow or in Paris and a lot more humane. This does not mean that Americans cannot accomplish a much better job than they are performing now, and your own foundation can search out good institutions with strong leadership; give them sustained, generous, general backing; as well as put up risk capital for new approaches.

We live at the end of a century that has been ravaged by ideology. A new socialist society cannot be created when agricultural production remains in the hands of a backward, hostile peasantry. Out of that logical theory came Stalin's war of extermination against the kulaks of the Ukraine. A dynamic national state with its own identity cannot tolerate a selfish, alien minority. Revolutionary Turkey cleanses itself of its Armenians, Germany of its Jews, Indonesia of its Chinese, Kenya of its Indians, and on and on. An efficient capitalist economy, which eventually will improve everyone's standard of living, can grow only by maximizing profits and minimizing costs, unimpeded by outmoded traditions of land ownership, labor management, and community autonomy. Therefore, factories close in Cleveland and new factories open in Taiwan, the corner store is replaced by the supermarket, family farm by agricorp, and private business by conglomerate. The skilled workman becomes a short-order cook at McDonald's.

Given these wonderful ideals that we have shared over the last decades, what new ones would you propose? Two options are popularly offered.

Measure identity and happiness by what one buys—up the ladder from bicycle, wrist watch, fountain pen, and radio to blue jeans, television and tape recorder, computer and word processor, vacations abroad, dacha and condo, cocaine and Chivas Regal. At a more vicarious level there are airports, highways, champion sports teams, and weapons systems. One can go anywhere, do anything. The cities, hotels, boutiques, television programs, diseases, and people become more and more similar. It is a tedious subject. We have read about it too often.

Or, frightened of the present and its cities, we can go back to hardline, authoritarian nostalgia. Much as they hate each other, these angry Christians, Jews, Moslems, and Communists speak the same language. They sing the same hymn: Gimme that old time religion . . . it was good enough for father, and it's good enough for me. They share the same primary target: the emancipated young woman in tight jeans. Take care of that—get her back in the home, get her pregnant, cover her rear end, her hair, and if appropriate her face, and then on to other matters such as organizing an educational system that encourages technological progress without permitting deviant ideas.

Modern times, accordingly, help work out a rationale for philanthropy, even for outfits as rambling as the Merrill Trust. The true believers tithe themselves for charity, but that means only their own widows and orphans. Compassion is as disciplined as curiosity. Those outside the stockade are sinners and deserve what they get.

In a privatized society the human unit is not the citizen, equal to every other citizen, but the bill payer, whose worth and authority are measured by the size of the bills he pays. The hardcore consumerists are too occupied in upscaling their private worlds to give any thought to what brings other folk pleasure on a Sunday afternoon: a pretty park or an interesting museum. They also box themselves into such a narrow time frame, as far as next summer's vacation, that they give no thought to what waits around the corner ten years from now—whether a mob of inner-city desperates or the pollution and exhaustion of their ground water.

I feel uncomfortable when private funds are expected to carry responsibilities like basic scientific research, good public education, adequate housing, and humane, reasonably priced medical care for the poor that should be the concern of the state. Why do we pay taxes? What does this great nation stand for? The United States becomes as maimed as state-controlled nations like Czechoslovakia, Turkey, and Brazil whose dissidents dream of seizing that state and setting it toward other goals but cannot imagine any real power being employed outside state control.

Accordingly, if one wanders, checkbook in hand, around this zoo of social values, there are plenty of useful things to do in partnership with the current ethos or in opposition to it. Try out odd approaches. The MacArthur Foundation's gamble of making huge string-free gifts to genuine geniuses is an intriguing novelty. "The very rich have such a touching faith in the efficacy of small sums," complained Tennessee Williams, and here is a crowd ready to travel in the opposite direction. I am an agnostic about methodology, however. Running a school or running a foundation, well, can be done in all sorts of ways.

When I started Commonwealth in 1958 I had planned to center our intellectual focus around Russian, more important than any other language if we are to communicate with our primary rival or partner. To my chagrin I kept hiring excellent Latin teachers, and gradually Latin pushed out Russian. Negro seniors used to tell younger peers to sign up for Latin. Mrs. Chatfield really taught you what language was like. She made you work hard, and she couldn't be conned, but if you played by the rules she was willing to hand out high grades, and if you got in trouble with The Man she'd fight for you. That moral tale made a big impact upon my theories of administration.

What is more important, in a school or foundation, is a certain set of attitudes. Despite all our disagreements, I think the Merrill trustees respected pluralism. If we had not, we couldn't have gotten through our meetings, but there was a willingness, not always spontaneous, to listen to each other's arguments: to examine different values for measuring a school, an urban or environmental program, and to recognize the ecology of institutions that make up a society. Slightly different is the concept of equilibrium. In our respect for known leadership, although that too is a worthy criterion, perhaps we gave too much money to Stanford and Harvard, but we also tried to look for obscure, worthwhile colleges, orchestras, clinics, and museums in small-town and unfashionable cities that give balance to America and work against the destructive centralizations of twentieth-century life.

What holds a society together? A frank recognition of the reality of class war, a taboo subject for our countrymen but as American as apple pie, will force intelligent argument about what can be shared between rich and poor, educated and ignorant. That was the intellectual foundation behind the large grants we made for zoos and parks. We also made grants to inner-city hospitals and public-school music programs and new lab equipment purchased for large parochial schools so that those at the bottom of the ladder didn't feel ignored. Aid to public libraries? Perhaps, if we believe that poor people still read. There should be a continued search for new leadership, the education of new additions to the ruling class. The Morehouse graduate may simply race off to a job at Merrill Lynch and be concerned only with earning enough money to buy a house in the suburbs. Nevertheless, if enough black professionals keep coming out of Morehouse and Yale and the rest go into positions of status and authority, then what is taken for granted in the running of American society begins to change, as has been true in city governance over the past twenty years.

What are the causes without a constituency? Fish don't vote. (Neither do children.) Take up the role of trouble-making outsider: the Good Samaritan, Theodore Roosevelt and his love for animals, or Julius Rosenwald and his concern for Negro education. Worry about the future—beyond the next election, where politicians and yuppies do not venture.

The argument I have omitted is anger. Why do ye beat my people to pieces? If you are poor, America can really be an awful place. Nice people, by and large, are protected from this truth. When they get angry it is usually at the poor: muggers in the park, dumb pregnant teenagers, or cheating welfare mothers. Forget the deceitful rhetoric about opportunity. Standard policy is to pauperize the poor. Welfare supplies just enough to exist on. For an emergency, fill out a form and wait. A chance to get ahead and pay for a bit of extra education through a gift or a piece of good luck is offset by a cut in monthly payments. Before one can apply for Medicaid for a defective child or hospitalized parent, savings must be drawn far down. A welfare recipient who doesn't cheat is a chump. Yahweh, the primal administrator, set the standards in Exodus 16. In the wilderness each Hebrew fugitive from Egypt could gather one omer of manna (tapioca?) a day, enough for twenty-four hours. If he gathered any more, except on the Sabbath eve, it got maggoty and stank. Yahweh had obtained a totally dependent welfare population.

One welcomes the simplicity of Isaiah's anger: Woe to them that add field to field until they stand alone in the middle of the earth. Checkwriters are proud to help the ghetto boy through Morehouse to Merrill Lynch. But suppose the society itself, despite its ameliorations and safety valves, is too flawed and too destructive to be remedied by gifts from these kindly checkwriters and suppose the survival of those generous folk is not first priority? That is another taboo subject, sidetracked by (quite valid) tales of Stalin's and Castro's prisons and secret police and all-controlling bureaucracy. Foundation executives might take bigger risks than they do and be less afraid of what their peers and the journalists will say. Perhaps the fragile revolutionary movement that is concerned not only with schools and clinics and new factories but with the dignity and self-respect of its citizens will not have to go all the way to gulag and total control if it is treated generously.

That is a naive, gullible concept with which to end this long book. It may be even more naive to think we can face the crises that are coming down the road in all their strange costumes by using the standard operating procedures of American practice.

INDEX

Aaron, Henry, 301, 321, 332
A Better Chance, 41, 47, 198
abortion issue, 144, 164, 236, 281, 322, 507
Acción International programs, 413–14; in Brazil, 426; in Caribbean, 417; in Costa Rica, 421; in Honduras, 420; in Peru, 424–25
Adams, Abigail, 112
Addiction Research Foundation, 244
adoption agencies, 236–37
Advent School, 204
Afghan refugees, 438, 454
Africa: history, 190; projects supported in, 441–47
African-American Institute, 443
African refugees, 454
African Wildlife Leadership Foundation, 481
Afro-American arts, 205–9
Age Center of New England, 330–31
Agency for International Development, 445
Agent Orange, 281
Aging, *see* Elderly
Agnes Scott College, 124
Agnew, Spiro, 155
aid-blind admissions, 74, 77
AIDS, 297
Alaska Pacific University, 107
Albert Einstein College of Medicine, 305
Albert Einstein Medical Center, Philadelphia, 310–11
Albright-Knox Art Gallery, 351
Alcoholics Rehabilitation Association of San Francisco, 245
Alcoholism, 245, 246, 253
Aldrich, Donald, 7, 131
Alfred Sloan Foundation, 494

Alfred Steiglitz Collection, 357
Alinsky, Saul, 18–19, 156, 157, 158, 163, 304
allergy research, 295–96
Alliance College, 93, 128
Ambiance Inter-Action, 402
American Academy in Rome, 407–8
American Antiquarian Society, 389
American Association for Gifted Children, 67
American Ballet Theatre, 372
American Civil Liberties Union, 392
American Committee of the Weimann Institute of Science, 431
American Conservatory Theatre, 379–80
American Council of Learned Societies, 64
American Crafts Council, 365
American Friends of Covent Garden and the Royal Ballet, 404
American Friends of Maru a Pula School, 444–45
American Friends of the Haifa University, 431
American Friends of the Israel Museum, 431
American Friends Service Committee programs: in Africa, 446; Arab-Israeli Assistance Fund, 432; in Chile, 423–24; Dispute Resolution Clearinghouse, 253; exchange and hospitality programs, 451; in Mexico, 414; in Peru, 424; Volunteer and International Service program, 451
American Geological Institute, 195
American Historical Association, 400
American Horticultural Society, 472
American Hospital in Paris, 21, 407
American Hungarian Foundation, 410

517